Java Programming

From the Beginning

Java Programming

From the Beginning

K. N. KING
Georgia State University

W • W • Norton & Company

New York • London

Copyright © 2000 W. W. Norton & Company, Inc.

The text of this book is composed in Times
with the display set in Courier
Composition by K. N. King
Manufacturing by Courier Companies, Inc.
Book design by K. N. King
Cover background photographs: Batik fabrics characteristic of the island of Java, Indonesia, from
Batik Patterns, compiled by Pepin Van Roojen (Shambhala Agile Rabbit Editions, 1999)
Cover design: Joan Greenfield

Library of Congress Cataloging-in-Publication Data

King, K. N. (Kim N.)
    Java programming : from the beginning / K.N. King.
      p. cm.
    Includes bibliographical references and index.
    ISBN 0-393-97437-5 (pbk.)
     1. Java (Computer program language) I. Title.

    QA76.73.J38 K56 2000
    005.13'3--dc21   99-059403

ISBN 0-393-97437-5 (pbk.)

W. W. Norton & Company, Inc., 500 Fifth Avenue, New York, N.Y. 10110
www.wwnorton.com

W. W. Norton & Company Ltd., 10 Coptic Street, London WC1A 1PU

5 6 7 8 9 0

CONTENTS

PREFACE

When Java appeared in 1995, I immediately noticed its potential as a language for beginning programmers. Java satisfies today's need for early instruction in an object-oriented language, while avoiding the complexities of C++. At the same time, Java is similar enough to C++ to serve as a steppingstone to that language. (At my institution, Java is the first language introduced, immediately followed by C++.) With no pointers to cause problems, Java programs are immune to those frustrating crashes that are so common in C++. If a Java program does encounter an error at run time, the interpreter provides a stack trace that can often pinpoint the problem. And, last but not least, the software needed to write and execute Java programs can be downloaded from the Web at no charge.

Who could resist a language with this many advantages for teaching? Certainly not me! I put aside my plans for writing a C++ book, and devoted the next four years to the book that you now hold in your hands.

Goals

This book attempts to satisfy a number of goals:

- *Cover objects early.* It's now apparent that the entire software field will soon be "object-oriented," if it's not already. Students need to think in terms of objects and classes from the beginning of their studies.

- *Cover "traditional" computer science concepts*. Coverage of topics such as data types, conditionals, and loops is crucial to lay a foundation for future studies in computer science.

- *Teach problem-solving skills.* Student need to learn how to write algorithms and then translate those algorithms into working programs.

- ■ *Emphasize the importance of program design.* Once their programs are large enough to justify a discussion of design techniques, students need to be exposed to stepwise refinement and object-oriented design as tools for program design. Design is a difficult subject for beginners, whose programs are so small that the need for a good design isn't always apparent. In addition to incorporating discussions of design throughout the text, I've included a number of case studies, which allow a discussion of design in more depth than would be possible with smaller programs.

- ■ *Emphasize good style.* Although an appreciation for design takes time to develop, even beginners can quickly grasp the importance of style. I've included many discussions of style in the book. I've adopted a style that's consistent with industry practices, and I've been careful to use that style in all the examples and case studies.

- ■ *Introduce students to the culture of computer science*. The target audience for this book includes many students whose knowledge of the computing field is limited to word processing and game playing. I've tried to use this book as a springboard for introducing the terminology, concepts, and general culture of computer science.

- ■ *Prepare students to learn other languages.* At most colleges, Java won't be the only programming language that students will learn. Recognizing this fact, I've tried to prepare students for the transition to C++ and other languages.

- ■ *Make programming fun, not work.* By providing interesting programming projects—often involving graphics—I've tried to show students that they can have fun at the same time they're learning.

- ■ *Use real-world examples.* Rather than relying on simplistic examples, I emphasize practical, real-world problems. Using realistic examples helps motivate students and shows clearly how programming techniques are used in the real world.

- ■ *Emphasize understanding, not imitating.* I have little patience for books that take a cookbook approach to programming, allowing students to imitate rather than understand.

Approach

I've employed a spiral approach to many topics, gradually adding detail over the course of several chapters rather than covering each topic in a single place. The treatment of objects and classes is spread over Chapters 3, 7, 10, and 11, for example. Control structures are covered in Chapters 4, 5, and 8.

Unlike some Java texts, this book covers objects early and often, on the theory that if students don't know that objects are "hard," they'll quickly become accustomed to using them. To illustrate the use of objects, I rely heavily on the graphics portion of Java's Abstract Window Toolkit. To illustrate inheritance and polymorphism, I use examples from the GUI portion of the AWT.

Although GUI programming is an important part of developing software, it's not the central focus of this book. There's little point in subjecting beginners to the myriad of details that are required in developing professional GUI applications. Full GUI programming is postponed until Chapter 12, after inheritance and polymorphism have been explained. For simplicity, I've chosen to cover the older AWT classes instead of the newer Swing classes.

To make it easier for students to get started, I've written a package named jpb that can be downloaded from the book's Web site (*http://knking.com/books/java/*). This package provides classes for console input, displaying graphics in a window, and converting strings to floating-point numbers. I'm not a big fan of instructor-supplied classes, so I've kept the use of these classes to a bare minimum.

The book was designed to be compatible with version 1.1 of the Java Development Kit and all later versions. Some chapters briefly mention some of the newer classes and methods available in version 1.2. (For brevity, I've chosen to refer to the Java 2 SDK, Standard Edition, Version 1.2 as simply "JDK version 1.2.")

Applications Versus Applets

Although many introductory Java books focus on applets rather than applications, I've chosen to discuss only applications. There are several reasons for this decision:

- *Writing applets requires "magic."* I prefer that beginners understand what's going on as much as possible. With applets, there is no clear flow of control. Instead, methods are called by a Web browser when needed.

- *Writing applets requires an understanding of inheritance.* Writing an applet involves extending the Applet class, calling inherited methods, and overriding other methods. Many applications, on the other hand, require no use of inheritance, so a discussion of that topic can be postponed until students have a better understanding of classes.

- *Applets have no more power than applications.* Relying on applications doesn't mean that we can't use graphics, animation, or any other Java feature. An application can do virtually everything that an applet can.

- *Applets are restricted.* Restrictions on applets—especially where files are concerned—means that students will eventually need to write applications anyway.

- *Applications are more important than applets.* In the long run, the vast majority of Java programs will be applications, not applets. Java is a powerful, general-purpose language whose potential uses go far beyond applets.

- *Applets don't exist in other languages.* Java isn't the only language that students will be exposed to during their studies. The applet concept doesn't exist in other languages, so students who are primarily adept at writing applets won't be able to transfer their skills as well to those languages.

For instructors who wish to cover applets, Appendix D explains the mechanics of writing applets and shows how to convert applications into applets.

Q&A Sections

Each chapter ends with a "Q&A section"—a series of questions and answers related to material covered in the chapter. Topics addressed in these sections include:

- *Frequently asked questions.* I've tried to answer questions that come up frequently in my own courses, in other books, and on newsgroups related to Java.
- *Additional discussion and clarification of tricky issues.* Although some readers may be satisfied with a brief explanation and a couple of examples, others may want more detail.
- *Side issues that don't belong in the main flow.* Some questions raise technical issues that won't be of interest to all readers.
- *Material too advanced or too esoteric to interest the average reader.* Curious readers with previous programming experience may wish to delve into these questions immediately; others should skip them on a first reading.

Q&A Many questions in Q&A sections relate directly to specific places in the chapter; these places are marked by a special icon to signal the reader that additional information is available.

Other Features

In addition to Q&A sections, I've included a number of useful features, many of which are marked with simple but distinctive icons (shown at left).

- **Warnings** alert readers to common pitfalls. Although Java has fewer traps than many popular languages (C and C++ come to mind), Java programmers are not immune to them. I've tried to point out the pitfalls that are most common and/or most important.

- **Style tips** discuss stylistic issues, including naming conventions, indentation, brace placement, comment usage, `private` versus `public`, and more. Each tip provides a recommendation for establishing a consistent and logical style.

- **Design tips** are similar to style tips, but tackle larger issues, such as the proper use of class variables, the importance of using helper methods, and how to design a class. Design tips begin to appear starting with Chapter 7. Some sections of the book are devoted entirely to design issues; the "design tip" icon appears at the beginning of such a section.

cross-references ➤ *Preface*

- **Cross-references** provide a hypertext-like ability to locate information. Although many of these are pointers to topics covered later in the book, some point to previous topics that the reader may wish to review.
- **Debugging sections** offer tips for effective testing and debugging.
- **Sidebars** cover topics that aren't strictly part of Java but that every knowledgeable Java programmer should be aware of, including number bases, the IEEE

floating-point standard, and pseudorandom numbers. (See "Source Code" in the middle of this page for an example of a sidebar.)

Programs

Choosing illustrative programs isn't an easy job. If programs are too brief and artificial, readers won't get any sense of how the features are used in the real world. On the other hand, if a program is *too* realistic, its point can easily be lost in a forest of details. I've chosen a middle course, using small, simple examples to make concepts clear when they're first introduced, then gradually building up to larger, more realistic programs.

Source Code

Source code for all programs in this book is available via the Web at *http://knking.com/books/java/*. Updates, corrections, and news about the book are also available at this site.

Audience

This book is designed as a primary text for the college course traditionally known as CS1. No previous programming experience is necessary. The only prerequisites are a modest amount of computer literacy and the ability to think logically. The book can also be used with students who already have experience in a programming language. Students in this group should be able to progress much faster and cover more chapters.

Thanks to its Q&A sections and emphasis on practical problems, the book will also appeal to readers who are enrolled in a training class or who are learning Java by self-study.

Organization

One key principle behind the organization of this book was to cover objects early, but without full details. Later chapters provide reinforcement and fill in missing details. Chapter 3 provides the first introduction to objects and classes. Chapter 7 introduces class variables and methods. Chapter 10 emphasizes the development of instantiable classes, and shows how to integrate instance variables and methods with class variables and methods. Chapter 11 covers subclasses.

The first ten chapters are the core of the book. Students who complete these chapters should be well-prepared for further study in Java, C++, or other object-oriented languages. These ten chapters are meant to be covered in order.

Some instructors may prefer to skip Chapter 6, which deals with graphics. (I find graphics to be a great motivator, so I always cover the chapter in my own classes.) References to Chapter 6 appear in Chapters 7, 9, and 11, but the instructor can easily adjust for the missing material.

After the first ten chapters, instructors have some flexibility. Chapter 11 is a prerequisite for Chapters 12 and 14, and for parts of Chapter 13, but those three chapters can be covered in any order. Moreover, instructors can cover portions of Chapters 13 and 14 without feeling obligated to cover the entire chapter.

When this book is used as a CS1 text, a reasonable goal is to cover the first ten chapters in a semester. In a class whose students already know another programming language, the first chapter can be skipped and other early chapters can be covered rapidly, allowing additional chapters to be covered beyond the first ten. Students with previous exposure to object-oriented programming should be able to complete the entire book within a semester.

Exercises

Having a variety of good exercises is obviously essential for a textbook. I've provided over 700 exercises, which fall into three categories:

- *Review questions.* Most sections end with several review questions. Answers to review questions appear at the end of each chapter.
- *End-of-chapter exercises.* Exercises appear at the end of each chapter, grouped by section. Some exercises are quite easy, while others might take an hour or so to complete.
- *Programming projects.* Each chapter except the first contains programming projects. Some of these projects involve modifying programs given in the current chapter or in a previous chapter. Others are modifications to earlier projects. A substantial number are new projects. The difficulty varies considerably, from programs that can be completed in an hour or so to programs that might take several days to finish.

Instructor Resources

Instructors who use this book as a text will find a variety of useful resources at the book's Web site (*http://knking.com/books/java/*), including teaching notes, overheads, solutions to selected exercises and programming projects, additional programming projects, test questions (with answers), and technical updates.

Errors, Lack of (?)

I've taken great pains to ensure the accuracy of this book. Inevitably, however, any book of this size contains a few errors. If you spot one, please send a message to *knking@knking.com*. I'd also appreciate hearing about which features you found especially helpful, which ones you could do without, and what you'd like to see added. Errors will be listed at the book's Web site (*http://knking.com/books/java/*) and corrected in future printings.

Acknowledgments

First, I'd like to thank my editor at Norton, Joe Wisnovsky, for his patience and sage advice. Ann Koonce did an admirable job of copyediting the manuscript.

The following colleagues were kind enough to review some or all of the manuscript:

Manuel Bermudez, University of Florida
Richard Borie, University of Alabama
Jim Clarke, University of Toronto
Doug Cooper, Southeast Asian Software Research Center, Bangkok
Ronald Leach, Howard University
John Motil, California State University, Northridge
William Topp, University of the Pacific

Richard Borie deserves special thanks for reading the entire manuscript with great care.

I also received much valuable feedback from friends and colleagues in Atlanta. Alan Wright provided many useful comments on the early chapters. Joe Levine and Ali Khanmohamadi caught a number of mistakes. The support and encouragement of my department chairs, first Fred Massey and then Marty Fraser, was especially appreciated. A number of students provided feedback, including Steve Hilbun and Jeff Padia. I am especially indebted to Jeff, whose sharp eyes spotted many a slip.

My wife, Susan Cole, helped with the book in innumerable ways, including reading the manuscript and testing the programs. As always, I owe her a huge debt for her support and assistance. Our cats, Bronco and Dennis, provided a welcome distraction from the rigors of writing.

Java Programming

From the Beginning

1 Getting Started

Before you start writing programs in Java, you'll first need to learn a few basic concepts about the development of software. This chapter begins with a look at the role of software in a computer system and how humans interact with software. We'll then see how programs are built out of algorithms and data, and how algorithms are expressed. From there, we'll examine the concept of high-level languages, find out how programs written in a high-level language are executed, and see why Java is a good language to learn. Then, we'll look at the process of developing programs from beginning to end. The chapter ends with a discussion of what knowledge you'll need to have before proceeding to Chapter 2.

Objectives

- Understand the difference between hardware and software.
- Learn two different ways of interacting with a program: via a graphical user interface and via a text-based interface.
- Learn what an algorithm is and how algorithms are expressed.
- Learn how computers store data.
- Learn what a variable is.
- Understand the difference between machine language and high-level languages.
- Learn how a program is executed once it's been written.
- Find out why Java is a good language to learn.
- See what the entire programming process looks like.

1.1 What Do Computers Do?

When you sit down at your computer and crank up your favorite word processor or try out the latest game, you probably don't give much thought to the complex interactions taking place inside your computer. That's good, of course. Computers are among the most complex systems ever built by humans. If it were necessary to understand every aspect of them in order to use them, most people would never make the effort.

As a software developer, however, you'll need to know a lot more about computers than the average person. Fortunately, it's not hard to learn the basics of how a computer system operates.

We'll start with the computer on your desk. You may think of it as a single device, but it's actually a *computer system:* an integrated collection of hardware and software components.

Hardware refers to the electronics inside your computer. Hardware is tangible: it has mass and occupies space. *Software* consists of programs that tell the hardware what to do. Without software, your computer would be nothing more than an expensive paperweight. Unlike hardware, software has no mass and occupies no space. Software is like the words printed in a book—both are intellectual properties, not physical entities.

Some computer systems are embedded within other objects. For example, most modern automobiles contain embedded computers that monitor fuel consumption, control braking, and perform other valuable tasks. These types of computers—called *embedded systems*—are now a part of everyday life, and they're certain to become even more common in the future.

Other computer systems are intended for direct use by humans. (We'll refer to a person who's interacting with a computer system as a *user.*) Some systems support multiple simultaneous users, while others are limited to one user at a time. Systems in the latter category are usually called *personal computers,* although high-end single-user systems are often called *workstations.*

Personal Computers

Although personal computers are ubiquitous today, they haven't been around that long. When the computer industry was established in the early 1950s, the only computers you could buy were the size of a room. These *mainframe* computers dominated for decades, although smaller *minicomputers* started becoming popular during the late 1960s. The personal computer was developed in the mid-1970s. There were a number of early manufacturers, with Apple Computer being the most successful. The personal computer began to conquer the business world in the early 1980s, when IBM Corporation began selling the IBM Personal Computer. (The term "personal computer" is now used in a generic sense.)

Hardware

Most of the hardware in a computer system falls into one of three categories:

- *Processors.* The *central processing unit,* or *CPU,* is the "brains" of a computer system. The CPU is usually a single chip. The biggest CPU manufacturers are Intel and Motorola. In addition to the CPU, a computer system may contain additional, more-specialized processors, such as a graphics processor or a processor that performs certain types of arithmetic.

- *Memory.* Memory gives the computer the ability to remember (or, as we'll say, *store*) information. Some types of memory store information for a relatively brief period of time. A computer's *main memory,* or *RAM (random-access memory),* stores information only as long as the power is turned on. (We say that RAM is *volatile.*) Other types of memory can store information indefinitely, even when the computer is turned off. *ROM (read-only memory)* falls into this category, as do hard disks, floppy disks, and other storage media. Main memory is of particular interest because that's where a program is stored (along with its data) as it executes.

- *Peripheral devices.* As their name suggests, *peripheral devices* lie on the edges of the computer system. Their job is to provide a connection, or *interface,* to the world outside the computer system. Peripheral devices include keyboards, mice, monitors, printers, and modems.

In other words, a processor **processes** information, memory **stores** information, and peripheral devices **receive** information from the user or **send** information to the user. When you edit a document, for example, your computer system collects information from the keyboard and mouse, representing your commands and the text that you're entering. That information is processed by the CPU, which decides what your actions mean and updates the document accordingly. The document itself is stored in main memory and, if you save the document, on disk as well. When the document is complete, you might decide to print a copy, which causes the system to send the document to a printer.

Software

Software consists of *programs* that instruct the hardware how to perform operations. A program is simply a step-by-step set of instructions that tells a computer what to do.

Most software falls into one of two categories:

- *Operating systems.* An operating system is a rather large and elaborate collection of programs that interact directly with the computer's hardware. Common operating systems include DOS, Windows, MacOS, and Unix. (Linux, which is becoming increasingly popular, is a version of Unix.)

- *Applications.* An application is a program designed to perform a useful task for a human. For example, a word processing program is an application, and so is a program that allows a person to draw pictures, send electronic mail, or play a game. Applications include software development tools—programs that are used to develop other programs.

An operating system serves as a bridge between hardware and applications. It provides services that most applications will need: obtaining input from the keyboard and mouse, displaying text and graphics on the screen, storing data in files, sending data to the printer, and so on. Applications are then much easier to write because they don't need to deal with such low-level details. When an application needs to interact with the hardware, it sends a request to the operating system, which performs the operation on behalf of the application.

We can visualize the hardware as the core of a computer system. The operating system is a layer that surrounds the core, and the applications form another layer around the operating system:

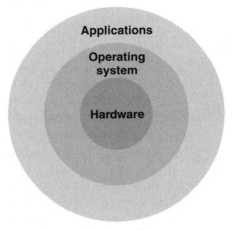

The combination of an operating system and a particular type of CPU is often called a *platform*. For example, Windows running on an Intel CPU is a platform. (This particular platform is so common that it's often shortened to just "Wintel.") The concept of a platform is an important one because software usually works only on a single platform. Making it run on a different platform can require a significant amount of work. (As we'll see later, one of the things that makes Java such an intriguing language is that Java programs—at least in theory—will run on multiple platforms without change.)

Most of the time, a computer system has only one operating system but many applications. The operating system is often preinstalled when a computer system is purchased, and it's not often changed, although it may be upgraded occasionally. Applications, on the other hand, are usually installed by the user, who can remove them and install new ones at any time.

An operating system often has a number of different versions, which can differ considerably. Common versions of Windows, for example, include Windows 3.1, Windows 95, Windows 98, Windows NT, Windows 2000, Windows CE, and whatever new versions Microsoft has released since this book was published. Applications are usually designed for one particular version of the operating system. Applications written for an older version of an operating system will often—but not always—work properly with a newer version.

Review Questions

1. An _____ _____ [two words] is a computer system that's part of some other device, such as an automobile or a washing machine.

2. Most of the hardware in a personal computer falls into one of three categories. The CPU and other processors represent one of these categories. What are the other two?

3. Operating systems constitute one major category of software. What is the other major category?

4. The combination of an operating system and a particular type of CPU is often called a _____.

1.2   Ways of Interacting with Computers

Most applications need to communicate, or "interface," with the user by displaying information for the user to see and accepting commands from the user. There are two primary types of user interfaces: *graphical user interfaces* and *text-based interfaces.* Let's take a look at the differences between these two types of interfaces. I'll use Windows as an example, but the principles are the same for other platforms.

Graphical User Interfaces

Most applications now rely on a *graphical user interface,* or *GUI* (pronounced "gooey") built out of visual components. When such a program is run, it displays a *window* on the screen. For example, if we run Microsoft Word—a word processor—we'll see a window similar to the one at the top of the next page. This window is composed of thousands of tiny *pixels* (picture elements), each with its own color. (The exact appearance of the window depends on the version of Word; your version may display a window that's somewhat different.)

Within a GUI window are visual components that display information to the user and (in most cases) allow the user to perform an action. In the Word window, we see the following components:

- *Buttons.* This program has two rows of buttons. Each represents a particular command, which can be selected by pointing at the button using the mouse and then clicking a mouse button. Usually the most common commands are assigned buttons.

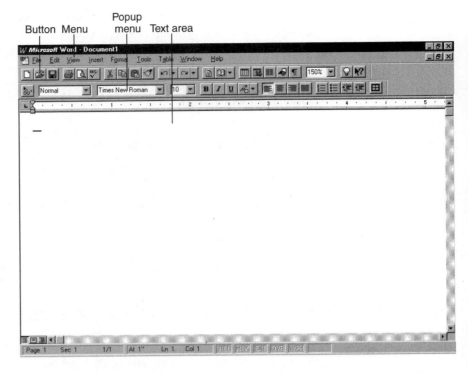

- **Menus.** Most programs have so many commands that there isn't enough room for each one to have a button. Instead, the user must click on one of the words listed at the top of the window. Doing so causes a menu of commands to appear. The user can then choose one of the commands from the menu by clicking a mouse button.

- **Popup menus.** In some cases, the user is allowed to make a choice from among a list of possibilities. One of Word's popup menus allows the user to choose a particular typeface (font). The user presses the tiny arrow button at the right side of the menu to view the choices and then selects one with the mouse.

- **Text areas.** The empty space in the middle of the window is a text area. The user can display a document here and make changes to it.

Performing certain actions will cause other windows to appear. These windows, known as *dialog boxes* or *dialogs,* are used to display information to the user and/or accept input from the user. For example, if we select the Open command from the File menu or simply click on the second button from the left, we'll see the dialog box shown at the top of the next page. This particular type of dialog box is called a *file dialog box* or a *file dialog.* A file dialog allows the user to choose a file name, either by typing it or by "browsing" the computer's disk drives and then making a selection.

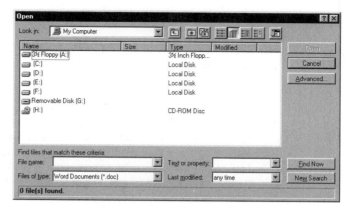

Basic window operations include:

- *Minimizing.* Clicking on the 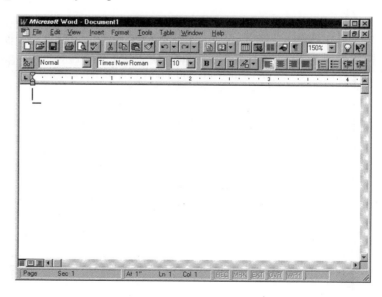 button makes a window disappear temporarily from the screen. In Windows, an icon representing the window appears in the taskbar, which is normally located at the bottom of the screen. By clicking on this icon, the user can later restore the window.

- *Maximizing.* Clicking on the ▢ button causes a window to expand to its maximum size.

- *Restoring.* Clicking on the ▣ button causes a window to return to its original size (before it was maximized).

- *Closing.* Clicking on the ☒ button closes a window.

For example, restoring the Microsoft Word window shown earlier has the following result on my computer:

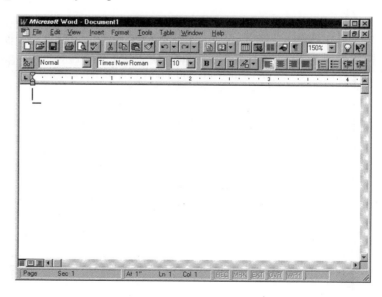

Notice that the window can't be reduced further without losing space for some of the buttons at the top.

Origin of the Graphical User Interface

Graphical user interfaces—as we know them—were developed during the 1970s at Xerox Corporation's Palo Alto Research Center (PARC). Researchers there developed the first workstation computer, the Xerox Alto. Unlike most computers of that era, the Alto was designed for a single person to use. The Alto had a high-resolution display that could show images as well as text. To allow the user to work with more than one program at a time, Xerox researchers came up with the idea of displaying multiple windows on the screen. Windows not currently displayed at their full size were represented by icons. To make it easier for the user to interact with the interface, a mouse was added. The result was quite similar to the graphical user interfaces of today.

Graphical user interfaces weren't an immediate success. Xerox's attempt to sell computers with graphical user interfaces was a failure. Apple Computer, headed by Steve Jobs at the time, saw the advantages of the GUI approach and incorporated it into a computer called the Lisa, which also flopped. Fortunately, Apple tried again and made a success of the Macintosh, the first widely used computer to support a graphical user interface. Users of the IBM Personal Computer and its clones had to wait a while longer, until Microsoft Corporation developed Windows, a graphical user interface for DOS users. Even then, many DOS users derided the GUI approach, referring to it as a WIMP (Windows, Icons, Mouse, Pointer) interface. Today, of course, graphical user interfaces are dominant, to the point that many users are able to avoid text-based interfaces entirely.

Text-Based Interfaces

Before the advent of graphical user interfaces, programs used a ***text-based interface,*** in which all input and output consisted of characters. In a text-based interface, no graphics are displayed, and user commands are entered from the keyboard. Programs that are written for DOS usually rely on a text-based interface.

Text-based programs are normally run from a ***command line.*** The operating system "prompts" the user to enter a command, which is then executed by the operating system. A command could represent a "built-in" operating system capability (listing the files in a directory, for example), or it could be a request to execute a program installed (or written) by the user. If the user enters the name of a program, the operating system will "load" the program and start it running.

The form of the prompt varies, depending on the operating system. In Unix and its variants, such as Linux, the prompt is often—but not always—a percent sign:

%

In DOS, the prompt is a > character, preceded by a letter indicating which disk drive is the "current" one:

```
C:>
```

The DOS prompt is often configured to display the "current directory" as well:

```
C:\WINDOWS>
```

Operating systems that provide a graphical user interface may still allow the user to run text-based programs from a command line. In Windows, for example, the user can open a "DOS window," which allows programs to be run from a DOS-like command line. Here's what a DOS window looks like:

A DOS window is normally capable of displaying up to 25 lines, with each line limited to 80 characters. Several DOS windows can be open at a time, which can be quite convenient.

We can run a text-based program within a DOS window by simply typing the name of the program. For example, DOS provides a program named `edit` that can edit files. To run the program, we would type `edit` and press the Enter key. The DOS window would now have the appearance shown at the top of the next page. The `edit` program may look "graphical," but it's still considered to be a text-based application. The lines that you see are actually formed out of special characters.

Java supports the creation of both GUI programs and text-based programs. We'll start off with text-based programs in Chapter 2. By Chapter 6, we'll begin to write programs that display their output in a window. In Chapter 12, we'll start to write full GUI programs.

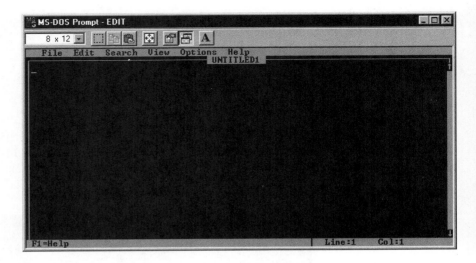

Review Questions

1. A window is composed of thousands of tiny _____.

2. In GUI programs, messages to the user (either displaying information or asking for input) are often displayed in separate windows. What are these windows called?

3. Which company was the first to create graphical user interfaces similar to the ones we use today?

4. Text-based programs are usually run from a _____ _____ [two words].

1.3   What Is Programming?

In a nutshell, ***programming*** means writing down a series of instructions that tell a computer what you want it to do. These instructions have the following properties:

- Computation proceeds in discrete steps.
- Each step is precisely defined.
- The order in which steps are performed may be important.

A set of instructions with these properties is said to be an ***algorithm.*** The steps in an algorithm can be short and simple, but they need not be:

- Some steps may involve a series of smaller steps.
- Some steps may involve making decisions.
- Some steps may repeat.

Algorithms are common in the real world. A cooking recipe is an algorithm, and so is a set of instructions that explains how to build a bookcase or establish an account with America Online.

A Real-World Algorithm

Here's an example of a real-world algorithm, taken from *Joy of Cooking* (1975 edition), a classic cookbook. The algorithm describes how to make Hollandaise sauce.

Melt slowly and keep warm:
   1/2 cup butter
Barely heat:
   1 1/2 tablespoons lemon juice, dry sherry, or tarragon vinegar
Have ready a small saucepan of boiling water and a tablespoon with which to measure it when ready. Place in the top of a double boiler over—not in—hot water:
   3 egg yolks
Beat the yolks with a wire whisk until they begin to thicken. Add:
   1 tablespoon boiling water
Beat again until the eggs begin to thicken. Repeat this process until you have added:
   3 more tablespoons water
Then beat in the warm lemon juice. Remove double boiler from heat. Beat the sauce well with a wire whisk. Continue to beat while slowly adding the melted butter and:
   1/4 teaspoon salt
   A few grains cayenne
Beat until the sauce is thick. Serve at once.

Let's reformat the recipe and number the steps:

1. Melt slowly and keep warm: 1/2 cup butter.
2. Barely heat: 1 1/2 tablespoons lemon juice, dry sherry, or tarragon vinegar.
3. Have ready a small saucepan of boiling water and a tablespoon with which to measure it when ready.
4. Place in the top of a double boiler over—not in—hot water: 3 egg yolks.
5. Beat the yolks with a wire whisk until they begin to thicken. Add: 1 tablespoon boiling water.
6. Beat again until the eggs begin to thicken. Repeat this process until you have added: 3 more tablespoons water.
7. Then beat in the warm lemon juice.
8. Remove double boiler from heat.
9. Beat the sauce well with a wire whisk. Continue to beat while slowly adding the melted butter and: 1/4 teaspoon salt; a few grains cayenne.
10. Beat until the sauce is thick.
11. Serve at once.

This recipe satisfies most of our requirements for an algorithm:

■ It involves discrete steps.

■ Each step is precisely defined—more or less. Several require the cook's judgment: What does "melt slowly" or "barely heat" mean?

■ The order of the steps matters. Still, we have some leeway. We could heat the lemon juice before melting the butter, for example. (Most computer algorithms also contain some flexibility.)

You'll also note that some steps require making decisions (step 2, for example, requires us to decide whether to use lemon juice, dry sherry, or tarragon vinegar) and repeating actions (steps 5, 6, 7, 9, and 10 require beating the mixture until some condition has been met).

Although this recipe is detailed enough for an experienced cook, it might pose problems for a novice. A computer is the ultimate novice—it does exactly what you tell it to do, even if you tell it to do something that's blatantly wrong. For that reason, our "recipes" (algorithms) will need to be much more precise than a *Joy of Cooking* recipe.

Computer Algorithms

Computer algorithms often involve obtaining input, performing a calculation, and producing output. Let's consider a simple problem that can be solved by a computer: converting a Fahrenheit temperature to Celsius. Here are the steps that we might use:

1. Display a message asking the user to enter a Fahrenheit temperature.
2. Obtain the input entered by the user.
3. Convert the user's input into numerical form.
4. Calculate the equivalent Celsius temperature, using the formula

    $C = (F - 32) \times (5 / 9)$
5. Convert the Celsius temperature into character form and display the result.

I've divided the algorithm into discrete steps. Most are reasonably precise, although it's not clear exactly how we're going to display information to the user and obtain the user's input. That will depend on what type of program we eventually write. In a GUI application, input usually takes the form of clicking a button, making a choice from a menu, or typing characters into a box. In a text-based application, input comes from the keyboard.

Another issue that's a bit fuzzy is step 3: converting the user's input to numerical form. What action do we take if the input is not in the form of a number? It would be nice to assume that users never make mistakes, but that's rarely the case in the real world. We'll have to decide whether the algorithm should stop at that point, or whether it should inform the user of the problem and ask for new input.

Expressing Algorithms

There are a number of ways to express algorithms; we'll use three of them in this book:

- *Natural languages.* Algorithms can be written in a natural (human) language—recipes in a cookbook are expressed in this way. The advantage of natural language is that anyone who understands that language can read the algorithm. However, natural language often lacks the precision that we'll need for expressing algorithms. Also, computers have trouble understanding natural language (although they're getting better at it!).

- ***Programming languages.*** In order for a computer to be able to execute our algorithm, we'll need to express it in a programming language. Programming languages provide the necessary precision that we'll need, and they're simple enough for computers to understand. (Whether they're simple enough for humans to understand is another matter.)

- ***Pseudocode.*** Pseudocode is a mixture of natural language and a programming language. An algorithm written in pseudocode is more precise than one written in natural language but less precise than one written in a programming language. On the other hand, a pseudocode algorithm is often easier to read (and to write) than one expressed in a programming language.

We'll often use pseudocode to express an algorithm first, so that we can focus on getting the algorithm correct. Later, we'll convert the pseudocode to a program in an actual programming language.

Review Questions

1. Most recipes found in cookbooks wouldn't be suitable as computer algorithms. Why not?

2. Algorithms can be expressed in a natural language, such as English. List two other ways to express algorithms.

1.4 Storing Data

The algorithms that we're interested in don't make dinner; instead, they manipulate data. The term ***data*** refers to information, particularly information that's stored in a uniform and systematic fashion. Our Fahrenheit-to-Celsius algorithm deals with several items of data, including a Fahrenheit temperature and its Celsius equivalent. Both are numbers, so let's consider for a moment how numbers are stored inside a computer.

Humans usually write numbers in ***decimal*** (base 10), using the ***digits*** 0 through 9. Computers, on the other hand, store numbers in ***binary*** (base 2). In binary, numbers consist of ***bits*** (binary digits), each of which is either 0 or 1. Inside a computer, each number, such as –97 or 31.125, is represented by a fixed number of 0s and 1s. Not all computers encode numbers the same way, but the following example is typical of many modern computers:

–97   11111111111111111111111110011110
31.125   01000001111110010000000000000000

The encoding scheme for integers (such as –97) is different from the one for nonintegers (such as 31.125). Numbers that contain a decimal point, such as 31.125, are often called *floating-point numbers,* because they're stored in a form of scientific notation that allows the decimal point to "float." Sections 9.2 and 9.3 discuss in greater detail how numbers are stored. The key thing to remember for now is that numbers are stored in binary, using a fixed number of bits.

Computers must be able to store character data as well. Each character is assigned a numeric code. This code, of course, is stored in binary. There are several codes in common use for representing characters; the one that Java uses is named *Unicode.* In Unicode, each character has a 16-bit code assigned to it. For example, the name "Susan Cole" would be represented by the following Unicode values:

S	0000000001010011
u	0000000001110101
s	0000000001110011
a	0000000001100001
n	0000000001101110
space	0000000000100000
C	0000000001000011
o	0000000001101111
l	0000000001101100
e	0000000001100101

Note that the space is considered to be a character.

A single bit doesn't contain much information, so most computers group bits into larger units called *bytes,* which usually contain eight bits. A number typically occupies four bytes (32 bits). A Unicode character occupies two bytes (16 bits).

Variables

Our Fahrenheit-to-Celsius algorithm needs to store three items of data:

> The input entered by a user
> The Fahrenheit temperature
> The Celsius temperature

Locations that are used to store data within a program are known as *variables.* Variables are given names by the programmer. We can choose whatever names we want, subject to the rules of the programming language.

It's best to choose a name that suggests what data the variable stores. For example, we might store the Fahrenheit temperature in a variable named `fahrenheit-Temperature`, `fahrenheitTemp`, or just `fahrenheit`. Shorter names are usually less descriptive and therefore undesirable. `fahr` would be worse than `fahrenheit` (what the heck does "fahr" mean, anyway?), and `f` would be worse still. Using a name that's completely unrelated to the value that it represents (such as `a` or `x`) would be in unspeakably poor taste; names such as these provide no useful information to anyone who might read the program in the future.

Avoid variable names that have more than one obvious interpretation. For example, `temp` wouldn't be a good name for a variable that stores a temperature, because `temp` could also mean "temporary." In fact, programmers often use `temp` as the name of a variable that will be used only temporarily. Also, it's not clear whether a variable named `temp` would store a Fahrenheit temperature or a Celsius temperature.

> When choosing a name for a variable, pick one that suggests what data the variable stores. Avoid names that are too short, are unrelated to the variable's value, or have more than one obvious interpretation.

Each variable will store a particular type of data. In the Fahrenheit-to-Celsius algorithm, the user's input will be a sequence of characters. The Fahrenheit and Celsius temperatures, on the other hand, will be numbers, possibly with digits after the decimal point.

Let's use the names `userInput`, `fahrenheit`, and `celsius` for the variables that we'll need in the Fahrenheit-to-Celsius algorithm. Here's what the algorithm looks like with the variables added:

1. Display a message asking the user to enter a Fahrenheit temperature.
2. Obtain the input entered by the user and store it into `userInput`.
3. Convert `userInput` into numerical form and store the result into `fahrenheit`.
4. Calculate the equivalent Celsius temperature using the formula
   `celsius = (fahrenheit − 32) × (5 / 9)`
5. Convert the value of `celsius` to character form and display the result.

Review Questions

1. In programming, numbers that contain a decimal point are called _____ numbers.

2. What is the name of the code that Java uses to represent characters?

3. Most modern computers group bits into larger units called _____, which typically contain eight bits.

4. Locations that store data are called _____.

1.5 Programming Languages

So far, we've described algorithms in English with the help of an occasional mathematical formula. That's not good enough for a computer, however. In order to create working programs, we'll need to express our algorithms in a highly precise language that's specifically designed for computers.

Every computer comes with such a language, known as ***machine language.*** Which machine language your computer supports depends on the type of CPU installed in it. Intel CPUs understand one language, Motorola CPUs use another, and so on. (The language used by different CPUs from the same manufacturer is often similar, although not exactly the same. For example, programs written for Intel's 486 CPU will run on a Pentium CPU, but not all Pentium programs will run on a 486.) Although it's possible to write programs in machine language, that's not what programmers typically do. Machine language is extremely primitive, making it difficult to write even simple programs.

Instead, most programmers use ***high-level languages*** that aren't tied to a particular computer. There are a number of high-level languages in common use; here are a few you may have heard of:

- *Ada* (named for Ada Lovelace, a 19th-century protégée of Charles Babbage, who invented a mechanical computer). Developed in the late 1970s for the U.S. Department of Defense, Ada is now widely used in the defense and aerospace industries.

- *BASIC* (Beginner's All-purpose Symbolic Instruction Code). Developed in the 1960s for programming novices, BASIC is now widely used for developing commercial applications. Many dialects of BASIC exist, of which Microsoft's Visual Basic is the most popular.

- *C.* Developed by Bell Laboratories in the 1970s in conjunction with the Unix operating system, C is often used for programs that need to be very fast or run in a limited amount of memory.

- *C++.* Developed during the 1980s at Bell Laboratories, C++ is a more modern, "object-oriented" version of C.

- *COBOL* (COmmon Business-Oriented Language). Developed in the early 1960s for business applications, COBOL has long been a mainstay of the business world.

- *FORTRAN* (FORmula TRANslation). Developed by IBM in the 1950s, FORTRAN was the first widely successful high-level programming language.

- *Pascal* (named after Blaise Pascal, a 17th-century mathematician and inventor of the first calculator). Designed by Swiss computer scientist Niklaus Wirth in the early 1970s, Pascal became the leading language for teaching computer science during the 1980s.

The high-level language that we're interested in, of course, is Java. Historically, it takes a number of years for a new language to gain widespread popularity. Java was the first exception to this rule. Within a year after its introduction in 1995, Java became one of the best-known programming languages on the planet. Java is famous for allowing Web developers to write cool "applets"—small programs embedded in Web pages. But Java's significance goes beyond that, as we'll see later.

History of Java

Java was developed by Sun Microsystems, a company famous for its Unix workstations and Internet servers. Around 1990, Sun began a project to develop software for consumer electronics. After examining popular languages of the day, including C and C++, Sun decided that a new language was needed. James Gosling, one of Sun's top software designers, created a language named Oak.

With the emergence of the Internet in the early 1990s, it became apparent that Oak would be suitable for Internet applications. Oak was given the more-marketable name "Java" in January 1995. The name was coined by Kim Polese, a Sun marketing person. Java isn't an acronym, by the way; the name was chosen because it's short and suggests a "hot" product.

Java was officially announced in May 1995. It immediately became popular, in part because of Sun's decision to make development tools available via the Internet at no charge. Another factor in Java's rapid acceptance was Netscape's decision to include Java support in version 2.0 of its popular Navigator browser. Before the end of 1995, Web users worldwide could use Navigator to view Java applets.

The first official release of Java occurred in February 1996, when Sun made available version 1.0 of the Java Development Kit, a collection of software tools used to write Java programs. Version 1.1 followed in 1997; version 1.2 (also known as Java 2) appeared in late 1998.

Writing and Executing a Program

Writing a program in a high-level language requires creating a file (or, in the case of a larger program, multiple files) containing *source code*—the program in a human-readable form. Source code is not *executable*—there is no direct way for a computer to follow the commands that it contains. *Executing* (or *running*) the program requires special software.

`Q&A`

There are two approaches to executing a program:

- *Compilation.* The program's source code is given to a program called a *compiler.* The compiler checks that the source code is valid (obeys the rules of the programming language) and translates it to machine instructions for a particular type of CPU. The compiled program is stored in a file, and it can be run as many times as desired. There's no need to compile the program a second time unless changes are made to it.

- *Interpretation.* The program's source code is given to a program known as an *interpreter.* The interpreter executes the program without first translating it to machine instructions (although the interpreter most likely will translate the program to some internal form). The interpreter itself is normally a compiled program, so it can execute machine instructions corresponding to the source code.

`Q&A`

Java employs a combination of the two techniques. Before a Java program can be executed, it must first be compiled. The compiler translates the original program

Q&A

into *bytecode instructions* for a computer called the *Java Virtual Machine.* The resulting *bytecode program* is then executed by an interpreter. The interpreter reads the bytecodes, determines which instructions they represent, and then executes those instructions. (The word "virtual" in Java Virtual Machine refers to the fact that this computer doesn't need to exist in hardware form. Instead, we can use software—the Java interpreter—to simulate its behavior.)

One advantage of Java's approach is that programs don't need a particular CPU or operating system. All that's needed is the interpreter, which has to be written once for each platform on which Java programs will need to run. Interpreters for all platforms should behave the same, because they're based on the published specifications for the Java Virtual Machine.

Review Questions

1. What high-level language was developed during the 1960s to teach programming to beginners?

2. The original, human-readable version of a program is called _____ _____ [two words].

3. Executing a Java program involves the use of: (a) a compiler, (b) an interpreter, or (c) both.

4. Java programs are translated to bytecode instructions for the _____ _____ _____ [three words].

1.6 Why Java?

With so many programming languages in existence, why start with Java? Why not learn C++, a language that's currently much more widely used than Java? It turns out that many of the properties that make Java a popular Internet language also make it a good language for learning to program. Let's look at some of these properties.

- *Simple.* Java is similar to C++, but much simpler. Because of the similarity between the two languages, knowing Java will give you a head start on learning C++. Although Java is smaller than C++, it's still more complicated than a lot of programming languages; learning Java isn't a trivial matter. Fortunately, you don't need to understand every aspect of Java in order to be able to write programs that are interesting and useful. Java is a good language to learn incrementally, piece by piece, over a period of time.

- *Object-oriented.* Java is an object-oriented language; programs manipulate *objects.* (An object is a collection of related data along with operations on that data.) C++ is object-oriented as well, but Java is closer to being a "pure" object-oriented language. As an object-oriented language, Java offers a number of advantages, including the ability to reuse existing programs to a much greater extent than is possible in older, non-object-oriented languages.

- *Distributed.* Java programs have the ability to retrieve information from across the Internet and interact with programs on other machines. Java programs can load files from anywhere on the Internet, including files containing graphics and sound.

- *Robust.* Java programs are more "robust" than those written in most other languages, such as C++. In a robust program, a programming error will not completely cripple the program or compromise the system on which it runs.

- *Architecture-neutral.* Java programs are platform-independent; they can run on any computer and operating system that supports the Java Virtual Machine. Software companies normally write different versions of their products for different platforms. One of Java's big attractions for these companies is the ability to write a single version of each of their products, rather than a Windows version, a Macintosh version, a Unix version, and so forth. In particular, Java provides a platform-independent way to write GUI applications.

- *Portable.* All aspects of Java are fully defined, so a Java program will behave the same on any platform that supports Java. As a result, programs written in Java are completely *portable*—a claim that few programming languages can make.

- *Interpreted.* Java programs are executed by an interpreter, so it's relatively easy to find errors in a program. When a running program encounters a problem, the Java interpreter will display a meaningful message and, if necessary, stop the program.

- *Multithreaded.* Java is one of the few programming languages to support *multithreading* (or *multitasking*), with multiple "threads" executing simultaneously within a single program. Each thread can be performing a different task, possibly (but not necessarily) related to what other threads are doing. One major reason for including threads in Java is to improve performance. When one part of the program is idle (perhaps the thread that detects user input), other threads can be performing useful activities, thus improving the overall performance of the program. Idle time is often abundant in programs with graphical user interfaces, as the user studies what's on the screen before pressing a key or clicking a mouse button.

Review Questions

1. Which other popular programming language is similar to Java?

2. An _____ is a collection of related data along with operations on that data.

3. What does it mean to say that Java programs are "robust"?

4. What was a major reason for giving Java the ability to support multiple threads?

1.7 The Programming Process

Now that we understand the role of a programming language in the development of software, let's take a look at the process of writing a program, from initial conception to completion. Later chapters will explain these steps in more detail and show how they're accomplished using the Java programming language.

The programming process can be divided into seven steps:

1. *Write a specification for the program.* The **specification** (or "spec") for a program is a detailed description of what the program is supposed to do. For a simple program—like many of the ones in this book—a specification may be only a few sentences. For a full-scale commercial program, the specification may be hundreds, or even thousands, of pages long.

2. *Design the program.* Like other man-made artifacts, programs generally require a design. The process of designing a program is similar to the process an architect goes through when designing a building.

3. *Choose algorithms and decide how data will be stored.* Once a program has been designed, the programmer must decide how the program's data is to be stored and what types of algorithms will be needed to manipulate that data.

4. *Write the program.* Next, the program is written in a specific programming language (Java, in our case). Some algorithms needed for the program may be common enough that the programmer can borrow from published sources such as books and articles or, even better, reuse existing code.

5. *Compile the program.* The program is compiled to a lower-level language. (This step is skipped if the language is interpreted.)

6. *Execute the program.* The program can now be executed and checked for correct behavior.

7. *Debug the program.* Unless we're very lucky, executing the program will reveal problems (*bugs*), which will need to be fixed. Fixing a program involves locating the problem, changing the program, compiling the program, and then executing the program to see if the bug has been fixed.

Most of the time, there's an additional step: *maintenance.* The vast majority of programs are designed to be used repeatedly over a period of time. During this period, the program will need to be changed occasionally to fix bugs, add enhancements, or adapt to changes in the program's specification. Maintenance is often the costliest step in the programming process. One reason for the high cost of maintenance is that the people who originally wrote the program are often not the ones who will be maintaining it. To reduce the cost of maintenance, it's vital for the original developers of the program to design it well, write it carefully, and document what they did.

The Y2K Problem

The Year 2000 problem (or Y2K problem, as it's often called) is undoubtedly the biggest maintenance problem in the history of computers. In programs that work with dates, years are often stored as a series of characters. Prior to the 1990s, it was common for programs to use two characters for each year (1985 would be stored as 85, for example). As the year 2000 approached, there was great concern about widespread software failures, because programs that compare dates would be in danger of confusing 2000 with 1900. A huge amount of money (untold billions of dollars in the United States alone) was spent to repair programs with the Y2K problem. Of course, all this trouble and expense would have been avoided by a more-careful design when the program was originally written. All too many programmers believed that their programs would no longer be in use by the time 2000 rolled around.

For now, we'll focus primarily on choosing an algorithm and then writing, compiling, executing, and debugging a program. As our programs grow longer, we'll need to begin worrying more about specification and design.

Review Questions

1. What is the "specification" for a program?

2. What is the second step in the programming process, after the specification is written?

3. A problem that prevents a program from working correctly is called a _____.

4. After a program is finished and put into service, changes are often made to the program later. What is this process called?

1.8 What You Need to Know

Writing simple Java programs isn't hard, as we'll see in Chapter 2. However, before you get started, you'll need some basic knowledge about your computer and its operating system. In this section, I'll list the prerequisites that you need. If you lack any of these prerequisites, you'll need to brush up before proceeding further.

First, you need to understand what a file is and how to perform simple file operations on your platform. A *file* is simply a collection of related data. A file could hold an executable program, a document, an image, or almost anything else. In many operating systems, a file name includes an *extension* that indicates the type of data stored in the file. In Windows, for example, the extension `.exe` indicates that the file contains an executable program. The extension `.doc` indicates that the file contains a document. Image files end with a variety of extensions (including `.gif` and `.jpg`), depending on the way the image is stored.

Next, you need to know how to perform basic file operations:

- **Create.** You can create a file with an editor or word processor. (An *editor* is a program that can create or modify a file containing *text*—letters, digits, punctuation, and so on. A *word processor* is an editor with the ability to format text, such as centering lines or putting words in italics.)

- **Edit.** Once a file has been created and saved, it can later be edited (changed) by using an editor or word processor, which doesn't have to be the same one used to create the file.

- **Copy.** Copying a file involves creating a new file that contains the same data as the original file but has a different name.

- **Rename.** Renaming a file changes the name of an existing file without changing its contents or creating a copy of the file.

- **Delete.** When a file is no longer needed, it's a good idea to delete it. Deleting a file releases the disk space that was used to store the file; that space can be used in the future by another file.

You'll also need to be able to use *directories*. A directory is a place where files can be kept. (Directories are also known as *folders*, especially on graphically oriented platforms such as Windows and the Macintosh. The term "folder" suggests a manila folder capable of holding documents, and the icon that represents a folder often resembles a manila folder.) Directories are normally organized in a tree-like fashion, with a "root" directory that contains other directories as well as files. These directories may contain files and directories, which may contain files and directories, and so on. You'll need to know how to create a directory, how to move from one directory to another, and how to obtain a list of all files in a particular directory.

Finally, you need to know how to execute programs on your computer. In a GUI environment, programs are *executed* (or *launched*) by clicking on an icon that represents the program or by choosing the program from a menu. In a text-based environment, a program is executed by typing its name. If the program isn't in the current directory, it can still be executed as long as the operating system knows where to look for the program.

Review Questions

1. How do most operating systems keep track of what type of data is stored in a file?

2. What kind of program would be used to create a file containing text?

3. Directories are called _____ in some operating systems.

4. Describe the difference between launching a GUI program and launching a text-based program.

Q & A

Q: **Which is better: compilation or interpretation? [p. 17]**

A: Neither is inherently better; each has advantages and disadvantages. A compiled program has been translated to machine instructions for a particular CPU, so it will normally execute much faster than an interpreted program. On the other hand, using an interpreter to execute a program can provide more feedback if the program contains an error. Also, interpreted programs tend to be more portable than compiled programs.

Q: **How does an interpreter work? [p. 17]**

A: Most interpreters convert source code to some more-convenient internal form that we never see. In this form, a program consists of a series of simple instructions. After converting the source code to this form, the interpreter selects the first instruction and executes it. The interpreter then repeats the process for the next instruction, the one after it, and so on.

Q: **Since a Java program is compiled to bytecodes, does that mean that we can't create a "normal" executable file from a Java program? [p. 18]**

A: That's probably not a good idea, but it can be done with the right tools. Executable files are platform-dependent; creating one sacrifices the portability that is Java's hallmark.

Q: **When I run a program in a text-based environment, how does the operating system know where the program is located? [p. 22]**

A: Unix and Windows rely on an *environment variable* named `path` (or `PATH`). This variable stores a list of directories to be searched when the user attempts to execute a program. As long as the program is located in one of these directories, the operating system can find it. Appendix A discusses this issue in the context of installing the Java Development Kit.

Summary

- A computer system is an integrated collection of hardware and software components.
- The major hardware components are processors, memory, and peripheral devices.
- Most software falls into two categories: operating systems and applications.

- There are two major types of interfaces between a program and its user: graphical user interfaces (GUIs) and text-based interfaces.
- A GUI provides the user with visual components, many of which the user can interact with using the keyboard or mouse.
- In a text-based interface, only characters are displayed on the screen.
- An algorithm is a step-by-step procedure for solving a problem.
- Algorithms can be expressed in a number of ways, including natural languages, programming languages, and pseudocode.
- Computers store data as binary (base 2) numbers.
- Characters in Java are stored using the Unicode character code.
- In a computer program, data is stored in variables.
- Programs can be written in machine language (the native language of a particular CPU) or in a high-level language.
- There are two approaches to executing a program written in a high-level language: compilation and interpretation.
- A compiler translates the source code of a program to machine instructions for a particular type of CPU.
- An interpreter executes a program directly, without first translating it to machine instructions.
- Executing a Java program requires two steps: compiling the program, which translates it into bytecodes, and then using an interpreter to execute the bytecodes.
- Java has a number of advantages that make it an excellent language for a beginner to learn.
- The programming process begins with writing a specification for a program. The remaining steps are designing the program, choosing algorithms and deciding how data will be stored, writing the program, compiling the program, executing the program, and debugging the program. For most programs, there's an additional step: maintenance.

Exercises

Section 1.3

1. Find a real-life algorithm (if you can't think of any, look in a cookbook!). Number the steps in the algorithm. Do the steps need to be performed in any particular order? Do any of the steps involve making decisions? Are any of the steps repeated?

2. Develop algorithms for performing the following tasks. Break each task into small, clearly defined steps.
    (a) Copying a file from a floppy disk to a directory named `java` on your computer. (Start with inserting the disk into the computer's floppy disk drive.)
    (b) Purchasing a ticket at a movie theater. (Start with walking up to the ticket window.)
    (c) Making 10 photocopies of a one-page document.

Section 1.4

3. For each of the following variable names, indicate what is wrong with the name and show how it could be improved.

    (a) `n` (stores the name of a file)
    (b) `dstnc` (stores the distance between two cities)
    (c) `anninc` (stores an annual income)

4. Create good names for variables that will store the following data items.

    (a) A sales tax rate
    (b) A street address
    (c) The number of days in the current month

Section 1.5

5. Pick one of the programming languages mentioned in Section 1.5 and locate information about it in a book or on the Internet. What was the language's intended use? (In other words, what types of programs were to be written in the language?) Is the language normally compiled or interpreted? How widely used is the language at present?

Section 1.6

6. Java's basic properties were enumerated in a famous Sun Microsystems document, "The Java Language: An Overview," which is available on the Web at

    http://java.sun.com/docs/overviews/java/java-overview-1.html

    Read this document and put together a list of Java's properties that were *not* mentioned in Section 1.6.

Section 1.7

7. Write a specification for a program that obtains a month, day, and year from the user and displays the number of days from January 1 to the user's month and day. (Note that the answer may depend on the year, because of leap years.) Include detailed information about the format of the date entered by the user, and describe what the program will do if the date is illegal.

Section 1.8

8. Section 1.8 mentioned the `.exe`, `.doc`, `.gif`, and `.jpg` file extensions. List five other extensions that are in use on your own system. What does each extension signify?

9. List the editors and/or word processors that are installed on your system.

10. Put together a list of commands for performing the following actions on your system.

    (a) Copy a file.
    (b) Rename a file.
    (c) Delete a file.
    (d) List the files in a particular directory.

Answers to Review Questions

Section 1.1

1. Embedded system
2. Memory, peripheral devices
3. Applications
4. Platform

Section 1.2

1. Pixels
2. Dialog boxes
3. Xerox

	4.	Command line
Section 1.3	1.	They're not precise enough.
	2.	Programming languages, pseudocode
Section 1.4	1.	Floating-point
	2.	Unicode
	3.	Bytes
	4.	Variables
Section 1.5	1.	BASIC
	2.	Source code
	3.	(c)
	4.	Java Virtual Machine
Section 1.6	1.	C++
	2.	Object
	3.	A programming error will not completely cripple the program or compromise the system on which it runs.
	4.	To improve performance
Section 1.7	1.	A detailed description of what the program is supposed to do
	2.	Design the program
	3.	Bug
	4.	Maintenance
Section 1.8	1.	By the file's extension
	2.	An editor or word processor
	3.	Folders
	4.	In a GUI environment, programs are launched by clicking on an icon that represents the program or by choosing the program from a menu. In a text-based environment, a program is executed by typing its name.

2 Writing Java Programs

In this chapter, we'll see how to write, execute, and debug simple Java programs. Along the way, we'll find out how to make a program accept input from the user, perform calculations, and display output on the screen. Much of the chapter is devoted to developing good programming habits, with advice on choosing names, laying out programs, and including documentation in programs.

Be aware that learning Java takes time and practice, so don't be dismayed if some aspects of Java seem obscure at first. Later chapters provide more information about many of the topics introduced in this chapter.

Objectives

- Learn how to write simple programs.
- Learn how to enter, compile, and execute programs.
- Learn how to use comments to embed explanatory information in a program.
- Learn how a compiler divides a program into tokens.
- Learn how indentation and proper brace placement can improve the appearance of a program.
- Learn how to declare variables and assign them values.
- Learn about several Java types and their literals.
- Learn the rules for creating identifiers.
- Learn how to build expressions from variables, literals, and operators.
- Learn the unary and binary arithmetic operators.

- Learn how Java uses precedence and associativity rules to determine the meaning of an expression.
- Learn how to declare constants.
- Learn how to call methods and use values that they return.
- Learn about several common mathematical methods.
- Learn how to use `System.out.print` and `System.out.println` to display information on the screen.
- Learn how to read user input using the `SimpleIO` class.
- Learn how to use packages.
- Learn how to debug a program.

2.1   A Simple Java Program

It's now time—finally!—for our first Java program.

PROGRAM   **Printing a Message**

The following program displays the message `Java rules!` on the screen. (The line numbers at the left are not part of the program.)

JavaRules.java

```
1  // Displays the message "Java rules!"
2
3  public class JavaRules {
4    public static void main(String[] args) {
5      System.out.println("Java rules!");
6    }
7  }
```

This program will be stored in a file named `JavaRules.java`, with the J and R capitalized. (Java is very picky about such matters.) At the beginning of each program in this book, I've listed its file name in the left margin. If you'd like to experiment with these programs, there's no need to type them yourself; just download them from *http://knking.com/books/java/*.

Let's go through the program line by line to see how it's put together. Line 1 is a *comment.* It provides information that might be useful to someone reading the program. Otherwise, this line is irrelevant: the compiler ignores it, and it doesn't affect the program's behavior. In this book, I've put comments in *italics* to make them stand out from the other lines in a program.

Line 3 is the beginning of the actual program. A Java program consists of one or more *classes.* This program has only one class, which I've named `JavaRules`. When a program consists of a single class, the name of that class also serves as the name of the program. After the class name comes the { symbol (called a *left curly brace*). Java uses curly braces to mark the beginning and end of a related series of program lines. In this case, the left brace indicates the beginning of the `Java-Rules` class.

Line 4 is a bit hard to explain at this early stage, so I'm not even going to try. (See the Q&A at the end of the chapter if you simply *must* find out now.) All you need to know at this point is that line 4 is the beginning of a ***method***—a chunk of program code that can be executed later when the program is run. This particular method is named `main`. Methods can have any name we want; however, a method named `main` has a special property: it is executed automatically when the program is run. The left curly brace at the end of the line marks the beginning of the `main` method.

Finally, we come to the heart of the program. Line 5 is a command (or ***statement,*** in programming terminology). Statements specify actions to be performed when the program is later executed. This particular statement causes the message `"Java rules!"` to be displayed on the screen. A series of characters enclosed in double quotes is said to be a ***string.*** When strings are displayed, the double quotes are not shown.

`System.out` is Java's name for the standard place to display messages (normally the user's screen). `println` is a method that displays output; its name is an abbreviation for "print and advance to the next line." After it displays `Java rules!` on the screen, this method will move the cursor to the beginning of the next line.

Notice the `;` (semicolon) at the end of line 5. Java requires most statements to end with a semicolon (just as each complete English sentence ends with a period or other punctuation mark).

The `}` symbol on line 6 is called the ***right curly brace.*** A right curly brace marks the end of some Java construct. In this case, the brace ends the `main` method. Notice that I've indented the brace the same number of spaces as the first line of `main`. The right curly brace on line 7 marks the end of the `JavaRules` class.

Although this program may look intimidating, there's some good news. Most of it is "boilerplate" that we'll be able to use—with little or no change—in later programs.

Java Programs in General

From our simple `JavaRules` program, it's not clear what the general appearance of a Java program is. That's a long story—one that we'll spend most of this book on—but it's not hard to give a rough description.

The building blocks of a Java program are:

- ***Classes.*** A class is a collection of related variables and/or methods (usually both). A Java program consists of one or more classes.

- ***Methods.*** A method is a series of statements. Each class may contain any number of methods.

- *Statements.* A statement is a single command. Each method may contain any number of statements.

We can visualize a Java program as a hierarchy:

Review Questions

1. A _____ provides information that might be useful to someone reading a program.

2. A series of characters enclosed in double quotes is said to be a _____.

3. What does `println` stand for?

4. A Java program consists of classes. What do classes consist of?

2.2 Executing a Java Program

OK, so we've written our first Java program. How can we get the computer to execute the program? The answer to that question depends on our platform as well as what Java system we're using. The basic steps are the same in any case, but the details are different. Here are the steps involved in executing a Java program:

ASCII ➤ 9.4

- *Enter the program.* First, we'll need to enter the program into the computer, using an editor or word processor. The source code for a program needs to be stored in an ordinary human-readable file, often called a "text file" or "ASCII file." The name of the file must match the name of the program (including capitalization), and the extension on the file must be `.java`. For example, the `JavaRules` program must be put in a file named `JavaRules.java`.

- *Compile the program.* The Java compiler will check the program for obvious errors (such as misspelled words, missing semicolons, and braces that don't match). If the compiler finds any errors, it will reject the program, and we'll need to go back and edit it. If the compiler finds no errors, it will translate the program into bytecode instructions, which are left in a *class file.*

- *Run the program.* The last step is to run the interpreter for the Java Virtual Machine, specifying that it should execute the bytecode instructions in the class file that was created by the compiler.

The figure at the top of the following page illustrates the process of creating and executing a program.

If you have an integrated development environment, you can perform all three steps within the environment itself. On the other hand, if you're using Sun's Java Development Kit (JDK), you have no such environment. The JDK has an attractive

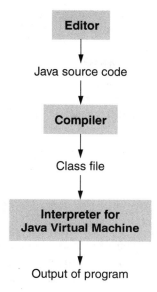

Output of program

price (it's free) and is easy to use, so that's what I'll discuss in this section. If you're not using the JDK, you'll need to read the documentation that comes with your Java system to find out how to perform the enter, compile, and run steps.

Integrated Development Environments

debuggers ➤ 2.12

An ***integrated development environment*** (IDE) is an integrated collection of software tools for developing and testing programs. A typical IDE includes at least an editor, a compiler, and a debugger. Some IDEs have other tools as well. One advantage of an IDE is that a programmer can write a program, compile it, and execute it, all without leaving the IDE. Another advantage is that the components of an IDE are designed to work together. For example, when the compiler detects an error in a program, it can arrange for the editor to highlight the line that contains the error. There are a number of IDEs for Java, including Borland's JBuilder and WebGain's Visual Café.

As a further simplification, I'm going to assume that you're working under Windows (sorry, Unix and Mac fans!). Consequently, my instructions will be Windows-specific, although the instructions for other platforms are similar. These instructions assume that the Java Development Kit is already installed on your computer. (See Appendix A for installation instructions.)

Entering a Java Program

The first step is to get the program into the computer. This step can be done in a number of ways. You can use any editor or word processor, including Notepad or

WordPad; if you use a word processor, be careful to save the file as a Text Document or as Text Only.

 Failing to save the program as text will cause errors during the compilation step. If you're not sure whether you saved the file correctly, try displaying it in a DOS window using the `type` command. If the file is in text form, it should look fine. If you see odd characters in the program, you've saved the file incorrectly.

You can also enter the program from a DOS window. Type `edit` to run the DOS `edit` program.

Compiling a Java Program

Compiling a program is done by running the Java compiler and specifying which file you want it to compile. In Windows, you'll need to open a DOS window in which to enter the command that runs the compiler. If you don't already have a DOS window visible on the screen, then do the following:

1. Click the **Start** button, which is usually located at the bottom left corner of the screen. A menu will appear.
2. Select **Programs** from the menu. A second menu will appear.
3. Select **MS-DOS Prompt** (or **Command Prompt**, in some versions of Windows) from the menu. A DOS window will open.
4. Use the `cd` (change directory) command to select the directory that contains the program. For example, if you've stored the `JavaRules.java` file in the directory `c:\myfiles\java\programs`, then you would enter

```
cd c:\myfiles\java\programs
```

To compile the program, type the following command in the DOS window:

```
javac JavaRules.java
```

`javac` is the name of the compiler that comes with the JDK. `JavaRules.java` is the name of the file containing the program.

 Be sure that the name of the file matches the name of the program, and be sure to include the file's extension. If the program is named `JavaRules`, then the file must be named `JavaRules.java`. The compiler will reject the program if its name doesn't match the file name. In particular, make sure that any letters that are capitalized in the program name are also capitalized in the file name.

If the compiler doesn't find any errors in the program, it will create a class file containing bytecode instructions. This file will have the same name as the program but with `.class` as the extension. For example, the bytecode instructions for the `JavaRules` program will be left in a file named `JavaRules.class`.

Running a Java Program

To run a program, you'll need to use the `java` interpreter, which is part of the JDK. `java` requires that the name of a class file be specified:

```
java JavaRules
```

(The `.class` extension *must* be omitted.) The class file must contain the byte-codes for a class with a `main` method.

Be careful not to type

```
java JavaRules.class
```

or

```
java JavaRules.java
```

The Java interpreter doesn't allow an extension after the program name.

Here's what you'll see in the DOS window when you compile and execute the `JavaRules` program:

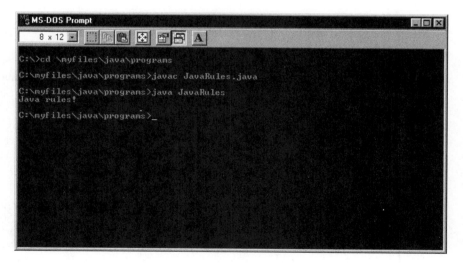

Using Multiple Windows

If you use `edit` to create and modify programs, it's a good idea to have two DOS windows open simultaneously. You can run `edit` in one window and use the other window to compile and test the program. That way, you won't have to leave the editor when compiling or testing.

It's also a good idea to enable the `doskey` utility by typing `doskey` when you go into a DOS window. `doskey` remembers previous commands that you've entered in that window. To repeat a command that you've entered previously, just press the up arrow key one or more times until you find the command, and then press Enter. You can even use the Backspace key to make changes to the command.

Review Questions

1. What does a Java class file contain?

2. The `javac` program is a compiler. What is the `java` program?

3. What command would we type to compile a program named `CourseAverage`?

2.3 Program Layout

Let's take a closer look at a couple of issues raised by our first program:

- Why do we put comments into programs, and what are the rules for doing so?
- How should we "lay out" a program? Does it matter where we put spaces and blank lines? Where should the curly braces go?

Comments

Although comments are ignored by the compiler, they are nonetheless an important part of every program. Comments provide information that's useful—even vital—for anyone who will need to read the program in the future. In most work environments, programs must be read by a number of people. These may be people working on the same team, or they may be people who have been given the program to maintain after the original author has left the organization. Even if you're writing a program strictly for your own amusement, comments are important. Without them, you may have trouble understanding the program after you put it aside for a while and then come back to it.

Most comments serve one of the following purposes:

- To document who wrote the program, when it was written, what changes have been made to it, and so on. The comments at the beginning of a commercial program may include a copyright notice, a list of restrictions on the program's use, and disclaimers to protect the program's owner from legal action. (It's amusing to read the comments in the demonstration programs that come with the Java Development Kit. Sun Microsystems prohibits anyone from using these programs "in a manner which is disparaging to Sun." Also, the comments note that the programs are not designed for controlling aircraft or nuclear facilities. Considering that the programs perform such tasks as making blinking text appear on the screen and playing tic-tac-toe, there seems to be little danger that they'll be used in such an inappropriate fashion!)

- To describe the behavior or purpose of a particular part of the program, such as a variable or method. This type of comment is important for someone who will need to understand how the program works and perhaps make changes to it.
- To describe how a particular task was accomplished, which algorithms were used, or what tricks were employed to get the program to work. In other words, the comment provides important information that might not be obvious to the reader.

Java gives us three ways to write comments. You've seen the first type already:

```
// Comment style 1
```

The comment begins with `//` and ends at the end of the line. I'll call this a "single-line comment."

The second type is enclosed between `/*` and `*/`:

```
/* Comment style 2 */
```

The advantage of style 2 is that comments can be many lines long:

```
/* Here's a long-winded comment that doesn't know when to
   stop; it just keeps rambling on and on and on until
   you're sick of reading it. */
```

I'll use the term "multiline comment" to refer to style 2.

The third type of comment starts with `/**` and ends with `*/`:

```
/** Comment style 3 */
```

This last style, known as a "doc comment," is special. Doc comments are designed to be extracted by a special program, `javadoc`, to produce on-line documentation for a program. I won't use doc comments in this book.

Be careful with multiline comments. Forgetting to terminate such a comment may cause the compiler to ignore part of your program. Consider the following example:

```
System.out.println("My");   /* forgot to close this comment...
System.out.println("cat");
System.out.println("has");  /* so it ends here */
System.out.println("fleas");
```

Because we've neglected to terminate the first comment, this example prints

```
My
fleas
```

The compiler ignores the middle two statements, which are inside a comment.

Many programmers prefer `//` comments to `/* ... */` comments, for several reasons:

- *Ease of use.* It's easier to type a // comment.
- *Safety.* Forgetting to terminate a /* ... */ comment is a common mistake. In many cases, the compiler won't notice the error.
- *Program readability.* If a program contains a long /* ... */ comment, it's possible that someone reading the program later might overlook the /* and */ symbols and think that what's inside the comment is actually part of the program.
- *Ability to "comment out" portions of a program.* During the development of a program, there may be times when we'll want to disable part of the program without removing it entirely. The easiest way to do so is by enclosing the part we don't want within a /* ... */ comment. (This technique is often called *commenting out.*) If the part that we're commenting out contains // comments, there's no problem. If it contains a /* ... */ comment, however, then we're in trouble, because Java prohibits this type of comment from being "nested."

Use // (single-line) comments rather than /* ... */ (multiline) comments.

Tokens

Before we can discuss program layout, we first need to understand what the compiler does when given a program to compile. Suppose that you were asked to read a document. You would start at the beginning of the document, look at the characters on the page, group them into words, and then collect the words into sentences. A Java compiler works much the same way. It begins compiling a program at the beginning. It groups the characters in the program into larger units, known as *tokens.* It then puts the tokens into larger groups (such as statements, methods, and classes).

Consider the JavaRules program, which is reproduced below:

```
// Displays the message "Java rules!"

public class JavaRules {
  public static void main(String[] args) {
    System.out.println("Java rules!");
  }
}
```

Here's what the program looks like after the compiler has divided it into tokens:

```
public   class   JavaRules   {   public   static   void   main   (
String   [   ]   args   )   {   System   .   out   .   println   (
"Java rules!"   )   ;   }   }
```

Altogether, there are 26 tokens in this program (count 'em!). The comment isn't a token; the compiler removes comments as it divides the program into tokens.

Notice that the compiler doesn't care how much space lies between tokens, or whether tokens are on different lines. To the compiler, the program is just a long series of tokens.

To avoid trouble, you need to follow two simple rules. First, be careful to leave at least one space between tokens that would otherwise merge together. The compiler would view the line

```
publicclassJavaRules {
```

as having just two tokens: `publicclassJavaRules` and `{`. Second, you can't put part of a token on one line and the other part on the next line:

```
pub
lic class JavaRules {
```

The compiler will treat the two pieces as separate tokens (`pub` and `lic`, in this case).

Indentation and Brace Placement

The compiler breaks a program into tokens anyway, so it doesn't really care how the program is laid out. As long as the tokens are in the proper order, the compiler is happy. That's good for us, because we're free to lay out a program so that it's easier for humans to understand.

Two important aspects of program layout are indentation and brace placement. Java programmers—as well as programmers in most other languages—use indentation to indicate nesting. An increase in the amount of indentation indicates an additional level of nesting. The `JavaRules` program consists of a *statement* nested inside a *method* nested inside a *class*. The following diagram illustrates this nesting:

```
public class JavaRules {

  public static void main(String[] args) {

    System.out.println("Java rules!");

  }

}
```

Although nearly all programmers agree that indentation is a good way to show nesting, there's considerable disagreement over how much to indent. My standard indentation is two spaces, because my programs need to fit within the confines of a book page. Most programmers use at least three spaces, and four is a common value. Here's what the `JavaRules` program would look like with an indentation of four spaces:

```
public class JavaRules {
    public static void main(String[] args) {
        System.out.println("Java rules!");
    }
}
```

Some people use eight spaces, but I don't recommend that practice: it makes lines so long that they become hard to read.

> Use three or four spaces as your standard amount of indentation. Always increase indentation by the same amount for each new level of nesting.

Programmers often use tabs to add indentation to a program, pressing the tab key once for a single indent, twice for a double indent, and so on. Tabs are easier to insert than spaces, but be careful: a program containing tabs may change appearance in different editors and may print differently on different printers. Many editors can convert tabs to spaces if you request this feature; doing so is a good idea.

Brace placement is another important issue. In the JavaRules program, I put each left curly brace at the end of a line. The matching right curly brace was then lined up with the first (nonblank) character on that line:

```
public class JavaRules {

  public static void main(String[] args) {

    System.out.println("Java rules!");

  }

}
```

Some programmers prefer to put left curly braces on separate lines:

```
public class JavaRules
{
  public static void main(String[] args)
  {
    System.out.println("Java rules!");
  }
}
```

The advantage of this placement scheme is that it's easier to verify by sight that left and right braces match up properly. The disadvantage is that program files become longer because of the additional lines. To avoid these extra lines, some programmers combine the line containing the left curly brace with the following line:

```
public class JavaRules
{ public static void main(String[] args)
  { System.out.println("Java rules!");
  }
}
```

The result is a bit too cluttered for my taste, but many programmers are happy with this style.

> There's no single "right" way to place curly braces. You'll need to experiment with various placements and see which one you're most comfortable with. As with many style issues, which placement scheme you choose is less important than picking one and using it consistently.

In a commercial environment, issues such as indentation and brace placement are often resolved by a "coding standard," which provides a uniform set of style rules for all programmers to follow.

Review Questions

1. How many kinds of comments are there in Java?

2. What symbol is used to indicate the beginning of a single-line comment in Java?

3. How many tokens does the following statement contain?

```
System.out.println("James Gosling");
```

4. Programmers use indentation to indicate _____ of one language construct inside another.

2.4 Using Variables

Section 1.4 discussed the importance of *variables* in the programming process. A variable is a location where a program can store an item of data for later use.

Declaring Variables

Java has an important rule concerning variables: *Every variable must be declared before it can be used.* Declaring a variable means informing the compiler of the variable's name and its properties. The most important of those properties is the variable's *type.* The type indicates what kind of data the variable will store. For example, int is a type in Java. Variables of type int can store integers (whole numbers).

A *variable declaration* has the following appearance:

- First comes the *type* of the variable we're declaring.
- Next comes the *name* of the variable.
- Finally, every variable declaration ends with a semicolon.

For example, the following declaration states that i is a variable of type int:

```
int i;  // Declares i to be an int variable
```

For convenience, Java lets us declare several variables at a time, provided that their names are separated by commas:

```
int i, j, k;
```

This example declares three variables—i, j, and k—each of which can store an integer. In many cases, it's better to declare variables one at a time, however. This practice makes it easier to change the program later, as well as leaving more space for a comment after each declaration.

Initializing Variables

Once a variable has been declared, we can begin using it to store data. A variable is given a value by using =, the ***assignment operator.*** For example, to give the variable i the value 0, we would use the following statement:

```
i = 0;
```

Be careful not to confuse the assignment operator with the = symbol in mathematics. The statement

```
i = 0;
```

doesn't say that i and 0 are equal; instead, it's a command that *changes* the value of i to 0. Also, make sure that the left side of an assignment is a single variable. Writing

```
i = j + k;
```

is fine, but writing

```
j + k = i;   // WRONG; left side must be a single variable
```

is not.

When we assign a value to a variable for the first time, we're said to be ***initializing*** the variable. Variables always need to be initialized before the first time their value is used. The Java compiler checks that variables declared in methods are initialized prior to their first use, rejecting any program that appears to violate this rule. (The compiler is very conservative, sometimes rejecting programs that *don't* violate the rule, but appear to.)

As a shortcut, Java allows variables to be initialized at the time they're declared. For example, the following statement declares i *and* gives i the value 0:

```
int i = 0;
```

We say that 0 is the ***initializer*** for i. If several variables are declared at the same time, each variable is allowed (but not required) to have its own initializer:

```
int i = 0, j, k = 1;
```

Here i has the value 0 and k has the value 1, but j has not been initialized yet.

Changing the Value of a Variable

The assignment operator can be used both to initialize a variable and to change the value of the variable later in the program. When a new value is assigned to a variable, the old value of the variable is lost, as the following example shows:

```
i = 1;  // Value of i is now 1
...
i = 2;  // Value of i is now 2
```

Be careful not to declare a variable more than once in a method. Writing

```
int i = 1;
...
i = 2;
```

is OK, because we're assigning a new value to an existing variable. Writing

```
int i = 1;
...
int i = 2;  // WRONG; i was previously declared
```

is illegal, because we're attempting to declare i a second time.

PROGRAM   ## Printing a Lottery Number

Here's a short program that uses a variable to store a lottery number.

Lottery.java

```
 1  // Displays the winning lottery number
 2
 3  public class Lottery {
 4    public static void main(String[] args) {
 5      int winningNumber = 973;
 6      System.out.print("The winning number ");
 7      System.out.print("in today's lottery is ");
 8      System.out.println(winningNumber);
 9    }
10  }
```

The first few lines of the program are essentially the same as in the JavaRules program. The first line that's different is line 5, which declares and initializes an integer variable named winningNumber.

Lines 6–8 display information on the screen. Two of these lines use System.out.print, while the last uses System.out.println. The only difference between print and println is that println advances to the next line after it's through printing. print, on the other hand, doesn't advance to the next line. Because the program prints three times before advancing to the next line, all the output will be on one line:

```
The winning number in today's lottery is 973
```

As this program shows, `println` (and `print`, as well) is capable of displaying a number as well as a character string. Both methods automatically convert the number to character form before displaying it.

Review Questions

1. What is the name of the = operator?

2. Suppose that `i` is a variable declared in a method. What happens if a statement tries to access the value of `i` (to print it, for example) before `i` has been initialized?

3. In the declaration
    ```
    int i = 0;
    ```
    we say that 0 is an _____.

2.5 Types

In Java, every variable has a type, which tells the compiler what kind of data the variable will store. In Section 2.4, all variables were declared to have `int` type, which means that they can store integers.

Java supports a variety of different types, which we'll learn more about in the chapters to come. For now, I'll simplify matters by discussing only four types:

- `int` — A variable of type `int` can store a single integer. The integer must lie between –2,147,483,648 and 2,147,483,647.

Q&A

- `double` — A variable of type `double` can store a single floating-point number. Floating-point numbers, unlike integers, may have digits after the decimal point. A floating-point number stored in `double` form can be as large as

float type ▸9.3

1.79×10^{308}. (Java has another floating-point type named `float`. `float` is slightly harder to use than `double`, so we won't discuss it until a later chapter.)

- `boolean` — A variable of type `boolean` can store one of two values: `true` or `false`.

Q&A

- `char` — A variable of type `char` can store a single character.

We've already seen examples of `int` variables. Here are examples showing how `double`, `boolean`, and `char` variables are declared:

```
double x, y;   // Declares x and y to be double variables
```

```
boolean b;    // Declares b to be a boolean variable
char ch;      // Declares ch to be a char variable
```

Notice that declarations always have the same form: first the type, then the variable name(s).

Literals

When we initialized an `int` variable in Section 2.4, we used a number such as 0 or 1. These are examples of ***literals***. A literal is a token that represents a particular number or other value. Literals, like variables, have specific types.

The following literals have `int` type:

```
0   297   30303
```

In English, we often use commas to punctuate large numbers. For example, we'd probably write 30,303 rather than 30303. Java, however, doesn't allow the use of commas in numeric literals. We'll also need to be careful not to exceed the maximum value for an `int` literal, which is `2147483647`.

`double` literals can be written in a variety of ways. For example, the number 48.0 could be written in any of the following ways (and many others as well):

```
48.0   48.   4.8e1   4.8e+1   .48e2   480e-1
```

The presence of the letter `e` indicates that the number is to be multiplied by 10 raised to the number after the `e` (the ***exponent***). For example, `4.8e1` represents 4.8×10^1 and `480e-1` represents 480.0×10^{-1}. A `double` literal is a single token, so it can't contain spaces.

The only `boolean` literals are `true` and `false`. `char` literals are enclosed within single quotes:

```
'a'   'z'   'A'   'Z'   '0'   '9'   '%'   '.'   ' '
```

The last literal, `' '`, represents the space character.

Literals are often used as initializers:

```
double x = 0.0, y = 1.0;
boolean b = true;
char ch = 'f';
```

Review Questions

1. Values of the _____ type are floating-point numbers that can be as large as 1.79×10^{308}.

2. The _____ type has only two values.

3. Values of the _____ type are single characters.

4. A _____ is a token that represents a particular number or other value.

2.6 Identifiers

As we're writing programs in Java, we'll often need to make up names. In Section 2.4, for example, I chose the name `Lottery` for the program itself and `winningNumber` for the variable that the program uses. Names that are chosen by the programmer are called *identifiers.* In Java, identifiers are subject to the following rules:

- *Identifiers may contain letters (both uppercase and lowercase), digits, and underscores (_).* Java actually allows a few other characters as well, but we won't use them in this book.

- *Identifiers begin with a letter or underscore.* For example, `THX1138` is a valid identifier because it begins with a letter and contains only letters and digits. On the other hand, `1138THX` is not legal because it begins with a digit. (This rule makes matters easier for the Java compiler, which can assume that any token beginning with a digit is a number.)

- *There's no limit on the length of an identifier.* Don't be afraid to use long, descriptive names. Some older programming languages put strict limits on the length of identifiers, forcing programmers to use cryptic abbreviations (for example, `pn` might represent a part name). Java doesn't have a length limit, so it's better style to use as many characters as you need to make a name readable. In other words, if you need a variable that represents a part name, call it `partName`, not `prtNm` or `pn`. Java itself uses some very long names. (The longest name I've found is `StringIndexOutOfBoundsException`, which is 31 characters long!)

- *Lowercase letters are not equivalent to uppercase letters.* For example, we could declare two variables, one named `i` and the other named `I`. Java would treat these as two independent variables, not related in any way. A language in which the case of letters matters is said to be *case-sensitive.*

Most of the time, our identifiers will consist solely of letters. In our struggle to find descriptive names, we'll often wind up with identifiers that consist of several words. When that happens, we'll need to be careful to mark the boundaries between the words. If we don't, the program's readability will suffer. One way to break up long identifiers is to use underscores between words:

```
last_index_of
```

Another technique is to capitalize the first letter of each word after the first:

```
lastIndexOf
```

The latter style is the one that's used by Java itself, so I'll adopt it for the rest of this book.

Conventions

A rule that we agree to follow, even though it's not required by the language, is said to be a **convention.** Capitalizing the first letter of each word in an identifier after the first is an example of a convention. Conventions vary from one programmer to another. The best conventions are the ones that most programmers observe, because they make it easier to read someone else's source code. A good source of general programming conventions is the book *Code Complete,* by Steve McConnell (Microsoft Press, 1993). Java has its own set of conventions, which are described in *The Java Language Specification,* by James Gosling, Bill Joy, and Guy Steele (Addison-Wesley, 1996).

Another convention that we'll use is beginning a class name with an uppercase letter:

```
Color
FontMetrics
String
```

Names of variables and methods, by convention, never start with an uppercase letter.

> If an identifier consists of more than one word, capitalize the first letter of each word after the first. If an identifier is the name of a class, capitalize the first letter of the identifier.

Keywords

Some words can't be used as identifiers because Java has already given them a meaning. For example, we can't use int and double as identifiers because they represent names of Java types. Words that are reserved in this fashion are called **keywords.** Table 2.1 shows the complete set of Java keywords.

Table 2.1
Keywords

abstract	double	int	super
boolean	else	interface	switch
break	extends	long	synchronized
byte	final	native	this
case	finally	new	throw
catch	float	package	throws
char	for	private	transient
class	goto*	protected	try
const*	if	public	void
continue	implements	return	volatile
default	import	short	while
do	instanceof	static	

*Not currently used in Java.

The words `null`, `true`, and `false` are also reserved in Java, although they aren't considered keywords.

 Be careful not to use keywords or other reserved words as names of classes, methods, or variables.

Review Questions

1. Which of the following names are not legal Java identifiers?

   `CSc2310   _Java_Rules_   100bottles   A_OK   S_and_P_500`

2. How long can identifiers be in Java?

3. A rule that programmers agree to follow, even though it's not part of the language, is said to be a _____.

4. Some words can't be used as identifiers because Java has already given them a meaning. Words that are reserved in this fashion are called _____.

2.7 Performing Calculations

So far, our programs haven't done anything beyond displaying a message on the screen. A more interesting (and more useful) program would perform a calculation of some sort. For example, Section 1.3 described an algorithm for converting a Fahrenheit temperature to Celsius. That algorithm used the following formula to perform the conversion:

$$C = (F - 32) \times (5 / 9)$$

We need to find a way to convert this formula into a Java statement.

In Section 2.4, we used assignment to give a value to a variable:

```
i = 0;
```

In this example, the value on the right side of the assignment is the literal 0. In general, the right side of an assignment can be an ***expression.*** A literal is an expression, and so is a variable. More complicated expressions are built out of ***operators*** and ***operands.*** In the expression 5 / 9, the operands are 5 and 9, and the operator is /. The operands in an expression can be variables, literals, or other expressions. For example, in the expression $(F - 32) \times (5 / 9)$, the operands are $(F - 32)$ and $(5 / 9)$, and the operator is $\times$.

Operators

We've discussed variables and literals already, so let's focus on operators. Table 2.2 lists Java operators that perform arithmetic. The first four operators in the table

Table 2.2
Binary Arithmetic
Operators

Symbol	Meaning
+	Addition
-	Subtraction
*	Multiplication
/	Division
%	Remainder

should look familiar. Let's see what values we get when we apply these operators to `int` operands:

```
6 + 2 ⟹ 8
6 - 2 ⟹ 4
6 * 2 ⟹ 12
6 / 2 ⟹ 3
```

The ⟹ symbol means "yields." This symbol isn't part of the Java language. It's merely a notation that I'll use to show what the value of an expression is.

So far there are no surprises, I hope. Here's a trick question for you, though: What's the value of `1/2`? If you answered 0.5, you lose. The value of `1/2` is 0, for the following reason: *The value of an integer divided by an integer is always an integer.* If the result of a division has a fractional part, Java throws it away (we say that it ***truncates*** the result). Thus, `1/2` has the value 0, because Java discards the fractional part of 0.5, the "real answer." This may seem a bit odd, but computer arithmetic doesn't always work the way you might expect.

The +, -, *, and / operators work equally well with `double` operands:

```
6.1 + 2.5 ⟹ 8.6
6.1 - 2.5 ⟹ 3.6
6.1 * 2.5 ⟹ 15.25
6.1 / 2.5 ⟹ 2.44
```

We can even mix `int` and `double` operands in the same expression. Java will convert each `int` value to the equivalent `double` value (2 becomes `2.0`, for example) before performing the operation. The result of the operation will be a `double` value:

```
6.1 + 2 ⟹ 8.1
6.1 - 2 ⟹ 4.1
6.1 * 2 ⟹ 12.2
6.1 / 2 ⟹ 3.05
```

The +, -, *, and / operators are said to be ***binary*** operators, because they require *two* operands. There's one other binary operator that's used for arithmetic: % (remainder). This operator divides its operands, but produces the remainder (what's left over after the division), instead of the quotient. For example, the value of `13 / 3` is 4 (because 3 goes into 13 four times), but the value of `13 % 3` is 1 (the remainder left over after the division). The % operator is normally used with integer operands, but Java allows it to have floating-point operands as well.

It's a good idea to put a space before and after each binary operator, although Java doesn't require spaces around operators. Expressions that don't contain spaces are often hard to read.

> To make expressions easier to read, put a space before and after each binary operator.

In addition to the binary arithmetic operators, Java has two **unary** arithmetic operators (Table 2.3). As the word "unary" suggests, these operators require just *one* operand.

Table 2.3
Unary Arithmetic
Operators

Symbol	Meaning
+	Plus
–	Minus

The astute reader will notice that our earlier discussion of integer literals said nothing about *negative* integer literals. There's a good reason for that omission: Java doesn't have negative integer literals. What we can do instead, though, is put a unary minus operator in front of an integer literal. For example, -3 is the same as -(3): the unary minus operator applied to the literal 3. The unary minus operator works with expressions in general, of course, not just literals, so we could write 3 * - (5 * 9). There's also a unary plus operator, which isn't all that useful; +3 is the same as 3.

Round-Off Errors

Calculations involving floating-point numbers can sometimes produce surprising results. For example, suppose that we perform the following calculation:

```
double d = 1.2 - 1.1;
```

In mathematics, the result would be 0.1. In programming, however, things don't always work the way you'd expect. If we use System.out.println to display the value of d, we'll get the following result:

```
0.09999999999999987
```

The answer is off by .00000000000000013. We call this a ***round-off error.*** Round-off errors occur because some numbers (1.2 and 1.1, for example) can't be stored in double form with complete accuracy. When these numbers are used later in a calculation, the result may be off slightly.

Integers aren't subject to round-off errors, by the way; only double and float values are. (The problem is even more common with float values, which are less accurate than double values.)

Precedence and Associativity

It's clear that the value of 6 + 2 is 8. But what's the value of 6 + 2 * 3? Is it (6 + 2) * 3, which yields 24, or 6 + (2 * 3), which yields 12? Most people (correctly) choose the latter interpretation, because they learned in algebra class that multiplication takes precedence over addition. In Java, the * operator does indeed take precedence over the + operator, so the compiler interprets 6 + 2 * 3 as 6 + (2 * 3). More generally, the * and / operators take precedence over the + and - operators, just as you'd expect from ordinary algebra. In the following examples, I've added parentheses to show how Java would interpret each expression.

```
5 + 2 / 2  ⟹  5 + (2 / 2)  ⟹  6
8 * 3 - 5  ⟹  (8 * 3) - 5  ⟹  19
6 - 1 * 7  ⟹  6 - (1 * 7)  ⟹  −1
9 / 4 + 6  ⟹  (9 / 4) + 6  ⟹  8
```

Although the concept of operator precedence should already be familiar to you, it's wise to pay close attention to it anyway. For one thing, Java has some operators that you didn't learn about in algebra. For example, what's the proper interpretation of 6 + 2 % 3? It turns out that the % operator has the same precedence as the * and / operators, so it takes precedence over + and -. As a result, Java will interpret 6 + 2 % 3 as 6 + (2 % 3), which has the value 8.

Now, here's a slightly tougher question: What's the value of 1 - 2 - 3? Should we interpret it as (1 − 2) − 3, which yields −4, or as 1 − (2 − 3), which yields 2? Again, algebra comes to our rescue. In algebra, subtractions are usually done from left to right—in other words, the subtraction operator is ***left associative.*** In Java, the binary +, -, *, /, and % operators are all left associative. The following examples illustrate how associativity works:

```
2 + 3 - 4  ⟹  (2 + 3) - 4  ⟹  1
2 * 3 / 4  ⟹  (2 * 3) / 4  ⟹  1
```

Associativity is a "tiebreaker" that's used only when precedence rules alone aren't enough to determine the meaning of an expression. The following example illustrates the combined effects of precedence and associativity:

```
2 + 4 * 6 - 8  ⟹  (2 + (4 * 6)) - 8  ⟹  18
```

The * operator takes precedence over + and -, which accounts for the parentheses around 4 * 6. The + and - operators have the same precedence, however, so associativity then comes into play, dictating that the addition be performed before the subtraction.

What if we don't want Java's interpretation of an expression? Then we'll be forced to use parentheses to state our intentions. For example, we can write (6 + 2) * 3 to force the addition to occur before the multiplication.

Parentheses in Expressions

How many parentheses should be used in an expression? That's not an easy question to answer. Many programmers *always* use parentheses, even when they're not strictly necessary, just to make sure that their expressions can never be misinterpreted. For example, the mathematical formula $x^2 + 2x - 1$ would be written

```
(x * x) + (2 * x) - 1
```

The parentheses aren't necessary; the expression would have the same meaning without them. Still, they make it easy to see how the expression will be evaluated.

One thing you don't want to do, however, is use parentheses when they serve no purpose. For example, there's no point in putting parentheses around variables or literals:

```
((x) * (x)) + ((2) * (x)) - (1)
```

This practice adds nothing to our understanding of the expression. All it does is make the expression appear more complicated than it really is.

Assignment Operators

Once we've performed a calculation, we'll often need to save the result in a variable. This is done by using the assignment operator (=), which we first encountered in Section 2.4. For example, to calculate the area of a rectangle, we might use the following statement:

```
area = height * width;
```

In general, the right side of an assignment can be any expression, provided that the type of the expression is appropriate for the type of the variable on the left side of the assignment. Section 9.5 describes Java's rules for determining whether an assignment is legal. For now, I'll just note that assigning a double value to an int variable is not legal. Assigning an int value to a double variable is OK, however. Assigning a double value to a double variable is fine, as is assigning an int value to an int variable.

Assignments often use the old value of a variable as part of the expression that computes the new value. For example, to add 1 to the variable i, we could write

```
i = i + 1;
```

This assignment looks a bit odd because we would never write $i = i + 1$ in mathematics. An assignment is not a mathematical equality, though, as we saw in Section 2.4. Instead, i = i + 1; is a command that means "add the current value of i and the number 1, then copy the result back into i."

Assignments that involve modifying the current value of a variable are so common that Java provides a couple of shortcuts to make them easier to do. One shortcut is to use the increment and decrement operators. The other shortcut

increment and decrement
operators ➤ 4.7

involves using alternative versions of the assignment operator, known as the ***compound assignment operators.*** Java has a number of compound assignment operators; Table 2.4 shows a partial list.

Table 2.4
Compound Assignment
Operators (partial list)

Symbol	Meaning
+=	Combines addition and assignment
-=	Combines subtraction and assignment
*=	Combines multiplication and assignment
/=	Combines division and assignment
%=	Combines remainder and assignment

Each compound assignment operator is a combination of assignment with some other operator. The += operator, for example, combines addition with assignment:

```
i += 2;   // Same as i = i + 2;
```

The other operators are similar:

```
i -= 2;   // Same as i = i - 2;
i *= 2;   // Same as i = i * 2;
i /= 2;   // Same as i = i / 2;
i %= 2;   // Same as i = i % 2;
```

PROGRAM **Converting from Fahrenheit to Celsius**

Our next program converts a Fahrenheit temperature to Celsius. The temperature to be converted will be stored in a variable named fahrenheit; the converted temperature will be stored in a variable named celsius.

Before we go any further, we'll need to make a decision: Should the program work only for integer temperatures, or should it allow temperatures that are not integers? In other words, should fahrenheit and celsius be int variables or double variables? The program could be made to work either way, so the question really boils down (ahem) to what the user wants and expects. Because humans often work with temperatures that aren't integers (does 98.6 degrees mean anything to you?), it seems that double variables are the proper choice.

FtoC.java

```
1   // Converts a Fahrenheit temperature to Celsius
2
3   public class FtoC {
4     public static void main(String[] args) {
5       double fahrenheit = 98.6;
6       double celsius = (fahrenheit - 32.0) * (5.0 / 9.0);
7       System.out.print("Celsius equivalent: ");
8       System.out.println(celsius);
9     }
10  }
```

The first significant departure from previous programs comes on line 5, which declares and initializes the fahrenheit variable. The most critical line in the program is the calculation of the Celsius temperature on line 6. There's a trap here. Suppose that we had used the following statement instead:

```
double celsius = (fahrenheit - 32) * (5 / 9);
```

The program would still compile without errors. However, we would find that `celsius` is always assigned the value 0, regardless of the value of `fahren-heit`. The problem is that `(5 / 9)` has the value 0 (remember our discussion of the / operator?). To fix the statement, we need to add a decimal point to either 5 or 9 (or both). There's nothing wrong with writing 32 instead of 32.0, by the way. `fahrenheit` is a `double` variable, so 32 will be converted to 32.0 automatically when it's subtracted from `fahrenheit`.

The statements on lines 7 and 8 display the string `"Celsius equiva-lent: "` and the value of the `celsius` variable, both on the same line:

```
Celsius equivalent: 37.0
```

Review Questions

1. Expressions are built out of operators and _____.

2. List two symbols that represent both unary and binary operators.

3. When the value of an expression contains a slight error because of the way in which float-ing-point numbers are stored, we call this a _____ error.

4. The += and -= operators are _____ _____ [two words] operators.

2.8 Constants

The `FtoC` program of Section 2.7 contains the numbers 32.0 (the freezing point of water on the Fahrenheit scale) and 5.0/9.0 (the ratio between one degree on the Celsius scale and one degree on the Fahrenheit scale). These numbers are exam-ples of ***constants:*** values that don't change during the execution of a program.

Q&A   It's often advantageous to create names for constants. One way to name a con-stant is to declare a variable and initialize it with the desired constant:

```
double freezingPoint = 32.0;
double degreeRatio = 5.0 / 9.0;
```

Using this technique, we could now write

```
double celsius = (fahrenheit - freezingPoint) * degreeRatio;
```

instead of

```
double celsius = (fahrenheit - 32.0) * (5.0 / 9.0);
```

Although this technique solves the problem of naming constants, it suffers from the disadvantage that `freezingPoint` and `degreeRatio` are variables. There's nothing to prevent them from being changed accidentally. More importantly, someone reading the program at a later date couldn't easily determine that `freezingPoint` and `degreeRatio` are used as constants.

Fortunately, Java provides a way for programmers to indicate when a variable is actually being used as a constant. The trick is to put the word `final` at the beginning of the variable's declaration:

```
final double freezingPoint = 32.0;
final double degreeRatio = 5.0 / 9.0;
```

The word `final` indicates that the *initial* value of the variable will also be its *final* value—in other words, the value of the variable won't change. A variable that's declared `final` isn't really a variable at all. The compiler will not allow a new value to be assigned to `freezingPoint` or `degreeRatio` later in the program. More importantly, someone reading the program can easily see that `freezingPoint` and `degreeRatio` are constants.

Many Java programmers follow the convention that names of constants are written entirely in uppercase letters, with underscores used to indicate boundaries between words. If we follow this convention (which I will from now on), the constants used in the `FtoC` program would be declared as follows:

```
final double FREEZING_POINT = 32.0;
final double DEGREE_RATIO = 5.0 / 9.0;
```

The advantage of this convention is that it's easy for someone to spot constants in the program, without having to locate declarations and check for the word `final`. Most (but not all) constants in Java follow the all-caps convention.

> Use uppercase letters in names of constants. When a constant consists of more than one word, use underscores to separate the words; for example, `WINDOW_SIZE` is better than `WINDOWSIZE`.

Here's what the `FtoC` program would look like with `FREEZING_POINT` and `DEGREE_RATIO` declared as constants.

FtoC2.java

```
 1  // Converts a Fahrenheit temperature to Celsius
 2
 3  public class FtoC2 {
 4    public static void main(String[] args) {
 5      final double FREEZING_POINT = 32.0;
 6      final double DEGREE_RATIO = 5.0 / 9.0;
 7      double fahrenheit = 98.6;
 8      double celsius =
 9        (fahrenheit - FREEZING_POINT) * DEGREE_RATIO;
10      System.out.print("Celsius equivalent: ");
11      System.out.println(celsius);
12    }
13  }
```

It's not clear that the `FtoC2` program is better than the `FtoC` program; it's two statements longer, and there are more names to keep track of. In such a small program, it makes little difference whether constants are given names. In larger programs, however, naming constants can have a big payoff:

- **Programs are easier to read.** The name of a constant—if well chosen—helps the reader understand the meaning of the constant. The alternative is a program full of "magic numbers" that can easily mystify the reader.

- **Programs are easier to modify.** We can change the value of a constant throughout a program by modifying a single declaration.

- **Inconsistencies and typographical errors are less likely.** If a numerical constant like 3.14159 appears many times in a program, chances are it will occasionally be written 3.1416 or 3.14195 by accident.

One last remark: make sure that you create meaningful names for your constants. There's no point in defining a constant whose name signifies its value:

```
final int TWELVE = 12;
```

The name `TWELVE` tells us nothing about the significance of the number 12. (Does it represent a dozen? The number of months in a year? Or something else?) Worse still, the name will be incorrect if we later change the value of the constant during program maintenance.

> The name of a constant should describe the *meaning* of the constant, not the *value* of the constant.

Review Questions

1. What keyword is used in Java to indicate that the value of a variable will not change (i.e., the variable is actually a constant)?

2. What is the Java convention for naming constants?

3. Name one advantage of creating names for constants.

4. Why is `TWENTY_FOUR` not a good name for the constant 24?

2.9 Methods

Methods play a key role in Java. A **method** is a series of statements that can be executed as a unit. In many cases, a method contains a complete (but usually small) algorithm. A method does nothing until it is activated, or **called.** To call a method, we write the name of the method, followed by a pair of parentheses. The method's **arguments** (if any) go inside the parentheses. For example, the `JavaRules` program of Section 2.1 contains the following call of the `println` method:

```
System.out.println("Java rules!");
```

There is one argument, `"Java rules!"`, in the call. Arguments are items of data that a method needs in order to do its job.

Some methods *return* a value when they have completed execution. Not all methods do; in particular, `println` does nothing but display information on the screen. Nearly all methods that perform a mathematical computation return a value, because the reason for calling such a method is to get an answer from it.

Methods in the `Math` Class

Java provides a number of methods for performing mathematical calculations. They belong to the `Math` class and are called by writing `Math.name`, where *name* is the name of the method. I'll describe a few of these methods here; Section 9.3 provides a more complete list.

Math.pow   The `pow` method raises a number to a power:

```
Math.pow(2.0, 3.0)  ⇒ 8.0
Math.pow(-2.0, 3.0) ⇒ −8.0
Math.pow(2.0, -1.0) ⇒ 0.5
```

I'm using the ⇒ symbol here to indicate the value returned by a method.

Math.sqrt   The `sqrt` method computes the square root of a number:

```
Math.sqrt(2.0)  ⇒ 1.4142135623730951
Math.sqrt(4.0)  ⇒ 2.0
```

Both `pow` and `sqrt` return values of type `double`.

Math.abs   The `abs` method computes the absolute value of a number:

```
Math.abs(2.0)  ⇒ 2.0
Math.abs(-2.0) ⇒ 2.0
Math.abs(2)  ⇒ 2
Math.abs(-2) ⇒ 2
```

Math.max   The `max` method finds the larger of two numbers:

```
Math.max(3.0, 5.5)   ⇒ 5.5
Math.max(10.0, -2.0) ⇒ 10.0
Math.max(12, -23)  ⇒ 12
Math.max(-5, -2)   ⇒ −2
```

Math.min   The `min` method finds the smaller of two numbers:

```
Math.min(3.0, 5.5)   ⇒ 3.0
Math.min(10.0, -2.0) ⇒ −2.0
Math.min(12, -23)  ⇒ −23
Math.min(-5, -2)   ⇒ −5
```

The value returned by `abs`, `max`, and `min` depends on the type of the argument. If the argument is an `int` value, then the methods return an `int` value. If the argument is a `double` value, then the methods return a `double` value.

Math.round   Finally, there are methods for rounding floating-point numbers to integers. The only one I'll mention here is `round`, which rounds a `double` value to the nearest integer:

```
Math.round(4.1)  ⇒ 4
Math.round(4.5)  ⇒ 5
Math.round(4.9)  ⇒ 5
Math.round(5.5)  ⇒ 6
Math.round(-4.1) ⇒ -4
Math.round(-4.5) ⇒ -4
Math.round(-4.9) ⇒ -5
Math.round(-5.5) ⇒ -5
```

Notice that `round` rounds up to the next larger integer when the number ends with .5. When used to round a `double` value, `round` returns a value of type `long` rather than an `int` value. The `long` type is similar to the `int` type but allows numbers to be much larger.

Q&A

long type ➤9.2

Using the Result of a Method Call

Methods that return a result correspond to functions in mathematics. To a mathematician, a function is a rule for computing a value when given one or more arguments. We can visualize a function as a box that transforms its arguments into a single value (the result):

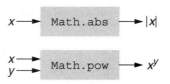

The value returned by a method can be used in a couple of ways. Often, we'll save it in a variable for later use:

```
double y = Math.abs(x);   // Save result in y
```

That's not our only option, though. We can use the result returned by a method directly, without first saving it in a variable. For example, suppose that we need to compute the square root of the absolute value of x. One alternative is to store the absolute value of x in a variable, then compute the square root in a separate statement:

```
double y = Math.abs(x);
double z = Math.sqrt(y);
```

However, we can combine the two steps if we choose:

```
double z = Math.sqrt(Math.abs(x));
```

As this example shows, the value returned by one method can be used as an argument in a call of another method. Schematically, here's what the process looks like:

Combining the two statements into one has the advantage of saving a statement and eliminating the variable y. Provided that y isn't needed later in the program, this transformation is worthwhile. However, if y (which contains the absolute value of x) is needed later, then the combination isn't a good idea. Also, nesting method calls should be done sparingly because it can hurt program readability.

Values returned by methods can also be used as operands in expressions, along with variables and literals. Consider the problem of finding the roots of the quadratic equation

$$ax^2 + bx + c = 0$$

The roots are given by the quadratic formula:

$$x = \frac{-b \pm \sqrt{b^2 - 4ac}}{2a}$$

Assuming that a, b, and c are all variables of type double, we could compute the roots as follows:

```
double root1 = (-b + Math.sqrt(b * b - 4 * a * c)) / (2 * a);
double root2 = (-b - Math.sqrt(b * b - 4 * a * c)) / (2 * a);
```

Because the square root of $b^2 - 4ac$ (known as the **discriminant**) is the same in both cases, it would be more efficient to compute it once and save it in a variable:

```
double discriminant = Math.sqrt(b * b - 4 * a * c);
double root1 = (-b + discriminant) / (2 * a);
double root2 = (-b - discriminant) / (2 * a);
```

The value of 2 * a is computed twice, so we might consider storing it in a variable as well. However, the savings would be small (one multiplication). Moreover, the Java compiler itself may notice that 2 * a is used twice and decide to save time by computing the value only once. (Yes, compilers are often smart enough to recognize this situation.)

Sometimes, we'll simply want to display the value returned by a method, rather than saving it in a variable or using it in a computation. In that case, the method call can be put inside a call of System.out.print or System.out.println:

```
System.out.println(Math.sqrt(2.0));
```

Review Questions

1. In a method call, the method's name is followed by its _____, which are enclosed in parentheses.

2. Methods such as `abs` and `sqrt` belong to the _____ class.

3. Methods that return a result correspond to _____ in mathematics.

4. Name three ways to use a value returned by a method.

2.10 Input and Output

Most programs require both input and output. *Input* is any information fed into the program from an outside source. For example, the user who's running the program could enter data, or the program could read data from a file stored on disk or obtain it from a network. *Output* is any data produced by the program and made available outside the program. Output can be displayed on the user's screen, written to a file, or sent to another computer over a network.

Displaying Output on the Screen

The only type of output that our programs have produced so far has taken the form of messages displayed on the user's screen. Our tools for displaying these messages have been `System.out.print` and `System.out.println`. Let's take a closer look at what these methods can do:

- Both methods can display any single value on the screen, regardless of type. Strings can be displayed, but so can `int`, `double`, `boolean`, and `char` values.

- The argument to `print` or `println` can be any expression, including a variable, literal, or value returned by a method.

- `println` always advances to the next line after displaying its argument. We can avoid advancing to the next line by using `print`, which is otherwise identical to `println`.

What if we want to display a line that's completely blank, containing no characters at all? There are two ways to accomplish that goal. One is to use a slightly different version of `println`, in which the parentheses are left empty:

```
System.out.println();
```

(Notice that parentheses are always required when a method is called, even if the method has no arguments.) If this statement follows another use of `println`, we'll end up with a blank line:

```
System.out.println("Hey Joe");
System.out.println();   // Write a blank line
```

The other technique is to insert \n into a string that's being displayed by print or println. Both recognize this combination—the **backslash** character followed by the letter n—as a command to advance to the next line. For example, suppose that a program contains the following statement:

```
System.out.println("do\nre\nmi");
```

When this statement is executed, we'll see the following output:

```
do
re
mi
```

One way to display a blank line is to use \n twice in a call of print or println:

```
System.out.println("A hop,\na skip,\n\nand a jump");
```

The double use of \n will cause Java to advance to a new line twice, producing the following output:

```
A hop,
a skip,

and a jump
```

Be careful not to confuse the *slash* character (/) with the *backslash* character (\). The statement

```
System.out.println("A hop,/na skip,/n/nand a jump");
```

will produce the output

```
A hop,/na skip,/n/nand a jump
```

The slash character has no special meaning; println treats it just like any other character.

Escape Sequences

escape sequences ➤9.4

The backslash character has a special meaning in Java, as we've just seen. It combines with the character after it to form an *escape sequence:* a combination of characters that represents a single character. The backslash character followed by n forms \n, the **new-line character.** Another common escape sequence is \ ", which represents " (double quote). We'll need this escape sequence if we want to print a double quote character. A statement such as

```
System.out.println("He yelled "Stop!" and we stopped.");
```

won't compile, because the compiler will match the first two double quotes, arriving at the string "He yelled ". The rest of the statement will look like gibberish to the compiler. By using \" instead of ", we'll be able to print the string correctly:

```
System.out.println("He yelled \"Stop!\" and we stopped.");
```

Because of the backslash character's unusual properties, we can't print it in the same way we print other characters. If we want to print a backslash character as part of a string, the string will need to contain *two* backslash characters. For example, in order to display the line

```
APL\360
```

we'd use the statement

```
System.out.println("APL\\360");
```

Printing Multiple Items

We'll often want to print more than one item on the same line. One way to accomplish this feat is to call `System.out.print` for each item except the last, and then call `System.out.println` for the last item. For example, the `FtoC` program of Section 2.7 contains the following lines:

```
System.out.print("Celsius equivalent: ");
System.out.println(celsius);
```

The goal was to display a single line of output:

```
Celsius equivalent: 37.0
```

Using multiple statements, one per item to be printed, isn't very convenient. Fortunately, Java provides a better way. The + operator can often be used to combine multiple items into a single item for printing purposes. Using +, the two statements from the `FtoC` program can be combined into one:

```
System.out.println("Celsius equivalent: " + celsius);
```

We'll learn more about this use of the + operator in Section 3.9. For now, I'll just mention that at least one of the two operands for the + operator must be a string. Otherwise, + will try to add the two operands, which isn't what we want. For example, the statement

```
System.out.println(3 + 5);
```

prints 8, not 35.

Obtaining Input from the User

Obtaining input in Java turns out to be a bit trickier than displaying output on the screen. In fact, we're not even going to read input the "standard" way. Instead, I've written a class named `SimpleIO` that we'll use instead.

Obtaining input from the user is done in two steps. First, we ***prompt*** the user to enter input by displaying a message on the screen. Then we ***read*** the input entered by the user. Prompting the user is done with the `SimpleIO.prompt` method. This method needs to know what the prompt should be, so we'll supply it to the method as a string:

```
SimpleIO.prompt("Enter Fahrenheit temperature: ");
```

On the screen, the user will see the message

```
Enter Fahrenheit temperature:
```

The cursor will be positioned at the end of the line, not on the next line. To read the user's input, we'll use the `SimpleIO.readLine` method, which reads the entire line of input entered by the user (all the characters the user types before pressing the Enter key). `SimpleIO.readLine` returns a string, which we'll probably want to save in a variable. In Java, a variable declared to have `String` type can store a string of any length. The following statement declares `userInput` to be a `String` variable and initializes it to contain the string returned by `SimpleIO.readLine`:

```
String userInput = SimpleIO.readLine();
```

At this point, the `userInput` variable might contain a string such as `"212"`, indicating that the user entered the characters 2, 1, and 2 before pressing the Enter key. Unfortunately, we want the number 212, not the string `"212"`. To make it easy to convert strings to numbers, I've written a class named `Convert`. One of the methods in this class is `toDouble`, which converts a string to a `double` value. Here's how we might use this method:

```
double fahrenheit = Convert.toDouble(userInput);
```

To convert a string to an integer, we'll use `Integer.parseInt`. This method, unlike `Convert.toDouble`, is part of standard Java. If `userInput` contains an integer in string form, we can convert the string to an integer as follows:

```
int n = Integer.parseInt(userInput);
```

Packages

The `SimpleIO` and `Convert` classes are designed to be used in a number of programs, not just a single program. Java provides a way of grouping related classes, making it easier to reuse them. This mechanism is the ***package.*** A package is simply a bunch of related classes that are grouped together and given a name. I've chosen the name `jpb` (*Java Programming: From the Beginning*) for the package that contains `SimpleIO` and `Convert`.

To access the classes that are contained within a package, we'll use an ***import declaration,*** which has the following form:

Q&A

String ►3.9

import declaration

```
import package-name . * ;
```

Import declarations go at the very beginning of a program. For example, if we need either the `SimpleIO` or `Convert` classes in a program, then we'll put the line

```
import jpb.*;
```

at the beginning of the program.

Java comes with a great many packages, some of which are documented in Appendix C. The `jpb` package is not one of these, so you'll need to install it on your computer before you can compile any program that uses this package. You can download the `jpb` package from *http://knking.com/books/java/*; see Appendix A for installation details.

Application Programming Interfaces

The packages that come with Java—as opposed to packages that you or I might write—belong to Java's ***Application Programming Interface*** (**API**). In general, an API consists of code that someone else has written but that we can use in our programs. Typically, an API allows an application programmer to access some lower level of software. In particular, an API often provides access to the capabilities of a particular operating system or windowing system.

PROGRAM **Converting from Fahrenheit to Celsius (Revisited)**

Using the `jpb` package, we can improve the `FtoC2` program by allowing the user to enter the temperature. The following program prompts the user to enter a Fahrenheit temperature; it then prints the equivalent Celsius temperature. The output of the program will have the following appearance (input entered by the user is shown in **bold**):

```
Enter Fahrenheit temperature: 212
Celsius equivalent: 100.0
```

The program will allow temperatures that aren't integers; that's why the Celsius temperature is displayed as `100.0` instead of `100`. Let's look first at the entire program and then see how it's put together.

FtoC3.java

```
1   // Converts a Fahrenheit temperature entered by the user to
2   // Celsius
3
4   import jpb.*;
5
6   public class FtoC3 {
7     public static void main(String[] args) {
```

```
 8        final double FREEZING_POINT = 32.0;
 9        final double DEGREE_RATIO = 5.0 / 9.0;
10
11        SimpleIO.prompt("Enter Fahrenheit temperature: ");
12        String userInput = SimpleIO.readLine();
13        double fahrenheit = Convert.toDouble(userInput);
14        double celsius =
15           (fahrenheit - FREEZING_POINT) * DEGREE_RATIO;
16        System.out.println("Celsius equivalent: " + celsius);
17     }
18  }
```

The FtoC3 program imports the jpb package in order to gain access to the SimpleIO and Convert classes. In addition to the fahrenheit and celsius variables, there's a new variable named userInput. The userInput variable will store the entire line of input typed by the user.

The main method consists of seven statements. Let's look at each of these in turn. Lines 8 and 9 declare constants. The statement on line 11 prompts the user for input. The statement on line 12 reads the user's input and assigns it to the userInput variable. The next statement converts the user's input into a number, which is then stored into the fahrenheit variable. The statement on line 14 calculates the equivalent Celsius temperature. The final statement displays the string "Celsius equivalent: " and the value of the celsius variable.

Review Questions

1. An _____ _____ [two words] is a combination of characters that represents a single character.

2. What operator can be used to combine multiple data items into a single string?

3. Before a program attempts to read user input, it should first _____ the user by displaying a message.

4. Java allows classes to be grouped into larger units known as _____.

2.11   Case Study: Computing a Course Average

Let's apply what we've learned so far toward writing a program of greater length than any of the previous examples in this chapter. We'll call this a "case study"; you'll find more case studies in later chapters. Case studies let us use language features in a more realistic setting. We'll get to apply the steps in the programming *programming process ▶1.7*   process. Also, we'll use the resulting program as a springboard for discussing style issues that haven't arisen previously.

Our first case study is one that's dear to the hearts of students everywhere: computing a course average from scores on assignments and tests. Our goal is to write a program named CourseAverage that calculates the overall class average for a student enrolled in CSc 2310 (the course that I taught while this book was being written). The average is calculated using the following percentages:

Programs	30%
Quizzes	10%
Test 1	15%
Test 2	15%
Final exam	30%

The user will be prompted to enter the grade for each program (0–20), the score on each quiz (0–10), and the grades on the two tests and the final exam (0–100). There will be eight program grades and five quiz grades.

The following example shows what the user will see on the screen:

```
Welcome to the CSc 2310 average calculation program.

Enter Program 1 score: 20
Enter Program 2 score: 19
Enter Program 3 score: 15
Enter Program 4 score: 18.5
Enter Program 5 score: 20
Enter Program 6 score: 20
Enter Program 7 score: 18
Enter Program 8 score: 20

Enter Quiz 1 score: 9
Enter Quiz 2 score: 10
Enter Quiz 3 score: 5.5
Enter Quiz 4 score: 8
Enter Quiz 5 score: 9.5

Enter Test 1 score: 78
Enter Test 2 score: 92
Enter Final Exam score: 85

Course average: 88
```

The previous two paragraphs will serve as the specification for the `Course-Average` program. Although this specification may seem to be pretty detailed, it fails to address several important points. (Specifications that are vague or ambiguous are equally common in the real world, unfortunately.) First, must the scores be integers, or can they contain digits after the decimal point? The example suggests that scores need not be integers, so that's what we'll assume. Second, what happens if the user enters invalid input? (Input could be bad in several different ways. The user might enter letters or other non-numeric input. Or the user might press the Enter key without entering any input. Or the user might enter a number that's outside the range we're looking for.) For now, we'll ignore this issue and simply assume that the user is friendly. In later chapters, we'll learn how to validate input, but that's beyond the scope of this chapter.

Now that we've nailed down the specification for the program, the next step is to design it. After studying the specification, we might decide to divide the program into eight steps:

1. Print the introductory message ("Welcome to the CSc 2310 average calculation program").
2. Prompt the user to enter eight program scores.
3. Compute the program average from the eight scores.
4. Prompt the user to enter five quiz scores.
5. Compute the quiz average from the five scores.
6. Prompt the user to enter scores on the tests and final exam.
7. Compute the course average from the program average, quiz average, test scores, and final exam score.
8. Round the course average to the nearest integer and display it.

Notice that we're simply outlining the program at this stage. We don't want to get bogged down with details; instead, we want to see the "big picture." This isn't the only possible design, by the way. Steps 3 and 5 could come after step 6, for example.

The next step is to choose algorithms and decide how the program's data will be stored—an easy task for a program this small. We can use `double` variables to store the various scores and averages, which aren't necessarily integers. The algorithms we'll need are simple ones. We already know how to prompt for input, read a line, and convert it to a `double` value. Computing the program average or quiz average is done by adding scores and dividing by the number of scores in the sum. Computing the course average will be the hardest part, because we'll need to scale the program average and quiz average so that they're expressed on a scale from 0 to 100, like the test scores and final exam score. The following formula should do the trick:

$$courseAverage = .30 \times programAverage \times 5 + .10 \times quizAverage \times 10 + .15 \times test1 + .15 \times test2 + .30 \times finalExam$$

The program average is multiplied by 5 (so that an average of 20 on the programs will be treated as an average of 100), and the quiz average is multiplied by 10. To round the course average to the nearest integer, we'll use the `Math.round` method.

The next step is to write the program. Here's my version.

CourseAverage.java

```
 1   // Program name: CourseAverage
 2   // Author: K. N. King
 3   // Written: 1998-04-05
 4   // Modified: 1999-01-27
 5   //
 6   // Prompts the user to enter eight program scores (0-20), five
 7   // quiz scores (0-10), two test scores (0-100), and a final
 8   // exam score (0-100). Scores may contain digits after the
 9   // decimal point. Input is not checked for validity. Displays
10   // the course average, computed using the following formula:
```

```
11    //
12    //     Programs     30%
13    //     Quizzes      10%
14    //     Test 1       15%
15    //     Test 2       15%
16    //     Final exam   30%
17    //
18    // The course average is rounded to the nearest integer.
19
20    import jpb.*;
21
22    public class CourseAverage {
23      public static void main(String[] args) {
24        // Print the introductory message
25        System.out.println("Welcome to the CSc 2310 average " +
26                           "calculation program.\n");
27
28        // Prompt the user to enter eight program scores
29        SimpleIO.prompt("Enter Program 1 score: ");
30        String userInput = SimpleIO.readLine();
31        double program1 = Convert.toDouble(userInput);
32
33        SimpleIO.prompt("Enter Program 2 score: ");
34        userInput = SimpleIO.readLine();
35        double program2 = Convert.toDouble(userInput);
36
37        SimpleIO.prompt("Enter Program 3 score: ");
38        userInput = SimpleIO.readLine();
39        double program3 = Convert.toDouble(userInput);
40
41        SimpleIO.prompt("Enter Program 4 score: ");
42        userInput = SimpleIO.readLine();
43        double program4 = Convert.toDouble(userInput);
44
45        SimpleIO.prompt("Enter Program 5 score: ");
46        userInput = SimpleIO.readLine();
47        double program5 = Convert.toDouble(userInput);
48
49        SimpleIO.prompt("Enter Program 6 score: ");
50        userInput = SimpleIO.readLine();
51        double program6 = Convert.toDouble(userInput);
52
53        SimpleIO.prompt("Enter Program 7 score: ");
54        userInput = SimpleIO.readLine();
55        double program7 = Convert.toDouble(userInput);
56
57        SimpleIO.prompt("Enter Program 8 score: ");
58        userInput = SimpleIO.readLine();
59        double program8 = Convert.toDouble(userInput);
60
61        // Compute the program average from the eight scores
62        double programAverage =
63          (program1 + program2 + program3 + program4 +
64           program5 + program6 + program7 + program8) / 8;
```

```
65
66      // Prompt the user to enter five quiz scores
67      SimpleIO.prompt("\nEnter Quiz 1 score: ");
68      userInput = SimpleIO.readLine();
69      double quiz1 = Convert.toDouble(userInput);
70
71      SimpleIO.prompt("Enter Quiz 2 score: ");
72      userInput = SimpleIO.readLine();
73      double quiz2 = Convert.toDouble(userInput);
74
75      SimpleIO.prompt("Enter Quiz 3 score: ");
76      userInput = SimpleIO.readLine();
77      double quiz3 = Convert.toDouble(userInput);
78
79      SimpleIO.prompt("Enter Quiz 4 score: ");
80      userInput = SimpleIO.readLine();
81      double quiz4 = Convert.toDouble(userInput);
82
83      SimpleIO.prompt("Enter Quiz 5 score: ");
84      userInput = SimpleIO.readLine();
85      double quiz5 = Convert.toDouble(userInput);
86
87      // Compute the quiz average from the five scores
88      double quizAverage =
89         (quiz1 + quiz2 + quiz3 + quiz4 + quiz5) / 5;
90
91      // Prompt the user to enter scores on the tests and final
92      // exam
93      SimpleIO.prompt("\nEnter Test 1 score: ");
94      userInput = SimpleIO.readLine();
95      double test1 = Convert.toDouble(userInput);
96
97      SimpleIO.prompt("Enter Test 2 score: ");
98      userInput = SimpleIO.readLine();
99      double test2 = Convert.toDouble(userInput);
100
101      SimpleIO.prompt("Enter Final Exam score: ");
102      userInput = SimpleIO.readLine();
103      double finalExam = Convert.toDouble(userInput);
104
105      // Compute the course average from the program average,
106      // quiz average, test scores, and final exam score.
107      // The program average (0-20) is multiplied by 5 to put
108      // it on a scale of 0 to 100. The quiz average (0-10) is
109      // multiplied by 10 for the same reason.
110      double courseAverage = .30 * programAverage * 5 +
111                             .10 * quizAverage * 10 +
112                             .15 * test1 +
113                             .15 * test2 +
114                             .30 * finalExam;
115
116      // Round the course average to the nearest integer and
117      // display it
```

```
118          System.out.println("\nCourse average: " +
119                              Math.round(courseAverage));
120     }
121  }
```

This program illustrates how to deal with some of the style issues that arise in programming:

- **Comment block.** The program begins with a fairly long block of comments (lines 1–18). These comments include the program name, the programmer's name, and the dates on which the program was written and modified. After that comes a concise description of what the program does.

> The longer the program, the larger and more detailed the comment block should be. Comment blocks in commercial programs are often quite lengthy.

- **Blank lines.** Blank lines play an important role in making programs readable. Programmers use blank lines to indicate a break between one group of related statements (such as lines 29–31) and the group that follows (lines 33–35). Trying to read a program that lacks blank lines is like trying to read a book that consists of one (very) long paragraph.

> Put blank lines between groups of related statements.

- **Short comments.** In addition to the comment block at the beginning, the program contains shorter comments interspersed with statements. Notice how these comments help to convey the program's design to the reader. The correct way to write a program is to do the design first, then write the comments. The actual statements in the program are written last.

> Use comments to reveal the overall structure of the program. Ideally, the reader should be able to understand the program's design without even reading the statements in the program.

- **Long lines.** One of the hassles of programming is that every program seems to contain lines that are uncomfortably long. There are several reasonable ways to split long lines; this program illustrates some of them. Lines 62–64 show one way to split a lengthy assignment. I've moved the expression on the right side of the = to a different line, indenting it by two spaces (my standard indentation). The expression inside the parentheses is too long for one line, so I put half of it on another line, aligning the variables `program1` and `program5`. Lines 110–114 show another way to divide a long assignment. In this case, I put the first part of the expression on the same line as the = operator itself. I then split up the rest of the expression, putting each piece on a different line and aligning the pieces. I chose to use this style because it emphasizes the weights that are being given to the different components of the average. My goal was the usual one: to make the program as easy to understand as possible.

There are several good techniques for splitting long lines. Regardless of which one you use, be sure to break lines at logical places and use a consistent method of alignment.

Improving the Program

Although the `CourseAverage` program works, it seems as though there should be a better way to write it: it contains a considerable amount of repetition and declares a huge number of variables. There's not much we can do about the repeated code until we learn more about Java. We'll return to this program in a later chapter and see how to simplify it. Let's concentrate instead on reducing the number of variables.

You'll notice that the values of most variables in the `CourseAverage` program are used only once. The `userInput` variable, for example, is assigned a value, which is then given to `Convert.toDouble`. After that, `userInput` is assigned a new value. When a variable's value is used only once, we can often eliminate the variable by substituting the value that's assigned to it. For example, instead of writing

```
String userInput = SimpleIO.readLine();
double program1 = Convert.toDouble(userInput);
```

we could simply write

```
double program1 = Convert.toDouble(SimpleIO.readLine());
```

It's not clear that this substitution makes the program easier to read, however, so I won't make this change.

Reducing the number of variables in a program is usually a good idea. However, avoid any reduction that makes the program harder to understand.

Our "substitution" technique won't help with most of the variables in `CourseAverage`. The `program1`, `program2`, ..., `program8` variables are needed to store program scores until all scores have been read and the average can be computed. Fortunately, we can use a different technique to reduce the number of variables. To compute the average of the program scores, we don't really need to know the individual program scores; all we need is the *total* of the scores. That observation suggests that we could declare a variable named `programTotal`, which will hold a "running total" of all the scores entered so far. Using this variable, we can modify lines 28–64 of the program in the following way (changes are in **bold**).

```
// Prompt the user to enter eight program scores.
SimpleIO.prompt("Enter Program 1 score: ");
String userInput = SimpleIO.readLine();
double programTotal = Convert.toDouble(userInput);

SimpleIO.prompt("Enter Program 2 score: ");
userInput = SimpleIO.readLine();
programTotal += Convert.toDouble(userInput);

SimpleIO.prompt("Enter Program 3 score: ");
userInput = SimpleIO.readLine();
programTotal += Convert.toDouble(userInput);

SimpleIO.prompt("Enter Program 4 score: ");
userInput = SimpleIO.readLine();
programTotal += Convert.toDouble(userInput);

SimpleIO.prompt("Enter Program 5 score: ");
userInput = SimpleIO.readLine();
programTotal += Convert.toDouble(userInput);

SimpleIO.prompt("Enter Program 6 score: ");
userInput = SimpleIO.readLine();
programTotal += Convert.toDouble(userInput);

SimpleIO.prompt("Enter Program 7 score: ");
userInput = SimpleIO.readLine();
programTotal += Convert.toDouble(userInput);

SimpleIO.prompt("Enter Program 8 score: ");
userInput = SimpleIO.readLine();
programTotal += Convert.toDouble(userInput);

// Compute the program average from the eight scores.
double programAverage = programTotal / 8;
```

Notice that the += operator is ideal for keeping a running total. We can use a similar technique to replace the quiz1, quiz2, quiz3, quiz4, and quiz5 variables by a single quizTotal variable.

Review Question

1. A program should begin with a _____ _____.

2.12 Debugging

Debugging is the process of finding bugs in a program and fixing them. Some of the chapters in this book, starting with this one, will end with a special section on debugging. This section will provide tips for quickly locating and fixing bugs. Reading this section will save you a lot of time during the debugging process.

Types of Errors

When your program contains a bug, it will show up in one of three ways:

- *Compile-time error.* The compiler may issue an error message when you attempt to compile the program. A bug of this type is usually minor and easy to fix, such as a missing semicolon or a variable that wasn't declared.

- *Run-time error.* A run-time error is a problem detected by the Java interpreter as the program is running. For example, perhaps the user was asked to enter an integer but entered nonnumeric input instead. When the program tries to convert the input into an `int` value, a run-time error will occur. In Java, run-time errors are called *exceptions.* Run-time errors can be caused by conditions that the programmer should have anticipated but failed to (the user entering the wrong type of input, for example). They can also be the result of a mistake in the original algorithm or in the way the algorithm was translated into Java.

- *Incorrect behavior.* A program may produce the wrong answer or misbehave in some way. Errors of this type are caused by the same things that cause run-time errors.

Fixing Compile-Time Errors

When you compile a program, the Java compiler will check your program thoroughly. If the program violates Java's many rules, the compiler will display a series of error messages. Each one describes a single error and tells you the point in the program at which the error was detected. It's not unusual to get a large number of error messages, especially when a program is compiled for the first time.

Q&A

Here are a few strategies for fixing compile-time errors:

- *Read error messages carefully.* Be sure that you understand what the compiler is trying to tell you. Consider the following two errors:

```
Buggy.java:8: Undefined variable: i
    System.out.println(i);
                       ^
Buggy.java:10: Variable j may not have been initialized
    System.out.println(j);
                       ^
```

The first message says that the variable `i` was not declared before line 8. The second message says that, although `j` was declared properly, the compiler was unable to determine that it was initialized before line 10.

- *Pay attention to line numbers.* Note that the compiler's error messages always include a line number. Most editors will display line numbers, allowing you to quickly locate the line at which the error was detected.

- *Fix the first error.* A single error in a program may trigger an avalanche of error messages. Be suspicious if the compiler reports a number of errors on the same line of the program. Fix the error that was reported first, and then compile the program again. The other error messages will often disappear.

- *Don't trust the compiler (completely).* Just because the compiler reports an error on line 10, don't assume that the error is actually on that line. Often, the error is on a previous line; the compiler just didn't detect it until line 10. Also, the compiler sometimes gets confused by an error and produces a message that doesn't accurately indicate the nature of the error. Consider the following statements:

```
System.out.print("Value of i: ")
System.out.println(i);
```

If you look closely, you'll notice that the first statement is missing a semicolon at the end. Here's what the compiler reported when I compiled a program that contained these statements:

```
Buggy.java:8: Invalid type expression.
    System.out.print("Value of i: ")
                    ^

Buggy.java:9: Invalid declaration.
    System.out.println(i);
                      ^

2 errors
```

The compiler detected an error on line 8, but it wasn't the "right" error, and it wasn't detected at the right place (the end of the line). Moreover, the error on line 8 triggered a second message concerning line 9, which contains no errors. When you get a confusing error message such as "Invalid type expression," the best you can do is examine the entire line carefully. Don't assume that the error is what the compiler says it is, and don't assume that it's located where the compiler shows it to be.

Fixing Run-Time Errors

When a run-time error occurs, a message will be displayed on the screen. The exact format of the message may vary, depending on which version of Java you're using. Here's a typical example:

```
Exception in thread "main" java.lang.NumberFormatException: foo
        at java.lang.Integer.parseInt(Compiled Code)
        at java.lang.Integer.parseInt(Integer.java:458)
        at Buggy.main(Buggy.java:11)
```

The first line of the message describes the type of error (NumberFormat-Exception, indicating that there was an illegal attempt to convert a string into a number) and the data that caused the exception to occur ("foo" was the string that was being converted). The next two lines mention the method that was executing at the time of the error (Integer.parseInt). The last line shows where Integer.parseInt was used in the program (in the main method, on line 11 of the file Buggy.java).

Once we know what the nature of the error is and where the error occurred, we can work backwards to determine what caused the error. In this case, we would check to see where the string "foo" came from. If the problem was caused by bad user input, there's not much we can do for now. In Section 8.1, we'll see that it's possible for a program to detect errors of this sort and take action (perhaps by asking the user to re-enter the input).

Fixing Behavioral Errors

Errors of behavior are the hardest problems to fix, because the problem probably lies either in the original algorithm or in the way we've translated the algorithm into a Java program. Either way, the problem may be a subtle one. Other than simply checking and rechecking the algorithm and the program, there are two approaches to locating the source of a behavioral problem, depending on whether we have a debugger available. Let's take a look at each of these approaches.

Using a Debugger

Despite its name, a *debugger* doesn't actually locate and fix bugs. Instead, it helps us see inside a program as it executes. As we watch the program execute, we're looking for two things:

- *Order of statement execution.* Are the statements in the program being executed in the proper order?
- *Values of variables.* Do the variables in the program have the proper values?

If you're using a commercial Java environment, it probably contains a debugger. I can't show you how to use your debugger, unfortunately, because the commands vary. You'll need to check your documentation for details. Here are the key features to look for:

- *Step.* A debugger will allow you to step through a program, executing one statement at a time. Usually there's a particular key that you'll need to press to cause a step to occur.
- *Breakpoint.* As our programs get longer, stepping through them from the beginning will become increasingly tedious. Most debuggers will allow you to set a breakpoint at any statement you choose. When you run the program, it will execute at full speed until the breakpoint is reached. You can then step through the program starting at that point.
- *Watch.* A debugger will allow you to watch a set of variables that you've selected. The values of the variables will be updated as you step through the program so you can see what's stored in each variable at all times.

Debugging Without a Debugger

If you're using the Java Development Kit, your debugging options are limited. The JDK includes a debugger, named jdb. However, it's a bit hard to use, so I don't recommend it, at least until you become more proficient in Java.

Fortunately, we won't need a debugger for most of the programs in this book. If we were using another programming language, we would find a debugger to be more important. With Java, on the other hand, we can often get by without a debugger, especially for short programs. For one thing, if a run-time error occurs, we'll get a message on the screen that describes the error and tells us where it was detected. That information may be enough to let us locate and fix the bug.

If you're having trouble finding a bug, the easiest—and often the best—course of action is to use `System.out.println` to print the values of any variables that you're interested in watching. For example, if you want to know the values of the variables a and b at some point in the program, you could insert the following statement into the program at that point:

```
System.out.println("Value of a: " + a + " Value of b: " + b);
```

Note that this statement prints the names of a and b along with their values. "Labeling" your debugging output in this way is a good idea. If you don't, you're likely to end up with an assortment of unidentifiable values as your output.

Choosing Test Data

When you test a program to see if it works correctly, you'll generally need to run the program a number of times, entering different input each time and checking that the program behaves according to its specifications. This is a painful but essential step in program development. It goes against human nature to try to cause your own program to fail. It's much easier on the psyche to test it once or twice and then assume that it works. Unfortunately, that practice is likely to get you into trouble. If you don't test a program before you turn it in, it probably contains bugs that your instructor will find. If you're working as a software developer and don't test your programs sufficiently, the customer may find the bugs for you—and the customer isn't likely to be in a forgiving mood.

Program testing is a subject in its own right. For now, I'm going to offer just one testing suggestion: *test at the boundaries.* Boundary-value testing involves entering input at the extremes of what the program considers to be legal. In the case of the `CourseAverage` program, we'll probably first test whether the program gives the correct answer with some randomly selected set of data (like the data in the example at the beginning of Section 2.11). Next, we should test at the boundaries: If we enter zero for all scores, does the program give 0 as the course average? If we enter the maximum value for each score (20 for each program, 10 for each quiz, and 100 for each exam), does the program give 100 as the course average? Boundary-value testing is both easy to do and surprisingly good at revealing bugs.

Review Questions

1. Attempting to convert a nonnumeric string into an integer causes: (a) a compile-time error, (b) a run-time error, or (c) incorrect behavior?

2. In Java, run-time errors are called _____.

3. What are the two major capabilities of a debugger?

4. What's the best way to debug without a debugger?

Q & A

Q: **What does the following line mean? [p. 29]**

```
public static void main(String[] args)
```

A: One of the methods in a program must be named `main`. The name `main` indicates that this method is the "main" one. When we later execute the program, it will always start at `main`. The words `public`, `static`, and `void` all describe properties of `main`. `public` says that `main` can be called from outside the class. Java has two types of methods: class methods and instance methods. `static` states that `main` is a class method. `void` says that `main` does not return a value. Inside the parentheses, `String[] args` states that `main` will be provided with an array of character strings when the program begins to execute. Even though our program doesn't use these strings, we're still required to acknowledge that they're available.

Q: **When I use Notepad or WordPad to create a Java source file, the file name has an extra `.txt` extension. How do I get rid of this? [p. 32]**

A: In Notepad, at least, there's an easy way to prevent this behavior. When you save the file for the first time, put quotation marks around the file name. For example, if you want the file to be named `Foo.java`, enter `"Foo.java"` as the file name. This trick doesn't work in WordPad, unfortunately. Either rename the file after you've created it, or don't use WordPad.

Q: **Where did the `double` type get its name? [p. 42]**

A: `double` is short for "double-precision." Numbers stored in `double` form have greater precision than numbers stored in `float` form, which is the alternative in Java. `float` is a contraction of "floating-point." The names `double` and `float` come from Java's predecessors, C and C++.

Q: **What's the proper way to pronounce `char`? [p. 42]**

A: There's no universally accepted pronunciation. Some people pronounce `char` in the same way as the first syllable of "character." Others say "char," as in

```
char broiled;
```

Q: **Should all constants in a program be given names? [p. 52]**

A: No. Everyday constants such as 0 and 1 shouldn't be given names unless there's a chance that they'll be replaced by other values during maintenance. Also, constants that are used only once in a program are often not named, since they'll be easy to change in the future and there's no chance of inconsistency.

Q: **The compiler gave me an error message when I tried to store the value returned by Math.round into an int variable. What did I do wrong? [p. 56]**

A: When we use Math.round to round a double value, it returns a long value, not an int value. A long value can't be assigned to an int variable, which explains the error message. There are two ways to avoid the problem. One is to declare the variable to have type long rather than int. The other is to convert the value returned by Math.round before storing it in the int variable. Here's an example:

```
double x = 3.5;
int i = (int) Math.round(x);
```

casting ➤9.5

By putting the word int in parentheses, we're telling Java to convert the value returned by Math.round to type int. This technique is called *casting.*

Q: **I don't understand why we need the SimpleIO.prompt method. Why not just use System.out.print to display the prompt? [p. 61]**

A: In Java, messages written to the screen don't always appear immediately. We definitely want the prompt message to appear immediately; otherwise, the user might end up staring at a blank screen, wondering what to do. The SimpleIO.prompt method displays the prompt using System.out.print, but then it issues a "flush" command, forcing the prompt to appear on the screen. See Appendix E for more information about how the SimpleIO class was written.

Q: **When I compile my program using the javac compiler, there are so many error messages that they scroll off the DOS window faster than I can read them. What should I do? [p. 71]**

A: There are several solutions to this problem, depending on your operating system and which version of the Java Development Kit you're using. Let's say that you're trying to compile the file named MyProg.java.

If you're using version 1.1 of the JDK and Windows NT, use the command

```
javac MyProg.java 2>errors.txt
```

The error messages will be saved in a file named errors.txt. (There's nothing magic about this name, by the way; feel free to choose a different one.) You can view this file in an editor or print it. You can also examine the file without using an editor by typing the command

```
more <errors.txt
```

more is a program that lets you view the contents of a file one screen at a time. You'll need to press a key after viewing each screen.

If you're using version 1.1 of the JDK and your operating system is Windows 95 or 98, use the following command instead:

```
javac -J-Djavac.pipe.output=true MyProg.java >errors.txt
```

Again, the error messages will end up in a file named `errors.txt`.

If you're using version 1.2 of the JDK, you can cause the scrolling to stop after each screen by using the command

```
javac -Xstdout MyProg.java | more
```

To save the error messages in a file named `errors.txt`, use the command

```
javac -Xstdout MyProg.java >errors.txt
```

Summary

- A class is a collection of related variables and/or methods. A Java program consists of one or more classes.
- A method is a series of statements.
- A statement is a command to be executed when the program is run.
- A small program consists of a class containing a single method named `main`. `main` is executed automatically when the program is run.
- Before a program can be executed, it must be entered and compiled.
- To compile a program using the Java Development Kit, use the `javac` command.
- To execute a program using the Java Development Kit, use the `java` command.
- Java has three kinds of comments: single-line comments, multiline comments, and "doc comments."
- A Java program consists of tokens. Tokens may be separated by any number of spaces and blank lines.
- Indentation is used to signify nesting: indentation increases as the amount of nesting increases.
- There are several methods of brace placement commonly used by Java programmers.
- Variables in a method must be declared before they can be used.
- Trying to use the value of a variable declared in a method before it has been initialized is an error in Java.
- The assignment operator can be used to assign an initial value to a variable or to change the value of a variable.
- Every variable must have a type.
- Java's types include `int`, `double`, `boolean`, and `char`.
- A literal is a token that represents a particular number or other value.
- A `double` literal may contain an exponent.

- `char` literals are written within single quotes.
- Identifiers consist of letters, digits, and underscores, with a letter or underscore at the beginning.
- There is no limit on the length of an identifier.
- Java is a case-sensitive language: lowercase letters are not considered equivalent to uppercase letters.
- By convention, when an identifier consists of more than one word, Java programmers capitalize the first letter of each word after the first.
- By convention, class names begin with an uppercase letter.
- Java's keywords cannot be used as identifiers.
- Expressions are constructed from operators and operands. Operands can be variables, literals, or other expressions.
- The binary arithmetic operators are + (addition), - (subtraction), * (multiplication), / (division), and % (remainder).
- The operands in an arithmetic expression can be integers or floating-point numbers, with mixing allowed.
- When an integer is divided by an integer, the result is truncated to an integer.
- The unary arithmetic operators are + and -.
- The *, /, and % operators take precedence over the binary + and - operators.
- The binary arithmetic operators are left associative.
- The result of a calculation involving floating-point numbers may not be entirely accurate because of round-off error.
- Assigning an `int` value to a `double` variable is legal, but assigning a `double` value to an `int` variable is not.
- The compound assignment operators (including +=, -=, *=, /=, and %=) combine assignment with another operation.
- It is often advantageous to create names for constants.
- A constant is declared in the same way as a variable, except that the word `final` appears at the beginning of the declaration.
- By convention, names of constants are written entirely in uppercase letters, with underscores used to indicate boundaries between words.
- A method is a series of statements that can be executed as a unit.
- A method is called by writing the name of the method, followed by a pair of parentheses. The method's arguments (if any) go inside the parentheses.
- Some methods return a value when they have completed execution. These methods correspond to functions in mathematics.
- Java provides a number of methods for performing mathematical calculations. These methods, which belong to the `Math` class, include `pow` (power), `sqrt` (square root), `abs` (absolute value), `max` (maximum), `min` (minimum), and `round`.

- The value returned by a method can be saved in a variable, used as an argument in another method call, or used as an operand in an expression.
- `System.out.print` and `System.out.println` can be used to display output on the screen. `println` advances to the next output line after printing; `print` does not.
- Printing the new-line character (\n) terminates the current output line and causes the cursor to move to the next line.
- To print the " (double quote) character as part of a string, put \" into the string.
- To print the \ (backslash) character as part of a string, put two \ characters into the string.
- The + operator can often be used to combine multiple items into a single item for printing purposes.
- Before attempting to read input entered by the user, always prompt the user first.
- A package is a collection of related classes.
- Java comes with a number of packages, known as the Java Application Programming Interface (API).
- Debugging is the process of finding bugs in a program and fixing them.
- A bug can show up in one of three ways: as a compile-time error, as a run-time error, or as incorrect behavior.
- In Java, run-time errors are known as exceptions.
- A program can often be debugged faster with the aid of a software tool called a debugger.
- In the absence of a debugger, `System.out.println` can be used to display the values of variables at key points in a program.

Exercises

Section 2.3

1. Locate the error in the following comment and show how to fix it.
```
/* CSc 2310
   Program 1: Basic interpreter
   Author: Billy Gates /*
```

2. How many tokens does the `Lottery` program (Section 2.4) contain?

Section 2.4

3. In each part below, locate the error and show how to fix it.
```
(a) int a = b = 0;
(b) int i = 1;
    int j = i + 2, k = i + 3;
    int i = j + k;
```

Section 2.5   4. Locate the error in each of the following declarations and show how to fix it.

(a) `double speedOfLight = 299,792,458.0;`
(b) `double pi = 3.14159e;`

5. Which one of the following `double` literals is not equivalent to the others?

(a) `1.23e+1`
(b) `1230.0e-3`
(c) `0.0123e3`
(d) `12.3e0`

Section 2.6   6. Locate the error in each of the following declarations and show how to fix it.

(a) `int students = 30, teacher = 1, class;`
(b) `double total-balance = 0, depositsFor2000;`
(c) `double expenses, net_profit, 2001revenues;`

Section 2.7   7. Give the *value* and *type* (`int` or `double`) of each of the following expressions.

(a) `- 1 + - 4.5`
(b) `4 - 5 - 6`
(c) `13 / 2 * 2.0`
(d) `1 % 2 + 3 % 2`
(e) `5 % 6 % 7`

8. Add parentheses to the following expressions to indicate how Java will interpret them. (An expression that contains *n* operators will need *n* – 1 sets of parentheses.)

(a) `a + - + b + - d`
(b) `a / b / c * d * e`
(c) `a + b - c + d`
(d) `a * b / c % d + e`
(e) `- a - b - c - d`

9. What is the output of the following program?

```java
public class Exercise2_9 {
    public static void main(String[] args) {
        int d1 = 11;
        int d4 = d1 % 2;
        d1 /= 2;
        int d3 = d1 % 2;
        d1 /= 2;
        int d2 = d1 % 2;
        d1 /= 2;
        System.out.println("Answer: " + d1 + d2 + d3 + d4);
    }
}
```

Section 2.10   10. Show the output produced by the following statement:

`System.out.println("\"a\n\\b\"");`

11. Locate the error in each of the following statements and show how to fix it.

(a) `System.out.println("Java directory: C:\JDK1.2");`
(b) `System.out.println("\"\\\");`
(c) `System.out.println("Who is this "Wisnovsky," anyway?");`

Section 2.11   12. Lines 110 and 111 of the `CourseAverage` program could be simplified further. Instead of `.30 * programAverage * 5`, we could write `1.50 * programAverage`. The expression `.10 * quizAverage * 10` could be replaced by `quizAverage`. Would it be a good idea to make these changes? Why or why not?

Programming Projects

1. Simplify the `CourseAverage` program as described on pages 69–70 by replacing the individual program and quiz variables by the `programTotal` and `quizTotal` variables.

2. Write a program named `ASCIIArt` that displays the following output on the screen:

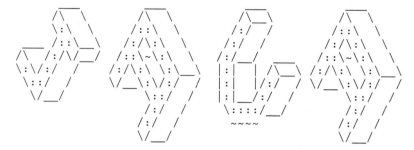

3. Write a program named `PrintJava` that displays the following output on the screen:

```
     /\___      ___      /\__      ___
     \:\    \    /::\    \    /:/  /    /::\    \
   ___/::\___\  /:/\:\    \  /:/  /    /:/\:\    \
  /\   /:/\/__/ /::\~\:\    \ /:/__/___ /:/  \~\:\    \
  \:\/:/  /    /:/\:\ \:\___\ |:|    | /\___\ /:/\:\ \:\___\
   \::/  /    \/__\:\/:/  / |:|    | |/:/  / \/__\:\/:/  /
   \/__/         \::/  / |:|__|_/:/  /       \::/  /
                 /:/  / \:::::/__/       /:/  /
                /:/  /   ~~~~          /:/  /
                \/__/                   \/__/
```

4. Write a program named `SellStocks` that calculates the value of a stock sale. The user will be prompted to enter the stock price, the number of shares to be sold, and the commission rate. The program will calculate the value of the shares by multiplying the stock price by the number of shares. It will also calculate the commission (the value of the shares multiplied by the commission rate) and the net proceeds (the value of the shares minus the commission). The following example shows what the user will see on the screen:

```
This program calculates the net proceeds from a sale of stock.

Enter stock price: 10.125
Enter number of shares: 11
Value of shares: $111.38

Enter commission rate (as a percentage): 1.5
Commission: $1.67
Net proceeds: $109.71
```

The stock price, number of shares, and commission rate may contain digits after the decimal point. Dollar amounts must be rounded to the nearest cent.

5.   Write a program named `DayOfWeek` that computes the day of the week for any date entered by the user. The user will be prompted to enter a month, day, and year. The program will then display the day of the week for that date as a number between 1 and 7, where 1 represents Sunday and 7 represents Saturday. The following example shows what the user will see on the screen:

`This program calculates the day of the week for any date.`

`Enter month (1-12):` **9**
`Enter day (1-31):` **25**
`Enter year:` **1998**

`The day of the week is 6 (1 = Sunday; 7 = Saturday)`

Hint: Use Zeller's congruence to compute the day of the week. Zeller's congruence relies on the following quantities:

J is the century (19, in our example)
K is the year within the century (98)
m is the month (9)
q is the day of the month (25)

The day of the week is determined by the following formula:

$$h = (q + 26(m+1)/10 + K + K/4 + J/4 + 5J) \bmod 7$$

where the results of all divisions are truncated. The value of h will lie between 0 (Saturday) and 6 (Friday). *Note:* Zeller's congruence assumes that January and February are treated as months 13 and 14 of the previous year; this affects the values of K and m, and possibly the value of J. Note that the value of h does not match the desired output of the program, so some adjustment will be necessary.

Answers to Review Questions

Section 2.1
1.   Comment
2.   String
3.   Print and advance to the next line
4.   Variables and/or methods

Section 2.2
1.   Bytecode instructions
2.   An interpreter
3.   `javac CourseAverage.java`

Section 2.3
1.   Three
2.   `//`
3.   Nine: `System`, `.`, `out`, `.`, `println`, `(`, `"James Gosling"`, `)`, and `;`
4.   Nesting

Section 2.4
1.   Assignment
2.   The compiler will issue an error message.
3.   Initializer

Section 2.5
1.   `double`
2.   `boolean`

	3.	`char`
	4.	Literal
Section 2.6	1.	All are valid except `100bottles`, which begins with a digit.
	2.	There is no limit on the length of an identifier.
	3.	Convention
	4.	Keywords
Section 2.7	1.	Operands
	2.	+ and -
	3.	Round-off
	4.	Compound assignment
Section 2.8	1.	`final`
	2.	Names of constants are written entirely in uppercase letters, with underscores used to indicate boundaries between words.
	3.	Helps the reader understand the meaning of the constant. Other answers: makes programs easier to modify; inconsistencies and typographical errors are less likely.
	4.	The name `TWENTY_FOUR` doesn't indicate the significance of the number `24`.
Section 2.9	1.	Arguments
	2.	`Math`
	3.	Functions
	4.	Store it in a variable, use it as an argument in another method call, or use it as an operand in an expression.
Section 2.10	1.	Escape sequence
	2.	The + operator
	3.	Prompt
	4.	Packages
Section 2.11	1.	Comment block
Section 2.12	1.	(b)
	2.	Exceptions
	3.	Checking whether statements are being executed in the proper order, and checking whether variables have the proper values.
	4.	Use `System.out.println` to print the values of variables.

3   Classes and Objects

Like many other modern programming languages, Java is "object-oriented"—
the "object" concept is central to the language. Objects play such an important
role in Java that I've chosen to devote this entire chapter to them. The chapter
explains what objects and classes are and shows how classes are declared. It
shows how objects are created from classes and how methods are used to perform operations on objects. It also explains how objects are stored in computer
memory.

The chapter develops two classes, `Account` and `Fraction`, as examples.
The `String` class—one of the most important of Java's standard classes—is also
introduced.

Objectives

- Learn what objects are.
- Learn how objects are represented by variables and methods organized into
  classes.
- Learn how to declare classes from which objects can be created.
- Learn how to create objects.
- Learn how to perform operations on objects by calling methods.
- Learn how to write programs that consist of more than one class.
- Learn how objects are stored in computer memory.
- Learn about Java's `String` class.

3.1 Objects as Models

Java is an ***object-oriented*** language. The ***object*** concept lies at the heart of Java, so it's crucial that you become familiar with objects. The sooner you become comfortable working with objects, the sooner you'll be able to write interesting programs in Java.

The word "object" suggests something in the physical world. (In the *American Heritage Dictionary,* one of the definitions of *object* is "something perceptible esp. to the sense of vision or touch.") Discussing objects in the context of writing software seems odd, because software appears to have little to do with the real world. In fact, however, a program can be thought of as a model of reality, with many objects in the program representing physical objects.

Objects have two properties:

- ***State.*** An object contains one or more items of information.
- ***Behavior.*** An object has behavior: it responds to operations that are performed on it. Some of these operations may change the state of the object.

In programming terminology, an object stores data, and it provides operations on that data.

Although this definition may seem far removed from everyday life, it's really not. There are objects all around you. Let's look at a few examples of real-world objects:

- ***Example 1: Ball-point pen.*** The state of a ball-point pen with a retractable point can be represented by two values:

  Is the point of the pen exposed?
  How much ink remains in the pen?

  Operations on a pen include:

  Press the button at the end of the pen. This action affects whether or not the point of the pen is exposed.
  Move the pen with the point held against a sheet of paper. This action reduces the amount of ink remaining in the pen.
  Replace the pen's cartridge. This action increases the amount of ink remaining in the pen.
  Determine how much ink remains in the pen. This action doesn't affect the state of the pen; it merely involves examining the level of ink remaining in the pen's cartridge.

- ***Example 2: Bank account.*** A real-world bank account contains a great deal of information: the account number, the balance, the transactions performed on the account since it was opened, and so forth. For simplicity, let's assume that a bank account stores only one piece of information: the balance. If we make this assumption, then relatively few operations are possible on a bank account. These operations include:

Deposit money into an account. This action increases the account's balance.

Withdraw money from the account. This action decreases the account's balance.

Check the balance in the account. This action returns the account's balance without changing it.

Close the account. This action reduces the account's balance to zero.

- ■ ***Example 3: Car.*** The state of a car is even more complex than the state of a bank account. It includes the amount of fluids in the car (fuel, oil, coolant, etc.), the state of the tires, and even the condition of each part in the car. For programming purposes, however, we can often simplify and focus on just a few elements of the state, such as whether or not the engine is on and how much fuel remains in the car's tank. Likewise, the operations that can be performed on a car are many: starting the engine, driving a certain distance, and so on.

As these examples suggest, nearly every "real-world" object can be modeled within a program, although we may have to simplify our computer model by ignoring details that aren't of interest. Objects in the software realm don't always correspond to real-world entities, however. In programming, we'll often work with artificial objects that don't model objects in the real world. However, like all objects, these artificial objects will have state and behavior.

Review Question

1. Objects have two properties. One is *state*. What is the other?

3.2 Representing Objects Within a Program

We saw in Section 3.1 that a real-world object has both *state* and *behavior*. In Java, the state of an object is stored in ***instance variables.*** (Some books use the term ***fields*** instead.) The behavior of an object is represented by ***instance methods.*** In Section 3.4, we'll see where this terminology comes from.

Instance Variables

Instance variables within an object keep track of the object's state. Some variables will store a single value, such as an integer or floating-point number. Others may store entire objects. (Yes, objects are allowed to contain other objects.) Let's see what instance variables we might need for the classes described in Section 3.1.

■ *Example 1: Ball-point pen.* We need to keep track of two items of data:

Is the point of the pen exposed?
How much ink remains in the pen?

We might store the first item in an instance variable named `pointIs-Exposed`. This variable will need only two values (`true` and `false`), so it would have type `boolean`. The amount of ink remaining could be stored in an instance variable named `inkRemaining`. This variable will store a number, probably with digits after the decimal point, so we could declare it to have type `double`.

■ *Example 2: Bank account.* In Section 3.1, we made the simplifying assumption that a bank account stores only one piece of information: the balance. Let's store the balance in an instance variable named `balance`; this will be a number with digits after the decimal point, so we could make it a `double` variable.

■ *Example 3: Car.* Again, we'll keep our model simple by storing only a few items of data. To keep track of whether or not the engine is on, we could use a `boolean` variable named `engineIsOn`. We might use a `double` variable named `fuelRemaining` to remember how much fuel remains in the car's tank.

Instance Methods

For each kind of object, we need to describe what operations can be performed on that object. In Java, operations on objects are represented by instance methods. To perform an operation on an object, we'll call one of the instance methods associated with the object.

Like the methods described in Section 2.9, an instance method may require arguments when it's called, and it may return a value. However, instance methods have an additional property that wasn't mentioned in Section 2.9: when asked to perform an operation on an object, an instance method can examine and/or change the values stored in any of the object's instance variables.

Returning to the examples of Section 3.1, let's identify the instance methods that we'll need for each kind of object.

■ *Example 1: Ball-point pen.* The `pressButton` method will "toggle" the `pointIsExposed` variable, changing it from `false` to `true` or from `true` to `false`. The `write` method will reduce the value of `inkRemaining`, based on the amount of time spent writing (an argument that will be supplied to the method). The `replaceCartridge` method will restore `inkRemaining` to its maximum value. The `checkInkRemaining` method will return the value of the `inkRemaining` variable.

■ *Example 2: Bank account.* The `deposit` method will add the amount of the deposit (an argument) to `balance`. The `withdraw` method will subtract the amount of the withdrawal (an argument) from `balance`. The `getBalance` method will return the current value of `balance`. The `close` method will store zero into `balance`.

■ *Example 3: Car.* The `startEngine` method will store `true` into the `engineIsOn` variable; the `stopEngine` method will store `false` into this variable. The `drive` method will reduce `fuelRemaining` by an amount calculated by dividing the distance traveled (an argument) by the expected fuel consumption. The `addFuel` method will increase `fuel-Remaining` by an amount specified as an argument.

Review Questions

1. The state of an object is stored in _____ _____ [two words].

2. The behavior of an object is represented by _____ _____ [two words].

3.3 Classes

The instance variables and instance methods that belong to a particular kind of object are grouped together into a *class.* For example, all ball-point pens might belong to a class named `BallpointPen`. All bank accounts might belong to a class named `Account`. All cars might belong to a class named `Car`.

This section describes the basics of creating classes in Java. To keep things simple, I'll postpone a number of details until Chapter 10.

Declaring a Class

A *class declaration* contains declarations of instance variables and instance methods. Most class declarations also contain declarations of one or more *constructors,* whose job is to initialize objects when they're created.

A class declaration typically has the following form:

class declaration

```
public class class-name {
    variable-declarations
    constructor-declarations
    method-declarations
}
```

The order of the declarations within a class usually doesn't matter. Some programmers prefer to put the variable declarations last, for example.

Let's develop a declaration for the `Account` class. Following this outline, the class will have the following overall appearance:

```
public class Account {
    variable-declarations
```

constructor-declarations
method-declarations
}

To complete the declaration of `Account`, we'll need to add instance variables, constructors, and instance methods.

The declaration of an instance variable, a constructor, or an instance method usually begins with an ***access modifier*** (one of the words `public` or `private`), which determines whether that entity can be accessed by other classes (`public`) or only within the class itself (`private`). The most common arrangement—and often the best one—is for instance variables to be private and constructors and instance methods to be public.

Declaring Instance Variables

Declaring instance variables is much like declaring variables in `main`. The primary difference is that declarations of instance variables normally begin with the word `private`, indicating that access to these variables from outside the class is forbidden. For example, here's a declaration of the `balance` variable, which would belong to the `Account` class:

```
private double balance;
```

The reason for making `balance` private rather than public is to make sure that the only access to the variable is through the instance methods in the `Account` class. By limiting access in this way, we can ensure that the value of `balance` is always legal. (In particular, we might want to prevent the value of `balance` from becoming negative!) The policy of making instance variables private rather than public is known as ***information hiding.*** Section 10.2 describes some additional advantages of this technique.

Declaring Instance Methods

The declaration of an instance method consists of an access modifier, a result type, the method's name, the parameters (if any), and the body (a series of statements to be executed when the method is called). Here's an outline of the `Account` class's `deposit` method:

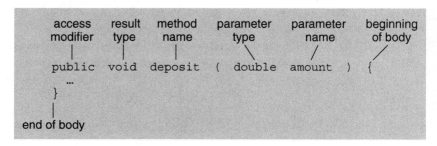

Let's take a closer look at each part of this declaration:

- *Access modifier.* For now, we'll use the word `public`, which specifies that the method can be called anywhere in a program, not just in the class. In later chapters, we'll see that `private` is sometimes more appropriate.

- *Result type.* The result type indicates what type of answer to expect when the method is called; if no value is returned, the result type is `void`. Depositing money into a bank account changes the balance in the account, but it doesn't cause a result to be returned, so `deposit`'s result type is `void`.

identifiers ➤*2.6* - *Method name.* The name of a method can be any legal identifier.

- *Parameters.* A method is allowed to have any number of *parameters*. Each parameter represents a single item of data that will be supplied when the method is called. For each parameter, we'll have to specify its *type* and its *name* (an identifier). (Arguments and parameters are very similar—the only difference is a matter of viewpoint. The names specified in a method declaration are *parameters*. The values supplied when a method is called are *arguments*.) If a method has no parameters, the parentheses will be empty. The `deposit` method has a single parameter, `amount`, which has type `double`.

- *Body.* The body of a method consists of a series of statements enclosed within curly braces. These statements will have access to all variables declared in the class. They will also have access to the method's parameters. The `deposit` method will have access to both the `balance` variable and the `amount` parameter.

Method Overloading

Java allows a class to contain several methods with the same name, provided that the methods have different numbers of parameters or there is some difference in the types of the parameters. For example, the `BallpointPen` class might have two `write` methods. One version of `write` would reduce the value of `ink-Remaining` based on the amount of time spent writing, so it would have a single parameter (`duration`, let's say). The second version of `write` might have two parameters (`duration` and `writingPressure`, perhaps), which would distinguish it from the original version. When there are several versions of a method
method overloading ➤ *10.3* within a single class, we say that the method is ***overloaded.***

Overloading is best used for methods that perform essentially the same operation. There will be fewer method names for us to remember, and we won't have to create different names for methods that do the same thing.

Declaring Constructors

When we create a new object, its instance variables are initialized by a ***constructor.*** Like a method, a constructor may have parameters, allowing us to supply data that the constructor will need.

A constructor looks like an instance method, except that it has no result type and its name is the same as the name of the class itself. A constructor for the Account class might have the following appearance:

```
public Account(double initialBalance) {
    ...
}
```

The initialBalance parameter will allow us to specify the initial balance to be stored in an Account object when it is created.

A class may have more than one constructor, provided that the constructors have different parameters. (In other words, constructors can be overloaded.) Having multiple constructors is often a good idea, because it gives us more options when creating objects. The Account class, for example, could benefit from having a second constructor with no parameters. This constructor would simply set the balance in a new account to zero.

Example: An Account Class

Here's a complete declaration of the Account class:

Account.java

```
 1  public class Account {
 2     // Instance variables
 3     private double balance;
 4
 5     // Constructors
 6     public Account(double initialBalance) {
 7        balance = initialBalance;
 8     }
 9
10     public Account() {
11        balance = 0.0;
12     }
13
14     // Instance methods
15     public void deposit(double amount) {
16        balance += amount;
17     }
18
19     public void withdraw(double amount) {
20        balance -= amount;
21     }
22
23     public double getBalance() {
24        return balance;
25     }
26
27     public void close() {
28        balance = 0.0;
29     }
30  }
```

return statement ►7.3
Note the use of the `return` statement in the `getBalance` method. This statement specifies what value a method will return. (In this case, `getBalance` returns the value stored in the `balance` variable.)

Review Questions

1. The job of a _____ is to initialize instance variables at the time an object is created.

2. Nested inside a class declaration are three kinds of declarations. What are they?

3. The words `public` and `private` are _____ _____ [two words].

4. A method is allowed to have _____, which represent data that will be supplied when the method is called.

3.4   Creating Objects

Once a class has been declared, we can create objects that belong to the class. We say that these objects are *instances* of the class. Each instance will contain its own copy of the instance variables declared in the class.

Most of the time, we'll want to store a newly created object in a variable. An object variable is declared in the same way as any other variable, with the class name serving to specify the type of the variable. For example, a variable that can store an instance of the `Account` class would have the following appearance:

```
Account acct;
```

Technically, the `acct` variable won't actually store an `Account` object. Instead, it will store a *reference* to an `Account` object. We'll explore this distinction further in Section 3.7.

We're now ready to create an `Account` object. The keyword `new`, when placed before a class name, causes an instance of the class to be created. We can then store the object (or, more precisely, a reference to the object) in a variable:

```
acct = new Account(1000.00);   // Create account with $1000
                               // balance
```

The `acct` variable now contains a reference to the newly created `Account` object. (We'll often ignore this distinction and just say that `acct` contains an `Account` object.) As a shortcut, we can declare the `acct` variable and create the `Account` object in a single step:

```
Account acct = new Account(1000.00);
```

The `Account` class provides a second constructor, so we have an alternative way to create an `Account` object:

```
acct = new Account();   // Create account with zero balance
```

This statement creates an `Account` object whose `balance` variable has been initialized to zero.

Now that we know what an instance is, the term "instance variable" begins to make sense. An instance variable is a variable that's stored in every instance of a class. For example, every instance of the `Account` class contains an instance variable named `balance`. The term "instance method" is used to describe methods that need access to instance variables (as all the methods in the `Account` class do). In Chapter 7, we'll see that not all variables in a class are necessarily instance variables, and not all methods are necessarily instance methods.

Review Questions

1. Once a class has been declared, we can create objects that belong to the class. We say that these objects are _____ of the class.

2. An object variable doesn't actually store an object. Instead, it stores a _____ to an object.

3. The keyword _____ is placed before a class name in order to create an object.

4. Where does the term "instance variable" come from?

3.5 Calling Instance Methods

Once an object has been created, we can perform operations on it by calling the instance methods in the object's class. Calling an instance method is done by writing the name of an object, a dot, and then the name of the method. After the method name comes a pair of matching parentheses containing the arguments (if any). The arguments provide the method with any data that it will need to complete its task.

instance method call

> *object* . *method-name* (*arguments*)

The parentheses are mandatory, even if there are no arguments.

Suppose that the `acct` variable contains an instance of the `Account` class. We could then perform the following method calls:

```
acct.deposit(1000.00);   // Deposit $1000 into acct
acct.withdraw(500.00);   // Withdraw $500 from acct
acct.close();            // Close acct
```

The reason that we have to mention `acct` each time is that there might be many different accounts in existence. We need to specify *which* account is the target of each action. We could have two accounts, for example, and write either

```
acct1.deposit(1000.00);   // Deposit $1000 into acct1
```

or

```
acct2.deposit(1000.00);   // Deposit $1000 into acct2
```

Let's take a closer look at how an instance method works. Recall that the `deposit` method consists of the following code:

```
public void deposit(double amount) {
  balance += amount;
}
```

Now, consider the following call of `deposit`:

```
acct1.deposit(1000.00);
```

`deposit` will add the value of `amount` (1000.00) to the `balance` variable *that belongs to the acct1 object.* If, instead, the call had been

```
acct2.deposit(1000.00);
```

then `deposit` would add 1000.00 to the `balance` variable *that belongs to the acct2 object.* Notice that the method itself doesn't specify which object's `balance` variable is being updated.

Some instance methods return a result when they're called, but others don't. For example, the `getBalance` method returns a `double` value, while the `deposit`, `withdraw`, and `close` methods don't return anything at all. When an instance method returns no result, a call of the method is an entire statement, so it ends with a semicolon:

```
acct.deposit(1000.00);
```

When an instance method *does* return a result, we'll probably want to make use of that result in one of the ways described in Section 2.9. Often, we'll store it in a variable:

```
double newBalance = acct.getBalance();   // Store acct balance
                                         // into newBalance
```

We could also use the value returned by `getBalance` in other ways, perhaps as an operand in an expression or as an argument to `System.out.println`:

```
System.out.println(acct.getBalance());   // Print acct balance
```

How Instance Methods Work

An instance method behaves much like a small program. It has a task that it's responsible for (the `deposit` method is responsible for updating an account's balance when money is deposited into the account) and possibly some data that it needs to accomplish that task (the amount of the deposit, in the case of `deposit`). It is activated by a method call. When an instance method is called, the program "jumps" to that method. The arguments in the call are copied into the method's corresponding parameters. The method then begins executing. When the method is finished, the program "returns" to the point at which the method was called.

Let's take a closer look at calls of deposit and getBalance, starting with the former:

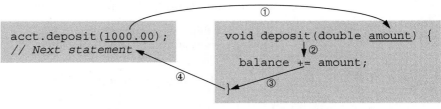

Method call   **Method declaration**

When the deposit method is called, the value of the argument (1000.00) is copied into the corresponding parameter, which is named amount (①). The first statement in the deposit method is then executed (②). There are no other statements in the method, so it reaches the end of its body (③). When a method has completed execution, it automatically returns to where it was called (④). The call of deposit is complete, so the statement after the call is executed next.

Now, suppose that we call getBalance:

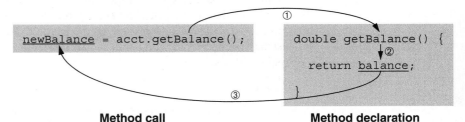

Method call   **Method declaration**

When getBalance is called, there's no argument to be copied. Instead, the program simply jumps to getBalance (①), and the first statement inside the method is executed (②). Executing a return statement causes the method to return immediately. The value specified by the return statement (the account's balance, in this example) is then stored into newBalance (③). After the assignment to newBalance has been performed, the next statement after the assignment is executed.

What deposit and getBalance have in common is that both are called by an object (acct in these examples) and both have access to the instance variables stored inside that object. When the acct object calls the deposit method, that method will increase the value of the balance variable, which is stored inside the acct object. When acct calls getBalance, it will return the value currently stored in acct's balance variable.

Review Question

1. To perform an operation on an object, we _____ one of the instance methods associated with the object.

3.6   **Writing Programs with Multiple Classes**

Let's write a small test program to check that the Account class works. We'll have the program create two Account objects and perform several operations on them. The program will check the balance after each operation to make sure it's being updated correctly.

TestAccount.java

```
1  public class TestAccount {
2    public static void main(String[] args) {
3      Account acct1 = new Account(1000.00);
4      System.out.println("Balance in account 1: " +
5                         acct1.getBalance());
6      acct1.deposit(100.00);
7      System.out.println("Balance in account 1: " +
8                         acct1.getBalance());
9      acct1.withdraw(150.00);
10     System.out.println("Balance in account 1: " +
11                        acct1.getBalance());
12     acct1.close();
13     System.out.println("Balance in account 1: " +
14                        acct1.getBalance());
15
16     Account acct2 = new Account();
17     System.out.println("Balance in account 2: " +
18                        acct2.getBalance());
19     acct2.deposit(500.00);
20     System.out.println("Balance in account 2: " +
21                        acct2.getBalance());
22     acct2.withdraw(350.00);
23     System.out.println("Balance in account 2: " +
24                        acct2.getBalance());
25     acct2.close();
26     System.out.println("Balance in account 2: " +
27                        acct2.getBalance());
28   }
29 }
```

Here's what the output of the program will look like:

```
Balance in account 1: 1000.0
Balance in account 1: 1100.0
Balance in account 1: 950.0
Balance in account 1: 0.0
Balance in account 2: 0.0
Balance in account 2: 500.0
Balance in account 2: 150.0
Balance in account 2: 0.0
```

The TestAccount class, together with the Account class, form a complete program. There are two ways to compile this program. One alternative is to put each class in a separate file: `TestAccount` would go into a file named `TestAccount.java` and `Account` would go into a file named `Account.java`. We can then compile the two files (if we're using the Java Development Kit) by entering the commands

```
javac Account.java
javac TestAccount.java
```

Actually, we can compile both files with a single command. If we simply type

```
javac TestAccount.java
```

the `javac` compiler will notice that the `Account` class is used in `Test-Account`, so it will look for a file named `Account.java`. When the compiler finds `Account.java`, it will check whether the file needs to be compiled and, if so, compile it automatically. `Account.java` needs to be compiled if either (a) no `Account.class` file is present, or (b) the `Account.class` file isn't current. To determine whether `Account.class` is up-to-date, the compiler will check the date and time at which the `Account.java` file was last modified. If the `Account.class` file is older, then it might not reflect any recent changes to `Account.java`. To be on the safe side, the compiler will create a new `Account.class` file.

In general, when a file is compiled, the compiler checks whether its dependent classes are up-to-date. If the `.java` file containing a dependent class has been modified since the `.class` file was created, `javac` will recompile the `.java` file automatically.

To execute the program, we'll use the command

```
java TestAccount
```

Notice that we don't mention the `Account` class. When the `java` interpreter loads the `TestAccount` program, it will notice that `Account` is missing and load it also.

For convenience, we might choose to put both the `Account` and `Test-Account` classes in the same file. If we do, the file will need to be named `TestAccount.java`, because `TestAccount` contains the `main` method, not `Account`. Also, we'll need to remove the `public` access modifier from the beginning of the `Account` class declaration. (The Java compiler allows only one class in a file to be declared `public`.) Compiling `TestAccount.java` causes two class files to be generated, `TestAccount.class` and `Account.class`, just as if the two classes had been put in different files.

Although either strategy (one file per class or all classes in one file) will work, it's often better to put only one class in each file. For one thing, that practice makes it easier to locate classes, because we can simply examine the names of the `.java` files until we find the desired class. Files are smaller and easier to edit if they contain only single classes. Also, if we make a change to a class declaration, we'll only have to recompile the class itself, not other classes that just happen to be in the same file.

Review Questions

1. Suppose that a program consists of two files: `BallpointPen.java` contains the declaration of the `BallpointPen` class, and `WriteLetter.java` contains a program that creates `BallpointPen` objects. What single command would compile both files?

2. What command would we use to execute the program described in Question 1?

3. Suppose that a program consists of more than one class. Which practice is usually better: putting all classes in one file, or putting each class in a separate file?

3.7 How Objects Are Stored

It's now time to take a look "under the hood" and see how objects are stored. So far, we've been able to avoid this detail. We can't postpone discussing it much longer, however, because it explains aspects of Java that would otherwise remain mysterious.

Consider the following declaration of an object variable:

```
Account acct;
```

This variable won't actually store an `Account` object. Instead, it will store a ***reference*** to an `Account` object. To help illustrate this difference, let's compare an ordinary `int` variable with an `Account` variable. Assume that the variable `i` is declared as follows:

```
int i;
```

We can visualize this variable as a box labeled `i`:

i [   ]

When we assign a value to `i`, that value is stored inside the box. For example, suppose that we perform the following assignment:

```
i = 0;
```

We'll now have the following picture:

i [0]

Similarly, we can visualize the `acct` variable as a box labeled `acct`:

acct [   ]

Suppose that we perform the following assignment:

```
acct = new Account(500.00);
```

The new `Account` object isn't stored in the `acct` box. Instead, the box contains a reference that "points to" the object. The object itself is drawn as a separate box:

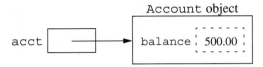

Instead of storing the object itself, the `acct` variable stores a value representing the *location* of the object.

In many programming languages, including C++, a variable such as `acct` would be called a ***pointer variable.*** In Java, however, it's known as a reference variable, because it has different properties than a pointer.

The `null` Keyword

To indicate that an object variable doesn't currently point to an object, we can assign the variable the value `null`. For example, to indicate that the `acct` variable isn't currently pointing to an `Account` object, we would use the statement

```
acct = null;   // acct doesn't point to an object
```

When an object variable has the value `null`, it's illegal to use the variable to call an instance method. If `acct` has the value `null`, executing the following statement will cause a run-time error (`NullPointerException`):

```
acct.deposit(500.00);   // Legal only if acct is not null
```

We'll encounter several uses for `null` in later chapters. For now, we'll use `null` primarily to initialize object variables without creating objects.

Object Assignment

One consequence of how objects are stored is that assignment of objects doesn't work the same as assignment of numbers. Suppose that `i` is an `int` variable with the value 10. Then suppose that we assign the value of `i` to another variable `j`:

```
j = i;
```

Both `i` and `j` now contain the number 10:

$$i \quad \boxed{10}$$

$$j \quad \boxed{10}$$

Next, let's assign a different value to `i`:

```
i = 20;
```

Here's the new picture:

$$i \boxed{20}$$

$$j \boxed{10}$$

Changing i had no effect on j, which still has the value 10.

Now, let's assume that acct1 contains a reference to an Account object with a balance of $500. Suppose that we assign the value of acct1 to another Account variable named acct2:

```
acct2 = acct1;
```

We'll end up with the following picture:

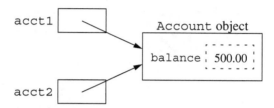

We haven't copied the Account object. Instead, both acct1 and acct2 refer to the *same* object. acct1 and acct2 are said to be *aliases,* because both represent the same object. Performing an operation that changes the acct1 object will also change the acct2 object, and vice-versa. For example, suppose that we deposit another $500 into acct1:

```
acct1.deposit(500.00);
```

The balance stored inside the Account object will change to $1000:

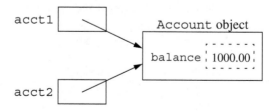

The balance for acct2 is now $1000.00 as well—a surprising outcome unless you understand that acct1 and acct2 represent the same object.

 Always keep in mind that copying an object variable using assignment never creates a new object. Forgetting this fact can lead to programming errors.

Some classes allow the creation of a new object that's identical to an existing object. The new object is said to be a ***clone*** of the old one. Clones are created by calling the `clone` method.

clone method ➤11.5

Garbage

Objects can become "orphaned" during program execution. Consider the following example:

```
acct1 = new Account(100.00);
acct2 = new Account(200.00);
acct1 = acct2;
```

After these assignments, we're left with the following picture:

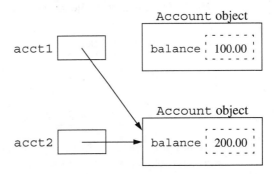

`acct1` refers to the same object as `acct2`, but what about the object that `acct1` *previously* referred to? No variable refers to that object, so we'll never be able to use it later in the program. The technical term for such an object is (believe it or not) ***garbage.*** Java provides automatic ***garbage collection:*** as a Java program runs, a software component known as the ***garbage collector*** watches for garbage and periodically "collects" it. The memory used by objects that have been garbage collected can be recycled and used for the creation of new objects. Garbage collection normally takes place when the program isn't doing any other useful activity, so it doesn't usually slow the program down.

Although garbage collection was invented decades ago, Java is the first widely used programming language to incorporate it. Most other popular languages (including Pascal, C, and C++) rely on the program to explicitly release memory that's no longer needed. Although this practice is potentially more efficient, it's also error-prone. Failing to recover garbage properly causes available memory to decrease, a condition known as a ***memory leak.*** After a period of time, a program with a memory leak may fail because it can't allocate memory that it needs. Releasing memory prematurely—when it's still in use—is even worse, often causing programs to crash. Garbage collection allows Java to avoid both problems.

Review Questions

1. Reference variables are known as _____ variables in other programming languages.

2. What value can we assign to an object variable to indicate that it doesn't currently store an object?

3. A new object that's been created by copying an existing object is said to be a _____.

4. An object that's no longer accessible through any object variable is said to be _____.

3.8 Developing a `Fraction` Class

So far, we've used `Account` as our primary example of a class. We'll now begin developing a second example, a class named `Fraction`. Instances of this class will represent mathematical fractions, such as 1/2 and 3/5. Creating this class will give us an opportunity to reinforce topics covered in previous sections, as well as introduce a few new topics. We'll also set the stage for future chapters, which will improve the `Fraction` class in several ways.

First, we need to consider the state and behavior of fractions:

- *State.* A `Fraction` object will need to store a numerator and a denominator. Both are integers.

- *Behavior.* There are many potential operations on fractions. (You undoubtedly learned a number of them at an early age.) Adding, subtracting, multiplying, and dividing are obvious choices, but we may want to add others later.

From this quick analysis, it's clear that the `Fraction` class will need two instance variables; `numerator` and `denominator` seem like logical names for these variables. The class will also need instance methods for performing arithmetic on fractions. Let's name these `add`, `subtract`, `multiply`, and `divide`. We'll also need a constructor or two.

Our first attempt at writing the `Fraction` class might look like this:

```
public class Fraction {
  private int numerator;    // Numerator of fraction
  private int denominator;  // Denominator of fraction

  public Fraction(int num, int denom) {  // Constructor
    numerator = num;
    denominator = denom;
  }

  // Methods will go here
}
```

The instance variables are declared, and the constructor is completely written, but the methods are missing.

To create a `Fraction` object, we'll use the `Fraction` constructor as follows:

```
Fraction f = new Fraction(4, 8);
```

The constructor will store 4 and 8, respectively, into the `numerator` and `denominator` variables of the new object. Although this strategy is a decent first attempt, it would be better if the constructor reduced fractions to lowest terms, so that 4/8 would be stored as 1/2. We'll add this improvement in Section 4.6.

Getters and Setters

Before we tackle `add`, `subtract`, `multiply`, and `divide`, we'll need to add a couple of other methods. The `Account` class has an instance method named `getBalance` that returns the balance stored in an account. The `Fraction` class will need similar methods named `getNumerator` and `getDenominator`. Here's what they'll look like:

```
public int getNumerator() {
   return numerator;
}

public int getDenominator() {
   return denominator;
}
```

An instance method that does nothing but return the value of an instance variable is said to be an *accessor* (or, more colloquially, a *getter*). By convention, names of getters start with the word `get`. Here are examples showing how `getNumerator` and `getDenominator` might be called, where `f` is a `Fraction` object:

```
int num = f.getNumerator();      // Get f's numerator
int denom = f.getDenominator();  // Get f's denominator
```

An instance method that stores its parameter into an instance variable is said to be a *mutator* (or *setter*). Names of setters begin with the word `set`, again by convention. For example, the `Account` class could have a setter named `setBalance`. The `Fraction` class could have methods named `setNumerator` and `setDenominator`:

```
public void setNumerator(int num) {
   numerator = num;
}

public void setDenominator(int denom) {
   denominator = denom;
}
```

Here's how the methods would be called:

```
f.setNumerator(5);    // Change f's numerator to 5
f.setDenominator(6);  // Change f's denominator to 6
```

Getters are often quite useful, because they provide safe access to an object's private instance variables. If the `Account` class didn't have a `getBalance` method, there would be no way to determine an account's balance.

Setters can also be useful, because they allow us to change data stored in private variables. In some cases, however, we may not want to allow changes to an object's instance variables. Such an object is said to be ***immutable*** (unchangeable). The advantage of making objects immutable is that they can be shared without problems. As we saw in Section 3.7, it's possible for more than one variable to refer to the same object. If the state of the object is later changed, the changes affect all the variables that refer to the object.

I've decided that instances of the `Fraction` class will be immutable: once a `Fraction` object has been created, its numerator and denominator will never change. Some of the classes in the Java API have this property, including the `String` class (Section 3.9).

Writing the `add` Method

To see how to write the `add`, `subtract`, `multiply`, and `divide` methods, let's first create a couple of `Fraction` objects:

```
Fraction f1 = new Fraction(1, 2);
Fraction f2 = new Fraction(3, 5);
```

Now, how would we add the two fractions to get a third fraction? It's tempting to say

```
Fraction f3 = add(f1, f2);   // WRONG
```

Unfortunately, this statement is illegal. `add` is an instance method, so it has to be called by an instance of the class. The correct way to call `add` is

```
Fraction f3 = f1.add(f2);   // Add f1 and f2
```

The `add` method will add the fraction stored in `f1` and the fraction stored in `f2`. The result will be a new fraction, which is then saved in `f3`. From this example, we see how the `add` method will look:

```
public Fraction add(Fraction f) {
   ...
}
```

The parameter `f` represents the second of the two fractions to be added.

Next, we need an algorithm for adding two fractions, but that's easy:

$$\frac{a}{b} + \frac{c}{d} = \frac{ad+bc}{bd}$$

With the help of this equation, we can now write the `add` method:

```
public Fraction add(Fraction f) {
  int num = numerator * f.getDenominator() +
            f.getNumerator() * denominator;
  int denom = denominator * f.getDenominator();
  Fraction result = new Fraction(num, denom);
  return result;
}
```

numerator and denominator refer to the numerator and denominator of the Fraction object that's calling add. To access the numerator and denominator of the parameter f, we use the getNumerator and getDenominator methods.

To see more clearly how the add method works, let's trace the execution of the following statement:

```
Fraction f3 = f1.add(f2);   // Add f1 and f2
```

1. The f2 argument is copied into the f parameter. As a result, all references to f in the body of the add method will actually refer to the f2 object.

2. The numerator of the new fraction is computed:

```
int num = numerator * f.getDenominator() +
          f.getNumerator() * denominator;
```

numerator contains the numerator of f1, the calling object. f.getDenominator() returns the denominator of f2. f.getNumerator() returns the numerator of f2, and denominator contains the denominator of f1.

3. The denominator of the new fraction is computed:

```
int denom = denominator * f.getDenominator();
```

denominator contains the denominator of f1 and f.getDenominator() returns the denominator of f2.

4. The new fraction is created and stored in the result variable:

```
Fraction result = new Fraction(num, denom);
```

5. The value of the result variable (the new fraction) is returned:

```
return result;
```

6. The new fraction is stored into f3.

We can shorten the add method slightly by combining the constructor call with the return statement:

```
public Fraction add(Fraction f) {
  int num = numerator * f.getDenominator() +
            f.getNumerator() * denominator;
  int denom = denominator * f.getDenominator();
  return new Fraction(num, denom);
}
```

If we choose, we can avoid the calls of getNumerator and getDenominator by having the add method access f's numerator and denominator variables directly:

```
public Fraction add(Fraction f) {
   int num = numerator * f.denominator +
             f.numerator * denominator;
   int denom = denominator * f.denominator;
   return new Fraction(num, denom);
}
```

Because it belongs to the Fraction class, the add method has access to the numerator and denominator variables of *any* Fraction object. Notice that accessing an instance variable belonging to an object is similar to calling an instance method: we write the name of the object, a dot, and then the name of the variable.

The subtract, multiply, and divide methods are similar to the add method, so I'll leave these as an exercise.

Adding a toString Method

To print the value stored in a Fraction object named f, we could use the following statement, which calls getNumerator and getDenominator:

```
System.out.println(f.getNumerator() + "/" +
                   f.getDenominator());
```

Although this statement works, it's not very convenient. To make it easier to print fractions, let's add an instance method to the Fraction class that returns a string of the form *"numerator/denominator"*. Here's what the method would look like:

```
public String toString() {
   return numerator + "/" + denominator;
}
```

toString method ➤ 11.5   In Java, the name toString is used for a method that returns the contents of an object as a string. With toString added to the Fraction class, we can now display the value stored in f by writing

```
System.out.println(f.toString());
```

In fact, we can shorten the statement even further:

```
System.out.println(f);
```

It turns out that System.out.println, when given an object as its argument, will automatically call the object's toString method. (That's why it's important to name the method toString.)

Review Questions

1. An instance method that returns the value of an instance variable is said to be an _____ .

2. An instance method that stores its parameter into an instance variable is said to be a _____ .

3. An object whose instance variables cannot be changed is said to be _____ .

4. A method that returns the contents of an object as a string should be named _____ .

3.9 Java's `String` Class

So far, we've seen what a class declaration looks like, and we've seen how to create objects and perform operations on them. Much of the time, however, we won't need to create our own classes, because the Java API provides a huge number of prewritten classes, ready for us to use.

Much of the effort in learning Java (or any other object-oriented language) is spent on mastering the classes that belong to its API. Of all the classes in the Java API, the `String` class is probably the most important. Instances of the `String` class represent strings of characters, which are used in virtually every Java program. Because of the importance of `String`, it will be the first of many API classes covered in this book.

The `String` class belongs to a package named `java.lang`. This package is automatically imported into every program, so we don't need an import declaration in order to use `String`. (`java.lang` is the *only* package that is automatically imported, by the way.)

Creating Strings

In Java, every string of characters, such as `"abc"`, is an instance of the `String` class. We can declare `String` variables, which can then be assigned `String` objects as their values:

```
String str1, str2;
```

`str1` and `str2` are each capable of storing a `String` object.

`String` objects can be created without using the word `new`. To create a `String` object, we can simply enclose the desired characters within double quotes:

```
str1 = "abc";
```

This statement creates a new `String` object containing the letters a, b, and c, and then assigns the object to the `str1` variable. `String` is the only class whose instances can be created without the word new. (This is an example of what programmers call *magic:* there's no reason for us to have suspected that instances of the String class could be created in this special way. Java treats the String class differently because of its importance and frequent use.)

We can visualize a String object as a series of characters, with each character identified by its position. The first character is located at position 0. The string "Java rules!", for example, has the letter J at position 0, a at position 1, and v at position 2:

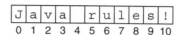

From now on, I'll use the term "string," which is more concise than "String object," but you should never forget that strings are in fact objects.

Common String Methods

The String class has a large number of instance methods. Table 3.1 lists some of the most commonly used methods. Notice that several of the methods in the table (indexOf, lastIndexOf, and substring) are overloaded.

To see what these methods do, let's look at a few examples. I'll assume that the following variable declarations are in effect:

```
String str1 = "Fat cat", str2;
char ch;
int index;
```

charAt   Let's start with the charAt method. This method returns the character stored at a specific position in a string:

```
ch = str1.charAt(0);   // Value of ch is now 'F'
ch = str1.charAt(6);   // Value of ch is now 't'
```

The argument to charAt must be an integer between 0 and $n - 1$, where n is the number of characters in the string.

indexOf   Both indexOf methods perform a search. The first version of indexOf searches for a string (the "search key") within a larger string, starting at the beginning of the larger string. To locate the string "at" within str1, we could use the following statement:

```
index = str1.indexOf("at");
```

After this assignment, index will have the value 1, indicating that the first occurrence of "at" within "Fat cat" begins at position 1. If "at" had not been found anywhere in str1, indexOf would have returned –1. The other version of indexOf begins the search at a specified position, rather than starting at position 0. This version is particularly useful when we need to repeat a previous search to find another occurrence of the search key. For example, after finding the first

Table 3.1

`String` Methods

Description	*Action*
`char charAt(int index)`	Returns the character at the specified index.
`int indexOf(String str)`	Returns the position of the first occurrence of `str` within this string.
`int indexOf(String str,` `        int fromIndex)`	Returns the position of the first occurrence of `str` within this string, with the search beginning at `fromIndex`.
`int lastIndexOf(String str)`	Returns the position of the last occurrence of `str` within this string.
`int lastIndexOf(String str,` `        int fromIndex)`	Returns the position of the last occurrence of `str` within this string; the search is performed in reverse, beginning at `fromIndex`.
`int length()`	Returns the length of this string.
`String substring(int beginIndex)`	Returns a substring of this string, starting at `beginIndex` and ending at the end of the string.
`String substring(int beginIndex,` `        int endIndex)`	Returns a substring of this string, starting at `beginIndex` and ending at `endIndex` − 1.
`String toLowerCase()`	Returns a similar string, with all letters converted to lowercase.
`String toUpperCase()`	Returns a similar string, with all letters converted to uppercase.
`String trim()`	Returns a similar string, with white-space characters removed from the beginning and end.

occurrence of `"at"` in `str1`, we could then use the following statement to find the second occurrence:

```
index = str1.indexOf("at", index + 1);
```

Starting the search at `index + 1` guarantees that we won't find the same occurrence of the search key. After this assignment, `index` will have the value 5, indicating that the second occurrence of `"at"` within `"Fat cat"` begins at position 5.

lastIndexOf   `lastIndexOf` is similar to `indexOf`, except that searches proceed backwards, starting from the end of the string. For example, let's search for the last occurrence of `"at"` in `str1`:

```
index = str1.lastIndexOf("at");
```

The value of `index` after the assignment will be 5. The second version of `lastIndexOf` begins the search at a specified position. To find the next-to-last occurrence of "at", we can call this version of lastIndexOf and have it start the search at index − 1:

```
index = str1.lastIndexOf("at", index - 1);
```

The value of index after the assignment will be 1.

The String class has additional versions of indexOf and lastIndexOf. They're similar to the ones shown in Table 3.1, except that the first argument is a single character rather than a string.

length

The length method returns the number of characters in a string. For example, str1.length() returns the length of str1, which is 7.

substring

One of the most important of these methods is substring, which returns a *substring:* a series of consecutive characters within a string. The substring is returned as a (new) String object. The first version of substring selects the portion of the string beginning at a specified position and continuing to the end of the string:

```
str2 = str1.substring(4);
```

After the assignment, str2 will have the value "cat". To select an arbitrary substring, we'd use the other version of substring, which accepts two arguments. The first argument specifies the position of the first character to include in the substring. The second specifies the position of the first character *after* the end of the substring. For example, the statement

```
str2 = str1.substring(0, 3);
```

assigns "Fat" to str2. In each case, substring creates a new string; the old string (str1 in our examples) isn't changed.

toLowerCase
toUpperCase

The toLowerCase and toUpperCase methods are useful for converting a string so that all letters in it are lowercase or uppercase. For example, after the assignment

```
str2 = str1.toLowerCase();
```

the value of str2 is "fat cat". After the assignment

```
str2 = str1.toUpperCase();
```

the value of str2 is "FAT CAT". Characters other than letters aren't changed by toLowerCase and toUpperCase. Also, the original string isn't affected by these methods.

trim

Finally, the trim method provides an easy way to remove spaces from both ends of a string. (Actually, trim will remove other invisible characters as well, including the tab character and the new-line character (\n).) Suppose that we perform the following two assignments:

```
str1 = "  How   now,   brown   cow?   ";
str2 = str1.trim();
```

Afterward, the value of `str2` will be

```
"How   now,   brown   cow?"
```

Spaces have been removed from the beginning and end of the string, but not between words.

Chaining Calls of Instance Methods

Suppose that we want to trim a string *and* convert it to lowercase. The obvious way to accomplish this effect is by two statements:

```
str2 = str1.trim();            // Trim str1
str2 = str2.toLowerCase();   // Convert str2 to lowercase
```

There's a shortcut available to us, however. When an instance method returns an object, that object can be used to call another instance method; we'll refer to this as "chaining" method calls. `trim` returns a string, so we can chain calls of `trim` and `toLowerCase`:

```
str2 = str1.trim().toLowerCase(); // Trim str1, then convert
                                  // the result to lowercase
```

The call `str1.trim()` returns an unnamed `String` object, which then calls `toLowerCase`. The string returned by `toLowerCase` is the one assigned to `str2`.

Using + to Concatenate Strings

One of the most common string operations is ***concatenation:*** joining two strings together to form a single string. The `String` class provides a `concat` method that performs concatenation, but it's rarely used. Concatenation of strings is so common that Java provides a shortcut. To concatenate strings, we simply put a plus sign (+) between them, as though we were adding two numbers. (Yes, this is also magic.) Here's an example:

```
str2 = str1 + "s";
```

The `str2` variable now contains the string `"Fat cats"`.

But that's not all! It turns out that the + operator works even if one of the operands isn't a `String` object. The non-`String` operand is converted to string form automatically before the concatenation is done. We first noticed this property in Section 2.10, where we were able to write

```
System.out.println("Celsius equivalent: " + celsius);
```

The + operator converts the value of `celsius` into a string, and then concatenates it to the end of `"Celsius equivalent: "`.

If the + operator is used to combine a string with any other kind of object, the object's `toString` method is called to convert the object into string form. As a result, we can write statements such as

```
System.out.println("Value of fraction: " + f);
```

where `f` is a `Fraction` object, instead of having to write

```
System.out.println("Value of fraction: " + f.toString());
```

Be careful with the + operator. In order for it to mean string concatenation, at least one of its two operands must be a string. Otherwise, it performs ordinary addition.

```
System.out.println("Java" + 1);      // Prints "Java1"
System.out.println(1 + "Java");      // Prints "1Java"
System.out.println(1 + 2);           // Prints "3"
```

If you apply the + operator several times in a row, hoping to concatenate all the operands into a single string, make sure that at least one of the first two operands is a string, or you may get an unexpected result:

```
System.out.println("Java" + 1 + 2);  // Prints "Java12"
System.out.println(1 + 2 + "Java");  // Prints "3Java"
```

In the second statement, the 1 and 2 were added to get 3, which was then concatenated with `"Java"` to form `"3Java"`.

The + operator is also useful for breaking up long strings into smaller, more manageable chunks. Suppose that we want to display the following message:

```
Bothered by unsightly white space? Remove it quickly and
easily with the new, improved trim method!
```

Instead of calling `System.out.println` twice, once for each line, we can join the two lines into a single string and then print that string with one call of `System.out.println`:

```
System.out.println("Bothered by unsightly white space? " +
                   "Remove it quickly and\neasily with " +
                   "the new, improved trim method!");
```

Section 2.7 discussed the compound assignment operators, which include +=. The += operator works for strings, as it turns out. By applying this operator, we can easily add characters to the end of an existing string:

```
String str = "The quick brown fox ";

str += "jumped over ";
str += "the lazy dog.";
```

The final value of the `str` variable will be `"The quick brown fox jumped over the lazy dog."`

One last tip: We can use the + operator as a quick and easy way to convert a number to string form—a technique that's handy when we're calling a method that requires a string but we want to pass a number instead. The secret is to use + to concatenate the number with an empty string—a string containing no characters. For example, if `i` is an `int` variable containing 37, then `i + ""` is the string `"37"`.

PROGRAM   **Decoding a Vehicle Identification Number**

When a vehicle is manufactured, the manufacturer assigns it a unique identifying number, called the *Vehicle Identification Number* (*VIN*). This number encodes a large amount of information about the vehicle in a 17-character string. You'll find the VIN in various places on a car. One location is the top of the dashboard, where the VIN is inscribed on a plate that can be read through the windshield.

Knowing how to decipher a VIN can be a useful skill, especially when buying a used car. (You don't want to pay for a 1999 model if the car was actually manufactured in 1996.) There are four parts to a VIN:

- *World Manufacturer Identifier* (3 characters)—Identifies the manufacturer and make of the vehicle.

- *Vehicle Description Section* (5 characters)—Describes characteristics of the vehicle.

- *Check digit* (1 character)—Helps verify that the VIN is correct.

- *Vehicle Identification Section* (8 characters)—Identifies the specific vehicle.

For example, consider JHMCB7658LC056658, the VIN from a Honda Accord that I once had. (If you now own this vehicle, congratulations—it was a great car.) Here's how the VIN is divided into sections:

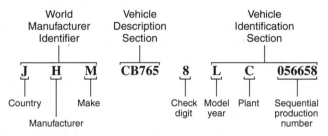

The World Manufacturer Identifier (WMI) consists of three single-character codes. The first character indicates the country of manufacture. J represents Japan; other codes include 1 (U.S.), 2 (Canada), and 3 (Mexico). The second character indicates the manufacturer; H is the code for Honda. The third character is the make and model. This code is assigned by the manufacturer; Honda uses M to indicate a passenger car built in Japan.

The Vehicle Description Section (VDS) contains information about the body type, transmission, restraint systems, and other characteristics of the vehicle. Decoding this information is difficult without tables supplied by the manufacturer.

By searching the Web, I was able to determine that CB7 indicates an Accord with a 2.2-liter engine, 6 indicates a four-door sedan with automatic transmission, and 5 indicates that the Accord is an LX model.

The Vehicle Identification Section (VIS) begins with a one-character code that represents the vehicle's model year. The code is A = 1980, B = 1981, C = 1982, and so on, except that I, O, and Q aren't used. (Those letters aren't used anywhere in a VIN, because they resemble the digits 1 and 0.) The letter L in the sample VIN represents 1990. The next character in the VIS indicates the plant at which the vehicle was built; for Hondas, the letter C indicates the Sayama plant in Japan. The rest of the VIS is a unique code assigned by the manufacturer. It may indicate the order in which the vehicle was manufactured, but it's not required to.

The check digit in a VIN is computed from the other characters in the VIN; its purpose is to help detect errors. (As you can imagine, it's quite easy to make a mistake when copying a VIN by hand.) For example, suppose that someone wrote JHMCB7658LC065658 instead of JHMCB7658LC056658. The check digit in the original VIN is 8, but the check digit computed from the modified VIN will not be 8, indicating an error in the VIN. The check digit algorithm used in vehicle identification numbers will catch most common errors, such as a single incorrect character or a transposition of two characters.

Vehicle identification numbers are obviously hard to read. The following program tries to help matters by splitting up a VIN into its constituent pieces. The VIN is entered by the user when prompted.

VIN.java

```
1   // Displays information from a VIN entered by the user
2
3   import jpb.*;
4
5   public class VIN {
6     public static void main(String[] args) {
7       // Prompt the user to enter a VIN
8       SimpleIO.prompt("Enter VIN: ");
9       String vin = SimpleIO.readLine();
10
11      // Extract the parts of the VIN
12      String manufacturer = vin.substring(0, 3);
13      String description = vin.substring(3, 8);
14      String checkDigit = vin.substring(8, 9);
15      String identification = vin.substring(9);
16
17      // Display the parts of the VIN
18      System.out.println("World manufacturer identifier: " +
19                          manufacturer);
20      System.out.println("Vehicle description section: " +
21                          description);
22      System.out.println("Check digit: " + checkDigit);
23      System.out.println("Vehicle identification section: " +
24                          identification);
25    }
26  }
```

The program's output will have the following appearance:

```
Enter VIN: JHMCB7658LC056658
World manufacturer identifier: JHM
Vehicle description section: CB765
Check digit: 8
Vehicle identification section: LC056658
```

The program would be much more useful if it could translate the codes into a form that's easier for humans to understand. That capability is beyond our current knowledge. However, we'll return to the program in later chapters and make several improvements to it.

We could condense the program by removing the manufacturer, description, checkDigit, and identification variables.

VIN2.java

```
1   // Displays information from a VIN entered by the user
2
3   import jpb.*;
4
5   public class VIN2 {
6     public static void main(String[] args) {
7       // Prompt the user to enter a VIN
8       SimpleIO.prompt("Enter VIN: ");
9       String vin = SimpleIO.readLine();
10
11      // Display the parts of the VIN
12      System.out.println("World manufacturer identifier: " +
13                          vin.substring(0, 3));
14      System.out.println("Vehicle description section: " +
15                          vin.substring(3, 8));
16      System.out.println("Check digit: " + vin.substring(8, 9));
17      System.out.println("Vehicle identification section: " +
18                          vin.substring(9));
19    }
20  }
```

Section 2.11 discussed this type of substitution in the context of the Course-Average program. Although I chose not to substitute variables in Course-Average, substitution makes more sense in the VIN program.

Before we leave the subject of vehicle identification numbers, let's take a moment to see how the check digit is computed. We don't need this information now, but exercises in future chapters will depend on it. Feel free to skip the rest of this section for the time being.

Computing the check digit for a VIN is a three-step process:

Step 1. Assign a numerical value to each character in the VIN (other than the check digit itself). The following table shows the numerical value for each letter. (The value of a digit is the digit itself.)

Letter:	A	B	C	D	E	F	G	H	J	K	L	M	N	P	R	S	T	U	V	W	X	Y	Z
Value:	1	2	3	4	5	6	7	8	1	2	3	4	5	7	9	2	3	4	5	6	7	8	9

I, O, and Q never appear in a VIN, so they have no corresponding numerical values.

Step 2. Multiply the value of each character by the weight factor shown in the following table. The first row indicates the position of the character within the VIN (note that position 8 is the check digit). The values in the second row are the weights.

Position:	0	1	2	3	4	5	6	7	9	10	11	12	13	14	15	16
Weight:	8	7	6	5	4	3	2	10	9	8	7	6	5	4	3	2

Step 3. Add the products to get a total. The remainder when the total is divided by 11 gives the check digit. If the remainder is 10, the check digit will be the letter X.

As an example, let's start with the VIN for the Honda Accord. After dropping the check digit, we have sixteen characters left:

J   H   M   C   B   7   6   5   L   C   0   5   6   6   5   8

Next, we assign a numerical value to each character, giving us the following series of numbers:

1   8   4   3   2   7   6   5   3   3   0   5   6   6   5   8

Next, we multiply each value by the weight factor corresponding to its position:

8   56   24   15   8   21   12   50   27   24   0   30   30   24   15   16

The sum of these numbers is 360. Dividing by 11 yields a remainder of 8, which is the check digit.

Review Questions

1. The act of joining two strings together to form a single string is called _____.

2. List two "magic" properties of the `String` class.

3. Which method is used to remove extra space from the beginning and end of a string?

4. What is the value of `11 + 38 + "THX"`?

3.10   Case Study: Checking an ISBN Number

Our case study for this chapter involves checking an ISBN (International Standard Book Number) for validity. An ISBN is a unique number assigned to a book when it's published. It can be found on the book's copyright page and back cover. For example, a certain popular C textbook has the following ISBN:

0–393–96945–2

The number 0 indicates that the book was published in English, 393 identifies the publisher (W. W. Norton), and 96945 identifies the particular book (*C Programming: A Modern Approach*). The number 2 at the end is a check digit that's calculated from the other digits in the ISBN.

Our goal is to write a program named `CheckISBN` that calculates the check digit for an ISBN entered by the user. The following example shows what the user will see on the screen:

```
Enter ISBN: 0-393-96945-2
Check digit entered: 2
Check digit computed: 2
```

"Check digit entered" is the last character in the ISBN entered by the user. "Check digit computed" is the check digit calculated by the program.

Now that we have a specification for the program, it's time to move to the design phase. After studying the output of the program, it seems clear that we'll need four steps:

1. Prompt the user to enter an ISBN.
2. Compute the check digit for the ISBN.
3. Display the check digit entered by the user.
4. Display the computed check digit.

Next, we'll need to choose algorithms and decide how our data will be stored. The ISBN will clearly be stored as a string, and the other variables we'll need will be integers. The sticky part is the algorithm for computing the check digit. Fortunately, this algorithm is a common one that can be found in many books.

To calculate the check digit, we begin by multiplying the first nine digits in the number by 10, 9, 8, ..., 2, respectively, and summing these products. Let's call this number *total*. The check digit is now determined by the expression

$$10 - ((total - 1) \textbf{ mod } 11)$$

where **mod** is the modulus operation (equivalent to the % operator in Java). The value of this expression is a number between 0 and 10. If the value is 10, the check digit is X. For example, the check digit for our sample ISBN would be calculated as follows. First, we compute the value of *total:*

$$total = 0 \times 10 + 3 \times 9 + 9 \times 8 + 3 \times 7 + 9 \times 6 + 6 \times 5 + 9 \times 4 + 4 \times 3 + 5 \times 2$$
$$= 0 + 27 + 72 + 21 + 54 + 30 + 36 + 12 + 10$$
$$= 262$$

Next, we calculate the check digit:

$$10 - ((262 - 1) \textbf{ mod } 11) = 10 - (261 \textbf{ mod } 11) = 10 - 8 = 2$$

Now, how do we implement this algorithm in Java? The first problem is extracting the digits from the ISBN. This problem is exacerbated by the fact that we don't know where all the dashes are. The third dash is guaranteed to be in position 11 of the ISBN, assuming that position 0 is the first character in the ISBN. The position of the other two dashes may vary, though. To simplify matters, I decided to have the program search for the dashes. Once their location is known, we can easily extract the parts of the ISBN that we'll need (the language code, publisher, and book number) and join these into a single string, the "reduced ISBN." (For example, if the original ISBN is `"0-393-96945-2"`, the reduced ISBN would be `"039396945"`.) All the tools we'll need are provided by the `String` class. Searching for the dashes can be done by calling the `indexOf` method. The `substring` method can extract a portion of the original ISBN, and the + operator can put the pieces together to form the reduced ISBN.

To extract a digit and convert it to a number, we can use the following expression:

```
Integer.parseInt(reducedISBN.substring(i, i + 1))
```

where i is the position of the digit in the reduced ISBN. (There's a better way to do the extraction and conversion, by the way, but it requires more knowledge of Java. We'll return to this point in Section 9.4.)

We need one last algorithm before we can write the program. Once we've computed the check digit, how do we display it? If the check digit is between 0 and 9, there's no problem. But the check digit might be 10, which means that we'll need to display the letter X. This problem can be solved by creating a string containing the digits from 0 to 9, plus the letter X:

```
final String DIGITS = "0123456789X";
```

We can now use the value of the check digit to select one of the characters in `DIGITS`. If the check digit is stored in the variable `checkDigit`, the expression will be

```
DIGITS.charAt(checkDigit)
```

Here's the finished program.

CheckISBN.java

```
1  // Program name: CheckISBN
2  // Author: K. N. King
3  // Written: 1998-04-17
4  // Modified: 1999-02-11
5  //
6  // Prompts the user to enter an ISBN number. Computes the
7  // check digit for the ISBN. Displays both the check digit
8  // entered by the user and the check digit computed by the
9  // program.
10
11 import jpb.*;
12
13 public class CheckISBN {
14   public static void main(String[] args) {
15     // Prompt the user to enter an ISBN
```

```
16        SimpleIO.prompt("Enter ISBN: ");
17        String originalISBN = SimpleIO.readLine();
18
19        // Determine location of dashes
20        int dashPos1 = originalISBN.indexOf("-");
21        int dashPos2 = originalISBN.indexOf("-", dashPos1 + 1);
22
23        // Remove dashes from ISBN
24        String reducedISBN =
25          originalISBN.substring(0, dashPos1) +
26          originalISBN.substring(dashPos1 + 1, dashPos2) +
27          originalISBN.substring(dashPos2 + 1, 11);
28
29        // Compute the check digit for the ISBN
30        int total =
31          10 * Integer.parseInt(reducedISBN.substring(0, 1)) +
32           9 * Integer.parseInt(reducedISBN.substring(1, 2)) +
33           8 * Integer.parseInt(reducedISBN.substring(2, 3)) +
34           7 * Integer.parseInt(reducedISBN.substring(3, 4)) +
35           6 * Integer.parseInt(reducedISBN.substring(4, 5)) +
36           5 * Integer.parseInt(reducedISBN.substring(5, 6)) +
37           4 * Integer.parseInt(reducedISBN.substring(6, 7)) +
38           3 * Integer.parseInt(reducedISBN.substring(7, 8)) +
39           2 * Integer.parseInt(reducedISBN.substring(8, 9));
40        int checkDigit = 10 - ((total - 1) % 11);
41
42        // Display the check digit entered by the user
43        System.out.println("Check digit entered: " +
44                           originalISBN.charAt(12));
45
46        // Display the computed check digit
47        final String DIGITS = "0123456789X";
48        System.out.println("Check digit computed: " +
49                           DIGITS.charAt(checkDigit));
50    }
51 }
```

Q & A

Q: **Is it legal for a string that's enclosed in double quotes to call a `String` instance method?**

A: Yes, strange as it may seem. A string enclosed in double quotes is a `String` object, so it's fully capable of calling instance methods in the `String` class. For example, instead of writing

```
String letterGrades = "FDCBA";
System.out.println(letterGrades.charAt(grade));
```

we could write

```
System.out.println("FDCBA".charAt(grade));
```

This statement will print either F, D, C, B, or A, depending on whether the grade variable has the value 0, 1, 2, 3, or 4.

Q: **How can I change the characters in a `String` object?**

A: You can't. Strings are immutable in Java. What you can do instead is convert the
StringBuffer class ▶*13.7* `String` object to a `StringBuffer` object, modify that object, and then convert the result back to a string.

Summary

- An object has two properties: state and behavior.
- In Java, an object's state is stored in instance variables. An object's behavior is represented by instance methods.
- Each object belongs to a class.
- The declaration for a class specifies the variables, constructors, and methods for a particular type of object.
- The declaration of an instance variable looks like the declaration of a variable inside a method, except for the presence of an access modifier (usually `private`) at the beginning.
- The declaration of an instance method includes an access modifier (usually `public`), a result type, the method's name, its parameters, and its body. Each parameter must have both a type and a name.
- A class may have more than one method with the same name, provided that the methods have different parameters. The methods are said to be overloaded.
- When an object is created, its instance variables are initialized by a constructor.
- A constructor looks like an instance method, except that it has no result type and its name is the same as the name of the class itself.
- Constructors can be overloaded.
- Once a class has been declared, instances of that class can be created by using the keyword `new`.
- To perform an operation on an object, we call one of the instance methods that belongs to the object's class.
- When a program consists of more than one class, we have the option of putting all the classes in one file or putting classes in separate files. The latter option is usually preferable.

- When a file is compiled, any other files containing classes that the file needs will be compiled automatically if the matching `.class` files aren't up-to-date.
- Object variables store references to objects, not objects themselves.
- The value `null` can be assigned to an object variable to indicate that the variable doesn't currently refer to any object.
- Assigning one object variable to another doesn't create a new object. Instead, it makes both variables refer to the same object.
- When there are no more references to an object, we say that the object has become garbage.
- Java provides automatic garbage collection to recycle the space occupied by objects that have become garbage.
- An instance method that returns the value of an instance variable is said to be an accessor (or getter). By convention, names of getters start with the word `get`.
- An instance method that stores its parameter into an instance variable is said to be a mutator (or setter). By convention, names of setters start with the word `set`.
- Objects whose instance variables cannot be changed are said to be immutable.
- The name `toString` should be used for a method that returns the contents of an object as a string. This method is called automatically when an attempt is made to print the object.
- A `String` object can be created without using the word `new`, by simply enclosing the desired characters in double quotes.
- The `String` class provides a number of instance methods that perform operations on strings, including `charAt`, `indexOf`, `lastIndexOf`, `length`, `substring`, `toLowerCase`, `toUpperCase`, and `trim`.
- Method calls can be "chained": when an instance method returns an object, that object can be used to call another instance method.
- The + operator can be used to concatenate two strings. If one of its operands is a string and the other isn't, the + operator converts the latter to a string and then concatenates the two strings. An object is converted to string form by calling its `toString` method.
- The += operator can be used to add characters to the end of an existing string.

Exercises

Section 3.1   1.   Suppose that we decide to model a soft-drink can as an object.

(a) List three significant items that will be part of the state of a soft-drink can.

(b) List three significant operations on a soft-drink can.

Section 3.3

2. Write a declaration for the `BallpointPen` class, using the variable names and method names mentioned in Section 3.2. Leave the bodies of the methods empty.

3. Write a declaration for the `Car` class, using the variable names and method names mentioned in Section 3.2. Leave the bodies of the methods empty.

Section 3.4

4. Locate the error in the following Java declaration and show how to fix it.

```
Account acct = Account(100.00);
```

Section 3.5

5. Assume that `pen` is a `BallpointPen` object. Using the class declaration from Exercise 2, write statements that perform the following operations on `pen`.

    (a) Press the button belonging to `pen`.
    (b) Write for 200 units using `pen`.
    (c) Replace `pen`'s cartridge
    (d) Determine how much ink remains in `pen`, and store that number into a `double` variable named `inkLeft`.

6. Assume that `car` is a `Car` object. Using the class declaration from Exercise 3, write statements that perform the following operations on `car`.

    (a) Start `car`'s engine.
    (b) Drive `car` for 120 miles (or kilometers, if you prefer).
    (c) Add 9.3 gallons (or liters) to `car`'s tank.
    (d) Stop `car`'s engine.

7. The following questions refer to the class at the end of this exercise.

    (a) How many constructors does this class have?
    (b) How many methods does this class have?
    (c) Write a declaration that declares a `Counter` variable named `ctr` and initializes it to contain a `Counter` object that contains the number 0.
    (d) Write a statement that increments the value stored in the `ctr` object.
    (e) Write a statement that changes the value stored in the `ctr` object to zero.
    (f) Write a statement that prints the value stored in the `ctr` object.

```
class Counter {
  private int count;

  public Counter(int initialCount) {
    count = initialCount;
  }
  public Counter() {
    count = 0;
  }
  public void increment() {
    count += 1;
  }
  public void reset() {
    count = 0;
  }
  public int getValue() {
    return count;
  }
}
```

Section 3.7

8. What balance will be stored in `acct1`, `acct2`, and `acct3` after the following statements have been executed?

    ```
    Account acct1 = new Account(500.00);
    Account acct2 = new Account(1000.00);
    Account acct3 = acct1;

    acct1.deposit(500.00);
    acct2.withdraw(250.00);
    acct3.deposit(100.00);
    ```

9. After the following statements have been executed, how many `Account` objects will exist, not counting garbage objects?

    ```
    Account acct1 = new Account();
    Account acct2 = new Account();
    Account acct3 = acct1;

    acct2 = acct3;
    acct1 = null;
    ```

Section 3.9

10. Suppose that `word` is a `String` variable containing a single word. Write a statement that capitalizes only the first letter of the word, leaving all other letters unchanged.

11. Write a series of statements that split up an email address stored in a `String` variable named `emailAddress`. Assume that the address has the form *name@domain2.domain1*. Store *name*, *domain2*, and *domain1* into variables with those names. For example, if `emailAddress` contains the string `"knking@gsu.edu"`, the `name` variable would be assigned `"knking"`, the `domain2` variable would be assigned `"gsu"`, and the `domain1` variable would be assigned `"edu"`.

12. Show the output of the following program.

    ```java
    public class Exercise3_12 {
      public static void main(String[] args) {
        String name = "Francis Albert Sinatra";

        int index1 = name.indexOf(" ");
        int index2 = name.lastIndexOf(" ");
        String str1 = name.substring(0, index1);
        String str2 = name.substring(index1 + 1, index1 + 2);
        String str3 = name.substring(index2 + 1);

        System.out.println(str3 + ", " + str1 + " " + str2 + ".");
      }
    }
    ```

Programming Projects

1. Modify the `Account` class (Section 3.3) so that the `balance` variable can never become negative. You'll need to change the primary constructor and the `deposit` and `withdraw` methods. If the balance threatens to become negative, set it to zero instead. *Hint:* Use the `Math.max` method to determine which is larger, the intended balance or zero.

2. Modify the `Account` class (Section 3.3) by adding two instance variables containing the customer's name and the account number. (Both will be `String` objects.) Modify the primary constructor for the `Account` class so that it takes three parameters: the balance, the customer's name, and the account number. Add instance methods named `getCustomer-Name` and `getAccountNumber` that return the customer name and account number. Modify the `TestAccount` class (Section 3.6) so it tests the new constructor and the two new methods.

3. Add `subtract`, `multiply`, and `divide` methods to the `Fraction` class (Section 3.8). Also, add two more constructors. One of the constructors will have no parameters; it initializes the fraction to 0/1. The other constructor will have one parameter, representing the numerator of the fraction; the denominator of the fraction will be 1. Write a `Test-Fraction` class (similar to the `TestAccount` class of Section 3.6) that creates two `Fraction` objects and tests the behavior of all constructors and instance methods in the `Fraction` class.

4. Using the `Fraction` class from Programming Project 3, write a program named `FractionMath` that prompts the user for two fractions, which are then combined using addition, subtraction, multiplication, and division. Here's what the user will see on the screen:

```
This program performs arithmetic operations on two fractions.

Enter first fraction: 3/5
Enter second fraction: 1/6

Sum: 23/30
Difference: 13/30
Product: 3/30
Quotient: 18/5
```

You can assume that the user always enters two integers separated by a slash (/). However, the user may enter any number of spaces before and after each integer. *Hint:* Use the `indexOf`, `substring`, and `trim` methods from the `String` class.

5. Write a program named `ConvertDate` that converts a date entered by the user into another form. The user's input will have the form

    month day, year

    The month will be one of the words `January`, `February`, ... The letters in the month may be lowercase, uppercase, or any mixture of the two. The day is a one- or two-digit number. The year is any number of digits. There may be any number of spaces (1) before the month, (2) between the month and the day, (3) between the day and the year, and (4) after the year. You may assume that there is at least one space between the month and day and between the day and year. You may also assume that there is a comma after the day. The converted date must have the form

    day month year

    with one space between the day and month and between the month and year. The first letter of the month must be uppercase, and the remaining letters must be lowercase. The following example shows what the user will see on the screen:

```
Enter date to be converted:    apRiL    28,    2003
Converted date: 28 April 2003
```

    Hint: Use the `indexOf` and `lastIndexOf` methods to locate the month, day, and year within the string entered by the user, and then use the `substring` method to extract them.

Answers to Review Questions

Section 3.1   1.   Behavior

Section 3.2   1.   Instance variables
                    2.   Instance methods

Section 3.3   1.   Constructor
                    2.   Variable declarations, constructor declarations, method declarations
                    3.   Access modifiers
                    4.   Parameters

Section 3.4   1.   Instances
                    2.   Reference
                    3.   `new`
                    4.   Instance variables are stored in each instance of a class.

Section 3.5   1.   Call

Section 3.6   1.   `javac WriteLetter.java`
                    2.   `java WriteLetter`
                    3.   Putting each class in a separate file

Section 3.7   1.   Pointer
                    2.   `null`
                    3.   Clone
                    4.   Garbage

Section 3.8   1.   Accessor (or getter)
                    2.   Mutator (or setter)
                    3.   Immutable
                    4.   `toString`

Section 3.9   1.   Concatenation
                    2.   (a) Instances can be created without the use of `new`. (b) Strings can be concatenated without
                          a method call.
                    3.   `trim`
                    4.   `"49THX"`

4 Basic Control Structures

Up to this point, our programs have consisted of statements to be executed one after the other, with no opportunities to choose between alternatives or repeat actions more than once. In this chapter, we'll see how Java's control structures make it possible to write much more sophisticated programs. A ***control structure*** is a statement that potentially changes the order in which other statements are executed.

The first control structure that we'll cover is the `if` statement. The `if` statement is capable of executing a statement conditionally, based on the outcome of a test condition. In addition to learning about the `if` statement, we'll also discover how to perform comparisons using the relational and equality operators, how to create more-complex conditions using the logical operators, and how to group statements using blocks. We'll also learn about the empty statement, as well as exploring possible uses for Java's `boolean` type.

The other control structures covered in this chapter are the `while` statement and the `break` statement. The `while` statement establishes a loop that repeatedly executes a statement or a series of statements. The `break` statement causes a loop to terminate prematurely. Our coverage of the `while` statement includes a discussion of counting loops—loops in which a variable is systematically increased or decreased. We'll also learn about Java's increment and decrement operators, which are frequently used in conjunction with counting loops.

The control structures described in this chapter aren't the only ones in Java, but they're the most fundamental, and they're powerful enough to let us write plenty of useful programs. Java's remaining control structures are described in Section 5.2 and Chapter 8.

Objectives

- Learn how to use the relational and equality operators to perform comparisons.
- Learn how to use the logical operators to combine the results of comparisons.
- Learn how to write `if` statements.
- Learn about the empty statement.
- Learn how to use blocks to group statements.
- Learn how to work with `boolean` data.
- Learn how a loop is built out of a controlling expression and a loop body.
- Learn how to use the `while` statement to write loops.
- Learn how to use a counter inside a loop.
- Learn how to use the increment and decrement operators.
- Learn how to use the `break` statement to exit from a loop.

4.1   Performing Comparisons

So far, our programs have been what programmers call "straight-line code." The statements inside `main` have been executed from first to last, with no side trips or excursions. Like life itself, however, programs rarely proceed on a straight path. Our programs will need the ability to test conditions and make decisions based on the outcomes of those tests. Our primary tool for testing conditions will be the `if` statement, which is introduced in Section 4.3. The `if` statement is designed to test whether a `boolean` expression has the value `true` or `false`. The behavior of the program will vary depending on the outcome of the test.

Most of the conditions in a program involve comparisons: Does one variable have a larger value than another? Does the user's input exceed the maximum allowable value? Have we repeated an operation the desired number of times? To perform comparisons such as these, we'll need relational operators and equality operators.

Relational Operators

Table 4.1 lists the ***relational operators,*** which test the relationship between two numbers, returning a `boolean` result.

Table 4.1
Relational Operators

Symbol	Meaning
<	Less than
>	Greater than
<=	Less than or equal to
>=	Greater than or equal to

Here are a few examples of the relational operators in action:

5 < 3 ⟹ *false*
5 > 3 ⟹ *true*
3 > 3 ⟹ *false*
5 <= 3 ⟹ *false*
5 >= 3 ⟹ *true*
3 >= 3 ⟹ *true*

The types of the operands don't need to be the same. If we compare an `int` value with a `double` value, the compiler will arrange for the `int` value to be converted to `double` before the comparison is performed.

The expressions being compared by a relational operator may themselves contain operators. The arithmetic operators take precedence over the relational operators, so we generally won't need parentheses around the expressions being compared. For example, Java would interpret the expression

```
a - b * c < d + e
```

as

```
(a - b * c) < (d + e)
```

Of course, it never hurts to use extra parentheses, especially when expressions are complicated.

Equality Operators

Testing whether two values are equal or not equal is done using the ***equality operators*** (Table 4.2).

Table 4.2
Equality Operators

Symbol	Meaning
==	Equal to
!=	Not equal to

Notice that the "equal to" operator is written with two = characters, not one. (One equals sign means assignment.) Although these operators are similar to the relational operators, they've been set apart for various reasons. They have lower precedence than the relational operators, for one thing. Also, the equality operators can be used in situations where the relational operators can't. In particular, we can test objects for equality and inequality, but we can't use a relational operator to test whether one object is "greater than" another.

The equality operators can be used to compare any two numbers. Here are a few examples:

6 == 2 ⟹ *false*
6 != 2 ⟹ *true*
2 == 2 ⟹ *true*
2 != 2 ⟹ *false*

As with the relational operators, the types of the operands don't need to be the same. If an `int` operand is compared to a `double` operand, the `int` value is converted automatically to `double` type before the comparison is performed:

$2 == 2.0 \Rightarrow$ *true*
$2 == 2.1 \Rightarrow$ *false*

Testing Floating-Point Numbers for Equality

Be careful when you test whether two floating-point numbers are equal. Because of round-off error, two numbers that seem as though they should be equal—at least according to the laws of mathematics—may in fact not be equal. For example, we would expect the condition

```
1.2 - 1.1 == 0.1
```

to be true. However, we saw in Section 2.7 that the value of `1.2 - 1.1` is 0.09999999999999987, not 0.1.

Q&A   One way to avoid problems with round-off error is to test whether floating-point numbers are close enough, rather than testing whether they're equal.

Testing Objects for Equality

Testing whether two objects are equal is a tricky business. If x and y are two object variables of the same type, we can test whether they're equal by writing

```
x == y
```

To test whether they're *not* equal, we'd write

```
x != y
```

object references ▶3.7   There's a snag here, however: in either case, what we're *really* testing are the references stored in x and y, not the contents of the objects that x and y refer to. The value of x == y will be `true` only when x and y both refer to the same object (or both x and y have the value `null`). In many cases, we're really interested in whether the objects to which x and y refer are "equal" in some other sense. For example, we would consider two `String` objects to be equal if they contain the same characters in the same order.

equals   To test whether two objects contain matching data, we'll need to use the `equals` method. The value of `x.equals(y)` is `true` if the objects that x and y represent are "equal." Every Java class supports the `equals` method, although the definition of "equals" varies from class to class.

 For some classes, the value of `x.equals(y)` is the same as x == y. Check the documentation for a class before assuming that `equals` compares the data stored in instances of the class.

Comparing Strings

`String` is one of the classes for which the `equals` method compares the contents of objects, so we can use `str1.equals(str2)` to test whether `str1` and `str2` contain the same series of characters.

 Strings are objects, so don't use the `==` operator to test whether two strings are equal.

equalsIgnoreCase   The `String` class has another method, named `equalsIgnoreCase`, that's also used frequently. The value of `str1.equalsIgnoreCase(str2)` is `true` if `str1` and `str2` contain the same characters, with upper- and lowercase letters considered equivalent. For example, if `str1` is `"hotjava"` and `str2` is `"HotJava"`, the value of `str1.equalsIgnoreCase(str2)` is `true`.

compareTo   Performing relational operations on objects is only possible if the objects belong to a class that provides methods for that purpose. `String` is one of the few classes in the Java API that support relational operations. Instead of providing separate methods for less than, greater than, and so on, the `String` class has a single method named `compareTo`. To compare the strings `str1` and `str2`, we'll write

```
str1.compareTo(str2)
```

The `compareTo` method returns an integer—not a `boolean` value—that's less than zero, equal to zero, or greater than zero, depending on whether `str1` is less than `str2`, equal to `str2`, or greater than `str2`, respectively.

`compareTo` performs a character-by-character comparison between the two strings, looking for the first position in which the strings are different. For example, `"aab"` is considered to be less than `"aba"`, because the first character of `"aab"` is the same as the first character of `"aba"`, but the second character of `"aab"` is smaller than the second character of `"aba"`. If the characters in the strings match, then `compareTo` considers the shorter of the two strings to be the smaller one; for example, `"ab"` is less than `"aba"`.

Unicode ➤9.4   To determine whether one character is less than another, the `compareTo` method examines the Unicode values of the characters. For now, I'll just make a few observations about the ordering of characters in Unicode:

- Digits are assigned consecutive values; 0 is less than 1, which is less than 2, and so on.
- Uppercase letters have consecutive values.
- Lowercase letters have consecutive values.
- Uppercase letters are less than lowercase letters.
- The space character is less than any printing character, including letters and digits.

Lexicographic Order

The `compareTo` method compares strings based on their **lexicographic** order. The term "lexicographic" comes from "lexicography"—the process of compiling a dictionary. It suggests that strings in Java are compared based on the order in which they would appear in a dictionary, which is essentially true. In a dictionary, *aardvark* would come before *ant*. Both start with the same letter, but the second letter of *aardvark* is less than the second letter of *ant*. When one word is a prefix of another, the shorter word precedes the longer one in a dictionary. For example, *ant* comes before *anteater*. The `compareTo` method would indicate that `"aardvark"` is less than `"ant"`, and that `"ant"` is less than `"anteater"`. Notice that the length of the strings being compared is usually irrelevant. Length is used only as a "tiebreaker," when a character-by-character comparison fails to find a difference between the strings.

Review Questions

1. To determine whether one number is greater than or equal to another, we would use a _____ operator.

2. The `==` and `!=` symbols are called _____ operators.

3. Why is it not a good idea to test whether two `double` variables are equal?

4. What method is used to test whether two objects are "equal"?

4.2 Logical Operators

In many cases, we'll need to combine the results of two or more comparisons that we've performed with the relational and equality operators. For example, suppose that we want to know whether `age` is greater than or equal to `18` *and* `age` is less than or equal to `65`. "age is greater than or equal to `18`" is written `age >= 18`, and "age is less than or equal to `65`" is written `age <= 65`, but how do we test that *both* conditions are true?

The solution is to use a ***logical operator,*** in this case the `&&` operator, which means "and." (The `&` character is pronounced "ampersand," by the way.) The following expression tests whether `age >= 18` is true *and* `age <= 65` is true:

```
age >= 18 && age <= 65
```

The `&&` operator has lower precedence than the relational and equality operators, so the `>=` and `<=` operations will be performed before the `&&` operation, which is what we want. Of course, we can always use parentheses to avoid confusion:

```
(age >= 18) && (age <= 65)
```

Watch out for logical expressions that look correct but aren't acceptable to Java. To test whether the value of `age` lies between 18 and 65, you can't write

```
18 <= age <= 65
```

The `<=` operator is left associative, so the compiler will treat this expression as (`18 <= age) <= 65`. It's illegal to compare the value of `18 <= age` (which has type `boolean`) to `65`, so you'll get a compilation error.

Table 4.3 shows the logical operators.

Table 4.3
Logical Operators

Symbol	Meaning
!	Logical *not*
&&	Logical *and*
||	Logical *or*

`!` is a unary operator (it has only one operand), while `&&` and `||` are binary operators (they require two operands). All logical operators expect `boolean` operands and produce `boolean` results. Let's take a closer look at each of these operators, starting with `&&`.

Performing the *And* Operation

We'll use the `&&` operator to test whether two `boolean` expressions are both true. When given two operands, the `&&` operator proceeds as follows:

> Evaluate the left operand. If it's false, return `false`. Otherwise, evaluate the right operand. If it's true, return `true`; if it's false, return `false`.

In other words, the `&&` operator always checks the left operand first. If that operand is false, then it ignores the right operand, because it has already determined that the entire expression must be false. This behavior is often called ***short-circuit evaluation***.

Q&A

Short-circuit evaluation can save time, because we won't always need to evaluate every operand in a `boolean` expression. Of greater importance, however, is the ability short-circuit evaluation gives us to avoid potential errors. For example, suppose that we want to test whether the value of `j` divided by `i` is greater than 0. Divisions are always dicey, because the divisor might have the value 0 at the time of the division, causing an error to occur. Short-circuit evaluation provides an easy way to ensure that no error can occur. The following expression illustrates the technique. This expression tests whether `i` is not 0 *before* checking whether `j / i` is greater than 0:

```
(i != 0) && (j / i > 0)
```

Let's consider two cases:

- ***i is equal to 0.*** The expression (i != 0) is false, so the entire expression is false. The right operand, (j / i > 0), was never tested, so the division wasn't performed and the error didn't occur.

- ***i is not equal to 0.*** The expression (i != 0) is true, so the value of the entire expression now depends solely on the value of the right operand, (j / i > 0).

 When we rely on short-circuit evaluation to guarantee that a program works, the order of the operands is important. Writing

```
(j / i > 0) && (i != 0)
```

would not protect the program against an error if i happened to be 0.

Performing the *Or* Operation

To test whether one (or both) of two conditions is true, we'll use the || ("or") operator. (The | character is called a "vertical bar" or "pipe.") The || operator, like the && operator, relies on short-circuit evaluation. When given two operands, the || operator performs the following actions:

> Evaluate the left operand. If it's true, return `true`. Otherwise, evaluate the right operand. If it's true, return `true`; if it's false, return `false`.

The || operator always checks the left operand first. If that operand is true, then it ignores the right operand, because it has already determined that the entire expression must be true.

Performing the *Not* Operation

I've saved the simplest of the three logical operators—the ! ("not") operator—for last. The ! operator allows us to reverse the outcome of a comparison. When applied to a false value, the ! operator returns `true`. When applied to a true value, it returns `false`. For example, the expression 9 < 11 has the value `true`, but the expression ! (9 < 11) has the value `false`.

One common use of the ! operator has to do with testing whether two objects are not equal. We can use the `equals` method to compare whether two objects are equal. There's usually no method for testing whether objects are *not* equal, though. Instead, we'll call the `equals` method and then apply the ! operator to the result. For example, to test whether two strings `str1` and `str2` are not equal, we'd write

```
!str1.equals(str2)
```

Using ! = to test whether two strings are not equal may not give the desired result. Use ! and `equals` instead.

Precedence and Associativity of *And, Or,* and *Not*

The ! operator takes precedence over the && operator, which in turn takes precedence over the | | operator. The relational and equality operators take precedence over && and | |, but have lower precedence than !. For example, Java would interpret the expression

```
a < b || c >= d && e == f
```

as

```
(a < b) || ((c >= d) && (e == f))
```

The ! operator is right associative; && and | | are left associative. For example, Java would interpret

```
a < b && c >= d && e == f
```

as

```
((a < b) && (c >= d)) && (e == f)
```

Simplifying `boolean` Expressions

We can often simplify `boolean` expressions that contain the ! operator by applying one of *de Morgan's Laws:*

de Morgan's Laws

> ! (*expr*$_1$ && *expr*$_2$) is equivalent to ! (*expr*$_1$) | | ! (*expr*$_2$)
> ! (*expr*$_1$ | | *expr*$_2$) is equivalent to ! (*expr*$_1$) && ! (*expr*$_2$)

expr$_1$ and *expr*$_2$ are arbitrary `boolean` expressions.

For example, we could write the condition "i is not between 1 and 10" as

```
!(i >= 1 && i <= 10)
```

Using one of de Morgan's Laws, we can rewrite the condition as

```
!(i >= 1) || !(i <= 10)
```

(The parentheses are necessary here because the ! operator takes precedence over the >= and <= operators.) We can now simplify the condition by replacing ! (i >= 1) by the equivalent expression i < 1, and replacing ! (i <= 10) by i > 10:

```
i < 1 || i > 10
```

This version of the condition is preferable to the original, not only because it has fewer operators, but also because it avoids the `!` operator, which can make `boolean` expressions harder to understand.

No matter how much we simplify our `boolean` expressions, they'll sometimes get complicated. Consider the rule for determining leap years. A leap year must be a multiple of 4. Centuries are special cases, however: if a year is a multiple of 100, then it must also be a multiple of 400 in order to be a leap year. For example, 2000 is a leap year because it's a multiple of 100 *and* a multiple of 400. However, 2100 isn't a leap year; it's a multiple of 100 but not a multiple of 400. We can write a single `boolean` expression that tests whether `year` is a leap year, but it's a bit tricky:

```
(year % 4 == 0) && (year % 100 != 0 || year % 400 == 0)
```

In order for this expression to be true, both operands of the `&&` operator must be true. For `(year % 4 == 0)` to be true, `year` must be a multiple of 4. For the other part of the test to be true, either `year % 100 != 0` must be true (`year` is not a multiple of 100) or `year % 400 == 0` must be true (`year` is a multiple of 400). In other words, it cannot be the case that `year` is a multiple of 100 but not a multiple of 400. In a case such as this, it's often a good idea to split the expression into smaller, easier-to-understand parts that are tested by separate `if` statements.

Review Questions

1. Which logical operator (`&&`, `||`, or `!`) has the highest precedence?

2. When a logical operator doesn't always compute the values of both its operands, we say that it performs _____ evaluation.

3. We can use _____ _____ [two words] Laws to simplify `boolean` expressions.

4. What is the correct way to test whether two strings `str1` and `str2` do *not* contain the same characters: (a) `str1 != str2`, (b) `!str1.equals(str2)`, or (c) `!(str1 == str2)`?

4.3　Simple `if` Statements

The `if` statement allows a program to test a condition and then vary its behavior based on the outcome of the test. In its simplest form, the `if` statement has the following appearance:

`if` statement

```
if ( expression )
    statement
```

expression (the condition being tested) must have `boolean` type. The parentheses around *expression* are mandatory. *statement* can be any valid Java statement. When the `if` statement is executed, the condition is evaluated. If it's true, then *statement* is executed. If it's false, *statement* is not executed.

For example, we could use the following `if` statement to print a message if the value of the `score` variable exceeds 100:

```
if (score > 100)
    System.out.println("** Error: Score exceeds 100 **");
```

Now suppose that we want to limit the value of `score` instead of printing an error message. That's easy as well—we'll change the "inner" statement, without changing the condition to be tested:

```
if (score > 100)
    score = 100;
```

Be careful not to use the = operator in an `if` statement's condition. The statement

```
if (i == 0) …
```

tests whether i is equal to 0. However, the statement

```
if (i = 0) …   // WRONG
```

attempts to assign 0 to i. When you try to compile the program, the compiler will produce an error message. Confusing == with = is a common mistake, because = means "is equal to" in mathematics (and in many programming languages).

Indentation

Each `if` statement contains an "inner statement"—the one to be executed if the condition is true. To make it clear that this statement is inside the `if` statement, programmers normally indent the inner statement, although that's not required by the compiler.

As we discussed in Section 2.3, programmers use indentation to indicate nesting. Every time a new level of nesting begins, the amount of indentation should increase. Each increase in indentation should be the same, regardless of the type of nesting. In other words, if you indent the statements inside a method by four spaces, you should indent an `if` statement's inner statement by an additional four spaces. The total amount of indentation for any statement should be a multiple of your usual indentation amount. For example, if you've chosen four spaces as your usual amount, then some lines will be indented four spaces, while the amount of indentation for more deeply nested lines will be 8, 12, 16, and so on.

The diagram on the next page shows what a properly nested program should look like. The dashes represent lines of code; I'm assuming that indentation is done in multiples of four spaces.

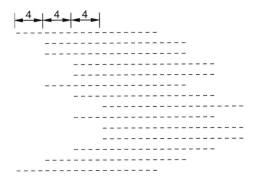

The Empty Statement

Java contains an amusing (?) trap for the unwary. Suppose that we put a semicolon immediately after the test condition in an `if` statement:

```
if (score > 100);   // WRONG
  score = 100;
```

It's easy to see why someone might do this, because most lines inside a method end with a semicolon. However, the correct rule to follow is not "put a semicolon at the end of each line," but rather "put a semicolon at the end of each *complete* declaration and each *complete* statement." An `if` statement isn't complete until we've specified what action should be performed when its condition is true.

So what happens when the compiler sees our faulty `if` statement? We won't get a compilation error, as you might expect. Instead, Java treats the semicolon as a command to do nothing—an ***empty statement.*** The assignment to the `score` variable is treated as a separate statement to be executed after the `if` statement. Here's how the compiler sees things:

```
if (score > 100)
  ;  // Empty statement--does nothing
score = 100;
```

If the value of `score` is greater than 100, the empty statement is executed (having no effect), and then `score` is assigned 100. On the other hand, if the value of `score` is less than or equal to 100, the empty statement is skipped, and then `score` is assigned 100. Either way, `score` ends up with the value 100, and the programmer ends up scratching his or her head.

The fact that Java treats a lonely semicolon as a statement is occasionally useful. Most of the time, though, it just makes life difficult for the beginner, who often isn't entirely sure where to put semicolons.

 Keep a close eye on the placement of semicolons. Never put a semicolon immediately after the test condition in an `if` statement. Follow the rule that a semicolon goes at the end of each *complete* declaration and each *complete* statement.

Blocks

Our description of the `if` statement makes it appear to be severely limited. An `if` statement can apparently contain only *one* inner statement to be executed if the condition is true. What if we need to perform two or more actions?

Java provides a feature known as the ***block*** to solve this problem. In its simplest form, a block is just a series of statements enclosed within curly braces:

block

```
{
    statements
}
```

declaring variables in blocks ➤*4.6*   We'll see later that a block may also contain declarations.

A block is considered to be one statement, even though it may contain any number of statements. As a result, we can use a block as the inner statement in an `if` statement. For example, suppose that we want to print an error message and reduce the score if it exceeds 100. The following `if` statement, which incorporates a block, will do just that:

Style 1
```
if (score > 100)
    {
        System.out.println("** Error: Score exceeds 100 **");
        score = 100;
    }
```

Q&A   Notice that each of the statements inside the block ends with a semicolon, but there's no semicolon after the block itself.

Let's take a look at how this `if` statement is put together. The following diagram illustrates the nesting of statements within statements:

```
if (score > 100)

    {

        System.out.println("** Error: Score exceeds 100 **");

        score = 100;

    }
```

The call of `println` and the assignment to `score` are statements. These are nested inside a block, which is itself a statement. Finally, the block is nested inside the `if` statement.

The ability to nest statements within other statements is a fundamental ability of most programming languages. For someone else to be able to read your program, it's important that you use visual cues to indicate how statements are nested.

Increasing the indentation at the beginning of each nesting level is important. Alignment is also important. Statements at the same level of nesting should be indented the same amount, not haphazardly scattered around. It takes a little more time to indent and align properly, but it's well worth the effort.

Unfortunately, indenting for each new level of nesting can cause program lines to become too long, which is a problem in itself. To avoid severe "indentation creep," it is customary to align braces with the statement that encloses them:

Style 2
```
if (score > 100)
{
   System.out.println("** Error: Score exceeds 100 **");
   score = 100;
}
```

To conserve vertical space, many programmers put the left curly brace at the end of the previous line:

Style 3
```
if (score > 100) {
   System.out.println("** Error: Score exceeds 100 **");
   score = 100;
}
```

This technique saves a line (the entire `if` statement now occupies four lines instead of the previous five). Notice that the right curly brace lines up with the word `if`, so we can easily see the beginning and end of the `if` statement.

From now on, I'll use Style 3 for nested statements. If you prefer Style 2, or even Style 1, feel free to use that instead. There's no single best way to format a program—being consistent is more important than choosing the "perfect" style.

Review Questions

1. Does the `if` statement require parentheses around the expression being tested, or is this a convention?

2. The _____ statement consists of nothing but a semicolon.

3. What is the effect of putting a semicolon after the test condition in an `if` statement?

4. Putting curly braces around a series of statements creates a single statement known as a _____.

4.4   `if` Statements with `else` Clauses

Sometimes we'll need to perform one action if a condition is true, but a different action if it's false. To achieve that effect in Java, we can add an `else` clause to the `if` statement:

**`if` statement with
`else` clause**

```
if ( expression )
    statement
else
    statement
```

There are now *two* inner statements. The first is executed if the expression is true; the second—the one after the word `else`—is executed if the expression is false.

For example, to determine the larger of the values stored in the variables a and b, we could use the following `if` statement:

```
if (a > b)
  larger = a;
else
  larger = b;
```

Note that both of the inner statements end with a semicolon. Also notice that I've aligned the word `else` with the word `if`. That's not necessary, of course, but it's considered good practice by most programmers because it clarifies which `if` statement the `else` clause belongs to. I've also put each assignment on a separate line and indented the assignments. I recommend that you do the same. Occasionally, if the statements inside the `if` statement are very short, programmers will put them on the same line as the `if` or `else`:

```
if (a > b) larger = a;
else larger = b;
```

Here's my recommended layout when the inner statements are blocks:

```
if (…) {
  …
} else {
  …
}
```

I prefer to align the right curly brace of each block with the `if` at the beginning of the statement. Other layouts are in common use, though. For example, some programmers put the word `else` at the beginning of a separate line:

```
if (…) {
  …
}
else {
  …
}
```

There are no restrictions on the statements nested inside an `if` statement; they can even be other `if` statements. Consider the problem of converting an hour expressed on a 24-hour scale (0–23) to a 12-hour scale. The following `if` statement first determines whether the hour is a.m. or p.m. In the former case, it then checks for midnight (a special case); in the latter case, it checks for noon.

```
if (hour <= 11)
  if (hour == 0)
    System.out.println("12 midnight");
  else
    System.out.println(hour + " a.m.");
else
  if (hour == 12)
    System.out.println("12 noon");
  else
    System.out.println((hour - 12) + " p.m.");
```

Notice the alignment of `if` and `else` in each `if` statement, even the inner ones. For clarity, it's probably a good idea to put braces around the inner `if` statements, even though they're not strictly necessary:

```
if (hour <= 11) {
  if (hour == 0)
    System.out.println("12 midnight");
  else
    System.out.println(hour + " a.m.");
} else {
  if (hour == 12)
    System.out.println("12 noon");
  else
    System.out.println((hour - 12) + " p.m.");
}
```

Using extra braces in statements is like using extra parentheses in expressions: it can't hurt and it sometimes keeps us out of trouble.

Cascaded `if` Statements

In many programs, we'll need to test a series of conditions, one after the other, until we find one that's true. This situation is best handled by nesting a series of `if` statements in such a way that the `else` clause of each is another `if` statement. We'll call this a *cascaded* `if` statement. For example, suppose that the variable `score` contains a number between 0 and 100. We need to print a letter grade that's based on the score:

90–100	A
80–89	B
70–79	C
60–69	D
0–59	F

The following cascaded `if` statement performs a series of tests until it can determine the letter grade:

```
if (score >= 90)
  System.out.println("A");
else
  if (score >= 80 && score <= 89)
    System.out.println("B");
  else
    if (score >= 70 && score <= 79)
      System.out.println("C");
    else
      if (score >= 60 && score <= 69)
        System.out.println("D");
      else
        System.out.println("F");
```

As you can see, a cascaded if statement that's laid out in the same way as other if statements will quickly suffer from indentation creep, as the indentation increases for each new level of nesting. To avoid this problem, programmers customarily put each else underneath the original if:

```
if (score >= 90)
  System.out.println("A");
else if (score >= 80 && score <= 89)
  System.out.println("B");
else if (score >= 70 && score <= 79)
  System.out.println("C");
else if (score >= 60 && score <= 69)
  System.out.println("D");
else
  System.out.println("F");
```

This layout saves vertical space as well as horizontal space because each else (except the last) has an if test on the same line.

In general, a cascaded if statement has the following appearance:

```
if ( expression )
  statement
else if ( expression )
  statement

...

else if ( expression )
  statement
else
  statement
```

The else clause at the end may or may not be present.

A cascaded if statement is nothing more than an if statement in which the else clause happens to be another if statement, whose else clause is another if statement, and so on. A cascaded if statement is not a new type of if statement, just a particular way of using the ordinary if statement.

Simplifying Cascaded `if` Statements

Because the conditions in a cascaded `if` statement are checked in order, from first to last, we can often simplify such a statement by removing conditions that are guaranteed (because of previous tests) to be true. Consider the "letter grade" example:

```
if (score >= 90)
  System.out.println("A");
else if (score >= 80 && score <= 89)
  System.out.println("B");
else if (score >= 70 && score <= 79)
  System.out.println("C");
else if (score >= 60 && score <= 69)
  System.out.println("D");
else
  System.out.println("F");
```

The first condition checks whether the score is at least 90. The second condition checks whether the score is between 80 and 89. Part of this test (`score <= 89`) is unnecessary; the score can't be greater than 89, or we would have already printed A as the grade. The later tests for `score <= 79` and `score <= 69` are also unnecessary. Here's what the simplified `if` statement would look like:

```
if (score >= 90)
  System.out.println("A");
else if (score >= 80)
  System.out.println("B");
else if (score >= 70)
  System.out.println("C");
else if (score >= 60)
  System.out.println("D");
else
  System.out.println("F");
```

Stay alert for ways to simplify your own cascaded `if` statements; you'll usually find plenty of opportunities to do so.

PROGRAM   ### Flipping a Coin

Let's write a program that asks the user to guess the outcome of a simulated coin flip. The program will first ask the user to enter either `heads` or `tails`. The user's input will then be compared with the result of the coin flip. If they match, the program will print the message `"You win!"`. If they don't match, the program will print `"Sorry, you lose."` (with no exclamation mark; it's not nice to gloat). Here's what the user will see on the screen:

```
Enter heads or tails: tails
Sorry, you lose.
```

To make the program more user-friendly, we'll have it ignore the case of the input: the user could enter HeAdS or hEADs, for example, instead of typing heads. If the user's input doesn't match heads or tails—even when case is ignored—then we'll have the program print an error message and terminate.

The only remaining question is how to simulate a coin flip. Fortunately, that's easy to do in Java with the help of the Math class. Math contains a method named random that returns a "random" number that's greater than or equal to 0.0 and less than 1.0. (The reason I've put the word "random" in quotation marks is that the value returned by the random method isn't *really* random. random actually uses a mathematical formula to calculate the values that it returns. Technically, random returns a ***pseudorandom*** number.) Let's adopt the rule that if random returns a number less than 0.5, the coin landed heads up; otherwise, it landed tails up.

pseudorandom numbers ➤9.3

Here's the finished program:

CoinFlip.java

```
1    // Asks the user to guess a coin flip
2
3    import jpb.*;
4
5    public class CoinFlip {
6      public static void main(String[] args) {
7        // Prompt user to guess heads or tails
8        SimpleIO.prompt("Enter heads or tails: ");
9        String userInput = SimpleIO.readLine();
10       if (!userInput.equalsIgnoreCase("heads") &&
11           !userInput.equalsIgnoreCase("tails")) {
12         System.out.println("Sorry, you didn't enter heads " +
13                            "or tails; please try again.");
14         return;
15       }
16
17       // Choose a random number
18       double randomNumber = Math.random();
19
20       // Determine whether user guessed correctly
21       if (userInput.equalsIgnoreCase("heads") &&
22           randomNumber < 0.5)
23         System.out.println("You win!");
24       else if (userInput.equalsIgnoreCase("tails") &&
25                randomNumber >= 0.5)
26         System.out.println("You win!");
27       else
28         System.out.println("Sorry, you lose.");
29     }
30   }
```

Let's do a line-by-line analysis of this program, starting with lines 8 and 9. The statements on these lines prompt the user to enter either heads or tails, then read the user's input. After reading the user's input, the next step is to *validate* it—to make sure that it meets the requirements of the program. In this case, we need to check whether the user entered either heads or tails. The expression userInput.equalsIgnoreCase("heads") on line 10 has the value true if the `userInput` variable contains a string that's equal to `"heads"`, ignoring case. If `userInput` isn't equal to `"heads"` and `userInput` isn't equal to `"tails"`, then the user's input isn't valid, and the program displays an error message (lines 12–13). The error message reminds the user what he or she *should* have entered, which is always a good idea. The `return` statement (line 14), when executed inside the `main` method, causes the program to terminate.

Line 18 declares the `randomNumber` variable and initializes it by calling `Math.random`. We're now ready to check whether the user guessed correctly. There are three possibilities: (a) the user guessed heads and the random number is less than 0.5, (b) the user guessed tails and the random number is greater than or equal to 0.5, or (c) neither of these cases applies. A cascaded `if` statement is the logical way to check for these three conditions.

If the user's input is `"heads"` (ignoring case) and the random number is less than 0.5 (which we interpret as "heads"), then the program prints the `"You win!"` message (lines 21–23). If the user's input is `"tails"` (ignoring case) and the random number is greater than or equal to 0.5 ("tails"), then the program prints `"You win!"` (lines 24–26). Finally, if neither of the `if` conditions is true, the program prints `"Sorry, you lose."` (lines 27–28).

The "Dangling `else`" Problem

When one `if` statement contains another, we'll sometimes get caught by the "dangling `else`" problem, a nasty trap that Java inherited from older languages.

Suppose that we want to add the value of the variable n to the variable `sum`. However, if n exceeds some maximum value `max`, we want to add `max` to `sum` instead. And, if n is less than or equal to 0, we'd like to ignore n and leave `sum` unchanged. The following `if` statement attempts to accomplish this effect:

```
if (n <= max)
  if (n > 0)
    sum += n;
else
  sum += max;
```

When we put this statement in a program and run the program, we quickly discover that the `sum` variable doesn't change if n is larger than `max`. What went wrong? The problem can be summed up in a single word: ***ambiguity.*** There are two ways to read the `if` statement, depending on whether we consider the `else` clause to belong to the outer `if` statement or the inner `if` statement:

Interpretation 1	*Interpretation 2*
```if (n <= max) { if (n > 0) sum += n; } else sum += max;```	```if (n <= max) { if (n > 0) sum += n; else sum += max; }```

We were expecting the first interpretation, but the compiler chose the second one instead. When `if` statements are nested, Java matches each `else` clause with the *nearest unmatched* `if`. To force the compiler to interpret the `if` statement our way, we'll need to enclose the inner statement in a block by adding curly braces:

```
if (n <= max) {
   if (n > 0)
      sum += n;
} else
   sum += max;
```

Notice that we wouldn't have gotten into trouble if we'd used braces in the first place.

Ambiguity

Ambiguity is common in programming languages. We encountered it in Section 2.7, as a matter of fact. An expression such as

```
a + b * c
```

is ambiguous, because it could mean either

```
(a + b) * c
```

or

```
a + (b * c)
```

Java resolves ambiguity in expressions by adopting rules for precedence and associativity. Because of precedence rules, we know that the correct interpretation of `a + b * c` is `a + (b * c)`. We can force the other interpretation by using parentheses, just as we can solve the dangling `else` problem by adding braces.

Review Questions

1. After reading an item of user input, the next step is to _____ it by checking whether it meets the requirements of the program.

2. A _____ if statement is created by nesting `if` statements in such a way that the `else` clause of each `if` statement is another `if` statement.

3. The dangling `else` problem may occur when an `if` statement has (a) more `if` clauses than `else` clauses; (b) more `else` clauses than `if` clauses; or (c) an equal number of `if` and `else` clauses.

4. When an expression or statement has two or more possible interpretations (as in the dangling `else` problem), we say that it suffers from _____.

4.5 The `boolean` Type

Java's `boolean` type clearly goes hand in hand with the `if` statement. When we perform a comparison using a relational or equality operator, the result is a `boolean` value. The logical operators require `boolean` operands and produce a `boolean` result. The `if` statement requires that its test condition be a `boolean` expression.

The `boolean` type has other uses, however. We can declare `boolean` variables and parameters, and methods can return `boolean` values. `boolean` variables are ideal for representing data items that have only two possible values. In Section 3.2, for example, we saw that a `boolean` variable named `pointIs-Exposed` would be useful for remembering whether or not the point of a pen is exposed.

`boolean` variables are often used to keep track of choices made by the user. For example, the `CoinFlip` program of Section 4.4 asks the user to choose between heads and tails. The user's decision could be recorded in a `boolean` variable. Let's name this variable `headsWasSelected`:

```
boolean headsWasSelected;
```

> Be careful to choose good names for `boolean` variables. Well-chosen names often contain a verb such as "is," "was," or "has."

`boolean` variables can be assigned either `true` or `false`:

```
headsWasSelected = true;
```

Assigning `true` to `headsWasSelected` indicates that the user chose heads rather than tails. The value assigned to a `boolean` variable often depends on the outcome of a test. For example, we might want to assign `true` to `headsWas-Selected` if the user's input was the string `"heads"` (ignoring case); otherwise, we want `headsWasSelected` to have the value `false`. One way to do the assignment is to use an `if` statement:

```
if (userInput.equalsIgnoreCase("heads"))
  headsWasSelected = true;
else
  headsWasSelected = false;
```

This approach certainly works, but there's a better way:

```
headsWasSelected = userInput.equalsIgnoreCase("heads");
```

The `equalsIgnoreCase` method returns a `boolean` value anyway, so we might as well store that value directly into the `headsWasSelected` variable.

Assigning the value of a `boolean` expression to a `boolean` variable is clearer and more efficient than testing the expression first, then performing the assignment.

> Avoid `if` statements that assign `true` and `false` to the same variable. Instead, assign the value of the test condition directly to the variable.

Once a value has been assigned to a `boolean` variable, we can test the variable using an `if` statement:

```
if (headsWasSelected) …
```

(Notice how nicely this statement reads—"if heads was selected …"—thanks to the name that we chose for the variable.) There's no need to write

```
if (headsWasSelected == true) …
```

Testing whether `headsWasSelected` is equal to `true` will work, but it's unnecessary.

Testing whether a `boolean` variable is equal to `true` is not only unnecessary but potentially dangerous as well. Suppose that we accidentally use the `=` operator to perform the test instead of the `==` operator:

```
if (headsWasSelected = true) …   // WRONG
```

The `headsWasSelected` variable will be assigned the value `true`, and then the `if` statement will test the value of `headsWasSelected`. It will always be `true`, of course, which isn't what we intended. This error is particularly insidious because the compiler can't detect it.

To test whether `headsWasSelected` is false, it's better to write

```
if (!headsWasSelected) …
```

rather than

```
if (headsWasSelected == false) …
```

> Avoid testing `boolean` variables for equality with `true` and `false`.

We'll occasionally need to display the value of a `boolean` variable, perhaps for debugging purposes. Fortunately, both the `System.out.print` and the `System.out.println` methods are capable of displaying a `boolean` value:

```
System.out.println(headsWasSelected);
```

Either the word `true` or the word `false` will be displayed.

PROGRAM   **Flipping a Coin (Revisited)**

Let's modify the `CoinFlip` program of Section 4.4 so that it uses a `boolean` variable to remember whether the user selected heads or tails. We'll name this variable `headsWasSelected`. If the user chooses heads, we'll have the program assign `true` to this variable. If the user chooses tails, `headsWasSelected` will have the value `false` instead.

CoinFlip2.java

```
1   // Asks the user to guess a coin flip
2
3   import jpb.*;
4
5   public class CoinFlip2 {
6     public static void main(String[] args) {
7       boolean headsWasSelected = false;
8
9       // Prompt user to guess heads or tails
10      SimpleIO.prompt("Enter heads or tails: ");
11      String userInput = SimpleIO.readLine();
12      if (userInput.equalsIgnoreCase("heads"))
13        headsWasSelected = true;
14      else if (!userInput.equalsIgnoreCase("tails")) {
15        System.out.println("Sorry, you didn't enter heads " +
16                              "or tails; please try again.");
17        return;
18      }
19
20      // Choose a random number
21      double randomNumber = Math.random();
22
23      // Determine whether user guessed correctly
24      if (headsWasSelected && randomNumber < 0.5)
25        System.out.println("You win!");
26      else if (!headsWasSelected && randomNumber >= 0.5)
27        System.out.println("You win!");
28      else
29        System.out.println("Sorry, you lose.");
30    }
31  }
```

As this program shows, it's often a good idea to assign a default value to a `boolean` variable. By initializing `headsWasSelected` to `false` on line 7, I was able to avoid testing whether the user's input was `tails`. Instead, I tested first for `heads`, and then—if the input wasn't `heads`—I checked whether the input wasn't `tails`. The only other possibility is that the user's input *was* `tails`, which matches the default value of `headsWasSelected`.

Review Questions

1. Which one of the following would *not* be a good name for a `boolean` variable: (a) `isBlue`, (b) `changeColor`, or (c) `colorWasSelected`?

2. What is the best way to test whether a `boolean` variable named b has the value `true`?

3. What is the best way to test whether a `boolean` variable named b has the value `false`?

4.6 Loops

Most algorithms contain steps that require an action to be repeated more than once. We first encountered repetition in our discussion of algorithms in Section 1.3. Step 5 of our recipe for Hollandaise sauce was

> 5. Beat the yolks with a wire whisk until they begin to thicken. Add: 1 tablespoon boiling water.

The first part of this step consists of an *action* to be repeated ("beat the yolks with a wire whisk") and a *condition* to be checked ("[the yolks] begin to thicken").

A language construct that repeatedly performs an action is called a ***loop.*** In Java, every loop has a statement to be repeated (the ***loop body***) and a condition to be checked (the ***controlling expression***). Each time the loop body is executed, the controlling expression is checked. If the expression is true, the loop continues to execute. If it's false, the loop terminates and the program continues with the next statement. A single cycle of the loop (executing the body and testing the condition) is called an ***iteration.***

Types of Loops

Java has three loop statements: the `while` statement, the `do` statement, and the `for` statement. All three have much in common. In particular, they all use a `boolean` expression to determine whether or not to continue looping. Also, all three require a single statement as the loop body. If we want the loop body to contain more than one statement, we'll need to enclose the statements in braces to form a block.

do statement ➤ 8.3

for statement ➤ 5.2

Which type of loop to use is mostly a matter of convenience. The `while` statement tests its condition *before* executing the loop body. The `do` statement tests its condition *after* executing the loop body, so it always executes the body at least once. The `for` statement is most convenient if the loop is controlled by a variable whose value needs to be updated each time the loop body is executed. For now, we'll focus on the `while` statement.

The `while` Statement

The `while` statement is the simplest of Java's loop statements. It has the following appearance:

`while` statement

```
while ( expression )
    statement
```

The controlling expression must have `boolean` type. The loop body can be any statement.

In the following `while` statement, the controlling expression is `i < n` and the loop body is `i *= 2;`.

```
while (i < n)    // Controlling expression
   i *= 2;       // Loop body
```

When a `while` statement is executed, the controlling expression is evaluated first. If it has the value `true`, the loop body is executed and the expression is tested again. The process continues in this fashion—first testing the controlling expression, then executing the loop body—until the controlling expression becomes false. The following diagram shows the flow of control within a `while` statement:

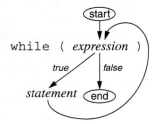

To see how `while` statements work, let's trace the execution of the following statements:

```
i = 1;
n = 10;
while (i < n)
   i *= 2;
```

Here's a step-by-step trace showing the result of executing each statement:

```
i = 1;      i is now 1.
n = 10;     n is now 10.
Is i < n?   Yes; continue.
i *= 2;     i is now 2.
Is i < n?   Yes; continue.
i *= 2;     i is now 4.
Is i < n?   Yes; continue.
i *= 2;     i is now 8.
Is i < n?   Yes; continue.
i *= 2;     i is now 16.
Is i < n?   No; exit from loop.
```

The loop continues executing as long as the controlling expression (`i < n`) is true. When the expression is false, the loop terminates. Because the expression `i < n` must be false when the loop terminates, we're guaranteed that i is greater than or equal to n. In other words:

> When a while statement terminates, the controlling expression is guaranteed to be false, which means that the logical negation of the controlling expression must be true.

This fact may seem too obvious to mention, but it's often an important aid in understanding how a program works.

One thing to notice about a while statement is that the loop body may not be executed at all. If the controlling expression is false to begin with, the loop will terminate immediately without executing the body even once. In our example, if i is initially greater than or equal to n, the loop won't do anything at all.

Blocks as Loop Bodies

Most loops will need more than one statement within the loop body. All we need to do is put braces around the statements to create a block.

Consider the problem of finding the greatest common divisor (GCD). The GCD of two integers is the largest integer that divides both numbers evenly, with no remainder. For example, the GCD of 15 and 35 is 5, because 5 is the largest integer that divides both numbers without a remainder. The classic algorithm for computing the GCD, known as Euclid's algorithm, goes as follows:

1. Let m and n be variables containing the two numbers.
2. If n is 0, then stop: m contains the GCD.
3. Divide m by n. Save the divisor in m, and save the remainder in n.
4. Repeat the process, starting at step 2.

The last line of the algorithm makes clear that we'll need a loop. The loop is supposed to terminate when n is 0, so it will need to have the form

```
while (n != 0) {
    ...
}
```

Inside the loop body, we'll need to execute the following statements:

```
m = n;       // Save divisor in m
n = m % n;   // Save remainder in n
```

Here we face a problem. If we assign n to m first, then m won't have the correct value when it comes time to compute m % n. On the other hand, if we switch the order of the two statements, the value of n assigned to m won't be the correct one. In order to solve this problem, we'll need a *temporary variable:* a variable that stores a value only briefly. Let's name this variable r (for remainder) and use it to store the value of the expression m % n. The body of the loop can now be written as follows:

```
r = m % n;   // Store remainder (temporarily) in r
m = n;       // Save divisor in m
n = r;       // Save remainder in n
```

The entire loop will look like this:

```
while (n != 0) {
  r = m % n;   // Store remainder (temporarily) in r
  m = n;       // Save divisor in m
  n = r;       // Save remainder in n
}
```

 Be careful to use braces if you need to put more than one statement in the body of a loop. Neglecting to do so may give you a program that compiles without an error, but goes into an infinite loop. An *infinite loop* occurs when a loop's controlling expression is always true, so the loop can never terminate.

For example, let's see what would happen if we neglected to put braces around the body of the Euclidean algorithm loop:

```
while (n != 0)   // WRONG; braces needed around loop body
  r = m % n;     // Loop ends here by mistake
  m = n;         // This statement and the next one
  n = r;         //   are outside the loop
```

The loop ends at the first semicolon, so the statements m = n; and n = r; aren't inside the loop. The program will compile with no problems. When we run the program, however, it will go into an infinite loop (if n is not equal to 0), repeatedly testing n and computing r. Because n never changes, the loop has no way to terminate.

If your program gets stuck in an infinite loop, you'll have to kill it from the keyboard. The method for doing so varies, depending on your platform and the Java system you're using. If you're using the Java Development Kit under Windows, hold down the Ctrl (Control) key and press the letter C.

Let's trace the behavior of the GCD loop. This loop is a bit more complicated, involving three variables, so I'll use a table to show how the variables change during the execution of the loop. Let's assume that m and n have the values 30 and 72, respectively, before the loop is executed.

	Initial value	*After iteration 1*	*After iteration 2*	*After iteration 3*	*After iteration 4*
r	?	30	12	6	0
m	30	72	30	12	6
n	72	30	12	6	0

The GCD of 30 and 72 is 6, the final value of m.

Declaring Variables in Blocks

A temporary variable can be declared at any point prior to where it's first used. In the GCD loop, we can declare r at the same time as m and n if we like. However, Java gives us another option—we can declare r inside the block itself:

```
while (n != 0) {
  int r = m % n;    // Store remainder (temporarily) in r
  m = n;            // Save divisor in m
  n = r;            // Save remainder in n
}
```

Any block may contain variable declarations, not just a block used as a loop body.

Be careful when declaring variables inside a block. Java prohibits such a variable from having the same name as a variable (or parameter) declared in the enclosing method. For example, if userInput is declared as a variable outside a block, you can't declare it a second time inside the block.

Declaring a variable inside a block isn't always a good idea. The variable can be used only within the block; it's not available to statements outside the block. Also, a variable declared in a block is created each time the block is entered and destroyed at the end of the block, causing its value to be lost. (As long as we're using the variable for temporary storage, that's no great loss.)

Example: Improving the Fraction Constructor

Section 3.8 introduced the Fraction class, which is a running example in this book. The original version of the class provides the following constructor:

```
public Fraction(int num, int denom) {
  numerator = num;
  denominator = denom;
}
```

This constructor could stand to be improved, because it makes no attempt to reduce fractions to lowest terms. For example, executing the statements

```
Fraction f = new Fraction(4, 8);
System.out.println(f);
```

will produce 4/8 as the output instead of 1/2.

To reduce a fraction to its lowest terms, the constructor will need to compute the GCD of the fraction's numerator and denominator. Then, it will divide both the numerator and the denominator by the GCD. While we're at it, we should have the constructor adjust the fraction so that the denominator is never negative. (If the denominator does happen to be negative, the constructor can simply change the sign of both the numerator and denominator.)

Here's a new version of the constructor with these improvements added:

```
public Fraction(int num, int denom) {
  // Compute GCD of num and denom
  int m = num, n = denom;
  while (n != 0) {
    int r = m % n;
    m = n;
    n = r;
  }

  // Divide num and denom by GCD; store results in instance
  // variables
  if (m != 0) {
    numerator = num / m;
    denominator = denom / m;
  }

  // Adjust fraction so that denominator is never negative
  if (denominator < 0) {
    numerator = -numerator;
    denominator = -denominator;
  }
}
```

If the GCD of num and denom is 0 (because both num and denom are 0), the constructor doesn't assign values to numerator and denominator. That's not a problem, because instance variables that represent numbers are automatically initialized to 0 in Java. (Section 10.5 discusses this point in more detail.)

Review Questions

1. The statement to be repeated within a loop is called the _____ _____ [two words].

2. A single cycle of a loop (executing the body and testing the condition) is called an _____.

3. The controlling expression for a loop must have _____ type.

4. A variable that stores a value for only a brief period of time is said to be a _____ variable.

4.7 Counting Loops

Many loops require a ***counter:*** a variable whose value increases or decreases systematically each time through the loop. Consider the problem of writing a loop that reads 10 numbers entered by the user and sums them. In order to know when the loop should terminate, we would need to have a variable that keeps track of how many numbers the user has entered so far. The variable would be assigned the value 0 before the loop is entered. Each loop iteration would then add 1 to this variable.

As a second example, consider the problem of writing a loop that displays a countdown, like the one used when a rocket is launched:

```
T minus 10 and counting
T minus 9 and counting
T minus 8 and counting
T minus 7 and counting
T minus 6 and counting
T minus 5 and counting
T minus 4 and counting
T minus 3 and counting
T minus 2 and counting
T minus 1 and counting
```

It's apparent that we'll need a counter that's assigned the values 10, 9, ..., 1 as the loop executes. If we name the counter i, our loop will look like this:

```
int i = 10;
while (i > 0) {
  System.out.println("T minus " + i + " and counting");
  i -= 1;
}
```

Before the `while` statement is executed, the variable i is assigned the value 10. Because 10 is greater than 0, the loop body is executed, causing the message T minus 10 and counting to be printed and i to be decremented. The condition i > 0 is then tested again. Because 9 is greater than 0, the loop body is executed once more. This process continues until the message T minus 1 and counting is printed and i becomes 0. The test i > 0 then fails, causing the loop to terminate.

Notice that I used i > 0 as the controlling expression, rather than i != 0. Either test will work, but i > 0 is more descriptive, because it suggests that i is decreasing until it reaches 0. The test i != 0, on the other hand, doesn't tell us whether i is increasing or decreasing.

Let's look now at a loop that counts *up* instead of *down*. Our goal is to display the numbers from 1 to n along with their squares. For example, if n is 5, we'd like to see the following output:

```
1 1
2 4
3 9
4 16
5 25
```

Clearly we need a counter variable i that takes on the values 1, 2, ..., n. Each time through the loop, we'll display the value of i along with the value of i * i. (Java has no special way to square numbers, so we'll simply multiply i by itself.) Here's a while loop that produces the desired output:

```
int i = 1;
while (i <= n) {
  System.out.println(i + " " + i * i);
  i += 1;
}
```

Variables used as counters should be integers, not floating-point numbers. (Using floating-point numbers is risky because of round-off errors that may accumulate over time.) Counters often have names like i, j, or k. (Notice that l—the letter "el"—isn't a good variable name, because it looks too much like the number 1.) Using these names is a tradition among programmers. Although such short names might seem to run contrary to our preference for descriptive variable names, they're actually not a bad idea. A counter is an artificial variable introduced for the purpose of controlling a loop, so there's often no more meaningful name for it than i.

Increment and Decrement Operators

Most loops that have a counter variable will probably either *increment* the variable (add 1 to it) or *decrement* the variable (subtract 1 from it). So far, we know two ways to increment or decrement a variable. The first is to use the + or - operator in conjunction with assignment:

```
i = i + 1;   // Increment i
i = i - 1;   // Decrement i
```

The second way is to use the += and -= operators:

```
i += 1;      // Increment i
i -= 1;      // Decrement i
```

The operation of incrementing a variable is so common that Java has a special operator for this purpose: ++, the *increment operator.* To increment a variable, we can write either

```
++i;
```

or

```
i++;
```

When it's placed before the variable to be incremented, we say that ++ is a *prefix* operator. When it's placed after the variable, it's a *postfix* operator.

Not surprisingly, Java also has an operator for decrementing a variable: --, the *decrement operator.* Again, we have a choice of putting the -- operator in front of the variable or after the variable:

```
--i;
i--;
```

When ++ and -- are used in isolation, as we've just done, it doesn't matter whether the operator goes before or after the variable. When these operators are used within some other type of statement, however, it usually *does* make a difference. Suppose that we want to print the value of the variable i and also increment i. The statement

```
System.out.println(++i);
```

will increment i and then print the new value of i. On the other hand, the statement

```
System.out.println(i++);
```

will print the old value of i, and then increment i. The value of i afterward is the same either way—it has increased by 1 as the result of the increment.

If we like, we can use ++ and -- in conjunction with other operators. Consider the following example:

```
i = 1;
j = ++i + 1;
```

After these statements are executed, i will have the value 2 (because it was incremented), and j will have the value 3. Now, let's put the ++ operator *after* i:

```
i = 1;
j = i++ + 1;
```

Afterward, i will have the value 2 and j will have the value 2. The old value of i was used during the computation of j's value; i was incremented later.

By now, you've probably noticed that the ++ and -- operators don't behave like normal arithmetic operators. Evaluating the expression i + j doesn't change either i or j. Evaluating ++i, on the other hand, causes a permanent change to i. We say that the ++ and -- operators have a *side effect,* because these operators do more than simply produce a result.

Using the Increment and Decrement Operators in Loops

The increment and decrement operators are used primarily to update loop counters. (In fact, that's all I'll use them for in this book.) Consider the countdown loop at the beginning of this section:

```
while (i > 0) {
  System.out.println("T minus " + i + " and counting");
  i -= 1;
}
```

We can modify the last statement in the loop body so that it uses the decrement operator:

```
while (i > 0) {
  System.out.println("T minus " + i + " and counting");
  i--;
}
```

Notice that it doesn't matter whether we use i-- or --i, because the decrement operation isn't part of some larger statement.

Likewise, we can use i++ (or ++i) in the "squares" example:

```
while (i <= n) {
  System.out.println(i + " " + i * i);
  i++;
}
```

Most of the time, the increment and decrement operators are nothing more than a minor convenience. Occasionally, though, they provide opportunities to simplify loops. In the countdown loop, for example, the counter could be decremented within the call of System.out.println:

```
while (i > 0) {
  System.out.println("T minus " + i-- + " and counting");
}
```

The braces around the loop body are no longer necessary, because the body is now a single statement. (Some programmers always put braces around the body of a loop, even when it's not necessary, so that statements can easily be added to the body in the future.)

The CourseAverage program of Section 2.11 would benefit greatly from counting loops. The portions of the program that prompt the user to enter the program scores and the quiz scores are highly repetitive, suggesting that loops should be used. The loops will need counters to control the number of repetitions (eight in the case of the program scores and five in the case of the quiz scores). Each counter should start at 1 and count up, because we'll want the current value of the counter to be part of the prompt ("Enter Program *i* score: "). For example, here's a new version of the code that reads the eight program scores and computes their total:

```
String userInput;
double programTotal = 0.0;
int i = 1;
while (i <= 8) {
  SimpleIO.prompt("Enter Program " + i + " score: ");
  userInput = SimpleIO.readLine();
  programTotal += Convert.toDouble(userInput);
  i++;
}
```

I declared the userInput variable outside the loop so that it can be reused later in the program.

PROGRAM **Counting Coin Flips**

The `CoinFlip` program of Section 4.4 showed how to flip a simulated coin. Let's modify that program so that it flips the imaginary coin any number of times, keeping track of the number of heads and tails. The modified program, which I'll name `CountFlips`, will ask the user to enter the number of flips. It will then print the number of heads and the number of tails. Here's what the user will see on the screen:

```
Enter number of flips: 10
Number of heads: 6
Number of tails: 4
```

As in the `CoinFlip` program, we'll use the `Math.random` method to generate a (pseudo-) random number between 0.0 and 1.0. If `Math.random` returns a number less than 0.5, we'll say that the coin landed heads up; otherwise, it landed tails up.

The `CountFlips` program will need a loop that flips the coin n times, where n is the number entered by the user. There are several ways to write such a loop. One is to initialize a counter to 1, and then increment the counter until it exceeds n. A slightly different approach is to decrement n itself until it reaches 0. Here's a side-by-side comparison of the two techniques:

Technique 1	*Technique 2*

`int i = 1;`
 `while (i <= n) {`
 `   ...`
 `   i++;`
 `}`
	`while (n > 0) {`
	 `   ...`
	 `   n--;`
	 `}`

The advantage of the first approach is that the value of n is preserved for use later in the program. The second approach has the advantage that no new counter variable is needed; n serves as the counter. I'll use the second approach in the `Count-Flips` program because the number of flips isn't needed after the loop terminates.

CountFlips.java

```
1  // Counts the number of heads and tails in a series of coin
2  // flips
3
4  import jpb.*;
5
6  public class CountFlips {
7    public static void main(String[] args) {
8      // Prompt user to enter number of flips
9      SimpleIO.prompt("Enter number of flips: ");
10     String userInput = SimpleIO.readLine();
11     int flips = Integer.parseInt(userInput);
12
```

```
13        // Flip coin for specified number of times
14        int heads = 0, tails = 0;
15        while (flips > 0) {
16          if (Math.random() < 0.5)
17            heads++;
18          else
19            tails++;
20          flips--;
21        }
22
23        // Display number of heads and tails
24        System.out.println("Number of heads: " + heads);
25        System.out.println("Number of tails: " + tails);
26      }
27    }
```

Lines 15–21 are the heart of the program. Line 15 tests whether the variable flips still has a value greater than 0. (If it doesn't, then we've completed the number of coin flips specified by the user.) Line 16 calls the Math.random method as part of the if statement's condition. If the random number returned by Math.random is less than 0.5, the heads variable is incremented; otherwise, the tails variable is incremented. Line 20 then decrements the flips variable.

The loop on lines 15–21 could also have been written in the following way:

```
while (flips-- > 0)
  if (Math.random() < 0.5)
    heads++;
  else
    tails++;
```

This version decrements the flips variable each time it's compared with 0. The decrement occurs *after* the test (because we're using the postfix version of the -- operator), so it doesn't affect the test's outcome. No braces are needed around the body of the loop (which is now a single if statement), although it wouldn't hurt to use them anyway.

Among other things, this program can be used to test whether Math.random actually returns numbers that appear to be random. If we ask for a large number of flips, we would expect the number of heads and tails to be extremely close. Table 4.4 shows what happened when I ran the program. (Your results may vary; there's no guarantee that the numbers generated by Math.random are the same each time.)

Table 4.4

Breakdown of Heads and Tails for Varying Numbers of Coin Flips

Number of Flips	Number of Heads	Number of Tails
100	54	46
1,000	501	499
10,000	4,974	5,026
100,000	49,788	50,212
1,000,000	500,170	499,830

As expected, the relative difference between the number of heads and the number of tails shrank as the number of flips increased. At 100 flips, the difference between the actual number of heads and the expected number of heads was 8%. By 1,000,000 flips, the difference was down to .034%.

Review Questions

1. A _____ is a variable that increases or decreases during each iteration of a loop.

2. When a unary operator is placed *after* its operand, we refer to it as a _____ operator.

3. ++ is called the _____ operator.

4. When an operator performs some action other than simply returning a value, we say that it has a _____ _____ [two words].

4.8 Exiting from a Loop: The `break` Statement

Although the `while` statement is a powerful tool for writing loops, we'll sometimes need more flexibility. In particular, we may need for a loop to terminate based on a condition that's tested *inside* the body of the loop, rather than at the beginning of the loop. Java's `break` statement allows a loop to terminate at any point, not just at the beginning. In this section, we'll see how the `break` statement is used inside the body of a loop. `break` statements are also used in conjunction with the `switch` statement.

switch statement ➤8.2

`break` is one of the simplest statements in Java. It has the following form:

break statement

```
break;
```

Executing a `break` statement inside the body of a loop causes the loop to terminate immediately. Because of this behavior, `break` statements don't normally appear by themselves. Instead, each `break` statement is usually nested inside an `if` statement, so that the enclosing loop will terminate only when a certain condition has been satisfied.

The `break` statement has several uses within loops:

- *Premature exit from a loop.* A loop may need to exit before its controlling expression becomes false. In some cases, the goal is simply to save time. In other cases, the correctness of the program depends on exiting from the loop as soon as possible.

- *Exit from the middle of a loop.* Normally the exit point in a loop is either at the beginning (the `while` and `for` statements) or at the end (the `do` statement). Some algorithms, however, are best implemented with a loop whose exit point is in the middle of the loop body. We can create such a loop by using `true` as the loop's controlling expression and relying on a `break` statement to terminate the loop.

■ *Multiple exit points within a loop.* Some loops require more than one exit point. A loop may contain any number of `break` statements, making multiple exit points possible.

To illustrate the need for premature exit from a loop, let's consider the problem of checking whether a number n is prime. Our plan is to write a `while` statement that divides n by the numbers between 2 and n − 1. We can break out of the loop as soon as any divisor is found; there's no need to try the remaining possibilities. After the loop has terminated, we can use an `if` statement to determine whether termination was premature (hence n isn't prime) or normal (n *is* prime):

```
int d = 2;
while (d < n) {
  if (n % d == 0)
    break;  // Terminate loop; n is not a prime
  d++;
}
if (d < n)
  System.out.println(n + " is divisible by " + d);
else
  System.out.println(n + " is prime");
```

Loops in which the exit point is in the middle of the body are fairly common. For example, loops that read user input, terminating when a particular value is entered, often fall into this category. Consider the following loop:

```
while (true) {
  SimpleIO.prompt("Enter a number (enter 0 to stop): ");
  String userInput = SimpleIO.readLine();
  int n = Integer.parseInt(userInput);
  if (n == 0)
    break;
  System.out.println(n + " cubed is " + n * n * n);
}
```

This loop prompts the user to enter a number and then prints the number and its cube. The process repeats until the user enters zero. The test for zero is done immediately after the input has been converted to integer form. If the test succeeds, a `break` statement causes the loop to terminate. Using `true` as the `while` loop's controlling expression forces the loop to repeat indefinitely, until the `break` statement is executed.

Review Questions

1.   How many `break` statements are allowed in a single loop?

2.   Name three reasons for using `break` statements in loops.

4.9 Case Study: Decoding Social Security Numbers

In the United States, nearly everyone has a Social Security Number (SSN), which is assigned by the government and used to track workers' Social Security contributions. SSNs have the form *ddd-dd-dddd*, where each *d* is a digit between 0 and 9. The first three digits form the "area number." This number is of particular interest because it indicates the state or U.S. territory in which the number was originally assigned. The area number usually indicates where a person was born or, in the case of an immigrant, where the person entered the United States. Area numbers between 1 and 680 are currently being used.

As our case study for this chapter, we'll develop a program named SSNInfo that asks the user to enter an SSN and then indicates where the number was issued. The following example shows what the user will see on the screen:

```
Enter a Social Security number: 078-05-1120
Number was issued in New York
```

In my examples, I'll use the number 078–05–1120, which doesn't belong to anyone. It was printed on sample cards inserted in thousands of wallets sold in the 1940s and 1950s. (Unfortunately, many people thought that this number was their own and supplied it to employers and the Selective Service, which kept track of young men who could be drafted for military service. At one point, there were at least 40 different people in the Selective Service database who used this SSN!)

We'll have SSNInfo check that the user's input is 11 characters long (not counting any spaces at the beginning or end) and contains dashes in the proper places. If either of these conditions is violated, the program will ask the user to re-enter the input. The process will repeat as many times as necessary, until the user enters satisfactory input:

```
Enter a Social Security number: 078051120
Error: Number must have 11 characters

Please re-enter number: 07805112000
Error: Number must have the form ddd-dd-dddd

Please re-enter number: 078-05-1120
Number was issued in New York
```

Note that the program won't completely validate the user's input: there's no check that the other characters are digits.

Let's start with an overall design for the program:

1. Prompt the user to enter an SSN and trim spaces from the input.

2. If the input isn't 11 characters long, or lacks dashes in the proper places, prompt the user to re-enter the SSN; repeat until the input is valid.
3. Compute the area number from the first three digits of the SSN.
4. Determine the location corresponding to the area number.
5. Print the location, or print an error message if the area number isn't legal.

Step 2 deserves a closer look. We'll clearly need to use a loop, but the conditions that we're testing will need to go inside the loop, so that we can print an appropriate message if either one is violated. If neither condition is true, then the input is valid, and we can use a `break` statement to terminate the loop. In pseudocode, the loop will look like this:

```
while (true) {
  if (user input is not 11 characters long) {
    print error message;
  else if (dashes are not in the right places) {
    print error message;
  else
    break;
  prompt user to re-enter input;
  read input;
}
```

Next, we'll need to choose algorithms and decide how the program's data will be stored. The input will be a single string, which we can trim by calling the `trim` method. The first three digits of this string can be extracted by calling `substring` and then converted to an integer by calling `Integer.parseInt`. This integer can then be tested by a cascaded `if` statement to see which location it corresponds to. Because ranges of area numbers correspond to the same location (for example, numbers 001 through 003 represent New Hampshire), we can use the technique described in Section 4.4 to simplify the cascaded `if` statement.

Here's the finished program.

SSNInfo.java

```
1   // Program name: SSNInfo
2   // Author: K. N. King
3   // Written: 1999-06-18
4   //
5   // Prompts the user to enter a Social Security number and
6   // then displays the location (state or territory) where the
7   // number was issued. The input is checked for length (should
8   // be 11 characters) and for dashes in the proper places. If
9   // the input is not valid, the user is asked to re-enter the
10  // Social Security number.
11
12  import jpb.*;
13
14  public class SSNInfo {
15    public static void main(String[] args) {
16      // Prompt the user to enter an SSN and trim the input
17      SimpleIO.prompt("Enter a Social Security number: ");
18      String ssn = SimpleIO.readLine().trim();
```

```
19
20      // If the input isn't 11 characters long, or lacks dashes
21      // in the proper places, prompt the user to re-enter
22      // the SSN; repeat until the input is valid.
23      while (true) {
24        if (ssn.length() != 11) {
25          System.out.println("Error: Number must have 11 " +
26                             "characters");
27        } else if (ssn.charAt(3) != '-' ||
28                   ssn.charAt(6) != '-') {
29          System.out.println(
30            "Error: Number must have the form ddd-dd-dddd");
31        } else
32          break;
33        SimpleIO.prompt("\nPlease re-enter number: ");
34        ssn = SimpleIO.readLine().trim();
35      }
36
37      // Get the area number (the first 3 digits of the SSN)
38      int area = Integer.parseInt(ssn.substring(0, 3));
39
40      // Determine the location corresponding to the area number
41      String location;
42      if        (area == 0)   location = null;
43      else if (area <= 3)   location = "New Hampshire";
44      else if (area <= 7)   location = "Maine";
45      else if (area <= 9)   location = "Vermont";
46      else if (area <= 34)  location = "Massachusetts";
47      else if (area <= 39)  location = "Rhode Island";
48      else if (area <= 49)  location = "Connecticut";
49      else if (area <= 134) location = "New York";
50      else if (area <= 158) location = "New Jersey";
51      else if (area <= 211) location = "Pennsylvania";
52      else if (area <= 220) location = "Maryland";
53      else if (area <= 222) location = "Delaware";
54      else if (area <= 231) location = "Virginia";
55      else if (area <= 236) location = "West Virginia";
56      else if (area <= 246) location = "North Carolina";
57      else if (area <= 251) location = "South Carolina";
58      else if (area <= 260) location = "Georgia";
59      else if (area <= 267) location = "Florida";
60      else if (area <= 302) location = "Ohio";
61      else if (area <= 317) location = "Indiana";
62      else if (area <= 361) location = "Illinois";
63      else if (area <= 386) location = "Michigan";
64      else if (area <= 399) location = "Wisconsin";
65      else if (area <= 407) location = "Kentucky";
66      else if (area <= 415) location = "Tennessee";
67      else if (area <= 424) location = "Alabama";
68      else if (area <= 428) location = "Mississippi";
69      else if (area <= 432) location = "Arkansas";
70      else if (area <= 439) location = "Louisiana";
71      else if (area <= 448) location = "Oklahoma";
72      else if (area <= 467) location = "Texas";
```

```
 73        else if (area <= 477) location = "Minnesota";
 74        else if (area <= 485) location = "Iowa";
 75        else if (area <= 500) location = "Missouri";
 76        else if (area <= 502) location = "North Dakota";
 77        else if (area <= 504) location = "South Dakota";
 78        else if (area <= 508) location = "Nebraska";
 79        else if (area <= 515) location = "Kansas";
 80        else if (area <= 517) location = "Montana";
 81        else if (area <= 519) location = "Idaho";
 82        else if (area <= 520) location = "Wyoming";
 83        else if (area <= 524) location = "Colorado";
 84        else if (area <= 525) location = "New Mexico";
 85        else if (area <= 527) location = "Arizona";
 86        else if (area <= 529) location = "Utah";
 87        else if (area <= 530) location = "Nevada";
 88        else if (area <= 539) location = "Washington";
 89        else if (area <= 544) location = "Oregon";
 90        else if (area <= 573) location = "California";
 91        else if (area <= 574) location = "Alaska";
 92        else if (area <= 576) location = "Hawaii";
 93        else if (area <= 579) location = "District of Columbia";
 94        else if (area <= 580) location = "Virgin Islands";
 95        else if (area <= 584) location = "Puerto Rico";
 96        else if (area <= 585) location = "New Mexico";
 97        else if (area <= 586) location = "Pacific Islands";
 98        else if (area <= 588) location = "Mississippi";
 99        else if (area <= 595) location = "Florida";
100        else if (area <= 599) location = "Puerto Rico";
101        else if (area <= 601) location = "Arizona";
102        else if (area <= 626) location = "California";
103        else if (area <= 645) location = "Texas";
104        else if (area <= 647) location = "Utah";
105        else if (area <= 649) location = "New Mexico";
106        else if (area <= 653) location = "Colorado";
107        else if (area <= 658) location = "South Carolina";
108        else if (area <= 665) location = "Louisiana";
109        else if (area <= 675) location = "Georgia";
110        else if (area <= 679) location = "Arkansas";
111        else if (area <= 680) location = "Nevada";
112        else                  location = null;
113
114        // Print the location, or print an error message if the
115        // area number isn't legal
116        if (location != null)
117          System.out.println("Number was issued in " + location);
118        else
119          System.out.println("Number is invalid");
120      }
121    }
```

Notice that the `location` variable is assigned the value `null` if the area number is zero or greater than 680. The `if` statement on line 116 can then test whether `location` is `null`; if so, the area number is invalid.

One annoying thing about the `SSNInfo` program is the size of the cascaded `if` statement. In later chapters, we'll discover better ways to keep track of the connections between area numbers and locations.

4.10 Debugging

When a program contains control structures such as the `if` and `while` statements, debugging becomes more challenging. For one thing, it will be necessary to run the program more than once, with different input data each time. (Each set of input data is called a ***test case***.) During a particular execution of the program, it's likely that only a portion of the statements in the program will actually be executed. For example, the `else` clause in an `if` statement won't be executed if the statement's controlling expression is true.

As you test a program, make sure that each statement in the program is executed by at least one test case. (This testing technique is called ***statement coverage***.) To make sure that every statement is tested at least once, check that the controlling expression in each `if` statement is true in some tests and false in others. For example, the `SSNInfo` program of Section 4.9 should be tested with test cases that force the condition on line 24 to be true, as well as test cases that make the condition false. The same is true for the conditions on lines 27–28 and 116. Ensuring statement coverage for this program will also require entering at least 71 Social Security numbers with different area numbers, to force each of the statements on lines 42–112 to be executed. (No one said testing was easy!) Testing every statement in a program doesn't guarantee that the program works, but it's a step in the right direction.

Loops also need more than one test case. Whenever possible, try to test each `while` loop with data that forces the controlling expression to be false initially (so the loop body is never executed), as well as data that forces the controlling expression to be true initially.

Loops are a rich source of bugs. Here are some of the varieties that you're likely to encounter:

- ***"Off-by-one" errors.*** An off-by-one error occurs when the number of iterations performed by a loop is one more (or one less) than the expected number. Off-by-one errors are often caused by using the wrong relational operator in the loop's controlling expression. If we write `i < n` when we should have written `i <= n`, the number of loop iterations will be one less than expected. If we write `i <= n` when we should have written `i < n`, the number of iterations will be one more than expected.

- ***Infinite loops.*** Infinite loops can occur in a variety of ways. One common cause is failing to increment (or decrement) a counter inside the body of the loop. Another is the accidental creation of an empty loop body by putting a semicolon in the wrong place.

■ *Never-executed loops.* Another common bug is a loop whose body is never executed. A never-executed loop is often caused by inverting the relational operator in the loop's controlling expression. If we write i > n instead of i < n, for example, then the loop may terminate immediately without executing the body. Another cause of a never-executed loop is using the == operator in a controlling expression. A condition such as i == n is probably false to start with, preventing the loop from ever getting off the ground.

A debugger is a great help in locating loop-related bugs. The "step" feature lets us execute statements one by one. By stepping through the statements in a loop body, we can quickly tell whether we have an off-by-one error, an infinite loop, or a never-executed loop. If you don't have a debugger, the tried-and-true approach—adding statements that print the values of variables—will usually give you the information that you need to find a loop-related bug. Put a call of System.out.println inside the loop and have it print the value of the counter variable (if the loop has one), plus any other important variables that change during the execution of the loop.

Review Questions

1. A set of input data used during the testing of a program is called a _____ _____ [two words].

2. The testing strategy of making sure that each statement is executed by at least one test case is called _____ _____ [two words].

3. List three common types of loop-related bugs.

━━━━━━━━━━

Q & A

Q: **What's a good way to test whether two floating-point numbers are sufficiently close? [p. 130]**

A: The following condition can be used to test whether a and b are "nearly" equal:

```
Math.abs(a - b) <= .000001 * a
```

The literal .000001 can be adjusted, depending on how close we want the numbers to be. Because we don't know whether a is larger than b or vice versa, it's safest to compute the absolute value of a - b using Math.abs. The test doesn't work if a can be less than or equal to zero, by the way. In that case, a more complicated test is required.

Notice that the test is not

```
Math.abs(a - b) <= .000001
```

This kind of test breaks down for very large or very small numbers. For example, if a is 1000001.0 and b is 1000000.0, then a - b is 1.0, which is not less than or equal to .000001. Yet a and b are close enough that the difference between the two might be round-off error. If a is .000001 and b is .000002, on the other hand, the absolute value of a - b is .000001, which is within our tolerance. But b is twice as large as a, so the difference between them is huge (relatively speaking) and probably not the result of round-off error.

Q: **The && and || operators perform short-circuit evaluation of their operands. Is there some way to avoid short-circuit evaluation and force both operands to be evaluated? [p. 133]**

A: Yes, there is. Most of the time, short-circuit evaluation is fine. It allows the left operand to protect the right operand, and it may also save a little time (because the right operand doesn't always need to be evaluated). Occasionally, however, we'll want to force both operands to be evaluated. Java's & and | operators will do just that. The & operator evaluates both its operands and then determines the value of the expression using Table 4.5.

Table 4.5
The & Operator

x	*y*	*x* & *y*
false	*false*	*false*
false	*true*	*false*
true	*false*	*false*
true	*true*	*true*

The | operator is similar, but uses Table 4.6 instead.

Table 4.6
The | Operator

x	*y*	*x* | *y*
false	*false*	*false*
false	*true*	*true*
true	*false*	*true*
true	*true*	*true*

Q: **You said that there should be a semicolon at the end of each complete declaration and each complete statement. But what about an if statement whose inner statement is a block? I don't see a semicolon at the end of the if statement. [p. 139]**

A: You're right. Every good rule needs one exception, and this is the exception to the rule that a semicolon goes at the end of each complete statement. When a statement contains a block, the right brace at the end of the block is enough to tell the compiler that the statement has ended. There's no need for a semicolon.

Q: **Does it cause any harm to put a semicolon after a block? [p. 139]**

A: Most of the time, no. However, it's not a good habit to develop. In fact, there's one situation in which putting a semicolon after a block causes a compilation error. Here it is:

```
if (score > 100) {
  System.out.println("** Error: Score exceeds 100 **");
  score = 100;
}; else
  System.out.println("Score is valid");
```

The compiler views the semicolon after the right brace as a separate statement that follows the `if` statement. The word `else` is treated as the beginning of a new statement. There's no such thing as an "`else` statement," so we'll get an error message such as

```
'else' without 'if'
```

Summary

- Numbers can be compared using the relational operators (`<`, `>`, `<=`, and `>=`) and the equality operators (`==` and `!=`).

- The relational and equality operators allow operands of different types.

- The arithmetic operators take precedence over the relational and equality operators.

- Testing floating-point numbers for equality or inequality may not always work correctly because of round-off error.

- The `==` and `!=` operators compare only *references* to objects, not the *contents* of the objects.

- To test whether two objects contain the same data, use the `equals` method.

- `String` objects can be compared using `equals`, `equalsIgnoreCase`, and `compareTo`. The value of `str1.compareTo(str2)` is negative if `str1` is less than `str2`, zero if `str1` is equal to `str2`, and positive if `str1` is greater than `str2`.

- The logical operators are `!` (not), `&&` (and), and `||` (or). All three require `boolean` operands and produce a `boolean` result.

- The `!` operator produces a true result if its operand is false; otherwise, it produces a false result.

- The `&&` operator produces a true result if both its operands are true.

- The `||` operator produces a true result if either one of its operands (or both) is true.

- Both the `&&` and `||` operators perform short-circuit evaluation, evaluating the left operand first and stopping as soon as the value of the expression is known.

- The relational and equality operators take precedence over the `&&` and `||` operators.

- The `!` operator takes precedence over the `&&` operator, which in turn takes precedence over the `||` operator.

- de Morgan's laws can often be used to simplify `boolean` expressions:

  ! (*expr*$_1$ && *expr*$_2$) is equivalent to ! (*expr*$_1$) || ! (*expr*$_2$).

  ! (*expr*$_1$ || *expr*$_2$) is equivalent to ! (*expr*$_1$) && ! (*expr*$_2$).

- In its simplest form, an `if` statement tests a `boolean` expression and then executes a particular statement if the expression is true.

- If a semicolon is placed at a point where Java expects a statement, the semicolon is treated as an empty statement—a command to do nothing.

- Whenever Java requires a single statement, we can substitute a series of statements, provided that the statements are enclosed in curly braces. The compiler treats the inner statements and the enclosing braces as a single statement, known as a block.

- An `if` statement may have an `else` clause. The statement following the word `else` is executed if the `if` statement's `boolean` expression is false.

- When `if` statements are nested so that the `else` clause of each is another `if` statement, the resulting statement is known as a cascaded `if` statement.

- The "dangling `else`" problem occurs when `if` statements are nested but not every `if` has a corresponding `else`. Java resolves the potential ambiguity by matching each `else` clause with the nearest unmatched `if`, which may not be what the programmer intended.

- The `boolean` type has only two values, `true` and `false`. `boolean` variables are useful for representing data items that have only two possible values.

- In Java, every loop has a body and a controlling expression.

- Java has three loop statements: the `while` statement, the `do` statement, and the `for` statement.

- A `while` statement repeatedly executes its loop body as long as the controlling expression is true. The controlling expression is tested at the beginning of each loop iteration, before the body is executed.

- To allow a loop body to contain more than one statement, we can use a block as the body.

- Temporary variables can be declared inside blocks.

- Many loops require a counter variable, whose value systematically increases or decreases during each loop iteration.

- The ++ (increment) and -- (decrement) operators are convenient for updating counter variables.

- When ++ is used as a prefix operator, its operand is incremented immediately. When ++ is used as a postfix operator, the increment is delayed. The -- operator behaves in a similar fashion.

- Because ++ and -- modify their operands in addition to producing a result, we say that these operators have side effects.

- Executing a `break` statement inside a loop body causes the loop to terminate.

- During the testing of a program, make sure that each statement in the program is executed by at least one test case.
- The most common kinds of loop bugs are off-by-one errors, infinite loops, and never-executed loops.

Exercises

1. Give the value of each of the following expressions. Assume that i has the value 5, j has the value 10, and x has the value 7.5.

   (a) `i * 2 >= j + 1`
   (b) `(i + j) / 2 == x`
   (c) `x * 2 < 3 * i`
   (d) `i * j != x * 6`

2. Add parentheses to the following expressions to indicate how Java will interpret them.

   (a) `a + b * c < d - e / f`
   (b) `a * b / c == - d * e + f`
   (c) `a * b >= c - d / e`
   (d) `a + b * c - d != e - f / g`

3. Which one of the strings `"tornado"`, `"tournament"`, and `"tomorrow"` would the compareTo method consider to be the *smallest*?

4. Write a boolean expression that tests whether str1 is less than str2, where str1 and str2 are strings.

5. The first Q&A at the end of the chapter describes how to test whether two floating-point numbers a and b are "almost equal." The test doesn't work if a is less than or equal to zero, however. Modify the test so that it works in that case as well.

6. Give the value of each of the following expressions. Assume that i has the value 5, j has the value 10, and x has the value 7.5.

   (a) `i - 2 != j + 2 && i + 3 >= x`
   (b) `3 * i > 2 * j || j / 2 >= i`
   (c) `i > j || j > x && x > i`
   (d) `i < j && j <= x || i < x`

7. Add parentheses to the following expressions to indicate how Java will interpret them.

   (a) `a * b < c && d >= e`
   (b) `a < b && b >= c || c == d`
   (c) `a == b || c - d < e && f != g`
   (d) `a && ! b || c && d`

8. Suppose that the value of the variable i is 0. How many arithmetic operations (additions, subtractions, multiplications, and divisions) will be performed when the following expression is evaluated?

   `(i * i - 1 >= 0) && (i * i + i - 12 <= j)`

9. Use de Morgan's laws to simplify the following `boolean` expressions. Each simplified expression must be equivalent to the original one but must not contain the `!` operator. (Using the `!=` operator is permissible, however.)

   (a) `!(i > 100 && i / 2 == 0)`
   (b) `!(x < 1.5 || x > 2.5)`
   (c) `!(i != 50 && i % 100 > 0)`
   (d) `!(i >= 10 && i <= 20 || i >= 30)`

10. The expression `(year % 4 == 0) && (year % 100 != 0 || year % 400 == 0)` tests whether the value of `year` is a leap year. Would the expression still be correct if the parentheses were removed? Justify your answer.

Section 4.3 11. Write an `if` statement that prints `Good-bye` if the value of the variable `str` is `"Hello"`.

12. Locate the error in each of the following statements and show how to fix it.

   (a) `if (day != "Sunday")`
       `System.out.println("Open for business");`
   (b) `if (grade = 4)`
       `System.out.println("A");`
   (c) `if (1 <= i <= 12)`
       `System.out.println("Month " + i + " was selected");`

Section 4.4 13. Locate the error in each of the following statements and show how to fix it.

   (a) `if (hour < 12);`
       `System.out.println("AM");`
   `else`
       `System.out.println("PM");`
   (b) `if (hour >= 7 && hour <= 10)`
       `System.out.println("Breakfast is served");`
   `else (hour >= 11 && hour <= 13)`
       `System.out.println("Lunch is served");`

14. What will the user see on the screen when the following statements are executed? What is the explanation for this behavior?

```
i = -1;
j = -2;
if (i >= 0)
  if (j < 0)
    System.out.println("j is negative");
else
  System.out.println("i is negative");
```

15. Assume that a, b, c, and `max` are `int` variables. Write a single `if` statement that determines which one of the numbers stored in a, b, and c is the largest one and stores it into `max`. *Hint:* Although you're allowed to write only one `if` statement, it may contain other `if` statements.

16. Modify the `toString` method in the `Fraction` class (Section 3.8) so that it returns only the numerator of a fraction (in string form) if the fraction's denominator is 1.

Section 4.6   17.   Show the output of the following program. Does the loop ever terminate?

```
public class Exercise4_17 {
  public static void main(String[] args) {
    int n = 40;
    while (n > 0) {
      if (n % 2 == 0)
        n /= 2;
      else
        n = 3 * n + 1;
      System.out.print(n + " ");
    }
  }
}
```

Section 4.7   18.   Suppose that i is an integer variable. Write three statements that increase the value of i by 1. Each statement must use a different operator.

19.   Show the values of the variables i and j after each series of statements has been executed.

```
(a) i = 5;
    j = --i + 1;
(b) i = 5;
    j = i++ - 1;
(c) i = 1;
    j = 2 * ++i;
(d) i = 1;
    j = 2 * i--;
```

20.   Which one of the following statements is not equivalent to the other two?

```
(a) if (++i > ++j) System.out.println(i);
(b) if (i++ > j++) System.out.println(i);
(c) if (++i > j++) System.out.println(i);
```

21.   What will be printed when the following statements are executed?

```
i = 1;
while (i == 5)
  System.out.println(i++);
```

22.   Show the values of the variables i and j after the following statements have been executed.

```
i = 0;
j = 0;
while (i < 5) {
  i++;
  j += i;
}
```

Programming Projects

1.   Make the following changes to the CourseAverage program (Section 2.11):

(a) Have the user enter six quiz scores instead of five. The revised program should drop the lowest of the six scores when computing the quiz average. *Hint:* Declare a variable (initialized to 10) whose job is to keep track of the lowest score entered so far. Each time the user enters a new quiz score, use an `if` statement to compare it with the lowest score so far; if the new score is lower, assign it to the "lowest score" variable. After all the quiz scores have been read, subtract the lowest score from the total. *Extra credit:* Write the program without using any `if` statements. (*Hint:* Use the `Math.min` method.)

(b) Use loops to read and calculate the program total and quiz total.

2. Make the following changes to the `SellStocks` program (Programming Project 4, Chapter 2):

(a) Add a loop so that, after displaying the net proceeds, the program will ask the user for another stock price, number of shares, and commission rate. The process will repeat indefinitely until the user enters zero as the stock price.

(b) Have the program put two digits after the decimal point when displaying dollar amounts. (The original program would display `$10.5` instead of `$10.50`.)

3. Make the following changes to the `VIN` program (Section 3.9):

(a) Add a loop so that, after displaying information about the VIN entered by the user, the program will ask the user for another VIN. The process will repeat indefinitely until the user enters an empty string for the VIN. (You can test this condition by writing either `vin.equals("")` or `vin.length() == 0`.)

(b) Have the program display the country of manufacture (Japan, United States, Canada, or Mexico) if the country code is J, 1, 2, or 3.

4. Make the following changes to the `CheckISBN` program (Section 3.10):

(a) If the user's input is not 13 characters long or does not contain exactly three dashes, have the program prompt the user to re-enter the input. The program will repeat the prompt as often as necessary until the input meets these criteria.

(b) Use a loop to calculate the value of the `total` variable.

(c) Instead of printing the original check digit and the computed check digit, have the program display either `ISBN is valid` (if the check digits match) or `ISBN is not valid` (if they don't).

5. Modify the `FractionMath` program (Programming Project 4, Chapter 3) so it performs a partial input validation. If either fraction does not contain exactly one slash, have the program prompt the user to re-enter the fraction. The program will repeat the prompt as often as necessary until the user enters a string containing one slash.

6. Make the following changes to the `CoinFlip2` program (Section 4.5):

(a) Use two `boolean` variables instead of one. The second variable will store the outcome of the coin flip.

(b) If the user fails to enter `heads` or `tails`, have the program prompt the user to re-enter the input. The program will repeat the prompt as often as necessary until the user enters either `heads` or `tails`.

7. Write a program that determines the number of digits in an integer:

```
Enter an integer: 374
The number 374 has 3 digits
```

Hint: Divide the integer by 10 repeatedly until it becomes 0. The number of divisions performed will be the number of digits in the integer.

8.   Write a program that asks the user for a 24-hour time, then displays the time in 12-hour form:

```
Enter a 24-hour time: 21:11
Equivalent 12-hour time: 9:11 PM
```

Be careful not to display 12:00 as 0:00.

9.   Here's a simplified version of the Beaufort scale, which is used to measure wind force:

Speed (knots)	Description
Less than 1	Calm
1–3	Light air
4–27	Breeze
28–47	Gale
48–63	Storm
Above 63	Hurricane

Write a program that asks the user to enter a wind speed (in knots), then displays the corresponding description.

10.   In one state, single residents are subject to the following income tax:

Income	Amount of tax	
Not over $750	1% of income	
$750–$2,250	$7.50	plus 2% of amount over $750
$2,250–$3,750	$37.50	plus 3% of amount over $2,250
$3,750–$5,250	$82.50	plus 4% of amount over $3,750
$5,250–$7,000	$142.50	plus 5% of amount over $5,250
Over $7,000	$230.00	plus 6% of amount over $7,000

Write a program that asks the user to enter the amount of taxable income, then displays the tax due.

11.   Write a program named `Fibonacci` that prints the Fibonacci sequence of numbers. The first two numbers in the Fibonacci sequence are 1. Every other number in the sequence is the sum of the two previous numbers. Your program should prompt the user to enter a limit; the program will stop when the current number in the sequence is greater than or equal to this limit. Here's what the user will see when the program is executed:

```
This program prints the Fibonacci sequence

Enter a limit on the largest number to be displayed: 50

1 1 2 3 5 8 13 21 34
```

Hint: Use three int variables to store the current number in the sequence, the previous number in the sequence, and the next number in the sequence.

Answers to Review Questions

Section 4.1

1.   Relational
2.   Equality
3.   Variables that should be equal may not test equal because of round-off error.
4.   `equals`

Section 4.2	1.	!
	2.	Short-circuit
	3.	de Morgan's
	4.	(b)
Section 4.3	1.	The parentheses are required.
	2.	Empty
	3.	This creates an empty statement. If the `if` statement's test condition is true, the empty statement (which has no effect) will be executed.
	4.	Block
Section 4.4	1.	Validate
	2.	Cascaded
	3.	(a)
	4.	Ambiguity
Section 4.5	1.	(b)
	2.	`if (b)` …
	3.	`if (!b)` …
Section 4.6	1.	Loop body
	2.	Iteration
	3.	`boolean`
	4.	Temporary
Section 4.7	1.	Counter
	2.	Postfix
	3.	Increment
	4.	Side effect
Section 4.8	1.	There is no limit.
	2.	Premature exit from a loop, exit from the middle of a loop, multiple exit points within a loop
Section 4.10	1.	Test case
	2.	Statement coverage
	3.	Off-by-one errors, infinite loops, never-executed loops

5 Arrays

Up to this point, we've worked with variables that are capable of storing a single number or object. In many programs, however, we'll need to store multiple data items of the same type. A bank doesn't have just one account, after all. A deck of cards consists of many cards, not a single card. Sometimes we'll know in advance how many items we'll need to store—for example, a standard deck of playing cards contains 52 cards. At other times, we won't know the number of items in advance; a bank would be unhappy if there were a limit on the number of accounts that could be opened.

In this chapter, we'll see how to store data in arrays. An array can store any number of data items, provided that all items have the same type. The elements of an array are accessed by position. As a result, loops are often used to process array elements. Arrays are closely related to one kind of loop, the `for` statement, which is covered in the chapter.

Arrays can be accessed either sequentially (visiting each element in sequence) or randomly (visiting the elements in no particular order). We'll see examples of both strategies. We'll also discuss two important applications for arrays: as vectors (in the mathematical sense) and as simple databases. Finally, we'll see that Java treats arrays as objects, which has important consequences for how we use arrays.

Objectives

- Learn how to create arrays and access their elements.
- Learn how to use the `for` statement to write counting loops.
- Learn the difference between sequential array access and random access.
- Learn how to use arrays as vectors.

181

- Learn how to store databases in arrays, using either parallel arrays or arrays of objects.
- Learn about the properties of arrays when used as objects.

5.1 Creating and Using Arrays

Most programs need to work with collections of data, rather than individual numbers and characters. In programming terminology, a collection of data items stored under a single name is known as a *data structure.* An object is one kind of data structure, because it can store multiple data items in its instance variables. The only other data structure that's supported by Java is the *array.* (The Java API provides additional data structures, some of which are covered in Chapter 13, but they're built out of objects and arrays.)

The data stored in an object can be a mixture of different types. In an array, on the other hand, all data items (known as *elements*) must have the same type. We can picture an array as a series of boxes, each capable of holding a single value belonging to this type:

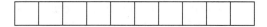

An array whose elements are arranged in a linear fashion is said to be *one-dimensional.* All arrays in this chapter will be one-dimensional. Section 13.1 discusses arrays with more than one dimension.

Creating Arrays

Declaring an array variable is similar to declaring any other type of variable, except that an array declaration always contains [and] symbols ("square brackets"):

```
int[] a;
```

This declaration states that a will be an array containing int values as its elements.

The elements of an array can be of any type. In particular, array elements can be objects. To declare an array of String objects, we would write

```
String[] b;
```

In an array declaration, it's legal to put the square brackets after the array name, instead of putting them after the element type:

```
int a[];
String b[];
```

Q&A It makes no difference which form you use to declare an array. I've chosen to put the brackets after the element type, because doing so emphasizes that the brackets are part of the variable's type.

Declaring an array variable doesn't cause Java to allocate any space for the array's elements. (Notice that we haven't yet said how many elements the array will have.) Before the array is good for anything, we'll need to allocate space, which means that we'll have to make a decision about the number of elements in the array. Suppose that we want the array a to have 10 elements. We can allocate space for the array by using the new keyword:

```
a = new int[10];
```

The expression new int[10] creates an array of 10 int values, which is then assigned to a. (It's no coincidence that this process resembles the one we use to create objects. Section 5.7 explores the resemblance in more detail.) The key thing to remember is that the creation of an array involves two steps: (1) declaring an array variable and (2) allocating space for the array.

 Be careful not to access the elements of an array before the array has been allocated. Neglecting to allocate space for an array is a common mistake in Java. The error will show up later when the program tries to access one of the elements in the array, causing a NullPointerException to occur.

If we want, the two steps—declaring the array and allocating space for its elements—can be combined:

```
int[] a = new int[10];
```

The value inside the square brackets can be any expression that evaluates to a single int value. In particular, we could use an int variable:

```
int n = 10;
int[] a = new int[n];
```

If we happen to know what values should be stored in an array, we can supply an initializer for the array:

```
int[] a = {3, 0, 3, 4, 5};
```

This time, a will contain five elements: 3, 0, 3, 4, and 5, in that order. Notice that the word new isn't used if we provide an initializer. The initializer must specify values for all elements of the array, so an array initializer isn't very useful except for small arrays.

When an array is created using new, the elements of the array are given default values. Numbers are set to zero. boolean elements are set to false. References to objects are set to null.

Array Subscripting

Each array element has an *index,* or *subscript,* that specifies the position of that element in the array. Like strings (and nearly everything else in Java, for that matter), arrays are indexed starting from 0. If an array has *n* elements, then only the numbers between 0 and *n* − 1 are valid indexes. Here's how we would visualize an array with 10 elements:

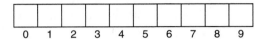

Sometimes we'll think of an array as being vertical rather than horizontal:

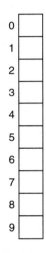

Arrays don't have an inherent orientation, so we can use whichever mental picture seems most appropriate.

The primary operation that we'll perform on an array is called *subscripting:* selecting a particular element by its position in the array. If a is an array, then a[i] represents the *ith* element in a. The expression a[i] is pronounced "a sub i."

An array subscript can be any expression, provided that it evaluates to an int value. The following are all legal ways of subscripting an array:

```
a[0]
a[i]
a[2*i-1]
```

Notice that—contrary to my usual convention—I've omitted the spaces in the expression 2 * i - 1. Expressions used as subscripts are usually fairly simple (most often consisting of a single variable), so leaving out the spaces isn't likely to hurt readability.

Be careful not to use an illegal subscript. A common error is trying to access element *n* in an array with *n* elements. Doing so is illegal, because the last element in the array is located at position *n* − 1, not position *n*. Attempting to access a nonexistent array element by using an index that's less than 0 or greater than *n* − 1 causes an error named `ArrayIndexOutOfBoundsException` (whew!).

When we subscript an array, the resulting array element behaves just like a variable of the element's type. For example, an element of an integer array behaves just like an ordinary integer variable. To assign the value 10 to `a[i]`, we would use the statement

```
a[i] = 10;
```

To print the value of `a[i]`, we would write

```
System.out.println(a[i]);
```

If the elements of an array are objects, they can call instance methods. For example, if the array b contains `String` objects, the call `b[i].length()` would return the length of the string stored in `b[i]`.

Most of the time, we won't do much with arrays other than storing values into their elements and later retrieving those values. However, Java does allow a limited number of other operations on arrays, as we'll see in Section 5.7.

Processing the Elements in an Array

In many cases, we'll need some systematic way to visit all the elements in an array. The elements are indexed by integers, so the logical approach is to set up a counting loop. Before the loop begins, the counter will be initialized to 0. Each time through the loop, the counter will be incremented. The loop will terminate when the counter reaches the number of elements in the array.

That brings up an interesting question: Is there an easy way to find out how long an array is? Fortunately, there is. If a is an array variable, the expression

Q&A `a.length` represents the length of a.

Armed with this information, we're ready to write a loop that visits every element in an array. The following statements will add up the elements in the array a, leaving the result in the `sum` variable:

```
int sum = 0;
int i = 0;
while (i < a.length) {
  sum += a[i];
  i++;
}
```

Let's trace the execution of this loop, assuming that a is the array {3, 5, 7}.

Action	Effect
Execute `int sum = 0.`	`sum` is assigned 0.
Execute `int i = 0.`	`i` is assigned 0.
Test `i < a.length.`	0 < 3 is true; loop continues.
Execute `sum += a[i].`	`a[0]` is 3, so 3 is added to `sum`, giving it the value 3.
Execute `i++.`	`i` is incremented to 1.
Test `i < a.length.`	1 < 3 is true; loop continues.
Execute `sum += a[i].`	`a[1]` is 5, so 5 is added to `sum`, giving it the value 8.
Execute `i++.`	`i` is incremented to 2.
Test `i < a.length.`	2 < 3 is true; loop continues.
Execute `sum += a[i].`	`a[2]` is 7, so 7 is added to `sum`, giving it the value 15.
Execute `i++.`	`i` is incremented to 3.
Test `i < a.length.`	3 < 3 is false; loop terminates.

The final value of `sum` is 15.

Because we know that `a` has three elements, we could have written the `while` loop as follows:

```
while (i < 3) {
  sum += a[i];
  i++;
}
```

However, our original test (`i < a.length`) is clearly better: if the length of `a` is later changed, the loop will still work correctly.

> To simplify program maintenance, always refer to the length of an array `a` as `a.length`.

PROGRAM   ## Computing an Average Score

The following program computes the average of a series of scores entered by the user. Here's what the user will see on the screen:

```
Enter number of scores: 5

Enter score #1: 68
Enter score #2: 93
Enter score #3: 75
Enter score #4: 86
Enter score #5: 72

Average score: 78
```

The scores are stored in an array named `scores`. To determine how large the array should be, the program first asks the user for the number of scores. That value is then used to set the length of the `scores` array.

AverageScores.java

```
1   // Computes the average of a series of scores
2
3   import jpb.*;
4
5   public class AverageScores {
6     public static void main(String[] args) {
7       // Prompt user to enter number of scores
8       SimpleIO.prompt("Enter number of scores: ");
9       String userInput = SimpleIO.readLine().trim();
10      int numberOfScores = Integer.parseInt(userInput);
11      System.out.println();
12
13      // Create array to hold scores
14      int[] scores = new int[numberOfScores];
15
16      // Prompt user to enter scores and store them in an array
17      int i = 0;
18      while (i < scores.length) {
19        SimpleIO.prompt("Enter score #" + (i + 1) + ": ");
20        userInput = SimpleIO.readLine().trim();
21        scores[i] = Integer.parseInt(userInput);
22        i++;
23      }
24
25      // Compute sum of scores
26      int sum = 0;
27      i = 0;
28      while (i < scores.length) {
29        sum += scores[i];
30        i++;
31      }
32
33      // Display average score
34      System.out.println("\nAverage score: " +
35                          sum / scores.length);
36    }
37  }
```

The astute reader will note that we don't really need an array in this program. The program could simply keep a running total of the scores entered so far by the user. (We saw this technique used in the improved version of the CourseAverage program in Section 2.11.)

Review Questions

1. The new keyword can allocate space for an array. What other technique is there for allocating space?

2. When an array is created using new, what values are stored in the array's elements?

3. A value used to select an array element is called an index or _____.

4. If a is an array, how can we determine how many elements a has?

5.2 The `for` Statement

The `AverageScores` program at the end of Section 5.1 contains two array-processing loops, one to store the user's input into elements of the `scores` array, and one to sum the elements of that array. Both loops have the same general form:

```
i = 0;
while (i < scores.length) {
  ...
  i++;
}
```

Because this kind of loop is so common, Java gives us a better way to write it: the `for` statement. Rewritten as `for` statements, our `while` loops would look like this:

```
for (i = 0; i < scores.length; i++) {
  ...
}
```

Of Java's loop statements, the `for` statement is the most powerful—and the most complicated. The `for` statement is ideal for counting loops, but it's versatile enough to be used for other kinds of loops as well.

The `for` statement has the following appearance:

`for` statement

> `for` (*initialization* ; *test* ; *update*)
> *statement*

The behavior of the loop is controlled by the *initialization, test,* and *update* parts, which are separated by semicolons and enclosed in parentheses. The body of a `for` loop is a single statement (which may, of course, be a block). In the following `for` statement, *initialization* is i = 0, *test* is i < scores.length, and *update* is i++:

```
for (i = 0; i < scores.length; i++) {
  ...
}
```

⚠ Note that the *initialization, test,* and *update* parts are separated by semicolons, not commas.

`for` Statements Versus `while` Statements

The `for` statement is closely related to the `while` statement. In fact, except in a couple of cases, a `for` loop of the form

```
for ( initialization ; test ; update )
    statement
```

is equivalent to the following `while` loop:

```
initialization ;
while ( test ) {
    statement
    update ;
}
```

Initialization is an initialization step that's performed only once, before the loop begins to execute. *Test* controls loop termination (the loop continues executing as long as *test* is true). *Update* is an operation to be performed at the end of each loop iteration.

The flow of control through a `for` statement is a bit tricky. Here's a diagram that shows the order in which the various parts of a `for` statement are evaluated or executed:

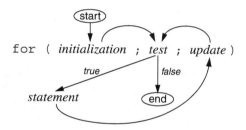

Consider the following `for` statement:

```
for (i = 10; i > 0; i--)
    System.out.println("T minus " + i + " and counting");
```

When this `for` statement is executed, the variable `i` is initialized to 10, then `i` is tested to see if it's greater than 0. It is, so the message `T minus 10 and count-ing` is printed, then `i` is decremented. The condition `i > 0` is then tested again. The loop body will be executed 10 times in all, with `i` varying from 10 down to 1.

If we convert the `for` statement to an equivalent `while` statement, we arrive at the following:

```
i = 10;
while (i > 0) {
    System.out.println("T minus " + i + " and counting");
    i--;
}
```

Studying the equivalent `while` statement can help us understand the fine points of a `for` statement. For example, suppose that we replace `i--` by `--i` in our `for` loop:

```
for (i = 10; i > 0; --i)
  System.out.println("T minus " + i + " and counting");
```

How does this change affect the loop? Looking at the equivalent `while` loop, we see that it has no effect:

```
i = 10;
while (i > 0) {
  System.out.println("T minus " + i + " and counting");
  --i;  // Same as i--;
}
```

The `for` statement has two advantages over the `while` statement. First, it's more concise; a `for` statement is typically two lines shorter than an equivalent `while` statement. A more important reason to use `for` statements is that they can make programs more readable. Consider the first `while` loop from the Average-Scores program:

```
int i = 0;
while (i < scores.length) {
  SimpleIO.prompt("Enter score #" + (i + 1) + ": ");
  userInput = SimpleIO.readLine().trim();
  scores[i] = Integer.parseInt(userInput);
  i++;
}
```

Notice how important information about the loop—the initial value of `i`, the test condition, and the increment of `i`—is scattered on different lines. If the loop were larger, the increment of `i` might be a considerable distance from the beginning of the loop, making it hard for someone reading the program to find. Now look at the corresponding `for` loop:

```
for (i = 0; i < scores.length; i++) {
  SimpleIO.prompt("Enter score #" + (i + 1) + ": ");
  userInput = SimpleIO.readLine().trim();
  scores[i] = Integer.parseInt(userInput);
}
```

All the vital information about the loop is collected in one place, at the beginning, making it much easier to understand the loop's behavior.

`for` Statement Idioms

The `for` statement is usually the best choice for loops that count up (increment a variable) or count down (decrement a variable). A `for` statement that counts up or down a total of n times will usually have one of the following forms:

- *Counting up from 0 to* n − 1:

  ```
  for (i = 0; i < n; i++) …        // 0, 1, ..., n - 1
  ```

- *Counting up from 1 to* n:

  ```
  for (i = 1; i <= n; i++) …        // 1, 2, ..., n
  ```

- *Counting down from* n − 1 *to* 0:

```
for (i = n - 1; i >= 0; i--) …  // n - 1, n - 2, ..., 0
```

- *Counting down from* n *to* 1:

```
for (i = n; i >= 1; i--) …       // n, n - 1, ..., 1
```

These loops are examples of ***idioms.*** An idiom is a conventional way of performing a common programming task. For any given task (counting from 0 to n − 1, for example), there are usually a variety of different ways to accomplish the task. Experienced programmers, however, tend to use the same idiom every time. Learning the idioms of a programming language is an important part of mastering the language and making your programs easy for other people to understand.

When you're writing a counting loop, your first choice should be the `for` statement, and it's likely that your `for` statement will have one of the forms shown above. Imitating these patterns will help you avoid the common loop errors described in Section 4.10.

Despite the existence of idioms for the `for` statement, there's no requirement in Java that a `for` statement's *initialization, test,* and *update* parts be related in any way. Most of the time, *initialization* will initialize a counter, *test* will compare the value of the counter with some stopping value, and *update* will increment or decrement the counter. However, that doesn't have to be the case. Consider the following example, which prints a table of the numbers between 1 and n and their squares:

```
i = 1;
odd = 3;
for (square = 1; i <= n; odd += 2) {
  System.out.println(i + " " + square);
  i++;
  square += odd;
}
```

The `for` statement in this example initializes one variable (`square`), tests another (`i`), and increments a third (`odd`). `i` is the number to be squared, `square` is the square of `i`, and `odd` is the odd number that must be added to the current square to get the next square. The tremendous flexibility of the `for` statement can sometimes be useful. The `for` statement can just as easily be misused, though, so don't go overboard.

> Avoid `for` statements in which the *initialization, test,* and *update* parts aren't related.

Omitting Expressions in a `for` Statement

The `for` statement is even more flexible than we've seen so far. Some `for` loops may not need all three of the parts that normally control the loop, so Java lets us omit any or all of them.

If *initialization* is omitted, no initialization is performed before the loop is executed:

```
i = 10;
for (; i > 0; i--)
  System.out.println("T minus " + i + " and counting");
```

In this example, i has been initialized by a separate assignment, so I've omitted the *initialization* step in the for statement. (Notice that the semicolon after *initialization* remains. Every for statement must have two semicolons inside the parentheses, even when some of the parts are omitted.)

If we omit the *update* part of a for statement, the loop body is responsible for ensuring that the value of *test* eventually becomes false. Our for statement example could be written like this:

```
for (i = 10; i > 0;)
  System.out.println("T minus " + i-- + " and counting");
```

To compensate for the missing *update,* the loop body now decrements i.

When both *initialization* and *update* are omitted, the resulting loop is nothing more than a while statement in disguise. For example, the loop

```
for (; i > 0;)
  System.out.println("T minus " + i-- + " and counting");
```

is the same as

```
while (i > 0)
  System.out.println("T minus " + i-- + " and counting");
```

The while version is clearer and therefore preferable.

If the *test* part is missing, it defaults to true, so the for statement doesn't terminate (unless stopped in some other fashion). For example, some programmers use the following for statement to establish an infinite loop:

```
for (;;) …
```

The break statement can be used to cause the loop to terminate.

Declaring Control Variables

In the examples we've seen so far, a variable used to control a for statement was declared separately, somewhere prior to the beginning of the loop. For convenience, Java allows a for statement to declare such a variable as part of *initialization:*

```
for (int i = 0; i < n; i++)
    …
```

A variable declared in this way can't be accessed outside the loop. (We say that it's not **visible** outside the loop.) Moreover, it's illegal for the enclosing method to declare a variable with the same name. (Section 4.6 mentioned a similar restriction on variables declared within a block.) It *is* legal for two `for` statements to declare the same variable, however; we'll see an example at the end of this section.

Having a `for` statement declare its own control variable is usually a good idea. It's convenient, and it can make programs easier to understand.

> A `for` statement should always declare its own control variable unless the variable will be needed once the loop terminates.

More than one variable can be declared in *initialization*, provided that all variables have the same type:

```
for (int i = 0, j = 0; i < n; i++)
   ...
```

Commas in `for` Statements

The `for` statement has another interesting option. Both *initialization* and *update* are allowed to contain commas:

```
for (i = 0, j = 0; i < n; i++, j += i)
   ...
```

Any number of expressions are allowed within *initialization* and *update*, provided that each can stand alone as a statement. (For example, `i++` changes the value of `i`, so it can stand alone as a statement. However, `i + j` can't be used as a statement, because it has no effect.) Normally, these expressions are either assignments or applications of the `++` and `--` operators. When expressions are joined using commas, the expressions are guaranteed to be evaluated from left to right. In this example, `i++` is guaranteed to be evaluated before `j += i`.

Using commas in a `for` statement isn't all that common. It's useful primarily when a loop has two or more counters to initialize and update.

PROGRAM | **Computing an Average Score (Revisited)**

Using `for` statements for the loops in the `AverageScores` program makes the program shorter and clearer. Most of the program is the same as before; the portions that were changed are shown in **bold.**

AverageScores2.java
```
1  // Computes the average of a series of scores
2
3  import jpb.*;
4
5  public class AverageScores2 {
6    public static void main(String[] args) {
7      // Prompt user to enter number of scores
8      SimpleIO.prompt("Enter number of scores: ");
```

```
 9      String userInput = SimpleIO.readLine().trim();
10      int numberOfScores = Integer.parseInt(userInput);
11      System.out.println();
12
13      // Create array to hold scores
14      int[] scores = new int[numberOfScores];
15
16      // Prompt user to enter scores and store them in an array
17      for (int i = 0; i < scores.length; i++) {
18        SimpleIO.prompt("Enter score #" + (i + 1) + ": ");
19        userInput = SimpleIO.readLine().trim();
20        scores[i] = Integer.parseInt(userInput);
21      }
22
23      // Compute sum of scores
24      int sum = 0;
25      for (int i = 0; i < scores.length; i++)
26        sum += scores[i];
27
28      // Display average score
29      System.out.println("\nAverage score: " +
30                          sum / scores.length);
31    }
32  }
```

Notice that the variable i is declared twice, once in each loop. Another possibility would have been to declare i just once and use it in both loops. However, since there's no connection between the two uses of i, it's better to declare it twice.

Review Questions

1. If a loop has a counter variable, would it normally be written as a while statement or a for statement?

2. Which of the *initialization, test,* and *update* parts are optional?

3. Which of the *initialization, test,* and *update* parts allow the use of commas?

4. An _____ is a conventional way of performing a common programming task.

5.3 Accessing Array Elements Sequentially

The AverageScores and AverageScores2 programs have one loop to initialize the elements of the scores array (using values obtained from the user) and a second loop to sum the elements of the array. Both loops are examples of *sequential access,* in which array elements are accessed in sequence, from first to last. Similar loops can be used to do many other common array operations. Let's take a look at some of these operations.

Searching for a Particular Element

One common array operation is searching an array to see if it contains a particular value. For example, the following statements search the scores array for the number 100:

```
int i;
for (i = 0; i < scores.length; i++)
  if (scores[i] == 100)
    break;
```

When the loop terminates, there are two cases: (1) The value of i is less than scores.length. In this case, the loop must have terminated prematurely, and the value of i indicates the position of the number 100 in the array. (2) The value of i is equal to scores.length, indicating that 100 was not found in the array. We can use an if statement to determine which case is the correct one:

```
if (i < scores.length)
  System.out.println("Found 100 at position " + i);
else
  System.out.println("Did not find 100");
```

Counting Occurrences

Counting the number of times that a particular value occurs in an array is similar to searching an array. The difference is that the loop increments a variable (which I'll call count) each time it encounters the desired value in the array.

For example, the following statements count the number of times the number 100 appears in the scores array:

```
int count = 0;
for (int i = 0; i < scores.length; i++)
  if (scores[i] == 100)
    count++;
```

Finding the Largest and Smallest Elements

Finding the largest (or smallest element) in an array is another common operation. The strategy is to visit each element in the array, using a variable to keep track of the largest element seen so far (let's name this variable largest). As each element is visited, it's compared with the value stored in largest. If the element is larger than largest, then it's copied into largest. Here's a first attempt at writing such a loop:

```
for (int i = 0; i < scores.length; i++)
  if (scores[i] > largest)
    largest = scores[i];
```

One question remains: What should be the initial value of largest, before the loop is entered? It can't be larger than any element in the array, or it will end up being chosen as the largest overall. In the case of the scores array, we can assume that the scores are between 0 and 100, so 0 is a safe choice as the initial value of largest. If the values in the array are arbitrary, however, 0 might not work. (What if all values in the array were negative?)

Fortunately, there's a way to initialize largest so that the loop will work in all cases, regardless of the values stored in the array. The secret is to choose one of the array elements—typically the one at position 0—and assign it to largest. Choosing an element from the array itself guarantees that the initial value of largest can't be larger than all the elements in the array. Here's the loop with this modification:

```
int largest = scores[0];
for (int i = 1; i < scores.length; i++)
  if (scores[i] > largest)
    largest = scores[i];
```

Notice that the loop now initializes i to 1 rather than 0. There's no point in comparing largest with scores[0], because that's the value largest contains initially.

Let's assume that the scores array contains the values 61, 78, 55, 91, and 72, in that order. The following table shows the values of largest, i, and scores[i] for each iteration of the loop:

	Initial value	*After iteration 1*	*After iteration 2*	*After iteration 3*	*After iteration 4*
largest	61	78	78	91	91
i	1	2	3	4	5
scores[i]	78	55	91	72	–

The technique for finding the smallest element in an array is similar. We start off by initializing the variable smallest with the value stored in scores[0]. The body of the for statement then compares smallest with each element of scores. Whenever an element of the array is smaller than smallest, its value is copied into smallest.

```
int smallest = scores[0];
for (int i = 1; i < scores.length; i++)
  if (scores[i] < smallest)
    smallest = scores[i];
```

Review Questions

1. Accessing the elements of an array in order, from first to last, is called _____ access.

2. Counting the number of times that a particular value occurs in an array is similar to _____ an array.

5.4 Accessing Array Elements Randomly

Although it's often convenient to write loops that process the elements of an array in order, arrays are good for more than just this kind of sequential processing. One of the biggest advantages of arrays, in fact, is that a program can access their elements in any order whatsoever. This capability is often called *random access,* in contrast to the sequential access that was described in Section 5.3. Random access is best illustrated by an example.

PROGRAM **Finding Repeated Digits in a Number**

Our next program, which I'll call `RepeatedDigits`, determines which digits in a number appear more than once. After the user enters a number, the program will print a list of digits that appear more than once in the number. The digits will be displayed in increasing order, from smallest to largest:

```
Enter a number: 392522459
Repeated digits: 2 5 9
```

If the user enters a number such as 361, the program will display the message No repeated digits.

The `RepeatedDigits` program uses an array of `int` values to keep track of how many times each digit appears in the user's number. The array, named `digitCounts`, is indexed from 0 to 9 to correspond to the 10 possible digits. Initially, every element of the array is 0. After converting the user's input into an integer, which is stored in a variable named `number`, the program examines `number`'s digits one at a time, incrementing one of the elements of `digit-Counts` each time. The statement used to do the increment is

```
digitCounts[number%10]++;
```

For example, if `number` is 392522459, the value of `number % 10` will be 9 (the last digit in `number`), so the increment is performed on `digitCounts[9]`. The next step is to divide `number` by 10, which effectively removes its last digit.

Eventually `number` will be reduced to zero. At this point, the `digitCounts` array will contain counts indicating how many times each digit appeared in the original number. If `number` is originally 392522459, the `digitCounts` array will have the following appearance:

0	0	3	1	1	2	0	0	0	2
0	1	2	3	4	5	6	7	8	9

The program next uses a `for` statement to visit each element of the `digit-Counts` array. If a particular element of the array has a value greater than 1, the index of that element is added to a string named `repeatedDigits`. After the loop terminates, the value of `repeatedDigits` is displayed. However, if the `repeatedDigits` string has no characters, the message `No repeated digits` is displayed instead.

RepeatedDigits.java

```
1   // Checks a number for repeated digits
2
3   import jpb.*;
4
5   public class RepeatedDigits {
6     public static void main(String[] args) {
7       // Prompt user to enter a number and convert to int form
8       SimpleIO.prompt("Enter a number: ");
9       String userInput = SimpleIO.readLine().trim();
10      int number = Integer.parseInt(userInput);
11
12      // Create an array to store digit counts
13      int[] digitCounts = new int[10];
14
15      // Remove digits from the number, one by one, and
16      // increment the corresponding array element
17      while (number > 0) {
18        digitCounts[number%10]++;
19        number /= 10;
20      }
21
22      // Create a string containing all repeated digits
23      String repeatedDigits = "";
24      for (int i = 0; i < digitCounts.length; i++)
25        if (digitCounts[i] > 1)
26          repeatedDigits += i + " ";
27
28      // Display repeated digits. If no digits are repeated,
29      // display "No repeated digits".
30      if (repeatedDigits.length() > 0)
31        System.out.println("Repeated digits: " +
32                             repeatedDigits);
33      else
34        System.out.println("No repeated digits");
35    }
36  }
```

This program clearly illustrates the dual nature of arrays. The `while` statement accesses the elements of the `digitCounts` array in a random fashion, depending on the digits that it finds in the user's number. The `for` statement then accesses the elements of `digitCounts` sequentially in order to generate the output message.

If you run the `RepeatedDigits` program, be careful not to enter a number larger than 2,147,483,647, which is the largest value of the `int` type. Also note that any leading zeros in the number will be ignored; `Integer.parseInt` removes these as it converts the user's input to integer form.

Review Question

1.   Accessing the elements of an array in no particular order is called _____ access.

5.5   Using Arrays as Vectors

Arrays are often vital for programs that perform mathematical calculations, in which they are used to model vectors and matrices. In fact, arrays were included in early programming languages solely for this purpose.

In mathematics, a ***matrix*** is a rectangular arrangement of numbers, displayed in rows and columns. A ***vector*** is a matrix with a single row or column. In Java, a vector can be stored in a one-dimensional array, and a matrix can be stored in a two-dimensional array.

two-dimensional arrays ➤ 13.1

Before we go further, a word of warning: The term "vector" normally has a different meaning in Java than it does in mathematics. In this section, I'll use "vector" in the usual mathematical sense. Vectors (in the Java sense) are discussed in Section 13.2.

In mathematics, a vector is often written in the following way:

$$\mathbf{A} = [\, a_1\ a_2\ \dots\ a_n \,]$$

To represent this vector in Java, we'd use an array containing floating-point numbers:

```
double[] a = new double[n];
```

Let's take a look at a few common vector operations and see how they would be implemented in Java. Assume in each case that **A** and **B** are vectors defined as follows:

$$\mathbf{A} = [\, a_1\ a_2\ \dots\ a_n \,]$$
$$\mathbf{B} = [\, b_1\ b_2\ \dots\ b_n \,]$$

Also assume that **A** and **B** are represented by arrays named a and b.

Scaling a Vector

One common vector operation is scaling a vector, which involves multiplying each element of the vector by the same number. In mathematical terms, we would write

$$\alpha\mathbf{A} = [\, \alpha a_1\ \alpha a_2\ \dots\ \alpha a_n \,]$$

where α is a constant. To perform this operation in Java, we would use a `for` statement:

```
for (int i = 0; i < a.length; i++)
  a[i] *= alpha;
```

I'm assuming that `alpha` is a `double` variable (possibly declared `final`). Notice that the loop starts at 0, rather than 1. Although the first element of a vector is element 1 in mathematics, it is element 0 in Java.

Adding Vectors

Another common operation is adding two vectors. The sum of **A** and **B** is defined as follows:

$$\mathbf{A} + \mathbf{B} = [\, a_1 + b_1 \; a_2 + b_2 \; \ldots \; a_n + b_n \,]$$

Let's assume that we want to store the sum of a and b into a new vector named c. The following code will do just that:

```java
double[] c = new double[a.length];
for (int i = 0; i < a.length; i++)
  c[i] = a[i] + b[i];
```

Vector subtraction is similar: just replace `a[i] + b[i]` with `a[i] - b[i]`.

Computing the Inner Product of Two Vectors

The last operation we'll consider is *inner product,* or *dot product*. The inner product of **A** and **B** is defined as follows:

$$\mathbf{A} \cdot \mathbf{B} = a_1 b_1 + a_2 b_2 + \ldots + a_n b_n$$

The following statements will calculate the inner product of the arrays a and b:

```java
double innerProduct = 0.0;
for (int i = 0; i < a.length; i++)
  innerProduct += a[i] * b[i];
```

Note that the inner product of two vectors is a number, not a vector.

Review Questions

1. In Java, a vector can be stored in a _____ array.

2. A matrix can be stored in a _____ array.

5.6 Using Arrays as Databases

In many real-world programs, data is stored as a collection of *records,* in which each record contains several related items of data, known as *fields.* Such collections are known as *databases.* Databases are ubiquitous in daily life. Airlines keep track of flights in databases. Banks keep track of customer accounts in databases. Even the humble phone directory is a database:

AARON Robin B	4011 Stone Mountain St	384-7110
ABBOTT C Michael	981 Glen Arden Way	776-5188
ABEL A B	343 Lakeshore Ct	871-7406
ABERCROMBIE Bill	5810 Lismoor Tr	844-9400
ABERNATHY C	2120 Martin Rd	779-7559
ABRAHAM Gary	585 Chandler Pond Dr	582-6630
⋮	⋮	⋮

Each record in a phone directory contains three fields: a name, an address, and a phone number.

There are many ways to store databases in Java, but the simplest is the array. In this chapter, we'll examine two ways to use arrays for storing databases.

Parallel Arrays

The first technique for storing a database is to use several arrays, one for each field. For example, to store the records in a phone directory, we would use three arrays. One array would store names, the second would store addresses, and the third would store phone numbers. Here's what the arrays would look like:

0	AARON Robin B	0	4011 Stone Mountain St	0	384-7110
1	ABBOTT C Michael	1	981 Glen Arden Way	1	776-5188
2	ABEL A B	2	343 Lakeshore Ct	2	871-7406
3	ABERCROMBIE Bill	3	5810 Lismoor Tr	3	844-9400
4	ABERNATHY C	4	2120 Martin Rd	4	779-7559
5	ABRAHAM Gary	5	585 Chandler Pond Dr	5	582-6630
	⋮		⋮		⋮

Even though the data is spread over three separate arrays, we still think in terms of "records." For example, the first record in the database (indicated by the oval in the diagram) consists of element 0 of the names array, element 0 of the addresses array, and element 0 of the phone numbers array.

When we store the records in a database using several arrays of the same length, with each array containing one field from each record, the arrays are said to be **parallel.**

For another example of parallel arrays, consider the problem of storing 100 points, where a point consists of an x coordinate and a y coordinate. We could store the points in two parallel arrays, one containing x coordinates and the other containing matching y coordinates:

```
int[] xCoordinates = new int[100];
int[] yCoordinates = new int[100];
```

The values of xCoordinates[i] and yCoordinates[i] represent a single point. For example, the first point's *x* coordinate would be stored in xCoordinates[0], and its *y* coordinate would be stored in yCoordinates[0].

Parallel arrays can be useful. (Indeed, some methods in the Java API rely on parallel arrays, as we'll see in Section 6.1.) However, they suffer from a couple of problems. First, we're forced to deal with several data structures rather than just one. It would be better to store the records in a single array rather then spreading them out over several arrays. Also, maintenance is more difficult. If we ever change the length of one of the parallel arrays, we'll have to be careful to change the lengths of the other arrays as well.

Arrays of Objects

The alternative to parallel arrays is to treat each record as an object, then store those objects in an array. For example, we could write a class named Phone-Record, where a PhoneRecord object stores a name, address, and phone number, and then create an array whose elements are PhoneRecord objects. To store 100 points, we could create a Point class with two instance variables, x and y, and then store a collection of Point objects in a single array:

```
Point[] points = new Point[100];
```

Point class ➤ 10.2 It turns out that the Java API already contains a Point class, so we won't need to define our own. Most of the time, however, we'll need to create our own record classes.

Creating a Database

To illustrate how databases are created and maintained, let's turn to a different example. Suppose that we need to keep track of the accounts in a bank. For simplicity, I'll assume that the only information that we need to store for each account is an account number and a balance. Our records will consist of a String object (the account number) and a double value (the account balance).

One way to store our database would be to use two parallel arrays:

```
String[] accountNumbers = new String[100];
double[] accountBalances = new double[100];
```

We would need a third variable to keep track of how many accounts are currently stored in the database:

```
int numAccounts = 0;
```

We could now add a new account to the database by executing the following statements:

```
accountNumbers[numAccounts] = newAccountNumber;
accountBalances[numAccounts] = newBalance;
numAccounts++;
```

Notice that `numAccounts` really serves two roles. It keeps track of the number of accounts, but it also indicates the next available "empty" position in the two arrays. `numAccounts` has the value 0 initially, so the first account number and balance will be stored in position 0 of the `accountNumbers` and `accountBalances` arrays. After the account number and balance have been stored, `numAccounts` is incremented, indicating both that the database now stores one record and that the next available position in the arrays is 1.

We could implement other operations on the database using the two-array representation, but, as we discussed earlier, it's usually best to avoid parallel arrays. Let's switch to a single array whose elements are `BankAccount` objects. I'll assume that the `BankAccount` class contains two instance variables (the account number and the balance) and provides the following constructors and methods:

```
public BankAccount(String accountNumber,
                   double initialBalance)
public void deposit(double amount)
public void withdraw(double amount)
public String getNumber()
public double getBalance()
```

This class is similar to the `Account` class defined in Section 3.3. The primary difference is that the `Account` class stores only a balance, while the `BankAccount` class also stores an account number.

Now we can declare the array that will hold the `BankAccount` objects:

```
BankAccount[] accounts = new BankAccount[100];
```

As before, I'll assume that the `numAccounts` variable tracks the number of accounts currently stored in the array. `numAccounts` will be zero initially.

Now that the database has been created, we'll need to perform operations on it. The fundamental operations on a database are adding a new record, deleting a record, locating a particular record, and modifying a record. Let's implement each of these operations, using the `accounts` array as our database.

Adding a Record to a Database

To add a record to a database, we can simply create a new object and store it in the array at the next available position:

```
accounts[numAccounts] = new BankAccount(number, balance);
numAccounts++;
```

We could combine the two statements into one if we wish:

```
accounts[numAccounts++] = new BankAccount(number, balance);
```

In some cases, we'll want the records in a database to be stored in a particular order. For example, we might want `BankAccount` objects to be stored so that the account numbers are in a particular order. This topic is covered in Section 13.4, so I won't discuss it any further here.

Removing a Record from a Database

When a record is removed from a database, it will leave a "hole" in the array—an element that doesn't contain a record. Such a hole is a nuisance when we want to perform later operations on the database. Fortunately, there's an easy way to fill the hole: just move the last record into the hole and then decrement `numAccounts`. Suppose that the record to be deleted is currently stored at position i in the `accounts` array. Here are the statements necessary to delete the record and replace it by the last record:

```
accounts[i] = accounts[numAccounts-1];
numAccounts--;
```

We could combine these into a single statement:

```
accounts[i] = accounts[--numAccounts];
```

Notice that this technique works even when the database contains only one record.

Searching a Database

When we search a database, we're usually looking for a record that matches a certain "key" value. In the case of our `accounts` database, we'll most likely be searching for a particular account number. (It's possible that we're looking for accounts with a particular balance, however. Accounts that have a zero balance might be of some interest to a bank.) Suppose that we need to search for the account whose number is stored in `number` (a `String` variable). The following statements will do the search:

```
int i;
for (i = 0; i < numAccounts; i++)
  if (accounts[i].getNumber().equals(number))
    break;
```

Once the loop has terminated, we can test whether i is less than `numAccounts`. If so, the value of i indicates the position of the record in the array.

Modifying a Record in a Database

If the records in our database are objects, we can update a record by calling a method that changes the object's state. For example, to deposit money into the account located at position i in the `accounts` array, we would write

```
accounts[i].deposit(amount);
```

There's another way to modify a record. Suppose that the variable `current-Account` has been assigned the value of `accounts[i]`, so that `current-Account` and `accounts[i]` both refer to the same `BankAccount` object. Any action that we perform on `currentAccount` will affect `accounts[i]`, because there's only one object involved. Here's an example:

```
BankAccount currentAccount = accounts[i];
currentAccount.deposit(amount);
```

This technique is sometimes more convenient.

Review Questions

1. A _____ is a single item of data in a record.

2. One way to store a collection of records is to use _____ arrays.

3. The other way to store a collection of records is to use a single array containing _____.

4. When a record is removed from a database, it will leave a "hole" in the array—an element that doesn't contain a record. Describe an easy way to avoid this problem.

5.7 Arrays as Objects

Like objects, arrays are created using the `new` keyword. But the similarities between arrays and objects don't end there. It turns out that arrays really *are* objects.

We saw in Section 3.7 that an object variable doesn't actually store an object. Instead, it stores a *reference* to an object. A `String` variable, for example, stores a reference to a `String` object. This fact explains many of the properties of object variables:

- When an object variable is declared, it's not necessary for the variable to refer to an object immediately. The object can be created later if desired.
- The value of an object variable can be changed as often as desired, allowing the variable to refer to different objects at different times.
- It's possible for several object variables to refer to the same object.
- It's possible that no variable refers to a particular object. The object is then said to be *garbage,* and it becomes eligible for garbage collection.
- Assigning one object variable to another causes only a reference to be copied; no new object is created.
- Testing whether two object variables are equal or not equal compares the references stored in the variables, not the objects themselves.

Java treats arrays as objects, so array variables have the same properties as object variables, including all those listed above. Let's explore these properties in the context of arrays.

An array variable contains a reference to where the array's elements are stored. For example, suppose that a is an array of 10 integers. Here's how a would be stored:

As this figure shows, a itself doesn't contain space for the integers. Instead, it contains a reference to the location where the integers are actually stored.

Arrays are "garbage collected" in the same way as other objects. When there are no more references to an array, the space occupied by the array can be reclaimed automatically.

Assigning one array variable to another is allowed. If a and b are array variables of the same type, it's legal to write

```
b = a;
```

The effect is that b now contains a reference to the same array as a:

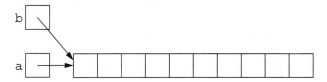

The assignment operator doesn't make a true copy of an array. You'll end up with two array variables that refer to the same array. Changes made to one array will show up in the other array as well.

To make a genuine copy of an array, there are two strategies. One is to create a new array of the same length as the old one, and then copy the elements from the old array to the new one. The other strategy is to use the clone method.

clone method ➤ *11.5*

Testing whether two array variables are equal (or not equal) is legal. However, such a test may not have the desired effect, because it really checks whether the two variables refer to the same array. To check whether two arrays contain identical elements, you'll need to write a loop that compares the elements of the arrays, one by one.

Resizing an Array

Although arrays have fixed sizes, it's possible to resize an array if it becomes full. The trick is to create an entirely new array to replace the old one. Consider the bank example of Section 5.6, in which accounts is an array of BankAccount objects and the `numAccounts` variable keeps track of the number of accounts currently stored in the array. If `numAccounts` ever becomes equal to `accounts.length`, then the array is full and no more accounts can be added. In order to allow the creation of additional accounts, we'll need to resize the array.

Resizing an array can be done in three steps:

1. Create a new array that's larger than the old one.
2. Copy the elements of the old array into the new array.
3. Assign the new array to the old array variable.

Here's what the code would look like to resize the `accounts` array, assuming that we want the new array to be twice as large as the old one:

```
BankAccount[] tempArray =
  new BankAccount[accounts.length*2];
for (int i = 0; i < accounts.length; i++)
  tempArray[i] = accounts[i];
accounts = tempArray;
```

Doubling the size of an array isn't a bad idea, by the way. It provides plenty of space for new elements, yet guarantees that there won't be too much unused space because the new array will be half-full to start.

Our code for resizing an array leaves a couple of nagging questions. One is the issue of what happens to the old array—the one originally stored in `accounts`. The answer is simple: the array becomes garbage, because the `accounts` variable no longer refers to it. If memory runs low, Java will automatically reclaim the space that the array occupies.

Another question involves efficiency. Copying elements from one array to another looks slow, but it's actually not bad. Even if the elements are objects, we're only copying references, not the objects themselves. For additional speed, Java provides a method named `System.arraycopy` that can be used to copy elements from one array to another. We could use the following call of `System.array-copy` instead of the `for` statement:

```
System.arraycopy(accounts, 0, tempArray, 0, accounts.length);
```

The first argument to `System.arraycopy` is the "source" array (the one whose elements are to be copied). The second argument is the position of the first element in the source array to be copied. The third and fourth arguments are the "destination" array and the position of the first element to be copied into. The last argument is the number of elements to be copied.

Vector class ▶ 13.2 Although we can resize arrays when needed, it's usually better to use Java's `Vector` class if we want a resizeable data structure. Instances of the `Vector` class behave like arrays that automatically grow when they become full.

Review Questions

1. If a and b are array variables, what is the effect of assigning a to b?

2.   What's the best way to determine whether two arrays contain the same elements?

3.   When resizing an array, it is a good idea to: (a) double the array's capacity, (b) triple the array's capacity, or (c) increase the array's capacity by a factor of 10?

4.   Describe two ways to copy the elements of one array into another array.

5.8 Case Study: A Phone Directory

In our next case study, we'll develop a program named `PhoneDirectory` that stores names and telephone numbers. The program will support two operations: (a) entering new names and numbers and (b) looking up existing names. Here's what the user will see on the screen:

```
Phone directory commands:
  a - Add a new phone number
  f - Find a phone number
  q - Quit

Enter command (a, f, or q): a
Enter new name: Abernathy, C.
Enter new phone number: 779-7559

Enter command (a, f, or q): a
Enter new name: Abbott, C. Michael
Enter new phone number: 776-5188

Enter command (a, f, or q): f
Enter name to look up: Abbott
Abbott, C. Michael 776-5188

Enter command (a, f, or q): f
Enter name to look up: ab
Abernathy, C. 779-7559
Abbott, C. Michael 776-5188

Enter command (a, f, or q): q
```

`PhoneDirectory` is an example of a menu-driven program. When the program begins to execute, it presents the user with a list of commands. The user can then enter as many commands as desired, in any order. The `a` command prompts the user to enter a name and a number, which are then stored in the program's database. The `f` command prompts the user to enter a name. The program then displays all matching names in the database, along with the corresponding phone numbers. Notice that the user doesn't need to enter an entire name. The program will display all names that begin with the characters entered by the user. For example, entering just `ab` causes the program to display all names that begin with `ab`.

(The user can even enter no characters at all, which will cause the program to display all names in the database.) The program will ignore the case of names entered in the f command; searching for ab is the same as searching for Ab.

Let's start with an overall design for the program:

1. Display a list of commands.
2. Read and execute commands.

Looks easy enough! Step 2 is obviously the heart of the program, so we'll need to sketch it in much more detail. This step will clearly require a loop. A loop that reads and executes commands is fairly common in programming, so there's an idiom that we can follow. In pseudocode, here's what it looks like:

```
while (true) {
    Prompt user to enter command;
    Execute command;
}
```

Notice that the controlling expression is true. There's nothing to test when the loop is entered, because we haven't read the first command yet. The loop appears to be infinite, but it's actually not. When the user enters the "quit" command, we can terminate the loop by executing a break statement or a return statement.

Inside the while loop, we'll need to test whether the command is a, f, q, or something else. A good way to implement a series of related tests is to use a cascaded if statement. Here's what the loop looks like with the addition of the if statement:

```
while (true) {
    Prompt user to enter command;
    if (command is "a") {
        Prompt user for name and number;
        Create a phone record and store it in the database;
    } else if (command is "f") {
        Prompt user for search key;
        Search the database for records whose names begin with the search key;
        Print these names and the corresponding phone numbers;
    } else if (command is "q") {
        Terminate program;
    } else {
        Display error message;
    }
}
```

Next, we'll need to choose algorithms and decide how the data will be stored. We saw in Section 5.6 that an array of objects is a good way to store a simple database. This section also showed how to create a new record and how to search an array of records, which are the only algorithms we'll need.

We'll need a class to represent the phone records that will be stored in the array. Let's name this class PhoneRecord. An instance of PhoneRecord will store a single name and phone number in name and number instance variables. The

PhoneRecord class will need a constructor to initialize the name and number instance variables. It will also need a couple of getters, getName and get-Number, which return the values of the instance variables. For simplicity, I'll put the PhoneRecord class in the same file as the PhoneDirectory class.

Here's the finished program.

PhoneDirectory.java

```
1  // Program name: PhoneDirectory
2  // Author: K. N. King
3  // Written: 1999-06-22
4  //
5  // Stores names and telephone numbers and allows phone
6  // numbers to be looked up. The user is given a menu of
7  // three commands:
8  //
9  //   a - Add a new phone number
10 //   f - Find a phone number
11 //   q - Quit
12 //
13 // The "a" command prompts the user to enter a name and a
14 // number, which are then stored in the program's database.
15 //
16 // The "f" command prompts the user to enter a name; the
17 // program then displays all matching names in the database,
18 // along with the corresponding phone numbers. It is not
19 // necessary to enter the entire name; all names that begin
20 // with the specified characters will be displayed. The "f"
21 // command ignores the case of letters when looking for
22 // matching names.
23 //
24 // The "q" command causes the program to terminate. All names
25 // and numbers are lost.
26
27 import jpb.*;
28
29 public class PhoneDirectory {
30   public static void main(String[] args) {
31     PhoneRecord[] records = new PhoneRecord[100];
32     int numRecords = 0;
33
34     // Display list of commands
35     System.out.println("Phone directory commands:\n" +
36                        "  a - Add a new phone number\n" +
37                        "  f - Find a phone number\n" +
38                        "  q - Quit\n");
39
40     // Read and execute commands
41     while (true) {
42
43       // Prompt user to enter a command
44       SimpleIO.prompt("Enter command (a, f, or q): ");
45       String command = SimpleIO.readLine().trim();
46
```

```
47          // Determine whether command is "a", "f", "q", or
48          // illegal; execute command if legal.
49          if (command.equalsIgnoreCase("a")) {
50
51              // Command is "a". Prompt user for name and number,
52              // then create a phone record and store it in the
53              // database.
54              if (numRecords < records.length) {
55                  SimpleIO.prompt("Enter new name: ");
56                  String name = SimpleIO.readLine().trim();
57                  SimpleIO.prompt("Enter new phone number: ");
58                  String number = SimpleIO.readLine().trim();
59                  records[numRecords] =
60                      new PhoneRecord(name, number);
61                  numRecords++;
62              } else
63                  System.out.println("Database is full");
64
65          } else if (command.equalsIgnoreCase("f")) {
66
67              // Command is "f". Prompt user for search key.
68              // Search the database for records whose names begin
69              // with the search key. Print these names and the
70              // corresponding phone numbers.
71              SimpleIO.prompt("Enter name to look up: ");
72              String key = SimpleIO.readLine().trim().toLowerCase();
73              for (int i = 0; i < numRecords; i++) {
74                  String name = records[i].getName().toLowerCase();
75                  if (name.startsWith(key))
76                      System.out.println(records[i].getName() + " " +
77                                         records[i].getNumber());
78              }
79
80          } else if (command.equalsIgnoreCase("q")) {
81              // Command is "q". Terminate program.
82              return;
83
84          } else {
85              // Command is illegal. Display error message.
86              System.out.println("Command was not recognized; " +
87                                 "please enter only a, f, or q.");
88          }
89
90          System.out.println();
91      }
92   }
93 }
94
95 // Represents a record containing a name and a phone number
96 class PhoneRecord {
97   private String name;
98   private String number;
99
```

```
100     // Constructor
101     public PhoneRecord(String personName, String phoneNumber) {
102       name = personName;
103       number = phoneNumber;
104     }
105
106     // Returns the name stored in the record
107     public String getName() {
108       return name;
109     }
110
111     // Returns the phone number stored in the record
112     public String getNumber() {
113       return number;
114     }
115   }
```

Line 75 uses a `String` method that we haven't seen before. The `startsWith` method returns `true` if the string that calls the method begins with the characters in another string (supplied as an argument).

The `PhoneDirectory` program has little practical use because the names and phone numbers are lost when the program terminates. In Chapter 14, we'll see how to fix this problem by saving the names and numbers in a file. There are numerous other ways in which the program could be improved; some of these improvements are described in a programming project at the end of this chapter.

Q & A

Q: Why are there two different places to put square brackets in an array declaration? [p. 183]

A: Putting square brackets after the name of the array variable is traditional:

```
int a[];
```

In fact, the C and C++ languages require that arrays be declared in this fashion. The designers of Java decided that it would be more logical to put the square brackets after the array's element type, so that all the type information is in one place:

```
int[] a;
```

This style emphasizes that the type of a is `int[]` (array of `int` values).

Q: Why do we write `a.length` instead of `a.length()` to get the length of an array? [p. 185]

A: `length` isn't the name of a method. Instead, it's the name of an instance variable that belongs to every array. Writing `a.length` allows us to retrieve the value stored in that variable. (You can't change the value of length, by the way; it's declared final.)

Q: **You said that for loops can be converted to while loops using a standard pattern, except in a couple of cases. What are those cases? [p. 188]**

A: One case occurs when the body of a for loop contains a continue statement. Consider the following example, which counts the number of nonzero elements in the array a:

continue statement ➤8.4

```
int[] a = {1, 0, 0, 1};
int zeroElements = 0;
for (int i = 0; i < a.length; i++) {
  if (a[i] != 0)
    continue;
  zeroElements++;
}
```

At first glance, it looks as though we could convert the for loop into the following while loop:

```
int[] a = {1, 0, 0, 1};
int zeroElements = 0;
int i = 0;
while (i < a.length) {
  if (a[i] != 0)
    continue;
  zeroElements++;
  i++;
}
```

Unfortunately, this loop isn't equivalent to the original one. If a[i] is not equal to 0, the new loop skips over the last two statements in the loop body, thanks to the continue statement. As a result, i doesn't get incremented, and the loop never terminates.

The second case stems from the ability of a for statement to declare its own control variable. A for statement that declares its own control variable isn't completely equivalent to any while statement, because the for statement's control variable can't be used after the loop terminates.

Summary

- A collection of data items stored under a single name is known as a data structure.
- An array is a data structure containing elements of a single type. All types are allowed, including classes.

- The declaration of an array variable must contain square brackets (`[]`), which can be placed after the type of the array's elements or after the array's name.

- Declaring an array variable doesn't cause Java to allocate space for the array's elements. Before an array can be used, space must be allocated, either by using the `new` keyword or by supplying an initializer in the array's declaration.

- When an array is created using `new`, the elements of the array are given default values: numbers are set to zero, `boolean` elements are set to `false`, and elements of a reference type are set to `null`.

- The elements of an array are accessed by position. Elements are numbered starting from 0.

- The primary array operation is subscripting: selecting an element by its position in the array. If `a` is an array, then `a[i]` represents the *i*th element in `a`.

- An array element behaves like a variable of the element's type.

- The length of an array `a` can be found by writing `a.length`.

- The behavior of a `for` statement is controlled by its *initialization, test,* and *update* parts. The *initialization* part is executed first. The *test* is evaluated next; if it is false, the loop terminates. Otherwise, the loop body is executed, *update* is performed, and *test* is evaluated again.

- Any or all of the parts of a `for` statement—*initialization, test,* and *update*—can be omitted.

- The *initialization* part of a `for` statement can be a declaration, allowing the statement to declare its own control variable(s).

- Both the *initialization* and *update* parts of a `for` statement may contain commas, allowing multiple initializations and/or updates.

- One way to process the elements of an array is by sequential access, in which the elements are visited in order, from first to last.

- Common sequential operations on arrays include searching for a particular value, counting the number of times that a particular value occurs, and finding the largest or smallest element.

- Another way to process the elements of an array is by random access, in which elements are visited in no particular order.

- Arrays are often used to model the mathematical concepts of vectors and matrices. A vector can be stored in a one-dimensional array, and a matrix can be stored in a two-dimensional array.

- A database is a collection of records. A record consists of related data items, known as fields.

- Arrays can be used as a simple way of implementing a database. One technique is to use several parallel arrays, one for each field. The alternative is to treat each record as an object and store those objects in an array.

- The fundamental operations on a database are adding a new record, removing a record, locating a record, and modifying a record.

- Arrays are objects in Java, so array variables have the same properties as object variables.
- An array variable contains a reference to where the array's elements are stored.
- Arrays are "garbage collected" in the same way as other objects.
- If a and b are array variables, assigning a to b doesn't copy the elements of a; instead, it causes b to refer to the same array as a.
- Testing whether two array variables are equal (or not equal) will compare only the references stored in the variables, not the elements of the arrays themselves.
- Resizing an array can be done by creating a new array that's larger than the old one, copying the elements of the old array into the new array, and then assigning the new array to the old array variable.
- Java provides a method named System.arraycopy that can be used to copy elements from one array to another.

Exercises

Section 5.1

1. Locate the error in the following declaration and show how to fix it.

```
int[] ages = new[20];
```

2. Write two (significantly) different declarations of an array a with five double elements, all initialized to 0.0.

3. Write a statement that assigns the value 33 to the last element of the array a.

Section 5.2

4. Use a table to track the values of the i, odd, and square variables as the following statements are executed. (Assume that n has the value 5.)

```
i = 1;
odd = 3;
for (square = 1; i <= n; odd += 2) {
  System.out.println(i + " " + square);
  i++;
  square += odd;
}
```

5. How many times will each of the following loops print the message "Foo"?

```
(a) for (int i = 0; i < 10; i += 2)
      System.out.println("Foo");
(b) for (int i = 1; i <= 10; i *= 2)
      System.out.println("Foo");
(c) for (int i = 10; i >= 0; i -= 2)
      System.out.println("Foo");
(d) for (int i = 10; i > 0; i /= 2)
      System.out.println("Foo");
```

6. Locate the error in each of the following code fragments and show how to fix it.

    (a) ```
        for (i = 10; i < 0; i--)
            System.out.println("T minus " + i + " and counting");
        ```
    (b) ```
        for (int i = 0; ; i++)
            if (i * i - 21 * i - 110 >= 0)
              break;
        System.out.println("Answer: " + i);
        ```
    (c) ```
        for (int age = 13; age <= 19;)
            System.out.println("A teenager can be " + ++age +
                                " years old");
        ```

7.  Which one of the following statements is not equivalent to the other two?

    (a) `for (int i = 0; i < 10; i++) System.out.println(i);`
    (b) `for (int i = 0; i < 10; ++i) System.out.println(i);`
    (c) `for (int i = 0; i++ < 10; ) System.out.println(i);`

8.  Which one of the following statements is not equivalent to the other two?

    (a) `for (int i = 5; i > 0; i--) System.out.println(i);`
    (b) `for (int i = 5; i >= 0; --i) System.out.println(i);`
    (c) `for (int i = 6; i-- > 0; ) System.out.println(i);`

9.  Convert the following code into a `for` statement:

    ```
    int i = 10;
    while (i > 0) {
       j += i;
       --i;
    }
    ```

10. What are the values of the variables m and n after the following statements have been executed?

    ```
    int m = 63;
    for (int n = 0; m > 0; n++)
       m = m / 2;
    ```

11. Write a `for` statement that computes $n! = n \times (n - 1) \times \ldots \times 1$. Assume that the variable n is already initialized. Have the `for` statement leave the value of n! in a variable named `factorial`.

12. Show the output of the following program.

    ```
    public class Exercise5_12 {
      public static void main(String[] args) {
        int[] a = new int[8];

        for (int i = 0; i < a.length; i++)
          a[i] = i + 1;

        int result = 0;
        for (int i = 0; i < a.length / 2; i++)
          result += a[i] * a[a.length-i-1];

        System.out.println("Result: " + result);
      }
    }
    ```
    ```

Section 5.3 13. Write a loop that finds the position of the *last* element containing 100 in the `scores` array. *Hint:* Search the array in reverse order.

Programming Projects

1. Modify the `SSNInfo` program (Section 4.9) by storing the area numbers and corresponding locations in parallel arrays. Here's what the arrays will look like:

```
int[] areaNumbers = {3, 7, 9, ... };
String[] locations = {"New Hampshire", "Maine", "Vermont", ...};
```

Use a loop to search `areaNumbers` for the first element that's greater than or equal to the area number entered by the user. The corresponding element of the `locations` array will contain the desired location.

2. Modify the `AverageScores2` program (Section 5.2) so that it also displays the highest score and lowest score. *Extra credit:* Have the program display the median score as well. (The median of a set of numbers is the number that would be in the middle if the numbers were placed in sorted order.)

3. Modify the `RepeatedDigits` program (Section 5.4) so that it prints a table showing how many times each digit appears in the number:

```
Enter a number: 41271092
Digit:        0   1   2   3   4   5   6   7   8   9
Occurrences:  1   2   2   0   1   0   0   1   0   1
```

4. Modify the `RepeatedDigits` program (Section 5.4) so that the user can enter more than one number to be tested for repeated digits. The program should terminate when the user enters a number that's less than or equal to 0.

5. Make the following changes to the `PhoneDirectory` program (Section 5.8):

    (a) Add a command named d (delete). It will prompt the user for a name and then delete all phone records that match the name. (As with the f command, partial matches are allowed.)

    (b) Set the initial size of the `records` array to 1, instead of 100, and have the program double the size of the array each time it becomes full.

    (c) Modify the f command so that it lines up names and numbers in columns:

```
Abernathy, C.              779-7559
Abbott, C. Michael         776-5188
```

Allow 25 characters for the name. *Hint:* Create a string containing 25 spaces. Use the `substring` method to select a portion of this string to display between the name and number.

6. Write a program named `ReverseNumbers` that prompts the user to enter 10 numbers, then writes the numbers in reverse order:

```
Enter 10 numbers: 34 82 49 102 7 94 23 11 50 31
In reverse order: 31 50 11 23 94 7 102 49 82 34
```

Hint: Store the numbers in an array, starting at position 0. When printing the numbers, visit the elements of the array in reverse order.

7. Write a program named `ClassifyScores` that classifies a series of scores into deciles (0–9, 10–19, and so forth). The scores will be numbers between 0 and 100, so the last decile will contain numbers from 90 to 100. Have the program prompt the user to enter each number separately. If an input is greater than 100, have the program display an error message and ignore the input. If the input is less than 0, the program should display a table showing how many scores fell into each decile. The table should have the following appearance:

```
Decile   Scores
------   ------
0-9        1
10-19      0
...
80-89      5
90-100     3
```

Hint: Create an array with 10 elements, one for each decile. After reading each score, divide it by 10 and increment the array element at that position. (For example, if the score is 56, increment the array element at position 5.) Note that the last decile will require special treatment.

8. Write a program named `Bank` that maintains a database of bank accounts. Each account will be stored in a `BankAccount` object. (See Section 5.6 for a description of the `BankAccount` class.) The following example shows what the user will see:

```
-------------------------------------------------
|Commands: o - Open account    c - Close account|
|          d - Deposit         w - Withdraw     |
|          s - Select account  q - Quit         |
-------------------------------------------------
Current account: None selected

Enter command: o
Enter new account number: 123-456
Enter initial balance: 100.00


-------------------------------------------------
|Commands: o - Open account    c - Close account|
|          d - Deposit         w - Withdraw     |
|          s - Select account  q - Quit         |
-------------------------------------------------
Current account: 123-456   Balance: $100.00

Enter command:
```

The program repeatedly prompts the user to enter commands, which it then executes. The program will not terminate until the user enters the command q. Note that the list of commands is redisplayed after each command has been executed, along with the current account and its balance. If there is no current account, the message `None selected` is displayed instead of the account number.

Here are descriptions of the other commands:

Open account. The user is prompted to enter a new account number and initial balance. This data is stored in a new `BankAccount` object. `BankAccount` objects for all existing accounts must be stored in an array. The new account becomes the current account.

Close account. If there is no current account, the message

```
Please select an account
```

is displayed. Otherwise, the current account is removed from the array. There is no current account after this operation is completed.

Deposit. If there is no current account, the message

```
Please select an account
```

is displayed. Otherwise, the user is prompted to enter the amount of the deposit:

```
Enter amount to deposit: 50.00
```

The amount entered by the user is added to the balance of the current account.

Withdraw. If there is no current account, the message

```
Please select an account
```

is displayed. Otherwise, the user is prompted to enter the amount of the withdrawal:

```
Enter amount to withdraw: 50.00
```

The amount entered by the user is subtracted from the balance of the current account.

Select account. The user is prompted to enter an account number:

```
Enter account number: 123-456
```

The array is then searched to see if any `BankAccount` object contains this number. If so, that object becomes the current account. If not, the following message is displayed:

```
Account number was not found
```

Here are a few other requirements for the program:

- The array used to store `BankAccount` objects must contain only one element initially. When the array becomes full, it must be doubled in size.
- Dollar amounts must be displayed correctly, with two digits after the decimal point. For example, make sure that your program displays $100.00, not $100.0.
- All user input may be preceded or followed by spaces. Commands may be entered as uppercase or lowercase letters. If the user enters a command other than o, c, d, w, s, or q, the program must display the following message:

    ```
    Command was not recognized; please try again.
    ```

9. Write a program named `CreateVIN` that creates a Vehicle Identification Number (VIN) from information entered by the user. (See Section 3.9 for more information about VINs.) The following example shows what the user will see on the screen:

   ```
   Enter 3-character world manufacturer identifier: JHM
   Enter 5-character vehicle description section: cb765
   Enter model year (1980-1999): 1990
   Enter 1-character plant code: C
   Enter 6-character sequential production number: 056658

   The VIN is JHMCB7658LC056658
   ```

   Notice that the user's input can be upper- or lowercase, but the VIN must contain only uppercase letters. The following table shows how to determine the code for the model year:

Year:	80	81	82	83	84	85	86	87	88	89	90	91	92	93	94	95	96	97	98	99
Code:	A	B	C	D	E	F	G	H	J	K	L	M	N	P	R	S	T	V	W	X

   Hint: Use arrays to store the table of model years, as well as the table of numerical values for characters and the table of weight factors. (The latter two tables appear in Section 3.9.)

Answers to Review Questions

Section 5.1
1. Initialize the array at the time it's declared.
2. Numbers are set to zero. `boolean` elements are set to `false`. Elements of a reference type are set to `null`.
3. Subscript
4. Use the expression `a.length`.

Section 5.2
1. A `for` statement
2. All three are optional.
3. *Initialization* and *update*
4. Idiom

Section 5.3
1. Sequential
2. Searching

Section 5.4
1. Random

Section 5.5
1. One-dimensional
2. Two-dimensional

Section 5.6
1. Field
2. Parallel
3. Objects
4. Move the last record into the hole.

Section 5.7
1. b now refers to the same array as a.
2. Write a `for` loop that compares corresponding elements in the two arrays.
3. (a)
4. Write a `for` loop that copies elements from one array to the other or call `System.arraycopy`.

6 Graphics

One of the advantages of using Java is that it allows programs to display graphics in a standard, platform-independent way. Most programming languages don't have this capability.

In this chapter, we'll learn about the `Graphics` class, whose instances are rectangular arrangements of pixels that can be modified by a program. Methods in the `Graphics` class are capable of drawing a variety of shapes (including lines, three kinds of rectangles, ovals, arcs, polygons, and polylines) as well as displaying text.

By default, all drawing is done in black. However, a program can change the drawing color at any time. Colors are represented by instances of the `Color` class. Similarly, a program can change the font in which text is displayed. Instances of the `Font` class represent particular fonts. By using the `FontMetrics` class, a program can obtain information about the sizes of characters in a font. This information is useful for aligning text with graphics.

Objectives

- Learn how to use `Graphics` methods to draw shapes (lines, rectangles, ovals, arcs, polygons, and polylines) and display text.
- Learn how to draw in different colors by creating `Color` objects.
- Learn how to display text in different fonts by creating `Font` objects.
- Learn how to use a `FontMetrics` object to obtain information about the sizes of characters in a font.

6.1 Creating a Drawing

Java's Abstract Window Toolkit (AWT) provides classes and other tools that we'll need to build programs that have a graphical user interface. Although we'll have to wait until Chapter 12 to see the full capabilities of the AWT, we can start using it on a smaller scale in this chapter.

The Graphics class, which belongs to the java.awt package, makes it possible for us to create line drawings on the screen. This class provides methods for drawing a number of shapes, including lines, rectangles, ovals, arcs, polygons, and polylines. There's also a method for displaying text.

An instance of the Graphics class is a rectangular area, called a *graphics context,* that's capable of storing an image. A graphics context consists of many tiny pixels (picture elements), each capable of displaying a single speck of color. Consider the following image, which I'll call "Bob":*

Looks pretty good, eh? Now, let's blow up Bob to six times his original size:

We now see that the image consists of tiny squares—pixels—colored either black or white.

The pixels in a graphics context are arranged in rows and columns (see the figure at the top of the next page). In this example (the upper-left corner of Bob's head), the graphics context consists of 300 pixels arranged in 15 rows and 20 columns. The rows are numbered from 0 to 14; the columns are numbered from 0 to 19. Each pixel can be identified by a pair of coordinates, with the *x* coordinate (column)

---

*This particular version of Bob is due to Doug Cooper.

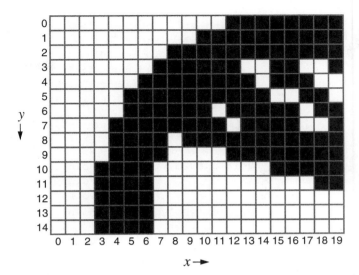

coming first. The pixel at the upper left corner is located at position (0, 0). (Technically, the coordinates refer to positions *between* pixels, but I'll ignore that fact in order to simplify the discussion.)

A graphics context typically contains an image that's being displayed on the user's screen. That's not always the case, however. A graphics context can also be printed or used to store an image that's not visible on the screen.

Using `Graphics` Methods

To change the pixels in a graphics context, we'll need to call one of the drawing methods that belongs to the `Graphics` class. Table 6.1 lists methods that display the outline of a shape. Table 6.1 contains only a brief description of what each method does; we examine each of these methods in detail later in the section. The methods in Table 6.2 on page 225 are similar to the ones in Table 6.1, except that they draw a *filled* shape, not just the outline of a shape.

drawLine   Before we can use the methods in the `Graphics` class, we need a graphics context to work with. Once we have a graphics context (named g, let's say), we can draw on it by calling one of the methods in Tables 6.1 or 6.2. For example, to draw a line, we would use a call of the form

```
g.drawLine(x1, y1, x2, y2);
```

where (x_1, y_1) is one of the line's endpoints and (x_2, y_2) is the other.

The `DrawableFrame` Class

To make it easy to experiment with the `Graphics` class, I've written a class named `DrawableFrame`. This class, like `SimpleIO` and `Convert`, belongs to the `jpb` package, which I wrote. A `DrawableFrame` object is a window containing

Table 6.1
Graphics Methods That
Draw the Outline of a
Shape

Description	Action

`void drawArc(int x, int y,`
`          int width, int height,`
`          int startAngle,`
`          int arcAngle)`
	Draws an arc.

`void drawLine(int x1, int y1,` `           int x2, int y2)`	Draws a line.
`void drawOval(int x, int y,` `           int width, int height)`	Draws an oval.

`void drawPolygon(int xPoints[],`
`              int yPoints[],`
`              int nPoints)`
	Draws a polygon when given arrays containing the coordinates of its vertices.

`void drawPolygon(Polygon p)`	Draws a polygon when given a `Polygon` object.

`void drawPolyline(int xPoints[],`
`               int yPoints[],`
`               int nPoints)`
	Draws a polyline (a series of connected lines).

`void drawRect(int x, int y,` `           int width, int height)`	Draws an ordinary rectangle.

`void drawRoundRect(int x, int y,`
`                int width,`
`                int height,`
`                int arcWidth,`
`                int arcHeight)`
	Draws a rectangle with rounded corners.

`void draw3DRect(int x, int y,`
`             int width, int height,`
`             boolean raised)`
	Draws a "3-dimensional" rectangle.

a graphics context. (In Java terminology, a "frame" is a window with a border and a title at the top. I chose the name `DrawableFrame` for the class because a `DrawableFrame` object is a window in which we can draw images.)

The first step in using `DrawableFrame` is to create an instance of the class:

```
DrawableFrame df = new DrawableFrame(title);
```

where *title* is a string containing the title that we want to appear at the top of the frame. By convention, we'll use the name `df` for a `DrawableFrame` variable, unless there's a more descriptive name available.

show   Creating a `DrawableFrame` object doesn't cause it to be displayed on the screen. To make a frame visible, we need to use the `show` method:

```
df.show();  // Make frame visible
```

setSize   The next step is to call `setSize` to specify how large we want the frame's graphics context to be:

```
df.setSize(width, height);  // Set width and height of
                            //   graphics context
```

Table 6.2
Graphics Methods That
Draw a Filled Shape

Description	*Action*

`void fillArc(int x, int y,`
`            int width, int height,`
`            int startAngle,`
`            int arcAngle)`
	Draws a filled arc.

`void fillOval(int x, int y,` `             int width, int height)`	Draws a filled oval.

`void fillPolygon(int xPoints[],`
`                int yPoints[],`
`                int nPoints)`
	Draws a filled polygon when given arrays containing the coordinates of its vertices.

`void fillPolygon(Polygon p)`	Draws a filled polygon when given a `Polygon` object.
`void fillRect(int x, int y,` `             int width, int height)`	Draws a filled ordinary rectangle.

`void fillRoundRect(int x, int y,`
`                  int width,`
`                  int height,`
`                  int arcWidth,`
`                  int arcHeight)`
	Draws a filled rectangle with rounded corners.

`void fill3DRect(int x, int y,`
`               int width, int height,`
`               boolean raised)`
	Draws a filled "3-dimensional" rectangle.

The values in the call of `setSize` don't determine the size of the frame itself, but rather the drawable area inside the frame. The frame itself will be somewhat larger because of its border. Here's what a drawable frame looks like on the Windows platform:

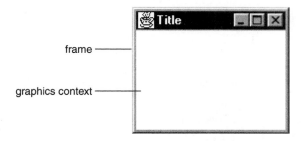

The title specified in the constructor will appear at the top of the frame, where the word "Title" currently is. The white rectangle in the center of the frame is the graphics context that we'll use for drawing.

getGraphicsContext   Before we can do any drawing within the frame, we'll need to call `get-GraphicsContext`:

```
Graphics g = df.getGraphicsContext(); // Get graphics context
```

getGraphicsContext returns the frame's graphics context. We'll need to save this object in a variable, which I'll name g by convention.

repaint   We're now ready to call the methods in Tables 6.1 and 6.2 to change the pixels in g. Any changes that we make to g won't necessarily show up on the screen, however. To guarantee that the user sees our changes to g, we'll need to call the repaint method:

```
df.repaint();   // Repaint frame
```

Calling repaint forces the entire frame to be redrawn, including the graphics context that g represents.

Be careful to follow the steps outlined here, in the order shown. In particular, be sure to call setSize before calling getGraphicsContext. Also, be sure to call repaint after changing the graphics context. Making DrawableFrame as easy to use as possible required making it less robust than I'd like; as a result, your program may not work if you deviate from the prescribed steps.

PROGRAM   **Drawing a Line**

The following program illustrates how to create a DrawableFrame object and draw a line within it.

DrawLine.java

```
 1  // Draws a line inside a frame
 2
 3  import java.awt.*;
 4  import jpb.*;
 5
 6  public class DrawLine {
 7    public static void main(String[] args) {
 8      // Create drawable frame
 9      DrawableFrame df = new DrawableFrame("Draw Line");
10      df.show();
11      df.setSize(150, 150);
12
13      // Obtain graphics context
14      Graphics g = df.getGraphicsContext();
15
16      // Draw line
17      g.drawLine(50, 50, 100, 100);
18
19      // Repaint frame
20      df.repaint();
21    }
22  }
```

The figure at the top of the next page shows what we'll see on the screen when we run this program. I've added marks along the left and bottom borders to indicate the *x* and *y* coordinates within the graphics context.

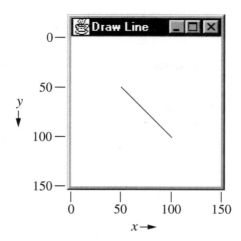

Let's analyze this program line by line, starting with the import declarations on lines 3 and 4. This program uses the `Graphics` class, which belongs to the `java.awt` package, and the `DrawableFrame` class, which belongs to the `jpb` package. The import declarations let us access the classes directly, without having to write `java.awt.Graphics` and `jpb.DrawableFrame`.

Line 9 creates a new `DrawableFrame` object, which is stored in the `df` variable. The argument `"Draw Line"` indicates what title should be displayed at the top of the frame. (The title can be any string; it doesn't have to match the name of the program.) Line 10 causes the frame to become visible. The statement on line 11 sets the size of the graphics context (150 pixels wide by 150 pixels high). The frame will now resize to accommodate these dimensions. (Note that the frame itself will be greater than 150 by 150.) Once the frame is established, line 14 calls `getGraphicsContext` and assigns the object that it returns to the g variable.

Line 17 calls the `drawLine` method to draw a line within the graphics context. The first two arguments are the *x* and *y* coordinates of the starting point (50, 50); the last two are the *x* and *y* coordinates of the ending point (100, 100). The line will be one pixel wide.

Q&A

Finally, line 20 calls the `repaint` method to make sure that the user sees the updated graphics context. The `main` method terminates at this point, but the frame remains visible on the screen until the user closes it by pressing the ☒ button.

Drawing Rectangles

The `Graphics` class provides methods to draw three types of rectangles:

Ordinary rectangles
Rectangles with rounded corners
"Three-dimensional" rectangles

For each type of rectangle, there's one method to draw the outline of a rectangle and another to draw a filled rectangle. Three-dimensional rectangles are tricky to do properly, so I'll focus on the other two types.

Rectangle methods take four arguments or more. The first two specify the coordinates of the rectangle's upper left corner. The next two specify the width and height of the rectangle.

Q&A

drawRect
fillRect

Ordinary rectangles. The `drawRect` method draws the outline of a rectangle; the `fillRect` method draws a filled rectangle:

```
g.drawRect(x, y, width, height);
g.fillRect(x, y, width, height);
```

The following figure illustrates how `x`, `y`, `width`, and `height` are interpreted:

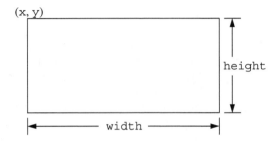

drawRoundRect
fillRoundRect

Rectangles with rounded corners. `drawRoundRect` draws an outline; `fillRoundRect` draws a filled rectangle:

```
g.drawRoundRect(x, y, width, height, arcWidth, arcHeight);
g.fillRoundRect(x, y, width, height, arcWidth, arcHeight);
```

Here's what a rounded rectangle looks like:

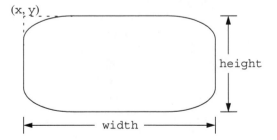

The `arcWidth` argument specifies the horizontal diameter of the arc at each corner; `arcHeight` is the vertical diameter. To understand what `arcWidth` and `arcHeight` mean, you have to visualize an oval enclosed within a rectangle with width `arcWidth` and height `arcHeight`. Each corner of the rectangle corresponds to one-fourth of that oval. In other words, the curvature of each corner extends `arcWidth`/2 pixels horizontally and `arcHeight`/2 pixels vertically. Here's an enlargement showing the upper-right corner of a rounded rectangle:

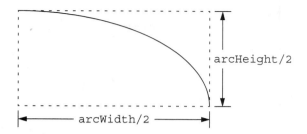

Drawing Ovals

drawOval
fillOval
The `drawOval` and `fillOval` methods will draw the outline of an oval (ellipse) or a filled oval, respectively:

```
g.drawOval(x, y, width, height);
g.fillOval(x, y, width, height);
```

`x` and `y` are the coordinates of the upper-left corner of an imaginary rectangle enclosing the oval. `width` and `height` are the measurements of this rectangle.

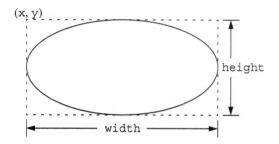

There's no method in the `Graphics` class designed specifically for drawing a circle. However, if the `width` and `height` arguments are equal, `drawOval` and `fillOval` will draw circles.

Drawing Arcs

drawArc
An arc, from the standpoint of the `Graphics` class, is a segment of an oval. The `drawArc` method requires six arguments:

```
g.drawArc(x, y, width, height, startAngle, arcAngle);
```

The first four arguments are the same ones that `drawOval` and `fillOval` require. The last two arguments specify the angle at which the oval starts and the "arc angle" of the oval. Angles are measured in degrees, with zero degrees at 3 o'clock. If the arc angle is positive, drawing is done in the counterclockwise direction. If the arc angle is negative, drawing is done in the clockwise direction.

The figure at the top of the next page illustrates the meaning of `x`, `y`, `width`, `height`, `startAngle`, and `arcAngle`.

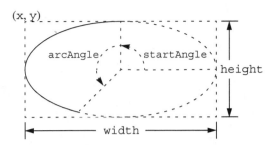

In this example, startAngle is 90 and arcAngle is 135.

fillArc   The fillArc method draws a filled arc, which resembles a slice of pie. The arguments to fillArc are the same as those for drawArc. The filled area is a portion of the oval described by the first four arguments to fillArc. The values of startAngle and arcAngle determine which portion is filled. If start-Angle is 90 and arcAngle is 135, fillArc will draw the following shape:

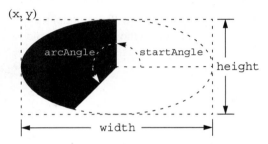

Drawing Polygons

drawPolygon   To draw a polygon, we first need to create two arrays, one containing the *x* coordinates of the polygon's vertices, and the other containing the *y* coordinates:

```
int[] xCoordinates = {0, 100, 200};
int[] yCoordinates = {100, 0, 100};
```

Next, we call the drawPolygon method, passing the two arrays, plus a third argument indicating the number of vertices:

```
g.drawPolygon(xCoordinates, yCoordinates,
              xCoordinates.length);
```

The result of this particular call will be a triangle whose corners are located at (0, 100), (100, 0), and (200, 100):

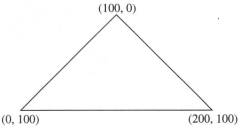

fillPolygon   Filling a polygon is similar to drawing one:

```
g.fillPolygon(xCoordinates, yCoordinates,
              xCoordinates.length);
```

Notice that I used xCoordinates.length as the third argument in the calls of drawPolygon and fillPolygon. Using yCoordinates.length would have given the same result, because both arrays have the same length. Using the number 3 would also work:

```
g.drawPolygon(xCoordinates, yCoordinates, 3);
```

Using a literal such as 3 isn't good practice, however. There's no easy way for someone reading the program to know that 3 is the correct number, short of going back to the definition of xCoordinates and yCoordinates. Also, if we ever change the number of values in the xCoordinates and yCoordinates arrays, we'll need to remember to replace 3 by the correct number. If we use xCoordinates.length or yCoordinates.length as the third argument, the call of drawPolygon won't need to be changed.

There's a second technique for drawing (or filling) a polygon. The java.awt package provides a class named Polygon. Instances of this class represent specific polygons. To create a Polygon object, we could write

```
Polygon p = new Polygon(xCoordinates, yCoordinates,
                        xCoordinates.length);
```

The Polygon constructor's arguments are the same as the arguments for draw-Polygon or fillPolygon: an array containing *x* coordinates, an array containing *y* coordinates, and the number of vertices in the polygon. We can now write

```
g.drawPolygon(p);
```

to draw the outline of p and

```
g.fillPolygon(p);
```

to draw a filled version of p.

The advantage of using Polygon objects is that the Polygon class provides several useful operations on polygons. For example, the translate method lets us change the position of a polygon, and the addPoint method lets us add another vertex to a polygon. Appendix C describes these and other Polygon methods.

Java's definition of "polygon" is fairly loose, by the way. A polygon in Java is any series of lines that form a closed region in two-dimensional space. The following figure is a polygon:

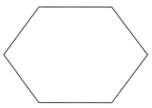

This polygon is *convex*—a line drawn from any corner to any other corner will stay within the polygon. Java doesn't require that polygons be convex, however. The following polygon is legal, even though it's not convex:

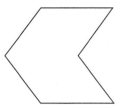

In fact, Java allows the lines that form a polygon to cross, which isn't allowed by the normal mathematical definition of "polygon." The following polygon was created from four points (the four corners). The crossing point in the center wasn't defined as one of the polygon's vertices.

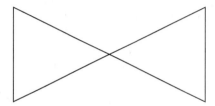

As this example shows, the order of the points in the two arrays makes a difference. To produce this figure, the points were placed in the order {upper-left, lower-right, upper-right, lower-left}. Other orders may result in different figures being drawn.

Drawing Polylines

A polyline is a series of lines, with each line after the first sharing an endpoint with the previous line. A polyline is the same as a polygon, except that Java doesn't automatically connect the last line back to the first to form a closed figure.

drawPolyline   Drawing a polyline is similar to drawing a polygon. The first step is to create arrays containing the x and y coordinates of the points in the polyline:

```
int[] xCoordinates = {0, 100, 200};
int[] yCoordinates = {100, 0, 100};
```

It takes $n + 1$ points to define a polyline with n lines. The next step is to call the `drawPolyline` method, passing the two arrays, plus a third argument indicating the number of points in the polyline:

```
g.drawPolyline(xCoordinates, yCoordinates,
               xCoordinates.length);
```

Here's what the resulting drawing will look like:

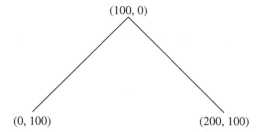

(100, 0)

(0, 100)   (200, 100)

Review Questions

1. Coordinates within a graphics context are expressed in _____.

2. What kinds of rectangles can be drawn using methods from the `Graphics` class?

3. In Java, an arc is: (a) a segment of a circle, (b) a segment of an oval, or (c) an arbitrary two-dimensional curve?

4. What is the difference between a polygon and a polyline?

6.2   Drawing in Color

The state of a `Graphics` object consists of more than just the pixels that it stores. Each `Graphics` object also has a "current color"; all drawing is done in that color until we call the `setColor` method. (By default, the drawing color is black.)

When we call `setColor`, we need to provide an instance of the `Color` class, which belongs to the `java.awt` package. A `Color` object can be created from three integers, indicating the red, green, and blue components of the color. Each component has a value between 0 (no contribution to the color) and 255 (maximum contribution). For example, the color "black" has red, green, and blue values of 0, whereas "white" has values of 255 for all three components.

Colors

The number of colors that can be created by choosing three integers between 0 and 255 is $256 \times 256 \times 256 = 16,777,216$. How many colors you can actually see on the screen depends on the video card that's installed in your system and how the card is currently configured. Some cards are capable of displaying a variety of different color ranges: 16 colors, 256 colors (or "8-bit color"), 65,536 colors ("16-bit color" or "high color"), and 16,777,216 colors ("24-bit color" or "true color" or "millions of colors"). Some even support 32-bit color, with over four billion possible colors. That's probably overkill, because humans can't distinguish that many colors. Java's 24-bit color is considered "photographic quality," because photographic images can be displayed on the screen with no discernible loss of color.

If your system isn't configured to display at least 24-bit color, you won't see the full range of colors that Java supports. Any color that Java tries to display will be converted to the nearest color that your system supports. The resulting image will still be recognizable but may not look as good as it could.

For our convenience, the Java API provides constants representing frequently used colors. These constants are defined inside the `Color` class itself. Table 6.3 shows the names of these constants and the red/green/blue combinations that they represent.

Table 6.3
Constants in the
`Color` Class

Name	Red Component	Green Component	Blue Component
black	0	0	0
blue	0	0	255
cyan	0	255	255
darkGray	64	64	64
gray	128	128	128
green	0	255	0
lightGray	192	192	192
magenta	255	0	255
orange	255	200	0
pink	255	175	175
red	255	0	0
white	255	255	255
yellow	255	255	0

setColor   To use a constant listed in Table 6.3, we must first write the name of the class (`Color`), then a dot, and then the name of the constant. For example, to change the current drawing color to magenta, we'd call `setColor` as follows:

```
g.setColor(Color.magenta);
```

If we need a color that's not in Table 6.3, we'll have to create a new `Color` object. For example, setting the color to light blue would require creating a `Color` object and then calling `setColor`:

```
Color lightBlue = new Color(64, 192, 255);
g.setColor(lightBlue);
```

We could save a step by creating the `Color` object and then passing it directly to `setColor`, without storing it in a variable first:

```
g.setColor(new Color(64, 192, 255));
```

Review Questions

1. What method is used to change the current drawing color for a graphics context?

2. A color is represented by three integers. What's the range of allowable values for these integers?

3. How many different colors can be created using Java's `Color` class?

4. Suppose that `myColor` has been declared as follows:

    ```
    Color myColor = new Color(255, 0, 255);
    ```

    The `Color` class already contains a constant representing this color. What's the name of that constant?

6.3 Displaying Text

drawString The `drawString` method lets us display text in a graphics context alongside lines, rectangles, and other shapes. `drawString` requires three arguments. The first argument is a string containing the text to be displayed. The other two arguments specify the *x* and *y* coordinates at which the text is to be displayed. For example, the following call of `drawString` displays the text `"Java rules!"` at location (x, y):

```
g.drawString("Java rules!", x, y);
```

x specifies the horizontal position of the first character in the string. y specifies the vertical position of the string's baseline (the invisible line on which the characters sit):

Java rules!
(x, y)

The **Font** Class

setFont When text is written using the `drawString` method, the appearance of the text depends on the "current font," which is stored in every `Graphics` object. The current font can be changed at any time by calling the `setFont` method:

```
g.setFont(newFont);
```

The argument to `setFont` must be a `Font` object.

  Font objects are created by calling the `Font` constructor, which requires three arguments: the font's name, style, and size.

- ■ *Font name.* The font name is a string, such as `"Monospaced"`, `"Serif"`, or `"SansSerif"`. (In a **monospaced** font, all characters have the same width. In a **serif** font, most letters have "serifs"—tiny lines added at the top and bottom. In a **sans serif** font, the letters lack serifs.) Other font names are allowed, but there's no guarantee that a particular font will be available on the user's computer. It's best to stick with these three fonts, which are nearly universal. If a program chooses a nonexistent font, Java will substitute another one (typically the monospaced font).

- **_Font style._** Possible styles are bold, italic, and plain, represented by the constants Font.BOLD, Font.ITALIC, and Font.PLAIN. To get both bold and italic, we can write Font.BOLD + Font.ITALIC.
- **_Font size._** Font sizes are measured in points. (A point is approximately 1/72" or 0.35 mm.)

The following statement creates a bold, 24-point, sans serif font:

```
Font f = new Font("SansSerif", Font.BOLD, 24);
```

 If the font name is stored in a variable (fontName, let's say), you can write

```
Font f = new Font(fontName, Font.BOLD, 24);
```

However, be careful not to write

```
Font f = new Font("fontName", Font.BOLD, 24);
```

The Font constructor will treat "fontName" itself as the name of the desired font. The Java compiler won't notice anything wrong, but the program won't behave as expected.

Passing f to the setFont method changes the current font:

```
g.setFont(f);
```

If desired, the font can be created within the call of setFont:

```
g.setFont(new Font("SansSerif", Font.BOLD, 24));
```

 Don't forget to call setFont. A common programming mistake is to create a Font object, but fail to pass it to setFont.

PROGRAM   **Displaying Text in Different Colors**

The following program displays text in three different colors and styles.

DisplayText.java

```
 1   // Displays text in three different colors and styles
 2
 3   import java.awt.*;
 4   import jpb.*;
 5
 6   public class DisplayText {
 7     public static void main(String[] args) {
 8       // Create drawable frame
 9       DrawableFrame df = new DrawableFrame("Display Text");
10       df.show();
11       df.setSize(210, 85);
12
13       // Obtain graphics context
14       Graphics g = df.getGraphicsContext();
```

```
15
16      // Display "Monospaced Bold"
17      g.setColor(Color.red);
18      g.setFont(new Font("Monospaced", Font.BOLD, 20));
19      g.drawString("Monospaced Bold", 15, 25);
20
21      // Display "SansSerif Italic"
22      g.setColor(Color.green);
23      g.setFont(new Font("SansSerif", Font.ITALIC, 20));
24      g.drawString("SansSerif Italic", 15, 50);
25
26      // Display "Serif Plain"
27      g.setColor(Color.blue);
28      g.setFont(new Font("Serif", Font.PLAIN, 20));
29      g.drawString("Serif Plain", 15, 75);
30
31      // Repaint frame
32      df.repaint();
33    }
34  }
```

Here's what the user will see when the program is run:

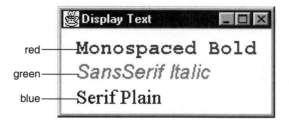

Review Questions

1. What method is used to display text in a graphics context?

2. When a string is displayed in a graphics context, we must specify *x* and *y* coordinates for the string. Explain the meaning of these coordinates.

3. The primary constructor for the Font class requires three arguments. What are they?

4. In a _____ font, all characters have the same width.

6.4   Combining Text with Graphics

We'll often need to combine text with graphics. Doing so isn't difficult, because the graphics methods (such as drawLine and drawRect) and the text method (drawString) all operate on a Graphics object. To combine text with graphics, we simply use both sets of methods in a single program. Here's an example.

PROGRAM   **Displaying a Stop Sign**

Our goal is to write a program that displays a stop sign:

red

The program will need to draw three figures:

- An eight-sided polygon (black).
- A filled eight-sided polygon (red).
- The word STOP in sans serif (white).

We can use the drawPolygon method to draw the black polygon and the fill-Polygon method to draw the filled red polygon. To display the word STOP, we'll use the drawString method.

StopSign.java

```
1   // Displays a stop sign
2
3   import java.awt.*;
4   import jpb.*;
5
6   public class StopSign {
7     public static void main(String[] args) {
8       // Create drawable frame
9       DrawableFrame df = new DrawableFrame("Stop Sign");
10      df.show();
11      df.setSize(125, 125);
12
13      // Obtain graphics context
14      Graphics g = df.getGraphicsContext();
15
16      // Define coordinates of outer polygon (edge of sign) and
17      // inner polygon (red portion)
18      int[] xOuter = {36, 87, 123, 123, 87, 36, 0, 0};
19      int[] yOuter = {0, 0, 36, 87, 123, 123, 87, 36};
20      int[] xInner = {37, 86, 118, 118, 86, 37, 5, 5};
21      int[] yInner = {5, 5, 37, 86, 118, 118, 86, 37};
22
23      // Draw edge of sign in black
24      g.setColor(Color.black);
25      g.drawPolygon(xOuter, yOuter, xOuter.length);
26
```

```
27        // Fill interior of sign with red
28        g.setColor(Color.red);
29        g.fillPolygon(xInner, yInner, xInner.length);
30
31        // Display "STOP" in white
32        g.setColor(Color.white);
33        g.setFont(new Font("SansSerif", Font.BOLD, 36));
34        g.drawString("STOP", 13, 76);
35
36        // Repaint frame
37        df.repaint();
38     }
39  }
```

Note that the inner polygon must be drawn before the word STOP; otherwise, the polygon would overwrite the word and make it disappear.

The `FontMetrics` Class

The `StopSign` program works, but it's quite limited. There's no easy way to display the stop sign in a different size, because all the data—the size of the frame, the vertices of the polygons, the font size, and the position of the word STOP—is "hard-coded" into the program as literals. A better version of the program would obtain the desired size of the stop sign from outside the program itself, perhaps by asking the user to enter the size. The coordinates of the vertices could then be computed by the program. Two questions remain, however: What should the size of the font be, and what should be the *x* and *y* coordinates for the word STOP? In order to answer these questions, we need to have an idea of the relationship between the size of a font (which is measured in points) and the sizes of characters on the screen (which are measured in pixels).

When we use `drawString` to display a string within a graphics context, the characters in the string are converted to pixels. Unfortunately, there's no simple relationship between the size of a font and the pixel sizes of the characters in the font. The designers of Java recognized our predicament and designed a class named `FontMetrics`. This class provides methods for computing the sizes of characters in a font. To use the `FontMetrics` class, we first create an object representing a particular font:

```
Font f = new Font("SansSerif", Font.BOLD, 24);
```

getFontMetrics   Next, we pass it to the `getFontMetrics` method:

```
FontMetrics fm = g.getFontMetrics(f);
```

Note that we don't use a constructor to create a `FontMetrics` object. Instead, we ask the graphics context `g` to provide the object. The reason for this process is that the sizes of characters in a particular font may depend on the graphics context. It's also legal to use a `DrawableFrame` object to obtain a `FontMetrics` object:

```
FontMetrics fm = df.getFontMetrics(f);
```

The result is the same either way. Using a `DrawableFrame` object can be convenient, because the `FontMetrics` object can be obtained as soon as the `DrawableFrame` object has been created, before the `Graphics` object is available.

Once we have a `FontMetrics` object, we can use it to call various query methods that return information about the size of the font. Here's a list of the information that's available:

- *Advance width*—The distance from the beginning of a character to the place where the next character would go in a line of text. So that characters don't touch, the advance width of a character is slightly larger than the character's actual width:

- *Ascent*—The distance from the baseline to the top of most alphanumeric characters. Some characters in the font may have a larger ascent.
- *Descent*—The distance from the baseline to the bottom of most alphanumeric characters. Some characters in the font may have a larger descent.
- *Leading* (pronounced "ledding")—The recommended amount of space between the descent of one line of text and the ascent of the next line.
- *Height*—The recommended distance between the baselines of adjacent lines of text. The height is the sum of the leading, ascent, and descent. There's no guarantee that lines of text spaced at this distance won't touch; overlap can occur if some characters exceed the font's normal ascent or descent.

The following figure illustrates the meaning of ascent, descent, leading, and height:

Table 6.4 lists several commonly used `FontMetrics` methods. Most of these methods have no arguments, because they return information about the font as a whole, not any particular character in the font. The exception is `stringWidth`, which returns the advance width of a particular string. All methods in the table return an integer, representing a measurement in pixels.

Table 6.4
FontMetrics Methods

Description	Action
int getAscent()	Returns the ascent for this font.
int getDescent()	Returns the descent for this font.
int getHeight()	Returns the height for this font.
int getLeading()	Returns the leading for this font.
int getMaxAdvance()	Returns the maximum advance width for any character in this font.
int stringWidth(String str)	Returns the advance width for str in this font.

getMaxAscent
getMaxDescent

To find the maximum ascent or descent for any character in a font, use the getMaxAscent and getMaxDescent methods. These methods are less commonly used than getAscent and getDescent, so I didn't put them in the table. (An amusing bit of trivia: When Java was originally released, the getMaxDescent method was named getMaxDecent because of a spelling error by someone at Sun Microsystems. The getMaxDecent method was still supported at the time this book was published, although Sun has "deprecated" it, which means that they intend to remove it eventually.)

PROGRAM   **Obtaining Font Information**

The following program creates a 20-point sans serif font and then displays information about the font in a frame. The text in the frame is displayed in the font itself.

FontInfo.java

```
 1   // Displays information about a font. Uses the FontMetrics
 2   // class to obtain the information to be displayed.
 3
 4   import java.awt.*;
 5   import jpb.*;
 6
 7   public class FontInfo {
 8     public static void main(String[] args) {
 9       // Create drawable frame
10       DrawableFrame df = new DrawableFrame("Font Information");
11       df.show();
12       df.setSize(215, 175);
13
14       // Get graphics context
15       Graphics g = df.getGraphicsContext();
16
17       // Create font, get metrics for font, and compute height
18       // of font
19       Font f = new Font("SansSerif", Font.PLAIN, 20);
20       FontMetrics fm = g.getFontMetrics(f);
21       int height = fm.getHeight();
22
```

```
23        // Display information about font
24        g.setFont(f);
25        g.drawString("Ascent: " + fm.getAscent(), 10, height);
26        g.drawString("Descent: " + fm.getDescent(), 10,
27                        height * 2);
28        g.drawString("Height: " + height, 10, height * 3);
29        g.drawString("Leading: " + fm.getLeading(), 10,
30                        height * 4);
31        g.drawString("Maximum advance: " + fm.getMaxAdvance(), 10,
32                        height * 5);
33        g.drawString("Width of \"Why?\": " +
34                        fm.stringWidth("Why?"), 10, height * 6);
35
36        // Repaint frame
37        df.repaint();
38    }
39 }
```

Here's what we might see on the screen when this program is executed:

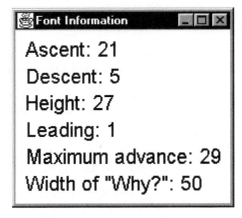

Notice that the *y* coordinates of the strings are `height`, `height * 2`, `height * 3`, and so on, where the `height` variable contains the font's height. Using the font's height—as returned by the `getHeight` method—guarantees that the distance between the lines will be appropriate for this font.

Review Questions

1. How does a program obtain a `FontMetrics` object for a particular font?

2. Explain the difference between the "advance width" of a character and the character's actual width.

3. The _____ of a font is the distance from the baseline to the bottom of most alphanumeric characters.

4. Suppose that a certain font has an ascent of 15, a descent of 3, and a height of 20. What is the font's leading?

6.5   Case Study: A Message Window

To illustrate the use of the various classes described in this chapter, we'll now develop a program that displays a message within a frame. The program, named `MessageWindow`, will prompt the user to enter the font (name and size) that will be used to display the message. The user will also be prompted to enter the number of lines in the message and, finally, the message itself, one line at a time:

```
Enter font name: Serif
Enter font size: 40
Enter number of lines in message: 3
Enter line 1: I'm the
Enter line 2: king of the
Enter line 3: world!
```

The program will allow spaces before and after each input item.

A frame labeled "Message Window" will now appear on the screen. The user's message will be displayed in blue against a white background, with the lines of the user's message centered within the frame:

The size of the frame will vary, depending on the message and the font. The distance between the baselines of consecutive lines will match the font's height. The distance from the top of the graphics context to the baseline of the first line will be the font's ascent plus its leading. The space below the last line's baseline will be equal to the font's descent. The amount of horizontal space on either side of the widest line will also match the font's descent.

Designing this program is a bit tricky, because we can't begin drawing without a graphics context, but we can't get a graphics context until we've determined the size of the frame. Determining the size of the frame requires knowing the entire message entered by the user. We'll need to know the number of lines in the message and the width of the widest line (in pixels). We'll also need to take into account the metrics of the font selected by the user. So, it seems that we can't display the message until we've read it all, which means that the program will need to store the entire message.

Let's tackle the design piece by piece. The first two steps seem clear enough:

1. Prompt the user to enter the font name.
2. Prompt the user to enter the font size and convert the input to an integer.

Before we read the message, we'll need the `FontMetrics` object for the user's font, so that we can determine the width of the widest line in the message. (We'll compute the width of each line as soon as it's read.) In order to get the `Font-Metrics` object, we first need to create the frame (a `DrawableFrame` object) and the `Font` object that corresponds to the user's font:

3. Create the frame and font objects and obtain the metrics for the font.

Now we're ready to read the message itself:

4. Prompt the user to enter the number of lines in the message and convert the input to an integer.
5. Read and store the lines in the message, computing the width of the widest line.

This step will provide the program with the information it needs to set the frame's size. The remaining steps are fairly clear:

6. Open the frame and set its size.
7. Obtain the graphics context; set the drawing color and the font.
8. Display the lines in the message.
9. Repaint the frame.

Next, we'll need to choose algorithms and decide how data will be stored. Step 5 requires the most thought. As the lines are read, the program will need to determine the width of the widest line. In Section 5.3, we discussed an algorithm for finding the largest number in an array; we can use a modified version of that algorithm here. We'll also need a way to store the lines in the message until they can be displayed in step 8; an array is the logical choice.

With these decisions made, step 5 can be written as a loop containing the following steps:

1. Prompt the user to enter a line; store the line in the array.
2. Compare the width of the line with the maximum width read so far, replacing the maximum width if necessary.

Here's the finished program.

MessageWindow.java

```
1  // Program name: MessageWindow
2  // Author: K. N. King
3  // Written: 1999-04-04
4  //
5  // Displays a message within a frame. Prompts the user to
6  // enter a font name and size, the number of lines in the
```

```
 7    // message, and the message to be displayed. Spaces are
 8    // allowed before and after each input item.
 9    //
10    // Once input is complete, a frame labeled "Message Window"
11    // will appear. The message will be displayed in blue against
12    // a white background, with the lines of the message centered
13    // within the frame. The size of the frame will depend
14    // on the message and the font. The distance between the
15    // baselines of consecutive lines will match the font's
16    // height. The distance from the top of the graphics context
17    // to the baseline of the first line will be the font's ascent
18    // plus its leading. The space below the last line's baseline
19    // will be equal to the font's descent. The amount of
20    // horizontal space on either side of the widest line will
21    // also match the font's descent.
22
23    import java.awt.*;
24    import jpb.*;
25
26    public class MessageWindow {
27      public static void main(String[] args) {
28        // Prompt user to enter font name
29        SimpleIO.prompt("Enter font name: ");
30        String fontName = SimpleIO.readLine().trim();
31
32        // Prompt user to enter font size; convert to integer form
33        SimpleIO.prompt("Enter font size: ");
34        String fontSizeString = SimpleIO.readLine().trim();
35        int fontSize = Integer.parseInt(fontSizeString);
36
37        // Create drawable frame and font objects;
38        // obtain font metrics
39        DrawableFrame df = new DrawableFrame("Message Window");
40        Font f = new Font(fontName, Font.PLAIN, fontSize);
41        FontMetrics fm = df.getFontMetrics(f);
42
43        // Prompt user to enter number of lines in message;
44        // convert to integer form
45        SimpleIO.prompt("Enter number of lines in message: ");
46        String numLinesString = SimpleIO.readLine().trim();
47        int numLines = Integer.parseInt(numLinesString);
48
49        // Read and store lines in message, computing width of
50        // widest line
51        String[] lines = new String[numLines];
52        int maxLineWidth = 0;
53        for (int i = 0; i < numLines; i++) {
54          // Prompt user to enter a line; store it in array
55          SimpleIO.prompt("Enter line " + (i + 1) + ": ");
56          lines[i] = SimpleIO.readLine().trim();
57
58          // Compare width of line with maximum width read so
59          // far, replacing maximum width if necessary.
60          int lineWidth = fm.stringWidth(lines[i]);
```

```
61            if (lineWidth > maxLineWidth)
62                maxLineWidth = lineWidth;
63        }
64
65        // Open frame and set its size
66        df.show();
67        int borderSize = fm.getDescent();
68        int height = fm.getHeight();
69        df.setSize(maxLineWidth + borderSize * 2,
70                    numLines * height + fm.getLeading());
71
72        // Obtain graphics context; set drawing color and font
73        Graphics g = df.getGraphicsContext();
74        g.setColor(Color.blue);
75        g.setFont(f);
76
77        // Display lines in message
78        int firstBaseline = fm.getLeading() + fm.getAscent();
79        for (int i = 0; i < numLines; i++) {
80            int lineWidth = fm.stringWidth(lines[i]);
81            g.drawString(lines[i],
82                        borderSize + (maxLineWidth - lineWidth) / 2,
83                        firstBaseline + i * height);
84        }
85
86        // Repaint frame
87        df.repaint();
88    }
89  }
```

The program closely follows the design sketched earlier. Note that line 78 computes the baseline of the first line in the message. The other lines are then positioned relative to the first line. Calculating the first baseline before entering the loop saves time, as well as simplifying line 83 of the program.

The call of `drawString` on lines 81–83 deserves special mention. The second argument to `drawString` is

```
borderSize + (maxLineWidth - lineWidth) / 2
```

Subtracting `lineWidth` from `maxLineWidth` and dividing by 2 yields the number of "extra" pixels on either side of line `i`. Adding this quantity to `border-Size`—the number of pixels on either side of the widest line—gives the *x* coordinate needed for line `i` to be centered within the frame.

6.6 Debugging

When we're working on a program that displays graphics in a frame, we can still display output using the `System.out.print` and `System.out.println` methods. This output will appear in the window from which we launched the program. The ability to display messages in the original window is quite valuable for debugging. For example, if we're not sure that the size of a frame was calculated correctly, we can have the program display the frame's height and width. If we're curious about the metrics of a particular font, we can have the program display those numbers.

Displaying information about a frame, font, or other object is often quite easy. In Section 3.8, we saw that `System.out.println`, when given an object as its argument, will automatically call the object's `toString` method. The resulting string is then displayed on the screen. (`System.out.print` has the same ability.) What Section 3.8 didn't mention was that *all* objects have a `toString` method. (If a class doesn't declare a `toString` method, Java supplies one automatically through a mechanism known as inheritance.) To obtain debugging information about an object, for example, all we may have to do is print the object.

inheritance ➤ *11.1*

Suppose that we print a `Color` object:

```
System.out.println(Color.lightGray);
```

We'll get the following output:

```
java.awt.Color[r=192,g=192,b=192]
```

The output shows the package that the `Color` class belongs to (`java.awt`), the name of the class, and the values stored inside this particular `Color` object (the red, green, and blue components are all 192).

Now, let's try printing a `Font` object:

```
Font f = new Font("SansSerif", Font.BOLD, 24);
System.out.println(f);
```

This time, the output is

```
java.awt.Font[family=SansSerif,name=SansSerif,style=bold,size=24]
```

We see the font's name, style, and size, as well as the family of fonts to which it belongs.

Printing an object variable can be a valuable way to check the behavior of a program. We can make sure that the variable actually contains an object and that the state of the object is what we expected. By the way, it's not necessary to test whether an object variable is `null` before printing it. If the value is `null` at the time the variable is printed, the word `null` will be displayed.

One caveat: Although printing the values of object variables can be helpful, it doesn't always provide much information. Any object can be printed, but the amount of information displayed varies from class to class. Section 11.5 discusses this point in more detail.

Review Questions

1. What information can we obtain by printing a `Color` object?

2.   What information can we obtain by printing a `Font` object?

3.   What happens if we print an object variable whose value is `null`?

Q & A

Q: How can I draw a single point?

A: Use the `drawLine` method. For example, to draw a single point at location (x, y), use the following call:

```
g.drawLine(x, y, x, y);
```

Q: How can I draw a thick line? The `drawLine` method only draws lines that are one pixel wide. [p. 227]

A: One way to solve this problem is to draw two or more lines next to each other (just one pixel apart), so that they appear to be a single line. If you need to draw a thick horizontal or vertical line, just draw a filled rectangle instead. In Java 2 (version 1.2 or later of the Java Development Kit), a new class named `Graphics2D` is available. This class is based on the `Graphics` class but provides more options for drawing. In particular, lines (and other shapes) can be more than one pixel wide.

Q: If I draw a rectangle with width 100 and height 100 in a drawable frame that has width 100 and height 100, the right and bottom sides of the rectangle are chopped off. Why is that? [p. 228]

A: It turns out that the call

```
g.drawRect(0, 0, 100, 100);
```

actually draws a rectangle that is 101 pixels wide and 101 pixels high. The left edge of the rectangle is located at $x = 0$, and the right edge is located at $x = 100$. The *distance* between the two edges is 100 (as we specified), but the number of pixels involved is 101 (one for the left edge, 99 for the interior pixels, and one for the right edge). You'll need to make your frame one pixel larger to compensate (or else make your rectangle one pixel smaller).

Summary

- A graphics context is a rectangular arrangement of pixels whose colors can be changed to create an image. Each graphics context is an instance of the `Graphics` class.

- Each pixel in a graphics context has an *x* coordinate and a *y* coordinate. The upper-left pixel in a graphics context is located at (0, 0).

- The `drawLine` method, which belongs to the `Graphics` class, is used to draw a line onto a graphics context.

- Rectangles can be drawn by calling `drawRect` and filled by calling `fillRect`.

- Rectangles with rounded corners can be drawn by calling `drawRoundRect` and filled by calling `fillRoundRect`.

- Ovals can be drawn by calling `drawOval` and filled by calling `fillOval`. There are no methods for drawing or filling a circle, but `drawOval` and `fillOval` can be used for this purpose.

- An arc is a segment of an oval. Arcs can be drawn by calling `drawArc` and filled by calling `fillArc`.

- A polygon is a series of lines that forms a closed region in two-dimensional space. Polygons are represented either by parallel arrays of *x* and *y* coordinates or by `Polygon` objects. Polygons can be drawn by calling `drawPolygon` and filled by calling `fillPolygon`.

- A polyline is a series of lines, with each line after the first sharing an endpoint with the previous line. Polylines can be drawn by calling `drawPolyline`.

- A graphics context has a "current color," which can be changed by calling the `setColor` method.

- Colors are represented by instances of the `Color` class.

- Text can be displayed in a graphics context by calling `drawString`.

- A graphics context has a "current font," which can be changed by calling the `setFont` method.

- Fonts are represented by instances of the `Font` class.

- The `FontMetrics` class provides methods for determining information about the sizes of characters in a particular font.

- The `getFontMetrics` method returns a `FontMetrics` object corresponding to a particular font.

- The `getAscent`, `getDescent`, `getLeading`, and `getHeight` methods return the ascent, descent, leading, and height for an entire font.

- The `getMaxAdvance` method returns the maximum width of any character in a font.

- The `stringWidth` method returns the width of a string in a particular font.

- `System.out.print` and `System.out.println` can be used to display the values of object variables for debugging purposes.

Exercises

Section 6.1

1. Assume that `g` is a `Graphics` object. Write a method call that will draw the outline of a rectangle whose upper-left corner is located at *x* = 10, *y* = 25, and whose width and height are 20 and 30, respectively.

2.   Assume that g is a Graphics object. Write a method call that will draw a filled rectangle whose upper-left corner is located at $x = 25$, $y = 40$, and whose lower-right corner is located at $x = 50$, $y = 60$.

3.   Suppose that g is a Graphics object with 200 rows and 200 columns. Do a drawing showing what g will look like after the following statements have been executed.

```
int[] a = {50, 100, 150};
int[] b = {75, 25, 75};
g.drawPolygon(a, b, a.length);
g.drawRect(50, 75, 100, 100);
g.drawRect(75, 100, 50, 75);
g.drawOval(88, 125, 25, 25);
```

4.   Write one or more method calls that will display the following figure. The figure should be 110 pixels wide and 90 pixels high.

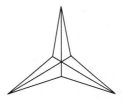

Section 6.2

5.   Declare a Color variable named violet and initialize it to contain a Color object whose red, green, and blue values are 100, 75, and 150, respectively.

Section 6.3

6.   Assume that g is a Graphics object, and suppose that the string "Java rules!" is 20 pixels high in the current font. Write a method call that displays "Java rules!" with 10 pixels of space above the string and 10 pixels of space to the left of the string.

7.   Locate the error in the following program fragment and show how to fix it.

```
SimpleIO.prompt("Enter font name: ");
String fontName = SimpleIO.readLine();
Font f = new Font("fontName", Font.PLAIN, 12);
```

Section 6.4

8.   Write a test program that determines the largest font size for which a plain serif font will have a height of no more than 20 pixels.

Programming Projects

1.   Modify the FontInfo program (Section 6.4) so that the user selects the font name, font style, and point size:

```
Enter font name: SansSerif
Enter font style: plain
Enter font size: 20
```

The font style can be either bold, italic, or plain. (The case of the input doesn't matter.) The size of the frame will depend on the font; leave 10 pixels of space at the borders of the graphics context. *Hint:* See the MessageWindow program (Section 6.5) for an example of how to determine the size of the frame based on the metrics of the font.

2. Modify the `MessageWindow` program (Section 6.5) so that the user enters the entire message as a single string, with backslashes used to indicate which words go on each line:

```
Enter font name: Serif
Enter font size: 40
Enter message: I'm the\king of the\world!
```

There can be any number of backslashes in the message, including none.

3. Write a program named `TicTacToe` that displays the following frame:

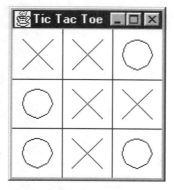

Each of the nine cells should be 50 pixels wide and 50 pixels high. Each X and O should be 30 pixels by 30 pixels.

4. Write a program named `NestedSquares` that displays the following frame:

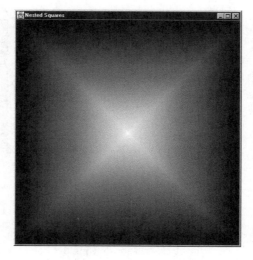

The frame contains 256 squares nested within each other. The outermost square is 512 pixels by 512 pixels. Its color has 0 as its red, green, and blue components. Inside this rectangle is a rectangle that's 510 pixels by 510 pixels. Its color has 1 as its red, green, and blue components. Each subsequent rectangle is 2 pixels smaller than the previous one, and has color components that are 1 unit larger.

5.   Write a program named `Checkerboard` that displays the following frame:

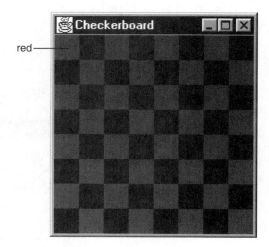

The frame contains 64 squares, each 25 pixels by 25 pixels. The colors of the squares alternate between red and black, starting with a red square in the upper-left corner.

6.   Write a program named `SignalAhead` that displays the following frame:

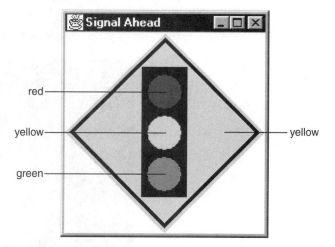

The overall size of the sign is 200 pixels by 200 pixels. The outer (yellow) edge of the sign is 5 pixels wide, and the black stripe is 5 pixels wide. The traffic signal (a black rectangle) is 46 pixels wide and 130 pixels high. Each traffic light is 34 pixels in diameter. *Hint:* Create the black stripe by drawing five polygons next to each other.

7.   Write a program named `RailroadCrossing` that displays the frame shown at the top of the next page. The overall size of the sign is 200 pixels by 200 pixels. The inner black circle is 186 pixels in diameter. The letters are in a bold, sans serif, 63-point font. *Hint:* The crossbars can be drawn as two overlapping polygons or as a single polygon.

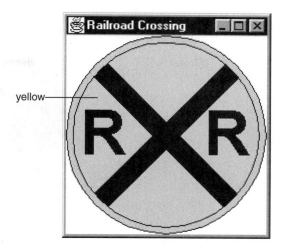

8. Write a program named `HeadsVsTails` that flips an imaginary coin and displays a bar chart showing the number of heads and tails. (The `CountFlips` program of Section 4.7 is similar.) The user will specify the number of coin flips:

```
Enter number of flips: 1000
```

A frame labeled `"Heads vs. Tails"` will now appear on the screen. The number of heads and tails will be displayed within the frame as colored bars:

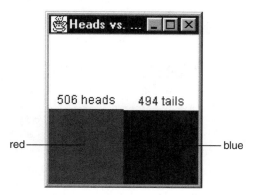

The frame's drawable area must be 150 pixels by 150 pixels. Each bar is 75 pixels wide. The height of the first bar is proportional to the number of heads. (If all flips were heads, the bar would be 150 pixels high.) Similarly, the height of the second bar is proportional to the number of tails. The left bar is red; the right bar is blue. The captions must be displayed in black in a plain, 12-point, sans serif font. Each caption must be centered above one of the bars, with a distance of 5 pixels between the baseline of the caption and the top of the bar.

9. Write the `HeadsVsTails` program as described in Programming Project 8, but with the results displayed as a pie chart (see the figure at the top of the next page). The frame's drawable area must be 150 pixels by 150 pixels. The circle in the center must be 100 pixels in diameter. The upper part of the circle, which indicates which portion of the coin flips were heads, must be red. The lower part of the circle, which indicates which portion of the coin flips were tails, must be blue. The captions must be displayed in black in a plain, 12-point,

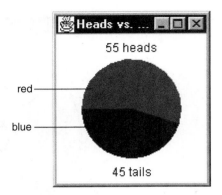

sans serif font. Each caption must be centered both horizontally and vertically. *Hint:* Use the
fillArc method to draw the red and blue "pie slices."

10.   Write a program named Display3DMessage that displays a one-line message in a
      frame. The user will select the background color of the frame, the font to be used to display
      the message, the size of the font, and the message to be displayed. The following example
      shows the program's interaction with the user:

      Enter background color: **Green**
      Enter font name: **SansSerif**
      Enter font size: **40**
      Enter message: **Mom's Old-Fashioned Robot Oil**

      A frame labeled Display 3D Message will now appear on the screen, with the user's
      message displayed in white at the center of the frame, with a shadow behind the message to
      give it a "three-dimensional" look:

      The amount of space around the message (at top, bottom, left, and right) must be equal to
      the sum of the font's ascent and descent divided by two. The background color can be any of
      the colors listed in Table 6.3. Case doesn't matter; green could be entered as green,
      GREEN, GrEen, and so on. If the user enters an unrecognized color, the program must use
      blue as a default. *Hint:* To achieve a three-dimensional effect, have the program compute the
      coordinates that would be used to center the message in the frame. Then have the program
      display the message in black, shifted one pixel down and to the right, relative to its centered
      position. Finally, have the program display the message in white, shifted one pixel up and to
      the left, relative to its centered position.

Answers to Review Questions

Section 6.1   1.   Pixels
                       2.   Ordinary rectangles, rectangles with rounded corners, three-dimensional rectangles

3. (b)
4. They are the same, except that Java doesn't automatically connect the last line in a polyline back to the first to form a closed figure.

Section 6.2

1. `setColor`
2. 0 to 255
3. $2^{24} = 16,777,216$
4. `magenta`

Section 6.3

1. `drawString`
2. The x coordinate represents the position of the left edge of the first character in the string. The y coordinate represents the string's baseline.
3. Font name, style, and size
4. Monospaced

Section 6.4

1. By calling `getFontMetrics`
2. The advance width is slightly larger than the actual width, because it includes the gap between consecutive characters.
3. Descent
4. 2

Section 6.6

1. Values of the color's red, green, and blue components
2. Font name, style, size, and family
3. The word `null` is displayed.

7 Class Variables and Methods

In Chapter 3, we saw that a class could contain *instance* variables and *instance* methods. In this chapter, we'll discover that a class may have *class* variables and *class* methods as well. Instance variables are stored in each instance of a class. Class variables, on the other hand, are stored only once within a program. Class variables are useful when data needs to be shared by more than one class. In particular, constants are often declared as `final` class variables.

An instance method is called by a specific object, and it has access to the instance variables inside that object. In contrast, a call of a class method doesn't involve an object. Class methods have a variety of uses, including serving as "helpers" for the `main` method.

The focus of this chapter is on defining and using class variables and methods. However, much of the discussion is relevant to instance methods as well as class methods. The `return` statement, which was introduced in Chapter 3, is covered here in detail. This chapter also explains how arguments are passed to methods and provides guidelines for designing methods.

A few of the topics in the chapter are only loosely related to class variables and methods. We'll discover how to access information provided by the user on the command line, and we'll learn about the standard streams, which provide a way for a program to communicate with the user. There's also a discussion of conditional expressions, which often appear in `return` statements.

Objectives

- Learn the difference between instance methods and class methods.
- Learn how to write class methods.

- Learn about the `return` statement and the conditional operator.
- Learn about how parameters are passed to methods.
- Learn how a program can access information provided by the user on the command line.
- Learn how class variables are used: as global variables, as constants, and as storage for class methods.
- Learn about the three standard streams: `System.in`, `System.out`, and `System.err`.
- Learn how to write helper methods.
- Learn how to design methods.

7.1 Class Methods Versus Instance Methods

Before we discuss class methods, let's start with a brief review of several topics from Chapter 3. In that chapter, we saw that a Java program consists of classes. Most classes contain both instance variables and instance methods. Any object created from a class will have its own copy of the class's instance variables, and that object will be capable of calling the class's (public) instance methods.

Two of the classes discussed in Chapter 3 were `Account` and `String`. We designed the `Account` class; it doesn't otherwise exist in Java. The `String` class, on the other hand, is part of the Java API. Both classes contain instance variables and methods. If `acct` is an `Account` variable, we can write

```
acct.deposit(1000.00);
```

to deposit $1000 into the `Account` object that `acct` represents. If `str` is a `String` variable, we can write

```
int len = str.length();
```

to find the length of the `String` object that `str` represents.

Both `deposit` and `length` are examples of instance methods. An instance method may simply access the instance variables in an object without changing them (as the `length` method does), or it may modify instance variables (as `deposit` does).

Class Methods

Not all methods require access to instance variables. For example, consider a method that computes the square root of a number. This method has nothing to do with objects. It doesn't need to access or modify the instance variables stored in an object. Methods that don't need access to instance variables are known as ***class methods***. (They're also known as ***static methods***, for reasons that will become apparent in Section 7.2.)

A class method—like all methods in Java—must belong to a class. If the method has been declared `public`, we can call it by writing the name of its class, a dot, the name of the method, and the method's argument list:

class method call

> *class* . *method-name* (*arguments*)

The class name is required because more than one class might have a class method with the same name. When a class method is called by another method in the *same* class, though, we can omit the class name and the dot.

We encountered several class methods in Chapter 2:

`SimpleIO.prompt`—Requires a string argument, which it displays on the screen as a prompt for the user to enter input.

`SimpleIO.readLine`—Returns a line of input entered by the user.

`Convert.toDouble`—Requires a string argument containing a number. Returns the value of the string as a `double`.

`Integer.parseInt`—Requires a string argument containing an integer. Returns the value of the string as an `int`.

`Math.abs`, `Math.max`, `Math.min`, `Math.pow`, `Math.round`, and `Math.sqrt`—Require one or two numeric arguments and return a number.

Although these methods perform a variety of tasks, they have one thing in common: they don't require access to an object's instance variables in order to do their jobs.

Class methods have several uses:

- *To provide a service to other classes.* Some class methods exist solely to provide a service to other classes. The methods that we encountered in Chapter 2 fall into this category, as do many other methods in the Java API. Methods in this category are declared `public` so that they can be called by methods in other classes.

- *To help other methods in the same class.* Section 7.7 shows how to write "helper" methods whose job is to provide assistance to other methods in the same class. Helper methods should be declared `private`, because they're not designed for use outside a single class.

- *To provide access to hidden class variables.* Some classes store data in class variables that are hidden inside the class. The only way for a method in a different class to determine the value of such a variable or to change its value is to call a class method that has permission to access the variable. (We'll have more to say about class variables in Section 7.5.) Methods in this category are declared `public`.

Class methods have another important purpose: to specify where a program begins execution. As we've seen already, every Java application must have a `main` method. `main` is a class method, so every Java application has at least one class method. Java requires that `main` be declared `public`.

Class methods play an important role in Java. A great many classes in the Java API provide class methods, including `Math`, `System`, and `String`. Let's take a closer look at these classes.

Example: The `Math` Class

Section 2.9 discussed six class methods that belong to the `Math` class, including `Math.pow` and `Math.sqrt`. This class contains other class methods in addition to these. In fact, *every* method in `Math` is a class method.

The `Math` class contains no instance variables and no instance methods; it's nothing more than a repository for mathematical functions (in the form of class methods) and mathematical constants. Having these constants and methods contained within a single class is convenient; when we need a mathematical constant or method, we know that the `Math` class is likely to have it.

Classes such as `Math` are used differently from the kind of classes that we discussed in Chapter 3. `Math` has no instance variables, so there's no point in creating instances of `Math`. A class from which objects can be created (such as the `Account` class) is said to be ***instantiable,*** because we can create instances of it. The `Math` class, on the other hand, is not instantiable. A class that is not instantiable exists solely as a haven for class variables and class methods.

Example: The `System` Class

System.exit The `System` class contains a number of class methods, including `exit`, which causes program termination. Here's how `System.exit` is called:

```
System.exit(0);
```

This method requires a single argument of type `int`, representing a status code that can be tested after program termination. By convention, 0 indicates normal termination. Any other value (–1 is a popular choice) indicates abnormal termination.

Calling `System.exit` is a more drastic way to terminate a program than simply returning from the `main` method. For example, if a program displays a frame on the screen, the program will not terminate until the frame is closed, even if `main` has completed execution. On the other hand, calling `System.exit` causes immediate program termination; any frames that are visible on the screen will be closed.

The `System` class, like the `Math` class, can't be instantiated. It's nothing more than a collection of class variables and methods related to the user's computer system.

Example: The `String` Class

String.valueOf Java's `String` class contains several overloaded class methods named `valueOf` that convert different types of data to string form. These methods don't operate on an existing `String` object; instead, they create a new `String` object and return it. Here are a couple of examples:

```
String intString = String.valueOf(607);
String doubleString = String.valueOf(4.5);
```

The value of `intString` will be `"607"` and the value of `doubleString` will be `"4.5"`.

   `String` is an example of a class that contains both instance methods *and* class methods. To keep things simple, I'll wait until Chapter 10 before designing a class that has both kinds of methods. Until then, my classes will be either instantiable (with instance variables and instance methods only) or not instantiable (with class variables and class methods only).

Summary

In this section, we've discussed both instance methods and class methods. Here's a summary of the differences between the two:

Instance Methods	*Class Methods*
■ Perform an operation on an object.	■ Do not perform an operation on an object.
■ Are called by an object.	■ Are not called by an object.
■ Have access to instance variables inside the calling object.	■ Do not have access to instance variables.

Review Questions

1. Which one of the following classes has class methods but no instance methods: (a) `FontMetrics`, (b) `Graphics`, (c) `Math`, or (d) `String`?

2. Which one of the following is *not* a class method: (a) `readLine` (`SimpleIO` class), (b) `indexOf` (`String` class), (c) `valueOf` (`String` class), or (d) `abs` (`Math` class)?

3. True or false: A class method has access to the instance variables in its class.

4. Suppose that a program contains the following statement:
   ```
   x = Foo.bar(y);
   ```
   Is `bar` more likely to be an instance method or a class method? Why?

7.2   Writing Class Methods

Q&A   Writing a class method is similar to writing an instance method. The primary difference is that the declaration of a class method must contain the word `static`, which tells the compiler that this is a class method and not an instance method. (Now you see why class methods are also known as static methods.)

The declaration of a class method consists of an optional access modifier, the word `static`, a result type, the method's name, the parameters (if any), and the body (a series of statements to be executed when the method is called). The `main` method itself has this form:

```
access                result              beginning
modifier              type  name    parameter  of body
  |                    |     |           |       |
public static void main(String[] args) {
  ...
}        indicates
  |      class method
end of body
```

Java requires that `main`'s result type be `void` and that `main` have one parameter of type `String[]` (array of `String` objects). Other class methods may have any number of parameters, including none. If a method has more than one parameter, each parameter except the last must be followed by a comma.

Java requires that the `main` method be declared `public`. Other class methods can be declared either `public` or `private`. We'll have to use `public` for any method that will need to be called outside its class. However, if a method is used only within its own class, it's best to use `private` instead. That way, we'll be able to modify the method in the future without having to worry about how the changes might affect other classes. For the rest of this chapter, all our class methods will be private. Starting with Chapter 10, we'll begin to make some class methods public.

> Class methods that are intended for use within a single class should be declared `private`. Class methods that are intended for use by other classes should be declared `public`.

Example: A Termination Method

When a program encounters an error condition, it may need to notify the user and terminate. To accomplish this task, we could use the following two statements:

```
System.out.println("Invalid input; consult manual.");
System.exit(-1);  // Terminate abnormally
```

Because these statements might appear many times in a program, with only minor changes (different messages to the user), it makes sense to put them into a class method. Here's how the method might be declared:

```
private static void terminate(String message) {
  System.out.println(message);
  System.exit(-1);   // Terminate abnormally
}
```

The message to be displayed is a parameter, allowing the method to display a different message each time it's called. The method is declared `private`, so it can be called only within the class to which it belongs. A call of `terminate` would have the following appearance:

```
terminate("Invalid input; consult manual.");
```

Because this call will be in the same class as the method itself, there's no need to mention the class name in the call.

Local Variables

In previous chapters, we've seen that variables can be declared inside the `main` method. In fact, Java allows all class methods—and instance methods as well—to declare variables. Variables declared within the body of a method are called *local variables.*

Local variables have the following properties:

- A local variable can be accessed only within the method that contains its declaration. Other methods cannot access the variable, although they are allowed to declare other variables with the same name.

- When a method returns, its local variables no longer exist, so their values are lost. When the method is called the next time, its local variables come into existence again, but without their old values.

- A method is not allowed to access the value stored in one of its local variables until the variable has been initialized. The Java compiler will check to make sure that each local variable has been assigned a value before an attempt is made to access the value of that variable. If the compiler can't verify that the variable has been initialized, you'll get a compilation error.

- A local variable can be declared `final` to indicate that its value doesn't change after initialization.

Review Questions

1. What keyword is used in Java to distinguish a class method from an instance method?

2. Class methods that are intended for use within a single class should be declared (a) `public`, (b) `private`, or (c) neither?

3. Variables that are declared within a method are known as _____ variables.

4. If a variable is declared within a method, how long will it continue to store a value that has been assigned to it?

7.3 The `return` Statement

When a method has a result type other than `void`, it must use the `return` statement to specify what value it returns. The `return` statement has the form

`return` statement

return *expression* ;

The expression is often just a literal or a variable:

```
return 0;
return n;
```

Expressions containing operators are also allowed:

```
return x * x - 2 * x + 1;
```

For example, the following class method computes the value of the polynomial $x^2 - 2x + 1$ each time it's called:

```
private static double poly(double x) {
   return x * x - 2 * x + 1;
}
```

We could have stored the value of the polynomial in a local variable first:

```
private static double poly(double x) {
   double y = x * x - 2 * x + 1;
   return y;
}
```

Using a local variable in this way doesn't cause any harm, but it makes the method longer. It's usually best to avoid variables that are assigned a value only once and then used in a `return` statement.

When you write a method that returns a result, make sure that there's no way to leave the method without executing a `return` statement. Be especially careful with cascaded `if` statements. Suppose, for example, that the body of a method consists entirely of the following cascaded `if` statement:

```
if (n > 0)
   return +1;
else if (n < 0)
   return -1;
```

Unfortunately, the method returns nothing if n is equal to 0. The Java compiler will detect this problem and issue an error message. To fix the problem, either add an `else` clause that returns a value, or put a separate `return` statement at the end of the method to guarantee that some value is returned.

We can use `return` statements even in methods whose result type is `void`. In those methods, however, the expression after the word `return` must be omitted:

```
return;
```

A `return` statement of this form provides a way to return from a method before it has executed all the statements in its body.

Example: A Dollar-Formatting Method

Programs that deal with money will often need to format monetary amounts according to local custom. In the United States, monetary amounts are normally displayed in the form *dollars.cents*, where *cents* is a two-digit number between 00 and 99. If we use a `double` variable to store a dollar amount and then simply print the variable using `System.out.print` or `System.out.println`, we won't always get the desired formatting: 10.50 will display as `10.5` and 10000000.00 will be printed as `1.0E7`. Moreover, amounts won't be rounded to cents, so we may end up printing values such as `10.50001`.

The Java API provides methods for formatting numbers, but let's pretend they don't exist and write our own instead. Here's the strategy we'll use to convert a dollar amount to a string that's suitable for printing:

1. Multiply the amount by 100 and round to the nearest integer (call this `roundedAmount`). `roundedAmount` will be the same as the original amount, except that it's expressed in cents and rounded to the nearest cent.
2. Determine the number of dollars (`roundedAmount` divided by 100) and the number of cents (the remainder when `roundedAmount` is divided by 100).
3. Build a string consisting of the number of dollars, a period, and the number of cents. If the number of cents is a single-digit number, put a zero between the period and the number of cents.

Here's what the finished method might look like:

```
private static String formatAsMoney(double amount) {
  long roundedAmount = Math.round(amount * 100);
  long dollars = roundedAmount / 100;
  long cents = roundedAmount % 100;

  String result;
  if (cents <= 9)
    result = dollars + ".0" + cents;
  else
    result = dollars + "." + cents;
  return result;
}
```

Note that the `roundedAmount`, `dollars`, and `cents` variables have type `long` instead of `int`, because the `Math.round` method returns a `long` value.

long type ►*9.2* `long` is similar to `int` but allows numbers to be much larger. I've used a variable named `result` to store the finished string, which is then returned by the `return` statement at the end of the method. Actually, we don't need the `result` variable. We can simplify `formatAsMoney` by replacing the `if` statement and the `return` statement with the following statement:

```
if (cents <= 9)
  return dollars + ".0" + cents;
else
  return dollars + "." + cents;
```

Once we've made this change, the declaration of `result` can be removed.

The `formatAsMoney` method might be called in the following way:

```
String formattedAmount = formatAsMoney(dollarAmount);
```

where `dollarAmount` is a `double` variable. Or we might choose to use the value returned by `formatAsMoney` without first storing it in a variable. For example, we could print the value returned by `formatAsMoney` by putting the method call inside a call of `System.out.println`:

```
System.out.println("$" + formatAsMoney(dollarAmount));
```

Conditional Expressions

Let's take another look at the `if` statement in the `formatAsMoney` method:

```
if (cents <= 9)
  return dollars + ".0" + cents;
else
  return dollars + "." + cents;
```

The two `return` statements are nearly identical, which suggests that there might be a way to simplify the code. Java has an operator that's often handy in such situations. The **conditional operator** is similar to Java's `if` statement: it tests a condition and performs one of two actions, depending on the outcome of the test. The difference is that the conditional operator produces a value (unlike an `if` statement, which doesn't). This property gives the conditional operator greater flexibility than the `if` statement.

The conditional operator consists of the symbols ? and :, which must be used together in the following way:

conditional expression

> *expr1* ? *expr2* : *expr3*

expr1 must be a `boolean` expression; *expr2* and *expr3* are normally expressions of the same type (both `int` or both `String`, for example). The resulting expression is said to be a **conditional expression**. The conditional operator is unique among Java operators in that it requires three operands instead of one or two; we say that it's a ***ternary*** operator.

The conditional expression *expr1* ? *expr2* : *expr3* should be read "if *expr1* then *expr2* else *expr3*." The expression is evaluated in stages: *expr1* is evaluated first; if its value is `true`, then *expr2* is evaluated, and its value is the value of the entire conditional. If the value of *expr1* is `false`, then the value of *expr3* is the value of the entire conditional.

Using the conditional operator, we can replace the `if` statement in the `formatAsMoney` method by the following `return` statement:

```
return (cents <= 9) ? (dollars + ".0" + cents) :
                      (dollars + "." + cents);
```

The parentheses aren't required; I added them for clarity. We could even condense the `return` statement further:

```
return dollars + (cents <= 9 ? ".0" : ".") + cents;
```

Here the parentheses are mandatory, because the + operator takes precedence over the conditional operator. In fact, the conditional operator has lower precedence than all other operators, with the exception of the assignment operators.

The conditional operator isn't used that much in Java. `return` statements are one of the few places where conditional expressions are often found. Occasionally a conditional expression is useful inside a call of `System.out.print` or `System.out.println`. For example, instead of writing

```
if (isLeapYear)
  System.out.println("February has 29 days");
else
  System.out.println("February has 28 days");
```

we could simply write

```
System.out.println("February has " +
                   (isLeapYear ? 29 : 28) + " days");
```

Java itself places few restrictions on the use of the conditional expression. As a rule, a conditional expression can be used just like any other kind of expression. For example, a conditional expression can appear on the right side of an assignment. Consider the following example:

```
int i = 1;
int j = 2;
int m = i > j ? i : j;         // m is 2
int n = (i >= 0 ? i : 0) + j;  // n is 3
```

In the declaration of m, the `i > j` comparison fails, so the value of the conditional expression `i > j ? i : j` is 2. In the declaration of n, the `i >= 0` comparison succeeds; the conditional expression `(i >= 0 ? i : 0)` has the value 1, which is then added to `j` to produce 3.

Review Questions

1. True or false: A method that returns nothing (whose result type is `void`) cannot contain a `return` statement.

2. The conditional operator has three operands, which makes it a _____ operator.

3. In what type of statement are conditional expressions most likely to appear?

7.4 Parameters

We saw in Chapter 3 that a method is allowed to have parameters, which represent values that will be supplied when the method is called. The values actually supplied to the method at the time of the call are said to be arguments. In this section, we'll examine some of the issues that arise when parameters are used. These issues are relevant to both instance methods and class methods.

How Arguments Are Passed

When a method is called, it is supplied with *copies* of the arguments that appear in the method call. (We say that the arguments are passed *by value,* because the *value* of each argument is given to the called method.) To understand what a "copy" is, though, we need to remember how variables are stored.

An object variable contains a *reference* to an object, not the object itself. For this reason, classes are said to be *reference types.* (Arrays are treated as objects in Java, so array types are also reference types.) All other types—including `boolean`, `char`, `double`, and `int`—are said to be *primitive types.* With this distinction in mind, let's see what happens when an argument is passed to a method:

- *Primitive type.* The value of the argument is copied into the corresponding parameter. For example, if the argument is the number 5, that value is copied into the parameter, which now has the value 5. There are two copies of the number 5: the original (stored in the argument) and the copy (stored in the parameter).

- *Reference type.* The value of the argument—a reference—is copied into the parameter. In other words, passing an object as an argument doesn't create a new copy of the object; instead, a new reference is created, but it points to the old object. We're still passing by value, but in this case the value happens to be a reference.

What happens when we change the value of a parameter? That depends. Assigning an entirely new value to a parameter is legal but has no effect on the corresponding argument. On the other hand, if the parameter refers to an object, then changes made to that object—for example, by calling a method that modifies the object—*will* be reflected in the argument. To see the difference, let's look at a couple of examples.

Example 1: Assigning a new value to a parameter. Consider the following class method, which writes a line consisting of stars (asterisks):

```
private static void printStars(int numStars) {
  while (numStars-- > 0)
    System.out.print('*');
  System.out.println();
}
```

Suppose that we execute the following statements, which contain a call of printStars:

```
int n = 30;
System.out.println("Value of n before call: " + n);
printStars(n);
System.out.println("Value of n after call: " + n);
```

The output will be

```
Value of n before call: 30
*****************************
Value of n after call: 30
```

Calling printStars had no effect on n. When printStars was called, the value of n was copied into the numStars parameter:

```
n    | 30 |

numStars | 30 |
```

Because numStars was merely a copy of n, decrementing numStars didn't change n. At the end of the method call, here's what n and numStars look like:

```
n    | 30 |

numStars | 0 |
```

Example 2: Modifying an object passed as an argument. The second example relies on the Account class of Section 3.3:

```
private static void transferBalance(Account oldAccount,
                                    Account newAccount) {
  newAccount.deposit(oldAccount.getBalance());
  oldAccount.close();
}
```

This method transfers the balance in oldAccount to newAccount, then closes oldAccount. The calls of deposit and close don't change the values of oldAccount and newAccount (they still refer to the same Account objects).

They do, however, change the *state* of the Account objects that oldAccount and newAccount represent.

To see how transferBalance works, let's assume that acct1 and acct2 are variables declared as follows:

```
Account acct1 = new Account(1000.00);
Account acct2 = new Account(500.00);
```

Here's how we would visualize acct1 and acct2:

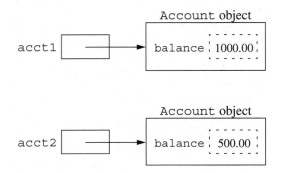

acct1 refers to an Account object whose balance variable stores 1000.00, and acct2 refers to an Account object whose balance variable stores 500.00. Now, let's execute the following statement:

```
transferBalance(acct1, acct2);
```

As the method begins to execute, acct1 is copied into the oldAccount parameter, and acct2 is copied into the newAccount parameter, giving us the following picture:

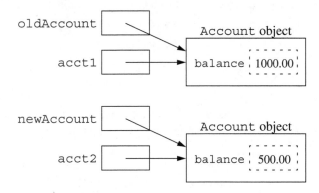

Because acct1 is a reference to an object, copying acct1 into oldAccount causes oldAccount to refer to the same object as acct1; no new object is created. Similarly, newAccount refers to the same object as acct2. Now the transferBalance method begins to execute. The first step is to execute the call `oldAccount.getBalance()`, which returns the value 1000.00. Next, this value is added to the balance stored in the `newAccount` object, causing its balance to increase to 1500.00. Finally, `oldAccount.close()` is executed, causing the balance in the `oldAccount` object to be set to zero. Here's the picture now:

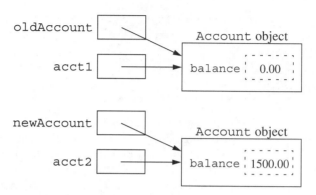

The call of `transferBalance` ended up changing the state of both the `acct1` and `acct2` objects.

Array Parameters

Passing arrays to methods is very much like passing objects. (This shouldn't be too surprising, because we saw in Section 5.7 that arrays actually *are* objects in Java.)

For example, suppose that we want to write a method named `findString` that searches an array of strings to see if it contains a particular string as one of its elements. One of the method's parameters will be the array to be searched. The other parameter will be the search key—the string that we're trying to locate. If it finds the key in the array, `findString` will return the key's position. If `findString` fails to find the key, it will return a number that can't possibly be an array index (−1 is the customary choice). Here's what the method will look like:

```
private static int findString(String[] strings, String key) {
   for (int i = 0; i < strings.length; i++)
      if (strings[i].equals(key))
         return i;
   return -1;
}
```

Notice that the argument supplied to `findString` can be any array of strings, no matter how long. The expression `strings.length` allows the method to determine the length of the argument. Each time `findString` is called, the value of `strings.length` could be different.

When an array is passed to a method, only a reference to the array is copied, just as a reference to an object is copied when an object is passed to a method. This fact has two important consequences. First, it means that passing an array to a method takes very little time, even when the array is huge. Second, it means that a method can modify the elements of any array passed to it, just as a method can change the state of an object passed to it. For example, the following method will assign zero to the elements of an array passed to it:

```
private static void setElementsToZero(int[] a) {
  for (int i = 0; i < a.length; i++)
    a[i] = 0;
}
```

Program Arguments

The `main` method has one parameter, an array of strings. We're now in a position to discuss what this parameter represents and what its uses might be.

In many operating systems, including Windows and Unix, the user can launch programs from a command line. (In Windows, we need to open a DOS window in order to run programs this way.) For example, to compile a program named `MyProgram`, we would launch the Java compiler by entering the following command:

```
javac MyProgram.java
```

The program that we're running is named `javac`, and the file that it's compiling is named `MyProgram.java`. Clearly, the compiler is obtaining the file name from the command line.

Some programs have *switches* or *options* that can be specified on the command line to affect the program's behavior. These usually begin with a distinctive character, such as - or /, so that the program won't confuse them with file names or other data. The programs in the Java Development Kit have many such options. `javac`, for example, has a `-O` option, which causes it to "optimize" a program for better performance. If we want this option, we would run the compiler as follows:

```
javac -O MyProgram.java
```

We'll use the term ***program arguments*** (or ***command-line arguments***) to refer to any data supplied by the user on the command line (not including the name of the program itself). Command-line arguments don't have to be options or file names, although in practice they usually are.

Our own programs are allowed to access command-line arguments supplied by the user. Doing so is easy. The `main` method is required to have a single parameter, which is customarily named `args`:

```
public static void main(String[] args) { ... }
```

Every time the program is executed, `args` will automatically contain the program's command-line arguments. `args` is an array of `String` objects, with each array element containing a single command-line argument. For example, suppose that `CopyFile` is a Java program that's been launched using the following command:

```
java CopyFile MyProgram.java MyProgram2.java
```

Inside `CopyFile`'s main method, the value of `args[0]` will be the string `"MyProgram.java"`. The value of `args[1]` will be `"MyProgram2.java"`. Notice that `"java"` and `"CopyFile"` aren't included in `args`.

There's nothing magical about the name `args` (short for "arguments"). You can choose any name you like, although `args` is the name used by most Java programmers. (`argv`—"argument vector"—is another popular choice.) Also, the square brackets can go after `args` instead of after `String`:

```
public static void main(String args[]) { … }
```

As we saw in Section 5.1, `String args[]` is equivalent to `String[] args`.

Because `args` is an array, we can easily determine the number of command-line arguments by writing `args.length`. Typically, a program will use a loop to examine and process the command-line arguments. The loop will be controlled by a counter that starts at 0 and stops at `args.length`, as in the program that follows.

PROGRAM ## Printing Command-Line Arguments

The following program prints each command-line argument on a line by itself:

PrintArgs.java

```
1  // Prints command-line arguments on separate lines
2
3  public class PrintArgs {
4    public static void main(String[] args) {
5      for (int i = 0; i < args.length; i++)
6        System.out.println(args[i]);
7    }
8  }
```

Suppose that we test the `PrintArgs` program as follows:

```
java PrintArgs Java rules
```

Here's what the program's output will be:

```
Java
rules
```

Review Questions

1. Arguments are passed by _____ in Java.

2. True or false: A method can change the elements of an array passed to it as an argument.

3.   How can a method determine the length of an array parameter named a?

4.   Data items supplied by the user on the command line are known as _____ _____ [two words].

7.5   Class Variables

In Chapter 3, we saw that objects store their state in instance variables. Every object has its own set of these variables. For example, every instance of the Fraction class contains its own copies of the numerator and denominator variables. Java doesn't require that all variables be stored in objects, however. Variables that belong to a class, but not to any particular *instance* of a class, are called ***class variables.*** (Some books use the terms ***static variables*** or ***static fields*** instead). Class variables are stored only once in the entire program, unlike instance variables, which are stored in individual objects.

Declaring Class Variables

Declarations of class variables look like declarations of instance variables, except that the word static is inserted between the access modifier (if present) and the type of the variable. Here are two examples of class variable declarations:

```
public static int numAccounts;
private static int windowHeight;
```

Variables that are declared public are accessible outside the class; variables declared private are hidden inside the class.

To use a public class variable outside its class, we must write the name of the class, followed by a dot, followed by the name of the variable. For example, if the numAccounts variable were declared in a class named Account, we could write

```
int accountsOpen = Account.numAccounts;
```

Within the class in which it's declared, a class variable can be accessed directly, without a class name or dot. For example, within the Account class, we could write

```
numAccounts++;
```

A private class variable can be accessed only within its own class, so the class name and dot aren't needed:

```
windowHeight = 200;
```

Uses for Class Variables

There are several common uses for class variables:

- **As global variables.** A *global variable* is a variable that can be used by any method in any class. (The term "global variable" is actually a relative term—any variable that can be shared by more than one method is "global" to those methods. In this section, however, I'll use the term only to refer to variables that are global to all methods in all classes.) In Java, class variables that have been declared `public` are global variables.

- **As constants.** In Section 2.8, we saw how to turn a local variable into a constant by adding the word `final` to its declaration. The same technique can turn a class variable into a constant. A constant declared as a class variable can be accessed by all the methods in a class and—if it is declared `public`—by methods in other classes as well.

- **To store data for class methods.** When a class method needs to store data for a long period of time, it must use a class variable. (Keep in mind that class methods don't have access to instance variables.) Also, when class methods need to share variables, those variables must be class variables.

(Class variables can also be used by instance methods, but we'll save that discussion for Chapter 10.) Let's look at each of these uses in turn.

Using Class Variables as Global Variables

Class variables are useful when a variable needs to be available to all classes in a program. In Java, there's no way to declare a variable that exists "outside" the classes in a program. Instead, a variable that must be universally available is put into some class (presumably one that's somehow related to the variable) and declared to be a public class variable.

> Well-designed programs have few global variables, and preferably none at all. Global variables make programs harder to test and harder to modify, so it's usually best to avoid them.

Actually, we've been using global variables ever since Chapter 2: every call of `System.out.print` or `System.out.println` involves a global variable. Let's take a closer look at the `System` class and its class variables.

Class Variables in the `System` Class

Inside the `System` class are three class variables, named `in`, `out`, and `err`. These variables are all public, which means that we can access them by writing

`System.in`, `System.out`, and `System.err`. Each variable represents a *stream*—a source of input or a destination for output.

- `System.in` represents the ***standard input stream***—the primary source of input for a Java program. By default, the standard input stream is attached to the user's keyboard. The `SimpleIO.readLine` method reads input from `System.in`.

- `System.out` represents the ***standard output stream.*** By default, data written to `System.out` is displayed in the window in which we started the program.

- `System.err` represents the ***standard error stream,*** which is a convenient place to write error messages. By default, data written to `System.err` is displayed in the same window as data written to `System.out`.

Operating systems often allow the user to ***redirect*** the standard streams. In Windows or Unix, for example, we can redirect the standard input stream so that data comes from a file instead of from the keyboard. Here's the command to use:

```
java MyProgram <myInputFile
```

This command tells the Java interpreter to execute the program named `MyProgram`, obtaining input from the file named `myInputFile`. (You can use any file name that you like, but the file must exist.) Likewise, the output of a program can be sent to a file, instead of having it displayed on the screen:

```
java MyProgram >myOutputFile
```

The output of the program will go into a file named `myOutputFile`. (The file will be created if it doesn't already exist.) It's even possible to have a program read from one file and write to another:

```
java MyProgram <myInputFile >myOutputFile
```

Because of redirection, writing error messages to `System.out` is a dicey proposition. If the user chooses to redirect the program's output to a file, error messages written to `System.out` won't appear on the screen, and the user may incorrectly assume that the program worked. By writing error messages to `System.err` instead, we can guarantee that they'll appear on the screen, because redirecting `System.out` has no effect on `System.err`. Writing to `System.err` is similar to writing to `System.out`:

```
System.err.println("Invalid data encountered");
```

`System.out` and `System.err` are instances of a class named `Print-Stream`, which provides the `print` and `println` methods. Armed with this knowledge, let's dissect a typical call of `System.out.println`:

```
System.out.println("Java rules!");
```

`System` is the name of a class. `System.out` is a class variable; it represents an instance of the `PrintStream` class. This object is invoking `println`, which is one of the instance methods in the `PrintStream` class.

Using Class Variables as Constants

Class variables are often used as constants. To turn a class variable into a constant, all we have to do is include the word `final` in its declaration.

Examples of class variables used as constants abound in the Java API. For example, Java's `Math` class contains declarations of two class variables, `E` and `PI`, both of which are `final`:

```java
public class Math {
  public static final double E = 2.7182818284590452354;
  public static final double PI = 3.14159265358979323846;
  ...
}
```

To use `E` and `PI`, we would write `Math.E` and `Math.PI`. Other examples can be found in the `Color` class (`Color.white`, `Color.black`, and so on), in the `Font` class (`Font.PLAIN`, `Font.BOLD`, and `Font.ITALIC`), and in many other classes. Most of the classes in the API follow our convention of using all uppercase letters for names of constants. (Unfortunately, some classes—including `Color`—do not.)

Like all class variables, constants can be declared `public` or `private`. Constants that are to be used by other classes—such as `E` and `PI`—must be declared `public`.

> Constants that are to be used within a single class should be declared `private` rather than `public`.

Using Class Variables to Store Data for Class Methods

We saw in Section 7.2 that local variables can only be used as long as the method to which they belong is executing. When the method returns, its local variables no longer exist. If a class method needs to store data where it will be safe after the method returns, it must use a class variable instead of a local variable.

Class variables are also used for sharing data among class methods in a class, because all methods in the class have access to its class variables. In the next section, we'll design a program in which two class methods share a class variable.

> Class variables that store data for class methods should be declared `private`.

Summary

The properties of class variables are different from those of instance variables and local variables. Here's a summary of the major differences:

Instance Variables	*Class Variables*	*Local Variables*
■ Declared in a class.	■ Declared in a class.	■ Declared in a method.
■ Created when an instance of the class is created.	■ Created when program begins to execute.	■ Created when method is called.
■ Retain values as long as object exists.	■ Retain values until program terminates.	■ Retain values until method returns.
■ Access controlled by `public` and `private`.	■ Access controlled by `public` and `private`.	■ Access limited to method in which declared.

Review Questions

1. Class variables are also known as _____ variables.

2. List three uses for class variables.

3. In order for a class variable to be global across a program that consists of more than one class, its declaration must contain the _____ keyword.

4. What are the names of the class variables that represent the standard streams?

7.6   Adding Class Variables and Methods to a Class

So far our programs have consisted of a single class method (the `main` method), giving them the following overall appearance:

```
public class class-name {
  public static void main(String[] args) {
    ...
  }
}
```

If we add class variables and methods to a program, it will now have the form

```
public class class-name {
  declarations of class variables
```

```
public static void main(String[] args) {
   ...
}
```

   declarations of class methods
```
}
```

My convention is to put declarations of class variables first, followed by the declaration of the `main` method, followed by declarations of other class methods. Java doesn't require this particular order, however.

Example: Modifying the `DisplayText` Program

To illustrate class variables and methods, let's add a class variable and a class method to the `DisplayText` program from Section 6.3. Here's the original program:

DisplayText.java

```
1   // Displays text in three different colors and styles
2
3   import java.awt.*;
4   import jpb.*;
5
6   public class DisplayText {
7     public static void main(String[] args) {
8       // Create drawable frame
9       DrawableFrame df = new DrawableFrame("Display Text");
10      df.show();
11      df.setSize(210, 85);
12
13      // Obtain graphics context
14      Graphics g = df.getGraphicsContext();
15
16      // Display "Monospaced Bold"
17      g.setColor(Color.red);
18      g.setFont(new Font("Monospaced", Font.BOLD, 20));
19      g.drawString("Monospaced Bold", 15, 25);
20
21      // Display "SansSerif Italic"
22      g.setColor(Color.green);
23      g.setFont(new Font("SansSerif", Font.ITALIC, 20));
24      g.drawString("SansSerif Italic", 15, 50);
25
26      // Display "Serif Plain"
27      g.setColor(Color.blue);
28      g.setFont(new Font("Serif", Font.PLAIN, 20));
29      g.drawString("Serif Plain", 15, 75);
30
31      // Repaint frame
32      df.repaint();
33    }
34  }
```

The similarity between lines 17–19, 22–24, and 27–29 suggests that we can write a single method to perform the setColor/setFont/drawString steps. Let's name this method displayFont.

The first step in designing the displayFont method is to determine what parameters it will need. The secret is to look for differences between the groups of statements. In most cases, the method will need one parameter for each difference. Here the differences are the drawing color, the font name, the font style, the string to be displayed, and the *y* coordinate of the string's baseline.

Next, we check to see if the method will need to return a result. Usually we can just check to see if any of the variables in the program are assigned new values as the statements are executed. In this example, the statements don't assign values to any program variables, so we won't need for displayFont to return a result.

Here's what the displayFont method will look like:

```
private static void displayFont(Color c, String fontName,
                                int fontStyle,
                                String message, int y) {
  g.setColor(c);
  g.setFont(new Font(fontName, fontStyle, 20));
  g.drawString(message, 15, y);
}
```

There's just one problem with this method. displayFont uses the variable g, which is declared in main. Variables declared inside a method are local to that method, which means that other methods don't have access to them. There are two ways to allow displayFont to use the graphics context that g represents. One technique is to add a Graphics parameter to displayFont. We would then have main supply g as the matching argument in each call of displayFont. The other technique is to move the declaration of g so that it becomes available to both main and displayFont—in other words, declare g as a class variable rather than a local variable. Let's adopt the latter technique—not because it's necessarily better, but because it will give us a chance to use a class variable.

Here's the modified program, with g declared as a class variable and displayFont declared as a class method. The declarations of g and displayFont are in **bold.**

DisplayText2.java

```
1   // Displays text in three different colors and styles
2
3   import java.awt.*;
4   import jpb.*;
5
6   public class DisplayText2 {
7     private static Graphics g;   // Class variable
8
9     public static void main(String[] args) {
10        // Create drawable frame
11        DrawableFrame df = new DrawableFrame("Display Text");
12        df.show();
13        df.setSize(210, 85);
14
```

```
15        // Obtain graphics context
16        g = df.getGraphicsContext();
17
18        // Display "Monospaced Bold"
19        displayFont(Color.red, "Monospaced", Font.BOLD,
20                    "Monospaced Bold", 25);
21
22        // Display "SansSerif Italic"
23        displayFont(Color.green, "SansSerif", Font.ITALIC,
24                    "SansSerif Italic", 50);
25
26        // Display "Serif Plain"
27        displayFont(Color.blue, "Serif", Font.PLAIN,
28                    "Serif Plain", 75);
29
30        // Repaint frame
31        df.repaint();
32    }
33
34    private static void displayFont(Color c, String fontName,
35                                    int fontStyle,
36                                    String message, int y) {
37        g.setColor(c);
38        g.setFont(new Font(fontName, fontStyle, 20));
39        g.drawString(message, 15, y);
40    }
41 }
```

Review Questions

1. True or false: In a class definition, declarations of class variables must come before declarations of class methods.

2. True or false: `main` must be the first method in a class definition.

7.7   Writing Helper Methods

So far, we've been putting all the code for a program into `main`, which isn't good practice if the program is more than a few lines long. It's better to parcel out some of the work that `main` would otherwise have to do, delegating portions of its responsibilities to smaller, more specialized methods. We'll call these **helper methods.** In general, a helper method is any method whose job is to assist another method, not necessarily the `main` method.

A helper for a class method such as `main` must be another class method, because class methods aren't allowed to call instance methods in the same class. Instance methods can have helpers as well. A helper for an instance method can be either an instance method or a class method. Section 10.3 explores helpers for instance methods.

Using helper methods has two primary advantages:

- ***Greater clarity.*** The structure of the program will be clearer, with a much shorter version of `main` providing an overview of how the program works and the other methods filling in the details.

- ***Less redundancy.*** Instead of repeating a block of code over and over with little or no change, we can move this code into a method and then call the method as many times as needed.

To see the advantages of helper methods, let's return to the case study of Section 2.11. In that section, we developed a program named `CourseAverage` that computes a student's course average. The `CourseAverage` program suffers from a great deal of repetitive code. By moving this code to class methods, we'll be able to shorten the program while simultaneously making it more understandable and easier to modify.

Improving Clarity

Here's the original design of `CourseAverage`:

1. Print the introductory message ("Welcome to the CSc 2310 average calculation program").
2. Prompt the user to enter eight program scores.
3. Compute the program average from the eight scores.
4. Prompt the user to enter five quiz scores.
5. Compute the quiz average from the five scores.
6. Prompt the user to enter scores on the tests and final exam.
7. Compute the course average from the program average, quiz average, test scores, and final exam score.
8. Round the course average to the nearest integer and display it.

Looking at this design, we see that most of the steps are fairly small, with the exception of steps 2 and 4. That suggests that we write helper methods to handle those steps. Let's name these methods `readProgramScores` and `readQuiz-Scores`. Each method computes a single number (the sum of the program scores or the sum of the quiz scores), so we'll declare the result type of each to be `double`. Here's what the methods will look like:

```
private static double readProgramScores() {
    ...
}

private static double readQuizScores() {
    ...
}
```

Neither method will need any parameters.

Reducing Redundancy

readProgramScores will consist of eight steps (one for each program score). Each step involves prompting the user to enter a number, reading the number as a string, and then converting the string to numeric form. Because the eight steps are nearly identical, it makes sense to write another helper method (let's name it readDouble) that performs a prompt/read/convert step for a single program score. The readQuizScores method will perform five prompt/read/convert steps. If we play our cards right, we should be able to use readDouble to help us write readQuizScores as well.

In the original CourseAverage program, a single prompt/read/convert step consists of statements such as the following:

```
SimpleIO.prompt("Enter Program 1 score: ");
String userInput = SimpleIO.readLine();
double program1 = Convert.toDouble(userInput);
```

The only difference between these statements and other, similar groups elsewhere in the program is the prompt ("Enter Program 1 score: ") and the name of the variable to which the converted input is assigned (program1). This observation suggests that we should make the prompt string a parameter to readDouble (so that we can supply different prompts). It also suggests that readDouble should return the converted input, so that we can assign it to any variable that we choose. In other words, our plan is to replace the three statements in the prompt/read/convert step by a single method call:

```
program1 = readDouble("Enter Program 1 score: ");
```

Here's what the readDouble method will look like:

```
private static double readDouble(String prompt) {
  SimpleIO.prompt(prompt);
  String userInput = SimpleIO.readLine();
  return Convert.toDouble(userInput);
}
```

readDouble has a single parameter (prompt), representing the prompt to be displayed for the user. The user's input will be stored in a local variable named userInput. The last line in the body of readDouble is a return statement that calls Convert.toDouble to convert the user's input into a double value, then returns that value.

The Revised CourseAverage Program

Here's the revised CourseAverage program with the three class methods—readProgramScores, readQuizScores, and readDouble—added. I made several other changes to the program as well. I defined a number of class variables, which are used as constants. I also added loops to read the program scores and grades, and I used the `readDouble` method to help read the test scores and the final exam score.

CourseAverage2.java

```
 1  // Program name: CourseAverage2
 2  // Author: K. N. King
 3  // Written: 1998-04-21
 4  // Modified: 1999-04-18
 5  //
 6  // Prompts the user to enter eight program scores (0-20), five
 7  // quiz scores (0-10), two test scores (0-100), and a final
 8  // exam score (0-100). Scores may contain digits after the
 9  // decimal point. Input is not checked for validity. Displays
10  // the course average, computed using the following formula:
11  //
12  //     Programs      30%
13  //     Quizzes       10%
14  //     Test 1        15%
15  //     Test 2        15%
16  //     Final exam    30%
17  //
18  // The course average is rounded to the nearest integer.
19
20  import jpb.*;
21
22  public class CourseAverage2 {
23
24    // Constants
25    private static final int NUM_PROGRAMS = 8;
26    private static final int NUM_QUIZZES = 5;
27    private static final int MAX_PROG_SCORE = 20;
28    private static final int MAX_QUIZ_SCORE = 10;
29    private static final double PROGRAM_WEIGHT = .30;
30    private static final double QUIZ_WEIGHT = .10;
31    private static final double TEST_WEIGHT = .15;
32    private static final double FINAL_EXAM_WEIGHT = .30;
33
34    public static void main(String[] args) {
35      // Print the introductory message
36      System.out.println("Welcome to the CSc 2310 average " +
37                         "calculation program.\n");
38
39      // Prompt the user to enter program scores and compute
40      // the average of the scores
41      double programAverage = readProgramScores() / NUM_PROGRAMS;
42
43      // Leave a blank line
44      System.out.println();
45
46      // Prompt the user to enter quiz scores and compute the
47      // average of the scores
48      double quizAverage = readQuizScores() / NUM_QUIZZES;
49
```

```
50        // Leave a blank line
51        System.out.println();
52
53        // Prompt the user to enter scores on the tests and final
54        // exam
55        double test1 = readDouble("Enter Test 1 score: ");
56        double test2 = readDouble("Enter Test 2 score: ");
57        double finalExam = readDouble("Enter Final Exam score: ");
58
59        // Compute the course average from the program average,
60        // quiz average, test scores, and final exam score
61        double courseAverage =
62          PROGRAM_WEIGHT * (programAverage / MAX_PROG_SCORE * 100) +
63          QUIZ_WEIGHT * (quizAverage / MAX_QUIZ_SCORE * 100) +
64          TEST_WEIGHT * test1 +
65          TEST_WEIGHT * test2 +
66          FINAL_EXAM_WEIGHT * finalExam;
67
68        // Round the course average to the nearest integer and
69        // display it
70        System.out.println("\nCourse average: " +
71                             Math.round(courseAverage));
72    }
73
74    //////////////////////////////////////////////////////////////
75    // NAME:       readProgramScores
76    // BEHAVIOR:   Prompts the user to enter program scores
77    //             and computes their total.
78    // PARAMETERS: None
79    // RETURNS:    Total of program scores
80    //////////////////////////////////////////////////////////////
81    private static double readProgramScores() {
82      double programTotal = 0.0;
83      for (int i = 1; i <= NUM_PROGRAMS; i++)
84        programTotal += readDouble("Enter Program " + i +
85                                     " score: ");
86      return programTotal;
87    }
88
89    //////////////////////////////////////////////////////////////
90    // NAME:       readQuizScores
91    // BEHAVIOR:   Prompts the user to enter quiz scores and
92    //             computes their total.
93    // PARAMETERS: None
94    // RETURNS:    Total of quiz scores
95    //////////////////////////////////////////////////////////////
96    private static double readQuizScores() {
97      double quizTotal = 0.0;
98      for (int i = 1; i <= NUM_QUIZZES; i++)
99        quizTotal += readDouble("Enter Quiz " + i + " score: ");
100     return quizTotal;
101   }
102
```

```
103     /////////////////////////////////////////////////////
104     // NAME:       readDouble
105     // BEHAVIOR:   Prompts the user to enter a number, reads
106     //             the user's input, and converts it to double
107     //             form.
108     // PARAMETERS: prompt - the prompt to be displayed
109     // RETURNS:    User's input after conversion to double
110     /////////////////////////////////////////////////////
111     private static double readDouble(String prompt) {
112       SimpleIO.prompt(prompt);
113       String userInput = SimpleIO.readLine();
114       return Convert.toDouble(userInput);
115     }
116   }
```

Notice the comment block that precedes each of the three helper methods. This block gives the name of the method and describes what the method does. It includes a description of each parameter and what value (if any) the method returns. The line of slashes at the beginning and end of each comment block helps the reader see the breaks between methods. It also helps distinguish the comment block from the code for the method.

> Each method in a program—other than main—should be preceded by a comment block containing the name of the method and descriptions of what the method does, what parameters it requires (if any), and what value it returns (if any).

The comment block for a method shouldn't mention how the method is used in the program. There should be no discussion of where the method is called or what is done with the method's return value. A single method may be used more than once in a program, and it would be too difficult to document each use. Also, the program is likely to be modified in the future; we don't want to have to change the comment block each time.

Reusing Helper Methods

Some helper methods (such as `readProgramScores` and `readQuizScores`) are specific to a particular program. Others, like `readDouble`, are potentially useful in other programs as well. In Section 10.8, we'll see how to create separate classes for helper methods, making them easier to reuse in other programs.

Review Questions

1. If we write a helper method for `main`, would it be an instance method or a class method?

2. What are the two primary advantages of using helper methods?

3. What information should go into a comment block for a helper method?

7.8 Designing Methods

In this section, we'll tackle some of the issues that you'll face as you begin to write your own methods: How do I know when to write a method? What should the name of the method be? What parameters will it need? We'll focus on class methods, although most of the issues are just as relevant for instance methods.

Cohesion

When you decide to write a method, make sure that it performs a single, clearly defined task. A method shouldn't be a hodgepodge of unrelated activities. Instead, it should have a well-defined responsibility that can be stated in a sentence or two. (If the explanation of what a method does is longer than a sentence or two, that's a good sign that the method wasn't properly designed.) A method that performs a single task is said to be *cohesive*—it "hangs together" well.

Writing a method is much like writing a small program. A well-designed method behaves like a program that we can run whenever we need to accomplish a specific task.

Stepwise Refinement

Requiring that a method perform a clearly defined task doesn't mean that the method will be small. As you begin to write a method, you may realize that it's going to be too large. At this stage, often the best thing to do is write helper methods for your method, delegating some of its work to these methods.

Dividing larger methods into smaller ones is part of a design strategy known as *stepwise refinement* or *top-down decomposition.* As we're designing a method, we sketch out the algorithm that the method will use and look for opportunities to spin off separate, helper methods. If we see that the same action will be performed two or more times (for example, `main` needs to read several numbers), that's a strong indication that the code for performing the action should go into a separate method. If an action is performed in just one place, but the action is rather long and complicated, it's often a good idea to move it to a separate method as well, just to simplify the method we're currently working on. Ideally, the final program will contain only methods that are fairly short, because any methods that would otherwise be too long will have been split into smaller pieces.

Stepwise refinement begins with the `main` method. A well-designed `main` method shouldn't be very long. Someone reading `main` should be able to understand the program's top-level design, rather than getting bogged down in details. In other words, `main` should be like the CEO of a corporation, who provides overall direction but isn't concerned with mundane details. Like a CEO, the `main` method should delegate most of its routine responsibilities to helper methods.

Stepwise refinement may require more than one iteration. Methods that were spun off from the `main` method may then need their own helper methods. Those methods may then need additional helper methods, and so on. We saw this process in the `CourseAverage2` program. After first identifying the need for the `readProgramScores` and `readQuizScores` methods, we then noticed that these methods needed a `readDouble` method as a helper.

> Use stepwise refinement to reduce the size of methods, including `main`.

Methods by Other Names ...

Simplifying a programming task by dividing it into smaller parts is one of the oldest ideas in the programming field. The first programming book ever published (Wilkes, Wheeler, and Gill, *Preparation of Programs for an Electronic Digital Computer,* 1951) is a collection of **subroutines,** which are similar to Java's class methods. Wheeler described the advantages of subroutines in a paper presented at the First ACM National Conference in 1952: "When a programme has been made from a set of sub-routines the breakdown of the code is more complete than it would otherwise be. This allows the coder to concentrate on one section of a programme at a time without the overall detailed programme continually intruding." (Quoted in Knuth, "Structured programming with go to statements," *ACM Computing Surveys* 6 (4), 1974, pp. 261-301.)

We can trace the subroutine concept back even further, though. In 1837, British mathematician and inventor Charles Babbage published a description of a mechanical computer called the Analytical Engine. Although it was never built, this machine is considered to be the forerunner of today's computers. The Analytical Engine was programmable, using punched cards. In Babbage's autobiography, *Passages from the Life of a Philosopher,* he discussed the ability to use the same cards each time a particular calculation needed to be done: "Every set of cards made for any formula will at any future time recalculate that formula with whatever constants may be required."

Choosing Method Names

Once you've decided what a method's responsibilities will be, it's time to choose a name for it. Choosing wisely will have a big impact on how readable your program is, so don't take this step lightly.

Here are some guidelines for picking an appropriate name for a method:

- *Start with a verb.* Methods are designed to *do* things—a method is a chunk of code that will be called and asked to perform some action. Actions are described by verbs in English, so method names will nearly always include a verb. I've been careful to include verbs in my method names: deposit, `withdraw`, `read`Line, `terminate`, `format`AsMoney, and so on. Note that getters and setters automatically obey this rule, because their names begin with `get` or `set`. If a method returns a `boolean` value, the method's name should begin with a verb such as `is` or `has`. For example, suppose that we *Fraction class ▶3.8* add an instance method to the `Fraction` class whose job is to test whether a fraction has a denominator of 1. A good name for this method would be `isInteger`.

- **If the verb isn't descriptive enough by itself, include a noun.** A method name that consists solely of a verb may not convey enough information about what the method does. In many cases, we'll need to include a noun in the method's name to indicate the target of the action. For example, `get`Balance is better than simply `get`, `read`Line is better than `read`, and `formatAs`Money is better than `format`.

- **Add adjectives if necessary to clarify the noun.** Adding a noun helps, but sometimes we'll need adjectives to help clarify the noun. For example, if we have two methods, one that converts British pounds to U.S. dollars and one that converts pounds to Canadian dollars, then `convertToDollars` isn't a good method name. Instead, we might use the names `convertToUSDollars` and `convertToCanadianDollars`.

Java's conventions sometimes deviate slightly from these guidelines. In particular, a method that converts an object to type *T* is customarily named `to`*T* (the verb "convert" is implied). The `toString` method is an example of this convention.

Parameters Versus Class Variables

Class methods have two ways to obtain any data that they need: through parameters and through class variables. In general, it's better for a method to obtain data via parameters. For one thing, a method that relies solely on parameters is self-contained; a method that accesses class variables is not.

> Use parameters—not class variables—to supply data to class methods.

Class variables are best used to maintain long-term information about the state of a class, rather than being used to supply data to class methods. There's a mitigating factor, however: we don't want methods to have so many parameters that they become difficult to use. The more parameters a method has, the harder it is to remember what the parameters are, and the harder it becomes to format the method's declaration and its calls.

How many parameters is too many is subject to debate; some people think that they should be limited to seven. (Why seven? Research shows that the human brain is able to deal with only about seven things at a time.) A few methods in the Java API require as many as 11 parameters, but most require two or fewer. When your methods begin to require an excessive number of parameters, or when you notice that the same variable will be needed by most of the methods in a class, it's time to consider using class variables.

Return Type

As you design a method, you'll need to decide whether or not the method returns a value (has a result type other than `void`). A method is allowed to return any value, whether it be a value of a primitive type (such as an `int` value or `double` value) or an object. Some methods obviously produce a result: `getBalance` returns the amount of money in an account; `readLine` returns the line of text that it read; `formatAsMoney` returns a string containing a dollar amount.

The only other way for a class method to leave data behind is to alter a class variable, which we'll try to avoid. It's easy for someone reading a program to see that a method has returned a value; it's much more difficult to detect that a method has changed class variables.

> Have a class method return a value rather than changing the values of class variables.

Review Questions

1. A method that performs a single, clearly defined task is said to be _____.

2. The process of dividing a larger method into smaller ones is called _____ _____ [two words].

3. Suppose that a method displays an error message on the screen when it is called. What would be wrong with naming the method `errorMessage`?

4. Is it better to provide data to a class method by using parameters or by using class variables?

Q & A

Q: Why do the declarations of class variables and methods contain the word `static`? And what does `static` mean, anyway? [p. 261]

A: The `static` keyword is used primarily for historical reasons. `static` has a long and colorful history, dating back at least as far as the C programming language. In C, declaring a variable to be `static` essentially makes it permanent—a value stored in a `static` variable will stay there indefinitely, until it is changed or the program terminates. Bjarne Stroustrup, who designed C++, decided to use `static` to differentiate class variables and methods from instance variables and methods. The designers of Java then simply followed the lead of C++.

Summary

- A class method (or static method) belongs to a class but isn't called by an instance of the class.
- A class method doesn't have access to instance variables inside its class.
- A class method is called by writing the name of the class, a dot, the name of the method, and the method's argument list. If it's called by another method in the same class, the class name and dot can be omitted.
- Class methods can provide a service to other classes, help other methods in the same class, or provide access to hidden class variables.
- The declaration of a class method must contain the word `static`.
- Class methods that are intended for use within a single class should be declared `private`. Class methods that are intended for use in more than one class should be declared `public`.
- All methods (class and instance) are allowed to declare local variables.
- A local variable can be accessed only within the method that contains its declaration.
- A value stored in a local variable is lost when the enclosing method returns.
- A method that has a result type other than `void` must use a `return` statement to return a value.
- A method whose result type is `void` can use a `return` statement to return prematurely.
- Conditional expressions are created by applying the conditional operator (`? :`) to three operands. A conditional expression returns one of two values, depending on the outcome of a Boolean test.
- Conditional expressions often appear in `return` statements.
- At the beginning of a method call, the arguments in the call are copied into the method's corresponding parameters. When an argument is an object, only the reference to the object is copied, not the object itself.
- A parameter can be changed within the body of a method by assigning it a new value. The corresponding argument isn't affected by such an assignment.
- When an object is used as an argument to a method, the body of the method can change the state of the object.
- Array parameters behave in much the same way as object parameters.
- The `main` method's parameter (customarily named `args`) provides access to program arguments, which are specified on the command line when a program is executed.
- A class variable (or static variable) belongs to a particular class but is stored just once in a program, not in each instance of the class.

- The declaration of a class variable must contain the word `static`.
- Class variables can be used as global variables, as constants, and as storage for class methods.
- A class variable that has been declared `public` is global to all classes in a program. Any method in any class can access the variable by giving the name of the variable's class, a dot, and the name of the variable.
- The `System` class contains three global variables named `in`, `out`, and `err`, which represent the standard input stream, standard output stream, and standard error stream, respectively.
- Class variables retain their values throughout the execution of a program.
- Class methods have access to all class variables in the same class, which allows methods to communicate through shared variables.
- Class variables and methods are declared inside a class, either before or after the `main` method.
- When a method becomes too large, it's often a good idea to delegate some of its work to helper methods. Using helper methods makes a program easier to understand and reduces the amount of redundancy in the program.
- Helper methods for `main` must be class methods.
- A well-designed method should perform a single, clearly defined task.
- Large methods should be divided into progressively smaller ones by the process known as stepwise refinement or top-down decomposition.
- A method name normally contains a verb. Many method names need a noun as well, and perhaps one or more adjectives.
- It's best to provide data to a class method through the method's parameters. Class variables are sometimes used as an alternative way to supply data.
- If a class method produces a result, it's usually best to return the value via a `return` statement. Occasionally, a method may alter class variables instead of (or in addition to) returning a value.

Exercises

Section 7.2

1. Write a class method named `capitalizeWords` that takes one parameter of type `String`. The method should print its parameter, but with the first letter of each word capitalized. For example, the call

```
capitalizeWords("abstract window toolkit");
```

will produce the following output:

```
Abstract Window Toolkit
```

Section 7.3

2. Show the output of the following program.

```
public class Exercise7_2 {
  public static void main(String[] args) {
```

```
      for (int i = 2; i < 50; i++)
        if (f(i) == i) {
           System.out.println("Found: " + i);
           return;
        }
      System.out.println("Sorry, none found.");
    }

    private static int f(int n) {
      int sum = 0;
      for (int d = 1; d < n; d++)
        if (n % d == 0)
          sum += d;
      return sum;
    }
  }
```

3. Locate the error in the following method and show how to fix it.

```
private static boolean isEven(int n) {
  if (n % 2 == 0)
    return true;
}
```

4. Simplify the following method as much as possible.

```
private static int cube(int n) {
  int result;
  result = n * n * n;
  return result;
}
```

5. What will be the value of k after the following statements are executed?

```
int i = 5;
int j = 7;
int k = (i / 2 >= j - 4) ? (i - 1) : (j - 2);
```

6. Write a class method named `addQuotes` that takes one parameter of type `String`. The method should return a string that's identical to its argument, but with a double quote character added at the beginning and end of the string.

7. Write a class method named `buildTime` that takes three `int` parameters (hours, minutes, and seconds) and returns a string of the form `"03:01:25 p.m."`. Assume that hours has a value between 0 and 23, `minutes` has a value between 0 and 59, and seconds has a value between 0 and 59.

8. Write a class method named `computeGrade` that takes an `int` parameter (a score between 0 and 100) and returns a one-character string containing a letter grade. The method will return `"A"` if the score is between 90 and 100, `"B"` if the score is between 80 and 89, and so on.

9. Write a class method named `gcd` that returns the greatest common divisor of two integers, which are parameters to the method.

10. Write a class method named `countDigits` that returns the number of digits in its parameter, which is of type `int`.

11. Write a class method named `convertStringToColor` whose parameter is a string containing the name of one of the 13 colors defined as constants in the `Color` class (see Table 6.3). The method will return the `Color` constant whose name matches the parameter. (The case of letters doesn't have to match.) If no match is found, the method will return `Color.black`.

Section 7.4   12. Suppose that `inc` is a class method that adds 1 to its parameter. What will be the value of n after the following statements have been executed?

```
n = 0;
inc(n);
```

13. Write an `if` statement that prints the message `"Try again"` if a program does not have exactly two command-line arguments.

14. Write a class method named `findFourLetterWord` that searches an array of words (`String` objects) for a word that's four characters long. The array will be the method's only parameter. `findFourLetterWord` will return the first four-letter word that it finds. If none of the words have the proper length, the method will return `null`.

15. Write a class method named `computeAverage` that returns the average of the numbers stored in its parameter, an array of `double` values.

16. Write a class method named `countOccurrences` that returns the number of times a particular integer occurs in an array of integers. The integer and the array will both be parameters.

17. Write a class method named `findLargest` that returns the largest number stored in its parameter, an array of `int` values.

18. Write a class method named `scaleVector` that multiplies each element of a vector by the same number (see Section 5.5). The method will have two parameters: the vector (an array of `double` values) and the scale factor (a `double`). `scaleVector` will modify the elements of the original vector, so it will not return a value.

19. Write a class method named `addVectors` that adds two vectors (see Section 5.5). The method will have two parameters, both arrays of `double` values. `addVectors` will not change the original arrays; instead, it will create and return a new array.

20. Write a class method named `computeInnerProduct` that computes the inner product of two vectors (see Section 5.5). The method will have two parameters, both arrays of `double` values, and will return a `double` value.

Section 7.5   21. Write a class method named `getCount` that returns a different integer each time it's called. The first call of `getCount` should return 1, the second call should return 2, and so on. *Hint:* Store the current integer in a private class variable.

Section 7.7   22. Write a `readInt` method that's similar to `readDouble`, except that it treats the user's input as an integer and returns an `int` value instead of a `double` value.

Section 7.8   23. Explain why each of the following method names is not well-chosen and give a better name for the method.

    (a) `closeWnd` — Closes a window.
    (b) `copy` — Creates a copy of a `Color` object.
    (c) `eraseanddrawnewboard` — Erases a chessboard and draws a new board.
    (d) `heading` — Prints a heading.

Programming Projects

1. Modify the CheckISBN program (Section 3.10) so that it uses class methods to create the reduced ISBN from the original ISBN and to compute the check digit from the reduced ISBN.

2. Modify the PhoneDirectory program (Section 5.8) so that it uses class methods to perform the a (add) and f (find) commands. records and numRecords will become class variables instead of local variables.

3. Modify the Bank program of Programming Project 8 (Chapter 5) so that it uses class methods to perform the o (open account), c (close account), d (deposit), w (withdraw), and s (select account) commands. The array that stores the bank accounts will become a class variable, as will the variables that keep track of the number of accounts and the currently selected account.

4. Modify the CreateVIN program of Programming Project 9 (Chapter 5) so that it uses class methods to determine the code for the model year and to compute the check digit.

5. Modify the Display3DMessage program of Programming Project 10 (Chapter 6) so that it uses a class method to find the Color object that corresponds to the user's choice of background color. (See Exercise 11 for a description of this method.)

6. Write a program named Reverse that displays its command-line arguments in reverse order. Running the program by typing

   ```
   java Reverse void and null
   ```

   should produce the following output:

   ```
   null and void
   ```

7. Write a program named SumIntegers that adds up its command-line arguments, which are assumed to be integers. Running the program by typing

   ```
   java SumIntegers 8 24 62
   ```

   should produce the following output:

   ```
   Total: 94
   ```

8. Write a program named StockChart that displays a bar chart representing the price of a stock over the course of a week. The user will specify the name of the stock, the price of the stock on each day, and the width and height of the chart:

   ```
   Enter stock name: Microstuff
   Enter Monday price: 20.125
   Enter Tuesday price: 19.50
   Enter Wednesday price: 22.375
   Enter Thursday price: 23
   Enter Friday price: 23.25
   Enter width of chart: 200
   Enter height of chart: 200
   ```

   A frame labeled "Chart for *stock name*" will now appear on the screen, with five colored bars representing the daily stock prices. The height of each bar will be proportional to the stock's price on the corresponding day (see the figure at the top of the next page).

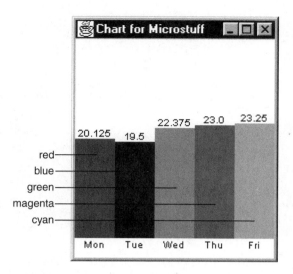

The program must satisfy the following requirements:

- The width of each bar must be (chart width)/5. The height of the Monday bar must be (chart height)/2. The distance from the base of each bar to the bottom of the frame must be (chart height)/10. The total height of the graphics context must be (chart height) + (chart height)/10.

- The colors of the bars must be red, blue, green, magenta, and cyan, in that order. The frame's background color must be white.

- The text must be displayed in black in a plain sans serif font. The point size must be (chart width)/20.

- Each text item (stock price or day) must be centered relative to the bar that it labels.

- The baseline of each stock price must be (chart height)/100 pixels above the bar that it labels.

- The baseline of each day must be (chart height)/20 pixels below the bar that it labels.

Hint: Use at least the following three class methods:

```
static int readInt(String prompt) { … }
static double readDouble(String prompt) { … }
static void drawBar(String day, double price, Color c) { … }
```

9. Write a program named PlotFunction that plots a function within a frame. The user will enter the size of the frame and the maximum *x* coordinate to be displayed (which will also serve as the maximum *y* coordinate):

```
Enter size of frame: 300
Enter maximum value for x: 2.5
```

A frame labeled "Plot Function" will now appear on the screen. A plot of the function $f(x) = x^3$ will be displayed within the frame (see the figure at the top of the next page). The frame must satisfy the following requirements:

- The width and height of the frame's drawing area must match the frame size entered by the user.

- The horizontal and vertical axes must be centered within the frame.

- Tick marks must divide each axis into 10 equal segments.

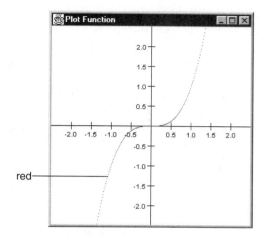

- The length of each tick mark must be 5 pixels on either side of an axis.
- Labels must be displayed in black in a plain sans serif font. The point size must be (frame size)/30.
- Labels must be rounded to two decimal places.
- The label for each tick mark on the *x* axis must be centered below the tick mark. The distance from the tick mark to the baseline of the label must be the ascent of the font plus the leading of the font.
- The label for each tick mark on the *y* axis must be centered to the left of the tick mark. The distance from the tick mark to the label must be 2 pixels.
- All drawing must be done in black, except for the curve being plotted, which must be drawn in red.

Hint: Write class methods that perform the following tasks:

- Draw and label the *x* axis.
- Draw and label the *y* axis.
- Display a single label on the *x* axis.
- Display a single label on the *y* axis.
- Plot the function.

Answers to Review Questions

Section 7.1
1. (c)
2. (b)
3. False
4. `bar` is more likely to be a class method. `Foo` begins with an uppercase letter, indicating that it's probably a class name.

Section 7.2
1. `static`
2. (b)
3. Local
4. Until the method returns (or the variable is assigned a new value)

Section 7.3
1. False
2. Ternary
3. `return` statements

Section 7.4
1. Value
2. True
3. By using the expression `a.length`
4. Program arguments (or command-line arguments)

Section 7.5
1. Static
2. Class variables can be used as global variables, as constants, and as places to store data for class methods.
3. `public`
4. `System.in`, `System.out`, and `System.err`

Section 7.6
1. False
2. False

Section 7.7
1. A class method
2. Improving clarity and reducing redundancy
3. The method's name, a description of what it does, a description of each parameter, and a description of what value the method returns

Section 7.8
1. Cohesive
2. Stepwise refinement (or top-down decomposition)
3. Method names should contain a verb. `displayErrorMessage` would be a better name.
4. By using parameters

8 More Control Structures

Chapter 4 covered Java's most basic control structures: the `if` statement, which is used to choose between alternative actions; the `while` statement, one of Java's three loop statements; and the `break` statement, which allows a program to jump out of a loop. Section 5.2 discussed the `for` statement, another kind of loop. This chapter is devoted to Java's remaining control structures.

First, we'll see how to write code that detects when an exception has occurred and performs some action in response. Next, we'll look at the `switch` statement, which can often be a convenient alternative to a cascaded `if` statement.

We'll then learn about the `do` statement, which is remarkably similar to the `while` statement. The `while` statement is used for loops whose controlling expression is tested *before* the loop body is executed. The `do` statement tests the expression *after* the loop body has been executed.

We'll also examine the `continue` statement, which is similar to `break` except that it skips a portion of a loop iteration rather than causing loop termination. Finally, we'll look at issues that arise when loops are nested inside each other. In some cases, we'll need to use special forms of the `break` and `continue` statements, known as the labeled `break` and the labeled `continue`.

Objectives

- Learn how to catch exceptions.
- Learn how to use the `switch` statement to choose from a list of possible actions.
- Learn how to use the `do` statement to write loops.

- Learn how to use the `continue` statement to skip part of a loop iteration.
- Learn how to use labeled `break` and labeled `continue` statements in nested loops.

8.1   Exceptions

When a Java program performs an illegal operation, a special event known as an *exception* happens. Exceptions occur during the execution of the program, not during compilation. They usually represent errors that the compiler was unable to detect.

If a program contains no special provisions for dealing with exceptions, then it will behave badly if an exception occurs. (In many cases, although not all, the program will terminate immediately.) Fortunately, Java provides a way for a program to detect that an exception has occurred and execute statements that are designed to deal with the problem. This process is called *exception handling.*

There are many kinds of exceptions, each with a different name. Common exceptions include `ArithmeticException` and `NullPointerException`. Trying to divide by zero causes an `ArithmeticException`:

```
i = j / k;   // ArithmeticException occurs if k = 0
```

Attempting to use zero as the right operand in a remainder operation also causes an `ArithmeticException`:

```
i = j % k;   // ArithmeticException occurs if k = 0
```

Trying to call a method using an object variable whose value is `null` causes a `NullPointerException`:

```
acct.deposit(100.00);
   // NullPointerException occurs if acct is null
```

Handling Exceptions

When an exception occurs (we say the exception is *thrown*), the program has the option of *catching* it. In order to catch an exception, we must anticipate where the exception might occur and enclose that code in a *try block.* After the `try` block, we'll put a *catch block* that catches the exception (if it occurs) and performs the desired action. Here's what the resulting code will look like:

```
try
   block
catch (exception-type identifier)
   block
```

The first block contains a series of statements that might throw the exception.

The second block contains statements to be executed if the exception is thrown. *exception-type* specifies what kind of exception the catch block should handle. *identifier* is an arbitrary name; we'll see what it's used for later. The try and catch blocks together form a single statement, which can be used anywhere in a program that a statement is allowed.

If an exception is thrown anywhere in the try block, and the exception matches the one named in the catch block, then the code in the catch block is executed. If the try block executes normally—without an exception—the catch block is ignored. Here's an example of try and catch:

```
try {
  quotient = dividend / divisor;
} catch (ArithmeticException e) {
  System.out.println("Error: Division by zero");
}
```

(Assume that quotient, dividend, and divisor are int variables that have been declared earlier.) If the value of divisor is zero, then an Arithmetic-Exception will be thrown when dividend is divided by divisor. The catch block will catch the exception and print an error message. If the value of divisor is not zero, the code in the catch block will be ignored. Either way, the program continues executing at the next statement after the catch block.

Variables and try Blocks

Although it's legal to declare variables inside a try (or catch) block, be careful if you do so. A variable declared inside a block is always local to that block. For example, suppose that we write

```
try {
  int quotient = dividend / divisor;
} catch (ArithmeticException e) {
  System.out.println("Error: Division by zero");
}
```

The quotient variable is local to the try block; we won't be able to use it outside the try block.

There's another trap associated with try blocks. Suppose that we declare the quotient variable immediately before the try block:

```
int quotient;
try {
  quotient = dividend / divisor;
} catch (ArithmeticException e) {
  System.out.println("Error: Division by zero");
}
```

The compiler won't let us access the value of the quotient variable later in the program, even though quotient was declared prior to the try block. The problem? The compiler notices that no value is assigned to `quotient` if the exception occurs. The solution is often to assign a default value to the variable:

```
int quotient = 0;   // Default value
try {
  quotient = dividend / divisor;
} catch (ArithmeticException e) {
  System.out.println("Error: Division by zero");
}
```

The `quotient` variable is now guaranteed to have a value even if `Arithmetic-Exception` is thrown.

Accessing Information About an Exception

One small mystery remains—what's the purpose of the identifier (typically e) that comes after the exception type? Here's the scoop: When an exception occurs, Java creates an "exception object" that contains information about the error. The identifier e (or whatever name we choose) represents this object.

getMessage   Every exception object contains a string. To access this string, we can call the `getMessage` method:

```
e.getMessage()
```

For example, when division by zero occurs, we could simply print the message stored inside the exception object, rather than printing our own message:

```
try {
  quotient = dividend / divisor;
} catch (ArithmeticException e) {
  System.out.println(e.getMessage());
}
```

If the exception is thrown, we'll get a message such as

```
/ by zero
```

The message is informative, although slightly cryptic.

Printing the value returned by `getMessage` can be useful in situations where we're not positive what the error is or what caused it. In our example, there's only one statement inside the `try` block, so if `ArithmeticException` is thrown, we can be pretty confident that it was as a result of dividing by zero. If the `try` block contained other statements, however, the `ArithmeticException` could have been thrown by one of them instead.

Terminating the Program After an Exception

When an exception is thrown, we may need to terminate the program. We've seen two ways to cause program termination. One is to execute a `return` statement in

System.exit method ►7.1 the `main` method. The other is to call the `System.exit` method, which causes immediate program termination no matter where it's called.

Let's add a call of `System.exit` to our `catch` block, so that the program will terminate if division by zero occurs:

```
try {
  quotient = dividend / divisor;
} catch (ArithmeticException e) {
  System.out.println("Error: Division by zero");
  System.exit(-1);
}
```

Note that I've used –1 rather than 0 as the argument to `System.exit`. A program that terminates abnormally should supply a nonzero argument to `System.exit`, and –1 is the value used by many programmers.

Converting Strings to Integers

In previous chapters, we've used the `Integer.parseInt` method, which converts a string to an `int` value. When we attempt to convert a string to a number, there's a chance that the conversion will fail. Attempting to convert `"123"` to an integer will succeed; attempting to convert `"duh"` into an integer will fail, causing a `NumberFormatException` to be thrown. A robust program should provide a `catch` block to handle the exception:

```
try {
  n = Integer.parseInt(str);
} catch (NumberFormatException e) {
  // Handle exception
}
```

Inside the `catch` block, we can take any action that seems appropriate. If the string contains user input, it's often a good idea to have the user re-enter the input. By putting the `try` and `catch` blocks in a loop, we can give the user multiple attempts to enter a valid number:

```
while (true) {
  SimpleIO.prompt("Enter an integer: ");
  String userInput = SimpleIO.readLine();
  try {
    n = Integer.parseInt(userInput);
    break;  // Input was valid; exit the loop
  } catch (NumberFormatException e) {
    System.out.println("Not an integer; try again.");
  }
}
```

We could even put this loop inside a class method that prompts the user to enter a number and then returns the user's input in integer form:

```
private static int readInt(String prompt) {
  while (true) {
    SimpleIO.prompt(prompt);
    String userInput = SimpleIO.readLine();
    try {
      return Integer.parseInt(userInput);
    } catch (NumberFormatException e) {
      System.out.println("Not an integer; try again.");
    }
  }
}
```

Multiple `catch` Blocks

A `try` block can be followed by more than one `catch` block. Here's an example:

```
try {
  quotient = Integer.parseInt(str1) / Integer.parseInt(str2);
} catch (NumberFormatException e) {
  System.out.println("Error: Not an integer");
} catch (ArithmeticException e) {
  System.out.println("Error: Division by zero");
}
```

When an exception is thrown inside a `try` block, the first matching `catch` block will handle the exception.

Checked Exceptions Versus Unchecked Exceptions

Exceptions fall into two categories:

- A *checked exception* is one that we can't ignore; the compiler will produce an error if we fail to use a `try` block and `catch` block to handle the exception.
- An *unchecked exception* can be ignored by the programmer; there's no need to use `try` and `catch` to handle the exception.

Both checked and unchecked exceptions are detected during program execution. The only difference between the two is whether or not the programmer is required to deal with the exception.

Unchecked exceptions sometimes represent disasters so severe that there's no hope of continuing program execution (for example, the program runs out of memory). They're also used for errors that could potentially occur at hundreds of places in a program, so that checking for all of them would be onerous. `Arithmetic-Exception`, `NullPointerException`, and `NumberFormatException` fall into this group.

Thread.sleep   Checked exceptions represent conditions that the programmer should be able to anticipate and deal with. One checked exception that we'll occasionally encounter is named `InterruptedException`. This exception can be thrown when we call the `Thread.sleep` method, which is part of the Java API. `Thread.sleep` allows us to put a delay in a program by having the program "go to sleep" for a specified time interval. When we call `Thread.sleep`, we're required to supply one argument, representing the "sleep time":

```
Thread.sleep(100);
```

The sleep time is measured in milliseconds, so the argument `100` indicates that the program should sleep for 100 milliseconds (1/10 of a second). Unfortunately, we can't simply put this call of `Thread.sleep` into a program. If we do, the compiler will give us an error message to the effect that "`InterruptedException` must be caught," because the compiler knows that `Thread.sleep` sometimes throws `InterruptedException`. To avoid getting an error from the compiler, we'll need to use a `try` block and `catch` block:

```
try {
  Thread.sleep(100);
} catch (InterruptedException e) {}
```

Notice that the `catch` block is empty. If the exception occurs, the sleep will end prematurely, but the program will otherwise continue in a normal fashion. Doing nothing is often the best thing when an `InterruptedException` occurs.

We won't see many checked exceptions prior to Chapter 14, which deals with files. Until then, we won't worry too much about checked exceptions.

Using Exceptions Properly

`try` and `catch` blocks aren't meant to be used as ordinary control structures. In most cases, it's better to test for an error before it occurs rather than wait until it happens and then catch the resulting exception.

Consider the following loop, which we first encountered in Section 4.6:

```
while (n != 0) {
  r = m % n;
  m = n;
  n = r;
}
```

Now that we know about exceptions, we could write the loop in the following way instead:

```
try {
  while (true) {
    r = m % n;
    m = n;
    n = r;
  }
} catch (ArithmeticException e) {}
```

The loop would still work correctly: when n becomes zero, performing the `%` operation will cause `ArithmeticException` to be thrown, and the loop will terminate. Is the loop better now? The answer is clearly no: it's harder to figure out when the loop will terminate, and the code is longer and more deeply nested.

Using exceptions when they're not strictly necessary can have another downside: it's possible that a `catch` block will catch exceptions that the programmer never anticipated. The program might then ignore the exception or deal with it incorrectly, rather than bringing it to the attention of the programmer. For example, a `catch` block that catches `ArithmeticException` may end up handling errors other than just division by zero. (Division by zero isn't the only error that triggers an `ArithmeticException`.)

The proper time to use exceptions is when you can't test for possible errors *before* performing an operation. It's easy to test whether the divisor is zero before performing a division, so `try` and `catch` shouldn't be used to detect that kind of error. On the other hand, there's no easy way to test whether the characters in a string form a valid integer. The best way to find out is to call a conversion method, such as `Integer.parseInt`; if the method detects a problem during the conversion, it throws an exception to notify the program of the error.

> Don't use exceptions to deal with error conditions that could have been checked beforehand.

Review Questions

1. When an exception occurs in a program, we say that the exception has been _____.

2. A `try` block is normally followed by a _____ _____ [two words].

3. Java's exceptions fall into two categories. What are they?

4. Which one of the following exceptions needs to be caught in order to avoid an error message from the compiler: (a) `ArithmeticException`, (b) `InterruptedException`, (c) `NullPointerException`, or (d) `NumberFormatException`?

8.2 The `switch` Statement

We'll often need to test whether the value of an expression matches one of a specific set of possible values. For example, suppose that the variable `day` contains a number between 1 and 7, representing a day of the week, and we'd like to display the name of that day. We could use a cascaded `if` statement to compare the value of `day` with the seven possible values that it might have:

```
if (day == 1)
  System.out.println("Sunday");
else if (day == 2)
  System.out.println("Monday");
```

```
else if (day == 3)
  System.out.println("Tuesday");
else if (day == 4)
  System.out.println("Wednesday");
else if (day == 5)
  System.out.println("Thursday");
else if (day == 6)
  System.out.println("Friday");
else if (day == 7)
  System.out.println("Saturday");
```

This statement works correctly, but there's a better way to accomplish the same effect. Java's `switch` statement is designed specifically for comparing a variable (or, more generally, an expression) against a series of possible values. Here's what an equivalent `switch` statement would look like:

```
switch (day) {
  case 1: System.out.println("Sunday");
          break;
  case 2: System.out.println("Monday");
          break;
  case 3: System.out.println("Tuesday");
          break;
  case 4: System.out.println("Wednesday");
          break;
  case 5: System.out.println("Thursday");
          break;
  case 6: System.out.println("Friday");
          break;
  case 7: System.out.println("Saturday");
          break;
}
```

When a `switch` statement is executed, the expression in parentheses (the *controlling expression*) is evaluated and its value is compared with the values listed after the word `case` (the *case labels*). If a match is found, the statements after the matching case label are executed. In our example, the value of `day` is compared with the values 1, 2, 3, 4, 5, 6, and 7. If `day` has the value 1, the string `"Sunday"` is printed. If `day` is 2, the string `"Monday"` is printed, and so on.

Notice that each case ends with a `break` statement. Executing a `break` statement inside a `switch` statement causes the `switch` statement to terminate. The program continues executing with the statement that follows the `switch` statement. The `break` statements are needed in order for the `switch` statement to work properly, as we'll see later.

Combining Case Labels

It's not unusual for several case labels to correspond to the same action. For example, instead of printing the name of a particular day, we might simply want to print an indication of whether it's a weekday or whether it belongs to the weekend. The following `switch` statement works, but it's a bit long:

```
switch (day) {
  case 1: System.out.println("Weekend");
          break;
  case 2: System.out.println("Weekday");
          break;
  case 3: System.out.println("Weekday");
          break;
  case 4: System.out.println("Weekday");
          break;
  case 5: System.out.println("Weekday");
          break;
  case 6: System.out.println("Weekday");
          break;
  case 7: System.out.println("Weekend");
          break;
}
```

We can shorten this statement considerably by combining cases whose actions are identical:

```
switch (day) {
  case 1:
  case 7: System.out.println("Weekend");
          break;
  case 2:
  case 3:
  case 4:
  case 5:
  case 6: System.out.println("Weekday");
          break;
}
```

To save space, we can put several case labels on the same line:

```
switch (day) {
  case 1: case 7:
    System.out.println("Weekend");
    break;
  case 2: case 3: case 4: case 5: case 6:
    System.out.println("Weekday");
    break;
}
```

The `default` Case

What happens if the value of the controlling expression in a `switch` statement doesn't match *any* of the case labels? In that event, the `switch` statement is skipped entirely, and the statement after it is executed next. In our weekend/weekday example, if the value of `day` is less than 1 or greater than 7, nothing will be printed.

At times, we may want some default action to occur whenever the controlling expression doesn't match any of the case labels. To indicate what that action is, we can use the word `default`: as a label. Any statements placed after `default:` are executed if the value of the controlling expression doesn't match any of the other case labels. For example, we could add a default case to our weekend/weekday example, using it to print an error message if the value of `day` isn't between 1 and 7:

```
switch (day) {
  case 1: case 7:
    System.out.println("Weekend");
    break;
  case 2: case 3: case 4: case 5: case 6:
    System.out.println("Weekday");
    break;
  default:
    System.out.println("Not a valid day");
    break;
}
```

The General Form of the `switch` Statement

In general, the `switch` statement has the following appearance:

`switch` **statement**

```
switch ( expression ) {
    case  constant-expression  :  statements
    ...
    case  constant-expression  :  statements
    default :  statements
}
```

The parentheses around the controlling expression are mandatory.

Case labels are subject to several rules:

- The word `case` must be followed by a ***constant expression***—an expression whose value can be determined by the compiler. For example, 6 is a constant expression, as is 1 + 2 + 3. Variables—and expressions that contain variables—don't qualify.

- Case labels don't have to go in any particular order, although it's good style to put the labels in a logical order. The `default` label doesn't have to go last, either, although that's where most programmers (wisely) put it.

- It's illegal for the same value to appear in two case labels. The compiler will catch such an error.

After each case label we're allowed to put any number of statements (including none at all). Normally, the last statement in each case is a `break` statement.

Layout of the `switch` Statement

There are at least two common ways to lay out a `switch` statement. One layout technique puts the first statement in each case on the same line as the case label:

```
switch (year) {
  case 1992: olympicSite = "Barcelona";
             break;
  case 1996: olympicSite = "Atlanta";
             break;
  case 2000: olympicSite = "Sydney";
             break;
  case 2004: olympicSite = "Athens";
             break;
}
```

When there's only one statement per case (not counting `break`), it's not unusual for programmers to save space by putting the `break` statement on the same line:

```
switch (year) {
  case 1992: olympicSite = "Barcelona"; break;
  case 1996: olympicSite = "Atlanta";   break;
  case 2000: olympicSite = "Sydney";    break;
  case 2004: olympicSite = "Athens";    break;
}
```

The other common layout involves putting the statements in each case under the case label, indenting them to make the case label stand out:

```
switch (year) {
  case 1992:
    olympicSite = "Barcelona";
    break;
  case 1996:
    olympicSite = "Atlanta";
    break;
  case 2000:
    olympicSite = "Sydney";
    break;
  case 2004:
    olympicSite = "Athens";
    break;
}
```

Although this layout allows longer statements, it also increases the number of lines required for the `switch` statement. This layout is best used when there are many statements in each case or the statements are lengthy.

Advantages of the `switch` Statement

The `switch` statement has two primary advantages over the cascaded `if` statement. One advantage is clarity: using `switch` statements instead of cascaded `if` statements can make a program easier to understand.

The other advantage of the switch statement is speed. When there are more than a few possibilities to be tested, the switch statement often outperforms the if statement. The conditions in a cascaded if statement must be tested in order, from first to last, until one is true. In a switch statement, however, it's often possible for the correct alternative to be selected without the need to examine the other alternatives. The speed advantage of the switch statement depends on various factors, including the number of cases. As the number of cases increases, the speed advantage of the switch becomes more significant.

Limitations of the switch Statement

Unfortunately, the switch statement isn't quite as useful as you might think. For one thing, it can't replace every cascaded if statement. To qualify for conversion to a switch statement, every test in a cascaded if statement must compare the *same* variable (or expression) for equality with a constant:

```
if (x == constant-expression₁)
    statement₁
else if (x == constant-expression₂)
    statement₂
else if (x == constant-expression₃)
    statement₃
...
```

If any of the values that x is being compared with aren't constant, we can't use a switch statement. Also, if the cascaded if statement tests a variety of different conditions (rather than testing the same variable or expression repeatedly), it's not eligible for switch treatment.

Q&A

byte type, short type ➤ *9.2*

Another limitation of the switch statement is that the controlling expression must have type char, byte, short, or int. Floating-point expressions aren't allowed. Objects aren't permitted either, so strings can't be tested in a switch statement.

The Role of the break Statement

Let's take a closer look at the role of the break statement. We've seen that executing a break statement causes a switch statement to terminate; the program moves on to the next statement after the switch. What would happen if break statements weren't present inside a switch?

The answer to that question is a bit surprising. At the end of a case, the switch statement would continue executing by "falling through" into the next case. The following example shows what would happen:

```
switch (sign) {
  case -1: System.out.println("Negative");
  case  0: System.out.println("Zero");
  case +1: System.out.println("Positive");
}
```

If `sign` has the value –1, the `switch` statement will print `"Negative"`, as desired. However, it will then continue onward, because there's no `break` statement at the end of the case. The statement will now print `"Zero"` and then fall into the final case, printing `"Positive"`.

The `switch` statement's ability to fall through from one case into the next is inherited from older languages. In the early days of programming, it was customary for a program to compute which case was applicable, "jump" directly to it, and then continue normal execution. The `switch` statement mirrors this behavior. The case labels in a `switch` statement are nothing more than markers that indicate possible places to enter the list of statements inside the braces. When the value of the controlling expression has been determined, the program "jumps into" the list of statements. The statements are then executed in order until the last one is reached or until one of the statements "jumps out" of the `switch`. Any case labels encountered along the way are simply ignored.

 Omitting the `break` statement is sometimes a useful programming technique, but most of the time it's simply a mistake.

 Be sure to put a `break` statement at the end of each case in a `switch` statement. Forgetting to use `break` statements is a common error in Java.

Although it's not necessary to put a `break` statement at the end of the last case, it's considered good style to do so. That way, it will be easier (and less risky) to add additional cases to the `switch` statement in the future. If we don't end the last case with a `break` statement, someone may come along later and add a new case to the end without noticing that the previous case—the one that used to be the last one—falls through into the new case.

> Always put a `break` statement at the end of the last case in a `switch` statement.

PROGRAM   **Determining the Number of Days in a Month**

To illustrate the `switch` statement, let's write a small program that asks the user for a month (represented by an integer between 1 and 12) and a year, then displays the number of days in that month:

```
Enter a month (1-12): 4
Enter a year: 2003
There are 30 days in this month
```

Months fall into three categories: those with 30 days, those with 31 days, and February, which is a special case. Our program will use a `switch` statement to determine into which category the user's month falls. If the month is February, we'll need an `if` statement to determine whether the year is a leap year. If so, February has 29 days. Otherwise, it has 28 days.

MonthLength.java

```
1   // Determines the number of days in a month
2
3   import jpb.*;
4
5   public class MonthLength {
6     public static void main(String[] args) {
7       // Prompt the user to enter a month
8       SimpleIO.prompt("Enter a month (1-12): ");
9       String userInput = SimpleIO.readLine();
10      int month = Integer.parseInt(userInput);
11
12      // Terminate program if month is not between 1 and 12
13      if (month < 1 || month > 12) {
14        System.out.println("Month must be between 1 and 12");
15        return;
16      }
17
18      // Prompt the user to enter a year
19      SimpleIO.prompt("Enter a year: ");
20      userInput = SimpleIO.readLine();
21      int year = Integer.parseInt(userInput);
22
23      // Determine the number of days in the month
24      int numberOfDays;
25      switch (month) {
26        case 2:   // February
27                  numberOfDays = 28;
28                  if (year % 4 == 0) {
29                    numberOfDays = 29;
30                    if (year % 100 == 0 && year % 400 != 0)
31                      numberOfDays = 28;
32                  }
33                  break;
34
35        case 4:   // April
36        case 6:   // June
37        case 9:   // September
38        case 11:  // November
39                  numberOfDays = 30;
40                  break;
41
42        default:  numberOfDays = 31;
43                  break;
44      }
45
46      // Display the number of days in the month
47      System.out.println("There are " + numberOfDays +
48                         " days in this month");
49    }
50  }
```

The `MonthLength` program only partially validates the user's input (by testing whether the month is between 1 and 12). Full validation is left as an exercise.

Review Questions

1. The `switch` statement can be used as an alternative to a _____ `if` statement.

2. A `switch` statement can have a clause that handles all cases not listed individually elsewhere in the statement. What keyword indicates the beginning of such a clause?

3. What types are permissible for the controlling expression in a `switch` statement?

4. One advantage of the `switch` statement is that it can make a program easier to understand. What is the other advantage of the `switch` statement?

8.3   The `do` Statement

Java has three loop statements: the `while` statement, the `do` statement, and the `for` statement. All three have much in common; in particular, they all use a `boolean` expression to determine whether or not to continue looping. Which type of loop to use is mostly a matter of convenience. So far, we've seen two of these loops: the `for` statement, which is convenient for counting loops, and the `while` statement, which is convenient for most other kinds of loops.

A `do` statement looks like a `while` statement in which the controlling expression and body have switched positions, with the word `do` added at the beginning:

do statement

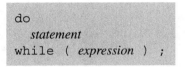

```
do
    statement
while ( expression ) ;
```

The loop body is a single statement, which can be a block. The controlling expression is required to be enclosed in parentheses, just as it is in a `while` statement.

The `do` statement behaves like the `while` statement, except that the controlling expression is tested *after* the body of the loop is executed. (The `while` statement tests the condition *before* the body of the loop is executed.) The following diagram shows the flow of control within a `do` statement:

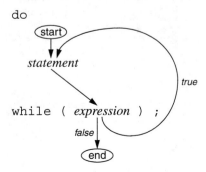

Notice that the body of a do statement is always executed at least once.

Let's rewrite the "countdown" example of Section 4.7, using a do statement this time:

```
i = 10;
do {
  System.out.println("T minus " + i + " and counting");
  --i;
} while (i > 0);
```

When the do statement is executed, the loop body is first executed, causing the message T minus 10 and counting to be printed and i to be decremented. The condition i > 0 is now tested. Because 9 is greater than 0, the loop body is executed a second time. This process continues until the message T minus 1 and counting is printed and i becomes 0. The test i > 0 now fails, causing the loop to terminate. As this example shows, the do statement is often indistinguishable from the while statement. The only difference between the two is that the body of a do statement is always executed at least once; the body of a while statement is skipped entirely if the controlling expression is false initially.

Although the do statement isn't used nearly as often as the while statement, it's handy in some cases. For example, suppose that we need to determine the number of digits in an integer. Our strategy will be to divide the integer by 10 repeatedly until it becomes 0; the number of divisions performed is the number of digits. Clearly we'll need some kind of loop, but should we use a while statement or a do statement? The do statement turns out to be the right choice, because every integer—even 0—has at least *one* digit.

Let's assume that the variable n contains the integer; our goal is to store the number of digits in a variable named numDigits. Here's what our do loop will look like:

```
numDigits = 0;
do {
  numDigits++;
  n /= 10;
} while (n > 0);
```

Here's a trace of the loop, assuming that n has the value 5392 initially:

	Initial value	*After iteration 1*	*After iteration 2*	*After iteration 3*	*After iteration 4*
numDigits	0	1	2	3	4
n	5392	539	53	5	0

When the loop terminates, numDigits has the value 4, which is the number of digits in 5392.

To see why the do statement is the right choice, let's see what would happen if we were to replace the do loop by a similar while loop:

```
numDigits = 0;
while (n > 0) {
  numDigits++;
  n /= 10;
}
```

If n is 0 initially, this loop won't execute at all, and numDigits will end up with the value 0.

A final remark about do statements: Many programmers use braces in *all* do statements, whether or not they're needed, because a do statement without braces around its body can easily be mistaken for a while statement:

```
do System.out.println("T minus " + i-- + " and counting");
while (i > 0);
```

A careless reader might think that the word while indicates the beginning of a while statement.

> Always put braces around the body of a do statement so that it's not mistaken for a while statement.

Review Questions

1. If a while statement is rewritten as a do statement (using the same controlling expression and loop body), the two loops will probably produce the same result: (a) all the time, (b) some of the time, or (c) never.

2. Putting braces around the body of a do statement is: (a) required, (b) not required but considered good style, or (c) not required and not considered good style.

8.4 The continue Statement

Java's continue statement is similar to the break statement. Like break, continue can be used inside a loop. Unlike break, however, executing a continue statement doesn't cause the loop to terminate. Instead, it causes the program to jump to the end of the loop body. The loop continues to execute, but part of the loop iteration is skipped. In other words, break transfers control just *past* the end of a loop, while continue transfers control to a point just *before* the end of the loop body. With break, control leaves the loop; with continue, control remains inside the loop. Unlike break, which can be used in loops and switch statements, the use of continue is limited to loops.

The continue statement is used much less often than the break statement. The primary advantage of continue is that it can simplify the body of a loop by reducing the amount of nesting inside the loop. Instead of writing

```
while (expr1) {
  if (expr2) {
    statements
  }
}
```

we can write

```
while (expr1) {
  if (!expr2)
    continue;
  statements
}
```

If *expr2* is false, the `continue` statement is executed and the program skips the rest of the statements in the loop body. Notice that the statements to be executed if *expr2* is true are indented just once now, instead of twice.

The `continue` statement is especially useful for checking whether input is valid. We can subject the input to a series of tests; if it fails any test, we can use `continue` to skip the remainder of the loop. Suppose, for example, that we want the user to enter a Social Security number. A valid Social Security number must contain a group of three digits, a dash, a group of two digits, a dash, and a group of four digits. The following loop won't terminate until the user enters an 11-character string with dashes in the right positions. (We won't verify that the remaining characters are digits, however. We'll see how to fix this omission in Section 9.4.)

```
while (true) {
  SimpleIO.prompt("Enter a Social Security number: ");
  ssn = SimpleIO.readLine();
  if (ssn.length() < 11) {
    System.out.println("Error: Number is too short");
    continue;
  }
  if (ssn.length() > 11) {
    System.out.println("Error: Number is too long");
    continue;
  }
  if (ssn.charAt(3) != '-' ||
      ssn.charAt(6) != '-') {
    System.out.println(
      "Error: Number must have the form ddd-dd-dddd");
    continue;
  }
  break;  // Input passed all the tests, so exit the loop
}
```

Review Questions

1. Which statement is used more often in Java: break or continue?

2. What is the primary advantage of the continue statement?

8.5 Nested Loops

When the body of a loop contains another loop, we say that the loops are ***nested.*** Nested loops are quite common, although the loops often aren't directly related to each other. For example, the PhoneDirectory program of Section 5.8 contains a while loop with the following form:

```
while (true) {
  ...
  if (command.equalsIgnoreCase("a")) {
    ...
  } else if (command.equalsIgnoreCase("f")) {
    ...
    for (int i = 0; i < numRecords; i++) {
      ...
    }
  } else if (command.equalsIgnoreCase("q")) {
    ...
  } else {
    ...
  }
  ...
}
```

A for loop is nested inside the while loop. The two loops aren't related, however, and the nesting is indirect. (The for statement is actually nested inside an if statement, which is then nested inside the while statement.)

In many cases, however, one loop is nested directly inside another loop, and the loops *are* related to each other. Here are a few typical situations:

- ***Displaying tables.*** Printing a table containing rows and columns is normally done by a pair of nested loops. The outer loop controls which row is currently being displayed, while the inner loop specifies the column. An example of this kind of nesting can be found at the end of this section.

- ***Working with multidimensional arrays.*** Processing the elements of a multidimensional array is normally done using nested loops, with one loop for each dimension of the array. We'll see examples of such loops in Section 13.1.

- ***Sorting.*** Nested loops are also common in algorithms that sort data into order. Section 13.4 discusses sorting algorithms.

When loops are nested, we'll need to take additional care with break and continue statements. Both statements normally affect only one loop—the loop that immediately encloses the break statement or continue statement—which isn't always what we want. Fortunately, Java has a solution to this problem: "labeled" break and continue statements.

Labeled `break` Statements

The `break` statement transfers control out of the *innermost* `while`, `do`, `for`, or `switch` statement that encloses the `break`. When these statements are nested, the normal `break` statement can escape only one level of nesting. Consider the case of a `switch` statement nested inside a `while` statement:

```
while (...) {
  switch (...) {
    ...
    break;
    ...
  }
}
```

The `break` statement transfers control out of the `switch` statement, but not out of the `while` loop. Similarly, if a loop is nested inside a loop, executing a `break` will break out of the inner loop, but not the outer loop. Unfortunately, that's not always the behavior that we want. At times, we'll need a `break` statement that can break out of multiple levels of nesting, not just a single level.

For example, suppose we're writing a program that prompts the user to enter a command. After executing the command, the program asks the user to enter another command. The loop might look like this:

```
while (true) {
  Prompt user to enter command;
  Execute command;
}
```

Before we can execute the command, we'll need to use a `switch` statement (or possibly a cascaded `if` statement) to determine which command the user entered:

```
while (true) {
  Prompt user to enter command;
  switch (command) {
    case command₁: Perform operation₁; break;
    case command₂: Perform operation₂; break;
    ...
    case commandₙ: Perform operationₙ; break;
    default: Print error message; break;
  }
}
```

The loop will terminate when the user enters a particular command ($command_n$, let's say). We'll need a `break` statement that can break out of the loop, not just the `switch` statement, when the user enters the termination command.

Fortunately, Java provides the labeled `break` statement for situations such as this. A labeled `break` statement has the following form:

labeled break statement

> `break` *identifier* ;

The identifier is a *label* that's chosen by the programmer. The label is placed just before the loop that we want to break out of. A colon must follow the label. Our command loop will now have the following appearance:

```
commandLoop:
  while (true) {
    Prompt user to enter command;
    switch (command) {
      case command₁: Perform operation₁; break;
      case command₂: Perform operation₂; break;
      ...
      case commandₙ: break commandLoop;   // Exit from loop
      default: Print error message; break;
    }
  }
```

Although `commandLoop` labels a `while` statement in this example, there's no requirement that it be attached to a loop. It could label any statement, including an `if` or `switch` statement.

Labeled `continue` Statements

The `continue` statement normally applies to the nearest enclosing loop. In other words, a `continue` statement inside an inner loop will skip the rest of the inner loop's current iteration; it will have no effect on any outer loops. Like the `break` statement, however, the `continue` statement is allowed to contain a label, to specify *which* enclosing loop the `continue` statement is trying to affect.

A labeled `continue` looks very much like a labeled `break`:

**labeled `continue`
statement**

> `continue` *identifier* ;

The label mentioned in the `continue` statement must precede one of the enclosing loops. Executing the `continue` statement causes the program to jump to the end of that loop, without causing the loop to terminate.

PROGRAM   ### Computing Interest

Our next program prints a table showing the value of $100 invested at different rates of interest over a period of years. The user will enter an interest rate and the number of years the money will be invested. The table will show the value of the money at one-year intervals—at that interest rate and the next four higher rates—assuming that interest is compounded once a year (see the figure at the top of the next page).

Clearly, we can use a `for` statement to print the first row. The second row is a little trickier, because its values depend on the numbers in the first row. The solution is to store the first row in an array as it's computed, then use the values in the array to compute the second row. Of course, this process can be repeated for the third and later rows. We'll end up with two `for` statements, one nested inside the other. The

```
Enter interest rate: 6
Enter number of years: 5

Years      6%     7%     8%     9%    10%
    1      106    107    108    109    110
    2      112    114    117    119    121
    3      119    123    126    130    133
    4      126    131    136    141    146
    5      134    140    147    154    161
```

outer loop will count from 1 to the number of years requested by the user. The inner loop will increment the interest rate from its lowest value to its highest value.

PrintInterest.java

```
1    // Prints a table showing the value of $100 invested at
2    // different rates of interest over a period of years
3
4    import jpb.*;
5
6    public class PrintInterest {
7      public static void main(String[] args) {
8        // Initialize array so that all amounts are equal
9        double[] amounts = new double[5];
10       for (int i = 0; i < amounts.length; i++)
11         amounts[i] = 100.00;
12
13       // Prompt user to enter interest rate
14       SimpleIO.prompt("Enter interest rate: ");
15       String userInput = SimpleIO.readLine();
16       int lowRate = Integer.parseInt(userInput);
17
18       // Prompt user to enter number of years
19       SimpleIO.prompt("Enter number of years: ");
20       userInput = SimpleIO.readLine();
21       int numYears = Integer.parseInt(userInput);
22
23       // Print a heading for the table. Each column represents
24       // a single interest rate. The lowest rate is the one
25       // entered by the user. Four other rates are shown; each
26       // is 1% higher than the previous one.
27       System.out.print("\nYears");
28       for (int i = 0; i < amounts.length; i++)
29         printField(lowRate + i + "%", 6);
30       System.out.println();
31
32       // Print contents of table; each row represents one
33       // year
34       for (int year = 1; year <= numYears; year++) {
35         printField(year + "   ", 5);
36         for (int i = 0; i < amounts.length; i++) {
37           amounts[i] += (lowRate + i) / 100.0 * amounts[i];
38           printField("" + Math.round(amounts[i]), 6);
39         }
40         System.out.println();
```

```
41        }
42    }
43
44    // Displays str in a field of the specified width, with
45    // spaces added at the beginning if necessary
46    private static void printField(String str, int width) {
47       for (int i = str.length(); i < width; i++)
48          System.out.print(" ");
49       System.out.print(str);
50    }
51 }
```

In order for the table to look good, the columns need to line up. To assist with that task, I wrote a helper method named `printField`, whose job is to print a string in a "field" of a certain width. If the string's length is less than the specified width, `printField` displays extra spaces before the string, so that the total number of characters printed (spaces plus the characters in the string) equals the width.

The following diagram shows how the table is arranged into fields. Each line begins with a single 5-character field, followed by five 6-character fields.

Years	●●●●6%	●●●●7%	●●●●8%	●●●●9%	●●●10%
●●1●●	●●●106	●●●107	●●●108	●●●109	●●●110
●●2●●	●●●112	●●●114	●●●117	●●●119	●●●121
●●3●●	●●●119	●●●123	●●●126	●●●130	●●●133
●●4●●	●●●126	●●●131	●●●136	●●●141	●●●146
●●5●●	●●●134	●●●140	●●●147	●●●154	●●●161

To make the diagram easier to read, I've used ● to represent the space character.

The nice thing about using fields is that the columns in the table will still line up properly when the years become two-digit numbers and the dollar amounts increase to four or five digits.

Review Question

1. To exit from multiple loops in a single step, we would use a _____ `break` statement.

8.6 Case Study: Printing a One-Month Calendar

Our next case study involves writing a program that prints a calendar for the current month. The program requires no input from the user. It automatically detects the current month and year, and then displays a calendar for that month:

```
       May 2000
--------------------
          1  2  3  4  5  6
    7  8  9 10 11 12 13
   14 15 16 17 18 19 20
   21 22 23 24 25 26 27
   28 29 30 31
```

The month and year are centered over the calendar.

Our initial design might look like this:

1. Determine the current month and year.
2. Determine on which day of the week the current month begins.
3. Display the calendar.

Step 1 is going to require some help from Java. Fortunately, the Java API provides a way for programs to determine the current date (and time). Step 2 can be done using a standard algorithm. (A formula known as Zeller's congruence can determine the day of the week for any given month, day, and year; see Programming Project 5 in Chapter 2.) However, Java provides an easy way to determine the day of the week, so we won't even need a separate algorithm. Step 3 will require further thought, so let's postpone it for a bit.

To determine the current month and year, we'll use a class named GregorianCalendar, which belongs to the `java.util` package. When a GregorianCalendar object is created using a constructor with no arguments, the object will contain the current time and date:

```
GregorianCalendar date = new GregorianCalendar();
```

get

The `get` method allows us to access the time and date stored inside a GregorianCalendar object. `get` is a general-purpose method that returns a single part of the time or date, encoded as an integer. To tell `get` what part we want, we must supply an argument. That argument is a constant defined in a different class, named Calendar (also part of `java.util`). Table 8.1 gives a partial list of the constants defined in the Calendar class.

Table 8.1
Partial List of Constants
in the Calendar Class

Name	Meaning	Range
DATE	Day of month	1–31
DAY_OF_WEEK	Day of the week	1–7
HOUR	Hour (12-hour clock)	0–11
HOUR_OF_DAY	Hour (24-hour clock)	0–23
MINUTE	Minutes	0–59
MONTH	Month	0–11
SECOND	Seconds	0–59
YEAR	Year	–

To obtain the current year, we would call `get` in the following way:

```
System.out.println("Current year: " +
                    date.get(Calendar.YEAR));
```

The value returned by `get` will fall within a certain range, depending on the constant passed to `get`. Table 8.1 shows the possible ranges. Notice that the months are numbered from 0 to 11 instead of from 1 to 12.

set

GregorianCalendar also provides a method named `set`, which lets us change the information stored inside a GregorianCalendar object. By using `set`, we can set the date to 1 (the first day of the month). If we now use `get` to retrieve `DAY_OF_WEEK`, we'll know the day of the week on which the current month began.

With the help of `GregorianCalendar`, we know how to tackle steps 1 and 2 of our design, but we still have step 3 to go. Let's break it into smaller steps:

1. Print a heading for the calendar.
2. Print the days in the current month.

Both steps will take a bit of work, so let's create two helper methods, `print-Heading` and `printDays`, each of which is responsible for one of the steps.

`printHeading` will need to perform the following steps:

1. Convert the month number to a name.
2. Determine how many spaces to display before the month.
3. Print the month, year, and a row of dashes.

Converting the month number to a name can be done by using the month number as an index into an array containing the names of all 12 months. The number of spaces to display before the month depends on the width of the calendar (20 characters), the length of the month name, and the number of characters needed for the year and the space between the month and the year (5 total). The formula is

(20 – (number of characters for year and space) – (length of month name))/2

which simplifies to

(15 – (length of month name))/2

`printDays` will need to perform the following steps:

1. Leave space for "empty days" at the beginning of the month.
2. Print the days in the current month.

We can use a loop for step 1, printing three spaces for each "empty day." The number of empty days depends on the day of the week for day 1 of the current month (which we determined earlier in the program).

Step 2 requires a loop with a counter going from 1 to the number of days in the month. (The algorithm for determining the number of days in the month can be borrowed from the `MonthLength` program in Section 8.2.) The loop body will print the value of the counter. If the counter has only a single digit, it will print a space before and after the number; otherwise, it will print a space after the number. After printing the value of the counter, the loop body will need to test whether it represented a Saturday. If so, it's time to advance to the next output line.

How do we know when a date falls on Saturday? That depends on what the first day of the month is. If the month begins on Sunday, then days 7, 14, 21, and 28 are Saturdays. If the month begins on Monday, then days 6, 13, 20, and 27 are Saturdays. In general, if `dayOfWeek` is the starting day for the month (where $0 \leq$ `dayOfWeek` ≤ 6) and `day` is the number of a particular day, then that day is a Saturday if `dayOfWeek` + `day` is a multiple of 7. To test for Saturday, all we need to do is check whether (`dayOfWeek` + `day`) % 7 is equal to 0.

The program follows. Note that the "day-of-week" value returned by `get` is reduced by 1, so that `dayOfWeek` will contain a number between 0 and 6.

PrintCalendar.java

```
 1  // Program name: PrintCalendar
 2  // Author: K. N. King
 3  // Written: 1998-05-07
 4  // Modified: 1999-07-07
 5  //
 6  // Displays a calendar for the current month. The calendar
 7  // has the following form:
 8  //
 9  //          May 2000
10  // --------------------
11  //    1  2  3  4  5  6
12  //    7  8  9 10 11 12 13
13  //   14 15 16 17 18 19 20
14  //   21 22 23 24 25 26 27
15  //   28 29 30 31
16  //
17  // The month name and year are centered over the calendar.
18
19  import java.util.*;
20  import jpb.*;
21
22  public class PrintCalendar {
23    public static void main(String[] args) {
24      // Determine the current date
25      GregorianCalendar date = new GregorianCalendar();
26
27      // Adjust to first day of month
28      date.set(Calendar.DATE, 1);
29
30      // Determine the current month and year
31      int month = date.get(Calendar.MONTH);
32      int year = date.get(Calendar.YEAR);
33
34      // Determine the day of the week for the first day of the
35      // current month
36      int dayOfWeek = date.get(Calendar.DAY_OF_WEEK) - 1;
37
38      // Print a heading for the calendar
39      printHeading(month, year);
40
41      // Print the body of the calendar
42      printDays(dayOfWeek, daysInMonth(month, year));
43    }
44
45    /////////////////////////////////////////////////////////////
46    // NAME:        printHeading
47    // BEHAVIOR:    Prints a heading for a one-month calendar.
48    //              The heading consists of a month and year,
49    //              centered over a row of 20 dashes.
50    // PARAMETERS:  month - number representing a month (0-11)
51    //              year - the year
```

```
52      // RETURNS:      Nothing
53      ///////////////////////////////////////////////////////////
54      private static void printHeading(int month, int year) {
55        // Convert the month number to a name
56        final String[] MONTH_NAMES =
57          {"January", "February", "March", "April", "May",
58           "June", "July", "August", "September", "October",
59           "November", "December"};
60        String monthString = MONTH_NAMES[month];
61
62        // Determine how many spaces to display before the month
63        int precedingSpaces = (15 - monthString.length()) / 2;
64
65        // Print the month, year, and row of dashes
66        System.out.println();
67        for (int i = 1; i <= precedingSpaces; i++)
68          System.out.print(" ");
69        System.out.println(monthString + " " + year);
70        System.out.println("--------------------");
71      }
72
73      ///////////////////////////////////////////////////////////
74      // NAME:        printDays
75      // BEHAVIOR:    Prints the days in a one-month calendar
76      // PARAMETERS:  dayOfWeek - day of week for first day in
77      //                          month (0-6)
78      //              monthLength - number of days in month
79      // RETURNS:     Nothing
80      ///////////////////////////////////////////////////////////
81      private static void printDays(int dayOfWeek,
82                                    int monthLength) {
83        // Leave space for "empty days" at the beginning of the
84        // month
85        for (int i = 0; i < dayOfWeek; i++)
86          System.out.print("   ");
87
88        // Display the calendar. Add a space before each
89        // single-digit day so that columns will line up. Advance
90        // to the next line after each Saturday date is printed.
91        for (int day = 1; day <= monthLength; day++) {
92          if (day <= 9)
93            System.out.print(" " + day + " ");
94          else
95            System.out.print(day + " ");
96          if ((dayOfWeek + day) % 7 == 0)
97            System.out.println();
98        }
99
100       // If the month did not end on a Saturday, terminate the
101       // last line of the calendar with a new-line
102       if ((dayOfWeek + monthLength) % 7 != 0)
103         System.out.println();
104     }
105
```

```
106   ///////////////////////////////////////////////////////////
107   // NAME:        daysInMonth
108   // BEHAVIOR:    Computes the number of days in a month.
109   // PARAMETERS:  month - number representing a month (0-11)
110   //              year - the year
111   // RETURNS:     Number of days in the specified month in the
112   //              specified year
113   ///////////////////////////////////////////////////////////
114   private static int daysInMonth(int month, int year) {
115      int numberOfDays = 31;
116
117      // Add 1 to month; the result will be between 1 and 12
118      switch (month + 1) {
119        case 2:   // February
120                  numberOfDays = 28;
121                  if (year % 4 == 0) {
122                    numberOfDays = 29;
123                    if (year % 100 == 0 && year % 400 != 0)
124                      numberOfDays = 28;
125                  }
126                  break;
127
128        case 4:   // April
129        case 6:   // June
130        case 9:   // September
131        case 11:  // November
132                  numberOfDays = 30;
133                  break;
134      }
135
136      return numberOfDays;
137   }
138 }
```

Note that the MONTH_NAMES array has been declared `final`, because the program doesn't change the array's elements.

Review Question

1. To find the current time and date, which class would we would create an instance of: (a) `Calendar`, (b) `CurrentTime`, (c) `GregorianCalendar`, or (d) `Time`?

8.7 Debugging

When a program fails to catch an exception, the Java interpreter will print information about the nature of the exception and the location at which it occurred. Knowing how to interpret this information makes debugging much easier and faster.

For example, consider what happens if line 121 of the `PrintCalendar` program (Section 8.6) happened to be

```
if (year % 0 == 4) {
```

instead of

```
if (year % 4 == 0) {
```

If the incorrect version of the statement is executed, the program will attempt to divide `year` by 0 in order to obtain the remainder. Here's what the Java interpreter displayed when I tried to run the modified `PrintCalendar` program:

```
Exception in thread "main" java.lang.ArithmeticException: / by zero
        at PrintCalendar.daysInMonth(PrintCalendar.java:121)
        at PrintCalendar.main(PrintCalendar.java:42)
```

Here's how to interpret this information:

- The exception named `ArithmeticException` occurred. This exception belongs to the `java.lang` package.

- The exception occurred on line 121 of `PrintCalendar.java`. The method that was executing at the time was `daysInMonth`.

- The `daysInMonth` method had been called on line 42 of `PrintCalendar.java` by the `main` method.

Q&A What the interpreter has displayed is often called a ***stack trace:*** a list showing what method was executing at the time of the exception, which method called it, which method called that method, and so on, all the way back to `main`.

The information printed when an exception occurs isn't always this easy to read. Sometimes an exception will be thrown inside one of Java's own methods, causing the interpreter to mention methods and files that belong to the Java API. The secret is to start at the top of the output and read down until you reach a line that refers to one of your own methods.

Review Question

1. When an exception is not caught, the Java interpreter will display a _____ _____ [two words] showing what method was executing at the time of the exception, which method called it, and so on.

Q & A

Q: **Why does Java require that the controlling expression in a `switch` statement be a value of type `char`, `byte`, `short`, or `int`? [p. 311]**

A: Restricting the type of the controlling expression simplifies the compiler and allows it to convert `switch` statements into more-efficient bytecode instructions. Many other programming languages have a similar restriction, for the same reasons.

Q: I don't understand how omitting `break` at the end of a case in a `switch` statement could be a "useful programming technique." Can you give an example? [p. 312]

A: Certainly. Assume that the variable `grade` contains either 1, 2, 3, 4, or 5, where a grade of 3 or better is considered "passing." Suppose that we're writing a program that counts the number of passing grades as well as the total number of grades. The following `switch` statement adds 1 to the variables `passingGrades` and `totalGrades` if the grade is passing. If the grade is failing, only `total-Grades` is incremented.

```
switch (grade) {
  case 3: case 4: case 5:
    passingGrades++;
  case 1: case 2:
    totalGrades++;
    break;
}
```

If you ever use this technique, be sure to document it with a comment:

```
switch (grade) {
  case 3: case 4: case 5:
    passingGrades++;
    // FALL THROUGH
  case 1: case 2:
    totalGrades++;
    break;
}
```

The comment is important to clarify what you're doing and discourage anyone from adding a `break` statement later.

Q: When an exception occurs in my program, I get a stack trace showing which methods had been called at the time of the exception. However, the trace doesn't show the line numbers for the method calls. Is there any way to see the line numbers? [p. 328]

A: Let's say that your program is named `MyProg`. If you're using an older version (1.1.x) of the Java Development Kit, use the following command to run the Java interpreter:

```
java -Dnojit MyProg
```

If you're using a more recent version (1.2 or later), use the following command instead:

```
java -Djava.compiler=none MyProg
```

Q: Many programming languages have a `goto` statement that causes the program to jump to a specified statement. Does Java have a `goto` statement?

A: Not at present. `goto` is a keyword in Java, however, which means that you can't use it as an identifier. One reason for making `goto` a keyword is that it enables a

Java compiler to produce better error messages if a programmer tries to include goto statements in a Java program. Although the goto statement is common in older languages, it's almost never needed in Java. Java's break, continue, and return statements are sufficient for nearly every situation that requires a "jump." The existence of Java's System.exit method (which terminates the program) and exceptions further reduce the need for goto statements.

Summary

- When a Java program performs an illegal operation, an exception is thrown.
- By using a try block together with a catch block, a program can catch an exception and perform any desired action.
- A single try block may be followed by any number of catch blocks.
- Exceptions are objects. The getMessage method returns the string stored inside an exception object.
- Exceptions are either checked or unchecked. Checked exceptions must be caught by a program; unchecked exceptions need not be.
- The Thread.sleep method allows a program to "sleep" for a specified number of milliseconds.
- The switch statement consists of a controlling expression, a series of case labels, and for each case label, a series of statements.
- When a switch statement is executed, the value of the controlling expression is compared with the case labels. If a match is found, the statements after the case label are executed.
- If the value of the controlling expression doesn't match any of the case labels, the statements following the default: label are executed. If there is no default: label, then the switch statement has no effect.
- Case labels can be combined if they represent identical actions.
- The value in a case label must be a constant expression.
- Case labels don't have to appear in any particular order.
- It's illegal to use the same value in two case labels within a single switch statement.
- A switch statement has two advantages over a cascaded if statement: clarity and speed. On the other hand, switch statements aren't as general as cascaded if statements. In particular, the controlling expression in a switch statement must have type char, byte, short, or int.
- Normally, each case in a switch statement ends with a break statement. If no break statement is present, the program "falls through" into the next case.
- A do statement repeatedly executes its loop body as long as the controlling expression is true. The expression is tested after the loop body is executed.

- Executing a `continue` statement inside a loop causes the rest of the loop body to be skipped.
- A normal `break` statement causes only the closest containing `switch` statement or loop to terminate. A labeled `break` statement can exit from nested `switch` statements and/or loops.
- A normal `continue` statement skips the rest of the body of the closest containing loop. A labeled `continue` statement can skip the rest of the body of any enclosing loop.

Exercises

Section 8.1

1. Locate the error in the following statement and show how to fix it.

```
try
    i = Integer.parseInt(str);
catch (NumberFormatException e)
    System.out.println("Input was not an integer");
```

2. (a) Show the output of the following program.

```
public class Exercise8_2 {
    public static void main(String[] args) {
        int a = 0, b = 5, c;

        try {
            c = a / b;
        } catch (ArithmeticException e) {
            System.out.println("Error in first division");
            return;
        }
        System.out.println("Finished first division");

        try {
            c = b / a;
        } catch (ArithmeticException e) {
            System.out.println("Error in second division");
            return;
        }
        System.out.println("Finished second division");
    }
}
```

(b) Suppose that we initialize a to 5 and b to 0 in part (a). What will be the output now?

3. What will be printed when the following statements are executed?

```
try {
    System.out.println("Starting to convert");
    int i = Integer.parseInt("Not a number");
    System.out.println("So far, so good");
} catch (NumberFormatException e) {
    System.out.println("Bad number");
}
System.out.println("All done");
```

Section 8.2

4. Locate the error in the following statement and show how to fix it.

```
switch (channel) {
  case 2:  System.out.println("WSB-TV");
  case 5:  System.out.println("WAGA-TV");
  case 11: System.out.println("WXIA-TV");
}
```

5. Consider the following `switch` statement:

```
switch (areaCode) {
  case 205: System.out.println("Alabama");
            break;
  case 334: System.out.println("Alabama");
            break;
  case 404: System.out.println("Georgia");
            break;
  case 601: System.out.println("Mississippi");
            break;
  case 678: System.out.println("Georgia");
            break;
  case 706: System.out.println("Georgia");
            break;
  case 770: System.out.println("Georgia");
            break;
  case 912: System.out.println("Georgia");
            break;
}
```

Rewrite this statement to make it as small as possible (using the fewest possible tokens). You may assume that `areaCode` always matches one of the values shown.

6. Convert each of the following cascaded `if` statements to an equivalent `switch` statement, if possible. If a particular `if` statement cannot be converted, explain why. Your `switch` statements should be as simple as possible. Assume that `letterGrade` is a `String` variable, `button` and `day` are `int` variables, and `average` is a `double` variable.

```
(a) if (letterGrade.equals("A"))
       grade = 4;
    else if (letterGrade.equals("B"))
       grade = 3;
    else if (letterGrade.equals("C"))
       grade = 2;
    else if (letterGrade.equals("D"))
       grade = 1;
    else
       grade = 0;

(b) if (button == 1)
       System.out.println("Account information");
    else if (button == 2)
       System.out.println("Transactions");
    else if (button == 3)
       System.out.println("Loan information");
    else if (button == 0)
       System.out.println("Speak to a representative");
```

```
(c) if (day == 2 || day == 9 || day == 16 ||
        day == 23 || day == 30)
      System.out.println("Saturday");
   else if (day == 3 || day == 10 || day == 17 ||
        day == 24 || day == 31)
      System.out.println("Sunday");
   else
      System.out.println("Weekday");
```

```
(d) if (60.0 <= average && average <= 100.0)
      System.out.println("Passing");
   else
      System.out.println("Failing");
```

7. Convert the first cascaded `if` statement of Section 4.4 to an equivalent `switch` statement. *Hint:* Use `score / 10` as the controlling expression.

Section 8.3

8. Show the output of the following program.

```
public class Exercise8_8 {
  public static void main(String[] args) {
    System.out.println("f(0) = " + f(0));
    System.out.println("f(15) = " + f(15));
    System.out.println("f(26) = " + f(26));
  }

  private static String f(int n) {
    String result = "";
    do {
      result += n % 2;
      n /= 2;
    } while (n > 0);
    return result;
  }
}
```

9. Locate the error in the following statement and show how to fix it.

```
do
  i /= 2
while (i > 10);
```

10. Which one of the following statements is not equivalent to the other two?

```
(a) while (i < 10) System.out.println(i);
(b) for (; i < 10;) System.out.println(i);
(c) do System.out.println(i); while (i < 10);
```

11. Which one of the following statements is not equivalent to the other two?

```
(a) while (--i > 0) j++;
(b) for (; --i > 0; j++);
(c) do j++; while (--i > 0);
```

12. Suppose that Java did not provide a `do` statement. Show how to get the same effect as the statement

```
do
   statement
while (expression);
```

where *expression* is an arbitrary `boolean` expression and *statement* is an arbitrary statement.

13. Suppose that Java did not provide a `while` statement. Show how to get the same effect as the statement

```
while (expression)
   statement
```

where *expression* is an arbitrary `boolean` expression and *statement* is an arbitrary statement. *Hint:* Use a combination of a `do` statement and an `if` statement.

14. Write a class method named `intToString` that converts an `int` value to string form. For example, `intToString(123)` should return `"123"` and `intToString(-123)` should return `"-123"`. Use a `do` loop that removes digits one by one from the parameter and adds them to a string that is later returned by the method. (A `do` loop is a good choice because every integer, including 0, has at least one digit.)

Section 8.4   15. Show the output of the following program.

```
public class Exercise8_15 {
  public static void main(String[] args) {
    int j = 0;

    for (int i = 1; i <= 100; i++) {
      if (i % 2 == 0)
        continue;
      if (i % 3 == 0)
        continue;
      if (i % 11 == 0)
        break;
      j += i;
    }

    System.out.println("Answer: " + j);
  }
}
```

Section 8.5   16. Show the output of the following program.

```
public class Exercise8_16 {
  public static void main(String[] args) {
    for (int i = 1; i <= 3; i++) {
      int k = 1;
      for (int j = 1; j <= 3; j++) {
        k *= i;
        System.out.print(f(k));
      }
      System.out.println();
    }
  }
}
```

```
    private static String f(int n) {
      if (n < 10)
        return "  " + n;
      else
        return " " + n;
    }
}
```

Programming Projects

1. Modify the MonthLength program (Section 8.2) so that it fully validates user input. If the month or year isn't an integer, the program must display the message "Not an integer; try again". If the month isn't between 1 and 12, the program must display the message "Month must be between 1 and 12; try again". If the year is less than 0, the program must display the message "Year cannot be negative; try again". In each case, the program must prompt the user to re-enter the input.

2. Modify the MonthLength program (Section 8.2) so that it accepts month names rather than numerical codes. The user's interaction with the program will have the following appearance:

```
Enter a month name: April
Enter a year: 2003
There are 30 days in this month
```

The case of the month name doesn't matter. If the month name isn't legal, the program must display the message "Illegal month name; try again". If the year isn't an integer, the program must display the message "Not an integer; try again". If the year is less than 0, the program must display the message "Year cannot be negative; try again". In each case, the program must prompt the user to re-enter the input.

3. Modify the PrintInterest program (Section 8.5) so that it fully validates user input. If the interest rate or number of years is not an integer, the program must display the message "Not an integer; try again" and then prompt the user to re-enter the input. If the interest rate or number of years is negative, the program must display the message "Number cannot be negative; try again" and then prompt the user to re-enter the number.

4. Modify the PrintCalendar program (Section 8.6) so that it asks the user to enter a month and year:

```
Enter a month name: May
Enter a year: 2000
```

The case of the month name doesn't matter. If the month name isn't legal, the program must display the message "Illegal month name; try again". If the year isn't an integer, the program must display the message "Not an integer; try again". If the year is less than 0, the program must display the message "Year cannot be negative; try again". In each case, the program must prompt the user to re-enter the input.

5. Modify the PrintCalendar program (Section 8.6) so that it displays the calendar in a frame (see the figure at the top of the next page). Each square must be 30 pixels wide and 30 pixels high. Days must be displayed in a plain, 15-point, sans serif font, with each day

centered within its square. The month and year must be displayed as the title for the frame. Note that the height of the frame may vary, because the calendar may have either 4, 5, or 6 rows.

6. Write a program named `NameForNumber` that asks the user for a two-digit number and then prints the English name for the number:

```
Enter a two-digit number: 45
You entered the number forty-five.
```

Hint: Split the number into two digits. Use one `switch` statement to print the word for the first digit ("twenty," "thirty," and so forth). Use a second `switch` statement to print the word for the second digit. Don't forget that the numbers between 11 and 19 require special treatment.

7. Legal documents are often dated in the following way:

Dated this _____ day of _____ , _____ .

Write a program named `LegalDate` that displays dates in this form. After asking the user to enter the year, month, and day, the program will display the date in legal form:

```
Enter year: 2003
Enter month (1-12): 4
Enter day: 28
Dated this 28th day of April, 2003.
```

Hint: Use a `switch` statement to print the day suffix (`th`, `st`, `nd`, or `rd`).

8. Write a program named `ComputeAge` that determines the user's age in years, months, and days. The user enters his or her birthday, and the program determines how old the person is on the current date. The following example shows what the user will see on the screen, assuming that the current date is July 9, 1999:

```
Enter the year you were born: 1980
Enter the month you were born (1-12): 7
Enter the day you were born: 26
You are 18 years, 11 months, and 13 days old
```

The words "years," "months," and "days" must be printed in singular form when appropriate.

Your program must detect the following input errors:

■ ***Input is not numeric.***
■ ***Input is too small.*** The year cannot be less than 1800. The month and day cannot be less than 1.

- ***Input is too large.*** The birth year cannot exceed the current year. The birth month cannot exceed 12. If the user was born in the current year, then the birth month cannot exceed the current month. The birth day cannot exceed the number of days in the specified birth month. (Note that the number of days may depend on the birth year as well.) Also, if the user was born in the current month of the current year, the day of birth cannot exceed the current day.

If any of these errors occur, the program must print an error message and ask the user to re-enter the offending input:

```
Enter the year you were born: 1700 AD
Input was not an integer
Enter the year you were born: 1700
Input must be at least 1800
Enter the year you were born: 2100
Input must be no more than 1999
Enter the year you were born: 1978
Enter the month you were born (1-12): 2
Enter the day you were born: 29
Input must be no more than 28
Enter the day you were born: 27
You are 21 years, 4 months, and 12 days old
```

Hints: 1. The number of days in the userís age may depend on the number of days in the birth month. If the birth month is February, your program will need to take into account whether the birth year is a leap year. 2. Write a helper method that prompts the user to enter an integer, validates the input, and then prompts the user to re-enter the input if necessary. The method should check that the input is an integer and that it falls within a specified range. 3. Use the `daysInMonth` method (Section 8.6) as a helper. 4. Write a method to help with the task of deciding whether or not to add an ìsî t o ìy ear,î ì month,î and ìda y.î

Answers to Review Questions

Section 8.1
1. Thrown
2. `catch` block
3. Checked and unchecked
4. (b)

Section 8.2
1. Cascaded
2. `default`
3. `char`, `byte`, `short`, and `int`
4. A `switch` statement can often be executed faster than a corresponding `if` statement.

Section 8.3
1. (b)
2. (b)

Section 8.4
1. `break`
2. It can simplify the body of a loop by reducing the amount of nesting.

Section 8.5
1. Labeled

Section 8.6
1. (c)

Section 8.7
1. Stack trace

9 **Primitive Types**

In previous chapters, we've used several of Java's primitive types, including `boolean`, `double`, and `int`. This chapter takes an in-depth look at all the primitive types, with the exception of `boolean`, which was discussed in Section 4.5. The remaining types fall into three groups: the integer types (`byte`, `short`, `int`, and `long`), the floating-point types (`float` and `double`), and the character type (`char`). The chapter also explains how a value of one primitive type can be converted to another primitive type. Such conversions sometimes occur automatically and sometimes at the programmer's request.

Objectives

- To learn about the integer types: `byte`, `short`, `int`, and `long`.
- To learn how integers are stored.
- To learn about the floating-point types: `float` and `double`.
- To learn how to use the special values of `float` and `double`: positive infinity, negative infinity, and NaN (not a number).
- To learn about the `Math` class, which provides mathematical constants and methods.
- To learn about the `char` (character) type.
- To learn about the ASCII and Unicode character sets.
- To learn about the `Character` class, which provides methods for classifying and converting characters.
- To learn how a value of one primitive type can be converted to another primitive type, either by implicit conversion or by casting.

9.1 Types

To a mathematician, there's no difference between the number 3 and the number 3.0. Both represent "three," a number that's both an integer and a real number. To a programmer, however, there's a big difference between 3 and 3.0. The problem is one of storage. Numbers, like all data, must be stored in computer memory. Computer memory, as we saw in Chapter 1, consists of bits (0s and 1s). These bits are grouped into larger units, known as bytes, each containing eight bits.

In Java, as in most other programming languages, the type of a data item determines how much space is used to store the item and how the bits in the item are interpreted. We saw in Section 7.4 that Java has two kinds of types: primitive types and reference types. A variable of a primitive type stores a data item directly. A variable of a reference type stores the *location* of the data, not the data itself. We've used both kinds of types in previous chapters; int and double are primitive types, whereas classes, such as String, are reference types. A String variable doesn't contain a String object; instead, it contains a reference to where a String object is stored.

The primitive types represent the smallest and simplest units of data: numbers, characters, and Boolean values. The term "primitive" doesn't mean that these types are remnants of some early civilization; instead, it indicates that they're the "building blocks" of Java. A chemist might call them "atomic types" instead, because they're used to build more-complex objects, in much the same way atoms are used to build molecules. Java's primitive types are "built into" the language—we don't define them ourselves.

The primitive types fall into two categories: numeric (the byte, short, int, long, float, double, and char types), and Boolean (the boolean type). Section 4.5 covered the boolean type; the next three sections describe the numeric types in some detail. We'll start with the byte, short, int, and long types, which are used to store integers. We'll then discuss the floating-point types, float and double. Finally, we'll cover the char (character) type. For each type, we'll look at the range of values that it includes and the operations that it supports.

Literals

When a value of a primitive type is written out in a program, we refer to the value's representation as a literal. For example, 12 is an int literal, and true is a boolean literal. For each primitive type, we'll see how to write literals that belong to that type.

When we discuss literals, it's important to keep in mind that there's usually no single way to represent a particular number. A "number," after all, is an abstract concept. 12 is not a number, but a particular way of representing the concept of "twelve." Mathematicians make this distinction by using the term "numeral" for the written representation of a number. Humans use different numerals to represent the same number; for example, the Romans wrote "twelve" as XII instead of 12. Similarly, programmers sometimes use different literals that represent the same number.

Review Questions

1. What does a variable of a reference type store?

2. What are the two categories of primitive types?

3. True or false: Two different literals may represent the same number.

9.2   Integer Types

A variable of type int can store any number between $-2,147,483,648$ and $+2,147,483,647$. Why such strange numbers? The explanation stems from the fact that computers store numbers in binary (base 2) rather than decimal (base 10).

Binary Numbers

Decimal numbers are written in a positional notation, with each digit corresponding to a power of 10. The number 153, for example, consists of a series of digits between 0 and 9. Each digit within the number is implicitly multiplied by a power of 10, depending on the digit's position. The last digit (3, in this example) is implicitly multiplied by 10 raised to the power 0, which is 1. The next-to-last digit is implicitly multiplied by 10^1, which is 10. The digit before that one is multiplied by 10^2, or 100. So the value of 153 can be expressed as

$$153 = 1 \times 10^2 + 5 \times 10^1 + 3 \times 10^0$$

Binary notation works much the same way. A binary number consists of a series of binary digits (bits), each of which is either 0 or 1. Each bit is implicitly multiplied by a power of 2, depending on its position in the number. For example, each bit in the binary number 10011001 represents a power of 2, from 2^0 (for the rightmost bit) to 2^7 (for the leftmost bit). We can use this fact to determine what decimal number 10011001 represents:

$$1 \times 2^7 + 0 \times 2^6 + 0 \times 2^5 + 1 \times 2^4 + 1 \times 2^3 + 0 \times 2^2 + 0 \times 2^1 + 1 \times 2^0 =$$
$$128 + 0 + 0 + 16 + 8 + 0 + 0 + 1 = 153$$

In other words, the number 10011001 (binary) is equivalent to 153 (decimal).

Inside the computer, numbers are stored using a fixed number of bits. The number of bits used depends on the type of the number. A number that has int type, for example, is stored using 32 bits. In `int` form, the number 153 would be stored as 00000000000000000000000010011001 rather than just 10011001.

The largest `int` value isn't 11111111111111111111111111111111, as you might expect. The leftmost bit of an integer is used to store the number's sign (whether it's positive or negative). If the leftmost bit is 0, the number is positive (or zero). If the leftmost bit is 1, the number is negative. Because of the presence of this *sign bit,* the largest `int` is actually 01111111111111111111111111111111, which has the value

$$1 \times 2^{30} + 1 \times 2^{29} + \dots + 1 \times 2^0 = 2^{31} - 1 = 2{,}147{,}483{,}647$$

Negative Integers

Java stores negative integers in a form known as *two's complement.* To determine the bits in a negative number, we'd use the following algorithm:

1. Write the positive version of the number in binary.
2. **Complement** the number (change each 0 bit to 1 and change each 1 bit to 0).
3. Add 1 to the result.

For example, let's see how Java would store the number −12 as an `int` value. First, we write the number 12 in binary:

00000000000000000000000000001100

Next, we complement the number:

11111111111111111111111111110011

Finally, we add 1 to the complement:

```
11111111111111111111111111110011
+                               1
```
11111111111111111111111111110100

Binary numbers are added bit by bit, using the following rules: 0 + 0 = 0, 0 + 1 = 1, 1 + 0 = 1, and 1 + 1 = 0 (with a carry into the next bit position). Notice that the sign bit of the result is 1, indicating that the number is negative.

Two's complement has several desirable properties. One is that the value of $N + (−N)$ is zero for all values of N. Also, the value of $−(−N)$ is equal to N. One final advantage is that 0 cannot be negative. (Try using our three-step algorithm to find the representation of −0.)

But what if we need to store a number that's larger than 2,147,483,647? Java has another type named `long`, which stores integers using 64 bits. The largest value that can be stored as a `long` is $2^{63} - 1$, which is big enough for nearly any application. (If that's *still* not big enough, though, Java doesn't leave us in the lurch; there's a class named `BigInteger` whose instances can store integers of *any* size whatsoever.)

When we're working with numbers that are known to be small, it's sometimes advantageous to use a "smaller" type than int. Java has two such types, byte and short. A byte value is stored in 8 bits, so its values range from -128 (-2^7) to $+127$ ($2^7 - 1$). A short value is stored in 16 bits; its values range from $-32{,}768$ (-2^{15}) to $+32{,}767$ ($2^{15} - 1$).

Table 9.1 summarizes Java's integer types.

Table 9.1
Integer Types

Type	Size	Smallest Value	Largest Value
byte	8 bits	-128	127
short	16 bits	$-32{,}768$	32,767
int	32 bits	$-2{,}147{,}483{,}648$	2,147,483,647
long	64 bits	-2^{63}	$2^{63}-1$

In this book, we'll rarely need the byte and short types. We'll use long sparingly, because we won't often need numbers larger than 2,147,483,647. Also, operations on long values may require more time than operations on int values, so it's a good idea to stick with int as much as possible.

One of the unique aspects of Java's primitive types is that they're completely defined. In most programming languages, the size and representation of most types aren't completely specified, allowing the language to "fit" different computers. In the C++ language, for example, an int value might be 16 bits long, 32 bits long, or some other size entirely, depending on what size the hardware supports most efficiently. Because it puts portability ahead of efficiency, Java must be much more specific: in Java, an int value must be exactly 32 bits long, with one bit reserved for the number's sign. As a result, Java's numeric types have fixed ranges that don't vary from one computer to another.

For each of the integer types, Java provides a corresponding class in the java.lang package. Section 13.3 describes the primary reason for these classes, which are named Byte, Short, Integer, and Long. For now, we'll simply note that each class provides constants named MIN_VALUE and MAX_VALUE, which represent the smallest and largest values of the corresponding primitive type. For example, the value of Byte.MIN_VALUE is -128 and the value of Byte.MAX_VALUE is 127.

Integer Literals

Java allows integer literals to be written in decimal (base 10), octal (base 8), or hexadecimal (base 16).

- *Decimal* literals contain digits between 0 and 9, but must not begin with a zero:

```
15   255   32767
```

- *Octal* literals contain only digits between 0 and 7, and *must* begin with a zero:

```
017   0377   077777
```

- *Hexadecimal* literals contain digits between 0 and 9 and letters between a and f, and always begin with 0x:

  ```
  0xf   0xff   0x7fff
  ```

  The letters in a hexadecimal literal may be either upper or lowercase:

  ```
  0xff   0xfF   0xFf   0xFF   0Xff   0XfF   0XFf   0XFF
  ```

  Keep in mind that octal and hexadecimal are nothing more than an alternative way of writing numbers; they have no effect on how the numbers are actually stored. (Integers are always stored in binary, regardless of what notation we've used to express them.) Whether we write 15, 017, or 0xf, we're still dealing with the same number (fifteen). We can switch from one notation to another at any time, and even mix them: 10 + 015 + 0x20 has the value 55 (decimal).

Octal and Hexadecimal

An octal number is written using only the digits 0 through 7. Each position in an octal number represents a power of 8 (just as each position in a decimal number represents a power of 10). Thus, the octal number 237 represents the decimal number $2 \times 8^2 + 3 \times 8^1 + 7 \times 8^0 = 128 + 24 + 7 = 159$.

A hexadecimal (or hex) number is written using the digits 0 through 9 plus the letters A through F, which stand for 10 through 15, respectively. Each position in a hex number represents a power of 16; the hex number 1AF has the decimal value $1 \times 16^2 + 10 \times 16^1 + 15 \times 16^0 = 256 + 160 + 15 = 431$.

Although integers are stored in binary form, we usually write them in decimal form within a program, because humans are more familiar with decimal. In some types of programs, however, we'll need to work directly with binary numbers. Unfortunately, writing numbers in binary is painful and error-prone. If you had to write the number 111111011110011110001111011110100, for example, it's likely that you'd get some of the bits wrong. Fortunately, there's a better way. Because of the close connection between the binary number system and the octal and hexadecimal systems, we can easily translate binary numbers to either octal or hexadecimal. The resulting octal or hexadecimal numbers can then be used as integer literals.

To translate a binary number into octal, we start by collecting the bits into groups of three, starting from the right end of the number:

```
011 111 101 111 001 111 000 111 101 110 100
```

(We'll add a zero or two to the leftmost group if necessary, so that all groups have three bits.) We now translate each group into a single octal digit; 000 becomes 0, 001 becomes 1, 010 becomes 2, and so on:

```
011 111 101 111 001 111 000 111 101 110 100
 ⇓   ⇓   ⇓   ⇓   ⇓   ⇓   ⇓   ⇓   ⇓   ⇓   ⇓
 3   7   5   7   1   7   0   7   5   6   4
```

When the digits are joined together, the result is an octal number that's equal to the original binary number. In this example, 111111011110011110001111011110100 (binary) is equivalent to 37571707564 (octal).

To translate a binary number into hexadecimal, we start by collecting the bits into groups of four, starting from the right end of the number:

1111 1101 1110 0111 1000 1111 0111 0100

We now translate each group into a single hexadecimal digit; 0000 becomes 0, 0001 becomes 1, 0010 becomes 2, and so on:

```
1111   1101   1110   0111   1000   1111   0111   0100
 ⇓      ⇓      ⇓      ⇓      ⇓      ⇓      ⇓      ⇓
 F      D      E      7      8      F      7      4
```

Joining the digits together gives us FDE78F74 (hexadecimal), which is equivalent to 11111101111001111000111101110100 (binary).

Here's an interesting question: what's the type of the literal 10? Is it byte, short, int, or long? On the one hand, who cares?—it's the same number regardless; the only difference is whether it's stored in 8 bits, 16 bits, 32 bits, or 64 bits. On the other hand, literals need to have types, just as variables do, so the compiler must assume *some* type for 10. Java's rule is that an integer literal always has type int, unless it ends with the letter L, in which case it has type long. The following literals have type int:

512   0777   0x10000000

The following literals have type long:

512L   0777L   0x10000000L

We can use a lowercase L if we like, although that's not a good idea—it's too easy to confuse the letter l with the digit 1. Any integer literal that's larger than 2147483647 (decimal) must have the L suffix, as must any integer literal whose value is less than –2147483648.

Converting Strings to Integers

Byte.parseByte
Integer.parseInt
Long.parseLong
Short.parseShort

We'll often need to convert a string that contains an integer into the actual value of the integer. There are four methods that perform such a conversion, one for each type of integer:

```
Byte.parseByte
Integer.parseInt
Long.parseLong
Short.parseShort
```

We've used Integer.parseInt in previous chapters. The other methods are called in the same way as Integer.parseInt. All four methods throw NumberFormatException if the string being converted doesn't contain a valid integer or the number that it represents falls outside the range of allowable values.

For example, `Byte.parseByte` would reject the string `"128"`, because the largest `byte` value is 127.

Review Questions

1. What's the largest number that can be stored in a `short` variable?

2. How many bits are used to store a value of type `long`?

3. What's the name of the form in which negative integers are stored in Java?

4. Java lets us write integer literals in decimal or in two other bases. What are those bases?

5. All but one of the following literals represent the same integer. Which literal is different from the others: (a) `15`, (b) `013`, (c) `0xf`, or (d) `0XF`?

6. What method would we use to convert a string such as `"2310"` into a `long` value?

9.3 Floating-Point Types

The integer types aren't suitable for all applications. Sometimes we'll need variables that can store numbers with digits after the decimal point, or numbers that are exceedingly large or small. In this situation, there are two types for us to choose from: `float` and `double`, the *floating-point types.*

Table 9.2 summarizes the characteristics of the floating-point types.

Table 9.2
Floating-Point Types

Type	Size	Smallest Positive Value	Largest Value	Precision
float	32 bits	1.40×10^{-45}	3.40×10^{38}	6 digits
double	64 bits	4.94×10^{-324}	1.79×10^{308}	15 digits

Which type to use depends on the size of the numbers we'll be working with and the amount of precision we'll need. `float` is suitable when accuracy isn't critical (calculating temperatures to one decimal point, for example). `double` provides greater precision—enough for nearly all applications. For numbers that must be stored even more precisely, the Java API provides a class named `BigDecimal`.

In most programming languages, the format of floating-point numbers isn't specified, because not all computers store floating-point numbers in the same way. For portability, however, Java requires that `float` and `double` values be stored in the format specified by IEEE Standard 754.

The IEEE Floating-Point Standard

IEEE Standard 754, developed by the Institute of Electrical and Electronics Engineers, provides two primary formats for floating-point numbers: single precision (32 bits) and double precision (64 bits). Numbers are stored in a form of scientific notation, with each number having three parts: a ***sign***, an ***exponent***, and a ***fraction***. The number of bits reserved for the exponent determines how large (or small) numbers can be; the number of bits in the fraction determines the precision. In single-precision format, the exponent is 8 bits long, and the fraction occupies 23 bits. As a result, a single-precision number has a maximum value of approximately 3.40×10^{38}, with a precision of about 6 decimal digits. In double-precision format, the exponent is 11 bits long, and the fraction occupies 52 bits. A double-precision number has a maximum value of approximately 1.79×10^{308}, with a precision of about 15 decimal digits.

Floating-Point Literals

When a literal represents a `float` or `double` value, it is said to be a ***floating-point literal.*** A floating-point literal can be written in a variety of ways. It may contain a decimal point:

```
2.9748    414.270984    .0008915
```

It may have an exponent instead, indicating the power of 10 by which the number should be scaled:

```
29748e-4   414270984e-6   8915e-7
```

Or it may have both a decimal point and an exponent:

```
297.48e-2   4.14270984e+2   89.15e-5
```

The + in the exponent is optional, and the e can be uppercase.

A floating-point literal may end with the letter f (or F), to indicate that it has type `float`, or it may end with d (or D), to indicate that it has type `double`. By default, a floating-point literal is treated as a `double` value. A floating-point literal must contain a decimal point and/or an exponent, unless f or d is appended to the literal. In other words, `597d` and `597f` are both floating-point literals, even though neither contains a decimal point or exponent.

Q&A

Java doesn't allow assignment of a `double` value to a `float` variable. As a result, a floating-point literal without a suffix can't be assigned to a `float` variable:

```
float x;
x = 1.0;   // WRONG; 1.0 has type double
```

There are two ways to fix this problem. One is to declare x as a `double` variable:

```
double x;
x = 1.0;   // Legal
```

The other is to put the letter f at the end of the literal, to indicate that it has type `float`:

```
float x;
x = 1.0f;   // Legal
```

Special Values

In Section 8.1, we saw that attempting to divide an integer by zero causes an exception to be thrown. Surprisingly, dividing a `float` or `double` value by zero does *not* cause an exception. To see why this is, we need to think like a mathematician. In mathematics, dividing a nonzero number by zero has a well-defined outcome: infinity. Java attempts to mirror mathematics by allowing division by zero to produce infinity.

Java's `float` and `double` types include three special values: +∞, −∞, and NaN (Not a Number). If a program divides a positive number by zero, the result will be +∞. Dividing a negative number by zero yields −∞. NaN is the result of a mathematically undefined operation, such as dividing zero by zero. Here are a few examples:

```
1.0 / 0.0 ⇒ +∞
-1.0 / 0.0 ⇒ −∞
0.0 / 0.0 ⇒ NaN
```

The IEEE 754 standard, which Java follows, allows special values to be used in computations. +∞ and −∞ have much the same properties as they do in ordinary mathematics. For example, dividing an ordinary floating-point number by infinity gives zero as the result:

```
1.0 / (1.0 / 0.0) ⇒ 0.0
1.0 / (-1.0 / 0.0) ⇒ −0.0
```

Notice that floating-point zero can be negative. (Integer zero is never negative.) Using NaN in a calculation always results in a value of NaN:

```
1.0 / (0.0 / 0.0) ⇒ NaN
0.0 * (0.0 / 0.0) ⇒ NaN
```

NaN can also result from multiplying infinity by zero:

```
(1.0 / 0.0) * 0.0 ⇒ NaN
(-1.0 / 0.0) * 0.0 ⇒ NaN
```

The `Float` and `Double` classes (in the `java.lang` package) provide constants named `POSITIVE_INFINITY`, `NEGATIVE_INFINITY`, and `NaN`, as well as a method named `isNaN` that tests whether a floating-point number is NaN. There's no other way to check for NaN; testing whether NaN is equal to any other number (including NaN) will yield `false`.

Expressions whose values are +∞, −∞, and NaN can be printed with `System.out.print` or `System.out.println`. Printing +∞ causes `Infinity` to be displayed, printing −∞ causes `-Infinity` to be displayed, and printing NaN causes `NaN` to be displayed:

```
System.out.println(1.0 / 0.0);    // Prints "Infinity"
System.out.println(-1.0 / 0.0);   // Prints "-Infinity"
System.out.println(0.0 / 0.0);    // Prints "NaN"
```

As we saw in an earlier example, the floating-point number 0.0 can be either positive or negative. Positive zero tests equal to negative zero, but the result of dividing a positive number by positive zero is $+\infty$; dividing by negative zero yields $-\infty$.

The `Math` Class

The `Math` class, which is part of the `java.lang` package, provides a number of methods that are useful when working with numbers, especially floating-point numbers. We saw in Section 7.5 that the `Math` class also defines two constants, named `E` and `PI`, which represent the familiar mathematical constants e and π. To use these constants, we must write `Math.E` and `Math.PI`.

Seven of the methods in the `Math` class are capable of computing trigonometric functions (Table 9.3).

Table 9.3
Trigonometric Methods

Description	*Action*
`double cos(double a)`	Returns the cosine of a.
`double sin(double a)`	Returns the sine of a.
`double tan(double a)`	Returns the tangent of a.
`double acos(double a)`	Returns the arc cosine of a.
`double asin(double a)`	Returns the arc sine of a.
`double atan(double a)`	Returns the arc tangent of a.
`double atan2(double a, double b)`	Returns the arc tangent of a/b.

Like most of the methods in the `Math` class, the trigonometric methods require parameters of type `double` and return a result of type `double`. Angles are measured in radians, not degrees.

Math.cos
Math.sin
Math.tan

The `cos`, `sin`, and `tan` methods compute the cosine, sine, and tangent functions:

```
Math.cos(Math.PI)  ⇒  –1.0
Math.sin(Math.PI)  ⇒  1.2246467991473532E-16
Math.tan(Math.PI)  ⇒  –1.2246467991473532E-16
```

Note that some of the results are slightly inaccurate because of round-off error. In particular, `Math.sin` and `Math.tan` returned small numbers instead of 0.

Math.acos
Math.asin
Math.atan
Math.atan2

The `acos`, `asin`, `atan`, and `atan2` methods compute inverse trigonometric functions:

```
Math.acos(1.0)  ⇒  0.0
Math.asin(1.0)  ⇒  1.5707963267948966
Math.atan(1.0)  ⇒  0.7853981633974483
Math.atan2(1.0, 1.0)  ⇒  0.7853981633974483
```

The `acos` method returns a value between 0.0 and π. The `asin` and `atan` methods return values between $-\pi/2$ through $\pi/2$. The `atan2` method returns a value between $-\pi$ and π.

Q&A

The Math class also provides methods that compute the exponential and logarithmic functions (Table 9.4).

Table 9.4
Exponential and
Logarithmic Methods

Description	Action
`double exp(double a)`	Returns *e* raised to the power a.
`double log(double a)`	Returns the logarithm (base *e*) of a.

Math.exp

The `exp` method computes the exponential function:

`Math.exp(1.0)` ⟹ 2.7182818284590455

Math.log

The `log` method computes the natural logarithm of its argument:

`Math.log(Math.E)` ⟹ 1.0

The `log` method's argument must be greater than zero. `log` returns $-\infty$ if the argument is zero; it returns NaN if the argument is less than zero.

The `pow` and `sqrt` methods compute powers and square roots (Table 9.5).

Table 9.5
Power Methods

Description	Action
`double pow(double a, double b)`	Returns a raised to the power b.
`double sqrt(double a)`	Returns the square root of a.

Math.pow
Math.sqrt

The `pow` method throws `ArithmeticException` if a is equal to 0.0 and b is less than or equal to 0.0, or if a is less than 0.0 and b is not a whole number. The `sqrt` method returns NaN if its argument is less than zero. See Section 2.9 for examples of how `pow` and `sqrt` are called.

The `abs`, `max`, and `min` methods compute the absolute value and the maximum and minimum of two numbers (Table 9.6).

Table 9.6
Absolute Value,
Maximum, and
Minimum Methods

Description	Action
`int abs(int a)`	Returns the absolute value of a.
`long abs(long a)`	
`float abs(float a)`	
`double abs(double a)`	
`int max(int a, int b)`	Returns the larger of a and b.
`long max(long a, long b)`	
`float max(float a, float b)`	
`double max(double a, double b)`	
`int min(int a, int b)`	Returns the smaller of a and b.
`long min(long a, long b)`	
`float min(float a, float b)`	
`double min(double a, double b)`	

Math.abs
Math.max
Math.min

Each method in Table 9.6 is overloaded. There are actually four different methods named `abs`, four named `max`, and four named `min`. One version of the `abs` method takes an `int` argument and returns an `int` value; the other versions take `long`, `float`, and `double` arguments, returning a value of the same type as the argument. The four versions of `max` and `min` are similar to the four versions of `abs`. Examples of `abs`, `max`, and `min` appear in Section 2.9.

The methods in the last group are used to round `float` and `double` values to integers (Table 9.7).

Table 9.7
Rounding Methods

Description	Action
`double ceil(double a)`	Returns a rounded up to the nearest integer.
`double floor(double a)`	Returns a rounded down to the nearest integer.
`double rint(double a)`	Returns a rounded to the nearest integer.
`int round(float a)`	Returns a rounded to the nearest `int` value.
`long round(double a)`	Returns a rounded to the nearest `long` value.

Math.ceil

The `ceil` method returns the smallest integer that's not less than the argument:

```
Math.ceil(4.1) ⇒ 5.0
Math.ceil(4.9) ⇒ 5.0
Math.ceil(-4.1) ⇒ -4.0
Math.ceil(-4.9) ⇒ -4.0
```

Math.floor

The `floor` method returns the largest integer that's not greater than the argument:

```
Math.floor(4.1) ⇒ 4.0
Math.floor(4.9) ⇒ 4.0
Math.floor(-4.1) ⇒ -5.0
Math.floor(-4.9) ⇒ -5.0
```

Math.rint

The `rint` method returns the integer closest to the argument:

```
Math.rint(4.1) ⇒ 4.0
Math.rint(4.5) ⇒ 4.0
Math.rint(4.9) ⇒ 5.0
Math.rint(5.5) ⇒ 6.0
Math.rint(-4.1) ⇒ -4.0
Math.rint(-4.5) ⇒ -4.0
Math.rint(-4.9) ⇒ -5.0
Math.rint(-5.5) ⇒ -6.0
```

If the argument to `rint` is equally close to two integers, `rint` returns the even one. In some older versions of Java, however, `rint` incorrectly returns the larger (more positive) integer.

Math.round   The two round methods behave exactly like rint; the only difference is that they return int or long values instead of double values. (Note that ceil, floor, and rint all return a double value.) One version of round rounds a float value to the nearest int value; the other rounds a double value to the nearest long value. Section 2.9 gives examples of the round method.

Math.random   The Math class also provides the random method, which returns a pseudo-random double value that's greater than or equal to 0.0 and less than 1.0. Several programs that use Math.random appear in Chapter 4.

Pseudorandom Numbers

We often need a source of numbers that appear to be random. Programs that play games may need to simulate the randomness of a card deal or a dice roll. Random numbers are also useful in programs that simulate real-world phenomena, from the behavior of subatomic particles to the behavior of big-city traffic.

Truly random numbers are hard to come by in the computer realm—after all, computers are built to behave predictably, not randomly—so programmers usually settle for **pseudorandom** numbers, which appear random but are actually generated by a mathematical formula. A pseudorandom sequence begins with a seed value; each value after that in the sequence is generated from the previous value. Pseudorandom numbers have one advantage over truly random numbers: a pseudorandom sequence can be reproduced as many times as desired—during the debugging of a program, say—by simply starting with the same seed.

The most popular method for generating pseudorandom numbers is also one of the oldest. The **linear congruential method,** devised in 1948 by mathematician D. H. Lehmer, uses the following formula:

$$X_{n+1} = (aX_n + c) \bmod m$$

X_n is the nth element in the sequence and a, c, and m are constants. Proper choice of a, c, and m is important; if they're poorly chosen, the sequence may begin repeating after relatively few numbers have been generated. (Pseudorandom sequences will always begin repeating after a certain point, but good ones will generate many thousands of numbers before repeating.)

Math.random uses the linear congruential method to generate a 53-bit integer, which is divided by 2^{53} to produce a double value between 0.0 and 1.0. The seed is based on the time of day at which the program is run, which means that the pseudorandom sequence will probably be different each time.

Math.random uses the services of a class named Random, which belongs to the java.util package. An instance of the Random class keeps track of a single pseudorandom sequence, generating new numbers in the sequence when asked.

Review Questions

1.   The double type is capable of representing larger numbers than the float type. What is the other advantage of the double type?

2. A floating-point number is stored in three parts: the sign, the fraction, and the _____.

3. What is the type of the literal `3.0e+10`?

4. If the `float` variable `f` contains positive infinity and the `float` variable `g` contains NaN, what is the value of `f + g`?

5. Which one of the following operations cannot be performed by calling a method that belongs to the `Math` class: (a) computing the square root of a `double` value, (b) finding the larger of two `double` values, (c) rounding a `double` value to the nearest integer, or (d) converting a `double` value to string form?

9.4 The `char` Type

The only remaining primitive type is `char`, the character type. A variable of type `char` can be assigned any single character:

```
char ch;

ch = 'a';  // Lowercase a
ch = 'A';  // Uppercase A
ch = '0';  // Zero
ch = ' ';  // Space
```

Notice that character literals are enclosed in single quotes, not double quotes.

The ASCII Character Set

To see what possible characters we can store in a `char` variable, we'll need to discuss the concept of a ***character set.*** A character set is simply a list of characters together with a unique code for each character. The most widely used character set is ***ASCII (American Standard Code for Information Interchange).*** There are 128 characters in the ASCII character set, which is shown in Table 9.8.

Don't bother trying to memorize Table 9.8. What's important is to get a feel for the relative positions of the most common characters. Notice that the space character (character 32) precedes the digits (48–57). The uppercase letters (65–90) come later in the table, before the lowercase letters (97–122).

The first 32 characters in ASCII (and the last character, *del*) are ***control characters.*** Control characters can't be displayed on the screen or printed; instead, they represent commands entered by the user or commands to be sent to an output device, such as a printer. The characters other than the control characters and the space character are said to be ***printing characters,*** because they're visible when displayed on the screen or sent to a printer.

Control characters can be entered at the keyboard by pressing special keys such as the backspace key (marked ← on many keyboards) and the Tab key. Pressing the

Decimal	Octal	Character										
0	0	*nul*		32	40		64	100	@	96	140	`
1	1	*soh* (^A)		33	41	!	65	101	A	97	141	a
2	2	*stx* (^B)		34	42	"	66	102	B	98	142	b
3	3	*etx* (^C)		35	43	#	67	103	C	99	143	c
4	4	*eot* (^D)		36	44	$	68	104	D	100	144	d
5	5	*enq* (^E)		37	45	%	69	105	E	101	145	e
6	6	*ack* (^F)		38	46	&	70	106	F	102	146	f
7	7	*bel* (^G)		39	47	'	71	107	G	103	147	g
8	10	*bs* (^H)		40	50	(	72	110	H	104	150	h
9	11	*ht* (^I)		41	51	)	73	111	I	105	151	i
10	12	*lf* (^J)		42	52	*	74	112	J	106	152	j
11	13	*vt* (^K)		43	53	+	75	113	K	107	153	k
12	14	*ff* (^L)		44	54	,	76	114	L	108	154	l
13	15	*cr* (^M)		45	55	-	77	115	M	109	155	m
14	16	*so* (^N)		46	56	.	78	116	N	110	156	n
15	17	*si* (^O)		47	57	/	79	117	O	111	157	o
16	20	*dle* (^P)		48	60	0	80	120	P	112	160	p
17	21	*dc1* (^Q)		49	61	1	81	121	Q	113	161	q
18	22	*dc2* (^R)		50	62	2	82	122	R	114	162	r
19	23	*dc3* (^S)		51	63	3	83	123	S	115	163	s
20	24	*dc4* (^T)		52	64	4	84	124	T	116	164	t
21	25	*nak* (^U)		53	65	5	85	125	U	117	165	u
22	26	*syn* (^V)		54	66	6	86	126	V	118	166	v
23	27	*etb* (^W)		55	67	7	87	127	W	119	167	w
24	30	*can* (^X)		56	70	8	88	130	X	120	170	x
25	31	*em* (^Y)		57	71	9	89	131	Y	121	171	y
26	32	*sub* (^Z)		58	72	:	90	132	Z	122	172	z
27	33	*esc*		59	73	;	91	133	[	123	173	{
28	34	*fs*		60	74	<	92	134	\	124	174	|
29	35	*gs*		61	75	=	93	135	]	125	175	}
30	36	*rs*		62	76	>	94	136	^	126	176	~
31	37	*us*		63	77	?	95	137	_	127	177	*del*

backspace key generates character 8, which is named *bs*. Pressing the Tab key produces character 9, which is named *ht* (horizontal tab).

We can also enter control characters by holding down the Control key (often marked Ctrl) and pressing a letter key. For example, holding down Control and pressing I is equivalent to pressing the Tab key. The third column in Table 9.8 indicates how to generate control characters from the keyboard (^A means to hold down Control while pressing the A key).

Because the largest ASCII value is 127, the code for any ASCII character will fit nicely in a single 8-bit byte, and that's the way characters are stored by most software applications. (Actually, only 7 bits are needed, but most computers are designed to work with data that's stored in multiples of 8 bits.) For example, the character A would be stored as 01000001, which is 65 in decimal or 101 in octal.

The Unicode Character Set

Instead of relying on ASCII to represent characters, Java uses a slightly different encoding known as **Unicode.** A Unicode character requires 16 bits instead of 7 or 8. Fortunately, though, Unicode is compatible with ASCII. Adding eight zero bits to the beginning of the ASCII code for any character gives the character's value in Unicode. For example, the Unicode version of the character A would be 0000000001000001.

The first 256 characters of Unicode match the **_Latin1_** character set. Latin1 is an extension of ASCII that includes the characters needed by European languages (such as é, ñ, and ô) plus a number of common symbols. Programs that need only ASCII (the first 128 characters of Unicode) or Latin1 can simply ignore the other Unicode characters. The following figure shows how ASCII, Latin1, and Unicode are related:

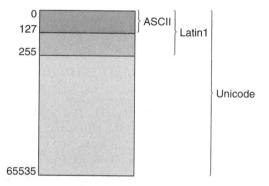

At first glance, Unicode seems rather silly. Why waste an extra eight bits per character? The answer is simple: Instead of being limited to 128 characters, Unicode can support up to 65,536 characters. That's important in many parts of the world, where the local language may require thousands of characters. Unicode contains the characters needed by all modern languages, including the Arabic, Chinese, Cyrillic, and Greek alphabets. Unicode also provides the characters needed for some archaic languages, such as Sanskrit. In addition, Unicode has special characters needed by mathematicians and scientists. (For a list of all characters available in Unicode, visit *www.unicode.org.*)

Java relies on Unicode throughout the language, both for writing programs and for storing character data within a program. This property makes it easier for non-English-speaking programmers to write Java, as well as making it possible to write Java programs that run nearly anywhere in the world. At the same time, programmers who don't need Unicode won't be affected by Java's support for it.

Although use of Unicode is increasing rapidly in the computer industry, ASCII is still by far the most popular character set. Some computers rely on even older character sets. IBM mainframes, for example, use a character set named **_EBCDIC_** (pronounced "eb-si-dic"), in which characters are represented by 8-bit codes.

Escape Sequences

A character literal is usually one character enclosed in single quotes, as we've seen in previous examples. However, the control characters can't be represented in this way. So that programs can deal with all characters—including control characters—Java provides a special notation, the **escape sequence** (or **escape,** for short). Escape sequences can be enclosed in single quotes to form character literals or embedded in string literals.

Table 9.9 lists the escape sequences that Java provides for use in character and string literals.

Table 9.9
Escape Sequences
for Character and
String Literals

Name	Escape Sequence
Backspace	\b
Form feed	\f
Line feed	\n
Carriage return	\r
Horizontal tab	\t
Backslash	\\
Single quote	\'
Double quote	\"
Octal escape	\0–\377

The \b, \f, \n, \r, and \t escapes represent common ASCII control characters. The \\ escape allows a character or string literal to contain the \ character. The \' escape allows a character literal to contain the ' character, and the \" escape allows a string literal to contain the " character. The remaining escapes are called *octal escapes.* Octal escapes let us represent any character whose Unicode value lies between 0 and 377 (octal).

To write an octal escape for a particular character, we first look up the character's octal value in a table such as Table 9.8. For example, the octal code for the escape character (the character produced when the user presses the Esc key) is 33. An octal escape consists of the \ character followed by an octal number with at most three digits. For example, the escape character could be written \33 or \033. Octal numbers in escape sequences—unlike octal numbers in integer literals—don't have to begin with 0.

Java also provides *Unicode escapes,* which have the form \u*dddd*, where each *d* is a hex digit. Unlike the other kinds of escapes, Unicode escapes are allowed anywhere in a program, not just in character and string literals. This property allows the use of Unicode characters in identifiers and comments. Although identifiers consist of letters, digits, and underscores, the definitions of "letter" and "digit" are fairly broad in Java. If some human language considers a particular character to be a letter or digit, Java probably does as well.

Operations on Characters

Working with characters in Java is easy, because the language treats characters as integers. The codes for Unicode characters range from 0000000000000000 to

1111111111111111, which we can think of as the integers from 0 to 65,535. The character 'a' has the value 97, 'A' has the value 65, '0' has the value 48, and ' ' has the value 32. In fact, Java considers char to be one of the *integral types,* along with byte, short, int, and long.

When a character appears in a computation, Java simply uses its integer value. Consider the following examples:

```
int i = 'a';    // i is now 97
char ch = 65;   // ch is now 'A'
ch++;           // ch is now 'B'
```

Characters can be compared, just as numbers can. The following if statement checks whether ch contains a lowercase letter:

```
if ('a' <= ch && ch <= 'z')
   ...
```

Comparisons such as 'a' <= ch are done using the integer values of the characters involved.

The fact that characters have the same properties as integers has some significant advantages. We can use a character variable as the controlling expression in a switch statement:

```
switch (letter) {
  case 'a': case 'e': case 'i': case 'o': case 'u':
    System.out.println("Vowel");
    break;
  case 'y':
    System.out.println("Possible vowel");
    break;
  default:
    System.out.println("Consonant");
    break;
}
```

We can also use a character variable as a counter in a loop. The following for statement steps through all the uppercase letters, assigning each in turn to the variable ch:

```
for (char ch = 'A'; ch <= 'Z'; ch++)
   ...
```

Although treating characters as numbers is convenient, there are disadvantages as well. We can write meaningless expressions such as 'a' * 'b' / 'c'. Moreover, a bug caused by accidentally using a character as a number won't be caught by the Java compiler.

Characters Versus Strings

There's a close relationship between the char type and the String class. A String object contains a series of characters, each of type char. We can retrieve any of the characters stored in a `String` object by calling `charAt`, an instance method provided by the `String` class. `charAt` requires a single argument, representing the position of the desired character. (Recall from Section 3.9 that the positions in a string range from 0 to *n* – 1, where *n* is the length of the string.)

We'll often need to write loops that visit all the characters in a string and perform some operation on each one. If `str` is the name of a `String` variable, a loop of this kind would have the following appearance:

```
for (int i = 0; i < str.length(); i++)
   ...
```

Inside the loop, we would write `str.charAt(i)` to access the character at position `i`. For example, the following loop will display an ISBN number (Section 3.10) with the dashes removed. (I'm assuming that `isbn` is a `String` variable containing an ISBN number.)

```
for (int i = 0; i < isbn.length(); i++) {
  char ch = isbn.charAt(i);
  if (ch != '-')
    System.out.print(ch);
}
```

The `Character` Class

The `Character` class, which belongs to the `java.lang` package, provides a number of useful methods for testing and converting characters. Table 9.10 lists the `Character` methods that test characters for various properties.

Table 9.10
Character-Testing
Methods

Description	*Action*
`boolean isDigit(char ch)`	Returns `true` if ch is a digit.
`boolean isISOControl(char ch)`	Returns `true` if ch is a control character.
`boolean isLetter(char ch)`	Returns `true` if ch is a letter.
`boolean isLetterOrDigit(char ch)`	Returns `true` if ch is a letter or digit.
`boolean isLowerCase(char ch)`	Returns `true` if ch is a lowercase letter.
`boolean isUpperCase(char ch)`	Returns `true` if ch is an uppercase letter.
`boolean isWhitespace(char ch)`	Returns `true` if ch is a white-space character.

Character.isDigit   The `isDigit` method checks whether its argument is a digit:

```
Character.isDigit('a') ⇒ false
Character.isDigit('0') ⇒ true
Character.isDigit(' ') ⇒ false
```

Character.isISOControl

The `isISOControl` method checks whether its argument is a control character:

```
Character.isISOControl('a') ⇒ false
Character.isISOControl('0') ⇒ false
Character.isISOControl('\n') ⇒ true
```

Character.isLetter

The `isLetter` method checks whether its argument is a letter:

```
Character.isLetter('a') ⇒ true
Character.isLetter('0') ⇒ false
Character.isLetter(' ') ⇒ false
```

Character.isLetterOrDigit

The `isLetterOrDigit` method checks whether its argument is a letter or a digit:

```
Character.isLetterOrDigit('a') ⇒ true
Character.isLetterOrDigit('0') ⇒ true
Character.isLetterOrDigit(' ') ⇒ false
```

Methods such as `isDigit`, `isLetter`, and `isLetterOrDigit` rely on the broad definitions of "letter" and "digit" used in Unicode. Letters include more than just the characters from A to Z, and digits are more than just 0 through 9.

Character.isLowerCase

The `isLowerCase` method checks whether its argument is a lowercase letter:

```
Character.isLowerCase('a') ⇒ true
Character.isLowerCase('A') ⇒ false
```

Character.isUpperCase

The `isUpperCase` method checks whether its argument is an uppercase letter:

```
Character.isUpperCase('a') ⇒ false
Character.isUpperCase('A') ⇒ true
```

Character.isWhitespace

The `isWhitespace` method checks whether its argument is a **white-space character**—a character that's invisible to the user. Some control characters—including the tab character and the line feed—are white-space characters, as is the space character itself.

```
Character.isWhitespace('a') ⇒ false
Character.isWhitespace(' ') ⇒ true
Character.isWhitespace('\n') ⇒ true
```

Character.digit

Table 9.11 lists the `Character` methods that perform conversions. When given a character ch and a radix (base) as its arguments, the `digit` method returns the integer equivalent of ch, provided that ch is a digit in the specified radix. (Legal radix values range from 2 to 36.) Here are a few examples, using base 8, base 10, and base 16:

Table 9.11
Character-Conversion
Methods

Description	Action
`int digit(char ch, int radix)`	Returns the integer form of ch in the specified radix.
`char forDigit(int i, int radix)`	Returns the character form of i in the specified radix.
`char toLowerCase(char ch)`	Returns the lowercase equivalent of ch.
`char toUpperCase(char ch)`	Returns the uppercase equivalent of ch.

```
Character.digit('5', 8) ⇒ 5
Character.digit('5', 10) ⇒ 5
Character.digit('A', 16) ⇒ 10
Character.digit('f', 16) ⇒ 15
```

If `radix` is illegal (not between 2 and 36) or `ch` is not a legal digit in the specified radix, `digit` returns –1. Notice that the digits after 9 can be uppercase or lowercase.

Character.forDigit   The `forDigit` method reverses the effect of the `digit` method, converting an integer in a specified radix to a single-digit character:

```
Character.forDigit(5, 8) ⇒ '5'
Character.forDigit(5, 10) ⇒ '5'
Character.forDigit(10, 16) ⇒ 'a'
Character.forDigit(15, 16) ⇒ 'f'
```

If `radix` isn't between 2 and 36 or `i` isn't between 0 and `radix – 1`, `forDigit` returns the ***null character***—the character whose integer code is 0. (*Note:* The null character is not the same as the `'0'` character, whose integer code is 48.) Digits above 9 are returned as lowercase letters.

Character.toLowerCase   The `toLowerCase` method accepts any character as its argument. If the argument is an uppercase letter, the lowercase version of the letter is returned; otherwise, the argument itself is returned:

```
Character.toLowerCase('a') ⇒ 'a'
Character.toLowerCase('A') ⇒ 'a'
Character.toLowerCase('5') ⇒ '5'
```

Character.toUpperCase   The `toUpperCase` method is similar to `toLowerCase`, converting lowercase letters to uppercase and returning all other characters unchanged:

```
Character.toUpperCase('a') ⇒ 'A'
Character.toUpperCase('A') ⇒ 'A'
Character.toUpperCase('5') ⇒ '5'
```

Review Questions

1.   The first 32 characters in ASCII are _____ characters.

2. Suppose that a Unicode character has the binary code 0000000001101010. What will be the binary code for this character in the ASCII character set?

3. Escape sequences of the form \0, \1, \2, and so on are called _____ escapes.

4. The first 256 characters in the Unicode character set are the same as those in: (a) ASCII, (b) EBCDIC, or (c) Latin1?

5. What value does `Character.toUpperCase('!')` return?

9.5   Type Conversion

The Java compiler checks the type of each variable and each expression to make sure they're being used in a safe and consistent fashion. Among other things, the compiler checks the types of operands in each expression. As long as the operands have the same type, there should be no problem. (Assuming, of course, that we don't try to perform an operation that's illegal for operands of that type.) If we mix operands of different types, however, we'll need to be careful.

Computers tend to be quite restrictive when it comes to arithmetic. For a computer to perform an arithmetic operation, the operands must usually be of the same size (the same number of bits) and be stored in the same way. A computer may be able to add two 32-bit integers, but not a 32-bit integer and a 64-bit integer or a 32-bit integer and a 32-bit floating-point number.

Java, on the other hand, allows primitive types to be mixed in expressions. We can combine integers, floating-point numbers, and even characters in a single expression. The Java compiler may then have to generate instructions that convert operands to different types so that the hardware will be able to evaluate the expression. If we add a 32-bit `int` and a 64-bit `long`, for example, the compiler will arrange for the `int` value to be converted to 64 bits. If we add an `int` and a `float`, the compiler will arrange for the `int` to be converted to `float` format. This conversion is a bit more complicated because `int` and `float` values are stored in different ways.

Because the compiler handles these conversions automatically, without the programmer's involvement, they're known as *implicit conversions*. Java also allows the programmer to perform *explicit conversions*. In this section, we'll look at both kinds of conversions, starting with the implicit variety.

Implicit Conversions

Java requires that implicit conversions be performed in the following situations:

- When the operands in a numeric expression don't have the same type.
- When the type of the expression on the right side of an assignment doesn't match the type of the variable on the left side.
- When the type of an argument in a method call doesn't match the type of the corresponding parameter.

- When a value needs to be converted to string form. (For example, this type of conversion occurs when we write "THX" + 1138, which causes 1138 to be converted automatically to a String object.)

Let's look at the rules that Java uses in the first three cases.

Numeric Promotion

Many Java operators allow operands of different types. For example, the + operator can add any two numbers, regardless of type. If the operands have different types, they must be converted to some common type before the operation can be performed.

Let's say that f is a float variable and i is an int variable. Clearly it's safer to convert i to type float (matching f's type) rather than convert f to type int (matching i's type). An integer can always be converted to float; the worst that can happen is a minor loss of precision. Converting a floating-point number to int, on the other hand, would cause us to lose the fractional part of the number. Worse still, we'd get a meaningless result if the original number were larger than the largest possible integer or smaller than the smallest integer.

Java's strategy is to convert operands to a type that will safely accommodate both values. This process is called ***numeric promotion.*** Here are the rules for numeric promotion:

1. If either operand is of type double, the other is converted to double.
2. If either operand is of type float, the other is converted to float.
3. If either operand is of type long, the other is converted to long.
4. Otherwise, both operands are converted to int.

For example, if we add a double value and an int value, the result has type double, which I'll show schematically as

double + int ⇒ double

Here are a few more examples:

int + double ⇒ double
float + int ⇒ float
long + float ⇒ float
short + long ⇒ long
byte + int ⇒ int
short + byte ⇒ int

The goal of numeric promotion is to change the way a number is stored, without changing the value of the number. For example, promoting an int value to long simply requires adding 32 zero bits to the beginning of the number. In a few cases, however—converting from int or long to float, or from long to double—some of the original number's precision may be lost (although its magnitude will be preserved).

The numeric promotions are applied to the operands of most binary operators, including the multiplicative operators (*, /, and %), the additive operators (+ and -), the relational operators (<, <=, >, and >=), and the equality operators (== and !=).

Conversion During Assignment

Numeric promotion doesn't apply to assignment. Instead, Java simply converts the expression on the right side of the assignment to the type of the variable on the left side, provided that the variable's type is at least as "wide" as the expression's type. The following list shows the numeric types, in order of increasing width:

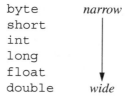

```
byte           narrow
short
int
long
float
double          wide
```

`byte` is considered to be the "narrowest" type; `double` is the "widest" type. As long as we're assigning to a variable that's at least as wide as the expression on the right side, the assignment will be legal. The following assignments, for example, are all legal:

```
short s;
int i;
float f;
double d;
...
i = s;   // s is converted to int
f = i;   // i is converted to float
d = f;   // f is converted to double
```

In addition, a `char` value can be assigned to a variable of type `int`, `long`, `float`, or `double`.

An assignment in which the expression on the right side has a wider type than the variable on the left side will be detected as an error by the compiler:

```
int i;
float f;
...
i = f;   // WRONG; int is narrower than float
```

The reason for this rule is that storing a value into a narrower variable can cause bugs in the program. In this example, the largest value that can be stored in `i` is 2,147,483,647; if `f` contains a value larger than this number (which is entirely possible), it would not be possible to assign `i` a meaningful value.

If you've been reading carefully, you've probably noticed that we've painted ourselves into a corner. Consider the following example:

```
byte b = 10;
short s = 127;
```

Because `10` and `127` have `int` type (remember the rules in Section 9.2?), it appears that we can't assign them to b and s, which belong to types that are narrower than `int`. As it turns out, these assignments *are* legal, thanks to a loophole in Java's rules for assignment. An `int` expression can be assigned to a `byte`, `short`, or `char` variable, provided that (a) the expression is constant and (b) the expression has a value that's legal for the variable. Thus, assigning `10` to b is OK, but assigning `128` to b would be an error.

Argument Conversion

What if we call a method, but give it an argument that doesn't match the type of the corresponding parameter? If the argument belongs to a primitive type, Java tries to convert the argument to the proper type. For example, suppose that we write

```
acct.deposit(100);
```

where `acct` is an `Account` variable. The `deposit` method expects a `double` argument, but `100` has type `int`. Java will convert the argument to `double` automatically.

The rules for converting arguments are nearly the same as the rules for conversion during assignment. Java converts each argument to the type of the matching parameter, provided that the parameter's type is at least as "wide" as the argument's type. There's just one difference. If a method has a `byte`, `short`, or `char` parameter, we can't use an integer literal (or, in general, any integer constant expression) as the corresponding argument.

Casting

Java's restriction on assignment can be annoying at times. If we happen to *know* that a `float` value can't exceed 2,147,483,647 in a particular program, there's no reason not to assign it to an `int` variable. We can solve this problem by explicitly converting the `float` value to `int` type prior to the assignment. A conversion that's done at the programmer's request is called a **cast**. To cast an expression to a particular type, all we need to do is enclose the type in parentheses and insert it before the expression:

```
int i;
float f;
...
i = (int) f;   // Cast f to int type
```

Here we're telling the compiler that f is to be converted to type `int`, and then the result of the conversion is to be assigned to i.

Casting a floating-point number to an integer type causes the number to be truncated rather than rounded. In our example, if f has the value 45.6, then i will be assigned 45. If f has the value −45.6, i will be assigned −45.

In general, a cast has the form

cast expression

$$(\textit{type-name}) \textit{ expression}$$

where *type-name* indicates the type to which *expression* should be converted. Cast expressions have many uses in Java. Let's look at a few of the more common reasons for casting values of a primitive type.

Truncating a floating-point number. Consider the problem of computing the fractional part of the number stored in a float variable f. We'll need to subtract the integer part of f from f itself, which is most easily accomplished with a cast:

```
float f, fractionalPart;
...
fractionalPart = f - (long) f;
```

The cast expression (long) f represents the result of converting the value of f to type long. Java will then automatically convert the value of (long) f back to type float before the subtraction can be performed. The difference between f and (long) f is the fractional part of f, which was dropped during the cast. I used long instead of int in the cast in order to reduce the chance that the value of f is too large to represent as an integer.

A similar use of casting lets us easily test whether a floating-point variable contains an integer value. If x is a float or double variable, the following if statement checks whether the value of x is an integer:

```
if (x == (long) x)
    ...
```

Notice that there's a chance of getting an incorrect result if the value of x exceeds the maximum value of the long type.

Truncating a floating-point number is also useful when we want to generate a pseudorandom integer. The Math.random method generates a random floating-point number between 0.0 and 1.0, which we can easily scale to any desired range of integer values. To generate a random integer between 0 and 9, for example, we could use the statement

```
int randomInteger = (int) (Math.random() * 10);
```

If Math.random returns a value that's less than 0.1, multiplying by 10 and casting to int will give a result of 0. If Math.random returns a value that's greater than 0.1 but less than 0.2, multiplying by 10 and casting to int will give a result of 1. In other words, we've divided the interval between 0.0 and 1.0 into 10 equal parts, each of which corresponds to a different integer.

Dividing integers without truncation. Consider the following example:

```
double quotient;
int dividend, divisor;
...
quotient = dividend / divisor;
```

As it's now written, the result of the division—an integer—will be converted to `double` form before being stored in `quotient`. We probably want `dividend` and `divisor` converted to `double` *before* the division, though, so that we get a more exact answer. A cast expression will do the trick:

```
quotient = (double) dividend / divisor;
```

Java regards (*type-name*) as a unary operator. Unary operators have higher precedence than binary operators, so the compiler interprets the expression

```
(double) dividend / divisor
```

as

```
((double) dividend) / divisor
```

`divisor` doesn't need a cast because casting `dividend` to `double` forces the compiler to convert `divisor` to `double` also.

We could also write the statement as

```
quotient = dividend / (double) divisor;
```

or

```
quotient = (double) dividend / (double) divisor;
```

The last version is probably the best; it makes clear that both `dividend` and `divisor` are being converted to `double` form.

Avoiding overflow during an arithmetic operation. Consider the following example:

```
long i;
int j = 1000000;

i = j * j;   // WRONG; product of two int values is an int
```

At first glance, this statement looks fine. The value of `j * j` is 1,000,000,000,000, and `i` is a `long`, which can easily store values of this size. The problem is that when two `int` values are multiplied, the result will have `int` type. But `j * j` is too large to represent as an `int`, so `i` is assigned the wrong value. Fortunately, using a cast avoids the problem:

```
i = (long) j * j;
```

Because the cast operator takes precedence over `*`, the first `j` is converted to `long` type, forcing the second `j` to be converted as well. Note that the statement

Q&A

```
i = (long) (j * j);  // WRONG; cast is done too late
```

wouldn't work, because the overflow would already have occurred by the time of the cast.

Performing arithmetic on byte, short, and char values. Consider the following example of arithmetic on `byte` values:

```
byte a, b, c;
...
c = a * b;  // WRONG; product of two byte values is an int
```

Looks perfectly innocent, right? Unfortunately, a and b are promoted to `int` before the multiplication is performed, so the result of the multiplication has type `int`, and `int` values, as we know, can't be assigned to `byte` variables. We'll need a cast to fix the problem:

```
c = (byte) (a * b);  // Legal
```

The same problem occurs when arithmetic is performed on `short` values or `char` variables. Java promotes the operands to `int`, so the result of the operation is an `int`, which can't be assigned to a `short` or `char` variable.

PROGRAM   **Encrypting a Message Using the Rot13 Technique**

One of the things that computers are ideally suited for is **encryption:** encoding a message in such a way that the original message can later be recovered. The "rot13" method is one of the simplest (but least effective!) ways to encrypt a message. To apply this algorithm, we replace each letter in the original message by the letter that comes 13 places after it in the alphabet:

```
A B C D E F G H I J K L M N O P Q R S T U V W X Y Z
↓ ↓ ↓ ↓ ↓ ↓ ↓ ↓ ↓ ↓ ↓ ↓ ↓ ↓ ↓ ↓ ↓ ↓ ↓ ↓ ↓ ↓ ↓ ↓ ↓ ↓
N O P Q R S T U V W X Y Z A B C D E F G H I J K L M
```

There's no letter 13 places after *N*, so we "wrap around" to the beginning of the alphabet. Rot13 is an abbreviation for "rotate alphabet 13 places."

Because it's so simple, the rot13 algorithm isn't suitable for encrypting state secrets. It *is* useful for making a message temporarily unreadable. It has long been used on the Internet, especially in newsgroups, where objectionable material can be hidden from people who may not want to see it. It's also good for concealing "spoilers," in which a message posted to a newsgroup reveals information about the plot of a movie or book.

Let's write a program named `Rot13` that asks the user for a message and then displays an encrypted version of the message:

```
Enter message to be encrypted: The truth is out there
Encrypted message: Gur gehgu vf bhg gurer
```

One of the useful properties of the rot13 method is that a message can be decrypted by applying the same algorithm to the encrypted message. If we run the `Rot13` program a second time and enter the encrypted message, we can recover the original message:

```
Enter message to be encrypted: Gur gehgu vf bhg gurer
Encrypted message: The truth is out there
```

The program will need a loop that visits each character in the user's message. The `charAt` method will allow us to extract the character at a particular position in the string. Then, we'll need to encrypt each character by applying the following algorithm:

1. If the character is not a letter, leave the character unchanged.
2. If the character is an uppercase letter, replace it by the uppercase letter that's 13 positions after it in the alphabet, wrapping around to the beginning of the alphabet if necessary.
3. Otherwise, the character must be a lowercase letter. Replace it by the lowercase letter that's 13 positions after it in the alphabet, wrapping around to the beginning of the alphabet if necessary.

To test whether a character is a letter or an uppercase letter, we can use the `Character.isLetter` and `Character.isUpperCase` methods.

Replacing a letter by the one that's 13 positions after in the alphabet is a bit tricky. The basic idea is simple (just add 13 to the letter), but that won't work correctly because of the "wrap-around" problem. One way to solve this problem would be to use an `if` statement, using one formula if the letter falls between *A* and *M* and a different formula if the letter lies between *N* and *Z*. As it turns out, an `if` statement isn't necessary. With the help of the `%` operator, we can write a single formula that handles all letters between *A* and *Z*.

Suppose that `ch` is an uppercase letter. (The technique will be similar for lowercase letters.) The value of

```
ch - 'A'
```

is a number between 0 and 25, indicating the position of `ch` in the alphabet. The value of

```
(ch - 'A') + 13
```

is a number between 13 and 38, indicating the position of the encrypted character. Of course, we really want a number between 0 and 25, so we apply the remainder operator:

```
((ch - 'A') + 13) % 26
```

The value of this expression lies between 0 and 25. Finally, we add the letter `'A'` to convert the result back to a Unicode value:

```
((ch - 'A') + 13) % 26 + 'A'
```

Unfortunately, this expression has type int, not char. We'll need to apply the cast operator to convert the expression to the desired type:

```
(char) (((ch - 'A') + 13) % 26 + 'A')
```

Here's the finished Rot13 program. To make the program easier to understand, I've written a helper method named encrypt whose job is to return the encrypted version of a single character.

Rot13.java

```
 1  // Uses the "rot13" algorithm to encrypt a message entered by
 2  // the user
 3
 4  import jpb.*;
 5
 6  public class Rot13 {
 7    public static void main(String[] args) {
 8      // Prompt the user to enter the message to be encrypted
 9      SimpleIO.prompt("Enter message to be encrypted: ");
10      String userInput = SimpleIO.readLine();
11
12      // Display the encrypted message
13      System.out.print("Encrypted message: ");
14      for (int i = 0; i < userInput.length(); i++)
15        System.out.print(encrypt(userInput.charAt(i)));
16      System.out.println();
17    }
18
19    // Returns the encrypted version of ch using the "rot13"
20    // algorithm
21    private static char encrypt(char ch) {
22      if (!Character.isLetter(ch))
23        return ch;
24      if (Character.isUpperCase(ch))
25        return (char) (((ch - 'A') + 13) % 26 + 'A');
26      return (char) (((ch - 'a') + 13) % 26 + 'a');
27    }
28  }
```

Review Questions

1. If a long value and a float value are added, what is the type of the result?

2. If a short value and a byte value are added, what is the type of the result?

3. If i is an int variable, what types of data can be assigned to i?

4. Which one of the following claims is true?

    (a) Each argument in a method call must have exactly the same type as the corresponding parameter.

    (b) An argument that does not match the corresponding parameter will always be converted to the type of the parameter.

(c) An argument that does not match the corresponding parameter will be converted, if possible, using rules similar to those for numeric promotion.

(d) An argument that does not match the corresponding parameter will be converted, if possible, using rules similar to those for assignment.

5. A conversion that's performed at the programmer's request is called a _____.

9.6   Case Study: Drawing Random Circles

Our case study for this chapter involves writing a program named `Random-Circles` that draws randomly generated circles within a frame. Each circle consists of 360 lines that share a common endpoint (the center of the circle). The circles are not drawn instantaneously. Instead, the program uses a "delay" to slow down the drawing process so that the user can see each circle being drawn. (This is an example of *animation*—changing the on-screen image at regular intervals to create the illusion of motion.)

The user will enter the size of the frame, the number of circles to be drawn, and the "delay time," which controls the drawing speed:

```
Enter frame size: 300
Enter number of circles: 10
Enter delay (in milliseconds): 5
```

After it reads an input value, the program will immediately check whether it is an integer. If it is not, the program will ask the user to re-enter the input:

```
Enter frame size: whatever
Not an integer; try again.
Enter frame size: 300
Enter number of circles: a bunch
Not an integer; try again.
Enter number of circles: 10
Enter delay (in milliseconds): 5
```

After the user has successfully entered all three input values, the program will display a frame on the screen. The width and height of the drawable portion of the frame will match the frame size entered by the user. Next, the program will select a random location within the frame, a random radius, and a random color. It will then begin drawing a circle with the chosen position, radius, and color. The lines that form the circle are to be drawn in clockwise order, starting from the 12 o'clock position. The delay time entered by the user determines the amount of delay between successive lines.

Here's a snapshot of the frame after four circles have been drawn and the fifth is currently being drawn:

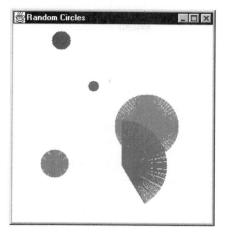

Here's what the frame looks like after 10 circles have been drawn (one of the circles is completely hidden by the others):

Here's an initial design for the program:

1. Prompt the user to enter the frame size, the number of circles, and the delay.
2. Create a frame titled "Random Circles" and set its size to the value entered by the user.
3. Get the frame's graphics context.
4. Draw a series of circles.

Because all three input values are integers, let's write a helper method named `readInt` that prompts the user to enter an integer, reads the user's input as a string, and converts it to an `int` value. If `NumberFormatException` occurs, the method will ask the user to re-enter the input value. Steps 2 and 3 are easy. That leaves Step 4, which I'll write as a separate method named DrawAllCircles.

DrawAllCircles will consist of a loop that executes once for each circle. Inside the loop body, we'll need to perform the following steps:

1. Select a color in which each component is a random number between 0 and 255.
2. Select a random radius between 0 and frameSize/4, where frameSize is the frame size chosen by the user; call this radius.
3. Select a random center whose coordinates fall between radius and frameSize - radius (to guarantee that the circle stays within the frame).
4. Display a circle with the chosen center, radius, and color.

Steps 1 through 3 aren't too hard. We'll need to use Math.random to choose random numbers between 0.0 and 1.0. These numbers can then be scaled to the ranges that we need. Step 4 looks to be rather long. Let's write another method, named DrawOneCircle, to implement this step.

After setting the drawing color, DrawOneCircle will need to display 360 lines inside a loop. Here's what we'll need to put inside the loop body:

1. Compute the coordinates of the current line's endpoint (the one at the edge of the circle).
2. Draw a line from the center of the circle to the edge of the circle.
3. Call repaint to update the screen.
4. Pause between successive lines.

Computing the coordinates of the current line's endpoint is a little tricky; we'll need to use Math.PI to help convert the line's angle from degrees to radians. Then we'll need to use the Math.cos and Math.sin methods to compute the x and y coordinates of the endpoint. In Step 4, we'll use Thread.sleep to add a delay between successive lines.

RandomCircles.java

```
1   // Program name: RandomCircles
2   // Author: K. N. King
3   // Written: 1998-05-19
4   // Revised: 1999-04-25
5   //
6   // Draws randomly generated circles within a frame. The user
7   // will enter the size of the frame, the number of circles to
8   // be drawn, and the "delay time," which controls the drawing
9   // speed. If the user enters a non-integer value, the program
10  // will ask the user to re-enter the input. The location,
11  // radius, and color of each circle is chosen randomly. The
12  // radius is at most the frame size divided by 4. The random
13  // location is chosen so that the circle is entirely contained
14  // within the frame. Each circle is drawn as 360 lines. The
15  // lines are drawn in clockwise order, starting from the 12
16  // o'clock position. The delay time entered by the user
17  // determines the amount of delay between successive lines.
18
```

```
19  import java.awt.*;
20  import jpb.*;
21
22  public class RandomCircles {
23    private static DrawableFrame df;  // Frame in which
24                                      //   circles are displayed
25    private static Graphics g;        // Graphics context for
26                                      //   frame
27    private static int delay;         // Delay between lines
28                                      //   (milliseconds)
29    private static int numCircles;    // Number of circles
30    private static int frameSize;     // Size of frame (pixels)
31
32    public static void main(String[] args) {
33      // Prompt the user to enter the frame size, the number of
34      // circles, and the delay
35      frameSize = readInt("Enter frame size: ");
36      numCircles = readInt("Enter number of circles: ");
37      delay = readInt("Enter delay (in milliseconds): ");
38
39      // Create a frame titled "Random Circles" and set its
40      // size to the value entered by the user
41      df = new DrawableFrame("Random Circles");
42      df.show();
43      df.setSize(frameSize, frameSize);
44
45      // Get the frame's graphics context
46      g = df.getGraphicsContext();
47
48      // Draw a series of circles
49      drawAllCircles();
50    }
51
52    ////////////////////////////////////////////////////////////
53    // NAME:       drawAllCircles
54    // BEHAVIOR:   Draws a series of circles with random
55    //             colors, sizes, and locations. The number of
56    //             circles is determined by numCircles. The
57    //             radius of each circle is at most
58    //             frameSize/4. The center of each circle is
59    //             chosen so that the circle stays within the
60    //             frame.
61    // PARAMETERS: None
62    // RETURNS:    Nothing
63    ////////////////////////////////////////////////////////////
64    private static void drawAllCircles() {
65      for (int i = 0; i < numCircles; i++) {
66        // Select a color in which each component is a random
67        // number between 0 and 255
68        int red = (int) (256 * Math.random());
69        int green = (int) (256 * Math.random());
70        int blue = (int) (256 * Math.random());
71        Color color = new Color(red, green, blue);
72
```

```
 73          // Select a random radius between 0 and frameSize/4
 74          int radius =
 75             (int) ((frameSize / 4 + 1) * Math.random());
 76
 77          // Select a random center with each coordinate between
 78          // radius and frameSize - radius.
 79          int xCenter = radius +
 80             (int) ((frameSize - 2 * radius + 1) * Math.random());
 81          int yCenter = radius +
 82             (int) ((frameSize - 2 * radius + 1) * Math.random());
 83
 84          // Display a circle with the chosen center, radius, and
 85          // color
 86          drawOneCircle(xCenter, yCenter, radius, color);
 87       }
 88    }
 89
 90    ///////////////////////////////////////////////////////////
 91    // NAME:        drawOneCircle
 92    // BEHAVIOR:    Draws one circle with the specified center,
 93    //              radius, and color. The circle is drawn as a
 94    //              series of 360 lines meeting at the center of
 95    //              the circle. Lines are drawn clockwise,
 96    //              starting from the 12 o'clock position. The
 97    //              amount of delay between successive lines
 98    //              (measured in milliseconds) is determined by
 99    //              the value of the delay variable.
100    // PARAMETERS: xCenter - x coordinate of center of circle
101    //              yCenter - y coordinate of center of circle
102    //              radius - radius of circle in pixels
103    //              color - color of circle
104    // RETURNS:     Nothing
105    ///////////////////////////////////////////////////////////
106    private static void drawOneCircle(int xCenter, int yCenter,
107                                      int radius, Color color) {
108       // Change drawing color
109       g.setColor(color);
110
111       for (int angle = 360; angle >= 1; angle--) {
112          // Compute coordinates of current line's endpoint (the
113          // one at the edge of the circle)
114          double radians = (angle + 90) * Math.PI / 180;
115          int xEdge =
116             xCenter + (int) (Math.cos(radians) * radius);
117          int yEdge =
118             yCenter - (int) (Math.sin(radians) * radius);
119
120          // Draw line from center of circle to edge of circle
121          g.drawLine(xCenter, yCenter, xEdge, yEdge);
122
123          // Call repaint to update the screen
124          df.repaint();
125
```

```
126            // Pause between successive lines
127            try {
128              Thread.sleep(delay);
129            } catch (InterruptedException e) {}
130          }
131        }
132
133        //////////////////////////////////////////////////////////////
134        // NAME:       readInt
135        // BEHAVIOR:   Prompts the user to enter a number, reads
136        //             the user's input, and converts it to int
137        //             form. If the conversion fails, the user is
138        //             prompted to re-enter the input. The process
139        //             repeats indefinitely until the user's input
140        //             represents a valid integer.
141        // PARAMETERS: prompt - the prompt to be displayed
142        // RETURNS:    User's input after conversion to int
143        //////////////////////////////////////////////////////////////
144        private static int readInt(String prompt) {
145          while (true) {
146            SimpleIO.prompt(prompt);
147            String userInput = SimpleIO.readLine();
148            try {
149              return Integer.parseInt(userInput);
150            } catch (NumberFormatException e) {
151              System.out.println("Not an integer; try again.");
152            }
153          }
154        }
155      }
```

Review Question

1. _____ is done by changing the on-screen image at regular intervals to create the illusion of motion.

Q & A

Q: **Now that computers have so much memory, is there any need to conserve memory by using types such as `byte` and `short`? [p. 343]**

A: First, you need to know that types such as `byte` and `short` are frequently used for reasons other than conserving memory. Java programs often need to interact with other hardware and software in a computer system, which means storing data in formats that are dictated by someone other than the programmer. In particular, the `byte` type is often used by programs that read data from files or write data to files. Also, some algorithms may require data to be stored in a particular number of bits.

Second, memory considerations remain relevant, even with today's larger memories. Some Java programs will be running on embedded systems, which often have a limited amount of memory. Even when memory is abundant, it pays to choose the best type for the job. The savings from using a `short` rather than an `int` may not seem like much, but keep in mind that data items are often stored in quantity. Storing a million integers as `short` values rather than `int` values saves two million bytes. Arrays that represent images are often extremely large, as we'll see in Section 13.1; programs that work with such images often have to be quite careful with memory.

Q: **Why are floating-point literals stored in `double` form by default rather than in `float` form? [p. 347]**

A: Java is following the lead of the C language, in which floating-point literals have type `double` by default. For historical reasons, C gives preference to the `double` type; `float` is treated as a second-class citizen.

Q: **What is the `Math.atan2` method used for? [p. 349]**

A: The `atan2` method is useful when converting from Cartesian coordinates to polar coordinates. Suppose that x and y are variables that represent the point (x, y) in Cartesian coordinates. The following statements compute the equivalent value (r, θ) in polar coordinates:

```
double r = Math.sqrt(x * x + y * y);
double theta = Math.atan2(y, x);
```

Q: **Why do we need `Math.atan2`? Isn't `Math.atan2(y, x)` the same as `Math.atan(y / x)`? [p. 349]**

A: Not always. `Math.atan` returns a value between $-\pi/2$ through $\pi/2$, whereas `Math.atan2` returns a value between $-\pi$ and π. For example, the value returned by `Math.atan(1.0)` is 0.7853981633974483, but the value returned by `Math.atan2(-1.0, -1.0)` is −2.356194490192345, which is the correct θ value when (−1.0, −1.0) is converted to polar coordinates.

Q: **What happens if numeric overflow occurs—for example, we multiply two numbers and the result is too large to store? [p. 366]**

A: That depends on whether the operands were integers or floating-point numbers. When overflow occurs during an operation on integers, the actual result is the "true" result with extra bits dropped from the beginning. When overflow occurs during an operation on floating-point numbers, the result is positive or negative infinity.

Summary

- The type of a data item determines how much space is used to store the item and how the bits in the item are interpreted.

- The primitive types fall into two categories: numeric (the byte, short, int, long, float, double, and char types), and Boolean (the boolean type).

- Inside the computer, numbers are stored in binary using a fixed number of bits.

- The leftmost bit of an integer is the sign bit.

- Java stores negative integers in two's complement form.

- The largest number that can be stored in an int variable is 2,147,483,647. Variables of type long can store much larger numbers, up to $2^{63} - 1$.

- To conserve space, small integers can be stored as byte values, which require 8 bits each, or short values, which require 16 bits.

- Integer literals can be written in decimal, octal, and hexadecimal. Octal literals begin with 0 (zero); hexadecimal literals begin with 0x or 0X.

- Integer literals have type int by default. A literal that ends with the letter L (or l) has type long instead.

- There are four methods that are capable of converting strings to integer form: Byte.parseByte, Integer.parseInt, Long.parseLong, and Short.parseShort. Each throws NumberFormatException if the conversion fails.

- Java has two floating-point types: float and double. The float type guarantees only six digits of accuracy; the double type guarantees 15.

- A floating-point literal may contain a decimal point, an exponent, or both.

- The letter f (or F) at the end of a floating-point literal indicates that the literal has type float. The letter d (or D) indicates that the literal has type double. If no letter is specified, the literal is a double by default.

- The float and double types contain three special values: $+\infty$, $-\infty$, and NaN (Not a Number), which can be used in computations.

- The Math class provides methods that compute many common mathematical functions, including trigonometric functions; exponential and logarithmic functions; power functions; absolute value, maximum, and minimum functions; and rounding functions.

- The Math.random method generates a sequence of pseudorandom numbers that lie between 0.0 and 1.0.

- A character set is a list of characters along with the code assigned to each.

- The most widely used character set is ASCII (American Standard Code for Information Interchange), which consists of 128 characters.

- The Latin1 character set is an extension of ASCII that includes characters needed by European languages plus a number of common symbols. Latin1 consists of 256 characters.

- In Java, values of type char are characters chosen from the Unicode character set.

- In Unicode, characters have 16-bit codes. The first 128 characters of Unicode match the ASCII character set. The first 256 characters of Unicode match the Latin1 character set.

- Escape sequences allow strings and character literals to contain any Unicode character.

- The escape sequences are \b (backspace), \f (form feed), \n (line feed), \r (carriage return), \t (horizontal tab), \\ (backslash), \' (single quote), \" (double quote), plus the octal and Unicode escapes.

- Octal escapes have the form *ddd*, in which the *d*s represent one to three octal digits.

- Unicode escapes have the form \u*dddd*, in which the *d*s represent four hex digits.

- Java treats char values as integers. char is one of the integral types, along with byte, short, int, and long.

- The Character class provides methods for testing and converting characters.

- Java performs an implicit conversion when the operands in a numeric expression don't have the same type; when the type of the expression on the right side of an assignment doesn't match the type of the variable on the left side; when the type of an argument in a method call doesn't match the type of the corresponding parameter; and when a value needs to be converted to string form.

- When the operands in a numeric expression don't have the same type, one or both of the operands are converted to a different type through a process known as numeric promotion.

- For an assignment to be legal, the type of the variable on the left side must be as least as "wide" as the type of the expression on the right side.

- If an argument of a primitive type doesn't have the same type as the corresponding parameter, Java will attempt to convert it automatically, using rules similar to those for conversion during assignment.

- A cast is a conversion that is performed explicitly, at the request of the programmer.

- Casting is a unary operation, so it takes precedence over all binary operations.

Exercises

Section 9.2

1. Suppose that the value of an integer variable i is 00000000000000000001101011001011 when written in binary.

   (a) Is the value of i positive or negative?

   (b) Is the value even or odd?

(c) What is the type of i?

2. (a) In what base is the literal 020 expressed?

   (b) Convert 020 to decimal.

Section 9.3

3. Why might the following declaration not be a good idea?

```
float f = 299792458.0f;
```

4. What are the values of the following expressions?

   (a) `-1.0 / (-1.0 / 0.0)`

   (b) `(0.0 / 0.0) * 0.0`

   (c) `1.0 - 0.0 / 0.0 - 1.0`

   (d) `0.0 / 0.0 - 0.0 / 0.0`

5. (a) Show the output of the following program.

```
public class Exercise9_5 {
  public static void main(String[] args) {
    double a = 0.0, b = 5.0, c;

    try {
      c = a / b;
    } catch (ArithmeticException e) {
      System.out.println("Error in first division");
      return;
    }
    System.out.println("Finished first division");

    try {
      c = b / a;
    } catch (ArithmeticException e) {
      System.out.println("Error in second division");
      return;
    }
    System.out.println("Finished second division");
  }
}
```

   (b) Suppose that we initialize a to 5.0 and b to 0.0 in part (a). What will be the output of the program now?

6. What are the *types* and *values* of the following expressions?

   (a) `Math.ceil(6.9)`

   (b) `Math.floor(6.9)`

   (c) `Math.rint(6.9)`

   (d) `Math.round(6.9)`

7. Use `Math.random` to write an expression that generates a random floating-point number between 1.0 and 10.0.

Section 9.4

8. Assume that ch is a char variable containing 'J'. What will be the value of ch after the following statement has been executed?

```
ch -= 9;
```

9. Show the output of the following program.

```java
public class Exercise9_9 {
  public static void main(String[] args) {
    String s = "Evil Empire";
    int aCount = 0, eCount = 0, iCount = 0, oCount = 0,
        uCount = 0;

    for (int i = 0; i < s.length(); i++) {
      char ch = s.charAt(i);
      switch (Character.toLowerCase(ch)) {
        case 'a': aCount++;
                  break;
        case 'e': eCount++;
                  break;
        case 'i': iCount++;
                  break;
        case 'o': oCount++;
                  break;
        case 'u': uCount++;
                  break;
      }
    }
    System.out.println(
        "A: " + aCount + "  E: " + eCount + "  I: " + iCount +
        "  O: " + oCount + "  U: " + uCount);
  }
}
```

10. Assume that ch is a variable of type char. Write an expression that has the value true if ch contains a letter between 'A' and 'F' and false otherwise.

Section 9.5   11. Assume that the following variable declarations are in effect:

```java
byte b;
int i;
short s;
long l;
float f;
double d;
```

For each of the following statements, indicate whether or not the statement is legal (will compile without an error).

(a) b = s;   (d) i = f;
(b) s = b;   (e) f = s;
(c) i = s;   (f) d = l;

12. Assume that the declarations of Exercise 11 are in effect. Give the type of each of the following expressions.

(a) b + b   (f) b + (int) b
(b) i + b   (g) i + (float) b
(c) s + l   (h) s + (int) l
(d) i + l   (i) i + (byte) l
(e) f + d   (j) f + (int) d

13. What are the values of the following expressions? Assume that i has the value 3, j has the value 8, and x has the value 6.9. (i and j are int variables; x is a double variable.)

(a) `j % (int) x + i`   (c) `j / (double) i`
(b) `(double) (j / i)`   (d) `(double) j < (int) x + 2`

14. What will be the value of c after the following statements have been executed?

```
double a = 3.5;
int b = 8;
double c = ((int) a + (double) b) / 2;
```

15. What will be the value of ch after the following statement has been executed?

```
char ch = (char) ('A' + 'z' - 'a');
```

16. Show the output of the following program.

```
public class Exercise9_16 {
  public static void main(String[] args) {
    double d = 521.125;
    double a = (int) d;
    double b = d - a;

    while (a > 1)
      a /= 10;
    while (b != (int) b) {
      b *= 10;
    }
    System.out.println(a + b);
  }
}
```

17. Write a class method named `generateRandomInt` that returns a random integer each time it's called. The method will have two parameters, `min` and `max`. The value returned by the method must lie between `min` and `max` (inclusive), with each integer in that range having equal probability.

Programming Projects

1. Modify the `SSNInfo` program (Section 4.9) so that it checks whether all characters in the user's input (other than the two dashes) are digits. If they're not, have the program display the message `"Error: Number must have the form ddd-dd-dddd"`.

2. Make the following changes to Programming Project 4 (Chapter 4):

(a) If the user's input is not 13 characters long, contains characters other than digits and dashes, or does not contain exactly three dashes, have the program prompt the user to re-enter the input. The last character (the check digit) can be either a digit or the letter X.

(b) In the loop that calculates the value of the `total` variable, use the `charAt` method to extract characters from the reduced ISBN, and use the `Character.digit` method to convert each character to numeric form.

3. Airline tickets are assigned lengthy identifying numbers, such as 47715497443. To be valid, the last digit of the number must match the remainder when the other digits—as a group—are divided by 7. (For example, 4771549744 divided by 7 yields the remainder 3.) Write a program that checks whether or not an airline ticket number is valid, displaying either "Valid" or "Not valid":

```
Enter ticket number: 47715497443
Valid
```

If the ticket number is not an integer, the program must display the message "Not an integer; try again" and then prompt the user to re-enter the ticket number. *Hint:* Ticket numbers are too large to store as int values, so you'll need to use the long type instead.

4. Write a program that prints a table of factorials, from 1! to 25!:

```
1! = 1
2! = 2
3! = 6
4! = 24
...
```

Use an int variable to store the value of each factorial, and determine the largest value of n for which the program prints the correct value of n!. Then switch to a long variable and determine the largest value of n again.

5. Some U.S. states operate a lottery game known as Fantasy 5. The person playing the game chooses five numbers between 1 and 35. Periodically, a drawing is held during which five numbers between 1 and 35 are chosen randomly. Winners of the lottery must have three, four, or five matching numbers. Write a program named Fantasy5 that prompts the user to enter five numbers between 1 and 35, picks five numbers between 1 and 35 randomly, displays the five numbers, and indicates how many of the user's numbers matched the computer's numbers:

```
Enter a number between 1 and 35: 28
Enter a number between 1 and 35: 18
Enter a number between 1 and 35: 5
Enter a number between 1 and 35: 4
Enter a number between 1 and 35: 23

The computer's numbers were 5 12 18 23 31
You have 3 matching number(s)
```

If any input is not an integer, the program must display the message "Not an integer; try again". If any number is not between 1 and 35, the program must display the message "Number must be between 1 and 35; try again". If the user attempts to enter the same number twice, the program must display the message "Duplicate numbers are not allowed; try again". In each case, the program must then prompt the user to re-enter the number. *Hint:* Use arrays of boolean values to keep track of which numbers were chosen by the program and by the user.

6. Write a program that translates an alphabetic phone number into numeric form:

```
Enter phone number: CALLATT
2255288
```

(In case you don't have a telephone nearby, here are the letters on the keys: 2=ABC, 3=DEF, 4=GHI, 5=JKL, 6=MNO, 7=PRS, 8=TUV, 9=WXY.) If the original phone number contains nonalphabetic characters (digits or punctuation, for example), leave them unchanged:

```
Enter phone number: 1-800-col-lect
1-800-265-5328
```

Notice that the alphabetic phone number may contain uppercase and/or lowercase letters.

7. In the SCRABBLE Crossword Game, players form words using small tiles, each containing a letter and a face value. The face value varies from one letter to another, based on the letter's rarity. (Here are the face values: 1: AEILNORSTU, 2: DG, 3: BCMP, 4: FHVWY, 5: K, 8: JX, 10: QZ.) Write a program that computes the value of a word by summing the values of its letters:

```
Enter a word: pitfall
Scrabble value: 12
```

Your program should allow any mixture of uppercase and lowercase letters in the word.

8. Write a program named `CondenseGrades` that "condenses" a series of letter grades. The user will enter any number of grades (either A, B, C, D, or F). The output of the program is a string whose elements consist of alternating grade counts and letter grades. Here's an example:

```
Enter a grade: b
Enter a grade: a
Enter a grade: C
Enter a grade: ff
Input must be a single letter
Enter a grade: f
Enter a grade: a
Enter a grade: x
Input must be A, B, C, D, or F
Enter a grade: b
Enter a grade:

Condensed grades: 2a2b1c1f
```

The final tally is 2 As, 2 Bs, 1 C, and 1 F. Note that input ends when the user enters an empty line. The program must produce an error message if the input is more than one character long or contains a character other than A, B, C, D, or F. The case of input letters doesn't matter. *Hint:* Use a loop that reads a line of input, checks it, and updates an array of grade counts. When an input line is illegal, use a `continue` statement to skip the rest of the loop.

9. Write a program named `CheckVIN` that checks a Vehicle Identification Number (Section 3.9) for validity:

```
Enter VIN: JHMCB7658LC056658
Valid
```

The letters in the VIN may be uppercase or lowercase. Your program must check the following conditions, producing the error message shown if the VIN violates any condition. The program must terminate as soon as any error in the VIN is discovered.

Condition 1: The VIN must consist of 17 characters.

```
Enter VIN: JHMCB7
Invalid; VIN must be 17 characters long
```

Condition 2: The VIN must contain only digits and letters other than I, O, and Q.

```
Enter VIN: JHMCB7-58LC0?6658
Invalid; illegal characters: - ?
```

Condition 3: The last four characters must be digits.

```
Enter VIN: JHMCB7658LC05665A
Invalid; last four characters must be digits
```

Condition 4: The check digit in the VIN must match the one computed from the rest of the VIN.

```
Enter VIN: JHMCB7659LC056658
Invalid; VIN check digit does not match computed check digit
```

10. Write a program named `ReadDouble` that reads a string entered by the user and converts it to a `double` value:

```
Enter a double: 123.456e+1
Value is: 1234.56
```

There is a Java method that performs the conversion, but your program must not use this method. The input must consist of the following groups of characters, in the order indicated:

    1. One or more digits
    2. A decimal point
    3. One or more digits
    4. The letter e or E
    5. A plus or minus sign (optional)
    6. One or more digits

If the input has the correct form, the program will display the value entered by the user after it has been converted to `double`. If the input does not have the correct form, the program will echo the input and place a caret (^) underneath the first illegal character:

```
Enter a double: 123.e+1
Error in: 123.e+1
             ^
```

If the input ends prematurely, the caret will be just past the last input character:

```
Enter a double: 123.
Error in: 123.
              ^
```

Hints: 1. Treat the input as three separate numbers: the part before the decimal point, the part after the decimal point, and the exponent. Store each number in a different variable, then combine the values of the variables once the number has been completely read. 2. Use the `charAt` method to extract characters from the input string. 3. Use methods in the `Character` class, such as `isDigit`. 4. Write a helper method that's called when an error is detected in the input string. After printing the error message, this method will call `System.exit` to terminate the program.

11. Write a program named `ChangeBase` that converts an integer expressed in one base to another base. Both the original base and the new base must be between 2 and 16, inclusive. Your program must prompt the user to enter the old base, the new base, and the number to be converted. The program will then print the answer and ask the user whether to convert another number:

```
Enter original base: 2
Enter new base: 10
Enter number to be converted: 1111111
Answer is: 127

Do another conversion (Y/N)? y
```

```
Enter original base: 8
Enter new base: 16
Enter number to be converted: 177
Answer is: 7f

Do another conversion (Y/N)? n
```

When asked whether or not to do another conversion, the program should terminate only if
the user enters n or N.

If the user enters invalid input, the program must prompt the user to re-enter the
requested input:

```
Enter original base: -1
Input must be between 2 and 16
Enter original base: 1
Input must be between 2 and 16
Enter original base: 10
Enter new base: ?%#$
Input was not an integer
Enter new base: 10G
Input was not an integer
Enter new base: 16
Enter number to be converted: 9FA
Illegal digit F
Enter number to be converted:
Number must have at least one digit
Enter number to be converted: 12!
Illegal digit !
Enter number to be converted: 100
Answer is: 64
```

Notice that a base could be illegal because it is not an integer or because it does not lie
between 2 and 16. The number to be converted could be illegal because it is empty or
because it contains characters other than digits that are legal in the original base (in base 8,
for example, only the digits between 0 and 7 are legal).

Hint: Use the Character.digit method to convert single digits from character
form to numeric form. Use Character.forDigit to convert single digits from numeric
form to character form.

12. Write a program named Bounce that displays an animated ball. The ball will move diago-
nally within a frame, bouncing off the edges. The user will enter the width and height of the
frame's drawable portion, the diameter of the ball (in pixels), and the "delay time," which
controls the ball's speed:

```
Enter width of frame: 300
Enter height of frame: 200
Enter diameter of ball: 5
Enter delay (in milliseconds): 10
```

After it reads an input value, the program will immediately check whether it is an integer. If
it is not, the program will ask the user to re-enter the input:

```
Enter width of frame: get lost
Input was not an integer; please try again.
Enter width of frame: buzz off
Input was not an integer; please try again.
Enter width of frame: 300
```

```
Enter height of frame: 200
Enter diameter of ball: 5
Enter delay (in milliseconds): 10
```

After the user has successfully entered all four input values, the program will display a frame on the screen, titled "Follow the Bouncing Ball." The width and height of the drawable portion of the frame must match the values entered by the user. The program will then draw a filled circle with the diameter specified by the user and with a randomly chosen position and color.

The program will now wait for the amount of time specified by the user. It next "moves" the ball one pixel down and to the right. (This step involves erasing the ball and redrawing it at a new position.) The process repeats until the ball touches one of the edges of the frame. If the ball touches the right edge, it begins moving one pixel to the left at each step. If the ball touches the bottom, it begins moving one pixel up at each step. Similar actions occur whenever the ball touches the left edge or top. In each case, the ball reverses its direction of movement, appearing to "bounce" off the edge. The ball will continue moving until the user closes the frame.

Hints: 1. Select the red, green, and blue components of the ball's color as three separate random numbers, each between 0 and 255. 2. Use `Thread.sleep` to let the program wait between steps. 3. Be sure to check that your program works even when the ball bounces in a corner.

Answers to Review Questions

Section 9.1	1.	The location of a data item
	2.	Numeric and Boolean
	3.	True
Section 9.2	1.	32,767
	2.	64
	3.	Two's complement
	4.	Octal and hexadecimal
	5.	(b)
	6.	`Long.parseLong`
Section 9.3	1.	It represents numbers more accurately.
	2.	Exponent
	3.	`double`
	4.	NaN
	5.	(d)
Section 9.4	1.	Control
	2.	01101010
	3.	Octal
	4.	(c)
	5.	`'!'`
Section 9.5	1.	`float`
	2.	`int`
	3.	`byte, short, char, and int`
	4.	(d)
	5.	Cast
Section 9.6	1.	Animation

10 Writing Classes

In Chapter 3, we saw how to write simple classes containing instance variables and instance methods. Chapter 7 then introduced class variables and class methods. In this chapter, we'll look at the process of designing and implementing larger and more-sophisticated classes that may contain both kinds of variables and both kinds of methods. Along the way, we'll learn more about the mechanics of writing classes, the Java features that support classes, and the issues that arise in class design.

The chapter also discusses how code that we've written for one program can be reused in other programs, which is one of the main tenets of modern-day programming. Java's packages play an important role in developing libraries of reusable classes. In this chapter, we'll see how to create our own packages.

Objectives

- Learn how object-oriented design and analysis are used to help determine which classes are needed for a program.
- Learn how to design classes.
- Learn how to choose instance variables for a class.
- Learn about the benefits of information hiding.
- Understand the scope rules for variables and parameters.
- Learn how to choose instance methods for a class.
- Learn how to write helpers for instance methods.
- Learn how methods can be overloaded.

- Learn how to use `this` in instance methods.
- Learn more about writing constructors.
- Learn how to use class variables and methods in instantiable classes.
- Learn how to reuse methods and classes in other programs.
- Learn how to write packages.

10.1 Designing Classes

So far, we've written only small programs, usually fewer than 200 lines long. Commercial programs are much larger, ranging from thousands of lines to millions of lines. As programs get larger, good design becomes increasingly important. One of the most popular techniques for designing Java programs is known as ***object-oriented design (OOD).*** The objective of OOD is to design a program by determining which classes it will need. A full treatment of OOD is beyond the scope of this book, but it's not hard to give a rough description of how the process works.

The first step of OOD is to identify an initial set of classes, along with the methods that these classes will need to provide. (I'll have more to say about this step in a moment.) These classes should be coherent, with each having a clearly defined set of responsibilities. Each class should represent a single type of object, whether it be a real-world object (such as a bank account) or an object that exists strictly in the computer realm (a window, for example).

As we're designing one of the initial classes, we'll often discover the need for other classes. For example, if we're designing a class that represents a bank account, we'll make a list of the data items that need to be stored for each account: the account number, information about the owner of the account, the balance in the account, the transactions that have been performed on the account, and so on. Some of these items can be stored in variables of a primitive type, such as `int` or `double`. Others can be stored as objects that belong to one of the classes in Java's API, such as the `String` class. But it's likely that we won't be able to store all the items in one of these two ways; some items will probably require new classes.

For example, we might decide to create a new class that stores information about the owner of an account. Or we might decide to create a class that stores a series of transactions. As we write those classes, we may discover the need for still more classes. While designing a class that represents a series of transactions, for example, we'll probably find that we need a class that represents a *single* transaction.

With OOD, the process of identifying new classes continues until no more classes are needed beyond the ones provided by the Java API. With small programs, the process will end quickly, but large programs will likely require several iterations.

Object-Oriented Analysis

The OOD process begins with a specification of what the program needs to do, written from the user's perspective. The initial classes are then identified by a process called *object-oriented analysis.*

There are many ways to do object-oriented analysis. One of the simplest involves finding nouns and verbs in the program's specification. Many of the nouns will represent *classes,* and many of the verbs will represent *methods.* Of course, this simple technique doesn't work perfectly; some of the nouns won't correspond to classes, and some of the verbs won't correspond to methods. Still, this technique can be useful for generating ideas.

For example, if we were handed a document describing a new software system to be built for a bank, it's likely that we would encounter nouns such as *customer* and *account.* Verbs in the document might include *open* (an account), *deposit* (money into an account), *withdraw* (money from an account), and *close* (an account). This analysis suggests that we'll need `Customer` and `Account` classes (among others), with the `Account` class having `open`, `deposit`, `withdraw`, and `close` methods.

Design Issues

Once we've identified the need for a class, a number of questions arise. What should the name of the class be? What variables will the class need? What methods should the class provide? Although there's no magic algorithm for designing classes, there are a number of guidelines that we can follow. Most are based on the experience that programmers have accumulated during the era of object-oriented programming. We'll discuss some of these guidelines in this section; later sections provide additional suggestions.

Naming Classes

One of the first decisions we'll have to make when designing a new class is choosing a name for it. Here are a couple of rules to follow:

- *Start with a noun.* A class represents a particular type of object, and objects are described by nouns in English. Many class names consist of nothing more than a single noun; `Account`, `Font`, `Fraction`, `Graphics`, and `String` are examples.

- *If the noun isn't descriptive enough by itself, include an adjective.* When a noun isn't enough by itself, add an adjective to help clarify the noun. `Metrics` is too fuzzy (metrics of what?); `FontMetrics` is better. If we have more than one type of account, `Account` by itself isn't enough, but `SavingsAccount` would be fine. A participle (a word ending in "ing") can also be used to clarify a noun (`CheckingAccount`).

Instantiable or Not?

Java's classes fall into one of two categories:

- *Used for object creation.* Classes in this group contain instance variables and (in most cases) instance methods. The vast majority of the classes in the Java API belong to this category, including Color, Font, FontMetrics, Graphics, and String.

- *Not used for object creation.* Classes in this category contain class variables and/or class methods, but no instance variables or methods. No instances of this kind of class will ever be created.

A class that will be used for creating objects is said to be *instantiable.* (We first encountered this term in Section 7.1.) When we're designing a class, one of the decisions that we'll need to make is whether or not the class will be instantiable. This decision is usually an easy one because classes that aren't instantiable have relatively few uses. Most of these classes fall into one of two categories:

- *Collections of related constants and/or methods.* Math is a prime example of this kind of class; it provides the constants E and PI as well as many methods that compute mathematical functions. The System class also falls into this category, although it goes a little further, providing several class variables (in, out, and err) in addition to class methods.

- *"Main programs."* A complete program needs a main method; many classes are created solely as a place to put main and its helper methods.

Chapter 7 discussed the design of classes that aren't instantiable. In this chapter, we'll focus on the design and implementation of instantiable classes.

Mutable or Immutable?

If a class is instantiable, the next decision we'll need to make is whether instances of the class will be *mutable* or *immutable.* The state of a mutable object can be changed (its instance variables can be assigned new values). The state of an immutable object cannot be changed after the object has been created.

Instances of most classes are mutable. For example, we can change the state of an Account object by depositing money or withdrawing money. Either action changes the account's balance. However, some classes produce immutable objects. Instances of Java's String class are immutable; there's no way to change the characters in a string after it's been created. Instances of our Fraction class (Section 3.8) are also immutable, because the Fraction class has no methods that change the numerator or denominator of an existing fraction.

The advantage of making objects immutable is that they can be shared safely. We saw in Section 3.7 that assigning one Account variable to another is risky because both variables will end up referring to the same Account object:

```
Account acct1 = new Account(1000.00);
Account acct2 = acct1;
```

Performing an operation such as

```
acct1.deposit(100.00);
```

will affect `acct2` as well, which is confusing and can lead to hard-to-find bugs. Because `String` objects are immutable, assigning one `String` variable to another is perfectly safe. Both variables will refer to the same `String` object, but the object's state will never change.

The disadvantage of making objects immutable is that programs are potentially less efficient. We can't change existing objects, so we'll have to create new objects frequently, which can be expensive. The class designer must weigh the safety of immutable objects against the greater efficiency of mutable objects.

Review Questions

1. The technique of designing a program by determining which classes it needs is called _____ _____ [two words].

2. In object-oriented analysis, what kind of words correspond to *classes?*

3. In object-oriented analysis, what kind of words correspond to *methods?*

4. Which one of the following would not be a good name for a class: (a) `Customer`, (b) `WithdrawMoney`, (c) `SavingsAccount`, or (d) `Teller`?

10.2 Choosing Instance Variables

Unlike other kinds of variables, instance variables are stored in every instance of a class. Every `Account` object contains a `balance` variable, and every `Fraction` object contains `numerator` and `denominator` variables.

Instance variables can be declared `public` or `private`. Variables declared `private` are visible only to methods in the same class; methods in other classes have no access to them. Variables declared `public` are visible to methods in other classes.

How Many Instance Variables?

The instance variables of a class will be used to store state information about each object that's later created from the class. Deciding what the instance variables should be depends mostly on what information is necessary to represent the state of an object. In some cases, the decision is simple: a fraction consists of a numerator and denominator; there's clearly no need to store any other information. On the other hand, a bank account is a much more complex object, and it can be hard to know how much state information to store.

It's usually best not to have a large number of instance variables in a class. Often the number of instance variables can be reduced by creating additional classes. For example, it's not a good idea for an `Account` class to use separate instance variables to store the owner's name, address, telephone number, and so on. It would be better to create a `Customer` class and have one of the instance variables in the `Account` class be a reference to a `Customer` object.

To help reduce the number of instance variables, be careful not to store unnecessary data in objects. For example, there's no point in storing an interest rate in every `SavingsAccount` object if all accounts have the same interest rate.

Fortunately, deciding which instance variables to put in a class turns out not to be as critical as you might think, because of an important principle known as information hiding—limiting access to the variables in a class by making them private. Before we explore the advantages of information hiding, though, let's look at the other side of the coin: making instance variables public.

Public Instance Variables

In previous chapters, I've always declared instance variables to be private rather than public. Doing so has definite advantages, which we'll discuss in a moment. However, in some cases it makes sense for a class to have public instance variables. Let's look at a couple of examples from the Java API.

We'll start with the `Point` class, which belongs to the `java.awt` package. A `Point` object represents a point in two-dimensional space. Every `Point` object contains two instance variables, x and y, which represent x and y coordinates. Both variables have type `int`, and both are public. Here's a small example that shows how to create a point and access its x and y variables:

```
Point p = new Point(10, 20);
System.out.println("x coordinate: " + p.x);
System.out.println("y coordinate: " + p.y);
```

As this example shows, we can access the value of a public instance variable by writing the name of an object, a dot, and then the name of the variable. The notation `p.x` means "the variable x belonging to the object p."

Our second example is the `Dimension` class, which also belongs to the `java.awt` package. A `Dimension` object contains two public instance variables, `width` and `height`, which are both of type `int`. `Dimension` objects are convenient for keeping track of the size of windows and other visual components.

getSize   We can determine the current size of a window by calling the `getSize` method. `getSize` returns a `Dimension` object containing the width and height of the window. `getSize` works with all kinds of windows, including the `DrawableFrame` objects that were introduced in Chapter 6. As an example, suppose that we want to determine the width and height of a particular frame. Assuming that the frame is represented by a `DrawableFrame` variable named `df`, we could proceed as follows:

```
Dimension dim = df.getSize();
System.out.println("Width of frame: " + dim.width);
System.out.println("Height of frame: " + dim.height);
```

Public instance variables make classes such as `Point` and `Dimension` easy to use; to get the `x` coordinate for a point `p`, we can write `p.x` instead of `p.getX()`. Also, we save a little time, because no method call is required to access or change the value of an instance variable.

Information Hiding

Despite the convenience of public instance variables, it's usually best for instance variables to be private. This technique, known as **information hiding**, has several significant advantages. The most important one is the flexibility that it gives us to make changes in the future. When instance variables are public, their names become freely available to any and all classes. The `Point` class will always have instance variables named `x` and `y`, because those names have been used in thousands—or maybe millions—of Java programs. Moreover, those variables will always have type `int`. Changing the type of `x` and `y` to `long`, let's say, would break untold numbers of existing programs.

Private instance variables, on the other hand, cannot be used outside their own class. As a result, we can make changes to those variables without affecting programs that rely on the class to which they belong. Private variables can be renamed, have their types changed, or even be removed without affecting program code outside the class.

Making variables private has several other important advantages:

- The variables are protected against corruption from methods outside the class.
- Classes are easier to test.
- Methods that modify the variables can check the new values for validity.

The last point deserves further discussion. In a well-designed class, methods that modify instance variables will check the validity of any values that are assigned to those variables. In addition, constructors will ensure that instance variables are initialized to reasonable values when an object is created. There should be no way to create an object whose state is undefined or illegal.

Information hiding is relevant for methods as well as variables. To get the greatest benefit from information hiding, there are two rules to follow:

- ***Make variables private.*** If access to a variable is needed outside the class, provide a method that returns the value of the variable and/or a method that changes the value of the variable.
- ***Make a method private if it's used only by other methods in the class.*** If there's no need for other classes to use a method—in other words, it's a helper designed for use only within the class—it should be declared `private`.

The "Hidden Variable" Problem

Each variable and parameter in a Java program has a **scope:** the region of the program in which it can be used. We say that the variable or parameter is **visible** within this region. Here are Java's visibility rules:

- Variables declared inside a class declaration—including both instance variables and class variables—are visible throughout the class declaration.
- A parameter is visible throughout the body of its method.
- A local variable is visible from the line on which it is declared to the end of its enclosing block.

The following example shows the scope of several variables in a program:

```
public class ScopeExample {
    …
    private int i;
    …
    public void f(int j) {
        …
        int k;
        …
        if (i > j) {
            …
            int n;
            …
        }
    }
}
```

i is an instance variable, so it's visible throughout the class declaration. j is a parameter, so it's visible throughout the body of its method. k is declared within a method, so it's visible from its declaration until the end of the method. n is declared within a block, so its scope ends at the end of the block.

When a variable in an inner scope has the same name as one in an outer scope, the inner variable temporarily "hides" the outer one. Consider the following example:

```
public class HiddenVariableExample {
    private static String str = "Original value";

    public static void main(String[] args) {
        String str = "New value";
        displayString();
    }

    private static void displayString() {
        System.out.println(str);  // Displays "Original value"
    }
}
```

The main method declares a local variable named str, which hides the class variable named str. (In this example, both versions of str have the same type, but that doesn't have to be the case for hiding to occur.) The assignment to str in the body of main changes the local variable named str; the class variable isn't affected by the assignment. When the `displayString` method is called, it will display `"Original value"`.

 Accidentally hiding a class variable or instance variable is a common bug in Java. Hidden variables aren't illegal, so the compiler won't point out the problem. When the program is run, however, it's likely to fail because the variable that's hidden won't have the expected value.

A parameter can also hide an instance variable or class variable. (Section 10.4 discusses this issue in more detail.) There's some good news, though: a variable declared in a block can't hide a variable in an enclosing block.

Review Questions

1. The technique of declaring variables to be private rather than public is called _____ _____ [two words].

2. The _____ of a variable is the region of the program in which the variable can be used.

10.3 Designing Instance Methods

 Deciding which instance methods to put in a class is more important—and more difficult—than deciding which instance variables to include. The public methods are especially important because they're the only ones that methods in other classes will be able to call. The public methods form the "interface" to the class, or the "contract" between the class and other classes that rely on it.

The public methods provided by a class should have two properties:

- *Complete.* Any reasonable operation on instances of the class should be supported, either by a single method call or by a combination of method calls.
- *Convenient.* Common operations should be easy to perform, usually by a single method call.

Consider the following version of the `Fraction` class, which has no instance methods:

```java
public class Fraction {
  private int numerator;
  private int denominator;

  public Fraction(int num, int denom) {
    ...
  }
}
```

The constructor allows us to initialize `Fraction` objects, but that's all. Once a `Fraction` object has been created, there's nothing that we can do with it. We can't add fractions, multiply fractions, or even print fractions. This version of `Fraction` is clearly not complete.

To give `Fraction` a complete set of methods, we could add two methods that return the numerator and denominator:

```
public int getNumerator() {
  return numerator;
}

public int getDenominator() {
  return denominator;
}
```

Believe it or not, we can now perform any conceivable operation on fractions. It won't be easy, though. For example, to multiply the fractions `f1` and `f2`, we'd have to write

```
f3 = new Fraction(f1.getNumerator() * f2.getNumerator(),
                  f1.getDenominator() * f2.getDenominator());
```

This looks ugly, and it takes four method calls, plus a call of the `Fraction` constructor. To make the `Fraction` class convenient to use, we'll need still more methods. But which ones?

Categories of Methods

Most instance methods fall into one of several categories:

- *Manager methods*—Methods that initialize objects and convert them to other types.
- *Implementor methods*—Methods that implement the important capabilities of the class.
- *Access methods*—Methods that allow access to private instance variables.
- *Helper methods*—Methods that are called only by other methods in the same class.

When we design a class, it's useful to check that it contains an adequate selection of methods in each category. If it doesn't, the class may be complete, but it probably won't be convenient to use. Let's take a closer look at each of these categories.

Manager Methods

Constructors fall into the category of manager methods. (Technically, constructors aren't methods, but we can ignore that distinction for design purposes.) Most classes will need at least one constructor, and many classes will benefit from having multiple constructors. (The `String` class, for example, has more than 10 constructors!) Having additional constructors provides more ways to create objects, which makes a class easier to use. I'll have more to say about constructors in Section 10.5.

Manager methods also include methods that convert an object to some other type. We've already seen a prime example of this kind of method: the `toString` method, which converts an object to string form. Section 3.8 showed how to write a `toString` method for the `Fraction` class. Most classes would benefit from having a `toString` method, which is handy for debugging, if nothing else. The `Account` class of Section 3.3 currently lacks a `toString` method, but we could easily add one. The only data stored in an `Account` object is the `balance` variable, so we'll have `toString` display the balance, formatted as a dollar amount:

```
public String toString() {
  long roundedBalance = Math.round(balance * 100);
  long dollars = roundedBalance / 100;
  long cents = roundedBalance % 100;

  return "$" + dollars + (cents <= 9 ? ".0" : ".") + cents;
}
```

We saw in Section 3.8 that `toString` is called automatically when an object is printed:

```
System.out.println(acct);   // Calls toString method for acct
```

`toString` is also called automatically when an object is concatenated with a string:

```
System.out.println("Balance: " + acct);   // Calls toString
```

`toString` may not be the only conversion method that a class needs to provide. The `Fraction` class should provide methods that convert fractions to `float` and `double` values. That way, we'll be able to write expressions that combine fractions with ordinary numbers. Here's what these methods will look like:

```
public float toFloat() {
  return (float) numerator / denominator;
}

public double toDouble() {
  return (double) numerator / denominator;
}
```

Casting `numerator` to `float` or `double` will cause Java to convert `denominator` to that type as well, as we saw in Section 9.5.

Implementor Methods

Implementor methods are the "meat" of a class. They represent useful operations that can be performed on instances of the class. In many cases, implementor methods change the state of an object or create a new object.

The Account class has three implementor methods: deposit, withdraw, and close, all of which are vital operations on accounts. Section 3.8 mentioned four implementor methods for the Fraction class: add, subtract, multiply, and divide. It's clear that we'll need at least these four if the Fraction class is to be convenient to use. For greater convenience, we might consider including implementor methods that compare fractions, find the reciprocal of a fraction, compute the absolute value of a fraction, determine the larger of two fractions, and so on. The more implementor methods we add, the more convenient the class will be.

Access Methods

Access methods fall into two categories:

- *Accessors* (or *getters*) — methods that *return* the value of a private variable.
- *Mutators* (or *setters*) — methods that *change* the value of a private variable.

In Section 3.8, we saw that Java has a convention for naming getters and setters: names of getters start with the word get; names of setters begin with set.

If it becomes necessary to allow access to an instance variable, it's usually best to provide a getter and/or a setter for the variable, rather than making the variable public. Most of the time, the advantages of information hiding outweigh the inconvenience (and potential overhead) of having to call a method each time we need to access the variable.

In the case of the Fraction class, it seems logical to provide getNumerator and getDenominator methods. More importantly, we need these methods in order for the class to have a complete set of methods. The Fraction class has no setters, however, because I've chosen to make Fraction objects immutable.

There's usually no need to provide an access method for every instance variable in a class. It's best to expose as little information as possible about the internal workings of a class.

Helper Methods

In Section 7.7, we saw how to write helper methods for main (and helper methods for those helpers). Our helper methods since then have been class methods, for good reason: main itself is a class method, so it can only call other class methods.

Instance methods can also benefit from helpers. A helper for an instance method can either be an instance method or a class method. Which choice is best depends on the situation; we'll see examples of both.

In Section 4.6, we developed the following version of the Fraction constructor:

```
public Fraction(int num, int denom) {
   // Compute GCD of num and denom
   int m = num, n = denom;
```

```
  while (n != 0) {
    int r = m % n;
    m = n;
    n = r;
  }

  // Divide num and denom by GCD; store results in instance
  // variables
  if (m != 0) {
    numerator = num / m;
    denominator = denom / m;
  }

  // Adjust fraction so that denominator is never negative
  if (denominator < 0) {
    numerator = -numerator;
    denominator = -denominator;
  }
}
```

Most of the statements in the constructor are devoted to reducing the fraction to lowest terms. It makes sense to move this code to a helper method that reduces a fraction to lowest terms. Doing so will not only simplify the constructor, but also give us a method that we might find useful as a helper for other instance methods.

Let's name the new method `reduce`. Our intent is that it will reduce the object that calls it. In other words, the call

```
f.reduce();
```

will cause the `reduce` method to reduce `f` to lowest terms, possibly changing its numerator and denominator. Here's what `reduce` will look like:

```
private void reduce() {
  // Compute GCD of numerator and denominator
  int m = numerator, n = denominator;
  while (n != 0) {
    int r = m % n;
    m = n;
    n = r;
  }

  // Divide numerator and denominator by GCD
  if (m != 0) {
    numerator /= m;
    denominator /= m;
  }

  // Adjust fraction so that denominator is never negative
  if (denominator < 0) {
    numerator = -numerator;
    denominator = -denominator;
  }
}
```

The `reduce` method will modify the `Fraction` object that calls it, so it needs no arguments and returns no value.

The `Fraction` constructor is much simpler now:

```
public Fraction(int num, int denom) {
  numerator = num;
  denominator = denom;
  reduce();
}
```

The constructor calls `reduce` once it has assigned values to the `numerator` and `denominator` instance variables. The `reduce` method will now reduce the fraction by modifying these two variables.

Notice how the constructor calls `reduce`. The fraction that we're trying to reduce has no name, so we can't write

```
f.reduce();
```

Instead, we simply write

```
reduce();
```

When a constructor or instance method calls another instance method in this way—without specifying which object is involved—the compiler assumes that the method is being called by the same object that the constructor (or instance method) is currently working with. (We'll explore this point more thoroughly in Section 10.4.)

Using Class Methods as Helpers

Instance methods are allowed to call class methods in the same class, which makes it possible for a class method to serve as a helper for an instance method. We don't have to look far for an example. The `reduce` method uses Euclid's algorithm to find the GCD of the fraction's numerator and denominator. To simplify `reduce` (and create a potentially useful helper method), let's move this code to a new method named `gcd`. Because `gcd` won't need access to the `numerator` and `denominator` variables, we can make it a class method.

Here's what `gcd` will look like:

```
private static int gcd(int m, int n) {
  while (n != 0) {
    int r = m % n;
    m = n;
    n = r;
  }
  return m;
}
```

Here's the new version of `reduce`:

```
private void reduce() {
  // Compute GCD of numerator and denominator
  int g = gcd(numerator, denominator);

  // Divide numerator and denominator by GCD
  if (g != 0) {
    numerator /= g;
    denominator /= g;
  }

  // Adjust fraction so that denominator is never negative
  if (denominator < 0) {
    numerator = -numerator;
    denominator = -denominator;
  }
}
```

Method Overloading

As we design the methods in a class, we'll need to decide whether it makes sense to give two or more methods the same name. This technique is known as ***overloading;*** the methods themselves are said to be ***overloaded.*** Both instance methods and class methods can be overloaded.

Overloading is normally done when two or more methods perform essentially the same operation. The advantage of overloading is that there are fewer method names to remember, which makes the class easier to use. The `String` class, for example, contains four methods named `indexOf`:

```
int indexOf(int ch)
int indexOf(int ch, int fromIndex)
int indexOf(String str)
int indexOf(String str, int fromIndex)
```

All four search for a key (a single character or a string) and return the index at which it was found. The only difference among the methods is the parameters that they require. (The `ch` parameters represent characters, despite the fact that they have type `int`.)

Every method has a ***signature,*** which consists of the name of the method and the number and types of its parameters. Methods within a class must have different signatures. In other words, two methods with the same name must have different numbers of parameters, or, if both have the same number of parameters, not all corresponding parameters can have the same type.

The familiar `print` and `println` methods are heavily overloaded, which makes them easy to use. The `print` method, for example, comes in many different versions:

```
void print(boolean b)
void print(char c)
void print(int i)
```

```
void print(long l)
void print(float f)
void print(double d)
void print(String s)
```

(I've omitted a couple of other versions that aren't relevant to our discussion.) For each `print` method, there is a corresponding `println` method.

In many cases, a call of an overloaded method could apply to any of several methods. For example, if we call `print` with an `int` value as the argument, this could (in theory) be a call of `print(int)`, `print(long)`, `print(float)`, or `print(double)`, because an `int` value can be converted to `long`, `float`, or `double`. We say that all these versions of `print` are ***applicable.*** The Java compiler then chooses the version that is ***most specific.*** In this example, `print(int)` is the most specific of the methods, because an `int` can be used as a `long`, `float`, or `double`, but not the other way around.

The Java compiler can't always find a most specific method. For example, suppose that a class contains the following two methods:

```
void f(int i, long j)
void f(long i, int j)
```

Calling `f` with two `int` values as arguments is illegal, because neither version of `f` is more specific than the other.

Review Questions

1.   The public methods of a well-designed class should satisfy two properties. What are they?

2.   Into what four categories do most instance methods fall?

3.   The _____ for a method consists of the method's name and the number and types of its parameters.

4.   When an overloaded method is called, the Java compiler chooses the version that is _____ _____ [two words].

10.4 The `this` Keyword

An instance method must be called by an object. For example, when we call the `getBalance` method in the `Account` class, we have to supply an object—an instance of the `Account` class—so that `getBalance` will know *whose* balance to return:

```
double balance = acct.getBalance();
```

In this example, `getBalance` returns the value of the `balance` variable in the `acct` object.

An instance method never knows the name of the object that called it. `getBalance` doesn't know if it's being called by the `acct` object or some other instance of the Account class. As it turns out, however, an instance method does have a "surrogate" name that it can use for the calling object: this, which is a keyword in Java. Inside an instance method, this has all the properties of an instance of the class. The rest of this section is devoted to exploring possible uses for this.

Using this to Access Hidden Variables

Occasionally, we might want an instance method to have a local variable (or, more likely, a parameter) with the same name as a variable that belongs to the enclosing class. The keyword this can be used to access the variable in the class, which would otherwise be hidden. For example, consider the constructor from the Account class:

```java
public Account(double initialBalance) {
  balance = initialBalance;
}
```

If we were to change the name of the parameter to balance, we'd be in trouble:

```java
public Account(double balance) {
  balance = balance;
}
```

This method is legal, but it won't have any effect, because it simply copies the value of the balance parameter back into the balance parameter. The bal-ance *variable* is hidden, so it won't be changed by the assignment. To clarify matters for the compiler, we need to write this.balance when we're referring to the balance variable:

```java
public Account(double balance) {
  this.balance = balance;
}
```

Some Java programmers *always* use this when referring to an instance variable, even when it's not needed. For example, they would write the getBalance method in the following way:

```java
public double getBalance() {
  return this.balance;
}
```

I don't follow this convention, although it certainly does no harm.

Using this to Call Instance Methods

Normally, a call of an instance method is preceded by an object. If f is an instance method, we could call f by writing

object.f();

However, if one instance method calls another in the same class, it's not necessary to specify the calling object. If we want f to call g, where g is another method in the same class, we can simply put the statement

```
g();
```

inside the body of f. The compiler will assume that g is being called by the same object that called f. We saw this behavior in Section 10.3, in which the Fraction constructor called the reduce method without specifying which fraction was to be reduced.

We can use the Account class as an example. Suppose that we decide to have the close method call the withdraw method instead of assigning 0.0 to balance directly. We would write

```
public void close() {
   withdraw(balance);
}
```

The compiler assumes that the withdraw method is being applied to the object that originally called close.

Java allows us to make the calling object explicit by using the word this:

```
public void close() {
   this.withdraw(balance);
}
```

Some programmers always use this whenever one instance method calls another in the same class, but I won't adopt this convention.

Using this as an Argument

Sometimes an instance method will need to pass the object that called it to another method. Using this as the argument to the call solves the problem of naming the object.

Let's use the Fraction class as an example. The divide method returns the quotient when two Fraction objects are divided. For example, if f1 is a Fraction object containing 2/3 (2 in the numerator variable and 3 in the denominator variable), and f2 is a Fraction object containing 5/3, then the value of f1.divide(f2) would be an object containing 2/5.

Now, let's assume that we want to write a method that computes the reciprocal of a fraction. The following method does just that, by dividing a Fraction object containing 1/1 by the object that calls reciprocal:

```
public Fraction reciprocal() {
   Fraction one = new Fraction(1, 1);
   return one.divide(this);
}
```

The argument to divide is this, which represents the object that called reciprocal in the first place. Of course, this example is a bit contrived. A better version of `reciprocal` would simply create a `Fraction` object in which the original numerator and denominator switch places:

```
public Fraction reciprocal() {
  return new Fraction(denominator, numerator);
}
```

Using `this` as a Return Value

`this` is also useful in `return` statements, when a method wants to return the object that called it.

For example, we might like to have a `Fraction` method that compares two fractions and returns the larger of the two. Here's how we intend to call the method:

```
f3 = f1.max(f2);   // f1, f2, and f3 are Fraction variables
```

The method will compare the two fractions and return the larger one. If the calling object (`f1` in this example) is the larger of the two fractions, the method will return the value of `this`:

```
public Fraction max(Fraction f) {
  if (numerator * f.denominator > denominator * f.numerator)
    return this;
  else
    return f;
}
```

Sometimes we'll have a method return `this` to allow method calls to be chained. For example, we could modify the `deposit` and `withdraw` methods of the `Account` class as follows:

```
public Account deposit(double amount) {
  balance += amount;
  return this;
}
```

```
public Account withdraw(double amount) {
  balance -= amount;
  return this;
}
```

We can now perform multiple deposits and withdrawals on the same `Account` object within a single statement:

```
acct.deposit(1000.00).withdraw(500.00).deposit(2500.00);
```

Review Question

1. Which one of the following is not a valid use of `this`: (a) to access a hidden variable, (b) to call an instance method in the same class, (c) to call a class method in the same class, or (d) as an argument in a method call?

10.5   Writing Constructors

If we don't provide a constructor for a class, Java supplies one automatically. This *default constructor* does nothing, however, so it's not very useful. Most of the time, we'll want to write a constructor—or perhaps several constructors—for our class.

A constructor's job is to initialize the instance variables inside a newly created object. If a class has *n* instance variables, we'll often need a constructor with *n* parameters, one for each instance variable. For example, suppose that we're writing a class named `Complex`, which is intended to model a complex number in mathematics. One way to represent a complex number is to store two `double` values, one for the number's real part and one for its imaginary part:

```
public class Complex {
  private double realPart;
  private double imaginaryPart;
  ...
}
```

When a `Complex` object is created, it would be logical to allow arbitrary values to be selected for `realPart` and `imaginaryPart`. The following constructor does just that:

```
public Complex(double real, double imaginary) {
  realPart = real;
  imaginaryPart = imaginary;
}
```

Although this constructor is the only one the `Complex` class really needs, it's often a good idea to provide additional constructors, purely as a matter of convenience. For example, we might allow a `Complex` object to be created from a real number alone, with the imaginary part set to zero by default:

```
public Complex(double real) {
  realPart = real;
  imaginaryPart = 0.0;
}
```

Using `this` in Constructors

It's not unusual for a Java class to have a large number of constructors. Often, these constructors are very similar: each one initializes some instance variables with values supplied as arguments and assigns default values to the other instance variables. To make it easier to write such constructors, Java allows one constructor to call another by using the word `this`:

```
public Complex(double real) {
  this(real, 0.0);
}
```

This constructor implicitly calls the two-argument constructor, giving it `real` as its first argument and `0.0` as its second argument. A constructor that relies on `this` may have other statements, but they must come after the call of `this`.

"No-Arg" Constructors

A *"no-arg" constructor* is a constructor that has no arguments. When we design a class, it's usually a good idea to include a no-arg constructor that assigns default values to the instance variables of a newly created object.

A no-arg constructor for the `Complex` class would have the following appearance:

```
public Complex() {
  realPart = 0.0;
  imaginaryPart = 0.0;
}
```

Or, if we like, we could simply write

```
public Complex() {
  this(0.0, 0.0);
}
```

At first glance, writing a no-arg constructor seems pointless, because Java should automatically create a default constructor that does nothing. (Default constructors are no-arg constructors, of course.) There are a couple of problems with that way of thinking, however. First, it's often better to initialize variables explicitly rather than let them assume the default values assigned by Java. Second, Java won't create a default constructor for a class if the class contains any other constructors.

Constructors Versus Instance Variable Initialization

In some cases, we can avoid writing a no-arg constructor for a class—or at least reduce the size of the no-arg constructor—by specifying initial values in the declarations of instance variables. Consider the `Fraction` class. The no-arg constructor for this class might set `numerator` and `denominator` to 0 and 1, respectively:

```
public class Fraction {
  private int numerator;
  private int denominator;

  public Fraction() {
    numerator = 0;
    denominator = 1;
  }
  ...
}
```

We can remove the assignments from this constructor if we simply initialize `numerator` and `denominator` at the time they're declared:

```java
public class Fraction {
  private int numerator = 0;
  private int denominator = 1;

  public Fraction() {}
  ...
}
```

What if the initial values of instance variables conflict with values assigned by constructors? To answer this question, we'll need to understand the process that Java goes through when an instance of a class is created:

1. Default values are assigned to all instance variables. Numeric variables—including `char` variables—are set to zero. `boolean` variables are set to `false`. Instance variables of a reference type are set to `null`.
2. For each instance variable whose declaration contains an initializer, the initializer is evaluated and assigned to the variable.
3. The constructor is executed, which may change the values of some or all of the instance variables.

These steps are done in the order indicated, so values assigned by the constructor take precedence over values in initializers, which in turn take precedence over default values.

As an example, let's suppose that the `Fraction` class specifies initial values for its variables, but the no-arg constructor assigns different values:

```java
public class Fraction {
  private int numerator = 1;
  private int denominator = 1;

  public Fraction() {
    numerator = 0;
    denominator = 1;
  }
  ...
}
```

When a `Fraction` object is created using the no-arg constructor, `numerator` and `denominator` are set to 0 by default. Then the initializers for `numerator` and `denominator` are evaluated and both variables are set to 1. Finally, the constructor is executed, assigning 0 to `numerator` and 1 to `denominator`.

Review Questions

1. If we don't write a constructor for a class, Java creates a _____ constructor automatically.

2. Describe three ways for an instance variable to be initialized to zero at the time an object is created.

10.6   Example: The `Fraction` Class

Section 3.8 described a rudimentary `Fraction` class. We're now in a position to develop the class more fully.

First, the `Fraction` class will need a constructor that initializes the numerator and denominator of a newly created fraction. To make the class easier to use, I'll include two other constructors that allow the denominator—or both the numerator and denominator—to be given default values.

Next, the class will need manager, implementor, access, and helper methods. The manager methods will be `toString`, which converts a fraction into a form suitable for printing, along with `toDouble` and `toFloat`, which convert a fraction into equivalent `double` and `float` values. The implementor methods will add, subtract, multiply, and divide fractions. For completeness, we'll need the `getNumerator` and `getDenominator` access methods. Finally, I'll include the `reduce` and `gcd` helper methods that were developed in Section 10.3.

Here's what the new class looks like. I've included comment blocks so that each method is fully documented.

Fraction.java

```
1   // Class name: Fraction
2   // Author: K. N. King
3   // Written: 1998-05-28
4   // Modified: 1999-07-12
5   //
6   // Represents a mathematical fraction, consisting of a
7   // numerator and a denominator, both of which are integers.
8
9   public class Fraction {
10    // Instance variables
11    private int numerator;      // Numerator of fraction
12    private int denominator;    // Denominator of fraction
13
14    //////////////////////////////////////////////////////////
15    // NAME:       Fraction
16    // BEHAVIOR:   Constructs a fraction with the specified
17    //             numerator and denominator
18    // PARAMETERS: num - numerator of fraction
19    //             denom - denominator of fraction
20    //////////////////////////////////////////////////////////
21    public Fraction(int num, int denom) {
22      numerator = num;
23      denominator = denom;
24      reduce();
25    }
26
```

```
27    ////////////////////////////////////////////////////////
28    // NAME:        Fraction
29    // BEHAVIOR:    Constructs a fraction with the specified
30    //              numerator and a denominator of 1
31    // PARAMETERS:  num - numerator of fraction
32    ////////////////////////////////////////////////////////
33    public Fraction(int num) {
34       this(num, 1);
35    }
36
37    ////////////////////////////////////////////////////////
38    // NAME:        Fraction
39    // BEHAVIOR:    Constructs a fraction with a numerator of 0
40    //              and a denominator of 1
41    // PARAMETERS: None
42    ////////////////////////////////////////////////////////
43    public Fraction() {
44       this(0, 1);
45    }
46
47    ////////////////////////////////////////////////////////
48    // NAME:        add
49    // BEHAVIOR:    Adds this fraction and another fraction
50    // PARAMETERS: f - the fraction to be added
51    // RETURNS:     The sum of this fraction and f
52    ////////////////////////////////////////////////////////
53    public Fraction add(Fraction f) {
54       int num = numerator * f.denominator +
55                  f.numerator * denominator;
56       int denom = denominator * f.denominator;
57       return new Fraction(num, denom);
58    }
59
60    ////////////////////////////////////////////////////////
61    // NAME:        divide
62    // BEHAVIOR:    Divides this fraction by another fraction
63    // PARAMETERS: f - the fraction to use as a divisor
64    // RETURNS:     The quotient of this fraction and f
65    ////////////////////////////////////////////////////////
66    public Fraction divide(Fraction f) {
67       int num = numerator * f.denominator;
68       int denom = denominator * f.numerator;
69       return new Fraction(num, denom);
70    }
71
72    ////////////////////////////////////////////////////////
73    // NAME:        getDenominator
74    // BEHAVIOR:    Returns the denominator of this fraction
75    // PARAMETERS: None
76    // RETURNS:     The denominator of this fraction
77    ////////////////////////////////////////////////////////
78    public int getDenominator() {
79       return denominator;
80    }
```

```
 81
 82    //////////////////////////////////////////////////////////
 83    // NAME:        getNumerator
 84    // BEHAVIOR:    Returns the numerator of this fraction
 85    // PARAMETERS:  None
 86    // RETURNS:     The numerator of this fraction
 87    //////////////////////////////////////////////////////////
 88    public int getNumerator() {
 89      return numerator;
 90    }
 91
 92    //////////////////////////////////////////////////////////
 93    // NAME:        multiply
 94    // BEHAVIOR:    Multiplies this fraction by another fraction
 95    // PARAMETERS:  f - the fraction to be multiplied
 96    // RETURNS:     The product of this fraction and f
 97    //////////////////////////////////////////////////////////
 98    public Fraction multiply(Fraction f) {
 99      int num = numerator * f.numerator;
100      int denom = denominator * f.denominator;
101      return new Fraction(num, denom);
102    }
103
104    //////////////////////////////////////////////////////////
105    // NAME:        subtract
106    // BEHAVIOR:    Subtracts a fraction from this fraction
107    // PARAMETERS:  f - the fraction to be subtracted
108    // RETURNS:     The difference between this fraction and f
109    //////////////////////////////////////////////////////////
110    public Fraction subtract(Fraction f) {
111      int num = numerator * f.denominator -
112                f.numerator * denominator;
113      int denom = denominator * f.denominator;
114      return new Fraction(num, denom);
115    }
116
117    //////////////////////////////////////////////////////////
118    // NAME:        toDouble
119    // BEHAVIOR:    Converts this fraction into a double value
120    // PARAMETERS:  None
121    // RETURNS:     A double value obtained by dividing the
122    //              fraction's numerator by its denominator
123    //////////////////////////////////////////////////////////
124    public double toDouble() {
125      return (double) numerator / denominator;
126    }
127
128    //////////////////////////////////////////////////////////
129    // NAME:        toFloat
130    // BEHAVIOR:    Converts this fraction into a float value
131    // PARAMETERS:  None
132    // RETURNS:     A float value obtained by dividing the
133    //              fraction's numerator by its denominator
134    //////////////////////////////////////////////////////////
```

```
135    public float toFloat() {
136      return (float) numerator / denominator;
137    }
138
139    ////////////////////////////////////////////////////////////
140    // NAME:        toString
141    // BEHAVIOR:    Converts this fraction into a string
142    // PARAMETERS:  None
143    // RETURNS:     A string of the form "num/denom". If the
144    //              denominator is 1, returns a string
145    //              containing only the numerator.
146    ////////////////////////////////////////////////////////////
147    public String toString() {
148      if (denominator == 1)
149        return numerator + "";
150      else
151        return numerator + "/" + denominator;
152    }
153
154    ////////////////////////////////////////////////////////////
155    // NAME:        reduce
156    // BEHAVIOR:    Reduces this fraction to lowest terms
157    // PARAMETERS:  None
158    // RETURNS:     Nothing
159    ////////////////////////////////////////////////////////////
160    private void reduce() {
161      // Compute GCD of numerator and denominator
162      int g = gcd(numerator, denominator);
163
164      // Divide numerator and denominator by GCD
165      if (g != 0) {
166        numerator /= g;
167        denominator /= g;
168      }
169
170      // Adjust fraction so that denominator is never negative
171      if (denominator < 0) {
172        numerator = -numerator;
173        denominator = -denominator;
174      }
175    }
176
177    ////////////////////////////////////////////////////////////
178    // NAME:        gcd
179    // BEHAVIOR:    Computes the greatest common divisor of two
180    //              integers
181    // PARAMETERS:  m - an integer
182    //              n - an integer
183    // RETURNS:     The greatest common divisor of m and n
184    ////////////////////////////////////////////////////////////
185    private static int gcd(int m, int n) {
186      while (n != 0) {
187        int r = m % n;
188        m = n;
```

```
189          n = r;
190        }
191        return m;
192     }
193   }
```

There's no universal agreement about the order in which variables and methods should appear in a class declaration, but—as with all matters of style—it helps to have some rules to follow for consistency. I've chosen the following arrangement for my class declarations:

1. Instance variables
2. Class variables
3. Constructors
4. Public instance methods
5. Public class methods
6. Private instance methods
7. Private class methods

I prefer to put variable declarations first, so that they'll be easy to find. Some programmers prefer to put variable declarations last, reasoning that variables are usually private and therefore of little interest to someone *using* the class.

I put the methods in each group into alphabetical order, to make it easier to locate a particular method. It's possible to do this for instance variables and class variables as well, but I usually don't bother unless there are more than a few.

Another way to arrange methods within a group is by role, with related methods kept together. For example, we might keep the `add`, `subtract`, `multiply`, and `divide` methods together, because they perform similar operations. The `getNumerator` and `getDenominator` methods would go together, as would the `toDouble`, `toFloat`, and `toString` methods.

Choose a consistent way of ordering the variables and methods in your classes.

10.7 Adding Class Variables and Methods

Instantiable classes often contain class variables and methods in addition to instance variables and methods. In this section, we'll explore some of the reasons for adding class variables and methods to an instantiable class.

Class Variables in Instantiable Classes

Sometimes a class will need to keep track of information about the instances that have been created so far. For example, the `Account` class might need to remember how many accounts have been created and the total amount of money stored in those accounts. These items of data aren't related to any particular account, but to all accounts in existence, so they would logically be stored as class variables. Here's what the `Account` class would look like with the addition of class variables named `totalDeposits` and `accountsOpen`:

```
public class Account {
  // Instance variables
  private double balance;

  // Class variables
  private static double totalDeposits = 0.0;
  private static int accountsOpen = 0;
  ...
}
```

`totalDeposits` will store the sum of the balances in *all* accounts. `accountsOpen` will keep track of how many accounts are open.

Notice that both `totalDeposits` and `accountsOpen` are private. If a class variable is public, it can be accessed by writing the name of the class, a dot, and the name of the variable. If `accountsOpen` were public, we would be able to access it by writing `Account.accountsOpen`:

```
System.out.println("Number of accounts open: " +
                    Account.accountsOpen);
```

The danger of making class variables public is that they're vulnerable to being changed outside the class. There's nothing to prevent us from adding 1000000 to `Account.accountsOpen`, making it look as though a million new accounts suddenly existed. In addition, we won't be able to change the name or type of a public class variable easily, because other classes may be affected by the change. As with instance variables, it's usually a good idea to make class variables private.

Constructors and instance methods have full access to all class variables in the same class, regardless of whether they're declared public or private. Here's a modified version of the `Account` class in which the constructors and instance methods keep the `totalDeposits` and `accountsOpen` variables up-to-date:

```
public class Account {
  // Instance variables
  private double balance;

  // Class variables
  private static double totalDeposits = 0.0;
  private static int accountsOpen = 0;

  // Constructors
  public Account(double initialBalance) {
    balance = initialBalance;
    totalDeposits += initialBalance;
    accountsOpen++;
  }
```

```java
public Account() {
  balance = 0.0;
  accountsOpen++;
}

// Instance methods
public void close() {
  totalDeposits -= balance;
  balance = 0.0;
  accountsOpen--;
}

public void deposit(double amount) {
  balance += amount;
  totalDeposits += amount;
}

public double getBalance() {
  return balance;
}

public void withdraw(double amount) {
  balance -= amount;
  totalDeposits -= amount;
}
}
```

Class Methods in Instantiable Classes

There are several reasons for adding class methods to an instantiable class. We've seen one already: Section 10.3 showed that a class method can be a helper for instance methods. Such a method would be declared `private`, because it's intended for use only within the class.

Another reason for having class methods in an instantiable class is to provide the ability to access and/or change class variables that belong to the class. These variables are usually private, so there's no direct way to access them from outside the class. Public class methods can provide indirect—and more controlled—access to class variables.

The new version of the `Account` class will need class methods. The `totalDeposits` and `accountsOpen` variables are private, so we can't access them directly from outside the class. In order to find out how much money is currently stored in all accounts, we'll need a class method that returns the value of `totalDeposits`:

```java
public static double getTotalDeposits() {
  return totalDeposits;
}
```

Similarly, we'll need a method that returns the number of accounts open:

```
public static int getAccountsOpen() {
  return accountsOpen;
}
```

These methods will be called in the same way as class methods in the Java API:

```
double deposits = Account.getTotalDeposits();
int numAccounts = Account.getAccountsOpen();
```

Restrictions on Class Methods

Be careful when you combine class methods and instance methods in the same class. Class methods have to obey a stricter set of rules than do instance methods:

Instance Methods	*Class Methods*
■ Are allowed to use `this` to refer to the calling object.	■ Are not allowed to use `this`.
■ Have access to all instance variables and class variables declared in the enclosing class.	■ Have access to class variables in the enclosing class, but not instance variables.
■ Can call any instance method or class method declared in the class.	■ Can call class methods, but not instance methods.

A bit of clarification is required for the last two restrictions on class methods. A class method isn't called by an object, which explains why it has no access to instance variables and can't call instance methods. However, if a class method is supplied with an instance of the class (through a parameter or class variable), the method *does* have access to that object's instance variables, and it *can* use the object to call instance methods.

Review Questions

1. Which one of the following is a class method allowed to do: (a) access instance variables in its class, (b) call instance methods in its class, (c) access class variables in its class, or (d) use the `this` keyword?

2. Which one of the following is an instance method *not* allowed to do: (a) access instance variables in its class, (b) access class variables in its class, (c) call instance methods in its class, (d) call class methods in its class, or (e) none of these?

10.8 Reusing Code

One of the biggest advantages of object-oriented programming is the ease with which code that was originally written for one program can be reused in other programs. In fact, Java programmers routinely assume that code will be reused, which affects how they write it in the first place.

When properly written, class methods and entire classes can be reused. (Instance methods can't be reused by themselves, without reusing the entire class to which they belong.) To make a method or class reusable, we need to write it in a general fashion, not tying it too closely to the program under development. In the case of a class, we might add extra methods that aren't needed in the current program, but which might be necessary if the class were to be reused in the future.

Reusing Class Methods

In order to reuse a class method, we need to find a home for it in an appropriate class. For example, consider the `gcd` method that we developed in Section 10.3. This method, which finds the greatest common divisor of two integers, is potentially useful for purposes other than reducing fractions. Instead of making `gcd` a private method in the `Fraction` class, we might put it in a different class, perhaps named `MathAlgorithms`, so that we'll be able to reuse it in other programs. Here's what the `MathAlgorithms` class would look like:

```
public class MathAlgorithms {
  public static int gcd(int m, int n) {
    while (n != 0) {
      int r = m % n;
      m = n;
      n = r;
    }
    return m;
  }
}
```

Although the class contains only one method at this point, we could easily add more methods in the future, gradually developing a highly useful utility class. Note that `gcd` has been declared `public` rather than `private`. `gcd` is no longer a helper method to be used in a single class. Instead, our goal is to make it available to *any* class, which requires that it be declared `public`.

Methods that read and validate user input are needed by many programs, so it's a good idea to make them reusable. For example, in Section 8.1, we developed a method named `readInt` that prompts the user to enter an integer, reads the user's input, and asks the user to re-enter the input if it is not an integer. To make this method reusable, we can put it in a class named `ValidIO`:

```
public class ValidIO {
  public static int readInt(String prompt) {
    while (true) {
      SimpleIO.prompt(prompt);
      String userInput = SimpleIO.readLine();
      try {
        return Integer.parseInt(userInput);
```

```
        } catch (NumberFormatException e) {
          System.out.println("Not an integer; try again");
        }
      }
    }
  }
}
```

`ValidIO` could easily contain other methods for reading and validating input, such as `readDouble`, `readLong`, and so on.

Reusing Classes

To understand how best to make classes reusable, we need to know more about packages. So far, all we know is that a package is a collection of classes. The Java API is divided into packages with names like `java.awt` and `java.lang`. We've also used the `jpb` package, which I wrote.

It turns out that every Java class belongs to a package. If we don't explicitly put a class into a particular package, the Java compiler adds it to a default package that has no name. Here's how we might visualize the `jpb`, `java.awt`, `java.lang`, and default packages:

default package	**jpb**	**java.awt**	**java.lang**
All the classes we've written so far	Convert DrawableFrame SimpleIO	Color Font FontMetrics Graphics ⋮	Character Integer Math String System ⋮

Classes that belong to the same package have privileges that classes in other packages don't enjoy. If we omit the access modifier (`public` or `private`) when declaring an instance variable or class variable, that variable becomes available to all classes in the same package as the class to which the variable belongs. The same is true of instance methods and class methods. Classes in other packages, however, have no access to such a variable or method.

We saw in Section 3.6 that each file in a package may contain multiple classes, but only one may be declared `public` (the one whose name matches the file name). It turns out that classes that aren't declared `public` aren't accessible to classes in other packages (which is another reason to put each class in a separate file).

Based on this information, we can formulate a strategy for making classes easily reusable in other programs:

- ***Make sure that the class is declared `public`.*** That way, all classes will have access to the class, not just classes in the same package.

- *Put the class into a package with related classes.* When two or more classes are related to each other, it often makes sense to bundle the classes into a package. Grouping classes into packages makes them easier to find and clarifies the relationships among the classes.

Writing Packages

Creating a package involves three steps:

1. Adding a package declaration to each file that contains classes belonging to the package.
2. Putting the files in a directory with the same name as the package.
3. Making sure that the Java compiler and interpreter can find the directory.

A *package declaration* has the form

```
package package-name ;
```

This line must come before any import lines and before the classes themselves. For example, if we decided to add the ValidIO class to the jpb package, we would have to put a package declaration at the beginning of the ValidIO.java file:

```
package jpb;

public class ValidIO {
  public static int readInt(String prompt) {
    while (true) {
      try {
        SimpleIO.prompt(prompt);
        String userInput = SimpleIO.readLine();
        return Integer.parseInt(userInput);
      } catch (NumberFormatException e) {
        System.out.println("Not an integer; try again");
      }
    }
  }
}
```

The files that belong to a package must be put in a directory with the same name as the package. The ValidIO.java file would go in the jpb directory, along with the other classes that belong to the jpb package. Package names may contain dots, which indicate directory structure. For example, the files for the java.awt package would be kept in a subdirectory named awt, which is located inside a directory named java.

The last step in creating a package is making sure that the Java compiler and interpreter can find the package. On the Windows platform, the Java compiler and interpreter locate package directories via the CLASSPATH environment variable. For example, the following definition of CLASSPATH would cause the compiler and interpreter to search for package names (subdirectories) in the current directory and in C:\MyPkgs:

SET CLASSPATH=.;C:\MyPkgs

The CLASSPATH variable must list the name of the directory in which the package directory is located, *not* the name of the package directory itself. Suppose that we create a package named foo. The files that belong to this package will be in a directory named foo. If foo happens to be located in the MyPkgs directory, the correct way to set the CLASSPATH variable is

SET CLASSPATH=.;C:\MyPkgs

Mentioning the name of the foo directory itself is wrong:

SET CLASSPATH=.;C:\MyPkgs\foo

We'll get error messages when we try to use the classes in the foo package.

Review Question

1. What line must we put at the beginning of a file to indicate that the classes in the file belong to a package named foo?

10.9 Case Study: Playing Blackjack

As an exercise in class design, let's develop a program that plays the card game known as Blackjack. We'll use the following rules for our version of this game:

- Blackjack is played with standard playing cards. The value of each numbered card is the card's number. The value of the jack, queen, and king is 10. The value of the ace can be either 1 or 11.

- The goal of the game is to accumulate cards whose total values come as close to 21 as possible, without exceeding 21.

- At the beginning of each hand, the dealer (the program) and the player (the user) are each dealt two cards. If the player's cards total to 21, the hand is over and the player wins (unless the dealer also has 21, in which case the hand is a tie).

- Otherwise, the player may now draw additional cards in an attempt to get closer to 21. If the player exceeds 21, the hand is over and the player loses.

- Once the player "stands" (stops drawing cards), the dealer begins drawing cards until reaching a total of 17 or more. If the dealer exceeds 21, the player wins. If the player's final count exceeds the dealer's final count, the player wins. If the dealer and the player have identical counts, the hand is a tie. Otherwise, the dealer wins.

The program will pick two cards randomly for both the dealer and the player. It will then display the player's cards and ask the user whether to stand or "hit" (request another card). The user will enter S (for stand) or H (for hit). Any input other than h or H is assumed to mean "stand." The process then repeats until the player's count exceeds 21 or the player decides to stand. If the player's count did not go over 21, the program now displays the dealer's cards and begins to draw additional cards until reaching 17 or exceeding 21.

At the end of each hand, the program will display the total number of wins for both the dealer and the player. The program will then ask the user whether or not to play again. When the user is shown the `"Play again (Y/N)?"` prompt, any input other than y or Y causes program termination. The example on the following page shows what a session with the program will look like.

From this description of the program, it seems clear that we'll need two classes. One class, which I'll name `Blackjack`, will contain the `main` method and its helpers. The other class, named `Card`, will be instantiable. Each instance of the `Card` class will represent a single playing card.

Let's start with the `Card` class. Each card has a rank and a suit, so we'll need `rank` and `suit` instance variables to store these values. I'll use integer codes to represent ranks and suits, with the numbers from 0 to 12 representing the thirteen possible ranks, and the numbers from 0 to 3 representing the four suits. (One of the programming projects at the end of the chapter explores another way to store ranks and suits.)

We'll need a constructor to initialize the `rank` and `suit` variables. Adding getters named `getRank` and `getSuit` will make the class complete. For convenience (and to follow Java conventions), we'll need a `toString` method that converts a card to string form. It will also be convenient to have a method that generates a random card. This method will need to be a class method because it creates a new card rather than performing an operation on an existing card. (As an alternative, we could write a no-arg constructor that creates a card containing a random rank and suit.)

Here's what the `Card` class will look like:

Card.java

```
1   // Class name: Card
2   // Author: K. N. King
3   // Written: 1998-05-26
4   // Modified: 1999-07-11
5   //
6   // Represents a playing card with a rank and a suit.
7
8   public class Card {
9     // Instance variables
10    private int rank;
11    private int suit;
12
13    // Names for ranks
14    public static final int TWO = 0;
15    public static final int THREE = 1;
16    public static final int FOUR = 2;
```

```
Your cards: 6S 5H
(S)tand or (H)it? h
You drew: 6H
(S)tand or (H)it? s
Dealer's cards: QC QS
Dealer wins
Dealer: 1 Player: 0
Play again (Y/N)? y

Your cards: 3C 2C
(S)tand or (H)it? h
You drew: JC
(S)tand or (H)it? s
Dealer's cards: 2D AS
Dealer drew: 2H
Dealer drew: AH
Dealer drew: KC
Dealer drew: 3C
Dealer wins
Dealer: 2 Player: 0
Play again (Y/N)? y

Your cards: JS AH
Dealer's cards: 5H TC
Player wins!
Dealer: 2 Player: 1
Play again (Y/N)? y

Your cards: 3H TS
(S)tand or (H)it? h
You drew: QH
Dealer wins
Dealer: 3 Player: 1
Play again (Y/N)? y

Your cards: 7C TD
(S)tand or (H)it? s
Dealer's cards: 4D 8C
Dealer drew: 2S
Dealer drew: 2D
Dealer drew: TH
Player wins!
Dealer: 3 Player: 2
Play again (Y/N)? y

Your cards: JS 7C
(S)tand or (H)it? s
Dealer's cards: TS 5D
Dealer drew: 2S
Tie
Dealer: 3 Player: 2
Play again (Y/N)? n
```

```
17   public static final int FIVE = 3;
18   public static final int SIX = 4;
19   public static final int SEVEN = 5;
20   public static final int EIGHT = 6;
21   public static final int NINE = 7;
22   public static final int TEN = 8;
23   public static final int JACK = 9;
24   public static final int QUEEN = 10;
25   public static final int KING = 11;
26   public static final int ACE = 12;
27
28   // Names for suits
29   public static final int CLUBS = 0;
30   public static final int DIAMONDS = 1;
31   public static final int HEARTS = 2;
32   public static final int SPADES = 3;
33
34   // Constants for use within the class
35   private static final String RANKS = "23456789TJQKA";
36   private static final String SUITS = "CDHS";
37
38   //////////////////////////////////////////////////////////
39   // NAME:       Card
40   // BEHAVIOR:   Constructs a card with the specified rank
41   //             and suit
42   // PARAMETERS: rank - rank of card
43   //             suit - suit of card
44   //////////////////////////////////////////////////////////
45   public Card(int rank, int suit) {
46     this.rank = rank;
47     this.suit = suit;
48   }
49
50   //////////////////////////////////////////////////////////
51   // NAME:       getRank
52   // BEHAVIOR:   Returns the rank of this card
53   // PARAMETERS: None
54   // RETURNS:    The rank of this card (0-12)
55   //////////////////////////////////////////////////////////
56   public int getRank() {
57     return rank;
58   }
59
60   //////////////////////////////////////////////////////////
61   // NAME:       getSuit
62   // BEHAVIOR:   Returns the suit of this card
63   // PARAMETERS: None
64   // RETURNS:    The suit of this card (0-3)
65   //////////////////////////////////////////////////////////
66   public int getSuit() {
67     return suit;
68   }
69
```

```
70     ///////////////////////////////////////////////////////////
71     // NAME:       toString
72     // BEHAVIOR:   Converts this card into a string
73     // PARAMETERS: None
74     // RETURNS:    A string of the form "rs", where r is a rank
75     //             (2, 3, 4, 5, 6, 7, 8, 9, T, J, Q, K, or A)
76     //             and s is a suit (C, D, H, or S)
77     ///////////////////////////////////////////////////////////
78     public String toString() {
79        return RANKS.charAt(rank) + "" + SUITS.charAt(suit);
80     }
81
82     ///////////////////////////////////////////////////////////
83     // NAME:       pickRandom
84     // BEHAVIOR:   Creates a new card containing a random rank
85     //             and suit
86     // PARAMETERS: None
87     // RETURNS:    A card containing a random rank and suit
88     ///////////////////////////////////////////////////////////
89     public static Card pickRandom() {
90        return new Card((int) (Math.random() * 13),
91                        (int) (Math.random() * 4));
92     }
93  }
```

Note that I included a number of constants in the class. The constants in the first group provide names for all the possible ranks, and the ones in the second group provide names for the suits. The existence of these constants makes it possible for methods in other classes to work with ranks and suits without referring to their numerical values. In addition, the resulting code is more readable. For example, we can write

```
Card c = new Card(Card.ACE, Card.SPADES);
```

instead of the less readable

```
Card c = new Card(12, 3);
```

As it turns out, the Blackjack program doesn't need names for suits. Still, by providing these names, the Card class becomes easier to reuse in other programs.

The pickRandom method deserves special mention. It doesn't keep track of which cards have been generated in the past, so it doesn't behave like a dealer with a single deck of cards. Instead, it behaves more like a dealer with an infinite number of decks that have been shuffled together.

One flaw in the Card class is the fact that the constructor will accept any integer as a rank or suit value. A constructor should ensure that it initializes a new object to a legal state, which the Card constructor fails to do. The Card constructor should probably throw an exception if it is given an illegal argument, but we haven't yet discussed how to throw exceptions.

Now, let's turn to the Blackjack class itself. The program can play multiple hands, so we'll need to put the game-playing code inside a loop. Here are the steps that will go inside the loop:

Choose two cards for both player and dealer;
Display player's cards;
Compute initial counts for player and dealer;
```
if (player's count is 21) {
   if (dealer's count is not 21)
      Dealer loses;
} else {
```
Ask player to draw additional cards and determine new value of player's hand;
```
   if (player's count exceeds 21)
      Player loses;
   else {
```
Show dealer's cards;
Draw additional cards for dealer and determine new value of dealer's hand;
```
      if (dealer's count exceeds 21)
         Dealer loses;
   }
}
```
Compare player's count with dealer's count to determine the winner; display the outcome
   and update the win counts;
Display the win counts;
See if user wants to play again; exit from loop if answer is no;

One of the trickier issues is how to keep track of whether the dealer or the player has lost during an early stage of the game (by exceeding 21, for example). We could use `boolean` variables for this purpose. However, after some experimentation, I found a simpler and more effective technique. To indicate that the dealer has lost, the program can simply set the dealer's count to 0. Similarly, the player's count can be set to 0 to indicate that the player has lost.

To simplify the `main` method, I created two helper methods named `get-DealerCards` and `getPlayerCards`. `getDealerCards` contains a loop that draws cards until the dealer's count reaches 17. `getPlayerCards` is similar, but it repeatedly asks the user whether or not to draw a card. The method returns when the player's count exceeds 21 or the user decides to stand. The hardest part of writing these methods is getting them to handle aces properly. The strategy I used is to start by assuming that the value of an ace is 11. However, whenever a count exceeds 21, the count is reduced by 10 if an ace is present. (This is tricky, because there could be more than one ace. The `getDealerCards` and `getPlayer-Cards` methods use a variable named `aceCount` to keep track of the number of aces that are still being valued at 11.)

Finally, I created an additional helper method, `getCount`, whose job is to determine the Blackjack value of a card. Here's the finished program.

Blackjack.java

```
1   // Program name: Blackjack
2   // Author: K. N. King
3   // Written: 1998-05-26
4   // Modified: 1999-07-11
5   //
6   // Plays the game of Blackjack. At the beginning of each hand,
7   // the dealer (the program) and the player (the user) are
8   // each dealt two cards. If the player's cards total to 21,
9   // the hand is over and the player wins (unless the dealer
```

```
10    // also has 21, in which case the hand is a tie). The player
11    // may now draw additional cards in an attempt to get close
12    // to 21. If the player exceeds 21, the hand is over and the
13    // player loses. Otherwise, the dealer begins drawing cards
14    // until reaching a total of 17 or more. If the dealer
15    // exceeds 21, the player wins. If the player's final count
16    // exceeds the dealer's final count, the player wins. If the
17    // dealer and the player have identical counts, the hand is
18    // a tie. Otherwise, the dealer wins.
19    //
20    // At the end of each hand, the program will display the
21    // total number of wins for both the dealer and the player.
22    // The player will then be asked whether or not to play
23    // another hand.
24
25    import jpb.*;
26
27    public class Blackjack {
28      public static void main(String[] args) {
29        int playerWins = 0;
30        int dealerWins = 0;
31
32        while (true) {
33          // Choose two cards for both player and dealer
34          Card playerCard1 = Card.pickRandom();
35          Card playerCard2 = Card.pickRandom();
36          Card dealerCard1 = Card.pickRandom();
37          Card dealerCard2 = Card.pickRandom();
38
39          // Display player's cards
40          System.out.println("Your cards: " + playerCard1 +
41                               " " + playerCard2);
42
43          // Compute initial counts for player and dealer
44          int playerCount = getCount(playerCard1) +
45                              getCount(playerCard2);
46          int dealerCount = getCount(dealerCard1) +
47                              getCount(dealerCard2);
48
49          // Check whether player's count is 21. If so, dealer
50          // must have 21 or lose automatically.
51          if (playerCount == 21) {
52            if (dealerCount != 21)
53              dealerCount = 0;
54          } else {
55            // Player's count was not 21. Ask player to draw
56            // additional cards and determine new value of
57            // player's hand.
58            playerCount = getPlayerCards(playerCard1,
59                                  playerCard2);
60
61            // Player loses if new count exceeds 21
62            if (playerCount > 21)
63              playerCount = 0;
```

```
 64                   else {
 65                     // Player's count does not exceed 21. Show dealer's
 66                     // cards.
 67                     System.out.println("Dealer's cards: " +
 68                                        dealerCard1 + " " + dealerCard2);
 69
 70                     // Draw additional cards for dealer and determine
 71                     // new value of dealer's hand
 72                     dealerCount = getDealerCards(dealerCard1,
 73                                                  dealerCard2);
 74
 75                     // Dealer loses if new count exceeds 21
 76                     if (dealerCount > 21)
 77                       dealerCount = 0;
 78                   }
 79                 }
 80
 81               // Compare player's count with dealer's count to
 82               // determine the winner; display the outcome and
 83               // update the win counts
 84               if (playerCount > dealerCount) {
 85                 System.out.println("You win!");
 86                 playerWins++;
 87               } else if (playerCount < dealerCount) {
 88                 System.out.println("Dealer wins");
 89                 dealerWins++;
 90               } else
 91                 System.out.println("Tie");
 92
 93               // Display the win counts
 94               System.out.println("Dealer: " + dealerWins +
 95                                  " Player: " + playerWins);
 96
 97               // See if user wants to play again; exit from loop if
 98               // answer is no
 99               SimpleIO.prompt("Play again (Y/N)? ");
100               String userInput = SimpleIO.readLine();
101               if (!userInput.equalsIgnoreCase("Y"))
102                 break;
103               System.out.println();
104             }
105           }
106
107     //////////////////////////////////////////////////////////////
108     // NAME:       getDealerCards
109     // BEHAVIOR:   Adds cards to the dealer's hand until the
110     //             value reaches 17 or more
111     // PARAMETERS: card1 - One of dealer's original two cards
112     //             card2 - The other original card
113     // RETURNS:    Value of the dealer's hand, including
114     //             original cards and new cards
115     //////////////////////////////////////////////////////////////
116     private static int getDealerCards(Card card1, Card card2) {
117       int dealerCount = getCount(card1) + getCount(card2);
```

```
118        int aceCount = 0;
119
120        // Determine number of aces among original pair of cards
121        if (card1.getRank() == Card.ACE)
122          aceCount++;
123        if (card2.getRank() == Card.ACE)
124          aceCount++;
125
126        while (true) {
127          // If the dealer's count exceeds 21 and the hand
128          // contains aces still valued at 11, then reduce the
129          // number of aces by 1 and reduce the count by 10
130          if (aceCount > 0 && dealerCount > 21) {
131            aceCount--;
132            dealerCount -= 10;
133          }
134
135          // Return if dealer's count is at least 17
136          if (dealerCount >= 17)
137            return dealerCount;
138
139          // Pick a new card and update the dealer's count
140          Card newCard = Card.pickRandom();
141          System.out.println("Dealer drew: " + newCard);
142          dealerCount += getCount(newCard);
143
144          // Check whether the new card is an ace
145          if (newCard.getRank() == Card.ACE)
146            aceCount++;
147        }
148      }
149
150      //////////////////////////////////////////////////////////
151      // NAME:       getPlayerCards
152      // BEHAVIOR:   Adds cards to the player's hand until the
153      //             value exceeds 21 or the player decides to
154      //             stand
155      // PARAMETERS: card1 - One of player's original two cards
156      //             card2 - The other original card
157      // RETURNS:    Value of the player's hand, including
158      //             original cards and new cards
159      //////////////////////////////////////////////////////////
160      private static int getPlayerCards(Card card1, Card card2) {
161        int playerCount = getCount(card1) + getCount(card2);
162        int aceCount = 0;
163
164        // Determine number of aces among original pair of cards
165        if (card1.getRank() == Card.ACE)
166          aceCount++;
167        if (card2.getRank() == Card.ACE)
168          aceCount++;
169
170        while (true) {
171          // If the player's count exceeds 21 and the hand
```

```
172          // contains aces still valued at 11, then reduce the
173          // number of aces by 1 and reduce the count by 10
174          if (aceCount > 0 && playerCount > 21) {
175            aceCount--;
176            playerCount -= 10;
177          }
178
179          // Return if player's count exceeds 21
180          if (playerCount > 21)
181            return playerCount;
182
183          // Ask user whether to stand or hit
184          SimpleIO.prompt("(S)tand or (H)it? ");
185          String userInput = SimpleIO.readLine();
186          if (!userInput.equalsIgnoreCase("H"))
187            return playerCount;
188
189          // Pick a new card and update the player's count
190          Card newCard = Card.pickRandom();
191          System.out.println("You drew: " + newCard);
192          playerCount += getCount(newCard);
193
194          // Check whether the new card is an ace
195          if (newCard.getRank() == Card.ACE)
196            aceCount++;
197        }
198      }
199
200      /////////////////////////////////////////////////////////////
201      // NAME:       getCount
202      // BEHAVIOR:   Returns the Blackjack value of a particular
203      //             card
204      // PARAMETERS: c - a Card object
205      // RETURNS:    The Blackjack value of the card c. The value
206      //             of a card is the same as its rank, except
207      //             that face cards have a value of 10 and aces
208      //             have a value of 11.
209      /////////////////////////////////////////////////////////////
210      private static int getCount(Card c) {
211        switch (c.getRank()) {
212          case Card.TWO:    return 2;
213          case Card.THREE:  return 3;
214          case Card.FOUR:   return 4;
215          case Card.FIVE:   return 5;
216          case Card.SIX:    return 6;
217          case Card.SEVEN:  return 7;
218          case Card.EIGHT:  return 8;
219          case Card.NINE:   return 9;
220          case Card.ACE:    return 11;
221          default:          return 10;  // TEN, JACK, QUEEN, KING
222        }
223      }
224    }
```

Review Question

1. What are the advantages of defining constants in the `Card` class to represent the names of ranks and suits?

10.10   Debugging

When a program consists of more than one component, it's important to test each component for proper behavior before trying to test the entire program. Testing a single component is known as ***unit testing.*** Testing the entire program, after each component has been tested individually, is known as ***integration testing.***

Unit testing helps us locate bugs and fix them at an early stage. If we attempt to test a large program without first testing its components, we're likely to be swamped with problems. Worse still, we may not have a clue about which part of the program is responsible for each problem.

Unit testing is important in the creation of any complex system, regardless of whether or not software is involved. Electrical and mechanical systems are often tested this way; small circuits or assemblies are checked before being combined into larger systems. Automobile manufacturers test engines separately before they're installed in new cars. That way, if the car won't start, the engine can be ruled out as a source of the problem.

In an object-oriented language such as Java, the components of a program are classes, so unit testing consists of verifying that the constructors and methods in each class work properly. One way to test the `Fraction` class would be to write a small test class (let's name it `TestFraction`). `TestFraction` will have a `main` method that creates two `Fraction` objects and performs operations on them. For greater testing power, we'll have `TestFraction` ask the user to enter the numerators and denominators of the fractions. Here's what `TestFraction` might look like:

TestFraction.java

```
1   // Tests the behavior of the Fraction class.
2
3   import jpb.*;
4
5   public class TestFraction {
6     public static void main(String[] args) {
7       while (true) {
8         // Prompt the user to enter the numerator and
9         // denominator of two fractions
10        int num = ValidIO.readInt("Enter first numerator: ");
11        int denom =
12          ValidIO.readInt("Enter first denominator: ");
13        Fraction f1 = new Fraction(num, denom);
14        System.out.println();
15
```

```
16        num = ValidIO.readInt("Enter second numerator: ");
17        denom = ValidIO.readInt("Enter second denominator: ");
18        Fraction f2 = new Fraction(num, denom);
19        System.out.println();
20
21        // Display the fractions after they've been stored in
22        // objects
23        System.out.println("First fraction: " + f1);
24        System.out.println("Second fraction: " + f2 + "\n");
25
26        // Compute and display the sum, difference, product,
27        // and quotient of the two fractions
28        System.out.println("Sum: " + f1.add(f2));
29        System.out.println("Difference: " + f1.subtract(f2));
30        System.out.println("Product: " + f1.multiply(f2));
31        System.out.println("Quotient: " + f1.divide(f2));
32
33        // Ask the user whether or not to test more fractions
34        SimpleIO.prompt("\nTest more fractions (Y/N)? ");
35        String userInput = SimpleIO.readLine();
36        if (!userInput.equalsIgnoreCase("Y"))
37          break;
38      }
39    }
40  }
```

`TestFraction` will ask the user for two fractions, which are then combined using addition, subtraction, multiplication, and division:

```
Enter first numerator: 3
Enter first denominator: 6

Enter second numerator: -100
Enter second denominator: -50

First fraction: 1/2
Second fraction: 2

Sum: 5/2
Difference: -3/2
Product: 1
Quotient: 1/4

Test more fractions (Y/N)? n
```

If the user enters y or Y, the program starts over again.

`TestFraction` uses the `readInt` method from the `ValidIO` class. If you run this program, you'll need to put `ValidIO.java` in the same directory as `TestFraction.java` (or else add `ValidIO` to the `jpb` package, as described in Section 10.8).

A class such as TestFraction is often called a ***test harness***. Although TestFraction is intended only for testing purposes, it's not a good idea to discard it once the Fraction class is done. Test harnesses should be retained for future use. If the Fraction class is modified in the future, we'll need to run TestFraction again to make sure that the changes haven't broken the Fraction class. Retesting a component after a change is known as ***regression testing.***

In Java, there's an easy way to create a test harness and make sure that it won't be lost in the future. The secret is to put a main method in the class that's being tested. This method will play the role of a test harness by creating instances of the class and performing operations on them.

For example, we could move the main method from TestFraction to the Fraction class itself. (The TestFraction class will no longer be needed.) Here's what the Fraction class would look like with the main method added:

```
public class Fraction {
  // Rest of Fraction class goes here

  public static void main(String[] args) {
    // Same code as in TestFraction
  }
}
```

I've put main at the end of the Fraction class because it's only present for testing purposes and won't be used otherwise.

It may seem odd for a class to have a main method that creates instances of the class, but look at it this way: the main method is the same, regardless of whether it's in the TestFraction class or the Fraction class. Java doesn't really care where the main method is located. We'll need to compile and execute the program a little differently (because Fraction, not TestFraction, contains the main method), but everything else will work the same.

One troubling question remains: If a program consists of several classes, and each class has its own main method, won't the compiler get confused about which main to use? Fortunately, the answer is no. When we execute the program, we must specify the name of the class whose main method we want to use. main methods in other classes are ignored. For example, suppose that we add a main method to the Card class for testing purposes. The Blackjack program will now have two main methods: one in the Blackjack class and one in the Card class. If we enter the command

```
java Blackjack
```

then the Java interpreter will execute the main method in the Blackjack class, and we'll play a game of Blackjack. But if we enter

```
java Card
```

the Java interpreter will execute the main method in the Card class, and we'll end up testing the behavior of the Card class.

Review Questions

1. Testing a single component is known as _____ testing.

2. Testing the entire program, after each component has been tested individually, is known as _____ testing.

3. A class that is created to test another class is often called a _____ _____ [two words].

4. Retesting a component after a change is known as _____ testing.

Q & A

Q: **Is there some way to indicate where packages are located without having to change the CLASSPATH variable? [p. 419]**

A: Yes. When you invoke `javac` or `java`, you can use the `-classpath` option to specify where your packages are located. For example, if your packages are in the directory `MyPkgs`, then you would compile the program `Demo.java` by typing

```
javac -classpath .;C:\MyPkgs Demo.java
```

To run the program, type

```
java -classpath .;C:\MyPkgs Demo
```

The class path in each case is `.;C:\MyPkgs`, which tells the compiler and interpreter to look in the current directory (`.`) first, and then search the directory `C:\MyPkgs`.

Summary

- The process of designing a program by breaking it down into classes is called object-oriented design.
- Object-oriented analysis is the process of identifying an initial set of classes for a program by examining the program's specification.
- The name of a class should consist of a noun, possibly modified by an adjective or participle.
- A class that will be used for creating objects is said to be instantiable. An instantiable class will contain instance variables and (in most cases) instance methods.
- An object is said to be mutable if its instance variables can be changed after the object is created; otherwise, the object is immutable.

- The advantage of making objects immutable is that they can be shared safely (more than one variable can safely refer to the same object). The disadvantage is that programs are potentially less efficient, because new objects will need to be created more often.

- Keep the number of instance variables in a class to a minimum. Avoid storing unnecessary data in objects.

- A public instance variable can be accessed outside its class by writing the name of an object, a dot, and the name of the instance variable.

- Instance variables should normally be declared private, thereby enforcing the design principle known as information hiding. Methods that are intended for use only within a class should also be declared private.

- Instance variables and class variables are visible throughout the class declaration. A parameter is visible throughout the body of its method. A local variable is visible from the line on which it is declared to the end of the enclosing block.

- A local variable or parameter will hide a class variable or instance variable with the same name.

- A well-designed class should provide a set of public methods that is both complete and convenient.

- Most methods fall into one of four categories: manager methods, implementor methods, access methods, and helper methods.

- Manager methods initialize objects and convert them to other types.

- It's a good idea for most classes to provide a manager method named `toString`, which returns a string representation of the data stored in an instance of the class.

- Implementor methods implement the important capabilities of a class.

- Access methods are either accessors (getters), which return the value of a variable, or mutators (setters), which change the value of a variable.

- An instance method can have helper methods, which may be either instance methods or class methods.

- A class may contain two or more methods with the same name; the methods are said to be overloaded.

- Overloaded methods must have different numbers of parameters or, if the number of parameters is the same, not all corresponding parameters can have the same type.

- When an overloaded method is called, the Java compiler chooses the method with the proper number of parameters. If more than one method has the same number of parameters, the compiler chooses the method that's most specific.

- The keyword `this` can be used in the body of an instance method to refer to the object that called the method.

- The expression this.*variable-name* allows access to an instance variable that's hidden by a local variable or parameter.

- The expression this.*method-name* (*arguments*) can be used to call an instance method in the same class.

- this can be used as an argument in a method call if it becomes necessary to pass the calling object to another method.

- this can be used in a return statement if a method needs to return the calling object.

- If a class has no constructor, Java provides a default constructor that does nothing.

- It's a good idea to write at least one constructor for each class. Providing multiple constructors makes the class easier to use.

- this can be used in a constructor to allow it to call another constructor in the same class.

- For convenience, it's usually a good idea for a class to provide a constructor with no arguments (a "no-arg" constructor).

- When an object is created, default values are assigned to each of its instance variables. If any instance variable has an initializer, the value of that initializer is assigned to the variable next. The constructor is executed last.

- An instantiable class may contain class variables and methods. One reason for adding a class variable to an instantiable class is to keep track of information that concerns all instances created so far.

- Class methods are not allowed to use the word this. Class methods may not access instance variables or call instance methods.

- To make a class method reusable in other programs, we can put it in a class by itself or add it to a class that contains other reusable methods.

- By default, every class belongs to a default package that has no name. To make a class more easily reusable, it can be put in a named package.

- When declared without an access modifier, variables and methods in a class can be accessed by other classes in the same package, but not by classes in other packages.

- Classes that are not declared public can be used only by other classes in the same package.

- Files that belong to a package must begin with a package declaration. These files must be in a directory with the same name as the package. Also, the enclosing directory (not the package directory itself) must be on the list of directories that is searched by the Java compiler and interpreter.

- Each component in a program should be tested individually before the components are assembled to form the complete program. Testing a single component is known as unit testing. Testing the entire program, after each component has been tested individually, is known as integration testing.

- In Java, unit testing consists of verifying that the constructors and methods in a class work properly.
- One way to test a class is to write a small test class (a test harness) containing a `main` method that creates objects and performs operations on them.
- Test harnesses are also used for regression testing (retesting a component after it has been changed).
- In Java, a class can serve as its own test harness by providing a `main` method that creates instances of the class and performs operations on them.
- When a program is executed, the Java interpreter is given the name of the class whose `main` method is to be used. `main` methods in other classes are ignored.

Exercises

Section 10.3

1. Pick a class in the Java API and classify its public methods as manager methods, implementor methods, or access methods.

2. Write a `toString` method for the `PhoneRecord` class of Section 5.8.

3. Suppose that a class contains the following instance methods:
   ```
   void f(short s)    // Version 1
   void f(float f)    // Version 2
   void f(double d)   // Version 3
   ```
   Which version of `f` (if any) will the compiler select, if the argument passed to `f` has type:
   (a) `char`
   (b) `int`
   (c) `long`

Section 10.4

4. Rewrite the final version of the `Fraction` constructor from Section 10.3 so that its parameters are named `numerator` and `denominator`.

Section 10.5

5. Write the following constructors for the `PhoneRecord` class of Section 5.8:
   (a) A constructor that initializes the name to a value specified by a parameter (defaulting the number to `null`).
   (b) A no-arg constructor that assigns `null` to both the name and number.
   Use `this` to simplify your constructors.

Section 10.6

6. Rewrite the `add`, `subtract`, `multiply`, and `divide` methods in the `Fraction` class so that the body of each is a single `return` statement.

7. The following questions refer to the program at the end of this exercise, which is assumed to be stored in a file named `TestMoney.java`.
   (a) What is the output of this program?
   (b) Would it be legal to add the word `public` to the beginning of line 12, without making any other changes?

(c) Would the program still compile if we replaced `this.amount` by `amount` on line 16? If so, would the program produce the same output?

(d) Would the program still compile if we replaced `this.amount` by `amount` on line 20? If so, would the program produce the same output?

(e) What is the Java name for a constructor such as the one on lines 19–21?

(f) Would the program still work if the constructor on lines 19–21 were removed?

(g) How many times is the `toString` method called inside the `main` method?

(h) Would the program still compile if we replaced `100.0` by `100` on line 32? If so, would the `toDouble` method still work correctly?

(i) Are Money objects mutable or immutable?

```
1 public class TestMoney {
2   public static void main(String[] args) {
3     Money m1 = new Money(56.789);
4     Money m2 = new Money(12.34);
5     System.out.println("Value of m1: " + m1);
6     System.out.println("Value of m2: " + m2);
7     System.out.println("Sum: " + m1.add(m2));
8     System.out.println("Difference: " + m1.subtract(m2));
9   }
10 }
11
12 class Money {
13   private long amount;
14
15   public Money(double amount) {
16     this.amount = Math.round(amount * 100);
17   }
18
19   public Money() {
20     this.amount = 0;
21   }
22
23   public Money add(Money m) {
24     return new Money(toDouble() + m.toDouble());
25   }
26
27   public Money subtract(Money m) {
28     return new Money(toDouble() - m.toDouble());
29   }
30
31   public double toDouble() {
32     return amount / 100.0;
33   }
34
35   public String toString() {
36     long cents = amount % 100;
37     if (cents < 10)
38       return amount / 100 + ".0" + cents;
39     else
40       return amount / 100 + "." + cents;
41   }
42 }
```

Programming Projects

1. Modify the `PhoneDirectory` program (Section 5.8) by adding a command named `c` (change). This command will first prompt the user for a name and then display all phone records that match the name. (As with the `f` command, partial matches are allowed.) If only one name matches, the command will then prompt the user for a new name and number, which will replace the old name and number. The user can leave the name unchanged by pressing Enter when prompted to enter the new name. (Similarly, the user can leave the number unchanged by pressing Enter when asked for the new number.) Here's an example of the desired behavior:

    ```
    Enter command (a, c, f, or q): c
    Enter name to look up: Abbott
    Abbott, C. Michael 776-5188

    Enter new name:
    Enter new number: 786-5188
    ```

    If no record matches the name initially entered by the user, or if more than one record matches, the program must display the message `"No unique matching record; try again"`. The user will not be prompted for a new name or number. *Hint:* You will need to add setters to the `PhoneRecord` class.

2. Add the following methods to the `Fraction` class (Section 10.6):

    (a) `abs()` — returns the absolute value of this fraction.

    (b) `compareTo(f)` — returns a negative integer, zero, or a positive integer, depending on whether this fraction is less than, equal to, or greater than `f` (a `Fraction` object).

    (c) `max(f)` — returns either this fraction or `f`, whichever is larger.

    (d) `min(f)` — returns either this fraction or `f`, whichever is smaller.

    (e) `reciprocal()` — returns the reciprocal of this fraction.

    Modify the `TestFraction` class (Section 10.10) so that it tests the new methods.

3. Modify the `Card` class (Section 10.9) so that `rank` and `suit` have type `char`. For example, the two of clubs would be stored as `'2'` in the `rank` variable and `'C'` in the `suit` variable. Does the `Blackjack` class have to be changed as a result of this change to `Card`? Which way of storing the rank and suit do you prefer?

4. Add a `main` method to the `Card` class (Section 10.9) for unit testing purposes. When executed, this method produces the following output:

    ```
    Full deck:
    2C 3C 4C 5C 6C 7C 8C 9C TC JC QC KC AC
    2D 3D 4D 5D 6D 7D 8D 9D TD JD QD KD AD
    2H 3H 4H 5H 6H 7H 8H 9H TH JH QH KH AH
    2S 3S 4S 5S 6S 7S 8S 9S TS JS QS KS AS

    100 random cards:
    AC TD JD KD JH 3H 7S 9C 4S AD
    QS 3D AD 2D TC 2D 8H QS QH 2S
    6C KD 9D 4S QC 7D JS TC KS 7H
    8S AH 3C JC 8H 4S 2C JC QH JC
    ```

```
2H AH 2S JD JC 7H 4H 8S AC 6S
2D 2S 4S 8D 9C TS 5H 2H 4C 4S
AC 7D KC 2H KD TS 9H KC 2S AS
7C 8C 7C 9C QH 7D QS QS JS AD
4S 4C TH 7D TD AS 8S 7S KD 7H
6H JS KD QD 3C 5C 5D 8S KC 3D
```

First, `main` creates 52 different `Card` objects and displays each one using `toString`. Next, `main` calls `pickRandom` 100 times and displays the cards that it returns.

5. Write a class named `Clock` that contains the following variables, methods, and constructors:

(a) Private instance variables that store hours (0–23), minutes (0–59), and seconds (0–59).

(b) A constructor that initializes the hours, minutes, and seconds to values specified by parameters.

(c) A constructor that initializes the hours and minutes to values specified by parameters (defaulting the seconds to 0).

(d) A constructor that initializes the hours to a value specified by a parameter (defaulting the minutes and seconds to 0).

(e) A no-arg constructor that sets the hours, minutes, and seconds to 0.

(f) A method that resets the hours, minutes, and seconds to 0.

(g) A method that advances the clock by one second.

(h) Getters and setters for hours, minutes, and seconds.

(i) A `toString` method that returns the hours, minutes, and seconds as a string of the form `"hh:mm:ss"`.

(j) A `main` method that tests all constructors and methods in the class.

Use the techniques described in the chapter to make the constructors and methods as short as possible. You may use helper methods.

6. Write a class named `Date` that contains the following variables, methods, and constructors:

(a) Private instance variables that store a year, month (1–12), and day (1–31).

(b) A constructor that initializes the year, month, and day to values specified by parameters.

(c) A no-arg constructor that sets the year, month, and day to match the date on which the program was run. *Hint:* Use the `GregorianCalendar` class (Section 8.6) to obtain this information.

(d) A method that advances the date by one day. *Note:* This method must work for all days, including the last day in a month or a year.

(e) Getters and setters for the year, month, and day.

(f) `compareTo(d)`, a method that returns a negative integer, zero, or a positive integer, depending on whether this date is earlier than, the same as, or later than d (a `Date` object).

(g) A `toString` method that returns the year, month, and day as a string of the form `"yyyy-mm-dd"`.

(h) A `main` method that tests all constructors and methods in the class.

Use the techniques described in the chapter to make the constructors and methods as short as possible. You may use helper methods.

7. Write a class named `Part` that contains the following variables, methods, and constructors:

   (a) Private instance variables that store a part number, a part name, and a quantity. The name is a string; the other variables are integers.

   (b) A constructor that initializes the part number, part name, and quantity to values specified by parameters.

   (c) A constructor that initializes the part number and part name to values specified by parameters (defaulting the quantity to 0).

   (d) A no-arg constructor that sets the part name to `"No name"` and the part number and quantity to 0.

   (e) Getters for the part number, part name, and quantity.

   (f) Methods that increase or decrease the quantity by an amount specified by a parameter.

   (g) A `toString` method that returns the part number, part name, and quantity as a string of the form `"number name quantity"`. The number is stored using 5 characters, with spaces at the end if necessary. The name is stored using 20 characters, with spaces at the end if necessary. (If the name exceeds 20 characters, only the first 20 are shown.)

   (h) A `main` method that tests all constructors and methods in the class.

   Use the techniques described in the chapter to make the constructors and methods as short as possible. You may use helper methods.

8. Write a class named `Odometer` that models the behavior of a car's odometer. An odometer is a counter with a fixed number of digits (let's call it n). The class must contain the following methods and constructors:

   (a) A constructor that sets n to a specified value.

   (b) A no-arg constructor that sets n to 6.

   (c) A method that resets the odometer's value to 0.

   (d) A method that adds 1 to the odometer's value. If the number of digits in the new value exceeds n, the odometer is reset to 0.

   (e) A `toInt` method that returns the odometer's value as an integer.

   (f) A `toString` method that returns the odometer's value as a string of n digits, with leading zeros added if necessary. For example, if n is 6, `toString` might return the string `"008124"`.

   (g) A `main` method that tests all constructors and methods in the class.

   You are free to use whatever instance variables seem most appropriate (two or three variables should be enough). Use the techniques described in the chapter to make the constructors and methods as short as possible.

9. Rewrite the `Odometer` class of Programming Project 8 so that it uses a different set of instance variables. The bodies of the constructors and instance methods will require modification, but the `main` method should not be changed.

10. Write a class named `Complex` that contains the following variables, methods, and constructors:

    (a) Private instance variables that store the real and imaginary parts of a complex number.

    (b) A constructor that initializes the real and imaginary parts to values specified by parameters.

    (c) A constructor that initializes the real part to a value specified by a parameter (defaulting the imaginary part to 0).

(d) A no-arg constructor that sets the real and imaginary parts to 0.

(e) Methods that add, subtract, multiply, and divide by another `Complex` object.

(f) A method that multiplies the real and imaginary parts by a `double` value.

(g) A method that returns the conjugate (a number with the same real part, but whose imaginary part is the negation of the original imaginary part).

(h) Getters for the real and imaginary parts.

(i) Methods that return the magnitude and angle of the number in polar coordinates.

(j) A `toString` method that returns a string of the form `"x+yi"`, where *x* is the real part and *y* is the imaginary part.

(k) Constants (class variables that have been declared `final`) that represent the complex numbers 0, 1, and *i*.

(l) A `main` method that tests all constructors and methods in the class.

Use the techniques described in the chapter to make the constructors and methods as short as possible. You may use helper methods.

11. Rewrite the `Complex` class of Programming Project 10 so that it stores the complex number using polar coordinates rather than Cartesian coordinates. The bodies of the constructors and instance methods will require modification, but the `main` method should not be changed.

Answers to Review Questions

Section 10.1	1.	Object-oriented design
	2.	Nouns
	3.	Verbs
	4.	(b)
Section 10.2	1.	Information hiding
	2.	Scope
Section 10.3	1.	They should be complete and convenient.
	2.	Manager methods, implementor methods, access methods, and helper methods
	3.	Signature
	4.	Most specific
Section 10.4	1.	(c)
Section 10.5	1.	Default
	2.	By default, by initialization in the variable's declaration, or by assignment in the constructor
Section 10.7	1.	(c)
	2.	(e)
Section 10.8	1.	`package foo;`
Section 10.9	1.	It is easier to work with names rather than numbers. Also, the code is more readable.
Section 10.10	1.	Unit
	2.	Integration
	3.	Test harness
	4.	Regression

11 Subclasses

The ability to define classes is one of Java's most powerful features, as we saw in Chapters 3 and 10. However, Java has two additional features that make classes even more useful. The first is the ability to define a new class by extending an existing class. The new class (the "subclass") inherits variables and methods from the old one (the "superclass"). This feature—one of the key principles of object-oriented programming—can save a significant amount of time and effort during the development of a program.

The second feature, known as polymorphism, is a little harder to describe. It turns out that Java allows an object variable to store a reference to more than one kind of object, provided that the objects are related. When we use this variable to call an instance method, which method is actually called depends on the object that's currently stored in the variable (a technique known as dynamic binding). Polymorphism is especially useful when objects of different types are stored in an array or other data structure.

This chapter explains inheritance and polymorphism and shows how they work in Java. It also covers a number of related topics, including the `protected` access modifier, which is an alternative to `public` and `private`. We'll see how to use the `instanceof` operator to test whether an object belongs to a particular class, and how to cast object references. We'll discover that all classes in Java are descendants of a special class named `Object` and therefore belong to the same "family tree." We'll also learn about the effect of declaring a class to be `abstract` or `final`.

The chapter concludes with a discussion of how the classes in Java's Abstract Window Toolkit are related by inheritance. This discussion provides a concrete example of the power of inheritance, as well as introducing many of the classes that we'll need in Chapter 12.

Objectives

- Learn about the concept of inheritance.
- Learn how to create a subclass of an existing class.
- Learn about the `protected` access modifier.
- Learn how to override inherited methods.
- Learn about the substitution principle, which allows an instance of a subclass to take the place of an instance of one of its superclasses.
- Learn how Java supports polymorphism by using dynamic binding for method calls.
- Learn about the `instanceof` operator.
- Learn how to cast object references.
- Learn about the `Object` class and the Java class hierarchy.
- Learn about abstract classes.
- Learn about declaring classes and methods to be `final`.
- Learn about the classes in Java's Abstract Window Toolkit and see how they're related by inheritance.

11.1 Inheritance

In the real world, objects aren't usually one-of-a-kind. Most objects have similarities to other objects. Cars, for example, are similar to trucks. Both cars and trucks are examples of *vehicles*—objects that can move and carry other objects. A car is a vehicle that has an engine and is designed to transport a small number of people. We can think of a car as a special type of vehicle, or a vehicle as a more general type of car.

In Java, relationships such as the one between cars and vehicles are expressed using a feature known as ***inheritance.*** The idea of inheritance is a natural one. As humans, we inherit from our parents. Like it or not, many of our properties are genetically influenced, from our hair color to our height. Inheritance is one of the basic tenets of object-oriented programming—a class is allowed to have a "parent" from which it inherits some of its state and some of its behavior.

Let's return to our car example. Cars have much in common, so there would be no point for a car designer to start from scratch when designing a new car. It can be taken for granted that a car has certain components: wheels, a steering wheel, an engine, and so forth. We can also assume certain behaviors: turn on engine, accelerate, press brake, and the like. So a car designer can focus on what distinguishes the new model from automobiles in general.

In programming using objects, we'll use inheritance for a similar reason.

When we need a new class, we'll try to create it from an existing class. That way, we won't be starting from scratch every time. Instead, we'll be able to inherit the variables and methods of the existing class, and then just specify what additional variables and methods we need to make the new class unique.

In Java, inheritance is accomplished by *extending* an existing class. To indicate that one class extends another, all we need to do is put the word `extends` in the class declaration, preceded by the name of the new class and followed by the name of the class that's being extended:

```
public class Car extends Vehicle {
    ...
}
```

Q&A

Car is said to be a *subclass* of `Vehicle`, and `Vehicle` is said to be the *superclass* of `Car`.

A subclass *inherits* the variables and methods of its superclass, with the exception of constructors, private variables, and private methods. Inherited variables and methods behave as though they were declared in the subclass. The subclass may define additional variables and methods that were not present in the superclass.

Writing a Subclass

The first step in writing a subclass, of course, is deciding what the superclass should be. The superclass can be any previously existing class, including one of the classes in the Java API, a class that we've obtained elsewhere, or a class that we've written ourselves.

As an example, let's develop a `SavingsAccount` class from the `Account` class of Section 3.3. A savings account has all the properties of an ordinary bank account: it has a balance, it can be opened or closed, money can be deposited or withdrawn, and so on. In addition, a savings account has an interest rate associated with it. At periodic intervals, money is added to the account based on the interest rate and the account balance.

Let's assume that different savings accounts can have different interest rates, which means that each `SavingsAccount` object will need to store an interest rate. (We're deviating a little from the real world here. Rather than storing the interest rate itself, a savings account would more likely store a code indicating the type of account, which would then indicate the appropriate interest rate.) We'll also need access methods to get and set the interest rate. Here's a preliminary version of the `SavingsAccount` class:

```
public class SavingsAccount extends Account {
  private double interestRate;

  public double getInterestRate() {
    return interestRate;
  }
```

```
    public void setInterestRate(double rate) {
      interestRate = rate;
    }
}
```

An instance of a subclass stores all the instance variables of the superclass, plus all the instance variables defined in the subclass. Even the superclass's private variables, which aren't inherited, are still stored in instances of the subclass. For example, a `SavingsAccount` object will contain two variables: `balance` and `interestRate`. Here's how we might visualize a `SavingsAccount` object:

SavingsAccount object

balance	500.00
interestRate	4.25

The methods that can be applied to `SavingsAccount` objects are `getInterestRate`, `setInterestRate`, `deposit` (inherited), `withdraw` (inherited), `getBalance` (inherited), and `close` (inherited). If `savingsAcct` is a `SavingsAccount` variable, the following statements are all legal:

```
System.out.println("Rate: " + savingsAcct.getInterestRate());
savingsAcct.setInterestRate(4.25);
savingsAcct.deposit(500.00);
savingsAcct.withdraw(100.00);
System.out.println("Balance: " + savingsAcct.getBalance());
savingsAcct.close();
```

When an instance method is called, Java looks first in the class to which the calling object belongs. If the method isn't found there, Java looks in the class's superclass. If the method isn't there either, Java looks in the superclass of *that* class, and so on. For example, when the statement

```
savingsAcct.deposit(500.00);
```

is executed, Java first looks for the `deposit` method in the `SavingsAccount` class, because `savingsAcct` is an instance of `SavingsAccount`. Because `SavingsAccount` doesn't have a `deposit` method, Java next looks in the superclass of `SavingsAccount`—the `Account` class—where it finds `deposit`.

Writing Subclass Constructors

A subclass doesn't inherit constructors from its superclass, so we'll need to write new constructors for the subclass. Writing a constructor for a subclass is much like writing the constructor for any class. The only problem is initializing the variables that belong to the superclass. These variables are likely to be private, so we can't initialize them directly.

For example, the constructor for the `SavingsAccount` class will need to initialize both the `balance` and `interestRate` variables. Here's a first attempt at writing the constructor:

```
public SavingsAccount(double initialBalance,
                      double initialRate) {
  balance = initialBalance;     // WRONG; balance is private
  interestRate = initialRate;
}
```

Unfortunately, this version of the constructor won't compile. The problem: `balance` was declared `private` in the `Account` class, so we have no access to it in the `SavingsAccount` class. There are two ways to solve this problem. One is for the `SavingsAccount` constructor to invoke the `Account` constructor. (Section 11.2 describes the other solution.)

Invoking a superclass constructor is done in a peculiar way, using the word `super` as though it were the name of the superclass constructor:

```
public SavingsAccount(double initialBalance,
                      double initialRate) {
  super(initialBalance);        // Invoke Account constructor
  interestRate = initialRate;
}
```

The `Account` constructor will initialize the `balance` variable to the value stored in `initialBalance`, solving our problem. When `super` is used to invoke a superclass constructor, Java requires that it come first, before the other statements in the body of the subclass constructor.

As a second example, consider the `DrawableFrame` class, which we began using in Chapter 6. I created this class by extending `Frame`, a class in the Java API. A `Frame` object is a window with a title at the top. When we create a `DrawableFrame` object, we need to specify the title for the frame:

```
DrawableFrame df = new DrawableFrame("Title goes here");
```

Sound familiar? The constructor for `DrawableFrame` must take the title that is given to it and pass it to the constructor for its superclass (`Frame`), which it does by using `super`:

```
public DrawableFrame(String title) {
  super(title);  // Invoke Frame constructor
  ...
}
```

If a subclass constructor fails to call `super`, the compiler will automatically insert `super();` at the beginning of the constructor, thereby invoking the no-arg version of the superclass constructor. If a subclass has no constructors at all, the compiler will create a no-arg constructor that contains `super();` but no other statements.

Illustrating Inheritance

There are various ways to indicate visually that one class is a subclass of another. One of the most common techniques is to place the superclass above the subclass and draw a line connecting the two:

Sometimes an arrow is drawn from the subclass to the superclass.

When two or more classes have the same superclass, we can draw a single diagram with the superclass at the top and the subclasses below it:

I'm assuming that the `CheckingAccount` class is similar to the `Account` class, except that it allows checks to be written on the account.

I'll often use a more compact notation in which the superclass is on the left and the subclasses are on the right:

```
               ┌ CheckingAccount
Account ──┤
               └ SavingsAccount
```

To show the ancestry of a particular class, I'll use a simpler notation:

`Account → CheckingAccount`

In this notation, the arrow points from the superclass to the subclass.

There's nothing to prevent us from creating a subclass of a subclass. By repeating this process, we can build up long chains of related—and increasingly specialized—classes. For example, we could create a `CheckingAccount` class by extending the `Account` class and then extend `CheckingAccount` to arrive at `InterestCheckingAccount`:

`Account → CheckingAccount → InterestCheckingAccount`

When a class is the result of a series of extensions, it has more than one superclass. The class will have a "direct superclass" (the class that it extends), as well as "indirect" superclasses. In this example, the direct superclass of `InterestCheckingAccount` is `CheckingAccount`. `Account` is an indirect superclass of `InterestCheckingAccount`.

When *Not* to Use Inheritance

It's easy to misuse inheritance. Inheritance is appropriate when the new class "is a" particular case of the old class. We'll refer to this as the *is-a* relationship. For example, a Car *is a* Vehicle, and a SavingsAccount *is an* Account. If the words "is a" (or "is an") don't fit between a potential subclass and its superclass, then inheritance shouldn't be used. For example, it wouldn't make sense to say that a SavingsAccount *is a* Vehicle. For the *is-a* relationship to exist, the subclass must have every property of the superclass.

It's tempting to extend a class in order to inherit the data that it contains. For example, suppose that we've defined a Money class, whose instances represent specific dollar amounts. We might now want to change the Account class so that it stores the account balance in a Money object instead of a double variable. It's tempting to have Account extend Money, so that every Account object can automatically store a monetary amount. That's not a good idea, though. For one thing, any public methods in the Money class would be inherited by Account, making it possible to apply operations to Account objects that were intended for Money objects instead. (Adding two Money objects makes sense; adding two Account objects doesn't.) The *is-a* rule tells us that Account shouldn't extend Money, because we can't legitimately say that an Account *is a* Money.

Instead of having Account extend Money, we should simply declare the type of the balance variable to be Money instead of double. Although the *is-a* relationship doesn't hold for Account and Money, there's clearly some connection between the two classes, because every Account object will contain a Money object in one of its variables. We'll call this the ***has-a*** relationship, because an Account object *has a* Money object stored within it.

> Use inheritance when the *is-a* relationship exists between the new class and the one that it extends. Don't use inheritance to model the *has-a* relationship.

Review Questions

1. In Java, inheritance is accomplished by _____ an existing class.

2. What does a subclass *not* inherit from its superclass?

3. How is a superclass constructor invoked?

4. Inheritance is appropriate when a new class is related to an existing class by the _____ relationship.

11.2   The protected Access Modifier

Up to this point, we've used two access modifiers: public and private. Declaring a variable or method to be public allows universal access to that variable or method. Declaring a variable or method to be `private` limits access to the class in which the variable or method is defined. (In this section, I'll use the term "method" to mean "method or constructor," because both are subject to the same access rules.)

Once we begin to use inheritance, it soon becomes clear that the public/private distinction is too restrictive, because it doesn't distinguish a subclass from classes in general. A subclass, like any class, can use the public variables and methods in its superclass, but it has no access at all to private variables and methods in the superclass. We need a way to give a subclass greater access to variables and methods in its superclass.

The situation is much like what we encounter in daily life with parents and children. Children are granted additional privileges beyond those available to the public. For example, a parent might accept a collect call from a child but not from an arbitrary person.

In Java, we can give subclasses access to superclass variables and methods by declaring them to be `protected` instead of `public` or `private`. Using `protected` provides an intermediate level of access—one that's more restrictive than `public` but less restrictive than `private`. Table 11.1 summarizes the differences between `private`, `protected`, and `public` when applied to a variable or method in a class.

Table 11.1
Access Modifiers

Access Modifier	*Meaning*
`private`	Can be accessed only in the same class
`protected`	Can be accessed in the same class or in a subclass
`public`	Can be accessed in any class
None	Can be accessed in any class in the same package

I've included one other option—"None"—in the table. We saw in Section 10.8 that omitting the access modifier allows access by all classes in the same package. Although it's not mentioned in Table 11.1, a class also has access to the protected variables and methods of all classes in the same package.

The ability to access protected variables and methods extends to subclasses of subclasses, their subclasses, and so on. For example, suppose that we have the following chain of classes:

`Vehicle → MotorizedVehicle → Car`

Methods in the `Car` class will have access to the protected variables and methods of both `Vehicle` and `MotorizedVehicle`.

The `protected` keyword gives us another way to solve the problem of writing the constructor for the `SavingsAccount` class. Suppose that we change the declaration of the `Account` class by declaring `balance` to be `protected` rather than `private`:

```
public class Account {
  protected double balance;

  ...
}
```

The SavingsAccount constructor—as well as the methods in the Savings-Account class—will now have direct access to the balance variable, so we can write the SavingsAccount constructor as we had originally intended:

```
public SavingsAccount(double initialBalance,
                      double initialRate) {
  balance = initialBalance;
  interestRate = initialRate;
}
```

Uses of protected

protected works with methods as well as variables. A protected method can be called within its own class and by methods in subclasses. When a class contains a helper method that might be useful to its subclasses as well, it's a good idea to declare the method protected rather than private.

protected can also be used with class variables and class methods. For example, consider the version of the Account class from Section 10.7. In this version, Account had a private class variable named totalDeposits:

```
public class Account {
  private static double totalDeposits = 0.0;
  ...
}
```

Now suppose that we want to add a creditInterest method to the Savings-Account class:

```
public class SavingsAccount extends Account {
  public void creditInterest() { ... }
  ...
}
```

This method will credit interest to a savings account, based on the balance in the account and the account's interest rate. Crediting interest will increase not only the balance in the account itself, but the total deposits for the entire bank. In order to allow creditInterest to update the totalDeposits variable directly, we could declare totalDeposits to be protected rather than private:

```
public class Account {
  protected static double totalDeposits = 0.0;
  ...
}
```

protected Versus private

Declaring instance variables to be protected exposes them to all subclasses—a potentially unlimited number of classes—possibly resulting in a maintenance nightmare. For this reason, we'll generally avoid protected variables. Instead, we'll make variables private and provide access methods to fetch and/or modify their values. These methods can be declared `protected` if they'll be needed only by subclasses, not by all classes.

> It's better to declare instance variables to be `private` rather than `protected`. If a subclass needs access to these variables, it should be able to call a getter or setter method. If there's no need to expose the getter or setter to all classes, it should be declared `protected`.

Review Questions

1. Which access modifier is more restrictive: `private` or `protected`?

2. True or false: The ability to access protected variables and methods extends to subclasses of subclasses, their subclasses, and so on.

3. Which of the following cannot be declared `protected`: (a) instance variables, (b) instance methods, (c) class variables, (d) class methods, or (e) none of these?

4. Why should protected variables usually be avoided?

11.3 Overriding

In Section 11.1, I assumed that a car always has a steering wheel, but that's not always true: some cars have had a steering *bar* instead. Does that mean that we couldn't classify these vehicles as cars? That would be unfortunate, because they clearly are, even though they deviate from what we consider "normal" for a car. Fortunately, the object-oriented view of the world can accommodate variation through a mechanism known as *overriding,* which lets a subclass replace some of its inherited behavior.

If we're unhappy with the behavior of an instance method that's been inherited by a subclass, we can simply have the subclass *override* the method by supplying one of its own. The new method must have the same name and return type as the inherited method. In addition, both methods must have the same number of parameters, and the types of corresponding parameters must be the same.

For example, suppose that the `Account` class has a method named `printStatement` that prints an account statement. A `CheckingAccount` class that extends `Account` might need a different `printStatement` method in order to display information that's unique to that type of account. To override the inherited `printStatement` method, all `CheckingAccount` has to do is have a `printStatement` method with the same return type and parameters as the one in the `Account` class.

There's one tricky situation that can arise when we're writing a subclass method, however. Suppose that we need to call a method that's inherited from the superclass but overridden in the new class. Calling it in the normal way won't work, because the compiler will assume that we want the new, overridden version. For example, suppose that the `CheckingAccount` version of `printStatement` tries to call the `Account` version. (A checking account statement might be identical to an account statement, with the addition of a list of checks that were honored during the statement period.) Here's our first attempt at writing the `CheckingAccount` version of `printStatement`:

```
void printStatement() {
  printStatement();   // Print regular statement
  ...                 // Then print list of checks
}
```

The compiler will assume that `printStatement` is calling *itself,* not the version that was inherited. To force the compiler to use the superclass version of `printStatement`, we'll need to add the word `super` to the call:

```
void printStatement() {
  super.printStatement();   // Print regular statement
  ...                       // Then print list of checks
}
```

This technique works even if the method we're calling doesn't belong to the direct superclass. When a method is called using `super`, Java looks first in the direct superclass. If the method isn't found there, Java looks in the superclass of *that* class, and so on.

Although class methods can't be overridden, it's possible for a class method to *hide* an inherited class method. The requirements for hiding a class method are the same as for overriding an instance method: The new method must have the same name and return type as the inherited method. Also, the methods must have the same number of parameters, and the types of corresponding parameters must be the same.

Review Questions

1. In order to override an inherited instance method, the new method must have the same name as the inherited method. What other requirements must be met?

2. Is it possible for a superclass method to be called if it has been overridden in the current class? If so, how?

3. Although an inherited class method can't be overridden, it's possible to _____ the method instead.

11.4 Polymorphism

Inheritance is a powerful idea by itself, but it becomes even more potent when combined with another concept: ***polymorphism.*** To see what polymorphism means, consider giving instructions to someone to operate a vehicle. We might write down a list such as:

1. Start vehicle
2. Release brake
3. Accelerate
4. Apply brake
5. Stop vehicle

Notice that these instructions will work for any type of vehicle, not just a car. That's good, because it means we won't have to prepare separate instructions for every kind of vehicle in existence. The exact meaning of each instruction may vary, however, depending on the vehicle. For a car, "accelerate" means "press on the accelerator." For a bicycle, "accelerate" means "turn the pedals."

The term "polymorphism" comes from the Greek *polus* (many) and *morphe* (shape). In biology, polymorphism is "the occurrence of different forms, stages, or color types in individual organisms or in organisms of the same species" (American Heritage Dictionary). In object-oriented programming, polymorphism refers to the ability of different kinds of objects to respond differently to the same commands, provided that the objects belong to classes with a common ancestor.

To allow polymorphism, Java has an interesting rule, which I'll call the ***Substitution Principle:***

> ***An instance of a subclass can take the place of an instance of any of its superclasses.***

At first glance, the Substitution Principle doesn't make sense, because it seems to blur the distinction between two different classes. However, further reflection shows that the Substitution Principle is actually quite logical:

- If we've used inheritance properly (by observing the *is-a* relationship), then the subclass is a more specialized version of the superclass, so substitution makes sense.

- An object that belongs to the subclass contains the same variables (plus possibly some more) as any instance of the superclass. Plus, an instance of the subclass responds to the same (public) methods as an instance of the superclass. Anything that we could possibly do with an instance of the superclass would make sense—and work properly—for an instance of the subclass.

Consider the following example:

```
Vehicle v = new Car();
```

This statement looks wrong, because the left side is a `Vehicle` variable, but the right side is a `Car` object. In the past, we've assigned objects only to variables of the same type. However, if `Vehicle` is a superclass of `Car` (not necessarily a direct superclass), the assignment is legal. After all, a car *is* a vehicle: it has all the properties and behaviors of a vehicle. Any operation that can be performed on a vehicle can be performed on a car. Some behaviors were inherited and left unchanged, while others were overridden, but—either way—they're guaranteed to exist.

In Java, our algorithm for operating a vehicle would have the following appearance:

```
v.start();
v.releaseBrake();
v.accelerate();
v.applyBrake();
v.stop();
```

It's not clear exactly what v is. It might be a car, or it might be a truck, or it might be some other type of vehicle. But it doesn't matter, because all vehicles are guaranteed to have these methods. The exact behavior of each method may depend on the type of vehicle, but that's fine, as long as the method has the desired effect. Our algorithm is polymorphic: it works for a variety of vehicles, not a single kind.

Notice that the object stored in v won't be known until the program is actually run. The compiler itself usually can't determine what kind of object v will refer to. As a result, it will be necessary to test v each time it calls an instance method. This process is known as ***dynamic binding,*** because the exact method that's being called won't be known until the program is run. If different objects are assigned to v during program execution, different versions of the method may be called:

```
v = new Car();
v.start();          // Calls start method in Car class
v = new Truck();
v.start();          // Calls start method in Truck class
```

The Substitution Principle applies to more than just assignment. A method whose parameter type is a class can be passed an instance of a subclass instead. A method whose result type is a class may return an instance of a subclass instead. We can even use the == and != operators to compare references to instances of different classes, provided that one class is a subclass of the other.

Casting Object References

Suppose that we write a method named updateAccount that has an Account object as its parameter:

```
static void updateAccount(Account acct) {
    ...
}
```

When updateAccount is called, it could be passed a SavingsAccount object or a CheckingAccount object instead of an Account object (thanks to the Substitution Principle). As long as updateAccount performs only operations on acct that are valid for any type of account, there won't be any problems.

It's possible, however, that updateAccount needs to determine what type of account it's dealing with. For example, updateAccount might need to credit interest to acct if it's a SavingsAccount object.

Java's instanceof operator can be used to solve problems such as the one faced by updateAccount. An expression of the form

object instanceof *class*

has the value true only if *object* is an instance of *class* or one of its subclasses. For example, if the variable savingsAcct contains a reference to a Savings- Account object, then savingsAcct instanceof SavingsAccount would have the value true, and savingsAcct instanceof Account would also have the value true.

Once we've determined that an object belongs to a particular class, however, we may not be able to use the full set of methods defined for that class. For example, after discovering that acct is in fact a SavingsAccount object, we'll still be restricted by the compiler to just the Account methods, because acct is declared to be of type Account. To get around this restriction, we'll need to *cast* acct to type SavingsAccount, thereby forcing the compiler to accept acct as a SavingsAccount object. We first used casts in Section 9.5, in conjunction with the primitive types, but casting can also be used with objects. Here's how we could cast acct to type SavingsAccount:

```
SavingsAccount savingsAcct = (SavingsAccount) acct;
```

We can now call creditInterest—or any other SavingsAccount method—using the savingsAcct variable.

Here's the code that we would need to add to updateAccount to test whether the acct object belongs to the SavingsAccount class and, if so, call the creditInterest method:

```
if (acct instanceof SavingsAccount) {
  SavingsAccount savingsAcct = (SavingsAccount) acct;
  savingsAcct.creditInterest();
}
```

Be careful when trying to cast an object to a subclass. If the object isn't an instance of the subclass, a ClassCastException will be thrown. It's often a good idea to use instanceof to test an object before attempting to cast it.

Advantages of Polymorphism

Polymorphism is especially useful when we need to store different types of objects in the same data structure. We'll be able to write general-purpose code that processes every object in the data structure without having to check each one first to see which class it belongs to. For example, if we have an array of Account objects, we can print statements for them all without first checking to see whether we're dealing with a checking account or a savings account.

Polymorphism becomes especially important during program maintenance. If we create a new subclass of Account, we won't have to go through the entire program to see how this change might affect code that performs operations on accounts. Likewise, if we remove an existing subclass of Account, most of the program should be unaffected.

Excessive use of the instanceof operator can negate the advantages of polymorphism, so it's best to use this operator sparingly. Avoiding instanceof is usually easy to do. Consider the updateAccount example. Suppose that we put an empty creditInterest method in the Account class. The Savings-Account class will override this method, but the CheckingAccount class will inherit the empty method from Account. Because both CheckingAccount and SavingsAccount now have a creditInterest method, we won't need to test whether acct refers to a SavingsAccount object before we call creditInterest:

```
acct.creditInterest();
```

If acct refers to a SavingsAccount object, the effect is to credit interest to the account. But if acct refers to a CheckingAccount object, then nothing happens, because the CheckingAccount version of creditInterest is empty.

Review Questions

1. In object-oriented programming, _____ refers to the ability of different kinds of objects to respond differently to the same commands.

2. A call of an instance method may require _____ _____ [two words], because the method being called may not be known until the program is run.

3. Is the following code legal? Explain why or why not.
```
SavingsAccount savingsAcct = new SavingsAccount(100.00, 5.0);
Account acct = savingsAcct;
```

4. Which of the following is allowed by the Substitution Principle: (a) assigning a subclass object to a superclass variable, (b) passing a subclass object to a method that has a superclass parameter, (c) returning a subclass object from a method with a superclass result type, or (d) all of these?

5. Which operator is used to test whether an object belongs to a particular class?

6. Casting an object to a subclass will cause a _____ exception to be thrown if the object doesn't belong to the subclass.

11.5   The Object Class

The idea of class extension pervades Java. In fact, every class—with one exception—is required to have a superclass. The exception is a class named Object, which plays a special role in Java. If we declare a new class without saying what its superclass is, Java uses `Object` as the default superclass. Because of this rule, all classes (other than `Object` itself) have `Object` as a superclass, either directly or indirectly. We can think of Java's classes as belonging to a single "family tree," known as a ***class hierarchy:***

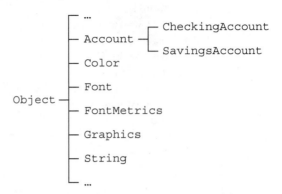

Notice that the class hierarchy includes both standard API classes and any classes that we write, such as `Account`, `CheckingAccount`, and `SavingsAccount`. Most of the standard classes that we've used so far have `Object` as their direct superclass. That's not always the case, however, as we'll see in Section 11.8.

The existence of a single class hierarchy has some important consequences:

- Every class (other than `Object` itself) inherits methods from the `Object` class. (Of course, some of these methods may have been overridden by another superclass.)
- A variable of type `Object` can store a reference to *any* object whatsoever. Similarly, a method with an `Object` parameter will accept any object as its argument.

Let's explore these points in more detail.

`Object` Methods

The `Object` class provides several methods, including:

- `clone()`—Returns a copy of this object.
- `equals(obj)`—Indicates whether the object `obj` is "equal" to this object.
- `toString()`—Returns a string representation of this object.

These methods are inherited by the subclasses of `Object`. Their subclasses then inherit the methods, and so on, so that every class in Java has these methods. However, these methods are frequently overridden; as a result, although every class has methods with these names, the behavior of the methods may vary.

The `clone` method is tricky to use, and not all classes support it, so I won't discuss it further. Let's take a closer look at the other two methods, `equals` and `toString`.

The `equals` Method

equals   The `equals` method is provided to solve the problem of testing whether two objects are equal. `equals` has one parameter, an arbitrary object, and returns a `boolean` result:

```
public boolean equals(Object obj) {
    ...
}
```

By default, the `equals` method behaves like the `==` operator. The call

```
x.equals(y)
```

returns true only if `x` and `y` refer to the same object. Because this test is often unsatisfactory, we may need to override `equals` and make it work properly for any classes that we write.

In the case of the `Fraction` class (Section 10.6), the `equals` method might look like this:

```
public boolean equals(Object obj) {
    if (!(obj instanceof Fraction))
        return false;
    Fraction f = (Fraction) obj;
    return (numerator == f.numerator &&
            denominator == f.denominator);
}
```

The method first checks whether `obj` is a `Fraction` object. If it's not, then the method immediately returns the value `false`. (We can't declare the parameter to be of type `Fraction`, because we're trying to override the version of `equals` in the `Object` class, and that version has an `Object` parameter.) If `obj` *is* a `Fraction` object, then the method casts `obj` and stores the result in a `Fraction` variable named `f`. Finally, the method checks whether the `Fraction` object that called `equals` has the same numerator and denominator as `f`.

If `f1` and `f2` are `Fraction` variables, we can test whether they represent identical fractions by writing

```
if (f1.equals(f2)) ...
```

The inherited version of `equals` would have tested whether `f1` and `f2` refer to the same object. The new version will test whether `f1` and `f2` have matching numerators and denominators.

> The `equals` method needs to behave in the manner expected of an equality test. In particular, if `x.equals(y)` returns `true`, then `y.equals(x)` should also.

We may not want to provide equality testing for a particular class, either because it may not be meaningful for that class or because it may not be worthwhile to take the time to write the `equals` method. If we don't provide an `equals` method for a class, it will inherit the method from its superclass.

The `toString` Method

toString   Section 3.8 discussed the `toString` method, which is used to convert an object into string form so that it can be displayed, often for debugging purposes. Because `toString` is declared in the `Object` class, all classes must have a `toString` method, even if it's the one inherited from `Object`.

We saw in Section 3.8 that if we use `System.out.print` or `System.out.println` to print an object, the object's `toString` method is called. It seemed like magic at the time, but there's a simple explanation for this phenomenon. The `print` and `println` methods are overloaded, with one version of each method requiring an `Object` parameter. We now know that a method with an `Object` parameter will accept any object as its argument. When supplied with an object as its argument, `print` (or `println`) in turn calls the `toString` method that belongs to the object and prints the string returned by `toString`.

What if we try to print an object whose class doesn't have a `toString` method? In that case, `print` will use an inherited version of `toString`. In the worst case, we'll end up using the version of `toString` declared in the `Object` class.

The version of `toString` in the `Object` class returns a string containing the name of the object's class, the @ character, and a hexadecimal number (the "hash code" for the object). For example, suppose that the `Fraction` class didn't contain a `toString` method. Let's see what happens when we print a `Fraction` object:

Q&A

```
Fraction f = new Fraction();
System.out.println(f);  // Calls the toString method
```

Because `Fraction` has no explicit superclass, Java will use `Object` as its superclass. When we call `toString` from a `Fraction` object, `Object`'s version of `toString` will be invoked, and we'll see output of the form

```
Fraction@1cc78a
```

This information isn't very useful, so it's a good idea for most classes to provide their own `toString` method.

Review Questions

1. If we declare a new class without specifying a superclass for it, what does Java use as its superclass?

2. All Java classes belong to a single _____ _____ [two words].

3. What is the behavior of the `equals` method if it's not overridden?

4. What is the behavior of the toString method if it's not overridden?

11.6 Abstract Classes

Some classes are purely artificial, created solely so that subclasses can take advantage of inheritance. Consider the Vehicle class, for example. We've never created a Vehicle object, and we never will. Vehicle was created for our convenience—in the real world, there are no "generic" vehicles, only specific types of vehicles. The same reasoning applies to the Account class. If you go to a bank and ask to open an account, you'll then be asked what type of account you want: checking, savings, and so on. If you insist that you don't want a specific type of account, you want only an "account," you'll likely end up being escorted out by the security guard.

Artificial classes like Vehicle and Account are actually pretty common. In Java, they're called ***abstract classes.*** Abstract classes have three distinguishing characteristics:

- The declaration of an abstract class must include the word abstract, which is usually placed just before the word class.
- Some of the methods in an abstract class may be ***abstract methods***. An abstract method is a "dummy" method that has no body:

```
public abstract double doubleValue();
```

  Note that an abstract method must contain the word abstract in its declaration. Also note that the declaration must end with a semicolon.
- It is illegal to create an instance of an abstract class.

Abstract classes are useful only as starting points for defining subclasses. They often arise from "bottom-up" design, in which we first identify which classes we'll need and then look for ways to "factor out" whatever those classes have in common. The result is an abstract class that we can extend to create the classes that we're really interested in.

For example, if we're in the process of designing classes that represent savings accounts and checking accounts, we'll probably notice that both types of accounts have a great deal in common. To take advantage of this commonality, it makes sense to create an abstract Account class first, then define SavingsAccount and CheckingAccount classes by extending Account. Account would define variables and methods that are common to both types of accounts.

Most of the time, subclasses of an abstract class will provide bodies for all inherited abstract methods. These subclasses are normal classes, and we'll be able to create objects from them. Occasionally, a subclass will fail to override all the abstract methods it inherits. In that case, the subclass is itself an abstract class, good only for defining further subclasses.

Example: A `Shape` Class

To illustrate abstract classes, suppose that we need to develop a series of classes that represent specific geometric shapes, such as `Circle` and `Rectangle`. These classes will have much in common, so we can save quite a bit of work by first creating a generic `Shape` class. We have no intention of creating actual `Shape` objects. Instead, the `Shape` class will serve solely as a starting point for defining more-specific shape classes. (*Note:* Classes named `Shape` and `Rectangle` already exist in the `java.awt` package; our `Shape` and `Rectangle` classes aren't related to these.)

First, we need to list the properties and behaviors that are common to all shapes. The properties will be represented by instance variables, and the behaviors will be represented by instance methods.

Let's start with the properties. Every shape has a location and a color, so our `Shape` class will need instance variables that store x and y coordinates and a `Color` object. Every shape will also have a width and a height. However, it might not be a good idea for the `Shape` class to have `width` and `height` variables, because that would force all subclasses to inherit these variables. Some subclasses won't need these variables, causing space to be wasted. In particular, the width and height of a circle are always the same, so a `Circle` object won't need two variables to keep track of its width and height.

Now, we'll turn to the behaviors. A shape can be displayed, so we'll need a `draw` method. A shape can be moved to a different location, so we'll need a `move` method. We'll also need getters named `getX`, `getY`, and `getColor`. Even though we won't store the width and height in the `Shape` class itself, it's a good idea for `Shape` to provide `getWidth` and `getHeight` methods, because every shape has a width and a height. For completeness, we should also include a `setColor` method.

Some of the methods that we've identified can be written without knowing exactly what kind of shape we're dealing with. The `draw`, `getHeight`, and `getWidth` methods can't be written, however, which suggests that `Shape` will need to be an abstract class. That way, we can avoid having to write the methods in the latter category.

Here's what the `Shape` class will look like:

Shape.java

```java
 1   // Represents a geometric shape that can be displayed in a
 2   // graphics context
 3
 4   import java.awt.*;
 5
 6   public abstract class Shape {
 7     // Instance variables
 8     private int x;
 9     private int y;
10     private Color color;
11
12     // Constructor
```

```
13    protected Shape(int x, int y, Color color) {
14      this.x = x;
15      this.y = y;
16      this.color = color;
17    }
18
19    // Abstract methods
20    public abstract void draw(Graphics g);
21    public abstract int getHeight();
22    public abstract int getWidth();
23
24    // Other instance methods
25    public Color getColor() {
26      return color;
27    }
28
29    public int getX() {
30      return x;
31    }
32
33    public int getY() {
34      return y;
35    }
36
37    public void move(int dx, int dy) {
38      x += dx;
39      y += dy;
40    }
41
42    public void setColor(Color color) {
43      this.color = color;
44    }
45  }
```

Notice that the Shape constructor has been declared `protected` rather than `public`. No instances of Shape can be created, so there's no need to make the constructor public.

We can now create subclasses of Shape that represent specific types of shapes. We'll define Circle and Rectangle classes here. Additional subclasses are left as exercises.

One difference between a circle and a shape in general is that a circle has a diameter. As a result, our Circle class will need a `diameter` instance variable. We'll also need to override the abstract methods that were inherited from the Shape class: draw, getHeight, and getWidth.

Circle.java

```
1  // Represents a circle that can be displayed in a graphics
2  // context
3
4  import java.awt.*;
5
6  public class Circle extends Shape {
7    // Instance variables
8    private int diameter;
```

```
 9
10      // Constructor
11      public Circle(int x, int y, Color color, int diameter) {
12        super(x, y, color);
13        this.diameter = diameter;
14      }
15
16      // Instance methods
17      public void draw(Graphics g) {
18        g.setColor(getColor());
19        g.fillOval(getX(), getY(), diameter, diameter);
20      }
21
22      public int getHeight() {
23        return diameter;
24      }
25
26      public int getWidth() {
27        return diameter;
28      }
29    }
```

Because x, y, and color are declared private in the Shape class, the draw method can't access these variables directly. Instead, it calls the getColor, getX, and getY methods that the Circle class inherited from Shape.

Our Rectangle class will need width and height instance variables. Like the Circle class, Rectangle will need to override the draw, get-Height, and getWidth methods.

Rectangle.java

```
 1    // Represents a rectangle that can be displayed in a graphics
 2    // context
 3
 4    import java.awt.*;
 5
 6    public class Rectangle extends Shape {
 7      // Instance variables
 8      private int width;
 9      private int height;
10
11      // Constructor
12      public Rectangle(int x, int y, Color color,
13                          int width, int height) {
14        super(x, y, color);
15        this.width = width;
16        this.height = height;
17      }
18
19      // Instance methods
20      public void draw(Graphics g) {
21        g.setColor(getColor());
22        g.fillRect(getX(), getY(), width, height);
23      }
24
```

```
25    public int getHeight() {
26       return height;
27    }
28
29    public int getWidth() {
30       return width;
31    }
32 }
```

Review Questions

1. What are abstract classes good for?

2. The declaration of an abstract method must contain the word `abstract`. What is the other distinguishing characteristic of an abstract method?

3. True or false: It is illegal to create an instance of an abstract class.

4. True or false: A subclass of an abstract class must override all abstract methods that it inherits.

11.7 Final Classes and Methods

In previous chapters, we've used the word `final` to indicate that the value of a variable won't change after it has been initialized. `final` can also be applied to a class or method. When `final` is present in a class declaration, it indicates that the class can't be extended. For example, we might decide to add `final` to the declaration of the `SavingsAccount` class:

```
public final class SavingsAccount extends Account {
   ...
}
```

As a result of this change, `SavingsAccount` is not allowed to have subclasses. Notice that a final class is—in some sense—the opposite of an abstract class. An abstract class is designed to be extended, whereas a final class can't be extended. Not surprisingly, declaring a class to be both `abstract` and `final` is illegal.

wrapper classes ➤ *13.3*   A number of classes in the Java API are declared to be `final`, including `Math`, `String`, and the "wrapper" classes, which include `Integer`, `Double`, and `Character`. The `String` class is declared `final` in order to guarantee that `String` variables always contain immutable objects. (If `String` could be extended, it would be possible to write a subclass whose instances were not immutable.)

In addition to preventing a class from being extended, `final` can have an important effect on program performance. Suppose that `x` is a variable of type `XClass`. Consider the following method call:

```
x.f();
```

When it sees the call of f, the compiler can't assume that x represents an instance of XClass; instead, x might store a reference to an instance of some subclass of XClass. As a result, the compiler inserts code to check x during program execution and call the appropriate version of f. If XClass were declared final, the compiler would know that x must contain a reference to an XClass object (because XClass could not have subclasses). The compiler would be able to produce simpler and faster code that calls f without first checking what kind of reference is stored in x.

Individual methods can be declared final without declaring the entire class to be final. It's illegal to override a final method, so declaring a method to be final provides the same performance enhancement for a single method that declaring an entire class to be final provides for all methods in the class.

Methods that are declared either static or private are automatically final, which means that we can't override a class method or a private instance method.

Review Questions

1. What is the effect of putting the word final at the beginning of a class declaration?

2. Name a class in the Java API that is declared final.

3. Explain how the use of final can improve the performance of a program.

4. Some methods are always final, even without the word final in their declaration. What methods are these?

11.8   Inheritance in the Abstract Window Toolkit

To provide a concrete illustration of inheritance—and to help convince you that it's a useful concept—this section is devoted to an overview of Java's AWT (Abstract Window Toolkit). The AWT provides classes that are used to write programs with a graphical user interface (GUI). Our goal in this section is not to design graphical user interfaces, but rather to learn a little about the AWT classes and see how they're related. Chapter 12 then discusses how to use these classes to write GUI programs.

Recall from Chapter 1 that a GUI program provides the user with various interactive graphical elements. For example, when we run a GUI program, we might see a window like the one at the top of the next page. This program stores names and telephone numbers, allowing the user to add, delete, and change the data. Within the program's window, we see several visual *components.* The four names are displayed in a *list.* The user can enter a new name and number in two *text fields.* Each text field is preceded by a *label.* Finally, there are three *buttons* at the bottom of the window.

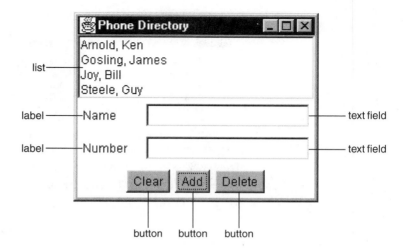

Components

In the AWT, each type of component is represented by a class. Let's take a quick look at the major classes and the component that each represents. (The components are shown with a Windows appearance. They may look somewhat different on other platforms.)

- `Button`—A labeled button:

The user can "press" a button by pointing to it with the mouse and pressing a mouse button. When a button is pressed, it changes appearance:

- `Checkbox`—A box that can be clicked "on" or "off":

☐ Enable sounds

Clicking on the box causes a check mark to appear:

☑ Enable sounds

Clicking on the box again causes the check mark to disappear.

- `Choice`—A choice menu (or "pop-up" menu) displays one of several items:

Clicking on the arrow button causes the full list to appear:

The user can now drag the mouse to move the highlight to any of the listed items. When the mouse button is released, the list disappears, and the selected item replaces the one originally displayed.

- Label—A text string that can be positioned next to other components.
- List—A list of items:

The user can choose an item by clicking on it:

If not all items are visible, a scrollbar appears to the right of the list:

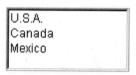

- Scrollbar—A sliding bar. Scrollbars can be either horizontal:

or vertical:

- `TextArea`—A multiline area in which text can be displayed:

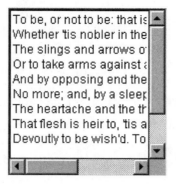

Scrollbars at the bottom and right side make it possible for the user to view text that's not otherwise visible. If desired, the user can edit the text.

- `TextField`—An area in which a single line of text can be displayed:

> Your name here

Like a text area, a text field can be made editable if desired.

Relationships Among Component Classes

The designers of the AWT decided to create a class named `Component` to represent the properties and behavior that all components have in common. For example, all components share the following properties (among others):

Position—The position of the component on the screen.
Size—The height and width of the component.
Visibility—Whether or not the component is currently visible on the screen.
Colors—The foreground and background colors for the component. (If the component is a button, for example, the button's label is displayed in the foreground color, and the area surrounding the label is displayed in the background color.)

The variables that keep track of these properties belong to the `Component` class, as do the access methods that let us test these properties and modify them.

`Component` is an abstract class. No instances of `Component` will ever be created. Instead, `Component`'s role is to serve as the superclass for more-specific component classes. The existence of the `Component` class means that the individual component classes are relatively small and easy to write. (The `Component` class has more than 100 constructors and methods. The `Button` class, on the other hand, has only a dozen constructors and methods.) We can also use the

`Component` class as a starting point for writing our own components, if we need any that aren't provided by the AWT.

Components don't stand on their own in Java; each component must belong to a window or some other kind of "container." The AWT provides several container classes:

- `Container`—Serves as a superclass for all the other container classes. (In other words, `Container` serves the same role for the container classes as `Component` does for the component classes.)
- `Dialog`—A dialog box.
- `FileDialog`—A file dialog box.
- `Frame`—A window with a title, a border, and possibly a menu.
- `Panel`—A container with no border.
- `Window`—A window with no title or border.

These classes are closely related. `FileDialog` is a subclass of `Dialog`, which is a subclass of `Window`, which is a subclass of `Container`. Also, `Frame` is a subclass of `Window`, and `Panel` is a subclass of `Container`. Notice that the *is-a* relationship holds in each case: a `FileDialog` *is a* `Dialog`, a `Dialog` *is a* `Window`, and so on.

The designers of the AWT decided to make `Container` a subclass of `Component`. This decision allows any container to be used as a component, thanks to the Substitution Principle. As a result, containers can be nested inside other containers. This feature has important consequences for GUI design, as we'll see in Section 12.6.

The following diagram shows how the component classes are related through inheritance:

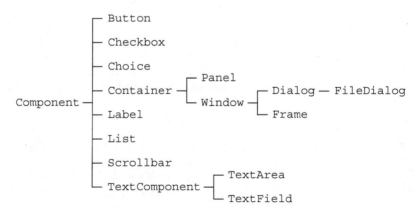

(This diagram shows only the classes that were mentioned in this section, not all classes that the AWT supports.) Notice that `TextArea` and `TextField` have a superclass named `TextComponent`. The designers of the AWT noticed that `TextArea` and `TextField` had many properties and methods in common, so they created `TextComponent` in order to simplify `TextArea` and `Text-Field`. The `TextArea` and `TextField` classes inherit many of their methods from `TextComponent`.

Review Questions

1. For each of the following components, name the corresponding AWT class:
    (a) A labeled button that can be pushed
    (b) A box that can be clicked "on" or "off"
    (c) A choice menu (or "pop-up" menu)
    (d) A label
    (e) A scrolling list of text items
    (f) A horizontal or vertical sliding bar
    (g) A multiline area in which text can be displayed
    (h) A single line of text

2. What class is the superclass for all component classes?

3. What class is the superclass for components that "contain" other components?

4. What class is the superclass for all window classes?

11.9 Case Study: "Nervous" Shapes

Our next case study illustrates the concepts of inheritance and polymorphism. The program that we'll develop, named `NervousShapes`, will perform an animation, much like the `RandomCircles` program of Section 9.6. The program will create a number of shapes (a random mixture of circles and rectangles) with random colors, sizes, and positions, which will be displayed in a frame. After a brief delay, the shapes will be moved to slightly different positions, with the direction of motion for each shape chosen randomly. The new x coordinate for each shape will either be the same as the old x coordinate, one pixel smaller, or one pixel larger; the new y coordinate will be computed in a similar manner. (Shapes will be constrained so that they don't move outside the drawing area.) The effect should be similar to Brownian motion—the shapes will "vibrate" without moving much from their original positions.

To keep the program reasonably short, I've chosen not to have it accept user input. Instead, the size of the frame's drawing area will be fixed at 200 pixels by 200 pixels, the number of shapes displayed will be 50, and the "delay time"—the interval between animation cycles—will be 10 milliseconds. The figure at the top of the next page shows what the frame will look like.

We can divide the program into three steps:

1. Create a frame labeled "Nervous Shapes."
2. Create 50 random `Circle` and `Rectangle` objects.
3. Display the shapes within an animation loop.

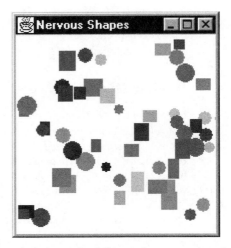

Let's write a separate helper method for each step, using the names `create-Window`, `createShapes`, and `animateShapes`. The `main` method will simply call these methods, one after the other.

`createWindow` is easy to write, so let's focus on `createShapes` and `animateShapes`. `createShapes` will need an array in which to store the 50 shapes that it creates. Let's name this array `shapes`. Because `animateShapes` will also need access to the `shapes` array, I'll make it a class variable. (As an alternative, `shapes` could be declared as a variable in `main` and then supplied to `createShapes` and `animateShapes` as an argument.) `shapes` will be declared as an array of `Shape` objects so that it can store both `Circle` objects and `Rectangle` objects, thanks to the Substitution Principle.

`createShapes` will consist of a loop that executes 50 times. Inside the loop body, the method will perform the following steps:

1. Select a color in which each component is a random number between 0 and 255.
2. Decide whether the new shape will be a circle or a rectangle. (The program can "flip" a simulated coin to make this decision.)
3. If the new shape is a circle, choose a random diameter between 10 and 20, choose a random position, create a `Circle` object, and store it in the `shapes` array. If the new shape is a rectangle, choose a random width and height between 10 and 20, choose a random position, create a `Rectangle` object, and store it in the `shapes` array.

We'll need to be careful when choosing a position for the new circle or square, because we want the entire shape to stay within the frame.

`animateShapes` will consist of an infinite loop that repeats the following steps:

1. Clear the frame's drawing area.
2. Move each shape in the `shapes` array to a new position and display it. The new *x* coordinate for each shape will be the same as the old one, one pixel

smaller, or one pixel larger; the new *y* coordinate is computed in a similar fashion. A move is not performed if it would cause a portion of the shape to go outside the frame's drawing area.

3. Call `repaint` to update the screen.
4. Pause briefly.

Step 2 shows the power of polymorphism. To display element `i` of the `shapes` array, `animateShapes` will call the `draw` method in the following way:

```
shapes[i].draw(g);
```

There's no need to test whether `shapes[i]` is a `Circle` object or a `Rectangle` object before calling the `draw` method. Thanks to dynamic binding, the correct version of `draw` will be selected automatically.

There are several places where the program will need to choose a random integer, so I decided to write an additional helper method named `generateRandomInt`. This method returns an integer that's chosen randomly from a specified range of integers.

NervousShapes.java

```
1   // Program name: NervousShapes
2   // Author: K. N. King
3   // Written: 1999-08-12
4   //
5   // Displays a frame containing a random mixture of circles
6   // and rectangles with random colors, sizes, and positions.
7   // The shapes periodically change position, with the
8   // direction of motion chosen randomly for each shape. The
9   // new x coordinate for each shape will either be the same
10  // as the old x coordinate, one pixel smaller, or one pixel
11  // larger; the new y coordinate will be computed in a
12  // similar manner. Shapes will be constrained so that they
13  // do not move outside the drawing area.
14
15  import java.awt.*;
16  import jpb.*;
17
18  public class NervousShapes {
19    // Constants
20    private static final int DELAY = 10;
21      // Animation delay (milliseconds)
22    private static final int MAX_SIZE = 20;
23      // Maximum width and height of a shape
24    private static final int MIN_SIZE = 10;
25      // Minimum width and height of a shape
26    private static final int NUM_SHAPES = 50;
27      // Number of shapes
28    private static final int WINDOW_SIZE = 200;
29      // Width and height of drawable portion of frame
30
31    // Class variables
32    private static DrawableFrame df;
33      // Frame in which shapes are displayed
```

```
34      private static Graphics g;
35        // Graphics context for frame
36      private static Shape shapes[] = new Shape[NUM_SHAPES];
37        // Array of shapes
38
39      public static void main(String[] args) {
40        createWindow();
41        createShapes();
42        animateShapes();
43      }
44
45      ////////////////////////////////////////////////////////////
46      // NAME:        createWindow
47      // BEHAVIOR:    Creates a frame labeled "Nervous Shapes",
48      //              displays the frame, and sets the size of
49      //              the frame (using the WINDOW_SIZE class
50      //              variable). Assigns the frame to the df
51      //              class variable, and assigns the frame's
52      //              graphics context to the g class variable.
53      // PARAMETERS: None
54      // RETURNS:    Nothing
55      ////////////////////////////////////////////////////////////
56      private static void createWindow() {
57        // Create a frame labeled "Nervous Shapes" and set its
58        // size
59        df = new DrawableFrame("Nervous Shapes");
60        df.show();
61        df.setSize(WINDOW_SIZE, WINDOW_SIZE);
62
63        // Get the frame's graphics context
64        g = df.getGraphicsContext();
65      }
66
67      ////////////////////////////////////////////////////////////
68      // NAME:        createShapes
69      // BEHAVIOR:    Creates enough Circle and Rectangle objects
70      //              to fill the shapes array. Each shape has a
71      //              random color, size, and position. The height
72      //              and width of each shape must lie between
73      //              MIN_SIZE and MAX_SIZE (inclusive). The
74      //              position is chosen so that the shape is
75      //              completely within the drawing area.
76      // PARAMETERS: None
77      // RETURNS:    Nothing
78      ////////////////////////////////////////////////////////////
79      private static void createShapes() {
80        for (int i = 0; i < shapes.length; i++) {
81          // Select a random color
82          int red = generateRandomInt(0, 255);
83          int green = generateRandomInt(0, 255);
84          int blue = generateRandomInt(0, 255);
85          Color color = new Color(red, green, blue);
86
```

```
 87            // Decide whether to create a circle or a rectangle
 88            if (Math.random() < 0.5)  {
 89               // Generate a circle with a random size and position
 90               int diameter = generateRandomInt(MIN_SIZE, MAX_SIZE);
 91               int x = generateRandomInt(0, WINDOW_SIZE - diameter);
 92               int y = generateRandomInt(0, WINDOW_SIZE - diameter);
 93               shapes[i] = new Circle(x, y, color, diameter);
 94            } else {
 95               // Generate a rectangle with a random size and
 96               // position
 97               int width = generateRandomInt(MIN_SIZE, MAX_SIZE);
 98               int height = generateRandomInt(MIN_SIZE, MAX_SIZE);
 99               int x = generateRandomInt(0, WINDOW_SIZE - width);
100               int y = generateRandomInt(0, WINDOW_SIZE - height);
101               shapes[i] = new Rectangle(x, y, color, width, height);
102            }
103         }
104      }
105
106      //////////////////////////////////////////////////////////////
107      // NAME:       animateShapes
108      // BEHAVIOR:   Establishes an infinite loop in which the
109      //             shapes are animated. During each loop
110      //             iteration, the drawing area is cleared and
111      //             the shapes are then drawn at new positions.
112      //             The new x and y coordinates for each shape
113      //             will either be the same as the old ones,
114      //             one pixel smaller, or one pixel larger. A
115      //             shape is not moved if doing so would cause
116      //             any portion of the shape to go outside the
117      //             drawing area. At the end of each animation
118      //             cycle, there is a brief pause, which is
119      //             controlled by the delay constant.
120      // PARAMETERS: None
121      // RETURNS:    Nothing
122      //////////////////////////////////////////////////////////////
123      private static void animateShapes() {
124         while (true) {
125            // Clear drawing area
126            g.setColor(Color.white);
127            g.fillRect(0, 0, WINDOW_SIZE - 1, WINDOW_SIZE - 1);
128
129            for (int i = 0; i < shapes.length; i++) {
130               // Change the x coordinate for shape i
131               int dx = generateRandomInt(-1, +1);
132               int newX = shapes[i].getX() + dx;
133               if (newX >= 0 &&
134                   newX + shapes[i].getWidth() < WINDOW_SIZE)
135                  shapes[i].move(dx, 0);
136
137               // Change the y coordinate for shape i
138               int dy = generateRandomInt(-1, +1);
139               int newY = shapes[i].getY() + dy;
```

```
140              if (newY >= 0 &&
141                  newY + shapes[i].getHeight() < WINDOW_SIZE)
142                shapes[i].move(0, dy);
143
144                // Draw shape i at its new position
145                shapes[i].draw(g);
146              }
147
148              // Call repaint to update the screen
149              df.repaint();
150
151              // Pause briefly
152              try {
153                Thread.sleep(DELAY);
154              } catch (InterruptedException e) {}
155            }
156          }
157
158          ////////////////////////////////////////////////////////
159          // NAME:       generateRandomInt
160          // BEHAVIOR:   Generates a random integer within a
161          //             specified range.
162          // PARAMETERS: min - the lower bound of the range
163          //             max - the upper bound of the range
164          // RETURNS:    A random integer that is greater than or
165          //             equal to min and less than or equal to max
166          ////////////////////////////////////////////////////////
167          private static int generateRandomInt(int min, int max) {
168            return (int) ((max - min + 1) * Math.random()) + min;
169          }
170        }
```

Q & A

Q: **Is it possible for a class to extend more than one class? In other words, can a class have more than one direct superclass? [p. 445]**

A: No. This feature, which is called *multiple inheritance,* is supported by some object-oriented languages, including C++, but not by Java. Multiple inheritance has some benefits, but it also has drawbacks. Java provides *interfaces* as an alternative. A class may have only one direct superclass, but it may implement any number of interfaces.

interfaces ➤ 12.3

Q: **What exactly is a "hash code"? [p. 460]**

A: A hash code is an integer that's used when storing an object in a *hash table.* The Java API provides a class named HashTable; an instance of this class is a data structure that can store a number of objects. A discussion of hash tables is beyond the scope of this book.

Summary

- A new class can be created by extending an existing class. The new class is said to be a subclass; the existing class is its superclass.

- A subclass inherits the variables and methods of its superclass, with the exception of constructors, private variables, and private methods. Inherited variables and methods behave as though they were declared in the subclass.

- A subclass may define additional variables and methods that were not present in its superclass.

- An instance of a subclass stores all instance variables—including private variables—defined in its superclass, plus all instance variables defined in the subclass.

- A constructor for a subclass can use the word `super` to invoke the constructor for its superclass.

- If a subclass constructor fails to call `super`, the compiler will automatically insert `super();` at the beginning of the constructor.

- If a subclass fails to declare any constructors, Java creates a default no-arg constructor that calls the no-arg version of the superclass constructor.

- Inheritance is appropriate when there is an "is-a" relationship between two classes. Inheritance is not appropriate when there is a "has-a" relationship between the classes.

- Variables that belong to a class can be declared `protected` instead of `public` or `private`. Protected variables can be accessed by methods in the class and in all its subclasses (direct and indirect).

- Methods can be declared `protected`. A protected method can be called within its own class and by methods in subclasses.

- A subclass can override an inherited method. The new method must have the same name and return type as the inherited method. In addition, the methods must have the same number of parameters, and the types of corresponding parameters must be the same.

- An overridden method can be called by using the word `super`.

- Java allows an instance of a subclass to take the place of an instance of any of its superclasses. If C is a class, then a variable of type C can be assigned an instance of a subclass of C. If a method has a parameter of type C, the corresponding argument can be an instance of a subclass of C. A method whose result type is C may instead return an instance of a subclass of C.

- Because methods can be overridden, the Java compiler can't always determine which version of a method is being called. Instead, the determination is made as the program is running, through a process known as dynamic binding.

- Because of dynamic binding, the same method call can perform different actions, depending on which object performs the call. This ability is called polymorphism.

- The expression *object* `instanceof` *class* has the value `true` only if *object* is an instance of *class* or one of its subclasses.

- The cast operator can be used to transform a reference to a class into a reference to one of its subclasses. If the referenced object is not an instance of that subclass, a `ClassCastException` will be thrown.

- Every class in Java—with the exception of the `Object` class—has a superclass.

- If a new class has no explicit superclass, Java uses `Object` as the default superclass.

- All Java classes—including the standard API classes and all classes that we write—belong to a single class hierarchy.

- A variable of type `Object` can store a reference to an instance of any class. A method with an `Object` parameter will accept any object as its argument.

- The `Object` class provides several methods, including `clone`, `equals`, and `toString`, which can be inherited by subclasses.

- The `equals` method is provided to solve the problem of testing whether two objects are equal. By default, `equals` behaves like the `==` operator. Many classes override the `equals` method.

- An abstract class is an artificial class that has been created solely as a starting point for defining subclasses. It is illegal to create an instance of an abstract class.

- Some of the methods in an abstract class may be abstract methods. An abstract method has no body.

- If a subclass of an abstract class overrides all the abstract methods it inherits, then it is a normal class from which instances can be created. If it doesn't, the subclass is itself an abstract class.

- A class that has been declared `final` can't be extended.

- Instance methods in a `final` class may execute slightly faster than ordinary instance methods.

- Individual methods can be declared `final`, which prevents them from being overridden.

- Methods that are declared either `static` or `private` are automatically final.

- Java's Abstract Window Toolkit provides classes that are used to design graphical user interfaces.

- Graphical user interfaces are built from components, which are placed into containers.

- The `Component` class, which is abstract, represents the properties and behavior that all components have in common.

- Subclasses of Component represent specific components. These subclasses include Button, Checkbox, Choice, Label, List, Scrollbar, TextArea, and TextField.
- Container is the superclass for all container classes, including Dialog, FileDialog, Frame, Panel, and Window.

Exercises

Section 11.1

1. Develop a hierarchical classification of vehicles based on the properties shared by each type of vehicle. Your hierarchy should include (but is not limited to) planes, boats, cars, trucks, buses, bicycles, skateboards, tractors, and horse-drawn carriages. Consider such factors as the medium in which the vehicle travels (air, land, or water), how the vehicles are powered, and what they transport.

2. Develop a hierarchical classification of writing instruments, which should include (but is not limited to) mechanical pencils, wooden pencils, ballpoint pens, fountain pens, felt-tip pens, and markers.

3. Create a CheckingAccount class by extending the Account class. The Checking-Account class will store the number of checks written against the account. It will need a method that returns the number of checks written so far and a method that writes a check for a given amount.

4. Create a Person class containing three instance variables: a last name, a first name, and a birth date. The names are strings, and the birth date is a Date object, where Date is the class described in Programming Project 6 of Chapter 10. Include a constructor, as well as getters and setters for the three variables. Then create an Employee class by extending the Person class. Employee will have two instance variables: a salary (of type double) and an employment date (a Date object). Include a constructor, as well as getters and setters for the two variables.

Section 11.4

5. Which of the following code fragments are legal?

```
(a) Account acct = new Account(100.00);
    SavingsAccount savingsAcct = acct;
(b) SavingsAccount savingsAcct =
        new SavingsAccount(100.00, 5.0);
    Account acct = (Account) savingsAcct;
(c) Account acct = new Account(100.00);
    SavingsAccount savingsAcct = (SavingsAccount) acct;
(d) Account acct = new SavingsAccount(100.00, 5.0);
    SavingsAccount savingsAcct = acct;
(e) SavingsAccount savingsAcct = new Account(100.00);
    Account acct = savingsAcct;
(f) Account acct = new SavingsAccount(100.00, 5.0);
    SavingsAccount savingsAcct = (SavingsAccount) acct;
(g) SavingsAccount savingsAcct = new Account(100.00);
    Account acct = (Account) savingsAcct;
```

Section 11.5

6. Write an equals method for the Complex class (Section 10.5). For two complex numbers to be equal, they must have the same real part and the same imaginary part.

7. Write a `toString` method for the `Complex` class (Section 10.5). Have the method return a string of the form "*a+bi*" or, when possible, a simpler string. For example, "`-i`" is simpler than "`0+(-1)i`". Other strings that might be returned include "`3+4i`", "`3-4i`", "`3`", "`4i`", "`-4i`", "`3+i`", "`3-i`", and "`0`".

Section 11.6

8. Java's `Point` class (Section 10.2) contains two instance variables, x and y. If the `Shape` class were to extend `Point`, it would inherit these variables (as well as the non-private methods of the `Point` class). Would this be a good way to define the `Shape` class? Explain why or why not.

9. Modify the `Shape` class by removing the x and y instance variables and replacing them by a single instance variable of type `Point`. Modify the instance methods accordingly.

10. Make the following changes to the `Shape`, `Circle`, and `Rectangle` classes:

    (a) Add an abstract method named `scale` to the `Shape` class and implement it in both the `Circle` and `Rectangle` classes. `scale` will increase the size of a shape by a specified factor of type `double` (supplied as an argument).

    (b) Add an abstract method named `area` to the `Shape` class and implement it in both the `Circle` and `Rectangle` classes. `area` will return the area of a shape as a `double` value.

    (c) Add `toString` methods to the `Shape`, `Circle`, and `Rectangle` classes. The version of `toString` in the `Shape` class will return a string of the form

    `"Position: (10, 50)   Color: (r=64, b=192, g=255)"`

    The version of `toString` in the `Circle` class will return a similar string, but with "`Diameter: ` *d*" added at the end, where *d* is the diameter of the circle. The version of `toString` in the `Rectangle` class will return a string with "`Width: ` *w* `Height: ` *h*" added at the end, where *w* is the width of the rectangle and *h* is the height of the rectangle. *Hint:* Have the `toString` methods in `Circle` and `Rectangle` call the `toString` method in `Shape`. Don't forget to use the word `super` in these calls.

11. Define a `Triangle` class by extending the `Shape` class. A `Triangle` object will represent an equilateral triangle, so the `Triangle` class will need only one instance variable, which will store the length of one of the triangle's sides.

Section 11.8

12. For each of the following classes, list all classes from which it potentially inherits methods. *Note:* The `Component` class is a subclass of `Object`.

    (a) `Checkbox`
    (b) `FileDialog`
    (c) `Panel`
    (d) `TextField`

Programming Projects

1. Modify the `Bank` program (Programming Project 8 in Chapter 5) so that it supports both savings and checking accounts. When the user opens an account, the program will ask whether it is a checking account or a savings account. The user will enter either c or s to make a selection. If the user enters s, the program will ask for the annual interest rate for that account. If the user enters a command other than s or c, the program will display the following message:

```
Input was not c or s; please try again.
```

The program will have two new commands: `r` (write a check) and `i` (credit interest). The `r` command is similar to the existing `w` command, except that it increments the number of checks written on the account. If the current account is not a checking account, the program will display the following message:

```
Please select a checking account
```

The `i` command credits one month of interest to each savings account, based on the interest rate for that account. (Checking accounts are not affected.)

Like the original `Bank` program, the new program will display information about the currently selected account. If the current account is a checking account, the information will have the following form:

```
Current account: 123-456  Balance: $100.00
Number of checks written: 25
```

If the current account is a savings account, the information will have a slightly different form:

```
Current account: 123-456  Balance: $100.00
Interest rate: 4.5%
```

Create two new classes, `CheckingAccount` and `SavingsAccount`, that extend the `BankAccount` class. The new program will store a mixture of `CheckingAccount` and `SavingsAccount` objects in a single array. The `CheckingAccount` class will store the number of checks written against the account. Its methods will include a getter for the number of checks written and a method that writes a check for a given amount. The `SavingsAccount` class will store the annual interest rate for the account. Its methods will include a getter and setter for the interest rate.

2. Modify the `NervousShapes` program (Section 11.9) so that it displays equilateral triangles as well as circles and rectangles. You'll need to define a `Triangle` class containing a single instance variable, representing the length of one of the triangle's sides. Have the program create circles, rectangles, and triangles with equal probability.

3. Write a program named `Personnel` that maintains wage information for the employees of a company. The following example shows what the user will see during a session with the program:

```
----------------------------------
|Commands: n - New employee       |
|          p - Compute paychecks  |
|          r - Raise wages        |
|          q - Quit               |
----------------------------------
Enter command: n
Enter name of new employee: Plumber, Phil
Hourly (h) or salaried (s): h
Enter hourly wage: 40.00

----------------------------------
|Commands: n - New employee       |
|          p - Compute paychecks  |
|          r - Raise wages        |
|          q - Quit               |
----------------------------------
Enter command: n
```

```
Enter name of new employee: Coder, Carol
Hourly (h) or salaried (s): s
Enter annual salary: 80000


-----------------------------------
|Commands: n - New employee        |
|          p - Compute paychecks    |
|          r - Raise wages          |
|          q - Quit                 |
-----------------------------------
Enter command: p
Enter number of hours worked by Plumber, Phil: 50
Pay: $2200.00
Enter number of hours worked by Coder, Carol: 50
Pay: $1538.46


-----------------------------------
|Commands: n - New employee        |
|          p - Compute paychecks    |
|          r - Raise wages          |
|          q - Quit                 |
-----------------------------------
Enter command: r
Enter percentage increase: 4.5

New Wages
---------
Plumber, Phil                $41.80/hour
Coder, Carol              $83600.00/year


-----------------------------------
|Commands: n - New employee        |
|          p - Compute paychecks    |
|          r - Raise wages          |
|          q - Quit                 |
-----------------------------------
Enter command: q
```

The program will repeatedly prompt the user to enter commands, which it then executes. The program will not terminate until the user enters the command q. Note that the list of commands is redisplayed after each command has been executed.

Write three classes that store information about an employee:

- Employee (abstract). Instances of this class will store an employee name (a string) and the employee's hourly wage (a double value). Methods will include getters and setters for the name and hourly wage, a method that increases the hourly wage by a given percentage, and an abstract method named computePay that computes the weekly pay for the employee when given the number of hours worked.

- HourlyEmployee, which extends Employee. The constructor will take a name and hourly wage as its parameters. Methods will include computePay and toString. To determine the employee's pay, computePay multiplies the first 40 hours (or fewer) by the employee's hourly wage. Hours worked beyond 40 are paid at time-and-a-half (1.5 times the hourly wage). toString returns a string containing the employee's name and hourly wage, formatted as shown in the example of the r command. Note that spaces are added between the name and wage so that the entire string is 40 characters long.

- SalariedEmployee, which extends Employee. The constructor will take a name and annual salary as its parameters. Methods will include a getter and a setter for the annual salary, along with computePay and toString. (Note that the salary will need to be converted to an hourly wage, because that's what the Employee class requires. To do this conversion, assume that a salaried employee works 40 hours a week for 52 weeks.) computePay always returns 1/52 of the annual salary, regardless of the number of hours worked. toString returns a string containing the employee's name and annual salary, formatted as shown in the example of the r command.

Use an array to store the employee records. Each element of the array will store a reference to an HourlyEmployee object or a SalariedEmployee object. The array used to store employee objects must contain only one element initially. When the array becomes full, it must be doubled in size.

Here are a few other requirements for the program:

- Dollar amounts must be displayed correctly, with two digits after the decimal point. For example, make sure that your program displays $100.00, not $100.0.
- All user input may be preceded or followed by spaces. Commands may be entered as uppercase or lowercase letters. If the user enters a command other than n, p, r, or q, the program must display the following message:

```
Command was not recognized; please try again.
```

- When asked if the employee is hourly or salaried, the user must enter either h or s (case doesn't matter). If the user enters any other input, the program must display the following message:

```
Input was not h or s; please try again.
```

To simplify your program, use a helper method that prompts the user to enter a number, reads the input, and converts it to double form. Also, use a helper method that converts a double value to a string containing a dollar amount.

Answers to Review Questions

Section 11.1

1. Extending
2. Constructors, private variables, and private methods
3. Using the word super
4. Is-a

Section 11.2

1. private
2. True
3. (e)
4. Declaring variables to be protected exposes them to all subclasses, which makes it more difficult to make changes during program maintenance.

Section 11.3

1. The new method must have the same return type as the inherited method. In addition, the methods must have the same number of parameters, and the types of corresponding parameters must be the same.
2. Yes, by using the word super
3. Hide

Section 11.4

1. Polymorphism
2. Dynamic binding
3. Yes. SavingsAccount is a subclass of Account, so it is legal to assign a SavingsAccount object to an Account variable.

4.   (d)
5.   `instanceof`
6.   `ClassCastException`

Section 11.5
1.   `Object`
2.   Class hierarchy
3.   It behaves like the `==` operator.
4.   It returns a string containing the name of the object's class, the @ character, and a hexadecimal number (the object's hash code).

Section 11.6
1.   Abstract classes are used as starting points for defining subclasses.
2.   An abstract method has no body.
3.   True
4.   False. If a subclass of an abstract class fails to override all abstract methods that it inherits, then it is also an abstract class.

Section 11.7
1.   It indicates that the class cannot be extended.
2.   Possible answers include `Math`, `String`, `Integer`, `Double`, and `Character`.
3.   If a class is declared `final`, its instance methods may execute slightly faster.
4.   Class methods and private instance methods

Section 11.8
1.   (a) `Button`, (b) `Checkbox`, (c) `Choice`, (d) `Label`, (e) `List`, (f) `Scrollbar`, (g) `TextArea`, and (h) `TextField`
2.   `Component`
3.   `Container`
4.   `Window`

12 The Abstract Window Toolkit

We first explored the differences between graphical user interfaces and text-based interfaces in Chapter 1. In the early chapters, our programs were all text-based. In Chapter 6, we began to write programs that could display graphics in a window. Until now, however, we haven't attempted to write a full-fledged GUI program. Writing GUI programs in Java requires knowledge about classes and inheritance that we didn't acquire until Chapters 10 and 11.

GUI programming in Java consists of creating AWT (Abstract Window Toolkit) components, putting them into containers, and arranging for the program to respond to events generated by the components. Frames will be our primary container. (A frame is a window with a border and a title.) The component and container classes that we'll need belong to the `java.awt` package, which is part of the Java API.

Much of the chapter is devoted to the issue of handling events. Events are handled in Java by "listener" objects, which are registered with components. When an event occurs that involves a particular component, any listener that is registered with the component will be notified (one of the listener's methods will be called).

In addition to discussing GUI programming, this chapter introduces two Java features: interfaces and inner classes. Interfaces are patterns for creating classes. Inner classes are classes that are nested inside other classes. Although interfaces and inner classes are used for a variety of purposes in Java, they're especially relevant to GUI programming: listener classes are normally created by "implementing" interfaces, and they're often nested inside container classes.

Layout managers are objects whose job is to control the size and position of components within a container. This chapter describes three of Java's layout manager classes: `BorderLayout`, `FlowLayout`, and `GridLayout`. It also discusses panels, which are used to create groups of components for layout purposes.

Section 11.8 set the stage for this chapter by introducing most of the AWT components. In this chapter, we'll take a closer look at these components, with an emphasis on learning how to create each kind of component, write a listener for that component, and check the state of the component.

Objectives

- Learn how to write programs that have a graphical user interface.
- Learn how to use frames (windows with a border and a title).
- Learn how to add components to a frame.
- Learn how to write listener classes by implementing interfaces and extending adapter classes.
- Learn how to register listener objects with components.
- Learn how to use inner classes as listeners.
- Learn how layout managers are used to control the size and position of components within a container.
- Learn how to use three layout managers: `BorderLayout`, `FlowLayout`, and `GridLayout`.
- Learn how to use panels to group multiple components into a single component.
- Learn how to use AWT components, including buttons, checkboxes, choice menus, labels, lists, scrollbars, text areas, and text fields.

12.1 Overview

Java's Abstract Window Toolkit provides classes and other tools that we'll need to build programs that have a graphical user interface. The term "Abstract" refers to the AWT's ability to run on multiple platforms. To build a GUI, we'll create "abstract" components such as buttons and windows, which are then mapped to "concrete" components for a specific platform.

The AWT is too large to cover completely in a single chapter, so I've had to be selective. The chapter doesn't cover all the components that the AWT supports, nor does it describe all the AWT containers. In particular, dialog boxes aren't covered, and there's no discussion of adding menus to a frame.

Swing

Java has a newer library for building graphical user interfaces, known as "Swing." Swing is more powerful and sophisticated than the AWT, giving professional programmers the tools they need to build elaborate user interfaces. We'll focus on the older AWT library instead, because Swing offers no significant advantages for the beginner. In fact, Swing is built around the existing AWT, so it helps to understand the AWT before learning Swing. Also, Swing is relatively new, so it's not available on as many platforms as the AWT.

Swing is similar enough to the AWT that you'll be able to make the switch easily if the need arises. Many of the Swing classes correspond to classes that we'll discuss. For example, Swing has a class named `JButton`, which corresponds to the `Button` class in the AWT.

Creating a Graphical User Interface

Creating a GUI in Java requires a knowledge of three concepts:

- *Components.* A component is an object that the user can see on the screen and—in most cases—interact with, such as a button or scrollbar.
- *Containers.* A container is a component that's capable of holding other components. Windows (including frames) are containers.
- *Events.* An event is an action triggered by the user, such as a key press or mouse click.

Designing a graphical user interface involves creating components, putting them into containers, and arranging for the program to respond to events.

Components are objects, so they're created in the same way as all objects in Java: by invoking a constructor. For example, to create a button, we would use one of the constructors belonging to the `Button` class. The most commonly used constructor has one argument, which represents the button's label:

```
Button b = new Button("Testing");
```

Creating a component doesn't make it visible on the screen. To make a component visible, we'll need to call the `add` method to add the component to a container. Frames will be our primary container, although Section 12.6 provides a brief introduction to panels.

To detect when an event occurs, we'll need to attach a special "listener" object to a component. When the user performs an action that involves the component, a method belonging to the listener object will be called automatically.

Review Questions

1. Java has a library for building graphical user interfaces that is newer than the AWT. What is its name?

2. A _____ is a component that's capable of containing other components.

3. An _____ is an action triggered by the user, such as a key press or mouse click.

4. To detect when the user performs an action involving a particular component, we'll need to attach a _____ object to the component.

12.2 Frames

In Java terminology, a *frame* is a window with a title and a border. A frame may also have a menu bar, although I won't discuss that aspect of frames. Frames play an important role in the AWT because a GUI program normally displays a frame when it's executed. We've seen frames before; the `DrawableFrame` objects that we've used in previous chapters are examples of frames.

To create a frame, we'll need one of the constructors in the `Frame` class. Typically, we'll use the constructor that takes one argument (the title to be displayed at the top of the frame):

```
Frame f = new Frame("Title goes here");
```

Although the `Frame` object now exists, it's not visible on the screen. Before we make it visible, we'll need to call a method that sets the size of the frame. We may also want to specify the frame's location on the screen.

Frame Methods

Table 12.1 lists some frequently used `Frame` methods. These methods are inherited from `Window` (`Frame`'s superclass) or from `Component` (`Window`'s superclass).

Table 12.1
Frame Methods

Description	*Action*
`Point getLocation()`	Returns the coordinates of the frame's upper-left corner.
`Dimension getSize()`	Returns the width and height of the frame.
`void pack()`	Shrinks the frame around the components that it contains.
`void setLocation(int x,` `              int y)`	Moves the frame so that its upper-left corner has the specified coordinates.
`void setSize(int width,` `            int height)`	Resizes the frame to the specified width and height.
`void setVisible(boolean b)`	Makes the frame visible if b is `true` or hides it if b is `false`.

setSize

The `setSize` method sets the width and height of a frame:

```
f.setSize(width, height);  // Sets size of f
```

If we fail to call `setSize` or `pack` before displaying a frame, it will assume a default size, which is usually quite small.

getSize

The size of a frame can be changed at any time by a call of `setSize`. Also, the user can drag the frame by the edge or by the corner and manually change its size. To find the current width and height of a frame, we can call getSize:

```
Dimension frameSize = f.getSize();   // Gets size of f
```

Dimension class ► 10.2

getSize returns a Dimension object, which I've saved in the variable frame-Size. The width of f will be stored in frameSize.width, and the height will be stored in frameSize.height.

setVisible

The setVisible method controls whether or not a frame is currently visible on the screen. To make it visible, we would call setVisible with true as the argument:

Q&A

```
f.setVisible(true);   // Makes f visible
```

Later, we might decide to make the frame disappear from the screen:

```
f.setVisible(false);  // Makes f invisible
```

The Frame object still exists, so we can always make it reappear later by calling setVisible again.

Creating a Frame

To illustrate the use of setSize and setVisible, let's look at a simple program that creates a Frame object and displays it on the screen.

FrameTest.java

```
 1  // Displays a frame on the screen.
 2  // WARNING: Frame cannot be closed.
 3
 4  import java.awt.*;
 5
 6  public class FrameTest {
 7    public static void main(String[] args) {
 8      Frame f = new Frame("Frame Test");
 9      f.setSize(150, 100);
10      f.setVisible(true);
11    }
12  }
```

This program illustrates three key steps: (1) using the Frame constructor to create a frame, (2) setting the size of the frame, and (3) displaying the frame on the screen.

When we run this program, the following frame will appear on the screen:

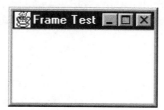

(As with the other AWT components, the appearance of a frame will depend on your platform; the Windows appearance is shown here.) The frame is empty because we didn't add any components to it. If you click on the ☒ button to close the frame, you'll get a small surprise: nothing happens! By default, there's no action associated with the ☒ button on a frame. If you run this program, you'll have to close the frame the hard way, by killing the program. (In Windows, click on the DOS window from which the program was launched, hold down the Ctrl key, and press the letter C.)

Setting the Location of a Frame

setLocation

By default, all windows (including frames) are displayed in the upper-left corner of the screen, which has coordinates (0, 0). To specify a different location, we would use the setLocation method:

```
f.setLocation(50, 75);   // Sets location of f
```

This call will position the frame f so that its upper-left corner is 50 pixels from the left edge of the screen and 75 pixels from the top of the screen.

Q&A

getLocation

The location of a frame, like its size, can change after the frame has been created. The program may call setLocation again, or the user may drag the frame to a different place on the screen. To find the current location of a frame, we can call getLocation:

```
Point frameLocation = f.getLocation();   // Gets location of f
```

Point class ➤ 10.2

getLocation returns a Point object, which I've saved in the variable frame-Location. The coordinates of f's upper-left corner will be stored in frame-Location.x and frameLocation.y.

Adding Components to a Frame

The Frame class is rarely used to create objects directly, as we did in the Frame-Test program. Instead, it's customary to define a subclass of Frame and then create an instance of the subclass. That way, we can tailor the subclass to our needs. In particular, we can have the constructor for the subclass put components into the frame.

add

To add a component to a frame (or any kind of container, for that matter), we'll use the add method. This method belongs to the Container class, so it's inherited by Frame and the other container classes. To add a button to a frame, for example, we could use the following statements:

```
Button b = new Button("Testing");
add(b);
```

These statements would normally go in the constructor for the frame class.

Here's a modified version of the FrameTest program. Instead of creating a

Frame object, the new program defines a subclass of Frame named Button-TestFrame, and then creates an instance of ButtonTestFrame. The constructor for ButtonTestFrame does four things:

1. Invokes the superclass constructor (the constructor for Frame), passing it the title of the frame.

setLayout method ➤ 12.6

2. Calls setLayout to specify how the components inside the frame will be laid out.
3. Creates a Button object.
4. Calls add to add the button to the frame.

ButtonTest.java

```
1   // Displays a frame containing a single button.
2   // WARNING: Frame cannot be closed.
3
4   import java.awt.*;
5
6   // Driver class
7   public class ButtonTest {
8     public static void main(String[] args) {
9       Frame f = new ButtonTestFrame("Button Test");
10      f.setSize(150, 100);
11      f.setVisible(true);
12    }
13  }
14
15  // Frame class
16  class ButtonTestFrame extends Frame {
17    public ButtonTestFrame(String title) {
18      super(title);
19      setLayout(new FlowLayout());
20      Button b = new Button("Testing");
21      add(b);
22    }
23  }
```

Notice that the program assigns a ButtonTestFrame object to a Frame variable on line 9. Doing so is legal because ButtonTestFrame is a subclass of Frame. We could have declared the variable to have type ButtonTestFrame, of course. Also note that I've omitted the word public at the beginning of the ButtonTestFrame class declaration, because Java allows only one public class in a file.

Here's what we'll see on the screen when this program is executed:

Pressing the "Testing" button has no effect. As before, we can't close the frame because the ☒ button doesn't work. In order for a program like this one to be useful, we'll need to know how to detect events, which is the subject of the next section.

pack   In `ButtonTest`, the `main` method calls `setSize` to specify the size of the frame. As an alternative, we could have used `pack`, which makes the frame just large enough to display the components within it. Suppose that we replace line 10 of the program by the following statement:

```
f.pack();
```

Here's what the frame will look like now:

Regardless of whether we use `setSize` or `pack`, the user can manually resize the frame once it's displayed on the screen.

One final remark: It's not necessary to have two separate classes, as we did with `ButtonTest` and `ButtonTestFrame`. By moving the `main` method from `ButtonTest` to `ButtonTestFrame`, we could condense the program to a single class (`ButtonTestFrame`). We've seen this technique before; in Section 10.10, we added a `main` method to an instantiable class for testing purposes. This technique is a bit confusing, however, so I'll continue to use two classes for each GUI program: a class that extends `Frame`, and a "driver" class containing a `main` method.

Review Questions

1. The _____ method controls whether or not a frame is currently visible on the screen.

2. By default, where are windows displayed on the screen?

3. Adding a component to a frame (or other container) is done by calling the _____ method.

4. The _____ method makes a frame just large enough to display the components within it.

12.3 Event Listeners

In Java, events are represented by objects. When the user performs an action—pressing a key, clicking a mouse button, or the like—Java creates an object containing information about the event. If we're interested in that kind of event, we'll need to write a method that can be called when the event occurs. Here's a step-by-step breakdown of what will happen:

1. The user performs an action, causing an event to be triggered (or *fired*).
2. An object is created to represent the event. The object contains information about the event, including an indication of which component was involved (for example, which button was pressed).
3. A method that belongs to a listener object is called. The event object created in step 2 is passed to the method as its argument. Because we'll be writing the method, we can make it do anything we want.

Let's now go over each of these steps in detail.

Events

When an event occurs, an object is created that contains information about the event. This object will belong to one of several different classes, depending on the nature of the event. These classes all belong to the `java.awt.event` package.

Java divides events into two groups. One group consists of "high-level" events, such as clicking on a button or choosing an item on a list (Table 12.2).

Table 12.2
High-Level Events

Class Name	Description of Event
`ActionEvent`	A significant action has been performed on a component (a button was pressed, a list item was double-clicked, or the Enter key was pressed in a text field).
`AdjustmentEvent`	The state of an adjustable component (such as a scrollbar) has changed.
`ItemEvent`	An item has been selected (or deselected) within a checkbox, choice menu, or list.
`TextEvent`	The contents of a text area or text field have changed.

The second group consists of "low-level" events, such as moving the mouse or pressing a key. Low-level events aren't always of interest. We may not always want to know if the user has moved the mouse, for example. The only low-level event that we'll discuss in this chapter is `WindowEvent`, which occurs when the status of a window has changed. In particular, a `WindowEvent` occurs when the user attempts to close a window.

Interfaces

Q&A

Before we can discuss how events are handled in Java, we'll need to introduce a Java feature known as an ***interface.*** An interface looks a lot like a class, except that its methods aren't fully defined. Each method in an interface has a name, a parameter list, and a result type, but no body. One of the interfaces we'll use in this chapter is named `ActionListener`; here's what it looks like:

```
public interface ActionListener extends EventListener {
  public void actionPerformed(ActionEvent evt);
}
```

The declaration of `ActionListener` resembles a class declaration, except that the word `class` has been replaced by `interface`, and the `actionPerformed` method has no body.

An interface is nothing but a pattern that will be used later to define "real" classes. A class *implements* an interface by agreeing to provide bodies for all methods in the interface. For example, a class that implements the `ActionListener` interface would have to provide a method named `actionPerformed` with one parameter of type `ActionEvent` and a result type of `void`.

The keyword `implements` is used to tell the compiler that a class will implement a particular interface. A class that implements the `ActionListener` interface would have the following appearance:

```
class class-name implements ActionListener {
  public void actionPerformed(ActionEvent evt) {
    ...
  }
  ...  // Variables, constructors, and methods, if desired
}
```

The class may contain any number of variables, constructors, and methods. The only difference between this class and any other is that it must declare the `actionPerformed` method, as dictated by the interface.

Creating Event Listeners

To handle an event, we'll need to create an *event listener* object. This object will be "registered" with a component; when an event occurs that involves the component, one of the listener's methods will be called.

An event listener will be an instance of a "listener class" that we've defined. A listener class must implement one of the interfaces that belong to the `java.awt.event` package. There are four listener interfaces for high-level events (Table 12.3).

Table 12.3
Listener Interfaces for
High-Level Events

Interface Name	Required Method
ActionListener	actionPerformed(ActionEvent evt)
AdjustmentListener	adjustmentValueChanged(AdjustmentEvent evt)
ItemListener	itemStateChanged(ItemEvent evt)
TextListener	textValueChanged(TextEvent evt)

Each interface contains a single method, which is also shown in Table 12.3. The access modifier for each method is `public`, and the result type is `void`.

There's a similar set of listener interfaces for the low-level events. The only low-level listener that we'll need is `WindowListener`.

For example, pressing a button is an action event, so the listener class for a button would need to implement the `ActionListener` interface. To implement this interface, the class must define a `public void` method named `action-Performed` with a parameter of type `ActionEvent`. Let's use the name `ButtonListener` for our listener class. Here's what the class will look like:

```
class ButtonListener implements ActionListener {
  public void actionPerformed(ActionEvent evt) {
    ...
  }
}
```

Once we've written a listener class, the next step is to create an instance of the class and connect it to a particular component. In the simplest case, we'll attach a single listener object to a single component. For example, suppose that we create a `Button` object named `b`:

```
Button b = new Button("Change Color");
```

The next step is to create a `ButtonListener` object:

```
ButtonListener listener = new ButtonListener();
```

addActionListener   Finally, we register `listener` as an action listener for the button:

```
b.addActionListener(listener);
```

We can sometimes save a statement by combining the creation of the listener object with the call of `addActionListener`:

```
b.addActionListener(new ButtonListener());
```

Calling `addActionListener` creates a link between the `Button` object and its listener. Here's how we might visualize this link:

Button object   ButtonListener object

When the user presses the button, the `ButtonListener` object's `action-Performed` method will be called. Because `ButtonListener` implements the `ActionListener` interface, the compiler can verify that it does indeed have an `actionPerformed` method. The `ActionListener` interface acts as a sort of contract that `ButtonListener` agrees to honor. It's an error to pass an object to `addActionListener` unless the object belongs to a class that implements `ActionListener`.

Let's return to the `ButtonTest` program of Section 12.2. In order for the "Testing" button to have any effect, we need to define a listener class that implements the `ActionListener` interface, create an instance of the class, and attach it to the button.

Here's the modified program. Changes to the `ButtonTest` program are highlighted in **bold.**

ButtonTest2.java

```
 1  // Displays a frame containing a single "Close window"
 2  // button. The frame can be closed by pressing the button.
 3
 4  import java.awt.*;
 5  import java.awt.event.*;
 6
 7  // Driver class
 8  public class ButtonTest2 {
 9    public static void main(String[] args) {
10      Frame f = new ButtonTestFrame("Button Test");
11      f.setSize(150, 100);
12      f.setVisible(true);
13    }
14  }
15
16  // Frame class
17  class ButtonTestFrame extends Frame {
18    public ButtonTestFrame(String title) {
19      super(title);
20      setLayout(new FlowLayout());
21      Button b = new Button("Close window");
22      add(b);
23      b.addActionListener(new ButtonListener());
24    }
25  }
26
27  // Listener for button
28  class ButtonListener implements ActionListener {
29    public void actionPerformed(ActionEvent evt) {
30      System.exit(0);
31    }
32  }
```

Notice that I changed the label on the button to "Close window." Here's what the new frame will look like:

Pressing the "Close window" button causes a call of the `actionPerformed` method for the button's listener object. This method calls `System.exit`, which causes the program to terminate and the frame to disappear. (When a program terminates, any windows that it created are automatically closed.)

We now have a way to close a frame. However, it would be better if the user could do so by pressing the ☒ button. Let's tackle that problem next.

Adapter Classes

In order to make the ☒ button work, we need a `WindowEvent` listener. The obvious way to get such a listener is to write a listener class that implements the `WindowListener` interface. That turns out to be a bad idea, though. Implementing this interface requires writing seven methods, one for each type of window event. We're interested in just one of these events, so we'd end up writing six methods for events that we don't care about. Fortunately, Java provides an easier way to write a `WindowEvent` listener.

The `java.awt.event` package contains a class named `WindowAdapter`. This class implements the `WindowListener` interface, although the methods that it provides are all empty. All we have to do is extend the `WindowAdapter` class and override the `windowClosing` method, which is the only one we're interested in. Our listener class will then inherit all the other methods it needs. Clever, eh?

`WindowAdapter` is an example of an *adapter* class—a class that we can extend instead of implementing an interface. Java provides matching adapter classes for most interfaces that have two or more methods. When an interface contains only one method, there's no need for an adapter class.

addWindowListener

Here's a modified version of `ButtonTest2`, with changes in **bold.** At the end of the program, there's a new `WindowCloser` class, which extends `WindowAdapter` and provides a `windowClosing` method of its own. The constructor for `ButtonTestFrame` now calls `addWindowListener` to install a `WindowCloser` object as a listener for window events.

ButtonTest3.java

```
1   // Displays a frame containing a single "Close window"
2   // button. The frame can be closed by pressing either the
3   // "Close window" button or the frame's "close" button.
4
5   import java.awt.*;
6   import java.awt.event.*;
7
8   // Driver class
9   public class ButtonTest3 {
10    public static void main(String[] args) {
11      Frame f = new ButtonTestFrame("Button Test");
12      f.setSize(150, 100);
13      f.setVisible(true);
14    }
15  }
16
17  // Frame class
18  class ButtonTestFrame extends Frame {
19    public ButtonTestFrame(String title) {
20      super(title);
```

```
21        setLayout(new FlowLayout());
22        Button b = new Button("Close window");
23        add(b);
24        b.addActionListener(new ButtonListener());
25
26        // Attach window listener
27        addWindowListener(new WindowCloser());
28    }
29 }
30
31 // Listener for button
32 class ButtonListener implements ActionListener {
33    public void actionPerformed(ActionEvent evt) {
34        System.exit(0);
35    }
36 }
37
38 // Listener for window
39 class WindowCloser extends WindowAdapter {
40    public void windowClosing(WindowEvent evt) {
41        System.exit(0);
42    }
43 }
```

When a window event occurs, one of the methods in the `WindowCloser` class will be called. If the event is caused by the user attempting to close the window, the `windowClosing` method is called, and the program terminates. Any other window event will cause one of `WindowCloser`'s inherited methods to be called. These methods are empty, so nothing will happen.

Review Questions

1. Which package contains classes that represent specific kinds of events?

2. When a button is pressed, Java creates an instance of the _____ class.

3. An _____ looks a lot like a class, except that none of its methods has a body.

4. To create a listener class, we can sometimes extend an _____ class instead of implementing an interface.

12.4 Inner Classes

By the end of Section 12.3, we were able to create a frame with a single button and define listeners to detect when the button was pressed or the frame was closed. Now let's see how to make the button do something more interesting.

Our next program, `ChangeColor`, will also have a single button. Pressing the button will change the background color of the frame. We'll start with a white background. Pressing the button once will change the background to black. Pressing it again will cause the background to return to white. Here's what the frame will look like in its original state and after the button has been pressed once:

setBackground

Changing the background color of a frame is done by calling the `setBackground` method, which is inherited from the `Component` class. For example, to select a black background, we would use the following call of `setBackground`:

```
setBackground(Color.black);
```

getBackground

The `getBackground` method (also inherited from `Component`) returns the current background color.

The new program looks easy to write; the only difference between it and `ButtonTest3` is that the button listener will change the frame's background color instead of causing the program to terminate. The new listener will look like this:

```
class ButtonListener implements ActionListener {
  public void actionPerformed(ActionEvent evt) {
    if (getBackground() == Color.white)
      setBackground(Color.black);
    else
      setBackground(Color.white);
  }
}
```

There's just one problem: The compiler won't let us call `getBackground` or `setBackground`, because those methods don't belong to the `ButtonListener` class or its superclass (`Object`). The `actionPerformed` method needs to get (and set) the background for the *frame,* not the background for the `ButtonListener` object itself (which doesn't have a background, anyway).

Problems of this sort are common when writing a listener class because listeners often need access to variables or methods that belong to the frame. Fortunately, there's an easy way to solve such a problem: put the listener class *inside* the frame class. A class that's nested inside another class is said to be an ***inner class.*** The methods in an inner class have access to the variables and methods of the enclosing class, allowing the inner class to serve as a "helper" for the enclosing class.

Here's what the `ChangeColor` program looks like with the `ButtonListener` class nested inside the frame class:

ChangeColor.java

```
1  // Displays a frame containing a single button. Pressing the
2  // button causes the background of the frame to change from
3  // white to black or from black to white.
```

```
4
5   import java.awt.*;
6   import java.awt.event.*;
7
8   // Driver class
9   public class ChangeColor {
10    public static void main(String[] args) {
11      Frame f = new ChangeColorFrame("Change Color");
12      f.setSize(160, 100);
13      f.setVisible(true);
14    }
15  }
16
17  // Frame class
18  class ChangeColorFrame extends Frame {
19    public ChangeColorFrame(String title) {
20      // Set title, layout, and background color
21      super(title);
22      setLayout(new FlowLayout());
23      setBackground(Color.white);
24
25      // Add "Change color" button to frame and attach listener
26      Button b = new Button("Change color");
27      add(b);
28      b.addActionListener(new ButtonListener());
29
30      // Attach window listener
31      addWindowListener(new WindowCloser());
32    }
33
34    // Listener for button
35    class ButtonListener implements ActionListener {
36      public void actionPerformed(ActionEvent evt) {
37        if (getBackground() == Color.white)
38          setBackground(Color.black);
39        else
40          setBackground(Color.white);
41      }
42    }
43
44    // Listener for window
45    class WindowCloser extends WindowAdapter {
46      public void windowClosing(WindowEvent evt) {
47        System.exit(0);
48      }
49    }
50  }
```

I also nested the WindowCloser class inside the ChangeColorFrame class. There was no need to do so, because WindowCloser doesn't need access to anything inside ChangeColorFrame. However, this nesting makes it clear that WindowCloser is used only by ChangeColorFrame.

Review Questions

1. The _____ method changes the background color of a frame.

2. A class that's nested inside another class is said to be an _____ class.

12.5 Attaching Listeners to Multiple Components

Now, let's consider what to do if we want to write a program with two buttons (or more). One possibility is to attach the second button to the same `Button-Listener` object:

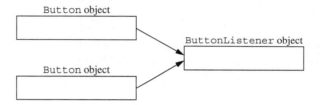

The `ButtonListener` object's `actionPerformed` method will be called when either button is pressed. (That raises an interesting question: how will the method know which button was pressed?) The other possibility is to create a different listener object for the second button:

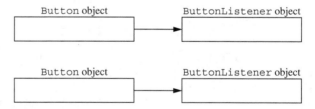

The second listener could be an instance of the same class, or it could be an instance of a different listener class:

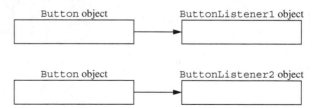

If we connect two or more buttons to a single listener object, we'll need some way to determine which button is involved when the listener's `action-Performed` method is called. There are two ways to solve this problem:

- By comparing the *source* of the event (the component that triggered the method call) to see which `Button` object it matches.
- By testing the event's ***action command*** to see which button label it matches.

getSource   If `evt` is an instance of any event class (not just `ActionEvent`), we can find the source of the event by calling `getSource`:

```
Object source = evt.getSource();
```

Because events can be caused by a variety of components, `getSource` returns an `Object` reference. To determine which component fired the event, we can compare the value returned by `getSource` with the variables containing the components. For example, if `testButton` is a `Button` object, we could check whether `testButton` was the source of the event by writing

```
if (source == testButton) …
```

getActionCommand   The other way to determine the origin of a button press is to use the `getActionCommand` method. This method can be used only with action events, such as button presses. It returns the name associated with an action event:

```
String label = evt.getActionCommand();
```

In the case of a button press, `getActionCommand` returns the label on the button. To check whether the button labeled "Testing" was pressed, we would use the following statement:

```
if (label.equals("Testing")) …
```

Example: A Single Listener

Let's modify the `ChangeColor` program so that it displays two buttons, labeled "Lighter" and "Darker":

Pressing the "Lighter" button will lighten the background slightly:

Pressing "Darker" will darken it:

Each button can be pressed more than once, causing the background to become successively lighter or darker.

We have a choice of using a single listener object for both buttons or creating two listeners, one for each button. Let's try a single listener first. The listener's `actionPerformed` method will determine which button was pressed by testing the string returned by `getActionCommand`. There are only two buttons, so the string will be either `"Lighter"` or `"Darker"`.

Here's what the program looks like with a single listener. Changes are indicated in **bold.**

ChangeColor2.java

```
1   // Displays a frame containing two buttons. Pressing the
2   // "Lighter" button lightens the background of the frame.
3   // Pressing the "Darker" button darkens the background.
4
5   import java.awt.*;
6   import java.awt.event.*;
7
8   // Driver class
9   public class ChangeColor2 {
10    public static void main(String[] args) {
11      Frame f = new ChangeColorFrame("Change Color");
12      f.setSize(160, 100);
13      f.setVisible(true);
14    }
15  }
16
17  // Frame class
18  class ChangeColorFrame extends Frame {
19    public ChangeColorFrame(String title) {
20      // Set title, layout, and background color
21      super(title);
22      setLayout(new FlowLayout());
23      setBackground(Color.gray);
24
25      // Create button listener
26      ButtonListener listener = new ButtonListener();
27
28      // Add "Lighter" button to frame and attach listener
29      Button b = new Button("Lighter");
30      add(b);
31      b.addActionListener(listener);
32
```

```
33        // Add "Darker" button to frame and attach listener
34        b = new Button("Darker");
35        add(b);
36        b.addActionListener(listener);
37
38        // Attach window listener
39        addWindowListener(new WindowCloser());
40      }
41
42      // Listener for both buttons
43      class ButtonListener implements ActionListener {
44        public void actionPerformed(ActionEvent evt) {
45          Color currentBackground = getBackground();
46          String buttonLabel = evt.getActionCommand();
47
48          // Test label on button and change background color
49          if (buttonLabel.equals("Lighter"))
50            setBackground(currentBackground.brighter());
51          else
52            setBackground(currentBackground.darker());
53        }
54      }
55
56      // Listener for window
57      class WindowCloser extends WindowAdapter {
58        public void windowClosing(WindowEvent evt) {
59          System.exit(0);
60        }
61      }
62    }
```

Color class ➤ 6.2   The brighter and darker methods belong to the Color class. brighter returns a brighter version of the Color object that called it; darker returns a darker version.

Example: Separate Listeners

Now, let's rewrite the ChangeColor2 program so that it uses separate listeners for the "Lighter" and "Darker" buttons. Using separate listeners will force us to write an additional listener class. On the other hand, the actionPerformed method in each class will be very short, because there won't be any need to test which button was pressed.

Here's what the program looks like with a separate listener for each button. Changes are indicated in **bold**.

ChangeColor3.java
```
1    // Displays a frame containing two buttons. Pressing the
2    // "Lighter" button lightens the background of the frame.
3    // Pressing the "Darker" button darkens the background.
4
5    import java.awt.*;
6    import java.awt.event.*;
```

```
7
8    // Driver class
9    public class ChangeColor3 {
10     public static void main(String[] args) {
11       Frame f = new ChangeColorFrame("Change Color");
12       f.setSize(160, 100);
13       f.setVisible(true);
14     }
15   }
16
17   // Frame class
18   class ChangeColorFrame extends Frame {
19     public ChangeColorFrame(String title) {
20       // Set title, layout, and background color
21       super(title);
22       setLayout(new FlowLayout());
23       setBackground(Color.gray);
24
25       // Add "Lighter" button to frame and attach listener
26       Button b = new Button("Lighter");
27       add(b);
28       b.addActionListener(new LighterButtonListener());
29
30       // Add "Darker" button to frame and attach listener
31       b = new Button("Darker");
32       add(b);
33       b.addActionListener(new DarkerButtonListener());
34
35       // Attach window listener
36       addWindowListener(new WindowCloser());
37     }
38
39     // Listener for "Lighter" button
40     class LighterButtonListener implements ActionListener {
41       public void actionPerformed(ActionEvent evt) {
42         setBackground(getBackground().brighter());
43       }
44     }
45
46     // Listener for "Darker" button
47     class DarkerButtonListener implements ActionListener {
48       public void actionPerformed(ActionEvent evt) {
49         setBackground(getBackground().darker());
50       }
51     }
52
53     // Listener for window
54     class WindowCloser extends WindowAdapter {
55       public void windowClosing(WindowEvent evt) {
56         System.exit(0);
57       }
58     }
59   }
```

Review Questions

1. If a program contains two buttons, how many listener objects will be needed? How many listener classes will be needed? (Give all possible answers.)

2. The _____ method returns the source of an event.

3. The _____ method returns the name associated with an action event.

4. In the case of a button press, what does the method in Question 3 return?

12.6 Layout

One issue that we haven't yet covered is the layout of components within a container. Consider the two-button version of the `ChangeColor` program, which displays the following frame:

Why are the two buttons placed side by side instead of being stacked one above the other? And why are the buttons centered within the frame instead of being aligned at the left or right? These decisions—and all others that affect the layout of components—are made by an object known as a ***layout manager.***

Every container has a default layout manager, whose job is to determine the sizes and positions of components within the container. If the default layout manager doesn't meet our needs, we can specify a different layout manager.

One reason that Java uses layout managers, rather than having us specify a size and position for each component, is so that containers can be resized gracefully. Each time a container is resized, the container's layout manager springs into action, determining new sizes and positions for the components in the container.

Layout Manager Classes

The `java.awt` package provides five layout manager classes (Table 12.4), each of which uses a different strategy to arrange components.

`FlowLayout` and `GridLayout` are the easiest layout managers to understand. `BorderLayout` and `CardLayout` are somewhat harder to use. `GridBagLayout` is the most powerful layout manager, but it's also the most complicated. We'll discuss only `FlowLayout`, `GridLayout`, and `BorderLayout`.

Table 12.4
Layout Manager Classes

Class Name	Behavior
BorderLayout	Arranges components along the sides of the container and in the middle.
CardLayout	Arrange components in "cards." Only one card is visible at a time.
FlowLayout	Arranges components in variable-length rows.
GridBagLayout	Aligns components horizontally and vertically; components can be of different sizes.
GridLayout	Arranges components in fixed-length rows and columns.

setLayout   Choosing a layout manager is done by calling the `setLayout` method and passing it an instance of a layout manager class. (`setLayout` belongs to the `Container` class, so it's inherited by all container classes.) To select `Flow-Layout` as the layout manager for a frame, we would put the following call of `setLayout` in the frame's constructor:

```
setLayout(new FlowLayout());
```

If we don't specify a layout manager for a frame, the default is `BorderLayout`.

The `FlowLayout` Class

The `FlowLayout` layout manager can handle any number of components. The components are laid out side by side from left to right. When no more components will fit in a row, `FlowLayout` starts a new row.

For example, suppose that we add seven buttons to a frame whose layout manager is `FlowLayout`. The number of buttons that can be squeezed into a row depends on how wide the frame is. Here are two examples:

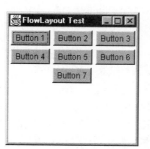 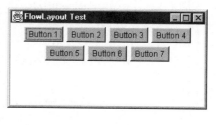

The number of rows changes as the frame is resized, but the buttons remain in the same order.

The simplest way to use `FlowLayout` is to call its no-arg constructor and pass the resulting object to `setLayout`:

```
setLayout(new FlowLayout());
```

By default, components will be separated by five pixels of space and centered in each row. The alignment can be specified explicitly by passing either `Flow-Layout.LEFT`, `FlowLayout.RIGHT`, or `FlowLayout.CENTER` to the constructor:

```
setLayout(new FlowLayout(FlowLayout.LEFT));
```

The horizontal and vertical gaps between components can also be passed to the constructor:

```
setLayout(new FlowLayout(FlowLayout.LEFT, 20, 10));
```

This example specifies a horizontal gap of 20 pixels and a vertical gap of 10 pixels.

The `GridLayout` Class

The `GridLayout` layout manager places components in rows, with each row (except possibly the last) having an equal number of components. Here's what our seven-button example would look like with `GridLayout` as the layout manager:

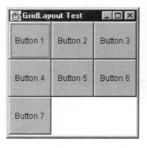 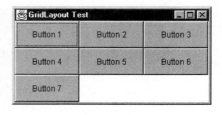

Notice that the buttons are arranged in a fixed number of rows and columns. If the frame is resized, the buttons change size as well.

The `GridLayout` constructor requires that the number of rows and columns be specified:

```
setLayout(new GridLayout(4, 5));
```

Components will be arranged in four rows and five columns, with no space between components.

If space is desired between components, two more arguments—the horizontal gap and the vertical gap—are supplied to the constructor. For example, the following statement specifies that the `GridLayout` manager should leave 20 pixels of space between components horizontally and 10 pixels vertically:

```
setLayout(new GridLayout(4, 5, 20, 10));
```

`GridLayout` works best when all components in the container are the same kind (all buttons, for example), because it forces the components to be the same size. If the container contains a mixture of components, some components may end up appearing too large while others look too small.

The `BorderLayout` Class

The `BorderLayout` layout manager can handle up to five components. Four of the components can be positioned against the sides of the container, with the fifth occupying the center of the container. The positions in a `BorderLayout` are named North, South, East, West, and Center, as the following diagram shows:

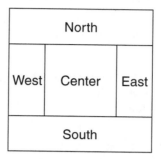

The North and South components are stretched to the width of the container. The West and East components are stretched vertically to fill the gap between North and South. The Center component expands in both directions to fill any remaining space.

If we use the no-arg version of the `BorderLayout` constructor, there will be no space between components:

```
setLayout(new BorderLayout());
```

To leave 20 pixels of horizontal space and 10 pixels of vertical space between components, we can use a different constructor:

```
setLayout(new BorderLayout(20, 10));
```

When a container uses `BorderLayout` as its layout manager, we must use a different version of the add method to add components to the container. The new version has two arguments: the position of the component (one of the strings `"North"`, `"South"`, `"East"`, `"West"`, or `"Center"`) and the component itself. Here's an example:

```
add("Center", new Button("Test"));
```

The following example shows the effect of putting five buttons into a frame with `BorderLayout` as the layout manager:

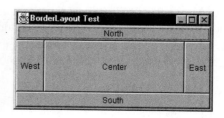

Notice that the heights of the "North" and "South" buttons don't change as the frame is resized. The widths of the "East" and "West" buttons also remain the same.

BorderLayout doesn't require that all five positions be used; unused positions are filled by neighboring components. This property makes BorderLayout a surprisingly versatile layout tool, as we'll see in Section 12.8.

Preferred Sizes

To understand how layout managers work, it's important to know that every component has a "preferred size." For example, the preferred size of a button is determined by the size of the label on the button—the longer the label, the wider the button.

Each layout manager has a different way of dealing with preferred sizes:

- FlowLayout: Honors the preferred sizes of all components.
- GridLayout: Ignores the preferred sizes of all components.
- BorderLayout: Honors the preferred *widths* of the East and West components. Honors the preferred *heights* of the North and South components. Ignores the preferred size of the Center component.

We can see this behavior in the examples given earlier in this section. The buttons in the FlowLayout example stayed the same size (their preferred size), no matter what the size of the frame was. The buttons in the GridLayout example expanded to fill the entire frame. In the BorderLayout example, the "North" and "South" buttons kept their preferred height, while the "East" and "West" buttons kept their preferred width.

Panels

A panel—an instance of the Panel class—is another kind of container. A panel is rectangular but has no border. When a panel is placed inside another container (a frame, for example), it blends in seamlessly. The user sees the components inside the panel, but not the panel itself. Each panel has its own layout manager.

Panels are used to create more-sophisticated layouts. Using a panel, we can create a group of components that—for layout purposes—is treated as a single component. (If you've ever used a drawing program, you're probably familiar with this concept. Most drawing programs allow the user to "group" lines, rectangles, and other shapes into a single unit.)

Panel objects can be created by using the no-arg version of the Panel constructor:

```
Panel p = new Panel();
```

By default, the layout manager for a panel is FlowLayout. We can switch to a different layout manager by calling `setLayout`:

```
p.setLayout(new BorderLayout());
```

If desired, the layout manager can be passed to the `Panel` constructor, avoiding a separate call of `setLayout`:

```
Panel p = new Panel(new BorderLayout());
```

Once a panel has been created, we can add components to it by calling the `add` method:

```
p.add("Center", new Button("Test"));
```

The panel itself will need to be added to a frame or other container.

To see how panels are used, consider the problem of creating a frame with the following appearance:

None of the standard layout managers are capable of arranging components in this way. In order to create this layout, we'll need to group the top 12 buttons into a single component using a panel. The panel will use a `GridLayout` to force the buttons into four rows and three columns. To make sure that this panel is positioned above the "Dial" button, we'll need to use a `BorderLayout` for the frame itself. We can put the "Dial" button at the South position and the panel at the Center position; that way, the panel will expand to fill the frame.

We're not done yet, though. If we simply put the "Dial" button at the South position, it will expand to the width of the frame. To keep the "Dial" button at the correct size, I'll put it into a panel of its own, which is then placed at the South position. This panel will have a `FlowLayout` manager—the default for panels— which will center the button and keep it at its preferred size, which is what we want. The panel containing the 12 buttons will also need to be put inside another panel, to keep the buttons from growing if the frame is resized.

Let's use the name `buttonPanel` for the panel containing the 12 buttons; it will use `GridLayout` as its layout manager. `buttonPanel` will then go into another panel named `centerPanel`, which will use `FlowLayout`. Finally, there will be a third panel, named `bottomPanel`, containing the "Dial" button; it will also use `FlowLayout`. The following figure shows the panels (which are normally invisible) as dashed rectangles:

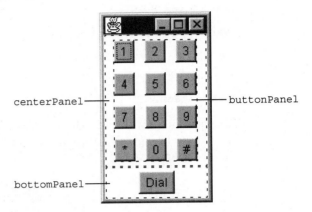

Here are the statements that would be used to create the phone layout:

```
Panel buttonPanel = new Panel();
buttonPanel.setLayout(new GridLayout(4, 3, 10, 10));
for (int i = 1; i <= 9; i++)
  buttonPanel.add(new Button(i + ""));
buttonPanel.add(new Button("*"));
buttonPanel.add(new Button("0"));
buttonPanel.add(new Button("#"));

Panel centerPanel = new Panel();
centerPanel.add(buttonPanel);
add("Center", centerPanel);

Panel bottomPanel = new Panel();
bottomPanel.add(new Button("Dial"));
add("South", bottomPanel);
```

The order in which the steps are performed usually isn't critical. For example, we could have added `centerPanel` to the frame before adding `buttonPanel` to `centerPanel`.

Review Questions

1. Choosing a layout manager for a container is done by calling the _____ method.

2. The _____ layout manager places components in rows, with each row possibly having a different number of components.

3. The _____ layout manager places components in rows, with each row (except possibly the last) having an equal number of components.

4. The _____ layout manager can position four components against the sides of a container, with the fifth occupying the center of the container.

5. Every component has a _____ size, which is the component's "natural" size.

6. A _____ is a container with no border; it is used for grouping components so that they can be treated as a single component.

12.7   Creating and Using Components

So far, we've relied on buttons as our only components. Now it's time to see how the other AWT components are used in a GUI program. In this section, we'll look at each of the components that were introduced in Section 11.8, focusing on three things: how to create the component, what kind of event(s) it fires, and how to determine the current state of the component.

Checkboxes

A *checkbox* is a small box that the user can "check" by clicking with the mouse:

☐ Enable sounds

Clicking on the box causes a check mark to appear:

☑ Enable sounds

Clicking a second time removes the check mark from the box.

A checkbox normally has a label, which is passed to the `Checkbox` constructor as an argument:

```
Checkbox cb = new Checkbox("Enable sounds");
```

If we don't want a label, we can use the no-arg version of the `Checkbox` constructor:

```
Checkbox cb = new Checkbox();
```

By default, a new checkbox is in the "off" state (no check mark). To create a checkbox that's "on" instead, we would use a constructor that takes the desired state as its second argument:

```
Checkbox cb = new Checkbox("Enable sounds", true);
```

When a checkbox is clicked, an item event occurs. To detect this event, we'll need to write a listener class that implements the `ItemListener` interface. Implementing this interface requires that we write a method named `itemStateChanged`:

```
class CheckboxListener implements ItemListener {
  public void itemStateChanged(ItemEvent evt) {
    ...
  }
}
```

addItemListener   To attach a listener to the checkbox, we can use the `addItemListener` method:

```
cb.addItemListener(new CheckboxListener());
```

getState   We may not need a listener for every checkbox. Sometimes we'll wait for some other event to occur (a button press, for example) and then examine the checkboxes to see which ones are currently checked. The `getState` method lets us easily determine the state of a checkbox:

```
boolean state = cb.getState();  // true if box is checked
```

setState   The `setState` method changes the state of a checkbox:

```
cb.setState(true);  // Set state to "on" (checked)
```

Checkbox Groups

We'll sometimes need a group of checkboxes in which only one box can be checked at a time:

Checkboxes that are related in this way are often referred to as ***radio buttons.***

Checkboxes that belong to a group often have a different appearance than individual checkboxes. Under Windows, for example, boxes in a group are round instead of square.

To create a group of checkboxes, we'll need to use the `CheckboxGroup` class. The first step is to create a `CheckboxGroup` object:

```
CheckboxGroup musicGroup = new CheckboxGroup();
```

The next step is to create the checkboxes, supplying the `CheckboxGroup` object as the second argument to the `Checkbox` constructor. (The third argument specifies whether the box is to be checked initially.)

```
Checkbox rockBox = new Checkbox("Rock", musicGroup, true);
Checkbox jazzBox = new Checkbox("Jazz", musicGroup, false);
Checkbox classicalBox =
          new Checkbox("Classical", musicGroup, false);
```

Choice Menus

A ***choice menu*** (or ***popup menu***) displays one of several items:

When the user presses on the arrow button with the mouse, the full list of choices pops up:

The user can now drag the mouse to move the highlight to any of the listed items. When the mouse button is released, the list disappears, and the selected item replaces the one originally displayed.

Creating a choice menu requires two steps. The first step is to create a `Choice` object:

```
Choice countryChoice = new Choice();
```

add   The second step is to add menu items using the `add` method:

```
countryChoice.add("U.S.A.");
countryChoice.add("Canada");
countryChoice.add("Mexico");
```

The order in which the items are added determines the order in which they'll appear on the menu.

getSelectedItem   When the user pops up the menu and makes a choice, an item event occurs, which means that our listener class will need to implement the `ItemListener` interface. We can find which item was selected by calling `getSelectedItem`:

```
String itemSelected = countryChoice.getSelectedItem();
```

getSelectedIndex   To find out the position of the selected item, we can call `getSelectedIndex`:

```
int itemIndex = countryChoice.getSelectedIndex();
```

Not surprisingly, the first item in the list has index 0.

Labels

A *label* is a rectangular area containing a text string:

> :Enter last name: :

A label has no border around it; the user sees nothing but the text. (The dashed line around the label is mine; the user doesn't see it.) Labels are often placed next to other components to indicate their meaning or function. The user can't change a label's text; there are no events defined for labels.

One of the `Label` constructors takes a single argument, the text to be displayed within the label:

```
Label lastName = new Label("Enter last name:");
```

By default, the text is left-justified within the label. (In other words, if the label is stretched by a layout manager, the text will stay at the left side of the label.) The desired alignment can be passed as a second argument to the `Label` constructor:

```
Label lastName = new Label("Enter last name:", Label.CENTER);
```

The possible values for this argument are `Label.CENTER`, `Label.LEFT`, and `Label.RIGHT`.

getText   The `getText` method returns the text of a label:

```
String labelContents = lastName.getText();
```

setText   The `setText` method changes the text of a label:

```
lastName.setText("Enter first name:");
```

Lists

A *list* is a rectangle containing a series of items:

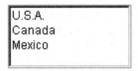

The user can choose an item by clicking on it:

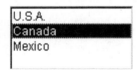

If not all list items are visible, a scrollbar appears to the right of the list:

Creating a list is similar to creating a choice menu. First, we create a `List` object:

```
List countryList = new List();
```

By default, the list will be large enough so that four items are visible at a time. If we want, we can specify the number of visible items:

```
List countryList = new List(5);
```

add   Once the list has been created, we can use the `add` method to add items to it:

```
countryList.add("U.S.A.");
countryList.add("Canada");
countryList.add("Mexico");
```

getSelectedIndex
getSelectedItem   Single-clicking on a list item causes an item event. Double-clicking causes an action event. (As a result, it's not unusual for a list to have two listeners, one for each kind of event.) We can determine which item was selected by calling either `getSelectedIndex` or `getSelectedItem`, just as we did for a choice menu.

Scrollbars

A *scrollbar* is a sliding bar. Scrollbars can be either horizontal:

or vertical:

Each scrollbar represents a number chosen from a range of integers, which we get to specify. For example, we might decide that a scrollbar represents the numbers between 0 and 100 or between 32 and 212. We also get to choose the width of the sliding portion of the scrollbar (the "scroll box" or "bubble"). The scroll box must have a width of at least 1 (measured in the scrollbar's own units, not in pixels), but it can be wider if desired. The width of the scroll box affects the largest value that the user can select, which is the maximum value of the scrollbar's range minus the width of the scroll box. For example, if the scrollbar has a range of 0 to 100, and the scroll box has a width of 10, then the largest value that the user can select is $100 - 10 = 90$.

The user can change the value of a scrollbar in several ways. One possibility is to drag the scroll box to a different position. Another is to click on the arrow buttons, which changes the value of the scrollbar by a small amount, known as the "unit increment." (By default, the unit increment is 1.) Finally, by clicking in the area between an arrow button and the scroll box, the user can change the value of the scrollbar by a larger amount, known as the "block increment." (By default, the block increment is 10.)

The `Scrollbar` constructor that we'll use has five arguments:

```
Scrollbar sb =
  new Scrollbar(Scrollbar.HORIZONTAL, 50, 1, 0, 100);
```

The first argument (either `Scrollbar.HORIZONTAL` or `Scrollbar.VER-TICAL`) specifies the scrollbar's orientation. The fourth and fifth arguments specify the minimum and maximum values of the scrollbar's range. The second argument is the initial value of the scrollbar. The third argument is the width of the scroll box, which must be at least 1.

When the user adjusts a scrollbar, an adjustment event occurs. To handle the event, we would write a class that implements the `AdjustmentListener` interface. This class must contain a method named `adjustmentValue-Changed`:

```
class ScrollbarListener implements AdjustmentListener {
  public void adjustmentValueChanged(AdjustmentEvent evt) {
    ...
  }
}
```

addAdjustmentListener
To attach a listener to the scrollbar, we would use the `addAdjustment-Listener` method:

```
sb.addAdjustmentListener(new ScrollbarListener());
```

getValue
The `getValue` method returns the current value of a scrollbar:

```
int value = sb.getValue();
```

setValue
The `setValue` method changes the value of a scrollbar:

```
sb.setValue(newValue);
```

Text Areas

A *text area* is capable of displaying multiple lines of text:

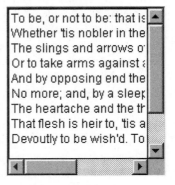

Scrollbars at the bottom and right side make it possible for the user to view text that's not otherwise visible.

There are four ways to create a `TextArea` object, depending on (a) whether or not text is to be displayed initially and (b) whether we want to specify the number of rows and columns in the text area. In the examples that follow, assume that quote is the following string:

```
String quote =
    "To be, or not to be: that is the question:\n" +
    "Whether 'tis nobler in the mind to suffer\n" +
    "The slings and arrows of outrageous fortune,\n" +
    "Or to take arms against a sea of troubles,\n" +
    "And by opposing end them? To die: to sleep;\n" +
    "No more; and, by a sleep to say we end\n" +
    "The heartache and the thousand natural shocks\n" +
    "That flesh is heir to, 'tis a consummation\n" +
    "Devoutly to be wish'd. To die, to sleep;\n" +
    "To sleep: perchance to dream: ay, there's the rub;\n" +
    "For in that sleep of death what dreams may come";
```

Notice that new-line characters are used to separate lines.

To create an empty text area with a default size, we would use the no-arg constructor:

```
TextArea ta = new TextArea();
```

To create a text area containing specified text, we would use the following constructor:

```
TextArea ta = new TextArea(quote);
```

 If we need a text area with a particular size, we can specify the number of rows and columns we want:

```
TextArea ta = new TextArea(10, 20);
```

Finally, we can specify values for both the text and the rows and columns:

```
TextArea ta = new TextArea(quote, 10, 20);
```

setEditable   A text area can be made editable or not editable by calling setEditable and passing either true or false:

```
ta.setEditable(false);   // Not editable
```

Text areas are editable by default.

A text event occurs whenever the user changes any of the text in a text area. (The text area must be editable, of course.) To detect this event, we'll need to write a class that implements the TextListener interface. Implementing this interface requires that we write a method named textValueChanged:

```
class TextAreaListener implements TextListener {
    public void textValueChanged(TextEvent evt) {
        ...
    }
}
```

addTextListener   To attach a listener to the text area, we would use the `addTextListener` method:

```
ta.addTextListener(new TextAreaListener());
```

getText   To fetch the current contents of a text area, we can call the `getText` method:

```
String text = ta.getText();
```

`getText` returns the entire contents of a text area as a single string, with new-line characters marking breaks between lines.

setText   The `setText` method replaces the contents of a text area:

```
ta.setText("Line 1\nLine 2\nLine 3");
```

append   To add text to the end of a text area—without replacing what's already there—we would call the `append` method:

```
ta.append("\nLine 4");
```

Text Fields

A *text field* contains a single line of text:

```
Your name here
```

The `TextField` class has four constructors, which allow us to specify the contents of the text field and/or the number of columns in the text field:

```
TextField tf = new TextField();
TextField tf = new TextField("Your name here");
TextField tf = new TextField(40);
TextField tf = new TextField("Your name here", 40);
```

Text fields are editable by default. To make a text field not editable, we would call the `setEditable` method with `false` as the argument:

```
tf.setEditable(false);   // Not editable
```

Like a text area, a text field can fire text events, which occur when the user modifies the contents of the text field. In addition, an action event occurs when the user presses the Enter key after entering data into a text field. (Both text events and action events are possible only if the text field is editable.)

The methods for text fields, which include `getText` and `setText`, are similar to those for text areas. This similarity isn't surprising, because the `TextArea` and `TextField` classes inherit much of their behavior from their superclass, `TextComponent`. Text fields don't support the `append` method, however.

Review Questions

1. The _____ method returns the state of a checkbox.

2. Checkboxes that are grouped so that only one box can be checked at a time are often called _____ _____ [two words].

3. The _____ method is used to put items into a choice menu or list.

4. The _____ method returns the index of an item selected by the user from a choice menu or list.

5. The _____ method returns the text of a label, text area, or text field.

6. The _____ method returns the current value of a scrollbar.

7. A text area can be made editable or not editable by calling the _____ method.

8. The _____ method can be used with text areas but not text fields.

12.8 Examples

It would be hard to develop a case study that uses more than a few of the GUI components, so I've decided to substitute several smaller programs, each using two different kinds of components. To save space, these programs don't have the full comments that are provided for case studies.

Using Labels and Text Fields: Temperature Conversion

In Chapter 2, we developed several versions of a program that converts Fahrenheit temperatures to Celsius. We'll now develop a GUI version of this program. As a bonus, the new version will be able to convert temperatures not only from Fahrenheit to Celsius, but also from Celsius to Fahrenheit.

The program will display the following frame:

If the user enters a value in the Fahrenheit field and presses the Enter key, the corresponding Celsius temperature will appear in the Celsius field:

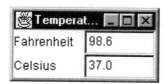

Likewise, if the user enters a value in the Celsius field and presses the Enter key, the corresponding Fahrenheit temperature will appear in the Fahrenheit field:

Temperatures displayed by the program will be rounded to two decimal places.

To design this program, we'll need to confront two issues: layout and event-handling. The GUI components we'll need are two labels and two text fields. For a layout manager, we can use `GridLayout` with two rows and two columns. `GridLayout` will make the labels and text fields all the same size, which should give a satisfactory result. The text fields will need to be declared as instance variables so that a listener will be able to modify one of the text fields when the other is changed.

As far as event-handling goes, we'll need at least two listeners. One listener will cause the program to terminate when the user closes the frame. We'll also need a listener that's called when the user enters data into either one of the text fields. Although one listener is enough for this purpose, the program is easier to understand if we use two listeners, one for each field. Let's name the listener classes `FahrenheitListener` and `CelsiusListener`. Each will have an `actionPerformed` method. This method will retrieve the user's input from one of the text fields and convert it to `double` form. Then it will convert from one temperature scale to the other. Finally, it will round the result to two decimal places and display it in the other text field.

ConvertTemp.java

```
1   // Converts a Fahrenheit temperature entered by the user to
2   // Celsius, or vice versa
3
4   import java.awt.*;
5   import java.awt.event.*;
6   import jpb.*;
7
8   // Driver class
9   public class ConvertTemp {
10    public static void main(String[] args) {
11      Frame frame =
12        new ConvertTempFrame("Temperature Conversion");
13      frame.setSize(150, 75);
14      frame.setVisible(true);
15    }
16  }
17
18  // Frame class
19  class ConvertTempFrame extends Frame {
20    private TextField fahrenField = new TextField();
21    private TextField celsiusField = new TextField();
22
```

```
23      // Constructor
24      public ConvertTempFrame(String title) {
25        // Set title for frame and choose layout
26        super(title);
27        setLayout(new GridLayout(2, 2));
28
29        // Add Fahrenheit label and text field to frame; attach
30        // listener to text field
31        add(new Label("Fahrenheit"));
32        add(fahrenField);
33        fahrenField.addActionListener(new FahrenheitListener());
34
35        // Add Celsius label and text field to frame; attach
36        // listener to text field
37        add(new Label("Celsius"));
38        add(celsiusField);
39        celsiusField.addActionListener(new CelsiusListener());
40
41        // Attach window listener
42        addWindowListener(new WindowCloser());
43      }
44
45      // Listener for fahrenField
46      class FahrenheitListener implements ActionListener {
47        public void actionPerformed(ActionEvent evt) {
48          String fahrenheitString = fahrenField.getText();
49          double fahrenheit = Convert.toDouble(fahrenheitString);
50          double celsius = (fahrenheit - 32.0) * 5.0 / 9.0;
51          celsius = Math.rint(celsius * 100.0) / 100.0;
52          celsiusField.setText(celsius + "");
53        }
54      }
55
56      // Listener for celsiusField
57      class CelsiusListener implements ActionListener {
58        public void actionPerformed(ActionEvent evt) {
59          String celsiusString = celsiusField.getText();
60          double celsius = Convert.toDouble(celsiusString);
61          double fahrenheit = celsius * 9.0 / 5.0 + 32.0;
62          fahrenheit = Math.rint(fahrenheit * 100.0) / 100.0;
63          fahrenField.setText(fahrenheit + "");
64        }
65      }
66
67      // Listener for window
68      class WindowCloser extends WindowAdapter {
69        public void windowClosing(WindowEvent evt) {
70          System.exit(0);
71        }
72      }
73    }
```

For simplicity, I used the Convert.toDouble method (from the jpb package) to convert the user's input into a `double` value. This method will cause the program to terminate if the input isn't a valid number.

Using Lists and Text Areas: Showing Definitions

Our next program illustrates the use of lists and text areas. The program will display the following frame:

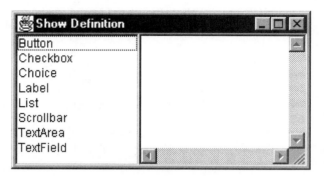

The list at the left contains terms to be defined. (I've used the names of AWT components, but you could easily substitute other terms.)

The user can click on any of the terms displayed in the list. The program will display the definition of the term in the text area at the right. For example, we'll have the following picture if the user clicks on "TextArea":

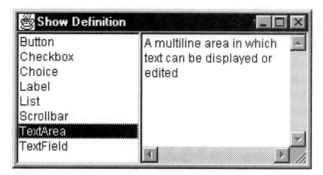

To make the text area as large as possible, I'll use a `BorderLayout`, with the list of terms at West and the text area at Center. (`BorderLayout` is the default layout manager for a frame anyway, so there won't be any need to call `setLayout` in this program.) Single-clicking on a list item causes an item event, so we'll need a listener class that implements the `ItemListener` interface. The text area won't be editable, so it won't need a listener.

For convenience, I'll store the terms and definitions in two parallel arrays named `terms` and `definitions`. When the user clicks on a list item, we can use the `getSelectedIndex` method to get the position of the selected term. We'll then display the definition at the same position in the `definitions` array.

ShowDefinition.java

```
1    // Shows the definition of a term
2
3    import java.awt.*;
4    import java.awt.event.*;
5
6    // Driver class
7    public class ShowDefinition {
8      public static void main(String[] args) {
9        Frame f = new ShowDefinitionFrame("Show Definition");
10       f.setSize(300, 160);
11       f.setVisible(true);
12     }
13   }
14
15   // Frame class
16   class ShowDefinitionFrame extends Frame {
17     private List termList = new List();
18     private TextArea definitionArea = new TextArea();
19     private String[] terms =
20       {"Button", "Checkbox", "Choice", "Label",
21        "List", "Scrollbar", "TextArea", "TextField"};
22     private String[] definitions =
23       {"A labeled button that can\nbe pressed",
24        "A box that can be clicked\n\"on\" or \"off\"",
25        "A menu that displays one\nitem at a time",
26        "A string that can be\npositioned next to " +
27          "other\ncomponents",
28        "A scrolling list of items",
29        "A sliding bar that can be\neither horizontal or " +
30          "vertical",
31        "A multiline area in which\ntext can be displayed " +
32          "or\nedited",
33        "A single line of text that\ncan be displayed " +
34          "or\nedited"};
35
36     // Constructor
37     public ShowDefinitionFrame(String title) {
38       // Set title for frame
39       super(title);
40
41       // Put terms in term list; add term list to frame
42       for (int i = 0; i < terms.length; i++)
43         termList.add(terms[i]);
44       termList.addItemListener(new ListListener());
45       add("West", termList);
46
47       // Make definition area not editable and add to frame
48       definitionArea.setEditable(false);
49       add("Center", definitionArea);
50
51       // Attach window listener
52       addWindowListener(new WindowCloser());
53     }
54
```

```
55    // Listener for termList
56    class ListListener implements ItemListener {
57      public void itemStateChanged(ItemEvent evt) {
58        int index = termList.getSelectedIndex();
59        definitionArea.setText(definitions[index]);
60      }
61    }
62
63    // Listener for window
64    class WindowCloser extends WindowAdapter {
65      public void windowClosing(WindowEvent evt) {
66        System.exit(0);
67      }
68    }
69  }
```

Using Labels and Scrollbars: Picking Colors

Our last program illustrates the use of labels and scrollbars. The program will display a frame containing three scrollbars, representing the colors red, green, and blue, and three labels. Initially, each scrollbar will be in its middle position, representing the color gray (red = 128, green = 128, blue = 128):

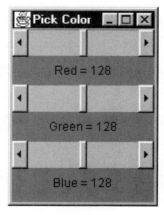

By moving the scrollbars, the user can experiment with different color combinations. For example, the user might select a light blue color by moving the scrollbars to the positions shown in the figure at the top of the next page.

As the user moves the scrollbars, the background colors of the labels will change to reflect the currently selected color combination. The text of each label will also change to indicate the current value of the corresponding scrollbar.

We can achieve the desired layout by using a `GridLayout` with six rows and one column. We'll create the three labels with the `Label.CENTER` attribute, forcing them to be centered.

We'll need a listener class that implements `AdjustmentListener`. It's not clear whether to use a separate listener for each scrollbar or just have one listener for all three. After some experimentation, I found that using a single listener led to

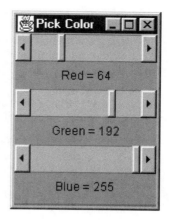

the shortest program (although perhaps not the most efficient one).

The three labels will have to be stored in instance variables because we'll need to change the labels' background color and text from within the listener. The three scrollbars will also need to be stored in instance variables. The reason here isn't so obvious. With a single listener object connected to all three scrollbars, the listener's adjustmentValueChanged method will be called when the user adjusts any one of the scrollbars. The listener can then call each scrollbar's getValue method to find the current value of the scrollbar. (Notice that we never know which scrollbar was actually changed, but we don't need to.)

PickColor.java

```java
1  // Allows the user to pick a color by moving three scrollbars
2
3  import java.awt.*;
4  import java.awt.event.*;
5
6  // Driver class
7  public class PickColor {
8    public static void main(String[] args) {
9      Frame f = new PickColorFrame("Pick Color");
10     f.setSize(150, 200);
11     f.setVisible(true);
12   }
13 }
14
15 // Frame class
16 class PickColorFrame extends Frame {
17   private Label redLabel =
18     new Label("Red = 128", Label.CENTER);
19   private Label greenLabel =
20     new Label("Green = 128", Label.CENTER);
21   private Label blueLabel =
22     new Label("Blue = 128", Label.CENTER);
23   private Scrollbar redBar =
24     new Scrollbar(Scrollbar.HORIZONTAL, 128, 1, 0, 256);
25   private Scrollbar greenBar =
26     new Scrollbar(Scrollbar.HORIZONTAL, 128, 1, 0, 256);
```

```
27    private Scrollbar blueBar =
28      new Scrollbar(Scrollbar.HORIZONTAL, 128, 1, 0, 256);
29
30    // Constructor
31    public PickColorFrame(String title) {
32      // Set title, background color, and layout
33      super(title);
34      setBackground(new Color(128, 128, 128));
35      setLayout(new GridLayout(6, 1));
36
37      // Create scrollbar listener
38      ScrollbarListener listener = new ScrollbarListener();
39
40      // Add red scrollbar and label to frame; attach
41      // listener to scrollbar
42      add(redBar);
43      redBar.addAdjustmentListener(listener);
44      add(redLabel);
45
46      // Add green scrollbar and label to frame; attach
47      // listener to scrollbar
48      add(greenBar);
49      greenBar.addAdjustmentListener(listener);
50      add(greenLabel);
51
52      // Add blue scrollbar and label to frame; attach
53      // listener to scrollbar
54      add(blueBar);
55      blueBar.addAdjustmentListener(listener);
56      add(blueLabel);
57
58      // Attach window listener
59      addWindowListener(new WindowCloser());
60    }
61
62    // Listener for all scrollbars
63    class ScrollbarListener implements AdjustmentListener {
64      public void adjustmentValueChanged(AdjustmentEvent evt) {
65        int red = redBar.getValue();
66        int green = greenBar.getValue();
67        int blue = blueBar.getValue();
68
69        redLabel.setText("Red = " + red);
70        greenLabel.setText("Green = " + green);
71        blueLabel.setText("Blue = " + blue);
72
73        Color newColor = new Color(red, green, blue);
74        redLabel.setBackground(newColor);
75        greenLabel.setBackground(newColor);
76        blueLabel.setBackground(newColor);
77      }
78    }
79
```

```
80    // Listener for window
81    class WindowCloser extends WindowAdapter {
82      public void windowClosing(WindowEvent evt) {
83        System.exit(0);
84      }
85    }
86  }
```

Note that the scrollbars are declared to have ranges from 0 to 256 rather than 0 to 255. The maximum value of a scrollbar is affected by the width of its scroll box, which is 1 for the scrollbars in this program. A scrollbar with a declared range of 0 to 256 is really limited to a maximum of 255.

Q & A

Q: **The `DrawableFrame` class has a method named `show`. Can this method be used with `Frame` objects as well? [p. 489]**

A: Yes. Calling `show` has the same effect as calling `setVisible` with `true` as the argument. The `show` method belongs to the `Window` class. `Frame` inherits it from `Window` (and `DrawableFrame` inherits it from `Frame`).

Q: **How can I position a frame so that it's in the center of the screen? [p. 490]**

A: First, you need to find out the size of the user's screen. The following call of `getScreenSize` will provide that information in the form of a `Dimension` object:

```
Dimension screenSize =
  Toolkit.getDefaultToolkit().getScreenSize();
```

Suppose that the variable `f` contains the frame that you want to center. The following statements will position `f` in the center of the screen:

```
Dimension frameSize = f.getSize();
f.setLocation((screenSize.width - frameSize.width) / 2,
              (screenSize.height - frameSize.height) / 2);
```

Q: **Interfaces seem to resemble abstract classes. Are the two concepts related? [p. 493]**

A: Yes. An interface is essentially an abstract class in which all methods are abstract. Interfaces and abstract classes also differ with respect to what variables they allow; see the answer to the following question.

Q: **Can an interface have variables? [p. 493]**

A: Yes, but they're highly restricted. Variables defined in an interface must be `static` and `final`—in other words, they're really constants. An interface can't declare any instance variables, nor can it have class variables that aren't `final`.

When a class implements an interface containing variables, those variables are "inherited" by the class.

Q: **Can I get rid of the scrollbars that are normally attached to a text area? [p. 518]**

A: Yes. When you create the text area, use the `TextArea` constructor that takes four arguments, and pass `TextArea.SCROLLBARS_NONE` as the last argument:

```
TextArea ta =
  new TextArea(text, 10, 40, TextArea.SCROLLBARS_NONE);
```

Q: **I created a text area with 40 columns, but it seems to be smaller than I expected. What's going on? [p. 519]**

A: The width of a column is based on the width of an "average" character. The text that you're displaying in the text area may contain characters that are wider than average.

Summary

- Java's Abstract Window Toolkit (AWT) provides classes and other tools for building programs that have a graphical user interface.
- Java has a newer library for building graphical user interfaces, known as "Swing." Swing is more powerful and sophisticated than the AWT, giving professional programmers the tools they need to build elaborate user interfaces.
- Designing a graphical user interface involves creating components, putting them into containers, and arranging for the program to respond to events.
- A frame is a window with a title and a border, and possibly a menu bar.
- After a frame is created, either `pack` or `setSize` should be called to select a size for the frame. The `pack` method makes the frame just large enough to display the components within it.
- The `setLocation` method sets the position of a frame's upper-left corner. By default, frames are displayed in the upper-left corner of the screen.
- The `setVisible` method controls whether or not a frame is currently visible on the screen.
- The `getLocation` method returns the position of a frame's upper-left corner. The `getSize` method returns the size of a frame.
- Instead of using the `Frame` class to create objects directly, it's customary to define a subclass of `Frame` instead. The constructor for this subclass will create components and add them to the frame.
- The `add` method is used to add a component to a frame (or any kind of container).

- When the user performs an action on a component, Java creates an object containing information about the event. If a listener object has been registered with the component, one of the listener's methods will be called automatically and given the event object as its argument.

- An event object is an instance of one of the classes in the `java.awt.event` package. These classes include `ActionEvent`, `AdjustmentEvent`, `ItemEvent`, `TextEvent`, and `WindowEvent`.

- A listener object must belong to a class that implements one of the interfaces in the `java.awt.event` package, which include `ActionListener`, `AdjustmentListener`, `ItemListener`, `TextListener`, and `WindowListener`.

- An interface is a pattern that will be used later to define "real" classes. The methods in an interface have no bodies.

- A class implements an interface by agreeing to provide bodies for all methods in the interface.

- Pressing a button is an action event, so the listener class for a button would need to implement the `ActionListener` interface.

- The `addActionListener` method connects an action listener to a component. When an action event occurs involving the component, the listener's `actionPerformed` method will be called.

- It's common for a window listener class to extend the `WindowAdapter` class instead of implementing the `WindowListener` interface. `WindowAdapter` provides empty bodies for the methods required by the `WindowListener` interface.

- To detect when a window is closed, a window listener must have a `windowClosing` method.

- An inner class is a class that's nested inside another class. The methods in an inner class have access to the variables and methods of the enclosing class.

- Listener classes are often inner classes so that they have access to variables and methods within a frame class.

- When a listener is notified of an event, it can determine which component was the source of the event by calling the `getSource` method. If the event is an action event, the `getActionCommand` method returns the "action command" associated with the component. (In the case of a button, the action command is the label on the button.)

- Every container has a layout manager, whose job is to determine the sizes and positions of components within the container.

- The `java.awt` package provides five layout manager classes: `BorderLayout`, `CardLayout`, `FlowLayout`, `GridBagLayout`, and `GridLayout`.

- Choosing a layout manager for a container is done by calling `setLayout` and passing it an instance of a layout manager class.

- The `FlowLayout` layout manager can handle any number of components. The components are laid out side by side from left to right. By default, the components are separated by five pixels of space and centered in each row.

- The `GridLayout` layout manager places components in rows, with each (except possibly the last) having an equal number of components. By default, there is no space between components.

- The `BorderLayout` layout manager can handle up to five components. Four of the components can be positioned against the sides of the container, with the fifth occupying the center of the container. By default, there is no space between components.

- `BorderLayout` doesn't require that all five positions be used; unused positions are filled by neighboring components.

- Every component has a "preferred size." For example, the preferred size of a button is determined by the size of the label on the button—the longer the label, the wider the button.

- `FlowLayout` honors the preferred sizes of all components. `GridLayout` ignores the preferred sizes of all components. `BorderLayout` honors the preferred widths of the East and West components and the preferred heights of the North and South components but ignores the preferred size of the Center component.

- A panel is a rectangular container with no border. By default, the layout manager for a panel is `FlowLayout`.

- Panels are used to create a group of components that—for layout purposes—is treated as a single component.

- A checkbox is a small box that the user can "check" by clicking with the mouse. A checkbox may or may not be accompanied by a label.

- When a checkbox is clicked, an item event occurs. A listener class for this event must implement the `ItemListener` interface. The `addItemListener` method is used to attach a listener to a checkbox.

- The `getState` method returns the state of a checkbox. The `setState` method changes the state of a checkbox.

- The `CheckboxGroup` class is used to create radio buttons—a group of checkboxes in which only one box can be checked at a time.

- A choice menu (or popup menu) displays one of several menu items.

- Setting up a choice menu involves creating a `Choice` object and then adding menu items using the `add` method.

- When the user makes a selection from a choice menu, an item event occurs. A listener class for this event must implement the `ItemListener` interface.

- The `getSelectedItem` method returns the menu item selected by the user. The `getSelectedIndex` method returns the position of the selected item.

- A label is a rectangular area containing a text string. By default, text is left-justified within a label.

- The user can't change a label's text; there are no events defined for labels.
- The `getText` method returns the text of a label. The `setText` method changes the text of a label.
- A list is a rectangle containing a scrolling list of items.
- Setting up a list involves creating a `List` object and then using the `add` method to add items to it. By default, a list will be large enough so that four items are visible at a time.
- Single-clicking on a list item causes an item event. Double-clicking causes an action event. The `getSelectedIndex` and `getSelectedItem` methods can be used to determine which item was selected.
- A scrollbar is a horizontal or vertical sliding bar.
- Each scrollbar represents a number chosen from a range of integers.
- When the user adjusts a scrollbar, an adjustment event occurs. A listener class for this event must implement the `AdjustmentListener` interface. The `addAdjustmentListener` method is used to attach a listener to a scrollbar.
- The `getValue` method returns the current value of a scrollbar. The `setValue` method changes the value of a scrollbar.
- A text area is capable of displaying multiple lines of text.
- A text area can be made editable or not editable by calling `setEditable` and passing either `true` or `false`. Text areas are editable by default.
- A text event occurs when the user modifies the text in a text area. A listener class for this event must implement the `TextListener` interface. The `addTextListener` method is used to attach a listener to a text area.
- The `getText` method returns the current contents of a text area. The `setText` method replaces the contents of a text area. The `append` method adds text to the end of a text area.
- A text field contains a single line of text.
- A text field can be made editable or not editable by calling `setEditable` and passing either `true` or `false`. Text fields are editable by default.
- A text event occurs when the user modifies the contents of a text field. An action event occurs when the user presses the Enter key after entering data into a text field.
- The methods for text fields are similar to those for text areas, except that text fields don't support the `append` method.

Exercises

Section 12.2

1. Write a call of `setLocation` that places the frame `f` in the lower-right corner of the screen. *Hint:* See the Q&A section.

Section 12.4

2. For each of the following actions, write a `ButtonListener` class whose `action-Performed` method performs the specified action. (Assume that `ButtonListener` is an inner class, so it has access to `Frame` methods.)

    (a) Increase the frame's width and height by five pixels.

    (b) Make the frame move to a random location on the screen. *Hint:* See the Q&A section.

    (c) Make the frame disappear for two seconds and then reappear.

Section 12.6

3. Indicate which layout managers (`BorderLayout`, `FlowLayout`, or `GridLayout`) have each of the following properties.

    (a) By default, puts no space between components.

    (b) Requires an `add` method with two arguments.

    (c) Keeps all components at their preferred sizes.

    (d) Forces all components to be the same size.

    (e) Keeps components in the same relative positions when the container is resized.

    (f) Can accommodate any number of components.

4. Write calls of `setLayout` that specify each of the following layouts.

    (a) A `FlowLayout` in which components are right-justified, with a 10-pixel horizontal gap and a 15-pixel vertical gap.

    (b) A `GridLayout` in which components are arranged in three rows and four columns, with a 5-pixel horizontal gap and a 10-pixel vertical gap.

    (c) A `BorderLayout` with a 15-pixel horizontal gap and a 5-pixel vertical gap.

Section 12.7

5. Indicate which components have each of the following properties. (Possible answers are buttons, checkboxes, choice menus, labels, lists, scrollbars, text areas, and text fields.)

    (a) Can fire action events.

    (b) Can fire adjustment events.

    (c) Can fire item events.

    (d) Can fire text events.

    (e) Cannot fire any events.

    (f) Can be grouped to form radio buttons.

    (g) Supports the `getSelectedIndex` and `getSelectedItem` methods.

    (h) Supports the `getState` and `setState` methods.

    (i) Supports the `getText` and `setText` methods.

    (j) Supports the `getValue` and `setValue` methods.

    (k) Supports the `setEditable` method.

6. Write statements that create each of the following components.

    (a) A button labeled `"Print"`.

    (b) A checkbox labeled `"Remember password"` in the "on" state.

    (c) A group of three checkboxes labeled `"Red"`, `"Green"`, and `"Blue"`.

    (d) A choice menu containing the items `"Standard Shipping"`, `"2nd Day Air"`, and `"Next Day Air"`.

    (e) A right-justified label containing the text `"Email address: "`.

    (f) A list containing the items `"Career"`, `"Casual"`, `"Active"`, and `"Contemporary"`.

    (g) A vertical scrollbar whose values range from –500 to +500. The initial value of the scrollbar should be 0, and the width of the scroll box should be 10.

    (h) A text area with 5 rows and 30 columns.

    (i) A text field with 20 columns containing the text `"Country"`.

Programming Projects

1. Modify the `DayOfWeek` program (Programming Project 5, Chapter 2) so that it has a graphical user interface. The program will display the following frame:

The user can now select a month and day from the choice menus, and enter a year in the text field. Whenever the user chooses from a choice menu or presses Enter in the year field, the program will attempt to calculate the day of the week. If the year field contains a valid integer, the program will display the day of the week in the lower part of the frame:

If the year field is empty or contains a non-integer, no message is displayed.

2. Modify the `Rot13` program (Section 9.5) so that it has a graphical user interface. The program will display the following frame:

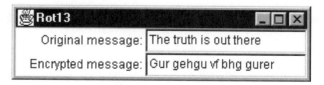

The text fields are initially empty. When the user enters a message into the upper text field and presses Enter, the encrypted message will appear in the lower text field.

3. Modify the `ConvertTemp` program (Section 12.8) by adding a button labeled "Reset":

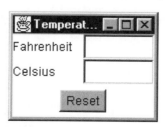

Pressing this button clears both text fields.

4.   Modify the `PickColor` program (Section 12.8) so that it has three listener classes—one
for each scrollbar—rather than one. *Hint:* Write a helper method that sets the background
for the three labels and have all three listeners call this method. Which version of `Pick-
Color` do you prefer: the original version or the three-listener version?

5.   Modify the `PickColor` program (Section 12.8) so that it displays the following frame:

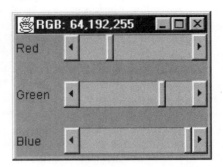

Notice that the red, green, and blue values are displayed in the frame's title. *Hints:* Put the
labels into one panel and scrollbars into another panel. Call `setBackground` separately
for each panel and each label.

6.   Modify the `PickColor` program (Section 12.8) so that it displays the following frame:

To pick a color, the user first selects one of the radio buttons. The user then adjusts the
scrollbar to choose a value for the corresponding color. (The "Blue" button is currently
selected, so changes to the scrollbar affect the blue component of the color.) *Hints:* Put the
buttons into a panel. Call `setBackground` separately for each button, the panel containing the buttons, and the label underneath the scrollbar.

7.   Write a program named `Lottery` that chooses winning lottery numbers. The program will
display the following frame:

Initially, no lottery number is shown. Each time the user presses the "Choose number" button, a randomly chosen four-digit number will be displayed above the button.

8. Write a program named `Dial` that simulates the behavior of a telephone. The program will display the following frame:

The layout is the one described in Section 12.6, except that a text field has been added at the top. When the user presses a numbered button, the corresponding digit will be added to the text field, so that the number being dialed is gradually spelled out. (Pressing the "*" and "#" buttons has no effect.) When the user presses the "Dial" button, the text field will display the message "Dialing..." for two seconds. The text field will then go blank, and the user can enter another phone number.

9. Write a program named `ScrollingList` that highlights words in a list. The program will display a frame containing an empty text field and a list of words in sorted order (see the figure at left). The user can now enter a word (or a portion of a word) in the text field. Each time the user changes the text field, the program will highlight the first word in the list that begins with the letters in the text field. For example, if the user enters *abdo* in the text field, the word *abdomen* will be highlighted (see the figure at right).

If the user enters letters that don't match any word in the list, the highlight should remain where it was previously. *Hints:* When a text event occurs, have the text field's listener search the word list in reverse order. If the word at position i begins with the letters entered by the user, move the highlight to that word by calling the `select` method:

```
wordList.select(i);  // wordList is a List object
```

The `String` class has a method named `startsWith` that returns `true` if a string begins with the characters in another string (supplied as an argument to `startsWith`).

10. Write a program named `PhoneDirectory` that stores a database of names and phone numbers. The program will display the following frame:

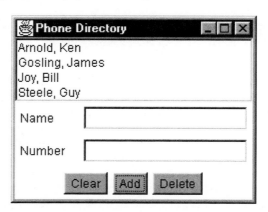

The names will appear in a list at the top of the frame; this list is initially empty. The user can perform the following actions:

(a) *Add a name and number.* Entering a name and number in the text fields and then pressing the "Add" button adds this information to the program's database. The name is displayed at the end of the list, and the fields go blank.

(b) *View a number.* Clicking on one of the names in the list causes the name and corresponding number to appear in the text fields.

(c) *Modify a name or number.* After a name has been selected and displayed, the name and/or number can be modified. The change goes into effect when the Enter key is pressed in either field.

(d) *Delete a name and number.* After a name has been selected and displayed, the name and number are removed from the program's database if the "Delete" button is pressed. The name disappears from the list and the fields go blank.

(e) *Clear the name and number fields.* Pressing the "Clear" button clears the name and number fields but has no effect on the stored names and numbers.

Hint: Store the numbers in an array whose elements are "parallel" to the names in the list.

Answers to Review Questions

1. Swing
2. Container
3. Event
4. Listener

Section 12.2
1. `setVisible`
2. In the upper-left corner
3. `add`
4. `pack`

Section 12.3
1. `java.awt.event`
2. `ActionEvent`
3. Interface
4. Adapter

Section 12.4
1. `setBackground`
2. Inner

Section 12.5
1. One or two listener objects will be needed. They may belong to the same listener class or to two different classes.
2. `getSource`
3. `getActionCommand`
4. The label on the button

Section 12.6
1. `setLayout`
2. `FlowLayout`
3. `GridLayout`
4. `BorderLayout`
5. Preferred
6. Panel

Section 12.7
1. `getState`
2. Radio buttons
3. `add`
4. `getSelectedIndex`
5. `getText`
6. `getValue`
7. `setEditable`
8. `append`

13 Data Structures

A collection of data items stored under a single name is known as a data structure. Objects are data structures, because an object may have multiple instance variables. Arrays are also data structures, because an array is a collection of elements. In this chapter, we'll delve into data structures in much greater depth than in previous chapters. We'll also examine some common algorithms that are used in conjunction with data structures.

Chapter 5 explored one-dimensional arrays in some detail; in this chapter, we'll discuss arrays with two or more dimensions. We'll also look at applications for multidimensional arrays, which include using arrays as matrices and using arrays to represent gray-scale and color images.

The `java.util` package includes several data structure classes. We'll examine two of these classes: `Vector` and `BitSet`. A vector behaves like an array that automatically resizes itself when it becomes full. Bit sets are used to model the mathematical concept of a set: an unordered collection of values with no duplicates.

Vectors, unlike arrays, are only capable of storing objects, not values of the primitive types. To work around this restriction, we can use "wrapper" classes, which let us create objects that contain a single value of a primitive type. These objects can then be stored in vectors.

The other data structure covered in the chapter is the string buffer. A string buffer is similar to a string, except that its characters can be modified. (Ordinary strings are immutable.)

In addition to its coverage of data structures, the chapter includes a discussion of algorithms for solving two common problems: sorting an array and searching an array for a particular value. We'll focus on the insertion sort algorithm, which is easy to understand but not very efficient, and the binary search algorithm, which is highly efficient.

Objectives

- Learn about multidimensional arrays and some of their applications.
- Learn about vectors, which are similar to arrays but more flexible.
- Learn how to use wrapper classes to create "wrapper objects" for values of a primitive type.
- Learn how to insert into a sorted array and how to sort an array using the insertion sort algorithm.
- Learn how to use the binary search algorithm to locate a key in a sorted array.
- Learn how to use bit sets, which resemble vectors of `boolean` values.
- Learn how to use string buffers for string manipulation.

13.1   Multidimensional Arrays

Chapter 5 explored one-dimensional arrays in considerable detail. It's now time to look at *multidimensional arrays*—arrays with more than one dimension. Java allows arrays to have any number of dimensions. In practice, however, arrays rarely have more than two dimensions. Arrays with three or more dimensions are hard to visualize, so programmers tend to avoid them, instead using one- or two-dimensional arrays containing objects.

Creating and Initializing a Multidimensional Array

A multidimensional array is declared in the same way as a one-dimensional array, except that the declaration will contain more than one set of square brackets. For example, the declaration

```
int[][] a;
```

states that a is a two-dimensional array whose elements have `int` type. It's legal to put some or all of the brackets after the array name:

```
int[] a[];
int a[][];
```

Both declarations of a are equivalent to the original one.

We saw in Section 5.1 that declaring an array variable doesn't cause Java to allocate any space for the array's elements. To allocate space, we can use the `new` keyword:

```
a = new int[5][10];
```

For a two-dimensional array, the number inside the first set of brackets specifies the number of rows in the array; the number in the second set specifies the number of columns. In this example, the array a will have 5 rows and 10 columns.

As a shortcut, we can combine the declaration of a multidimensional array with the allocation of space for the array:

```
int[][] a = new int[5][10];
```

We can visualize the array a as a table with 5 rows and 10 columns:

	column →									
	0	1	2	3	4	5	6	7	8	9
0										
1										
row 2										
3										
4										

We'll see later that a is actually stored in a different way. Still, visualizing a two-dimensional array as a table is fine most of the time.

In Section 5.1, we saw that the elements of a one-dimensional array are given default values at the time storage for the array is allocated. Numbers are set to zero, boolean elements are set to false, and elements of a reference type are set to null. The same rules apply to multidimensional arrays, which means that the array a will be full of zeros initially:

	0	1	2	3	4	5	6	7	8	9
0	0	0	0	0	0	0	0	0	0	0
1	0	0	0	0	0	0	0	0	0	0
2	0	0	0	0	0	0	0	0	0	0
3	0	0	0	0	0	0	0	0	0	0
4	0	0	0	0	0	0	0	0	0	0

Instead of using new to allocate space for a multidimensional array, we have the option of providing an initializer instead. For example, suppose that we wanted to create a 3×3 array whose elements are initialized in the following way:

	0	1	2
0	8	3	4
1	1	5	9
2	6	7	2

Here's how we could declare and initialize this array:

```
int[][] square = {{8, 3, 4}, {1, 5, 9}, {6, 7, 2}};
```

The elements in each row of the array are enclosed in curly braces, and there's another set of curly braces around the entire initializer. As this example shows, the initializer for a two-dimensional array looks like a series of one-dimensional array initializers. The initializer for a three-dimensional array would look like a series of two-dimensional array initializers.

Subscripting a Multidimensional Array

Selecting an element of a multidimensional array requires more than one subscript. If a is a two-dimensional array, for example, we could access the element in row i, column j by writing

```
a[i][j]
```

As with a one-dimensional array, each subscript can be a literal, a variable, or any expression that produces an int value.

 Be careful not to write a[i, j] to access the element of a in row i and column j. Java requires square brackets around each subscript.

Processing the Elements in a Multidimensional Array

As with one-dimensional arrays, we can access the elements of a multidimensional array sequentially, or we can access elements in no particular order. When we need to access the elements of a two-dimensional array sequentially, we'll typically visit the elements in row order, visiting all elements in row 0, then all elements in row 1, and so on. Occasionally we'll need to visit the elements in column order, visiting all elements in column 0, then all elements in column 1, and so on.

For example, suppose that we need to sum the elements in a 3 × 3 array named a, whose elements have type int. The following statements visit the elements row by row, computing the total in the process:

```
int sum = 0;
for (int row = 0; row < 3; row++)
  for (int col = 0; col < 3; col++)
    sum += a[row][col];
```

The outer loop controls which row is currently being visited, and the inner loop controls the column. Because the loops are nested, the row and col variables will take on all possible combinations of values, and we'll end up visiting the elements of a in the following order:

```
a[0][0]
a[0][1]
a[0][2]
a[1][0]
a[1][1]
a[1][2]
a[2][0]
a[2][1]
a[2][2]
```

Just as `for` loops go hand in hand with one-dimensional arrays, nested `for` loops are ideal for processing multidimensional arrays.

How Multidimensional Arrays Are Stored

Although our mental picture of a two-dimensional array as a table is useful, it isn't all that accurate. In Java, a two-dimensional array is actually a one-dimensional array whose elements are other one-dimensional arrays. For example, assume that the array a has been declared as follows:

```
int[][] a = new int[5][10];
```

Here's how a is really stored:

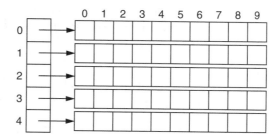

In this figure, we see a one-dimensional array with five elements. Each element contains a reference to another one-dimensional array with 10 elements. This latter array stores one complete row of the two-dimensional array.

Because a is really a one-dimensional array, it's legal to write a.length to find the number of rows in a. To find the number of columns, we'll need to use the expression a[0].length. (The choice of 0 is arbitrary; other subscripts would also work.) The length of the next dimension—if a had more than two dimensions—would be a[0][0].length, and so on.

We can now improve our previous example, which used nested loops to sum the elements of a two-dimensional array. In the new version, the literals representing the number of rows and columns are replaced by a.length and a[0].length:

```
for (int row = 0; row < a.length; row++)
  for (int col = 0; col < a[0].length; col++)
    sum += a[row][col];
```

Using Two-Dimensional Arrays as Matrices

In Section 5.5, we explored the uses of one-dimensional arrays as vectors (in the mathematical sense, not the Java sense). Multidimensional arrays also play an important role in mathematical calculations, because we can use a two-dimensional array to store a matrix. Consider the following matrices:

$$\mathbf{A} = \begin{bmatrix} a_{11} & a_{12} & a_{13} \\ a_{21} & a_{22} & a_{23} \end{bmatrix} \qquad \mathbf{B} = \begin{bmatrix} b_{11} & b_{12} \\ b_{21} & b_{22} \\ b_{31} & b_{32} \end{bmatrix}$$

To represent these matrices in Java, we can use the following two-dimensional arrays:

```
double[][] a = new double[2][3];
double[][] b = new double[3][2];
```

The subscripts will be off by 1, however, as they were for vectors. For example, element a_{ij} of the matrix **A** will be stored in element a[i-1][j-1] of the array a.

There are a number of common operations on matrices, including addition, subtraction, and multiplication. The exercises at the end of the chapter explore some of these operations. Let's focus on matrix multiplication, one of the most important matrix operations. If **A** and **B** are the matrices defined earlier, the product of **A** and **B** is defined as follows:

$$\mathbf{AB} = \begin{bmatrix} a_{11}b_{11} + a_{12}b_{21} + a_{13}b_{31} & a_{11}b_{12} + a_{12}b_{22} + a_{13}b_{32} \\ a_{21}b_{11} + a_{22}b_{21} + a_{23}b_{31} & a_{21}b_{12} + a_{22}b_{22} + a_{23}b_{32} \end{bmatrix}$$

In general, **A** and **B** can be multiplied only if the number of columns in **A** matches the number of rows in **B**.

The following statements will multiply arrays named a and b, storing the result in a new array named c. There are no restrictions on a and b, other than the requirement that the number of columns in a be equal to the number of rows in b.

```
double[][] c = new double[a.length][b[0].length];
for (int row = 0; row < a.length; row++)
  for (int col = 0; col < b[0].length; col++) {
    c[row][col] = 0.0;
    for (int i = 0; i < b.length; i++)
      c[row][col] += a[row][i] * b[i][col];
  }
```

Notice that the for loops are nested three deep. The outer loops range over all possible row and column subscripts in the c array. The innermost loop performs the summation that's necessary to calculate the value of c[row][col].

Using Two-Dimensional Arrays to Store Images

Two-dimensional arrays are often used to store images. (A graphics context, after all, is a two-dimensional arrangement of pixels.)

Images are sometimes stored in ***gray scale***, rather than in color. In a gray-scale image, each pixel is a shade of gray. Typically there are 256 shades, represented by integers between 0 (black) and 255 (white). Consider the following gray-scale image:

(This image—a picture of the author—looks much better when viewed from a distance.) We could represent the image as a two-dimensional array of integers (see the figure at the top of the next page).

To store a full-color image, we could use three parallel two-dimensional arrays (storing the red, green, and blue components of the pixels), a single two-dimensional array of `Color` objects, or a three-dimensional array. If we decide to choose the last option, here's how the array might be declared:

```
int[][][] colorImage = new int[numRows][numColumns][3];
```

`numRows` is the number of rows in the image and `numColumns` is the number of columns. The red component of the pixel at position (*row*, *column*) would be stored in `colorImage[row][column][0]`, the green component would be stored in `colorImage[row][column][1]`, and the blue component would be stored in `colorImage[row][column][2]`.

Arrays can often occupy large amounts of memory, especially when they have more than one dimension. For example, if `numRows` and `numColumns` are both 1000, then the `colorImage` array will require 12,000,000 bytes of memory (1000 × 1000 × 3 × 4), because an `int` value occupies four bytes in Java. Arrays this large may exceed the limits of a Java interpreter, making it impossible to run the program. (Because of the way a multidimensional array is stored in Java—as a one-dimensional array whose elements are arrays—the `colorImage` array will actually require more than 12,000,000 bytes, but let's ignore that detail.)

	0	1	2	3	4	5	6	7	8	9	10	11	12	13	14	15
0	231	231	231	231	231	231	231	231	231	231	231	231	231	231	231	231
1	231	231	231	231	231	231	231	177	231	231	231	231	231	231	231	231
2	231	231	231	231	231	53	7	0	0	37	23	53	231	231	231	231
3	231	231	231	231	7	0	0	7	7	0	7	7	153	231	231	231
4	231	231	231	7	0	0	69	0	0	0	0	0	7	231	231	231
5	231	231	231	7	0	153	207	207	207	0	7	0	7	23	231	231
6	231	231	231	7	23	207	207	231	231	207	231	207	153	23	231	231
7	231	231	231	7	61	207	215	231	231	231	223	207	161	53	231	231
8	231	231	114	7	153	153	38	53	153	231	207	85	138	7	231	231
9	231	231	207	7	161	153	153	153	207	231	153	153	138	7	231	231
10	231	231	231	215	153	231	207	215	207	231	207	191	207	207	231	231
11	231	231	153	231	191	207	231	231	191	215	183	231	207	138	231	231
12	231	231	231	53	130	161	207	207	85	161	85	207	153	231	231	231
13	231	231	231	231	23	153	85	7	0	0	7	69	77	231	231	231
14	231	231	231	231	23	7	7	138	207	191	122	23	23	231	231	231
15	231	231	231	231	138	93	23	69	0	0	23	7	69	231	231	231
16	231	231	231	93	177	7	0	23	23	39	7	0	93	93	109	138
17	177	93	109	93	117	231	23	0	7	0	23	161	109	153	93	85
18	138	93	93	161	161	231	231	53	7	185	255	161	109	161	109	138
19	138	109	161	109	177	255	231	7	23	231	255	161	231	177	161	138

short type ➤9.2   We can often conserve memory by switching to a smaller element type (`short` instead of `int` or `float` instead of `double`). In the case of the `colorImage` array, switching from `int` to `short` will reduce the array's memory requirements

byte type ➤9.2   by a factor of 2. If we're careful, we can even use the `byte` type. `byte` values range from −128 to 127, which isn't exactly what we want. However, by subtracting 128 from each color value when storing it into the array, we can scale the color values so that they become legal `byte` values. Switching to `byte` will reduce the size of the `colorImage` array by a factor of 4 (3,000,000 bytes instead of 12,000,000).

Ragged Arrays

Each row of a two-dimensional array is an array in its own right, so there's no reason that the rows can't have different lengths. If they do, the array is said to be *ragged.* Consider the problem of storing the following table containing distances between major American cities:

	Atlanta	Boston	Chicago	Houston	Los Angeles	New York	San Francisco	Washington
Atlanta	–	1110	710	790	2190	850	2480	620
Boston	1110	–	1000	1830	3020	210	3130	450
Chicago	710	1000	–	1090	2050	810	2170	710
Houston	790	1830	1090	–	1540	1610	1910	1370
Los Angeles	2190	3020	2050	1540	–	2790	390	2650
New York	850	210	810	1610	2790	–	2930	240
San Francisco	2480	3130	2170	1910	390	2930	–	2840
Washington	620	450	710	1370	2650	240	2840	–

We could obviously store the table as a two-dimensional array with eight rows and eight columns, using a total of 64 elements. However, it's possible to save space by using a ragged array instead. The elements on the diagonal aren't used, so there's no need to store them. Also, the values above the diagonal are symmetric to the values below the diagonal, so we don't need to store both groups.

If the elements of a ragged array are initialized at the time the array is declared, we can use an initializer in which the rows have different lengths. For example, the following declaration creates and initializes an array containing the distances between cities:

```
int[][] distances =
  {null,
   {1110},
   { 710, 1000},
   { 790, 1830, 1090},
   {2190, 3020, 2050, 1540},
   { 850, 210,   810, 1610, 2790},
   {2480, 3130, 2170, 1910,  390, 2930},
   { 620, 450,   710, 1370, 2650,  240, 2840}};
```

There's no need to store any of the information in the first row of the table, so we could get by with seven rows instead of eight. However, the array will be easier to work with if it has eight rows, corresponding to the eight cities. Putting `null` at the beginning of the array indicates that row 0 has no elements. Here's what the array will look like:

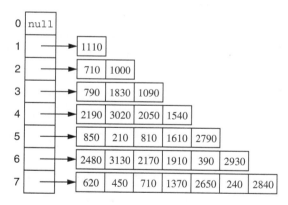

If we don't want to initialize the elements of a ragged array, creating the array is a little more difficult. For example, suppose that we want to allocate space for the `distances` array without specifying values for its elements. We'll first need to allocate storage for a one-dimensional array with eight elements, whose elements will be arrays of integers themselves. We'll then use a loop to allocate storage for each of the "inner" arrays. Here are statements that perform both steps:

```
int[][] distances = new int[8][];
for (int i = 1; i < distances.length; i++)
  distances[i] = new int[i];
```

The value of `distances[0]` will be `null` by default.

Another consequence of the way Java stores arrays is that we can change the length of a row during program execution. Each row is a separate one-dimensional array, so we have the ability to replace a row with another one-dimensional array of a different length.

Using Multidimensional Arrays as Parameters and Results

Multidimensional arrays, like one-dimensional arrays, can be passed to methods and returned by methods. The following method, for example, has a two-dimensional array of integers as its parameter. The method returns the sum of all the elements in the array.

```java
public static int sumElements(int[][] a) {
  int total = 0;

  for (int row = 0; row < a.length; row++)
    for (int col = 0; col < a[row].length; col++)
      total += a[row][col];

  return total;
}
```

Note that I used `a[row].length` as the limit on the inner loop, rather than `a[0].length`. That way, the method will work even if the array has rows of different lengths.

Methods that return multidimensional arrays are not uncommon in Java. The following method, for example, returns an identity matrix of a specified rank. (An *identity matrix* contains 1s on the main diagonal, where the row and column index are the same, and 0s everywhere else.)

```java
public static double[][] createIdentityMatrix(int rank) {
  double[][] matrix = new double[rank][rank];

  for (int row = 0; row < rank; row++)
    for (int col = 0; col < rank; col++)
      if (row == col)
        matrix[row][col] = 1.0;

  return matrix;
}
```

To save time, the `createIdentityMatrix` method assigns values only to elements on the main diagonal of `matrix`. Other elements will have the value 0.0 by default. Here's a sample call of `createIdentityMatrix`:

```java
double[][] identityMatrix = createIdentityMatrix(3);
```

The `identityMatrix` variable will contain a reference to the 3×3 array that `createIdentityMatrix` returns.

PROGRAM **Finding the Distance Between Two Cities**

Earlier in this section, we looked at a table of distances between cities. Let's build this table into a program named FindDistance that prompts the user for the names of two cities and then displays the distance between the cities. Here's what the user will see on the screen:

```
This program finds the distance between two cities.
Supported cities: Atlanta, Boston, Chicago, Houston,
Los Angeles, New York, San Francisco, Washington.

Enter starting city: San Francisco
Enter destination city: Atlanta

The distance from San Francisco to Atlanta is 2480 miles.
```

The program will validate the city names, prompting the user to re-enter the name of a city if it doesn't match any of the names supported by the program. I'll use a normal two-dimensional array to store the distances between cities. Modifying the program to use a ragged array is left as an exercise.

FindDistance.java

```
 1  // Finds the distance between two major American cities
 2
 3  import jpb.*;
 4
 5  public class FindDistance {
 6    private static final String[] CITY_NAMES =
 7      {"Atlanta", "Boston", "Chicago", "Houston",
 8       "Los Angeles", "New York", "San Francisco",
 9       "Washington"};
10
11    private static final int[][] DISTANCES =
12      {{   0, 1110,  710,  790, 2190,  850, 2480,  620},
13       {1110,    0, 1000, 1830, 3020,  210, 3130,  450},
14       { 710, 1000,    0, 1090, 2050,  810, 2170,  710},
15       { 790, 1830, 1090,    0, 1540, 1610, 1910, 1370},
16       {2190, 3020, 2050, 1540,    0, 2790,  390, 2650},
17       { 850,  210,  810, 1610, 2790,    0, 2930,  240},
18       {2480, 3130, 2170, 1910,  390, 2930,    0, 2840},
19       { 620,  450,  710, 1370, 2650,  240, 2840,    0}};
20
21    public static void main(String[] args) {
22      // Display initial message, including a list of legal
23      // cities
24      System.out.println(
25        "This program finds the distance between two cities.\n"
26      + "Supported cities: Atlanta, Boston, Chicago, Houston,\n"
27      + "Los Angeles, New York, San Francisco, Washington.\n");
28
29      // Call getCityCode to obtain codes for starting city
30      // and destination city
```

```
31          int start = getCityCode("Enter starting city: ");
32          int destination = getCityCode("Enter destination city: ");
33
34          // Display distance between chosen cities
35          System.out.println(
36            "\nThe distance from " + CITY_NAMES[start] + " to " +
37            CITY_NAMES[destination] + " is " +
38            DISTANCES[start][destination] + " miles.");
39        }
40
41        // Prompts user to enter city name; returns corresponding
42        // city code. If city name is not recognized, allows user
43        // to enter another name.
44        private static int getCityCode(String prompt) {
45          while (true) {
46            SimpleIO.prompt(prompt);
47            String cityName = SimpleIO.readLine().trim();
48
49            for (int i = 0; i < CITY_NAMES.length; i++)
50              if (cityName.equalsIgnoreCase(CITY_NAMES[i]))
51                return i;
52
53            System.out.println("City name was not recognized.");
54          }
55        }
56      }
```

Review Questions

1. What is the maximum number of dimensions for an array in Java?

2. If a is a two-dimensional array, which is the correct way to access the element of a in row i, column j: a[i, j] or a[i][j]?

3. If a is a two-dimensional array, how can we determine how many rows a has? How many columns?

4. Describe three ways to use a multidimensional array to store a color image.

5. Suppose that an array of double values has 50 rows and 40 columns. How many bytes of memory will be required to store the elements of the array?

6. A two-dimensional array whose rows have different lengths is said to be a _____ array.

13.2 The Vector Class

Although arrays play an important role in Java—and in many other programming languages—they suffer from a significant limitation. Every array has a fixed number of elements. We can make an array as large as we like (subject to memory restrictions, of course!), but once we've allocated the array, we can never change its size. If we need room for more elements, the best we can do is to allocate space for a new, larger array and then copy the values of the old array into the new one.

Fortunately, Java provides a class that we can use when we want an array that can grow (or perhaps shrink) during the execution of a program. That class is named `Vector`, and it belongs to the `java.util` package. `java.util` contains other data structure classes besides `Vector`—we'll meet one of them in Section 13.6—but `Vector` is probably the most important.

A *vector* (an instance of the `Vector` class, not a mathematical vector) is an array-like object that stores references to other objects. There's no limit on the number of objects that can be stored in a `Vector` object, nor is there any restriction on what type of objects can be stored. (Most of the time, the objects in a vector will belong to a single class, but that's not required.) The elements of a vector, like the elements of an array, are indexed from 0.

There are two key differences between vectors and arrays:

- *Vectors can grow or shrink as needed.* An array, once created, can't change its size.

- *Vectors must contain objects.* A vector can't store values of a primitive type (although there's a way to work around this restriction, as we'll see in Section 13.3).

Each vector has a *capacity* and a *capacity increment.* The capacity is the number of elements the vector can store without requiring additional memory. When a vector becomes full, Java will automatically increase its capacity by the amount of the capacity increment. The *size* of a vector—the number of items that it currently stores—is always less than or equal to its capacity. The following figure illustrates the difference between the size of a vector and its capacity:

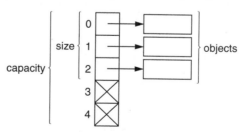

This vector's capacity is five, but its size is only three, because only three elements of the vector are currently being used. These elements contain references to objects. (Vectors *always* store references to objects, never values of primitive types.) The remaining two elements aren't in use, so their values are shown as ✕. Keep in mind that a vector is an object, although—for simplicity—I've drawn it in the same way as an array. A vector stores more than just a series of elements; it also has to keep track of its size, capacity, and capacity increment.

Table 13.1 on the next page shows the constructors for the `Vector` class.

Table 13.1
Vector Constructors

Description	Action
Vector()	Creates an empty vector.
Vector(int initialCapacity)	Creates an empty vector with the specified initial capacity.
Vector(int initialCapacity, int capacityIncrement)	Creates an empty vector with the specified initial capacity and capacity increment.

As an example, let's use the single-argument constructor to create a vector with an initial capacity of five elements:

```
Vector v = new Vector(5);
```

Here's how we might visualize the vector:

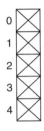

The vector consists of five elements, each of which is capable of storing a reference to an object. The size of the vector is currently 0.

The Vector class has a large number of methods. Let's look at some of the more commonly used methods, breaking these into groups of related methods. Table 13.2 shows the first group of methods, which let us store data into a vector.

Table 13.2
Vector Methods for
Storing Elements

Description	Action
void addElement(Object obj)	Adds an object to the end of this vector.
void insertElementAt(Object obj, int index)	Inserts an object into this vector at the specified position.
void setElementAt(Object obj, int index)	Stores an object into this vector at the specified position.

Notice that all three methods have a parameter named obj, which represents the object to be stored in the vector. obj is declared to be of type Object, which means that we can supply any kind of object as the argument when we call one of these methods. (We saw in Section 11.5 that Object parameters have this property because every class is—directly or indirectly—a subclass of Object.) I'll use String objects in my examples, but other kinds of objects will work just as well.

When we store an object in a vector, we'll have to decide whether we want to *add* the object after all objects currently stored in the vector (addElement), *insert* the object somewhere in the middle of the vector (`insertElementAt`), or *replace* an existing object with the new one (`setElementAt`). Let's try all three techniques, taking a look at the vector after each operation.

addElement   First, we'll add a few objects to the vector v that we created previously:

```
v.addElement("a");          // Stores "a" at position 0
v.addElement("b");          // Stores "b" at position 1
v.addElement("c");          // Stores "c" at position 2
```

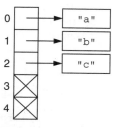

The size of the vector increases automatically each time `addElement` is called, going from 0 to 1 to 2 to 3. Notice that we don't have to tell `addElement` where to put the new object; it uses the vector's size to determine which slot will be the next to be filled.

insertElementAt   Next, we'll insert an object at position 1:

```
v.insertElementAt("d", 1);  // Inserts "d" at position 1
```

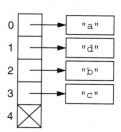

The objects stored at positions 1 and 2 were moved down one position to make room for "d". The `insertElementAt` method throws an `ArrayIndex-OutOfBoundsException` if the second argument isn't a number between 0 and the size of the vector.

setElementAt   Finally, let's replace the object stored at position 2:

```
v.setElementAt("e", 2);     // Stores "e" at position 2
```

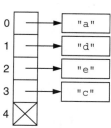

Notice that the "e" object has replaced the "b" object in the vector. The size of the vector (4) hasn't changed. Again, there's a possibility of an ArrayIndexOutOfBoundsException if the second argument to setElementAt is out of range.

 Be careful when using insertElementAt or setElementAt. The second argument in a call of insertElementAt (the index at which the new element is to be inserted) must be *less than or equal to* the vector's current size. The second argument in a call of setElementAt (the index at which the new element is to be stored) must be *less than* the vector's current size.

Storing objects into a vector is easy; retrieving them is slightly harder. The methods that we'll use are shown in Table 13.3.

Table 13.3
Vector Methods for
Retrieving Elements

Description	*Action*
Object elementAt(int index)	Returns the element at the specified index.
Object firstElement()	Returns the first element of this vector.
Object lastElement()	Returns the last element of this vector.

The problem with retrieving objects is that the methods in Table 13.3 are designed to retrieve *any* kind of object from a vector, and so their return type is Object. When we retrieve an element from a vector, we'll always get an Object value, which isn't quite what we want. If we want to save the element in a variable, it would have to be an Object variable. If we do that, however, we won't be able to call the object's methods, because the Java compiler will allow us to use only methods that belong to the Object class. The solution to our problem

casting objects ➤ 11.4

elementAt

is to cast the value returned by the retrieval methods.

Suppose that we call elementAt to obtain the element stored at a particular position in a vector. If we know that the vector contains only String objects, we would cast the return value to String:

```
String str = (String) v.elementAt(2);    // str will be "e"
```

If we're wrong, and the element turns out not to be a String object, a ClassCastException will be thrown.

firstElement

The firstElement method returns the first element in a vector:

```
String str = (String) v.firstElement();  // str will be "a"
```

lastElement

The lastElement method returns the last element in a vector:

```
String str = (String) v.lastElement();   // str will be "c"
```

The elementAt method throws ArrayIndexOutOfBounds if its argument is out of bounds (less than 0 or not less than the vector's current size). firstElement and lastElement throw ArrayIndexOutOfBounds if the vector is empty.

Table 13.4 lists the methods for removing elements from a vector.

Table 13.4
Vector Methods for
Removing Elements

Description	*Action*
`void removeAllElements()`	Removes all elements from this vector and sets its size to zero.
`boolean removeElement(Object obj)`	Removes the first occurrence of the specified object from this vector. Returns `true` if the object was found in the vector.
`void removeElementAt(int index)`	Removes the element at the specified index.

removeAllElements

The `removeAllElements` method removes all elements from a vector:

```
v.removeAllElements();   // Removes all elements from v
```

The size of `v` will be zero after this call.

removeElement

The `removeElement` method removes a single occurrence of a particular element. If the specified element occurs more than once in the vector, only the first occurrence is removed. `removeElement` returns a `boolean` value that can be tested to determine whether or not an element was removed. If `removeElement` returns `true`, then a matching element was found and removed. If it returns `false`, the vector is unchanged.

```
v.removeElement("a");   // Removes first occurrence of "a"
```

removeElementAt

The `removeElementAt` method removes the element stored at a particular index in the vector:

```
v.removeElementAt(1);   // Removes element at position 1
```

When an element is removed from a vector at position *i*, both `removeElement` and `removeElementAt` will fill the resulting "hole" by shifting the elements starting at position *i* + 1 to the next lower position.

The methods in the next group (Table 13.5) are used to search a vector.

Table 13.5
Vector Methods
for Searching

Description	*Action*
`boolean contains(Object elem)`	Returns `true` if the specified object is an element in this vector.
`int indexOf(Object elem)`	Returns the index of the first occurrence of the specified object.
`int indexOf(Object elem, int index)`	Returns the index of the first occurrence of the specified object, beginning the search at the specified position.
`int lastIndexOf(Object elem)`	Returns the index of the last occurrence of the specified object.
`int lastIndexOf(Object elem, int index)`	Returns the index of the last occurrence of the specified object, beginning the search at the specified position.

contains　　　The `contains` method searches a vector for a specified element, returning `true` if it finds the element and `false` otherwise:

```
if (v.contains("a")) ...          // Tests whether v contains "a"
```

indexOf　　　The `indexOf` method searches a vector for a specified element, returning the index of the element (or −1 if the element isn't found). There are two versions of `indexOf`. One version starts looking at the beginning of the vector; the other version begins its search at a specified index.

```
index = v.indexOf("a");           // Finds first occurrence of
                                  // "a" in v

index = v.indexOf("a", 10);       // Finds first occurrence of
                                  // "a" in v, starting at
                                  // position 10
```

lastIndexOf　　　The `lastIndexOf` method performs a reverse-order search for a specified element, returning the index of the element (or −1 if the element isn't found). There are two versions of `lastIndexOf`. One version starts looking at the end of the vector; the other version begins its search at a specified index.

```
index = v.lastIndexOf("a");       // Finds last occurrence of
                                  // "a" in v

index = v.lastIndexOf("a", 10);   // Finds last occurrence of
                                  // "a" in v, starting at
                                  // position 10
```

In these examples, I'm assuming that `index` is an `int` variable.

One important thing to know about the `contains`, `indexOf`, and `lastIndexOf` methods is that they use the `equals` method, not the `==` operator, to test whether an object in the vector matches the one we're looking for. For example, two strings will test equal if they contain the same characters; it's not necessary for the references to the strings to match.

The methods in the last group (Table 13.6) are related to the size and capacity of a vector.

Table 13.6

`Vector` Methods Related to Size and Capacity

Description	Action
`int capacity()`	Returns the capacity of this vector.
`void ensureCapacity` `  (int minCapacity)`	Increases the capacity of this vector, if necessary, to the specified value.
`boolean isEmpty()`	Returns `true` if this vector has no elements.
`void setSize(int newSize)`	Changes the size of this vector to the specified value.
`int size()`	Returns the size of this vector.
`void trimToSize()`	Reduces the capacity of this vector to its current size.

capacity　　　　The `capacity` method returns the current capacity of a vector:

```
int capacity = v.capacity();   // Gets current capacity of v
```

ensureCapacity　　　The `ensureCapacity` method increases the capacity of a vector, if necessary, to a specified value. If the vector's current capacity is greater than or equal to the desired capacity, the method does nothing.

```
v.ensureCapacity(100);          // Ensures capacity of 100
```

If we need to add a large number of additional values to a vector, increasing the vector's capacity in advance can be more efficient than allowing the vector to increase its capacity automatically.

isEmpty　　　　The `isEmpty` method returns `true` if a vector is empty (its size is zero) and `false` otherwise:

```
if (v.isEmpty()) …              // Tests whether v is empty
```

setSize　　　　The `setSize` method changes the size of a vector to a specified value. If the vector's current size exceeds the specified value, the excess elements are lost. If the vector's size is smaller than the specified value, `null` values are added at the end of the vector.

```
v.setSize(10);                  // Changes size of v to 10
```

size　　　　The `size` method returns the current size of a vector:

```
int size = v.size();            // Gets the current size of v
```

trimToSize　　　The `trimToSize` method reduces the capacity of a vector so it exactly matches the vector's current size:

```
v.trimToSize();                 // Reduces capacity of v to
                                // its current size
```

The only reason to use `trimToSize` is to conserve memory. The best time to call `trimToSize` is after the vector has reached its maximum size, at a time when no new elements will be inserted.

Arrays Versus Vectors

When we write a program that will need to store multiple items of data, we'll often need to choose between using an array to store the data and using a vector. Here are some of the factors we'll need to consider:

- *Flexibility.* Vectors clearly have the edge in this category because they can grow automatically. An array can be replaced by a larger array when it fills up (as we saw in Section 5.7), but we have to write code to allocate the new array and copy elements from the old array into the new one.

- *Ease of use.* Arrays are generally easier to use than vectors. Square brackets make it easy to select an element within an array; accessing an element of a vector requires a method call. The elements of a vector must be cast to the proper type when they are retrieved; arrays have no such disadvantage. The elements of an array can be of any (single) type, including both primitive types and object types; the elements of a vector must be objects, making life more difficult if we need to store values of a primitive type. (Section 13.3 shows the technique we'll need to use.) On the other hand, the Vector class provides useful methods such as insertElementAt, which take care of moving elements to make room for the one being inserted; if we were to use an array instead, we would have to write the code to move the elements.

■ *Efficiency.* Here we need to consider both space efficiency and time efficiency. If the number of elements is known in advance, arrays are more space efficient than vectors. If the number of elements isn't known, an array may be less efficient, because we'll probably end up making it too large. As far as time goes, arrays are slightly more efficient than vectors for comparable operations, but the difference is fairly small. However, if a vector becomes full and is forced to resize itself, there will be a time penalty.

Although vectors are useful in a lot of programming situations, they do have drawbacks. In particular, there's no way to force the elements of a vector to be of the same type. If a program stores objects of the wrong type in a vector because of a programming error, the compiler won't be able to detect the error.

PROGRAM   **Reversing a Series of Lines**

Let's write an application named ReverseLines that reverses a series of lines entered by the user. When we run the program, the user will enter any number of input lines, which the program will store. When the user enters a blank line (by pressing the Enter key without entering any characters on the line), the program stops accepting input. At that point, it will display—in reverse order—the lines originally entered by the user. For example, here's what will happen if the user enters a portion of Shakespeare's *Hamlet:*

```
Enter lines to be reversed, ending with a blank line.
To be, or not to be: that is the question:
Whether 'tis nobler in the mind to suffer
The slings and arrows of outrageous fortune,
Or to take arms against a sea of troubles,
And by opposing end them? To die: to sleep;
No more; and, by a sleep to say we end
The heartache and the thousand natural shocks
That flesh is heir to, 'tis a consummation
Devoutly to be wish'd. To die, to sleep;
To sleep: perchance to dream: ay, there's the rub;
For in that sleep of death what dreams may come
                                    ← user enters a blank line
```

```
For in that sleep of death what dreams may come
To sleep: perchance to dream: ay, there's the rub;
Devoutly to be wish'd. To die, to sleep;
That flesh is heir to, 'tis a consummation
The heartache and the thousand natural shocks
No more; and, by a sleep to say we end
And by opposing end them? To die: to sleep;
Or to take arms against a sea of troubles,
The slings and arrows of outrageous fortune,
Whether 'tis nobler in the mind to suffer
To be, or not to be: that is the question:
```

ReverseLines can't begin displaying the reversed lines until the user has finished entering the original lines. As a result, the program will need to store the lines (as strings) in a data structure. Using an array for this purpose doesn't sound too appealing, because we'd have to put some arbitrary limit on the number of lines entered by the user (or have the program resize the array each time it becomes full). It's usually best to avoid arbitrary restrictions—they tend to make users unhappy. (You never know—perhaps someone with too much time on his or her hands will try to enter the entire text of *Hamlet,* which exceeds 4000 lines.) Storing the lines in a vector will let us avoid placing a limit on the number of input lines.

ReverseLines.java

```
 1  // Reverses a series of lines entered by the user
 2
 3  import java.util.*;
 4  import jpb.*;
 5
 6  public class ReverseLines {
 7    public static void main(String[] args) {
 8      // Prompt user to enter lines
 9      System.out.println("Enter lines to be reversed, " +
10                          "ending with a blank line.");
11
12      // Create vector to hold lines
13      Vector lines = new Vector();
14
15      // Read lines and store in vector
16      while (true) {
17        String inputLine = SimpleIO.readLine();
18        if (inputLine.length() == 0)
19          break;
20        lines.addElement(inputLine);
21      }
22
23      // Display elements of vector in reverse order
24      for (int i = lines.size() - 1; i >= 0; i--)
25        System.out.println(lines.elementAt(i));
26    }
27  }
```

Review Questions

1. How many elements can a vector store?

2. What kinds of objects can be stored in a vector?

3. What is the difference between the *capacity* of a vector and the *size* of a vector?

4. Why do we usually need to cast the value returned by `firstElement`, `lastElement`, or `elementAt`?

5. List two advantages of vectors over arrays.

6. List two advantages of arrays over vectors.

13.3   Wrapper Classes

Although vectors have several advantages, they appear to suffer from a serious flaw: their elements must be objects. Apparently, a vector of integers or floating-point numbers is out of the question. As it turns out, however, we can get around this restriction, thanks to ***wrapper classes.*** An instance of a wrapper class is an object that contains a single value of a primitive type. Instead of storing an integer into a vector, for example, we can store an object that *contains* an integer as its only instance variable.

Java's wrapper classes belong to the `java.lang` package. Each primitive type has a corresponding wrapper class (Table 13.7).

Table 13.7
Wrapper Classes

Primitive Type	*Wrapper Class*
boolean	Boolean
byte	Byte
char	Character
double	Double
float	Float
int	Integer
long	Long
short	Short

Notice that the primitive type names don't always match the wrapper class names (`char` versus `Character` and `int` versus `Integer`).

Using Wrapper Classes to Create Objects

To convert a value of a primitive type into an object, we use the constructor for the matching wrapper class. For example, suppose that `x` is a `double` variable. To convert the value of `x` to an object, we would use the `Double` constructor:

```
Double d = new Double(x);
```

doubleValue The object d will contain the value of x as an instance variable. To retrieve the value later, we would call the doubleValue method:

```
double y = d.doubleValue();
```

The other wrapper classes work in a similar fashion. Each has a constructor that converts a value of a primitive type into a wrapper object, and each has one or more methods that will return the stored value upon request. Table 13.8 shows the names of these methods.

Table 13.8
Retrieval Methods for
Wrapper Classes

Wrapper Class	*Retrieval Method(s)*
Boolean	booleanValue
Byte	byteValue, doubleValue, floatValue, intValue, longValue, shortValue
Character	charValue
Double	byteValue, doubleValue, floatValue, intValue, longValue, shortValue
Float	byteValue, doubleValue, floatValue, intValue, longValue, shortValue
Integer	byteValue, doubleValue, floatValue, intValue, longValue, shortValue
Long	byteValue, doubleValue, floatValue, intValue, longValue, shortValue
Short	byteValue, doubleValue, floatValue, intValue, longValue, shortValue

Note that each numeric class (Byte, Double, Float, Integer, Long, Short) has six retrieval methods, allowing the stored value to be retrieved with any desired type. If the value isn't retrieved in its "natural" form (for example, if we retrieve an int value from a Double object), the value stored inside the object is cast to the desired type.

Using the Wrapper Classes with Vectors

Suppose that we need a vector whose elements belong to a primitive type, such as double. We can't store double values in a vector directly, but we can store Double objects instead.

If x is a double variable, we can use the following statement to store the value of x in the vector v at position i:

```
v.setElementAt(new Double(x), i);
```

To retrieve the number later, we can use the doubleValue method:

```
Double d = (Double) v.elementAt(i);
double y = d.doubleValue();
```

Or, at the risk of some confusion, we can combine the two statements:

```
double y = ((Double) v.elementAt(i)).doubleValue();
```

Other Uses of Wrapper Classes

Wrapper classes serve a second purpose in Java. In addition to allowing values of primitive types to be treated as objects, each wrapper class provides class variables and methods that are related to the corresponding primitive type.

Each wrapper class (other than `Boolean`) contains constants named `MIN_VALUE` and `MAX_VALUE`, which represent the smallest and largest values of the corresponding primitive type. For example, the value of `Short.MIN_VALUE` is –32768 and the value of `Short.MAX_VALUE` is 32767. The `Double` and `Float` classes also provide constants named NaN, `NEGATIVE_INFINITY`, and `POSITIVE_INFINITY`.

Each wrapper class (other than `Boolean` and `Character`) also provides a class method that converts a string into a value of the corresponding primitive type. We've used these methods, especially `Integer.parseInt`, on many occasions. Prior to JDK version 1.2, the `Double` and `Float` classes lacked such a method, however. Starting with version 1.2, the `Double` class provides a `parseDouble` method, and the `Float` class provides a `parseFloat` method.

Review Questions

1. What restriction on vectors do wrapper classes let us circumvent?

2. Name two wrapper classes whose names don't match the names of the corresponding primitive types.

3. Each wrapper class (other than `Boolean`) contains constants that represent the smallest and largest values of the corresponding primitive type. What are the names of these constants?

4. Each wrapper class provides class methods that are related to the corresponding primitive type. Name a frequently used class method that belongs to the `Integer` class.

13.4 Sorting

One of the most fundamental (and common) operations in programming is *sorting:* putting a list of data items in order. Magazine publishers sort their mailing lists by zip code in order to get the most favorable postal rate. Libraries sort books by their Library of Congress numbers so patrons can easily locate a particular book.

Defining the meaning of "sorted" is trickier than you might think. Consider the following lists of data, which are all sorted:

Numbers: −53 −38 9 16 45 66 89
Characters: *0 1 A B a b*
Strings: *aardvark ant anteater bat cat*

Numbers have a natural ordering, so it's clear that −53 comes before −38, which comes before 9, and so forth. Characters are a little trickier; it's not clear that *0* and *1* are less than *A*, for example. In Java, the ordering of characters is based on their Unicode values. In Unicode, digits come before letters, which explains why *0* and *1* are listed ahead of *A*, *B*, *a*, and *b*. Uppercase letters come before lowercase letters, so *A* and *B* precede *a* and *b*. Strings are normally sorted into lexicographic order.

Unicode ➤*9.4*

lexicographic order ➤*4.1*

Although data items are typically sorted into ***ascending*** order (with smaller values coming before larger ones), it's sometimes necessary to sort in ***descending*** order instead:

Ascending order: −53 −38 9 16 45 66 89
Descending order: 89 66 45 16 9 −38 −53

Sorting can be very time consuming if not done properly. (If you don't believe this, try sorting—by hand—a pile of a hundred cards containing numbers or names.) Fortunately, sorting is such a common operation that it's been studied extensively over the past forty or so years, and a number of good sorting algorithms are known. A full discussion of sorting algorithms is beyond the scope of this book, but it's not hard to describe one of the simplest algorithms, which is known as insertion sort. Before we tackle that algorithm, though, let's start by solving a slightly easier problem: how to insert a value into an array that's already sorted.

Inserting into a Sorted Array

Suppose that we want to insert items into an empty array one by one, keeping the items in sorted order at all times. We'll store the first item at position 0 in the array. If the next item to be stored is smaller than the one at position 0, we'll move the one at position 0 to position 1, and then insert the new item at position 0. On the other hand, if the next item is larger than the one at position 0, we'll simply store it at position 1. In general our algorithm will look like this:

1. For all positions in the array, from 0 to $n - 1$ (where n is the number of items stored in the array), test whether the item to be inserted is less than the one stored at position i. If so, break out of the loop.
2. Insert the new item at position i after moving the items at positions i through $n - 1$ down one position.

Here's what the algorithm looks like as Java code, where a is the name of the array, n is the number of items currently stored in the array, and `itemToInsert` is the item to be inserted into the array:

```
int i;
for (i = 0; i < n; i++)
  if (itemToInsert < a[i])
    break;
for (int j = n; j > i; j--)
  a[j] = a[j-1];
a[i] = itemToInsert;
n++;
```

If the array contains values other than numbers, we'll need to change the condition in the `if` statement. If a contains strings, for example, we'll need to change the test condition to `itemToInsert.compareTo(a[i]) < 0`.

Wait a second. Doesn't this algorithm fail if the new item is larger than all the ones already in the array? In this situation, the first loop would never execute the `break` statement, instead terminating with i equal to n. The second loop will then terminate immediately (because j > i is false). The new item will be inserted at position n, which is the correct place.

But what happens when the first item is inserted? If there are no items in the array, n must be 0, so the first loop won't execute. We'll end up in the second loop with i having the value 0. The condition j > i will be false, because j is also 0, so the second loop won't execute either. The new item will be stored at position 0, where it belongs.

Our technique for inserting items into an array illustrates an important principle of algorithm design:

> When you're designing an algorithm, don't worry about special cases at first. Design the algorithm to work in the typical case. After you've completed the algorithm, go back and check to see if it correctly handles the special cases. If it doesn't, add additional tests for those cases.

In other words, don't waste time and complicate your algorithms by worrying about all the special cases before you've designed the general algorithm.

Here are snapshots of an array as the numbers 83, 24, 56, 90, and 17 are inserted:

0 83	0 24	0 24	0 24	0 17
1	1 83	1 56	1 56	1 24
2	2	2 83	2 83	2 56
3	3	3	3 90	3 83
4	4	4	4	4 90
(a)	(b)	(c)	(d)	(e)

At step (a), 83 is inserted into the array at position 0. (The values of the other array elements are irrelevant, so I didn't show them.) At step (b), 24 is compared with 83 and found to be smaller. 83 is moved down one position and 24 is inserted in its place. At step (c), 56 is compared first with 24 and then with 83. It is smaller than 83, so 83 is moved down one position and 56 takes its place. At step (d), 90 is compared with 24, 56, and 83. It is larger than all three, so it goes after them, at position 3. At step (e), 17 is compared with 24 and found to be smaller. The values stored at positions 0 through 3 are all moved down one position, and 17 is stored at position 0.

Insertion Sort

The idea of inserting a new item into a set of items that's already in order can be used to sort an array even if all the items are already stored in the array prior to sorting.

Suppose that a is an unsorted array of integers. Our strategy for sorting a will be to insert the element at position i into the ones at positions 0 through $i - 1$ (which will already be in order). In other words, we insert the element at position 1 into the elements at positions 0 through 0, then insert the element at position 2 into the elements at positions 0 through 1, then insert the element at position 3 into the elements at positions 0 through 2, and so on. This sorting algorithm is known as *insertion sort*.

In the past, we've started at the beginning when inserting an item into a sorted array. When doing an insertion sort, however, the algorithm is simpler if we compare the element to be inserted (the one at position i) with the elements at positions $i - 1, i - 2, \ldots, 0$, working backward instead of forward. If a comparison indicates that the element to be inserted is smaller than the one at position j, then we can move the element at position j down one place in the array.

Here's a series of snapshots, showing how insertion sort sorts an array of five integers:

	(a)		(b)		(c)		(d)		(e)
0	83	0	24	0	24	0	24	0	17
1	24	1	83	1	56	1	56	1	24
2	56	2	56	2	83	2	83	2	56
3	90	3	90	3	90	3	90	3	83
4	17	4	17	4	17	4	17	4	90

Shaded elements are not yet in sorted order. Initially, we think of the element at position 0 as forming a sorted list of length 1. At step (a), the algorithm compares 24 (the first shaded element) with 83. Because 24 is smaller, 83 is moved down one position and 24 is inserted in its place, taking us to step (b). The algorithm next compares 56 with 83; because 56 is smaller, 83 is moved down one position. The algorithm now compares 56 with 24. Because 24 is smaller, it is left in place and 56 is stored at position 1. At step (c), 90 is compared with 83. Because 90 is larger, it is left in its original position. At step (d), 17 is compared with 90, 83, 56, and 24, in that order. Each element is larger than 17, so each is moved down one position and 17 is stored at position 0. The final sorted array is shown in (e).

Here's what insertion sort looks like in Java, where a is the array to be sorted:

```java
for (int i = 1; i < a.length; i++) {
  int itemToInsert = a[i];
  int j = i - 1;
  while (j >= 0 && itemToInsert < a[j]) {
    a[j+1] = a[j];
    j--;
  }
  a[j+1] = itemToInsert;
}
```

If the array contains values other than numbers, we'll need to change the condition in the while statement. If a contains strings, for example, the while statement will have the following appearance:

```java
while (j >= 0 && itemToInsert.compareTo(a[j]) < 0) {
  ...
}
```

Although insertion sort is an easy algorithm to implement in Java (and in other programming languages), it's not all that efficient. In the worst case, each element will need to be compared with all the elements that precede it in the array, for a total of

$$1 + 2 + 3 + ... + (n-1) = n(n-1)/2$$

comparisons, where n is the number of elements in the array. Table 13.9 shows the value of this formula for various array sizes.

Table 13.9
Worst-Case Number of Comparisons Performed by Insertion Sort

Array Size	Number of Comparisons
10	45
100	4,950
1,000	499,500
10,000	49,995,000
100,000	4,999,950,000

The worst-case number of comparisons is approximately $n^2/2$, so the time required to sort grows rapidly as n increases. For sorting small arrays (up to 100 elements or so), insertion sort is usually fast enough. For larger arrays, better algorithms are necessary.

Q&A

PROGRAM   **Sorting a Series of Lines**

Let's write a program named SortLines that sorts a series of lines entered by the user. When the user enters a blank line, SortLines will display the lines entered by the user, sorted into lexicographic order. Here's an example:

Enter lines to be sorted, ending with a blank line.
To be, or not to be: that is the question:
Whether 'tis nobler in the mind to suffer
The slings and arrows of outrageous fortune,
Or to take arms against a sea of troubles,
And by opposing end them? To die: to sleep;
No more; and, by a sleep to say we end
The heartache and the thousand natural shocks
That flesh is heir to, 'tis a consummation
Devoutly to be wish'd. To die, to sleep;
To sleep: perchance to dream: ay, there's the rub;
For in that sleep of death what dreams may come
                                    ← *user enters a blank line*
And by opposing end them? To die: to sleep;
Devoutly to be wish'd. To die, to sleep;
For in that sleep of death what dreams may come
No more; and, by a sleep to say we end
Or to take arms against a sea of troubles,
That flesh is heir to, 'tis a consummation
The heartache and the thousand natural shocks
The slings and arrows of outrageous fortune,
To be, or not to be: that is the question:
To sleep: perchance to dream: ay, there's the rub;
Whether 'tis nobler in the mind to suffer

Because the number of lines isn't known in advance, a vector would seem to be the right data structure. And because the lines are read one by one, we can insert them into the vector so that it remains sorted at all times. The algorithm for inserting into a sorted vector is nearly the same as the one for inserting into a sorted array. The only difference is that we won't need a loop to move existing elements. Instead, we can call the `insertElementAt` method to insert each new line, which will automatically shift existing elements to make room for the new one.

SortLines.java

```
1   // Sorts a series of lines entered by the user
2
3   import java.util.*;
4   import jpb.*;
5
6   public class SortLines {
7     public static void main(String[] args) {
8       // Prompt user to enter lines
9       System.out.println("Enter lines to be sorted, " +
10                          "ending with a blank line.");
11
12      // Create vector to store lines
13      Vector v = new Vector();
14
15      // Read lines and insert into vector; elements will be
16      // kept in order at all times
17      while (true) {
18
```

```
19        // Read a line; exit loop if line is empty
20        String inputLine = SimpleIO.readLine();
21        if (inputLine.length() == 0)
22          break;
23
24        // Determine where line should be stored in vector
25        int i;
26        for (i = 0; i < v.size(); i++)
27          if (inputLine.compareTo((String) v.elementAt(i)) < 0)
28            break;
29
30        // Insert line at this position. Existing elements will
31        // be moved to make room for the new element.
32        v.insertElementAt(inputLine, i);
33      }
34
35      // Display elements of vector
36      for (int i = 0; i < v.size(); i++)
37        System.out.println(v.elementAt(i));
38    }
39  }
```

Review Questions

1. When data items are sorted so that smaller values come before larger ones, we say that the data is in _____ order.

2. When data items are sorted so that larger values come before smaller ones, we say that the data is in _____ order.

3. The _____ _____ algorithm sorts an array by inserting the element at position i into the ones at positions 0 through $i - 1$.

4. When the algorithm in Review Question 3 is used to sort an array with 20 elements, how many comparisons does it perform (in the worst case)?

13.5 Searching

In Section 5.3, we saw how to search an array sequentially to locate a particular element. That's the best we can do if the elements of the array aren't in any particular order. If the elements of an array (or vector) are sorted, however, then a more efficient strategy, **binary search,** becomes possible.

Suppose that a is an array whose elements have been sorted into ascending order and that key is a value that we're trying to locate in the array. The binary search algorithm compares key with the element in the middle of a. If key is smaller than the middle element, the algorithm can limit its search to the first half of a; if key is larger, the algorithm searches only the last half of a. The algorithm simply repeats this process until it finds the key or runs out of elements to search.

To implement the binary search algorithm in Java, we can use two variables to keep track of which array elements are still under consideration. Let's name these variables `low` and `high`. We'll use a third variable, `mid`, to indicate the halfway point between `low` and `high`—the midpoint of the elements that are still under consideration.

Here's a Java version of the binary search algorithm:

```java
int low = 0;
int high = a.length - 1;

while (low < high) {
  int mid = (low + high) / 2;
  if (a[mid] < key)
    low = mid + 1;
  else
    high = mid;
}
```

If a contains values other than numbers, we'll need to change the condition in the `if` statement. If the elements of a are strings, for example, the statement becomes

```java
if (a[mid].compareTo(key) < 0) …
```

If the key is present in the array, the final value of `low` indicates its position in the array. If we don't know in advance that the key is present, then we'll need to add a test whether the key was found. This test can be done after the `while` loop terminates:

```java
if (a[low] == key)
  // Key was found
else
  // Key was not found
```

Here's a series of snapshots that shows how the binary search algorithm would search an array for the number 40:

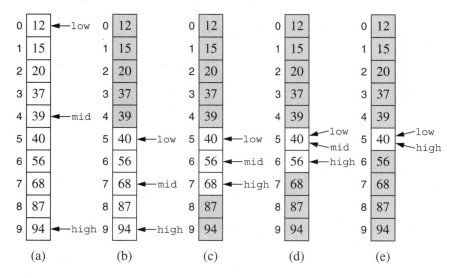

(a) (b) (c) (d) (e)

At step (a), `low` is 0 and `high` is 9, so `mid` will have the value 4. The search key, 40, is greater than the middle element (the one whose index is `mid`). As a result, we know that the elements in the first half of the array can't be equal to the key. (I've shaded elements that are known not to match the key.) At step (b), `low` has been assigned the value `mid` + 1, and a new value of `mid` has been calculated. The key is less than the middle element this time, so the elements at positions `mid` + 1 and higher can't match the key. At step (c), `high` has been assigned the value of `mid`. The key is less than the new middle element. At step (d), `high` has been assigned the value of `mid`. The key is equal to the new middle element. At step (e), `high` has been assigned the value of `mid`. The values of `low` and `high` are now equal, so the algorithm terminates. The value stored in `low` indicates where the key must be in the array, if it's there at all.

Binary search works by repeatedly dividing the array in half, so it is extremely efficient. In the worst case, it performs $\log_2 n$ comparisons, rounded up to the nearest integer, where n is the number of elements in the array. (Informally, $\log_2 n$ is the number of times we can divide n by 2 before reaching 1.) As Table 13.10 shows, the number of comparisons performed remains small even for very large values of n, because $\log_2 n$ is such a slow-growing function.

Table 13.10
Worst-Case Number of Comparisons Performed by Binary Search

Array Size	Number of Comparisons
10	4
100	7
1,000	10
10,000	14
100,000	17

PROGRAM   **Determining Air Mileage**

Let's use the binary search algorithm in a program named `AirMileage` that finds the air mileage between New York City and other international cities. The program will ask the user to enter a city name and then display the mileage to that city:

```
This program finds the air mileage between
New York and major international cities.

Enter city name: Oslo
Oslo is 3671 miles from New York City.
```

The `AirMileage` program will store the names of 36 cities in an array. A parallel array will store the distances from New York to each of the cities in the first array. Instead of using sequential search to locate the city name entered by the user, we can save a little time by using binary search.

AirMileage.java

```
1    // Determines air mileage from New York to other cities.
2    // Mileages are from The New York Public Library Desk
3    // Reference, Second Edition (New York: Prentice-Hall, 1993).
```

```
4
5   import jpb.*;
6
7   public class AirMileage {
8     // Names of international cities
9     private static final String[] CITY_NAMES =
10      {"acapulco",      "amsterdam",   "antigua",
11       "aruba",         "athens",      "barbados",
12       "bermuda",       "bogota",      "brussels",
13       "buenos aires",  "caracas",     "copenhagen",
14       "curacao",       "frankfurt",   "geneva",
15       "glasgow",       "hamburg",     "kingston",
16       "lima",          "lisbon",      "london",
17       "madrid",        "manchester",  "mexico City",
18       "milan",         "nassau",      "oslo",
19       "paris",         "reykjavik",   "rio de janeiro",
20       "rome",          "san juan",    "santo domingo",
21       "st. croix",     "tel aviv",    "zurich"};
22
23    // Distances from New York to other cities
24    private static final int[] DISTANCES =
25      {2260, 3639, 1783, 1963, 4927, 2100,  771, 2487, 3662,
26       5302, 2123, 3849, 1993, 3851, 3859, 3211, 3806, 1583,
27       3651, 3366, 3456, 3588, 3336, 2086, 4004, 1101, 3671,
28       3628, 2600, 4816, 4280, 1609, 1560, 1680, 5672, 3926};
29
30    public static void main(String[] args) {
31      // Display initial message
32      System.out.println(
33        "This program finds the air mileage between\n" +
34        "New York and major international cities.\n");
35
36      // Prompt user for city name
37      SimpleIO.prompt("Enter city name: ");
38      String cityName = SimpleIO.readLine().trim();
39
40      // Use binary search to locate name in CITY_NAMES array
41      int i = binarySearch(CITY_NAMES, cityName.toLowerCase());
42
43      // If name was found in array, display distance from New
44      // York to chosen city
45      if (cityName.equalsIgnoreCase(CITY_NAMES[i]))
46        System.out.println(cityName + " is " + DISTANCES[i] +
47                           " miles from New York City.");
48      else
49        System.out.println(cityName + " wasn't found.");
50    }
51
52    // Uses the binary search algorithm to locate key in the
53    // array a. Returns the index of key if it is found in a.
54    private static int binarySearch(String[] a, String key) {
55      int low = 0;
56      int high = a.length - 1;
57
```

```
58      while (low < high) {
59        int mid = (low + high) / 2;
60        if (a[mid].compareTo(key) < 0)
61          low = mid + 1;
62        else
63          high = mid;
64      }
65      return low;
66    }
67  }
```

Review Questions

1. What requirement is necessary in order to be able to use binary search with a particular array?

2. When the binary search algorithm terminates, what does the final value of the `low` variable indicate?

3. Why is binary search so efficient?

4. In the worst case, how many comparisons will binary search perform when searching an array of 500 elements?

13.6 Sets

In mathematics, a **set** is an unordered collection of values, with no duplicates. Sets are usually enclosed in curly braces. For example, {3, 9, 11} would be a set consisting of three elements: 3, 9, and 11.

Sets are just as useful to programmers as they are to mathematicians. What distinguishes sets from other data structures are the following properties:

- A set has no duplicate elements.
- The elements of a set don't have to be stored in any particular order.
- Operations on sets are different from those on other data structures.

Typical set operations include:

- Storing a value into a set. If the value is already an element of the set, this operation has no effect.
- Removing a value from a set. If the value is not an element of the set, this operation has no effect.
- Testing whether a value belongs to a set.
- Computing the union of two sets (the set of all elements that belong to either, or both, of the sets).
- Computing the intersection of two sets (the set of all elements that belong to both sets).

For example, sets might be useful if we were writing a program that plays a card game; we could use a set to keep track of which cards are in a player's hand.

In a program that works with English text, we could use a set to keep track of which letters appear in a word or sentence.

Bit Sets

Some programming languages—Pascal in particular—provide sets as a language feature. Java doesn't go that far, but it does give us the `BitSet` class, whose instances (***bit sets***) can be used to represent sets. The `BitSet` class, like the `Vector` class, belongs to the `java.util` package.

At first glance, a bit set doesn't look much like a set. It behaves more like a vector whose elements are `boolean` values. However, by setting some of the elements of a bit set to `true` and the others to `false`, we can use it to keep track of the elements in a set. For example, suppose that we want a set that stores all positive integers no larger than 15 that are divisible by 2. In mathematical notation, this set would be written

$\{2, 4, 6, 8, 10, 12, 14\}$

A bit set that corresponds to this set would have the following appearance:

f	f	t	f	t	f	t	f	t	f	t	f	t	f	t	f
0	1	2	3	4	5	6	7	8	9	10	11	12	13	14	15

where f means `false` and t means `true`. Note that each element of a bit set has an integer index, starting at 0. The set of positive integers no larger than 15 that are divisible by 3 is

$\{3, 6, 9, 12, 15\}$

which would be represented by the following bit set:

f	f	f	t	f	f	t	f	f	t	f	f	t	f	f	t
0	1	2	3	4	5	6	7	8	9	10	11	12	13	14	15

Bit sets have several useful properties. Because the elements of a bit set have only two possible values (`true` or `false`), Java can store each element as a single bit (0 or 1). As a result, a bit set requires considerably less memory than an array or vector containing ordinary `boolean` values.

Another advantage of a bit set is that it will automatically increase its size as needed. If we change the value of a bit from `false` to `true`, and the position of that bit lies outside the bit set's current range, Java will increase the size of the bit set to accommodate the new bit.

To create a bit set, we'll need to use one of the `BitSet` constructors, which are shown in Table 13.11.

Table 13.11
`BitSet` Constructors

Description	Action
`BitSet()`	Creates a bit set with no specified size.
`BitSet(int nbits)`	Creates a bit set containing the specified number of bits.

For example, to create the sets described earlier, we can use the following declarations:

```
BitSet multiplesOf2 = new BitSet(16);
BitSet multiplesOf3 = new BitSet(16);
```

set

In a newly created bit set, all bits have the value `false`. To change some of the bits to `true`, we'll need to call the `set` method:

```
multiplesOf2.set(2);    // Sets the bit at position 2
multiplesOf2.set(4);
multiplesOf2.set(6);
multiplesOf2.set(8);
multiplesOf2.set(10);
multiplesOf2.set(12);
multiplesOf2.set(14);

multiplesOf3.set(3);
multiplesOf3.set(6);
multiplesOf3.set(9);
multiplesOf3.set(12);
multiplesOf3.set(15);
```

Setting a bit is one of the three basic operations on a bit set. The others are clearing a bit and retrieving the value of a bit (Table 13.12).

Table 13.12
Basic Operations
on Bit Sets

Description	*Action*
`void clear(int bit)`	Sets the bit with the specified index to `false`.
`boolean get(int bit)`	Returns the value of the bit with the specified index.
`void set(int bit)`	Sets the bit with the specified index to `true`.

clear

The `clear` method "clears" a bit by setting it to `false`:

```
multiplesOf2.clear(2);       // Clears the bit at position 2
```

get

The `get` method returns the value stored at a specific bit position. We'll typically call `get` as part of an `if` statement:

```
if (multiplesOf2.get(2)) …  // Tests the bit at position 2
```

Bit sets support several Boolean operations—*and, or,* and *exclusive or*—which correspond to the set operations of intersection, union, and symmetric difference. (The symmetric difference of two sets is the set of all elements that belong to one set but not the other.) Table 13.13 lists the `BitSet` methods that perform Boolean operations. Notice that all three methods are `void`—they modify the calling object rather than returning a new bit set.

Table 13.13
Boolean Operations
on Bit Sets

Description	*Action*
`void and(BitSet set)`	Modifies this bit set by *and*ing it with the argument.
`void or(BitSet set)`	Modifies this bit set by *or*ing it with the argument.
`void xor(BitSet set)`	Modifies this bit set by *xor*ing it with the argument.

and   The `and` method combines two bit sets by performing a logical *and* operation on all corresponding bits in the sets. For example, suppose that we call the `and` method as follows:

```
multiplesOf2.and(multiplesOf3);
```

`multiplesOf2` will be modified so that it has `true` values only in those positions where both `multiplesOf2` and `multiplesOf3` originally had `true` values (positions 6 and 12).

or   The `or` method is similar to the `and` method, except that it performs a logical *or* operation on the two bit sets. If we call the `or` method as follows, the resulting set will have `true` values only in those positions where `multiplesOf2` or `multiplesOf3` (or both) has a `true` value (positions 2, 3, 4, 6, 8, 9, 10, 12, 14, and 15).

```
multiplesOf2.or(multiplesOf3);
```

xor   The `xor` method is similar to the `or` method, except that it produces a `true` result only in those positions where one of the original sets (but not both) has a `true` value. If we call the `xor` method as follows, the resulting set will have `true` values in positions 2, 3, 4, 8, 9, 10, 14, and 15:

```
multiplesOf2.xor(multiplesOf3);
```

PROGRAM   **Finding Primes Using the Sieve of Eratosthenes**

The Greek mathematician Eratosthenes (c. 276–194 B.C.) devised an efficient way to find prime numbers, known as the ***sieve of Eratosthenes.*** (A number is ***prime*** if it is evenly divisible only by itself and 1.) To use his strategy with pencil and paper, we would first write down a list of the integers from 2 to some maximum value. We would then cross off every second number after 2. (These numbers are all divisible by 2, so they can't be primes.) We would next look for the first number after 2 that wasn't crossed off (3, in this case) and cross off all multiples of 3, starting at 6. By repeating the process enough times, all non-primes would be crossed off, leaving only the primes:

$$2 \quad 3 \quad \cancel{4} \quad 5 \quad \cancel{6} \quad 7 \quad \cancel{8}\,\cancel{9}\,\cancel{10} \quad 11 \quad \cancel{12} \quad 13 \quad \cancel{14}\,\cancel{15}\,\cancel{16} \quad 17 \quad \cancel{18} \quad 19 \quad \cancel{20}\,\cancel{21}\,\cancel{22} \quad 23 \quad \cancel{24}\,\cancel{25}$$

To implement the sieve of Eratosthenes in Java, we can use a bit set to keep track of which numbers have been crossed off. Initially, all bits at positions 2 and higher will be set, indicating that these numbers are potential primes. (0 and 1 aren't primes, so we'll ignore those positions in the bit set.) "Crossing off" a number will consist of clearing the corresponding bit.

Sieve.java

```
1  // Finds primes using the sieve of Eratosthenes
2
3  import java.util.*;
4  import jpb.*;
5
```

```
 6   public class Sieve {
 7     public static void main(String[] args) {
 8       // Prompt user to enter a bound on the largest prime
 9       SimpleIO.prompt("Enter bound on largest prime: ");
10       String userInput = SimpleIO.readLine().trim();
11       int bound = Integer.parseInt(userInput);
12
13       // Create a bit set; bits 0 and 1 will not be used
14       BitSet primes = new BitSet(bound + 1);
15
16       // Set all bits, starting at position 2
17       for (int i = 2; i <= bound; i++)
18         primes.set(i);
19
20       // Clear bits that correspond to multiples of a prime
21       for (int i = 2; i * i <= bound; i++)
22         if (primes.get(i))
23           for (int j = 2 * i; j <= bound; j += i)
24             primes.clear(j);
25
26       // Display all numbers whose bits are still set
27       System.out.println("Primes: " + primes);
28     }
29   }
```

Note that the `for` statement on line 21 tests the condition $i * i <= bound$, terminating when it is false (in other words, when the value of i exceeds the square root of `bound`). Any number that isn't prime must have a divisor that's no larger than its square root, allowing us to use this test, instead of a less efficient condition such as $i <= bound$.

Here's what the output of the program looks like:

```
Enter bound on largest prime: 25
Primes: {2, 3, 5, 7, 11, 13, 17, 19, 23}
```

Notice that the statement on line 27 implicitly uses the `toString` method to convert the `primes` bit set into a string. As this output shows, `toString` returns a string containing the contents of a bit set in mathematical notation. This string lists the positions of all `true` elements, separated by commas and enclosed in curly braces.

Review Questions

1.   Which does a bit set more closely resemble: an array or a vector?

2.   What advantage does a bit set have over an array or vector?

3.   What are the values of the bits in a newly created bit set?

4.   To what set operations do the `and`, `or`, and `xor` methods correspond?

13.7 The `StringBuffer` Class

`String` objects are immutable: once a `String` object has been created, the characters in it can never be changed. Fortunately, Java provides another class, `StringBuffer`, that we can use in conjunction with the `String` class. A `StringBuffer` object (or *string buffer,* as we'll call it) is similar to a `String` object, except that we can change the characters in a string buffer.

In the computing field, a *buffer* is a place where data is stored temporarily, usually on its way from one place to another. For example, when a program reads data from a disk, the data is placed in a buffer first, and the program then obtains the data from the buffer. A string buffer is a temporary place to store a string as it's being changed. Because `String` objects can't be modified directly, changing a `String` object requires three steps: (1) converting it to a string buffer, (2) changing the characters in the string buffer, then (3) converting the buffer back to a `String` object.

Each string buffer has a *capacity*—the maximum number of characters it can store. If an operation on the buffer causes the capacity to be exceeded, the capacity is increased automatically. In other words, a string buffer behaves a lot like a vector of characters.

The `StringBuffer` class, like the `String` class, belongs to the `java.lang` package. Table 13.14 lists the constructors for the `StringBuffer` class.

Table 13.14
`StringBuffer`
Constructors

Description	Action
`StringBuffer()`	Creates an empty string buffer with a capacity of 16 characters.
`StringBuffer(int length)`	Creates an empty string buffer with the specified capacity.
`StringBuffer(String str)`	Creates a string buffer containing the same sequence of characters as the specified string. The capacity of the string buffer is the length of the string plus 16.

The following examples show how these constructors would be used:

```
StringBuffer stringBuf1 = new StringBuffer();
StringBuffer stringBuf2 = new StringBuffer(100);
StringBuffer stringBuf3 =
  new StringBuffer("antidisestablishmentarianism");
```

`strBuf1` will have a capacity of 16 characters. The capacity of `strBuf2` will be 100, and the capacity of `strBuf3` will be 28 + 16 = 44. `strBuf1` and `strBuf2` are currently empty, but `strBuf3` contains `antidisestablishmentarianism`.

The primary operations on a string buffer are appending characters and inserting characters. *Appending* characters means adding characters to the end of the string that's currently stored in the string buffer. *Inserting* characters involves moving some of the characters already in the string and then putting additional characters in the middle of the string. Both operations will automatically increase the capacity of the buffer if necessary.

append   Appending is done by calling one of the `append` methods that the `String-Buffer` class provides. There are 10 different versions of `append`, but they all do the same thing: append characters to the end of a string buffer. Almost any kind of data can be appended, including a string, a value of a primitive type, or an object:

```
StringBuffer stringBuf = new StringBuffer();
stringBuf.append("abc");   // stringBuf now contains "abc"
stringBuf.append(123);     // stringBuf now contains "abc123"
```

If the data to be appended isn't a string, the `append` method will automatically convert it to string form (just as `System.out.println` converts data to string form before displaying it).

The result type of the `append` method is `StringBuffer`, because `append` returns the string buffer on which the operation was performed. This property is handy, because it lets us "string" (ahem) together a series of `append` calls:

```
stringBuf.append("abc").append(123);
```

We've actually seen this behavior before, in a disguised form. To join strings together, we've used the + operator. It turns out that the + operator is actually a shorthand notation for the `append` method. For example, the statement

```
str = str1 + str2 + str3;
```

is equivalent to

```
StringBuffer stringBuf = new StringBuffer();
stringBuf.append(str1).append(str2).append(str3);
str = stringBuf.toString();
```

toString   Note that the `toString` method can be used to convert a string buffer back to ordinary string form. If we just want to print the contents of a string buffer, we don't need to call `toString` explicitly; the `System.out.print` and `System.out.println` methods will automatically call `toString`, as they do for any object.

insert   The `insert` methods that `StringBuffer` provides are similar to the `append` methods. Most versions of `insert` require two arguments. The first argument specifies an "offset" in the string buffer. The second argument is the data item to be inserted. After the insertion, the first character of this item will occupy the specified offset.

```
StringBuffer stringBuf = new StringBuffer("TH8");
stringBuf.insert(2, "X");   // stringBuf now contains "THX8"
stringBuf.insert(3, 113);   // stringBuf now contains "THX1138"
```

Any kind of data can be inserted into a string buffer, including values of primitive types as well as objects.

All the `insert` methods return the string buffer on which the operation was performed, which allows chaining:

```
stringBuf.insert(2, "X").insert(3, 113);
```

`insert` will throw `StringIndexOutOfBoundsException` if the offset is less than 0 or greater than the length of the string stored in the string buffer. Note that inserting at the end of a string is legal:

```
StringBuffer stringBuf = new StringBuffer("abc");
stringBuf.insert(3, "d");   // stringBuf now contains "abcd"
```

Here `"d"` is simply appended to `"abc"`; no existing characters will be moved.

Besides inserting and appending, the other major operations on a string buffer are accessing a character and changing a character (Table 13.15).

Table 13.15
`StringBuffer`
Methods for Accessing
and Changing a Character

Description	Action
`char charAt(int index)`	Returns the character at the specified index in this string buffer.
`void setCharAt(int index, char ch)`	Sets the character at the specified index in this string buffer to the specified character.

charAt   The `charAt` method returns the character at a specified position in a string buffer:

```
char ch = stringBuf.charAt(2);   // Returns char at position 2
```

setCharAt   The `setCharAt` method stores a character into a string buffer at a specified position:

```
stringBuf.setCharAt(2, 'a');   // Changes char at position 2
```

Several other `StringBuffer` methods are related to the length and capacity of a string buffer (see Table 13.16 on the next page).

capacity   The `capacity` method returns the current capacity of a string buffer:

```
int capacity = stringBuf.capacity();   // Gets current capacity
```

ensureCapacity   The `ensureCapacity` method increases the capacity of a string buffer, if necessary, to a specified value. If the buffer's current capacity is greater than or equal to the desired capacity, the method does nothing.

```
stringBuf.ensureCapacity(100);        // Ensures capacity of 100
```

Table 13.16
`StringBuffer`
Methods Related to
Length and Capacity

Description	*Action*
`int capacity()`	Returns the capacity of this string buffer.
`void ensureCapacity` `    (int minimumCapacity)`	Increases the capacity of this string buffer, if necessary, to the specified value.
`int length()`	Returns the length of the string stored in this string buffer.
`void setLength(int newLength)`	Sets the length of this string buffer.

length

The `length` method returns the current length of the string stored in a string buffer:

```
int length = stringBuf.length();       // Gets current length
```

setLength

The `setLength` method changes the length of a string buffer to a specified value. If the length of the string that's currently stored in the buffer is larger than the specified value, characters are removed from the end of the string. If the string's length is smaller than the specified value, null characters are added to the end of the string.

```
stringBuf.setLength(10);               // Changes length to 10
```

PROGRAM   **Sorting the Characters in a String**

Our next program illustrates the capabilities of string buffers. The program is similar to the `SortLines` program in Section 13.4, except that it sorts the characters in a string rather than the lines in a vector. The user will enter a string of characters, and the program will print the sorted version of those characters:

```
Enter a string: folderol
Sorted version of string: deflloor
```

The user's input will be stored in a string, as usual. Because we can't change that object directly, however, we'll need to create a string buffer. We'll fetch characters one by one from the original string and insert them into the string buffer, using the same algorithm we used in the `SortLines` program. We'll then print the string buffer.

SortCharacters.java

```
1  // Sorts the characters in a string
2
3  import jpb.*;
4
5  public class SortCharacters {
6    public static void main(String[] args) {
7      // Prompt user to enter a string
8      SimpleIO.prompt("Enter a string: ");
```

```
9       String userInput = SimpleIO.readLine();
10
11      // Create a string buffer to hold the sorted string
12      StringBuffer stringBuf = new StringBuffer();
13
14      // Insert characters from the user's input into the
15      // string buffer, keeping the characters in the buffer
16      // sorted at all times
17      for (int i = 0; i < userInput.length(); i++) {
18        char ch = userInput.charAt(i);
19        int j;
20        for (j = 0; j < stringBuf.length(); j++)
21          if (ch < stringBuf.charAt(j))
22            break;
23        stringBuf.insert(j, ch);
24      }
25
26      // Display contents of string buffer
27      System.out.println("Sorted version of string: " +
28                          stringBuf);
29    }
30  }
```

Review Questions

1. What purpose does the `StringBuffer` class serve?

2. In what way is a string buffer similar to a vector?

3. What are the two primary operations on a string buffer?

4. How can a `StringBuffer` object be converted back to an ordinary `String` object?

13.8 Case Study: Finding Anagrams

The idea of "sorting" is one of the most potent weapons in the programmer's arsenal; it can be used to solve a surprising number of problems, many of which initially appear to be unrelated to sorting.

As an example of the power of sorting, we'll use it to solve the problem of finding anagrams in a list of words. An ***anagram*** of a word is a permutation of the letters in that word; for example, *stop* is an anagram of *tops*. Our goal in this section is to write a program named `FindAnagrams` that prompts the user to enter a series of words and then determines which words in the list are anagrams of each other.

The `FindAnagrams` program will repeatedly prompt the user to enter words; input stops when the user presses the Enter key without entering a word. The program will then display the words, with anagrams grouped together on the same line:

```
Enter a word: pans
Enter a word: pots
Enter a word: opt
Enter a word: snap
Enter a word: stop
Enter a word: tops
Enter a word:

Anagrams:
---------
1. pans snap
2. pots stop tops
3. opt
```

We'll have the program ignore punctuation in a word (*it's* is an anagram of *sit*) and we'll have it ignore the case of letters in a word (*Pots, STOP,* and *tops* are anagrams).

Jon Bentley's excellent book, *Programming Pearls* (Second Edition, Addison-Wesley, 2000) poses the problem of finding anagrams and discusses how to solve it. Finding a good solution is harder than you might expect. As Bentley notes, "many approaches to this problem are surprisingly ineffective and complicated." Good solutions do exist, however, and one of them is based on sorting.

One problem we'll face is determining whether two words are anagrams. Without an efficient strategy, this test can require enormous amounts of time. As Bentley points out, the word *cholecystoduodenostomy* has 22! (roughly 1.124×10^{21}) permutations. Computing all permutations of *cholecystoduodenostomy* and comparing them against *duodenocholecystostomy* (an anagram) could take decades, even assuming (optimistically) that we can test a trillion permutations a second.

There's an easy way to test whether two words are anagrams, however. The trick is to compute a "signature" for each word in such a way that two words will have the same signatures if (and only if) the words are anagrams. One way to compute such a signature is to sort the letters in a word. For example, the signature of *pans* is *anps,* and the signature of *snap* is also *anps,* demonstrating that *pans* and *snap* are anagrams. Here's a table showing our words and their signatures:

Word	Signature
pans	anps
pots	opst
opt	opt
snap	anps
stop	opst
tops	opst

Uppercase letters are converted to lowercase before the signature is computed. Punctuation marks are ignored when computing signatures.

Creating signatures for words makes it easy to check whether two words are anagrams. However, we still have the problem of (apparently) having to compare every word against every other word. Actually, all we need to do is sort the lines in the table by their signatures:

Word	Signature
pans	anps
snap	anps
pots	opst
stop	opst
tops	opst
opt	opt

We next make a pass over the table from top to bottom, printing the words. Words that have the same signature are anagrams, so we print them on the same line:

```
pans snap
pots stop tops
opt
```

I've chosen to have the `FindAnagrams` program store the words and their signatures in two separate vectors named `words` and `signatures`. For each index *i*, the signature stored in position *i* of the `signatures` vector will correspond to the word stored at index *i* in the `words` vector. (The vectors are parallel, much like the parallel arrays discussed in Section 5.6.) As an alternative, I could have defined a new class, whose instances contain both a word and its signature, and then stored those objects in a single vector.

We can divide the program into two steps:

1. Read words from the user, storing the words into the `words` vector and the signatures of the words into the `signatures` vector.
2. Print the words in the `words` vector, putting words that are anagrams of each other on the same line.

Both steps appear to be fairly substantial, so let's turn them into class methods named `readWords` and `printAnagrams`.

`readWords` will need a loop that repeatedly prompts the user to enter words, stopping when the user enters an empty word. `readWords` will compute the signature of each word, storing the signature in the `signatures` vector in such a way that the vector is always sorted in ascending order. It will also store each word in the `words` vector at the same position as the signature in the `signatures` vector. Here's the pseudocode for `readWords`:

```
while (true) {
    Prompt the user to enter a word; return if the word is empty;
    Compute the signature of the word;
    Determine where the signature belongs in the signatures vector;
    Insert the signature into the signatures vector;
    Insert the word at the corresponding location in the words vector;
}
```

The printAnagrams method will print the contents of the words vector, putting words that are anagrams of each other on the same line. The method will use the signatures vector to determine which words are anagrams. Here's the pseudocode for printAnagrams:

Return if the signatures *vector is empty;*
Print a heading, followed by the first word in the words *vector;*
Print the remaining words in the words *vector, placing words on the same line if they have the same signature;*

We'll need a helper method that computes the signature of a word. Let's name this method computeSignature. Here's the pseudocode for the method; word is the word whose signature is being computed.

Create a new string buffer;
```
for (int i = 0; i < word.length(); i++) {
```
    Extract the character at position i *in* word;
    If the character is not a letter, ignore it; otherwise, convert it to lowercase;
    Insert the character into the string buffer, keeping the characters in the buffer sorted at all times;
```
}
```
Convert the string buffer into a string and return it;

Here's the finished program.

FindAnagrams.java

```
1   // Program name: FindAnagrams
2   // Author: K. N. King
3   // Written: 1998-08-19
4   //
5   // Prompts the user to enter a series of words. When the
6   // user presses the Enter key without entering a word, the
7   // program will then display the original words, with
8   // anagrams displayed on the same line.
9   //
10  // When determining whether two words are anagrams, the
11  // program will ignore punctuation and the case of the
12  // letters in the words.
13  //
14  // To find anagrams, the program computes a "signature" for
15  // each word, consisting of the letters in the word after
16  // they have been sorted. The words and their signatures are
17  // stored in parallel vectors, sorted by signature. After
18  // all words have been read, anagrams are located by
19  // looking for identical signatures. Because the signatures
20  // are sorted, identical signatures must be adjacent in the
21  // signatures vector.
22
23  import java.util.*;
24  import jpb.*;
25
26  public class FindAnagrams {
27    private static Vector words = new Vector();
28    private static Vector signatures = new Vector();
29
```

```
30     public static void main(String[] args) {
31       readWords();
32       printAnagrams();
33     }
34
35     //////////////////////////////////////////////////////////
36     // NAME:        readWords
37     // BEHAVIOR:    Repeatedly prompts the user to enter words,
38     //              stopping when the user enters an empty
39     //              word. Computes the signature of each word,
40     //              storing the signature in the signatures
41     //              vector in such a way that the vector is
42     //              always sorted in ascending order. Stores
43     //              each word in the words vector at the same
44     //              position as the signature in the
45     //              signatures vector.
46     // PARAMETERS: None
47     // RETURNS:     Nothing
48     //////////////////////////////////////////////////////////
49     private static void readWords() {
50       while (true) {
51         // Prompt the user to enter a word; return if the word
52         // is empty
53         SimpleIO.prompt("Enter a word: ");
54         String word = SimpleIO.readLine().trim();
55         if (word.length() == 0)
56           return;
57
58         // Compute the signature of the word
59         String signature = computeSignature(word);
60
61         // Determine where the signature belongs in the
62         // signatures vector
63         int i;
64         for (i = 0; i < signatures.size(); i++) {
65           String signatureInVector =
66             (String) signatures.elementAt(i);
67           if (signature.compareTo(signatureInVector) < 0)
68             break;
69         }
70
71         // Insert the signature into the signatures vector.
72         // Insert the word at the corresponding location in the
73         // words vector.
74         signatures.insertElementAt(signature, i);
75         words.insertElementAt(word, i);
76       }
77     }
78
79     //////////////////////////////////////////////////////////
80     // NAME:        printAnagrams
81     // BEHAVIOR:    Prints the contents of the words vector,
82     //              putting words that are anagrams of each
83     //              other on the same line. Uses the signatures
```

```
84    //                    vector to determine which words are
85    //                    anagrams. Assumes that the i-th element of
86    //                    the signatures vector is the signature of
87    //                    the i-th word in the words vector. Also
88    //                    assumes that the elements of the signatures
89    //                    vector are in sorted order.
90    // PARAMETERS: None
91    // RETURNS:    Nothing
92    //////////////////////////////////////////////////////////////
93    private static void printAnagrams() {
94      int anagramNumber = 1;
95      int signatureCount = signatures.size();
96
97      // Return if the signatures vector is empty
98      if (signatureCount == 0)
99        return;
100
101      // Print a heading, followed by the first word in the
102      // words vector
103      System.out.println("\nAnagrams:\n---------");
104      System.out.print("1. " + words.firstElement());
105
106      // Print the remaining words in the words vector, placing
107      // words on the same line if they have the same signature
108      for (int i = 1; i < signatureCount; i++) {
109        if (signatures.elementAt(i).equals
110            (signatures.elementAt(i-1)))
111          System.out.print(" ");
112        else
113          System.out.print("\n" + ++anagramNumber + ". ");
114        System.out.print(words.elementAt(i));
115      }
116      System.out.println();
117    }
118
119    //////////////////////////////////////////////////////////////
120    // NAME:        computeSignature
121    // BEHAVIOR:    Computes the signature of a word by sorting
122    //              the letters in the word. Characters other
123    //              than letters are ignored, and uppercase
124    //              letters are converted to lowercase.
125    // PARAMETERS: word - the word whose signature is to be
126    //                    computed
127    // RETURNS:     String object containing the same letters
128    //              as the original word, but in sorted order
129    //////////////////////////////////////////////////////////////
130    private static String computeSignature(String word) {
131      // Create a new string buffer
132      StringBuffer stringBuf = new StringBuffer(word.length());
133
134      for (int i = 0; i < word.length(); i++) {
135        // Extract the character at position i in word.
136        // If the character is not a letter, ignore it;
137        // otherwise, convert it to lowercase.
```

```
138        char ch = word.charAt(i);
139        if (!Character.isLetter(ch))
140          continue;
141        ch = Character.toLowerCase(ch);
142
143        // Insert the character into the string buffer, keeping
144        // the characters in the buffer sorted at all times
145        int j;
146        for (j = 0; j < stringBuf.length(); j++)
147          if (ch < stringBuf.charAt(j))
148            break;
149        stringBuf.insert(j, ch);
150      }
151
152      // Convert the string buffer into a string and return it
153      return stringBuf.toString();
154    }
155 }
```

Q & A

Q: **If sorting is such a common operation, why doesn't the Java API provide a method that does sorting? [p. 568]**

A: Actually, the Java API *does* provide a sorting method, at least in the most recent versions. In the Java 2 platform (version 1.2 or later of the Java Development Kit), the `java.util` package has a class named `Collections`, which provides a class method named `sort`. The `sort` method can sort vectors (and some other data structures as well). To sort a vector v, all you have to do is write

```
Collections.sort(v);
```

Easy enough, eh? Calling `sort` is not only less work than writing your own sorting method, but it's also much more efficient. The `sort` method uses a fast sorting algorithm that's been fine-tuned for best performance.

The `Collections.sort` method doesn't work for arrays. There's another class, named `Arrays`, that provides methods for sorting arrays. To sort an array named a, use the following statement:

```
Arrays.sort(a);
```

The elements of a can be numbers, characters, or objects.

Q: **Does the Java API have a binary search method? [p. 570]**

A: Yes, starting with version 1.2 of the JDK. The method is named `binarySearch`. There are versions of it in both the `Collections` class and the `Arrays` class. If v is a vector and key is the element you're looking for, use the following call of `binarySearch`:

```
int index = Collections.binarySearch(v, key);
```

If `index` is greater than or equal to 0, it indicates the position of the key within the vector. If `index` is negative, the key wasn't found. In that case, the value of `index` indicates where the key could be inserted into the vector (the value of `index` will be one less than the negation of the insertion point). For example if `index` is –3, the key belongs in the vector at position 2. If `index` is –1, the key belongs at position 0.

To perform a binary search on an array `a`, use the following call of `binary-Search`:

```
int index = Arrays.binarySearch(a, key);
```

Q: **Is there some way to find out how large a bit set is? [p. 575]**

A: Sort of. The `size` method returns a value indicating how much memory is currently being used to store a bit set. This value depends on how bit sets are stored, so we can't rely on it too much. Bit sets are often stored in "chunks" of 64 bits, so the number that `size` returns is usually a multiple of 64. If we create a bit set containing 25 bits and then call the `size` method, it will probably return 64. Note that the value returned by `size` has nothing to do with the number of bits that currently have the value `true`.

Starting with version 1.2 of the JDK, the `BitSet` class provides a more useful method named `length`. This method returns the index of the highest `true` bit plus 1. For example, if the bits in positions 2, 6, and 8 are `true`, the `length` method would return 9. If all bits in the set have the value `false`, then `length` returns 0.

Summary

- Java allows an array to have any number of dimensions. In practice, arrays rarely have more than two dimensions.

- A multidimensional array is declared in the same way as a one-dimensional array, except that the declaration will contain more than one set of square brackets.

- The elements of a multidimensional array are given the same default values as the elements of a one-dimensional array.

- The initializer for a two-dimensional array is a series of single-dimensional initializers, with another set of curly braces around the entire initializer.

- When an element of a multidimensional array is selected by subscripting, each subscript must be enclosed in a separate pair of square brackets.

- Nested `for` loops are ideal for processing multidimensional arrays.

- A multidimensional array is treated as a one-dimensional array whose elements are arrays.

- In a multidimensional array a, the length of the first dimension is a.length. The length of the second dimension is a[0].length. The length of the next dimension—if a has more than two—is a[0][0].length, and so on.

- If the rows of a two-dimensional array have different lengths, the array is said to be ragged. Ragged arrays are sometimes useful for conserving memory.

- Multidimensional arrays, like one-dimensional arrays, can be passed to methods and returned by methods.

- The java.util package contains classes that represent data structures, including the Vector class and the BitSet class.

- A vector—an instance of the Vector class—is an array-like object. Unlike an array, a vector can grow or shrink automatically as elements are added to it or removed from it.

- The elements of a vector are arbitrary objects that can belong to any class. The elements of a single vector can even belong to different classes.

- The elements of a vector, like the elements of an array, are indexed from 0.

- Each vector has a capacity and a capacity increment. When the capacity is reached, additional storage is allocated based on the capacity increment.

- The size of a vector—the number of items that it currently stores—is always less than or equal to its capacity.

- The addElement, insertElementAt, and setElementAt methods are used to store data into a vector.

- The elementAt, firstElement, and lastElement methods are used to retrieve elements from a vector. All three methods return an Object value, which can then be cast to the actual type of the retrieved element.

- The removeAllElements, removeElement, and removeElement-At methods are used to remove elements from a vector.

- The contains, indexOf, and lastIndexOf methods are used to search a vector for a particular element.

- The capacity method returns the current capacity of a vector. The ensureCapacity method increases the capacity of a vector, if necessary, to a specified value.

- The isEmpty method returns true if a vector is empty and false otherwise. The setSize method changes the size of a vector to a specified value. The size method returns the current size of a vector. The trimToSize method reduces the capacity of a vector so it exactly matches the vector's current size.

- For each primitive type, the Java API has a corresponding wrapper class. An instance of a wrapper class stores a single value of a primitive type.

- By creating instances of a wrapper class, it becomes possible to store values of a primitive type in a vector.

- Sorting—putting a list of data items in order—is one of the most fundamental operations in programming.

- Data items are normally sorted into ascending order, with smaller values coming before larger ones. The alternative is descending order, with larger values coming first.

- If the elements of an array are already in order, the order can easily be maintained when a new value is inserted. After determining where the new value belongs in the array, existing elements at that position and all later positions are shifted down one place to make room for the new value.

- There are many ways to sort an array. One algorithm—known as insertion sort—inserts the element at position i into the ones at positions 0 through $i - 1$, repeating this operation for $i = 1, 2, \ldots$

- Insertion sort is easy to implement but not very efficient.

- If the elements of an array aren't in any particular order, there's no better searching strategy than examining the elements sequentially. If the elements are sorted, a more efficient algorithm known as binary search can be used.

- Binary search compares the search key against the element in the middle of a sorted array. Based on the outcome of this comparison, the search can be narrowed to half of the original array. The process repeats until the key is found or there are no elements left to search.

- A bit set—an instance of the `BitSet` class—behaves like a vector of `boolean` values.

- Bit sets are useful for simulating the mathematical concept of a set. `true` elements in a bit set correspond to values that are members of the set; `false` elements indicate values that are not members.

- The elements of a newly created bit set are all `false`.

- The `set` method sets one of the bits in a bit set to `true`. The `clear` method clears a bit by setting it to `false`. The `get` method returns the value stored at a specific bit position.

- Bit sets support the Boolean *and*, *or*, and *exclusive or* operations, which correspond to the set operations of intersection, union, and symmetric difference. The methods that perform these operations are named `and`, `or`, and `xor`.

- A string buffer—an instance of the `StringBuffer` class—is similar to a `String` object, except that the characters in a string buffer can be modified.

- Because `String` objects can't be modified directly, changing a `String` object requires three steps: (1) converting it to a string buffer, (2) changing the characters in the string buffer, then (3) converting the buffer back to a `String` object (by calling the `toString` method).

- Each string buffer has a capacity—the maximum number of characters it can store. If an operation on the buffer causes the capacity to be exceeded, the capacity is increased automatically.

- The primary operations on a string buffer are appending characters to the end of the buffer and inserting characters into the middle of the buffer. These operations are performed by methods named `append` and `insert`.

- The charAt method returns the character at a specified position in a string buffer. The setCharAt method stores a character into a string buffer at a specified position.

- The capacity method returns the current capacity of a string buffer. The ensureCapacity method increases the capacity of a string buffer, if necessary, to a specified value.

- The length method returns the current length of the string stored in a string buffer. The setLength method changes the length of a string buffer to a specified value.

Exercises

Section 13.1

1. Write class methods that perform the following operations on matrices (two-dimensional arrays). All data necessary to perform an operation must be supplied to the method through its parameters. Assume that all numbers have type double.

   (a) Scale the elements of a matrix a by the value alpha. (The method's result type will be void.)
   (b) Add matrices a and b, returning the result as a new array. Assume that a and b have the same number of rows and columns.
   (c) Compute the additive inverse of a matrix a, returning the result as a new array. (The additive inverse of a matrix is the same as the original matrix, but with the sign of each element reversed.)
   (d) Compute the transpose of a matrix a, returning the result as a new array. (In the transpose, each column contains the same elements as the corresponding row of the original matrix. For example, the transpose of a 3×4 matrix is a 4×3 matrix.)
   (e) Return the trace of a square matrix a. (The trace of a matrix is the sum of the elements on the main diagonal.)

2. Assume that g is a graphics context and image is a two-dimensional array of integers representing a gray-scale image. Write a series of statements that display the image on the graphics context. *Hint:* Write nested loops that visit each element in the image array. In the inner loop, set the drawing color to the value specified by the current element, then call drawLine to display a single pixel on the graphics context. The value stored in the image array will determine the red, green, and blue components of the drawing color. (In a gray-scale image, all three components have the same value).

3. Assume that colorImage is the three-dimensional array discussed in Section 13.1. Write a loop that copies the data in colorImage into a two-dimensional array of Color objects.

Section 13.2

4. Using the indexOf method and removeElementAt methods, write a loop that removes all occurrences of the string "Java" from a vector named v.

5. Repeat Exercise 4, using the removeElement method instead of the indexOf and removeElementAt methods. Which technique is simpler? Which one is more efficient?

6. Write loops that perform the following actions on a vector whose name is names. Assume that names contains strings.

(a) Locate the first element that stores the string `"Java"`.

(b) Count the number of times that the string `"Java"` occurs in the vector.

(c) Find the largest element in the vector. ("Largest" refers to a lexicographic ordering of the strings in the vector, not to the lengths of the strings.)

Section 13.3   7. Rewrite the loops described in Exercise 6, using a vector named `scores` whose elements are `Integer` objects. Instead of looking for the string `"Java"` in parts (a) and (b), write the loops so that they search for the number 100.

Section 13.4   8. Draw a series of diagrams tracing the execution of the insertion sort algorithm, assuming that the array being sorted contains the following integers:

86 13 27 56 21 34

How many comparisons does the algorithm perform during the sort?

9. How many comparisons will the insertion sort algorithm perform when used to sort an array of length n whose elements are already arranged in ascending order?

10. The `SortLines` program uses the following statements to insert a new item into a sorted vector:

```
for (i = 0; i < v.size(); i++)
  if (inputLine.compareTo((String) v.elementAt(i)) < 0)
    break;
v.insertElementAt(inputLine, i);
```

Suppose that we modify these statements as follows:

```
for (i = 0; i < v.size(); i++)
  if (inputLine.compareTo((String) v.elementAt(i)) < 0) {
    v.insertElementAt(inputLine, i);
    break;
  }
```

Would the modified version work correctly? If so, which version is better? If not, explain why not.

11. One alternative to insertion sort is an algorithm known as **bubble sort**. This algorithm works by making repeated passes over the array to be sorted. During a pass, each element is compared with the one after it. If the elements are out of order (the current element is greater than the one after it), then the algorithm exchanges the elements. Here's a series of snapshots showing the contents of an array during a bubble sort:

```
Before sorting: 93 43 75 36 59 20
After pass 1:    43 75 36 59 20 93
After pass 2:    43 36 59 20 75 93
After pass 3:    36 43 20 59 75 93
After pass 4:    36 20 43 59 75 93
After pass 5:    20 36 43 59 75 93
```

(a) Write a class method named `bubbleSort` that sorts an array of integers supplied as a parameter. Have the method perform $n - 1$ passes over the entire array, where n is the length of the array.

(b) Bubble sort has an interesting property: After i passes, the elements in the last i positions of the array are in their final positions and need not be examined during later passes. Use this fact to improve the performance of the `bubbleSort` method in part (a).

(c) Improve the `bubbleSort` method further by having it return as soon as the array is sorted, even if fewer than *n* − 1 passes have been done. *Hint:* Use a `boolean` variable to keep track of whether any elements have been exchanged during the current pass. If no exchanges are done during a particular pass, then the array is sorted.

Section 13.5   12. Draw a series of diagrams tracing the execution of the binary search algorithm, assuming that the search key is 12 and the array being searched contains the following integers:

4 6 9 12 14 17 20 25 38 42 48 50

Show the values of `low`, `high`, and `mid` during each iteration of the `while` loop. How many comparisons are performed during the search?

13. If the search key matches several elements of an array, which one will the binary search algorithm find? (In other words, which one of the elements will be stored at the position indicated by the final value of the `low` variable?)

14. Modify the binary search algorithm so that the `while` loop terminates as soon as the search key is found.

15. Modify the binary search algorithm so that, if the key isn't found, the final value of the `low` variable indicates where the key could be inserted into the array. More specifically, inserting the key just before the position indicated by `low` should keep the elements of the array in sorted order.

16. Modify the binary search algorithm so that it searches a vector named v rather than an array. Assume that the objects in the vector have a `compareTo` method similar to the one in the `String` class.

Section 13.6   17. Write the following class methods, which perform operations on bit sets. Each method has either one `BitSet` parameter (named `set`) or two (`set1` and `set2`).

(a) A `not` method that changes each element of `set` to the opposite of its original value (`true` elements become `false` and vice versa).
(b) A `difference` method that computes the difference between two sets. The method will modify `set1` so that it contains `true` values in each position where `set1` originally stored a `true` value and `set2` stored a `false` value.
(c) A `cardinality` method that returns the number of `true` elements in `set`.
(d) An `isSubset` method that tests whether `set1` is a subset of `set2`, returning a `boolean` result.

18. The `Sieve` program uses the `toString` method to convert the `primes` bit set into a string for display purposes. Suppose that we wanted the output of the program to have the following form instead:

Primes: 2 3 5 7 11 13 17 19 23

Write a series of statements that will display the contents of `primes` in this form.

Section 13.7   19. Write a class method named `removeDashes` that has one parameter, a string, and returns the same string with all dashes (hyphens) removed. *Hint:* Convert the parameter into a string buffer, remove the dashes, and then convert the string buffer back to string form.

20. Rewrite the `formatAsMoney` method (Section 7.3) so that it works in a different way. Have the new version of the method convert `roundedAmount` into a string, which is then stored in a string buffer. After inserting the decimal point into the correct position, the method will convert the string buffer back into a string, which it then returns. Be sure that your method correctly handles amounts that are less than $1.00.

Section 13.8   21.   Without running the `FindAnagrams` program, find the anagrams among the following words. *Hint:* Compute the signatures of the words by hand and look for matches.

```
caret    laser    reins    salad    star
cater    least    resin    siren    steal
crate    rates    rinse    slate    trace
dials    react    risen    stale    track
```

Programming Projects

1.   Modify the `PhoneDirectory` program (Section 5.8) so that it stores the phone records in a vector, keeping them sorted by name at all times.

2.   Modify the `Bank` program (Programming Project 8, Chapter 5) so that it stores the bank accounts in a vector, keeping them sorted by account number at all times. Have the `s` (select) command use a binary search to locate the desired account quickly.

3.   Modify the `PhoneDirectory` program (Programming Project 10, Chapter 12) so that it uses vectors rather than arrays, with the names kept sorted at all times.

4.   Modify the `FindDistance` program (Section 13.1) so that it uses a ragged array to store the distances between cities.

5.   Modify the `SortLines` program (Section 13.4) so that the inner loop goes backward through the vector, comparing the new line with each element of the vector, starting with the last element. If the new line is less than the current element in the vector, move the element down by one position.

6.   Modify the `SortCharacters` program (Section 13.7) so that it copies the original string into a string buffer and then sorts the string buffer using the insertion sort algorithm.

7.   The `FindAnagrams` program (Section 13.8) uses two parallel vectors named `words` and `signatures`. Modify the program by introducing a new class named `WordPair`. A `WordPair` object will store a word and its signature, both as strings. Replace the `words` and `signatures` vectors with a single vector whose elements are `WordPair` objects.

8.   Write a program named `FindMedian` that finds the median of a set of positive integers entered on the command line. Running the program by typing

```
java FindMedian 9 87 43 10 2 66 52 68 45 21 71
```

should produce the following output:

```
Median: 45
```

Hint: Have the program store the numbers in a sorted vector. The median will be the integer in the middle. (If the user enters an even number of integers, there will be two "middle" values. Have the program display the average of these two integers.)

9.   Write a program named `SortStrings` that displays its command-line arguments in sorted order. Running the program by typing

```
java SortStrings The quick brown fox jumped over the lazy dog
```

should produce the following output:

```
In sorted order: The brown dog fox jumped lazy over quick the
```

10. Write a program named `SortIntegers` that displays its command-line arguments—a series of integers—in sorted order. Running the program by typing

    `java SortIntegers 9 87 43 10 2 66 52 68 45 21 71`

    should produce the following output:

    `In sorted order: 2 9 10 21 43 45 52 66 68 71 87`

    Have the program ignore any command-line arguments that are not integers or have values that are less than zero. You may assume that no integer appears twice on the command line. *Hint:* A bit set can be used to sort a series of integers, provided that the integers are unique. Have the program keep track of which integers have been seen by setting bits in a bit set. After it has finished processing the command-line arguments, have the program visit all elements in the bit set, printing the index of all elements that are `true`.

11. Write a program named `LetterCounts` that displays a list of all letters that appear in the program's command-line arguments, followed by a list of all letters that don't appear in the command-line arguments. Running the program by typing

    `java LetterCounts The quick brown fox jumped over the lazy dog`

    should produce the following output:

    `Letters used: abcdefghijklmnopqrtuvwxyz`
    `Letters missing: s`

    The letters in the output will be lowercase, regardless of the case of the letters in the command-line arguments. *Hint:* Use a bit set to keep track of which letters appear in the command-line arguments.

12. Calculators, watches, and other electronic devices often rely on seven-segment displays for numerical output. To form a digit, such devices "turn on" some of the seven segments while leaving others "off":

    ```
     _       _   _       _   _       _   _
    | |   |  _|  _| |_| |_  |_    | |_| |_|
    |_|   | |_   _|   |  _| |_|   | |_|  _|
    ```

    Write a program named `SevenSegmentDisplay` that displays its command-line argument as a series of seven-segment digits, with one space between each pair of digits. Have the program ignore any characters in the argument that are not digits. Running the program by typing

    `java SevenSegmentDisplay 491`

    should produce the following output:

    ```
         _
    |_| |_|   |
      |  _|   |
    ```

    Hint: Store the output in three string buffers, one for each output line. As each input digit is processed, append four characters to each buffer (three for the digit itself plus a space). For example, if the current input digit is 9, the program would append " _ " to the first buffer, "|_| " to the second buffer, and " _| " to the third buffer.

Answers to Review Questions

Section 13.1

1. There's no limit on the number of dimensions.
2. `a[i][j]`

3. `a.length` is the number of rows; `a[0].length` is the number of columns.
4. (1) three parallel two-dimensional arrays (storing the red, green, and blue components of the pixels). (2) Use a single two-dimensional array of `Color` objects. (3) Use a three-dimensional array.
5. Because a `double` value occupies 8 bytes, the memory required for the array's elements will be $50 \times 40 \times 8 = 16,000$ bytes.
6. Ragged

Section 13.2

1. There's no limit on the number of objects that can be stored in a vector.
2. Any object, regardless of which class it belongs to, can be stored in a vector.
3. The capacity of a vector is the maximum number of elements that can be stored in a vector without resizing it. The size of a vector is the current number of elements that are used to store data. The size is always less than or equal to the capacity.
4. These methods return an `Object` reference, regardless of the type of object actually stored in the vector. Casting is necessary in order to call any of the instance methods that belong to the object.
5. Vectors are more flexible than arrays because they can grow automatically and support methods such as `insertElementAt`. Also, using a vector avoids the problem of allocating more space for an array than will actually be used.
6. Arrays are easier to use than vectors. If the number of elements is known in advance, arrays are more space-efficient than vectors. Also, vectors are more error-prone than arrays: if a program stores objects of the wrong type in a vector because of a programming error, the compiler won't be able to detect the error.

Section 13.3

1. The elements of a vector must be objects, not values of a primitive type. However, we can create instances of a wrapper class, with each instance containing a single primitive value, and then store those instances in a vector.
2. `Character` and `Integer`
3. `MIN_VALUE` and `MAX_VALUE`
4. `Integer.parseInt`

Section 13.4

1. Ascending
2. Descending
3. Insertion sort
4. 190

Section 13.5

1. The elements of the array must be sorted into ascending order.
2. The position of the search key in the array (if the key is present in the array)
3. It repeatedly reduces the number of potentially matching elements by a factor of two.
4. 9

Section 13.6

1. A vector, because the size of a bit set will increase automatically as needed
2. The elements of a bit set have only two possible values, so Java can store each element as a single bit. As a result, a bit set requires considerably less memory than an array or vector.
3. `false`
4. Intersection, union, and symmetric difference

Section 13.7

1. `String` objects can't be changed directly. However, a string can be converted into a string buffer, which can then be modified and converted back to string form.
2. Each string buffer has a capacity. If an operation on the buffer causes the capacity to be exceeded, the capacity is increased automatically.
3. Appending characters and inserting characters
4. By calling the `toString` method

14 Files

It's often the case that a program will need to save data in a file so that another program—or perhaps even the same program—can read it later. The java.io package provides the classes that we'll need in order to write data to a file and later read the data back in. There are a vast number of classes in this package; we'll only be able to examine some of the most important.

Before we discuss the mechanics of reading and writing files, we'll need a better understanding of how files are stored. In particular, we'll need to learn the difference between text files, which store only characters, and binary files, which store arbitrary data.

One of the classes in the java.io package is File, which provides methods for checking the properties of a file, as well as methods for renaming and deleting files. The File class doesn't support reading from a file or writing to a file, however, so we'll need other classes for those purposes.

The FileInputStream and FileOutputStream classes allow a program to read and write individual bytes or blocks of bytes. In order to read and write specific types of data, such as integers or floating-point numbers, we'll need to use the DataInputStream and DataOutputStream classes. All four of these classes are designed to be used with binary files.

Working with text files requires a different set of classes. To write characters to a text file, we'll use the FileWriter, BufferedWriter, and PrintWriter classes. To read characters from a text file, we'll use the FileReader and BufferedReader classes.

Entire objects can be written to a file via a process known as serialization. To read and write objects, we'll need yet another pair of classes, ObjectInputStream and ObjectOutputStream.

Many things can go wrong when working with files, so programs that use files must deal with a variety of exceptions. Section 8.1 discussed exceptions and showed how to use `try` and `catch` blocks to handle exceptions. In order to work with files, however, we'll need a deeper understanding of exceptions. In particular, we'll need to pay more attention to the order of `catch` blocks, and we'll need to learn about the `throws` clause.

Objectives

- Learn the difference between text files and binary files.
- Learn how the `Stream`, `Reader`, and `Writer` classes are related.
- Learn how to perform basic file operations, including opening a file, closing a file, reading from a file, and writing to a file.
- Learn how to use the `File` class to check the properties of a file and perform basic file operations, such as deleting a file and renaming a file.
- Learn how to use the `FileInputStream` and `FileOutputStream` classes for reading and writing bytes.
- Learn how the exception classes are related.
- Learn how to tell whether an exception is checked or unchecked.
- Learn why the order of `catch` blocks can be important.
- Learn how to put a `finally` block after a series of `catch` blocks.
- Learn how to use the `throws` clause in method declarations.
- Learn how to use the `DataInputStream` and `DataOutputStream` classes for reading and writing data of specific types.
- Learn how to use the `FileWriter`, `BufferedWriter`, and `Print-Writer` classes to write characters to a text file.
- Learn how to use the `FileReader` and `BufferedReader` classes to read characters from a text file.
- Learn how to use the `ObjectInputStream` and `ObjectOutput-Stream` classes for reading and writing objects.

14.1   Files and Streams

The idea of a file is central to most computer systems. A *file* is a collection of related data that is given a name and placed on a storage medium of some sort. We usually think of a file as a place to keep data for a long period of time, but that's not always the case. It's fairly common for a program to create a file, use it temporarily as a place to store data, and then delete the file before the program terminates.

Files can be stored on a variety of media, including hard drives, floppy disks,

CD-ROMs, and tapes. They can also be transmitted in various ways, such as over a computer network.

As we discussed in Section 1.8, a file can hold nearly any type of data imaginable. A file could contain the source code for a program (as our .java files do). It could contain a compiled program, such as our .class files. It could also contain a document, an image, a sound clip, or many other things.

How Files Are Stored

All files are the same in one important respect: they consist of bytes. The byte is the basic unit of storage as far as files are concerned. All files, no matter how large or small, consist of some number of bytes. Most operating systems will show you the size of the files on your computer. If you're a Windows user, for example, one way to see the sizes of your files is to enter the dir command in a DOS window. For example, here's what the dir command displayed for one of the directories on my PC:

```
Volume in drive C has no label
Volume Serial Number is 07CE-0C08
Directory of C:\programs\lottery

.              <DIR>        12-20-99  1:02p .
..             <DIR>        12-20-99  1:02p ..
LOTTER~1 JAV          283   12-20-99  1:04p Lottery.java
LOTTER~1 CLA          511   12-20-99  1:04p Lottery.class
         2 file(s)              794 bytes
         2 dir(s)        12,802.72 MB free
```

According to the dir command, the lottery directory contains two files, named Lottery.java and Lottery.class. The first file contains 283 bytes, and the second contains 511 bytes. Lottery.java is a program from Section 2.4, and Lottery.class is the class file created when Lottery.java was compiled.

Wait a second—if all files consist of bytes, how can files contain so many different kinds of data? The answer is simple: the bytes in a file can mean anything we want them to mean. In some files, each byte represents a character. In other files, the bytes mean other things. Groups of bytes may represent integers, or floating-point numbers, or something else.

To see how this works, suppose that we create a file consisting of four bytes. Here's how the file will look internally:

| 01001010 | 01100001 | 01110110 | 01100001 |

Let's assume that the bytes represent ASCII characters. Consulting Table 9.8, we see that the first byte represents the letter J, the second represents a, the third represents v, and the fourth represents a. But it's possible that the bytes have some other meaning. Perhaps the four bytes represent a single integer. (Recall from Section 9.2 that int values are 32 bits long—four bytes—in Java.) Or perhaps the first two bytes represent a short integer, and the second two represent another short integer. Or maybe the four bytes represent a single float value. Or—well, you get the idea: bytes can represent numbers, characters, or any type of data.

That raises an interesting question. If someone were to give us a file, how would we know what kind of data is stored in the file? The answer is: *we don't know.* A file is just a series of bytes, and the bytes could mean anything. Fortunately, there are ways to leave hints about the contents of a file. The extension on a file name is an important hint. For example, a file with the .java extension is normally assumed to contain the source code for a Java program. When you create a file or rename one, it's critical that you give it the proper extension. Otherwise, programs that use the file may make the wrong assumption about the format of data in the file.

Another way to leave a hint about the contents of the file is to store a "marker" of some sort in the file itself, usually at the beginning. In Windows, for example, an executable file begins with two special bytes containing the ASCII codes for the letters *M* and *Z*. In Unix, an executable file begins with a "magic number." When the user tries to execute a program, Unix first checks for the magic number. If the number isn't present, Unix will refuse to let the program run.

Text Files Versus Binary Files

All files fall into one of two categories. In a ***text file,*** the bytes represent characters in some character set, such as ASCII or Unicode. In a ***binary file,*** the bytes don't necessarily represent characters (although some of them may).

Text files have two characteristics that binary files don't possess:

- ***Text files are divided into lines.*** Each line in a text file normally ends with one or two special characters that mark the end of the line. Which character(s) is used depends on the operating system. In Windows, the end-of-line marker is a carriage-return character ('\r') followed immediately by a line-feed character ('\n'). In Unix, the end-of-line marker is a single line-feed character. The Macintosh operating system uses a single carriage-return character.

- ***Text files may contain a special "end-of-file" marker.*** Some operating systems allow a special byte to be used as a marker at the end of a text file. In Windows, the marker is '\u1a' (Ctrl-Z). There's no requirement that Ctrl-Z be present, but if it is, it marks the end of the file. Any bytes after Ctrl-Z are to be ignored.

Binary files aren't divided into lines. In a binary file, there's no "end-of-line" or "end-of-file" marker; all bytes are treated equally.

It's not difficult to write a program that will display the individual bytes in a file (see Programming Project 20 at the end of this chapter). Such a program can be useful for understanding how data is stored in files. Suppose that we create a Windows text file containing the following two lines:

```
Java
rules!
```

If we examine the bytes in the file, here's what we'll see:

4A	61	76	61	0D	0A	72	75	6C	65	73	21	0D	0A
J	a	v	a	*cr*	*lf*	r	u	l	e	s	!	*cr*	*lf*

(To save space, I've shown the byte values as hexadecimal numbers rather than as binary numbers.) Notice that each line ends with two characters, a carriage return (0D in hex) followed by a line feed (0A in hex). In Unix, the file would be two bytes shorter, because the carriage returns would not be present.

Streams

In order to work with files, we'll need to use the `java.io` package, which is part of the Java API. ("io" stands for "input/output.") However, the names of many `java.io` classes don't include the word "file"; instead, they refer to "streams." A *stream* is an abstraction that represents any "file-like" source of input or destination for output. The term "stream" is meant to indicate that these classes and their methods are capable of doing more than just file input/output. A stream object may be capable of reading from anything that resembles a file or writing to anything that resembles a file.

`java.io` contains a dizzying assortment of classes, which can sometimes make it difficult to determine which class is best for a particular purpose. In this chapter, we'll examine only the most fundamental—and most widely used— classes.

Some classes in `java.io` have names that end with `Stream`, such as `FileInputStream` and `DataOutputStream`. These classes are subclasses of `InputStream` and `OutputStream`:

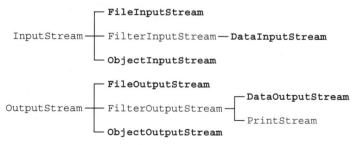

(Not all subclasses of `InputStream` and `OutputStream` are shown.) The classes whose names are in bold are discussed in this chapter. The `PrintStream` class was discussed in Section 7.5; `System.out` and `System.err` are instances of this class.

Other classes have names that end with `Reader` or `Writer`, such as `BufferedReader` or `PrintWriter`. These classes are subclasses of `Reader` and `Writer`:

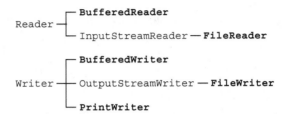

(Again, not all subclasses of `Reader` and `Writer` are shown.) The classes whose names are in bold are discussed in this chapter.

The various reader and writer classes are designed to help with a common problem: Java stores characters in Unicode, using two bytes per character, whereas most software assumes that characters are stored in ASCII form, with one byte per character. If we were to write characters to a file in the same way that they're stored in a Java program, then programs written in other languages wouldn't be able to read the file easily. (Not to mention the fact that files would be twice as large as necessary!) Similarly, Java programs would have difficulty reading files containing ASCII characters. An instance of a `Reader` class solves the problem by automatically converting bytes to Unicode characters during input. Similarly, an instance of a `Writer` class will convert Unicode characters to single bytes during output.

Stream Layering

To work with a file, we'll need to create an object that represents the file. We can then perform operations on the file by calling instance methods. In the simplest case, we'll need just a single object. Much of the time, however, it's not that simple. Many of the classes in the `java.io` package are designed to be "layered," with two or more objects involved. Calling a method that belongs to one object triggers a call to an "underlying" object, which may in turn call a method that belongs to a third object.

For example, to write characters to a file, we'll need to create an instance of the `FileWriter` class. However, this class isn't very efficient by itself, so we'll need to create a `BufferedWriter` object that's built on top of the `FileWriter` object. The methods in the `BufferedWriter` class aren't very convenient to use, however, so we'll want to create a `PrintWriter` object that's built on top of the `BufferedWriter` object. Here's how we might visualize the layering of the three classes:

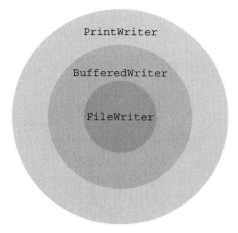

When we call a method that belongs to `PrintWriter`, it in turn calls a method (or methods) belonging to `BufferedWriter`, which then calls a method(s) belonging to `FileWriter`. The advantage of this layering is flexibility: the programmer can combine classes in many different ways to get the right blend of efficiency and convenience. The disadvantage is that working with files is more complicated in Java than in many programming languages.

Working with Files

Working with a file involves three steps: opening the file, performing operations on the file, and closing the file. Let's look at each step in turn.

- **Open the file.** Opening a file requires specifying the file's name and possibly its location (such as the drive on which the file is located and the directory it's in). Once we have the name of a file, we can open it by creating an instance of an appropriate stream class (or—in the case of a text file—a reader or writer class). This object will represent the file within the program. For example, to open a binary file for writing, we would create an instance of the `File-OutputStream` class:

```
FileOutputStream out = new FileOutputStream(filename);
```

- **Perform operations on the file.** The primary file operations are reading data from a file and writing data to a file. These operations—as well as all other file operations—are performed by calling instance methods that belong to the stream object's class. In the case of the `out` object, the operations that we can perform are dictated by the methods in the `FileOutputStream` class (and its superclasses). One of these methods, named `write`, is capable of writing a single byte:

```
out.write(b);   // Writes the byte b
```

Q&A ■ *Close the file.* When we're through with a file, we'll need to close it. Closing a file is done by calling the `close` method:

```
out.close();
```

close   The `InputStream`, `OutputStream`, `Reader`, and `Writer` classes all have a `close` method, which forces all stream, reader, and writer classes to support this method (either by providing it or inheriting it). Because `close` is so ubiquitous, I didn't include it in any of the tables of methods later in the chapter. It's safe to assume that any class whose name ends with "`Stream`", "`Reader`", or "`Writer`" supports the `close` method.

Opening a file for input will fail—causing an exception to be thrown—unless the file already exists. Opening a file for output is a different story. When we open an existing file for output, the file is normally ***truncated***—the bytes already in the file are lost. Attempting to open a nonexistent file for output will cause the file to be created. Either way, the file is empty to begin with.

Obtaining File Names

In order to open a file, we'll need to know its name. There are three primary ways to supply a file name to a program:

■ ***Build the name into the program.*** The easiest way to supply a file name to a program is to put the name in the program's source code. Some programs indeed work this way, requiring that a file with a certain name be present when the program is run. For example, a program might access a file containing configuration data or options previously chosen by the user. A game program might use a file to store the number of times the user has won or lost, or to keep track of where the user was when he or she last saved the game.

■ ***Have the program prompt the user to enter the name.*** A more flexible approach is to ask the user for the file name.

■ ***Have the program obtain the name from the command line.*** A third technique is to obtain the file name from the command line—the command that the user entered to run the program. For example, we could have the user enter the following command to copy one file into another:

command-line arguments ➤ 7.4

```
java CopyFile file1 file2
```

The `CopyFile` program assumes that `args[0]` contains the name of the file to be copied and `args[1]` contains the name of the file that will store the copy.

We'll see examples of all three approaches in this chapter.

Buffering and Flushing

We first encountered the concept of a "buffer" in Section 13.7, which covered the `StringBuffer` class. A buffer is a place where data is stored temporarily, usually on its way from one place to another.

Buffers are quite common when working with files. When a program calls a method that writes to a file, the data being written usually goes into a buffer first. When the buffer is full, all the data in the buffer is then transferred to the file, and the buffer becomes empty. Similar actions take place when data is read from a file: a large chunk of data is first transferred to a buffer. The program then obtains small portions of the data from the buffer. When the buffer becomes empty, another large chunk is read from the file.

Using buffers for input and output can dramatically improve the performance of a program. Transferring information to or from a disk drive is a relatively slow operation. As a result, it isn't feasible for a program to access a disk file directly each time it wants to read or write data. On the other hand, reading a byte from a buffer or storing a byte into a buffer takes hardly any time at all. Of course, it takes time to transfer the buffer contents to or from disk, but one large data transfer is much faster than many small ones.

flush   Normally, we won't have to worry much about buffering. Java's stream classes are designed to perform buffering without any action on our part. Occasionally, though, we may need to take a more active role. In particular, we may sometimes want to ensure that data written to a file is actually stored in the file as soon as possible. Normally, data written to a file goes into a buffer first. The buffer is *flushed* (written to the file) automatically when it's full or the file is closed. Sometimes we may want to flush the buffer manually, however, which we can do by calling the `flush` method. If `out` is an output stream or writer object, we would call `flush` in the following way:

```
out.flush();
```

One reason for calling `flush` is to ensure that data is written to a file as soon as possible, where it will be safe, even if the program terminates unexpectedly, the operating system crashes, or the power goes off.

All output stream and writer classes support the `flush` method, so I didn't include it in any of the tables later in the chapter.

File Pointers

To understand how file operations work, it's important to know about *file pointers.* For each file that we have open, Java will automatically keep track of where we are in the file—which byte will be the next to be read or written. When a file is opened, the file pointer is normally at the beginning of the file. For example, suppose that we open an existing file for reading. The file pointer will be at the beginning:

If we now read one byte from the file, the file pointer will advance automatically to the next byte:

Reading another byte causes the file pointer to advance again. If we read enough bytes, the file pointer will eventually advance past the last byte in the file—a condition known as *end of file.* We'll need to test for this condition each time we read input from a file.

Writing to a file is similar. Java keeps track of our current position in the file and automatically advances the file pointer after each write operation. Normally, writing starts at the beginning of a file. In some cases, however, we may want to preserve the data that was originally stored in the file. In this situation, we would choose to *append* data to the end of the file, rather than replacing the data that the file already contains.

Reading or writing a file in the fashion I've just described is called *sequential access,* because we access the bytes in order, from beginning to end. Java also supports a different type of access, known as *random access.* Random access allows a program to move freely within a file, perhaps reading a few bytes in one place, jumping to a different location, and then writing a few bytes. The classes described in this chapter are designed for sequential access. Random access requires the use of the `RandomAccessFile` class, which is beyond the scope of this book.

Review Questions

1. Suppose that a file contains eight bytes. What could those bytes represent: (a) eight ASCII characters, (b) four Unicode characters, (c) two `int` values, (d) a `double` value, or (e) any of the above?

2. Files can be divided into two categories. What are they?

3. A _____ is an abstraction that represents any "file-like" source of input or destination for output.

4. What problem are `Reader` and `Writer` classes designed to solve?

5. Before we can read data from a file or write data to a file, we must _____ the file.

6. To avoid replacing the existing contents of a file, we can _____ data to the end of the file.

14.2 The `File` Class

We'll begin our exploration of the `java.io` package with one of the most fundamental classes: `File`. A `File` object represents a file stored on disk or some other medium. The `File` class lets us work with the *properties* of a file, not the *contents* of the file. Using a `File` object, we can determine whether a file is readable, whether it's a directory, and so on. We can also perform a few basic file operations, including deleting a file and renaming a file.

Using the `File` class is easy. First, we'll need to create a `File` object by invoking one of the `File` constructors (Table 14.1).

Table 14.1
File Constructors

Description	Action
`File(String path)`	Creates a `File` object representing the file located at the specified path.
`File(String path, String name)`	Creates a `File` object representing the file with the specified name, located in the specified directory.

The first constructor expects a `String` object containing the file's name:

```
File f = new File("Lottery.java");
```

Java will try to locate the file in the current directory. To work with a file in a different directory, we'll need to include path information in the string:

```
File f = new File("c:\\programs\\lottery\\Lottery.java");
```

Sometimes it's more convenient to supply the path and the file name as two separate arguments, which the `File` class allows:

```
File f = new File("c:\\programs\\lottery", "Lottery.java");
```

escape sequences ➤9.4

You'll notice that I used *two* backslash characters, not one, to separate directory names. Java would interpret a single backslash character as the beginning of an escape sequence. In the string `"c:\programs\lottery"`, for example, the Java compiler would try to treat `\p` and `\l` as escape sequences. (Neither is legal, so we would get an error message from the compiler.)

Another way to solve the backslash problem is to use a slash character instead of a backslash to separate directory names:

```
File f = new File("c:/programs/lottery/Lottery.java");
```

Although the backslash is the normal character for separating directory names in Windows, ordinary slashes will also work within Java programs.

File Properties

Once we've created a `File` object, we can call various methods that provide information about the file that the object represents. Table 14.2 on the next page lists some of the common "query" methods. The query methods are best understood by examples, so let's look at a couple of programs that use them.

Table 14.2
File Query Methods

Description	*Action*
`boolean canRead()`	Returns `true` if the program can read from this file.
`boolean canWrite()`	Returns `true` if the program can write to this file.
`boolean exists()`	Returns `true` if this file exists.
`boolean isDirectory()`	Returns `true` if this file is a directory.
`boolean isFile()`	Returns `true` if this file is normal (not a directory).
`long length()`	Returns the length of this file in bytes.
`String[] list()`	Returns an array of strings containing the names of the files in this directory (assuming that this file is a directory).

PROGRAM   **Determining the Properties of a File**

The following program prompts the user for the name of a file and then displays the file's properties.

FileProperties.java

```
1   // Displays the properties of a file
2
3   import java.io.*;
4   import jpb.*;
5
6   public class FileProperties {
7     public static void main(String[] args) {
8       // Prompt user to enter file name
9       SimpleIO.prompt("Enter a file name: ");
10      String fileName = SimpleIO.readLine();
11
12      // Create a File object
13      File f = new File(fileName);
14
15      // Display properties of file
16      if (f.canRead())
17        System.out.println("File can be read");
18      if (f.canWrite())
19        System.out.println("File can be written");
20      if (f.exists())
21        System.out.println("File exists");
22      if (f.isDirectory())
23        System.out.println("File is a directory");
24      if (f.isFile())
25        System.out.println("File is normal");
26      System.out.println("Length of file: " + f.length());
27    }
28  }
```

Here's the output if we ask about the properties of the `Lottery.java` file (see the example in Section 14.1):

```
Enter a file name: Lottery.java
File can be read
File can be written
File exists
File is normal
Length of file: 283
```

Q&A Here's the output if we ask about the properties of the *directory* containing Lottery.java:

```
Enter a file name: c:\programs\lottery
File can be read
File can be written
File exists
File is a directory
Length of file: 0
```

PROGRAM   **Listing the Files in a Directory**

list   The list method returns an array of String objects containing the names of all files in a particular directory. (This method should be called only by a File object that represents a directory.) The following program uses the list method to display the names of the files in the current directory.

ListFiles.java

```java
 1  // Displays a list of all files in the current directory
 2
 3  import java.io.*;
 4
 5  public class ListFiles {
 6    public static void main(String[] args) {
 7      // Obtain a list of all files in the current directory
 8      File currentDirectory = new File(".");
 9      String[] fileNames = currentDirectory.list();
10
11      // Display each name in the list
12      for (int i = 0; i < fileNames.length; i++)
13        System.out.println(fileNames[i]);
14    }
15  }
```

The file name " . " indicates the current directory. If we use the program to list the files in the c:\programs\lottery directory, we'll get the following output:

```
Lottery.java
Lottery.class
```

Notice that the list of files doesn't include the current directory (.) or the parent directory (. .).

File Operations

In addition to query methods, the `File` class also provides a few basic operations on files (Table 14.3). All three methods return `true` if they are successful and `false` if they are not successful.

Table 14.3
File Action Methods

Description	*Action*
`boolean delete()`	Deletes this file.
`boolean mkdir()`	Creates a directory corresponding to this `File` object.
`boolean renameTo(File dest)`	Renames this file to the name specified by `dest`.

PROGRAM

Renaming the Files in a Directory

Occasionally we'll need to rename a group of files, perhaps because they need to be copied to a different operating system that puts more restrictions on file names. The following program displays the names of all files in the current directory, one by one, and gives the user the opportunity to change the names of selected files. For each file, the program will display a prompt of the form

```
Rename foo (y/n)?
```

where `foo` is the file name. If the user responds with `y` or `Y`, the program then asks for the new name and then changes the file's name. Here's what a session with the program might look like:

```
Rename Lottery.java (y/n)? n
Rename Lottery.class (y/n)? y
Enter new name: Lottery2.class
```

Our strategy will be to construct `File` objects from both the old and new file names, then use the `renameTo` method to do the renaming.

RenameFiles.java

```
1   // Renames selected files in the current directory
2
3   import java.io.*;
4   import jpb.*;
5
6   public class RenameFiles {
7     public static void main(String[] args) {
8       // Obtain a list of all files in the current directory
9       File currentDirectory = new File(".");
10      String[] fileNames = currentDirectory.list();
11
12      // Process each name in the list
13      for (int i = 0; i < fileNames.length; i++) {
14
```

```
15        // Ask user whether or not to rename file
16        SimpleIO.prompt("Rename " + fileNames[i] + " (y/n)? ");
17        String response = SimpleIO.readLine();
18
19        // If the answer is "y" or "Y", ask for new name and
20        // then call renameTo
21        if (response.equalsIgnoreCase("y")) {
22          SimpleIO.prompt("Enter new name: ");
23          String newName = SimpleIO.readLine();
24          File oldFile = new File(fileNames[i]);
25          File newFile = new File(newName);
26          boolean successful = oldFile.renameTo(newFile);
27          if (!successful)
28            System.out.println("Could not rename " +
29                                fileNames[i] + " to " +
30                                newName);
31        }
32      }
33    }
34  }
```

Review Questions

1.   What is the purpose of the `File` class?

2.   What `File` method would we use to determine whether it's legal to write to a file?

3.   What `File` method returns an array containing the names of all files in a particular directory?

4.   What `File` method would we use to create a directory?

14.3   Reading and Writing Bytes

Beginning with this section, we'll focus on how to read data from files and write data to files. We'll start with the simplest possible way to read and write data—as single bytes or blocks of bytes. The classes that we'll discuss in this section, `FileInputStream` and `FileOutputStream`, are useful for writing file utilities, such as a program that makes a copy of a file. Such a program doesn't need to know what the bytes in a file mean; it simply creates a new file containing an exact copy of the bytes in the original file.

Writing Bytes

Let's start by seeing how we could write bytes to a file. We'll follow the standard series of steps described in Section 14.1: open the file, write data to the file, and then close the file.

To open a file for writing, we'll need to create a `FileOutputStream` object. Table 14.4 lists the most common `FileOutputStream` constructors.

Table 14.4

`FileOutputStream`
Constructors

Description	Action
`FileOutputStream(String name)`	Creates a `FileOutputStream` object representing the file with the specified name.
`FileOutputStream` `  (String name, boolean append)`	Creates a `FileOutputStream` object representing the file with the specified name. If append is `true`, bytes will be written to the end of the file rather than the beginning.
`FileOutputStream(File file)`	Creates a `FileOutputStream` object representing the specified `File` object.

The first constructor in the table is the one most frequently used:

```
FileOutputStream out = new FileOutputStream(fileName);
```

This constructor needs a file name as its argument. (The file name for all such constructors may contain path information, so I won't bother mentioning that detail again in this chapter.) The second constructor lets us specify that any bytes written to the file should be appended to the file, thereby preserving the file's original contents. The third constructor lets us supply a `File` object instead of a file name.

If the `FileOutputStream` constructor is given the name of an existing file, it will truncate the file, discarding its contents (unless we use the second constructor and the value of append is `true`). If the `FileOutputStream` constructor is given the name of a file that doesn't exist, the file will be created.

checked exception ►8.1

If the file can't be opened for writing, the `FileOutputStream` constructor will throw `IOException`. Because `IOException` is a checked exception, we'll need to enclose the constructor call within a `try` block. (Starting with version 1.2 of the JDK, the `FileOutputStream` constructor throws `FileNotFoundException` instead of `IOException`.)

The primary methods provided by `FileOutputStream` are all named `write` (Table 14.5). These methods throw `IOException` if an error occurs.

Table 14.5

`FileOutputStream`
Methods

Description	Action
`void write(int b)`	Writes the specified byte.
`void write(byte[] b)`	Writes the bytes in the specified array.
`void write(byte[] b, int off,` `            int len)`	Writes `len` bytes of the array `b`, starting at the position indicated by `off`.

write
(version 1)

The first version of `write` lets us write a single byte:

```
byte outputByte;
...
```

```
out.write(outputByte);
```

write
(version 2)

The second version lets us write a block of bytes stored in an array:

```
byte[] buffer = new byte[512];
...
out.write(buffer);
```

write
(version 3)

The third version is also designed to write a block of bytes. It requires two additional arguments:

```
byte[] buffer = new byte[512];
int count;
...
out.write(buffer, 0, count);
```

The second argument is an offset into the array; the value 0 indicates that the byte at position 0 will be the first to be written. By supplying a value other than 0, we can cause the `write` method to skip some of the bytes at the beginning of the array. The third argument is the number of bytes to write.

The `FileOutputStream` class (like stream classes in general) is very error-conscious; just about any operation that you perform on a `FileOutput-Stream` object might throw `IOException`. This fact reflects the uncertainty of working with files. An attempt to open a file for writing might fail for a variety of reasons: we've specified an invalid path, we don't have permission to write to the file, and so on. Attempts to write to the file could fail because the physical device has a problem (floppy disks, in particular, often go bad) or because the device is full.

When you write a program that works with files, you'll need to worry about potential failures and decide what action the program should take for each thing that could go wrong. Because `IOException` is a checked exception, you can't just ignore possible errors. Think carefully and decide what to do if an error should occur. In many cases, the program won't be able to continue execution, but you should at least have it display a meaningful error message to notify the user of the problem. In particular, it's a good idea to display the name of the file that has caused the problem.

Reading Bytes

In order to read bytes from a file, we'll need to create a `FileInputStream` object. Table 14.6 lists the most common `FileInputStream` constructors.

Table 14.6
`FileInputStream`
Constructors

Description	Action
`FileInputStream(String name)`	Creates a `FileInputStream` object representing the file with the specified name.
`FileInputStream(File file)`	Creates a `FileInputStream` object representing the specified `File` object.

Most of the time, we'll use the first constructor, which requires a file name:

```
FileInputStream in = new FileInputStream(fileName);
```

Both constructors throw `FileNotFoundException` if the specified file can't be opened for input.

The primary methods provided by `FileInputStream` are all named `read` (Table 14.7). All methods in the table throw `IOException` if an error occurs. If one of the methods fails to read any input because it has reached the end of the file, it returns −1.

Table 14.7
`FileInputStream`
Methods

Description	*Action*
`int read()`	Reads a byte, returning it in `int` form.
`int read(byte[] b)`	Reads bytes into b until the array is full or the end of the file has been reached. Returns the number of bytes read.

`int read(byte[] b,`
`         int off,`
`         int len)`
	Reads up to `len` bytes into the array b, starting at the position indicated by `off`. Returns the number of bytes read.

read
(version 1)

To read a single byte, we would use the first version of the `read` method:

```
int byteValue = in.read();
```

`read` returns an `int` value, not a `byte` value, so we'll need to store the return value in an `int` variable. We next need to test whether the variable is equal to −1 (indicating that no byte could be read). If the variable is not equal to −1, then we can cast its value to `byte` form. The following loop illustrates this process:

```
while (true) {
  int byteValue = in.read();
  if (byteValue == -1)
    break;  // End of file reached
  byte inputByte = (byte) byteValue;
  ...
}
```

In some cases, we can omit the cast and just leave the byte in the original `int` variable.

read
(versions 2 and 3)

The second version of the `read` method reads bytes into an array until the array is full or no more bytes can be read:

```
byte[] buffer = new byte[512];
...
int count = in.read(buffer);
```

The third version of `read` is similar, but it lets us specify where the bytes should be stored in the array. This version also lets us limit the number of bytes that can be read. After calling either version, it's important to test whether `count` has the value −1. If so, no bytes could be read because the method encountered the end of the file.

PROGRAM   **Copying a File**

To illustrate the use of the `FileInputStream` and `FileOutputStream` classes, let's write a program that makes a copy of a file. `FileInputStream` and `FileOutputStream` are perfect for this kind of program; we have no idea what the bytes in the original file represent, nor do we care.

The user will supply the names of the original file and the new file on the command line. To run the program, the user will enter the command

```
java CopyFile source destination
```

where *source* is the name of the original file, and *destination* is the name of the new file.

Here's the strategy we'll use:

- Check that there are two command-line arguments.
- Create a `FileInputStream` object to represent the source file.
- Create a `FileOutputStream` object to represent the destination file.
- Use a loop to read a block of bytes from the `FileInputStream` object and write the block to the `FileOutputStream` object.
- Close both files.

A number of checked exceptions can occur and must be dealt with:

- The `FileInputStream` constructor can throw `FileNotFoundException`.
- The `FileOutputStream` constructor can throw `IOException` (or `FileNotFoundException`, in more recent versions of Java).
- The `read` method in `FileInputStream` can throw `IOException`.
- The `write` method in `FileOutputStream` can throw `IOException`.
- The `close` methods in `FileInputStream` and `FileOutputStream` can throw `IOException`.

Instead of writing a separate `try` block and `catch` block for each exception, which would be cumbersome, I'll enclose most of the program within a single `try` block. After the `try` block will come two `catch` blocks, one for `FileNotFoundException` and one for `IOException`.

CopyFile.java

```
1   // Copies one file into another. The names of both files must
2   // be specified on the command line.
3
4   import java.io.*;
5
6   public class CopyFile {
7     public static void main(String[] args) {
8       // Terminate program if number of command-line arguments
9       // is wrong
```

```
10      if (args.length != 2) {
11        System.out.println("Usage: java CopyFile source dest");
12        System.exit(-1);
13      }
14
15      try {
16        // Open source file for input and destination file for
17        // output
18        FileInputStream source = new FileInputStream(args[0]);
19        FileOutputStream dest = new FileOutputStream(args[1]);
20
21        // Set up a 512-byte buffer
22        byte[] buffer = new byte[512];
23
24        // Copy bytes from the source file to the destination
25        // file, 512 bytes at a time
26        while (true) {
27          int count = source.read(buffer);
28          if (count == -1)
29            break;
30          dest.write(buffer, 0, count);
31        }
32
33        // Close source and destination files
34        source.close();
35        dest.close();
36
37      } catch (FileNotFoundException e) {
38        System.out.println("File cannot be opened");
39      } catch (IOException e) {
40        System.out.println("I/O error during copy");
41      }
42    }
43  }
```

Although the loop on lines 26–31 is designed to copy 512 bytes at a time, the program will probably eventually encounter a block of fewer than 512 bytes. (If the source file is 1271 bytes long, for example, the loop will read two blocks of 512 bytes followed by a block of 247 bytes.) When the read method reads this "small block," the loop won't terminate, because the count variable isn't –1 yet. Instead, the small block will be written to the destination file. When read is called the *next* time, it will return –1, and the loop will terminate.

Review Questions

1. Write a statement that opens a file named records.dat for writing without losing the original contents of the file.

2. What exception do the write methods in the FileOutputStream class throw?

3. How do the read methods in the FileInputStream class indicate when there are no more bytes to be read?

14.4 Advanced Exception-Handling

As the `CopyFile` program of Section 14.3 shows, programs that work with files must deal with a plethora of exceptions, because the constructors and methods of the stream classes tend to throw checked exceptions. Section 8.1 covered the rudiments of exception-handling, but we'll need a more detailed knowledge in order to write programs that use files.

The Hierarchy of Exception Classes

In Section 8.1, we saw that exceptions are objects. For each kind of exception, the Java API provides a corresponding class, such as `FileNotFoundException` and `IOException`. Section 11.5 showed that every class (except for `Object`) must have a superclass; as a result, all Java classes belong to a single class hierarchy. The exception classes have a hierarchy of their own, within the larger hierarchy headed by the `Object` class. A class named `Throwable` is the superclass (directly or indirectly) for all exception classes.

The `Throwable` class has only two direct subclasses: `Error` and `Exception`. Classes that represent specific kinds of exceptions are subclasses of either `Error` or `Exception`. Here's a diagram showing how the exception classes are descended from `Throwable`:

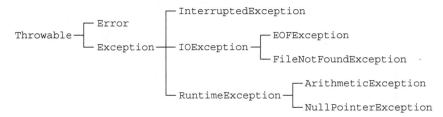

This diagram shows only a few of `Throwable`'s many subclasses. In particular, I've omitted all subclasses of `Error`.

Exception classes that extend `Error` represent unrecoverable errors, such as the Java interpreter failing to load a class or running out of memory. There's nothing that we can do about errors of this sort, so I won't say any more about them. Exception classes that extend `Exception` represent problems that can potentially be handled within a program. All the exceptions in which we're interested fall into this category.

We saw in Section 8.1 that there are two kinds of exceptions: checked and unchecked. What we didn't find out, however, was how to tell whether a particular exception is checked or unchecked. Here's the rule: Subclasses of `Error` or `RuntimeException` represent unchecked exceptions. Subclasses of `Exception` (but not `RuntimeException`) represent checked exceptions.

Using Multiple `catch` Blocks

The fact that exception classes are related to each other has some interesting consequences for writing `catch` blocks. Suppose that a `try` block is followed by two or more `catch` blocks:

```
try
    block
catch (exception-type  identifier)
    block
...
catch (exception-type  identifier)
    block
```

If an exception is thrown inside the `try` block, the first `catch` block whose exception type is compatible with the type of the exception will be allowed to handle the exception. By "compatible," we mean in the same sense as the argument passed to a method being compatible with the method's parameter.

Remember the Substitution Principle (Section 11.4)? Among other things, it allows us to pass an object to a method, even though the object doesn't have the same type as the method's parameter, provided that the object's type is a subclass of the parameter's type. `catch` blocks have "parameters," just like methods, and they behave like method parameters. For example, a `FileNotFoundException` would be compatible with `IOException`, because the `FileNotFoundException` class is a subclass of `IOException`. However, `IOException` would not be compatible with `FileNotFoundException`.

Because exception classes are often related by inheritance, it's quite possible that more than one `catch` block is capable of handling a given exception. Consider the following example:

```
try {
    ...
} catch (FileNotFoundException e) {
    ...
} catch (IOException e) {
    ...
}
```

If a `FileNotFoundException` occurs within the `try` block, both `catch` blocks can potentially handle the exception, because the `FileNotFoundException` class is a subclass of `IOException`. The `catch` block for `FileNotFoundException` comes first, however, so it will handle the exception.

It's important to pay attention to the order of `catch` blocks. If they're put in the wrong order, it's possible that an early `catch` block may end up catching exceptions that were meant for a later `catch` block. Consider what happens if we switch the order of the `catch` blocks in our example:

```
try {
    ...
} catch (IOException e) {
    ... // Catches FileNotFoundException as well as IOException
} catch (FileNotFoundException e) {
    ... // Never executed!
}
```

The second `catch` block can never be executed; if a `FileNotFoundException` occurs in the `try` block, the first `catch` block will handle the exception, because `FileNotFoundException` is compatible with `IOException`. Early Java compilers failed to detect this problem, leaving the programmer puzzling over why the second `catch` block was never executed. Today's compilers will issue an error message, such as "catch not reached."

 If the exception type in one `catch` block is a subclass of the exception type in another block, the `catch` block for the subclass must come first. Otherwise, that block can never be executed.

As we've just seen, a `catch` block for `IOException` will catch not only `IOException`, but also `FileNotFoundException`. In fact, a `catch` block for `IOException` will catch all exceptions that belong to subclasses of `IOException`. This fact suggests a way of simplifying our code: if we're not interested in distinguishing between different kinds of I/O exceptions, we can write a single `catch` block for `IOException`, and it will handle any kind of I/O exception that might arise. Doing so isn't always appropriate, however, because we lose the ability to have the program act differently based on the particular exception (print different messages, for example).

getMessage method ►*8.1* If we do write a single `catch` block for `IOException`, rather than `catch` blocks for specific exceptions, it's a good idea to use `getMessage` to display the message stored inside the `IOException` object. That way, we'll get a better idea of what caused the exception. For example, if the exception was really `FileNotFoundException`, the message stored inside the object might be

```
foo (The system cannot find the file specified)
```

where `foo` is the name of the file that couldn't be opened.

By the way, it's possible to write `catch` blocks that handle a wide variety of exceptions, not just I/O exceptions. In particular, a `catch` block for `Exception` will catch any exception that represents a recoverable error. Consider the following example:

```
try {
    ...
} catch (IOException e) {
    ... // Catches all I/O exceptions
} catch (Exception e) {
    ... // Catches all other exceptions
}
```

The first `catch` block will catch exceptions that belong to the `IOException` class or any of its subclasses. The second `catch` block will catch all other exceptions. Using `Exception` in a `catch` block can be dangerous, however: the block may catch exceptions that we never anticipated when designing the program.

> Whenever possible, use specific exception classes in `catch` blocks, rather than broader classes such as `Exception`.

`finally` Blocks

In our previous discussions of `try` and `catch`, I didn't mention one option. In general, a `try` block can be followed by any number of `catch` blocks. After the last `catch` block, we're allowed to add a ***finally block:***

```
try
    block
catch  (exception-type  identifier)
    block
...
catch  (exception-type  identifier)
    block
finally
    block
```

The `finally` block is executed after the `try` block terminates or the exception is caught by a `catch` block.

The `finally` block has a unique feature: it *must* be executed, no matter what else happens. The `finally` block must be executed even if the `try` block terminates prematurely because of a control statement (`break`, `continue`, or `return`).

Typically, the `finally` block contains code that closes files or performs other "cleanup" actions. We can even use `finally` without any `catch` blocks, just as a way to make sure that the code in the `finally` block is executed, regardless of how the `try` block terminates.

The `throws` Clause

Section 8.1 states that checked exceptions must always be caught. That's not the whole story, as it turns out. When there's a possibility that a checked exception might be thrown inside a method, we have two choices:

- ***Handle the exception within the method.*** We can enclose the affected statement(s) within a `try` block, which is then followed by a `catch` block that can handle the exception.

- ■ *Declare that the method throws the exception.* Any method that calls this one will now be responsible for handling the exception. In effect, we're "passing the buck," telling the compiler that this method won't handle the exception, but any method that calls it will.

To see the difference between the two techniques, consider the problem of writing a helper method named `sleep`, which calls Java's `Thread.sleep` method. We know from Section 8.1 that `Thread.sleep` throws a checked exception named `InterruptedException`. We have two choices. One is to handle the exception within our `sleep` method:

```
static void sleep(int time) {
  try {
    Thread.sleep(time);
  } catch (InterruptedException e) {}
}
```

The other possibility is to declare that our `sleep` method throws `Interrupted-Exception`:

```
static void sleep(int time) throws InterruptedException {
  Thread.sleep(time);
}
```

If `InterruptedException` occurs during a call of our `sleep` method, it will immediately return to wherever it was called. The method that called `sleep` will now be responsible for catching the exception. Of course, that method might also have a `throws` clause, allowing it to avoid handling the exception.

The Java compiler doesn't care which way we deal with the exception, as long as we use one of the two techniques. If a method fails to either catch a checked exception or declare it using `throws`, the compiler will issue an error message.

Which technique is better? That depends on whether or not we can meaningfully deal with the exception inside the method where it's thrown. If we can, then there's no reason for the calling method to know about the exception. If we can't, then it's better to let the calling method handle the exception. In the `sleep` example, it seems better to handle `InterruptedException` within the method itself, so that the rest of the program won't have to deal with this detail.

PROGRAM   **Copying a File (Revisited)**

The `throws` clause is sometimes used by programmers looking for a shortcut. For example, we could simplify the `CopyFile` program (Section 14.3) by not handling exceptions in the program itself, instead declaring that `main` throws `IOException`. (There's no need to mention that `main` throws `FileNot-FoundException`, because `FileNotFoundException` is a subclass of `IOException`.) Here's what the program would look like.

CopyFile2.java

```
1    // Copies one file into another. The names of both files must
2    // be specified on the command line.
3
4    import java.io.*;
5
6    public class CopyFile2 {
7      public static void main(String[] args) throws IOException {
8        // Terminate program if number of command-line arguments
9        // is wrong
10       if (args.length != 2) {
11         System.out.println("Usage: java CopyFile2 source dest");
12         System.exit(-1);
13       }
14
15       // Open source file for input and destination file for
16       // output
17       FileInputStream source = new FileInputStream(args[0]);
18       FileOutputStream dest = new FileOutputStream(args[1]);
19
20       // Set up a 512-byte buffer
21       byte[] buffer = new byte[512];
22
23       // Copy bytes from the source file to the destination
24       // file, 512 bytes at a time
25       while (true) {
26         int count = source.read(buffer);
27         if (count == -1)
28           break;
29         dest.write(buffer, 0, count);
30       }
31
32       // Close source and destination files
33       source.close();
34       dest.close();
35     }
36   }
```

If an IOException (or FileNotFoundException) occurs during the execution of CopyFile2, the program will terminate with an error message about an unhandled exception. From a design standpoint, this isn't very good. It's better to handle the exception within the program itself, displaying an appropriate error message and, if possible, taking steps to recover from the exception.

> Avoid using the throws clause in the main method. Instead, include code in main to deal with exceptions in an appropriate fashion.

Review Questions

1. What is the superclass for all exception classes?

2. How can we tell whether or not an exception is checked?

3. If a `try` block is followed by two `catch` blocks, one for `FileNotFoundException` and one for `IOException`, does it matter which block comes first?

4. What technique can be used to catch any exception that represents a recoverable error?

14.5 Reading and Writing Data Types

The `FileInputStream` and `FileOutputStream` classes (Section 14.3) are useful when we want to read and write single bytes or blocks of bytes. However, they're not very convenient if the bytes represent specific types of data, such as a four-byte `int` value or an eight-byte `double` value. For reading and writing specific data types, we'll need another pair of classes, `DataInputStream` and `DataOutputStream`.

`DataInputStream` and `DataOutputStream` are designed for use with binary files, not text files. Numbers and other types of data can be written to a text file, but only after they've been converted to character form. Section 14.6 discusses reading and writing text files.

Writing Data Types

A `DataOutputStream` object can't be created directly from a file name. Instead, we'll create a `FileOutputStream` object first, and then use that object to create a `DataOutputStream` object. (This is an example of stream layering, which was discussed in Section 14.1.) Here's an example:

```
FileOutputStream fileOut = new FileOutputStream(fileName);
DataOutputStream out = new DataOutputStream(fileOut);
```

The parameter for the `DataOutputStream` constructor has type `Output-Stream`, which is the superclass for several output stream classes, including `FileOutputStream`. As a result, the `DataOutputStream` constructor will accept several different kinds of stream objects as arguments.

To shorten the code (and avoid creating unnecessary variables), some programmers nest the `FileOutputStream` constructor inside the `DataOutput-Stream` constructor:

```
DataOutputStream out =
  new DataOutputStream(new FileOutputStream(fileName));
```

There's no name for the `FileOutputStream` object, but that's not a problem because we won't be using that object directly. Instead, we'll perform operations on the `DataOutputStream` object; these operations will indirectly affect the underlying `FileOutputStream` object.

The methods in the `DataOutputStream` class are capable of writing data of specific types. Table 14.8 on the next page lists some of these methods. All methods in the table throw `IOException` if an error occurs.

Description	Action
`void write(int b)`	Writes the value of b as a single byte.
`void write(byte[] b, int off,` `          int len)`	Writes `len` bytes of the array b, starting at the position indicated by `off`.
`void writeBoolean(boolean v)`	Writes the value of v as a byte containing either 1 (`true`) or 0 (`false`).
`void writeByte(int v)`	Writes the value of v as a single byte.
`void writeChar(int v)`	Writes the value of v as 2 bytes.
`void writeDouble(double v)`	Writes the value of v as 8 bytes.
`void writeFloat(float v)`	Writes the value of v as 4 bytes.
`void writeInt(int v)`	Writes the value of v as 4 bytes.
`void writeLong(long v)`	Writes the value of v as 8 bytes.
`void writeShort(int v)`	Writes the value of v as 2 bytes.

writeInt   To write data to a `DataOutputStream` object, we can use one of the methods from Table 14.8. For example, the following call of `writeInt` will write a single int value stored in the variable n:

```
out.writeInt(n);
```

The other methods in the table are called in a similar fashion. As a result of this call, four bytes (the value of n in binary) will be written to the stream.

Writing Strings

Writing strings to a `DataOutputStream` is a bit tricky, because a string—unlike a value of the primitive types—doesn't have a fixed size. It turns out that `DataOutputStream` has three different methods for writing strings (Table 14.9). All three methods throw `IOException` if an error occurs.

Description	Action
`void writeBytes(String s)`	Writes the specified string as a sequence of bytes.
`void writeChars(String s)`	Writes the specified string as a sequence of two-byte Unicode characters.
`void writeUTF(String s)`	Writes the specified string using UTF-8 encoding.

writeBytes   The `writeBytes` and `writeChars` methods are easy to understand. `writeBytes` writes a string as a series of single bytes. For example, the call

```
out.writeBytes("abc");
```

would write three bytes to the output stream, one for each character in the string `"abc"`.

writeChars   `writeChars` writes a string as a series of Unicode characters, each of which requires two bytes. For example, the call

```
out.writeChars("abc");
```

would write six bytes to the output stream.

writeUTF   Reading a string that's been written by either `writeBytes` or `write-Chars` could be difficult, because there's no indication in the file itself of how many characters are in the string. To avoid this problem, we can use the

Q&A   `writeUTF` method. This method uses an encoding scheme known as ***UTF-8*** to write a string in such a way that it can be read later. If all the characters in the string are ASCII characters, then the UTF-8 encoding of a string consists of a two-byte integer containing the length of the string, followed by the characters in the string, each as a single byte. For example, suppose that we use `writeUTF` to write two strings, one after the other:

```
out.writeUTF("so");
out.writeUTF("far");
```

The two calls will write a total of nine bytes (four bytes for `"so"` and five bytes for `"far"`). Here's what the bytes will look like:

00000000	00000010	01110011	01101111	00000000	00000011	01100110	01100001	01110010
2		's'	'o'	3		'f'	'a'	'r'

As long as we use `writeUTF` to write only strings containing ASCII characters, the number of bytes written will always be equal to the length of the string plus 2. In UTF, non-ASCII characters are stored using two or three bytes; the details are beyond the scope of this book. (To be completely accurate, there's one *null character* ▶9.4   ASCII character—the null character—that's also stored using two bytes. Fortunately, the null character rarely appears in strings.) When a string contains non-ASCII characters, the two bytes that are written ahead of the string represent the number of bytes in the string's encoding, not the original length of the string.

The big advantage of the `writeUTF` method is that each string is preceded by its size in bytes, making it easy to recover the original string when the file is later read. In fact, the `readUTF` method (in the `DataInputStream` class) is designed to do exactly that.

Reading Data Types

In order to read data that was written to a `DataOutputStream`, we'll need a `DataInputStream` object. Creating a `DataInputStream` object is similar to creating a `DataOutputStream` object. We'll need to layer the `Data-InputStream` object on top of a `FileInputStream` object:

```
FileInputStream fileIn = new FileInputStream(fileName);
DataInputStream in = new DataInputStream(fileIn);
```

The parameter for the DataInputStream constructor has type InputStream, which is the superclass for several input stream classes, including FileInput-Stream.

Table 14.10 lists some of the methods provided by the DataInput-Stream class. All methods in the table throw IOException if an error occurs. If one of the read methods fails to read any input because it reaches the end of the file, it returns –1. Each of the methods whose name mentions a primitive type (readBoolean and readByte, for example) throws EOFException if it fails to read the necessary number of bytes because it has reached the end of the file.

Table 14.10
DataInputStream
Methods

Description	Action
int read(byte[] b)	Reads bytes into b until the array is full or the end of the file has been reached. Returns the number of bytes read.
int read(byte[] b, int off, int len)	Reads up to len bytes of data into the array b, starting at the position indicated by off. Returns the number of bytes read.
boolean readBoolean()	Reads a single byte. Returns false if the byte is 0; returns true otherwise.
byte readByte()	Reads a single byte and returns it.
char readChar()	Reads a 2-byte char value and returns it.
double readDouble()	Reads an 8-byte double value and returns it.
float readFloat()	Reads a 4-byte float value and returns it.
int readInt()	Reads a 4-byte int value and returns it.
long readLong()	Reads an 8-byte long value and returns it.
short readShort()	Reads a 2-byte short value and returns it.
String readUTF()	Reads a string and returns it. The string is assumed to be stored using UTF-8 encoding.

readInt

We can use the methods in Table 14.10 to read a single data item. For example, we could call the readInt method to read a four-byte int value:

```
int n = in.readInt();
```

Review Questions

1. Are the DataInputStream and DataOutputStream classes designed for use with binary files or text files?

2. What is the advantage of using DataInputStream and DataOutputStream instead of FileInputStream and FileOutputStream?

3. What three ways does DataOutputStream provide to write strings?

4. If writeUTF is given a string containing five ASCII characters, how many bytes will the method write?

14.6   **Reading and Writing Characters**

To read and write text files—files that contain character data—the preferred technique is to use reader and writer classes. Reader objects are capable of translating single bytes into the two-byte Unicode characters that Java uses. Writer objects perform the opposite translation, converting Unicode characters to single bytes.

Writing to a Text File

The `FileWriter` class is similar to the `FileOutputStream` class of Section 14.3, except that it's designed for use with text files. As it writes characters to a file, a `FileWriter` object will automatically convert each Unicode character into a single byte.

The constructors for the `FileWriter` class (Table 14.11) resemble those for the `FileOutputStream` class. The constructors in the table throw `IOException` if the specified file can't be opened for output.

Table 14.11
`FileWriter`
Constructors

Description	Action
`FileWriter(String fileName)`	Creates a `FileWriter` object representing the file with the specified name.
`FileWriter(String fileName, boolean append)`	Creates a `FileWriter` object representing the file with the specified name. If append is `true`, bytes will be written to the end of the file rather than the beginning.
`FileWriter(File file)`	Creates a `FileWriter` object representing the specified `File` object.

The `FileWriter` class has no methods, although it does inherit methods for writing characters from its superclasses. In most cases, however, it's best to create a different kind of object to do the actual writing to a `FileWriter` object. The `BufferedWriter` class is designed for this purpose. Using `BufferedWriter` provides greater efficiency than using `FileWriter` directly.

We'll normally use the single-argument `BufferedWriter` constructor, which accepts a `FileWriter` object (as well as other kinds of writer objects) as its argument:

```
FileWriter fileOut = new FileWriter(filename);
BufferedWriter bufOut = new BufferedWriter(fileOut);
```

For a list of methods that `BufferedWriter` supports, see Appendix C. We'll usually find it to be more convenient to use the methods in yet another class, `PrintWriter`, instead of the `BufferedWriter` methods. `BufferedWriter` provides methods for writing characters, character arrays, and strings, but it lacks methods for writing other kinds of data. `PrintWriter`, on the other hand, provides the familiar `print` and `println` methods, which closely resemble the ones that we use with `System.out`. To create a `PrintWriter` object, we can supply a `BufferedWriter` object to the `PrintWriter` constructor:

```
PrintWriter out = new PrintWriter(bufOut);
```

In general, the argument to the `PrintWriter` constructor can be any writer or output stream object.

print   Once we have a `PrintWriter` object, we can call the `print` method, which is capable of writing objects as well as values of the primitive types:

```
out.print(3.14);
out.print("Testing...");
```

When we use `print` to write an object, the object's `toString` method is used to convert the object to string form. Table 14.12 lists the `print` methods in the `PrintWriter` class.

Table 14.12
print Methods in the
PrintWriter Class

Description	Action
void print(boolean b)	Writes the value of b as a series of characters.
void print(char c)	Writes the value of c.
void print(int i)	Writes the value of i as a series of characters.
void print(long l)	Writes the value of l as a series of characters.
void print(float f)	Writes the value of f as a series of characters.
void print(double d)	Writes the value of d as a series of characters.
void print(char[] s)	Writes the characters in s.
void print(String s)	Writes the characters in s.
void print(Object obj)	Writes the string returned by obj.toString().

println   The `PrintWriter` class also provides a number of `println` methods, which are used in the same way as `print`:

```
out.println(3.14);
out.println("Testing...");
```

Table 14.13 on the next page lists the `println` methods in the `PrintWriter` class.

Reading from a Text File

For reading characters from a text file, we'll use the `FileReader` class, which is similar to the `FileInputStream` class of Section 14.3. As it reads from a file, a `FileReader` object will automatically convert each byte into the corresponding two-byte Unicode character.

The `FileReader` constructors are analogous to the `FileInputStream`

Table 14.13
println Methods in the
PrintWriter Class

Description	Action
void println()	Finishes the line.
void println(boolean x)	Writes the value of x as a series of characters and then finishes the line.
void println(char x)	Writes the value of x and then finishes the line.
void println(int x)	Writes the value of x as a series of characters and then finishes the line.
void println(long x)	Writes the value of x as a series of characters and then finishes the line.
void println(float x)	Writes the value of x as a series of characters and then finishes the line.
void println(double x)	Writes the value of x as a series of characters and then finishes the line.
void println(char[] x)	Writes the characters in x and then finishes the line.
void println(String x)	Writes the characters in x and then finishes the line.
void println(Object x)	Writes the string returned by x.toString() and then finishes the line.

constructors (Table 14.6). Both constructors throw FileNotFoundException if the file can't be opened for reading.

The FileReader class has no methods, although it does inherit methods for reading characters from its superclasses. In most cases, however, it's best to create a different kind of object to do the actual reading from a FileReader object. The BufferedReader class is designed for this purpose. Using Buffered-Reader provides greater efficiency than using FileReader directly. Also, the BufferedReader class has methods to read whole lines of characters, not just single characters.

We'll normally use the single-argument BufferedReader constructor, which accepts a FileReader object (as well as other kinds of reader objects) as its argument:

```
FileReader fileIn = new FileReader(filename);
BufferedReader in = new BufferedReader(fileIn);
```

Table 14.14 lists some of the methods provided by the BufferedReader class.

Table 14.14
BufferedReader
Methods

Description	Action
int read()	Reads a character, returning it in int form.
int read(char[] cbuf, int off, int len)	Reads up to len characters of data into the array cbuf, starting at the position indicated by off. Returns the number of characters read.
String readLine()	Reads a single line of characters and returns it.

All methods in the table throw IOException if an error occurs. If one of the read methods fails to read any input because it reaches the end of the file, it returns −1.

read
(version 1)

The first version of the read method reads one character from a file. read returns an integer, so a cast is necessary before using the return value as a character. For example, we could use the following loop to read all the characters in a file:

```
while (true) {
  int charValue = in.read();
  if (charValue == -1)
    break;  // End of file reached
  char inputChar = (char) charValue;
  ...
}
```

readLine

The readLine method reads characters until it encounters a line feed ('\n'), a carriage return ('\r'), or a carriage return followed immediately by a line feed. (As a result, readLine will work correctly with Windows, Unix, and Macintosh files.) readLine returns a string containing all the characters it read, not including the line-feed and/or carriage-return character. readLine returns null if it was unable to read any characters at all because it reached the end of the input file.

The following example shows how we could use readLine to read all the lines in a file:

```
while (true) {
  String line = in.readLine();
  if (line == null)
    break;
  ...
}
```

PROGRAM   ## Converting Text to HTML

To illustrate the use of text files, we'll now write a program named ConvertTo-HTML that converts an ordinary text file into an HTML file. An *HTML* (Hypertext Markup Language) file is a text file that contains formatting commands, known as *tags.* These commands are used by a browser to format the file for display.

For example, suppose that the file norton.txt contains a title line plus three paragraphs (see the figure at the top of the next page). To convert this file to HTML form, we'll use the following command to run ConvertToHTML:

```
java ConvertToHTML norton.txt
```

The program will create a file with the same name as the one listed on the command line, but with the extension .html. (The name norton.txt is just an example; the user can supply any file name.) The figure at the bottom of the next page shows the contents of the norton.html file.

norton.txt

```
W. W. Norton & Company

W. W. Norton & Company, Inc., the oldest and
largest publishing house owned wholly by its
employees, strives to carry out the imperative of
its founder to "publish books not for a single
season, but for the years" in the areas of fiction,
nonfiction, and poetry.

The roots of the company date back to 1923, when
William Warder Norton and his wife, M. D. Herter
Norton, began publishing lectures delivered at the
People's Institute, the adult education division of
New York City's Cooper Union. The Nortons soon
expanded their program beyond the Institute,
acquiring manuscripts by celebrated academics from
America and abroad.

Norton now publishes about 300 books annually in
hardcover and paperback.
```

norton.html

start HTML file —	`<HTML>`
start head —	`<HEAD>`
title —	`<TITLE>W. W. Norton & Company</TITLE>`
end head —	`</HEAD>`
start body —	`<BODY>`
level 2 heading —	`<H2>W. W. Norton & Company</H2>`
start paragraph —	`<P>`
	`W. W. Norton & Company, Inc., the oldest and largest publishing house owned wholly by its employees, strives to carry out the imperative of its founder to "publish books not for a single season, but for the years" in the areas of fiction, nonfiction, and poetry.`
start paragraph —	`<P>`
	`The roots of the company date back to 1923, when William Warder Norton and his wife, M. D. Herter Norton, began publishing lectures delivered at the People's Institute, the adult education division of New York City's Cooper Union. The Nortons soon expanded their program beyond the Institute, acquiring manuscripts by celebrated academics from America and abroad.`
start paragraph —	`<P>`
	`Norton now publishes about 300 books annually in hardcover and paperback.`
end body —	`</BODY>`
end HTML file —	`</HTML>`

The tags that have been added indicate the file's title, heading, and paragraph structure. Here's what we might see if we view `norton.html` in a browser:

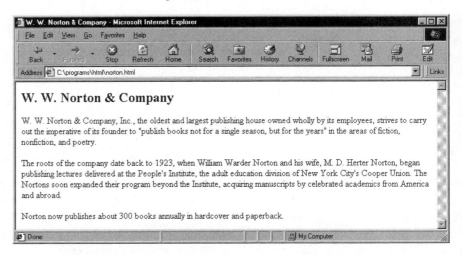

Notice that the text between `<TITLE>` and `</TITLE>` appears in the title of the window. The text between `<H2>` and `</H2>` is displayed as a heading, in a large bold font. Each `<P>` indicates the beginning of a new paragraph. This tag is needed because the browser normally ignores breaks between lines of text; without the `<P>` tags, the text would be displayed as one huge paragraph.

The `ConvertToHTML` program will use the first line in the original file as the text for both the `<TITLE>` and `<H2>` tags. Each blank line in the original file will be replaced by the line

```
<P>
```

in the output file. Nonblank lines after the first one are copied to the HTML file without change. (Certain characters have a special meaning in HTML, including &, <, and >. To be on the safe side, the program should replace these characters by special codes if they appear in the original file. For simplicity, I'll ignore this issue.)

ConvertToHTML.java

```
1   // Converts an ordinary text file to an HTML file
2
3   import java.io.*;
4
5   public class ConvertToHTML {
6     public static void main(String[] args) {
7       // Terminate program if number of command-line arguments
8       // is wrong
9       if (args.length != 1) {
10        System.out.println("Usage: java ConvertToHTML file");
11        System.exit(-1);
12      }
13
```

```
14      // Call the generateHTMLFile method, which converts the
15      // original file to an HTML file. Terminate the program
16      // if an exception occurs.
17      try {
18        generateHTMLFile(args[0]);
19      } catch (IOException e) {
20        System.out.println("Error: " + e.getMessage());
21        System.exit(-1);
22      }
23    }
24
25    // Returns a file name that is identical to fileName, but
26    // with the extension changed to .html
27    private static String createHTMLFileName(String fileName) {
28      int index = fileName.lastIndexOf(".");
29      if (index != -1)
30        fileName = fileName.substring(0, index);
31      return fileName + ".html";
32    }
33
34    // Generates an HTML file containing the contents of the
35    // original file, with HTML tags added
36    private static void generateHTMLFile(String originalFile)
37        throws IOException {
38
39      // Open the original file for reading
40      FileReader fileIn = new FileReader(originalFile);
41      BufferedReader in = new BufferedReader(fileIn);
42
43      // Determine the name of the HTML file by changing the
44      // extension of the original file name to .html
45      String newFile = createHTMLFileName(originalFile);
46
47      // Open the HTML file for writing
48      FileWriter fileOut = new FileWriter(newFile);
49      BufferedWriter bufOut = new BufferedWriter(fileOut);
50      PrintWriter out = new PrintWriter(bufOut);
51
52      // Read the first line of the original file. Terminate
53      // the program if the original file is empty.
54      String firstLine = in.readLine();
55      if (firstLine == null) {
56        System.out.println("File is empty");
57        System.exit(-1);
58      }
59
60      // Write a series of tags to the HTML file, using the
61      // first line of the original file for the <TITLE>
62      // and <H2> tags.
63      out.println("<HTML>");
64      out.println("<HEAD>");
65      out.println("<TITLE>" + firstLine + "</TITLE>");
66      out.println("</HEAD>");
```

```
67      out.println("<BODY>");
68      out.println("<H2>" + firstLine + "</H2>");
69
70      // Copy the remaining lines of the original file to the
71      // HTML file, replacing each empty line with a <P> tag
72      while (true) {
73        String currentLine = in.readLine();
74        if (currentLine == null)
75          break;
76        if (currentLine.length() == 0)
77          out.println("<P>");
78        else
79          out.println(currentLine);
80      }
81
82      // Write the closing tags to the HTML file
83      out.println("</BODY>");
84      out.println("</HTML>");
85
86      // Close both files
87      in.close();
88      out.close();
89    }
90  }
```

Notice that the program has no `catch` block for `FileNotFoundException`. If this exception occurs, it will be caught on line 19, because `FileNotFoundException` is a subclass of `IOException`.

Review Questions

1. Are the `FileReader` and `FileWriter` classes designed for use with binary files or text files?

2. Instead of writing data directly to a `FileWriter` object, it is more efficient to write to a _____ object instead.

3. What methods does the `PrintWriter` class provide for writing data?

4. What methods does the `BufferedReader` class provide for reading data?

14.7 Reading and Writing Objects

Because objects play such an important role in Java, it's not surprising that we can write objects to a file and later read them back in. A file that contains objects is always a binary file.

Storing objects in a file is a complicated process. Writing an object to a file involves saving the values of all the object's instance variables. In addition, some sort of "tag" will need to be saved so that the object's type is known when it's later read back in. But it's even more complicated than that. Some of the values stored in an object might be references to other objects. Those objects will need to be saved as well. Also, to conserve space, we want to avoid storing objects more than once.

Fortunately, Java handles all these details for us, thanks to a process known as *serialization.* When an object is written to a file, Java automatically adds information to identify its class. If the object contains references to other objects, those objects are stored as well. (Because objects can contain other objects, which contain other objects, and so forth, writing one object to a file may cause many other objects to be written as well.)

Each object is stored only once, regardless of the number of references to it. For example, suppose that we need to save `Account` objects. One of the instance variables in the `Account` class might store a `String` object containing the customer's name. If the same customer has two accounts, both `Account` objects might contain a reference to the same `String` object. When the `Account` objects are serialized, only one copy of the `String` object will be stored.

The `Serializable` Interface

interfaces ➤ *12.3*

Not all objects can be written to a file. In order to be serialized, an object must belong to a class that implements the `Serializable` interface. (Actually, the class could implement the `Externalizable` interface instead, but that's beyond the scope of this book.) `Serializable` belongs to the `java.io` package.

A number of classes in the Java API implement the `Serializable` interface, allowing instances of these classes to be serialized. If a class is serializable, then all its subclasses are as well. If you're checking to see if a class is serializable, don't forget to check whether any of its superclasses are.

We can declare one of our own classes to be serializable by adding the words `implements Serializable` to the class declaration:

```
class MyClass implements Serializable {
    ...
}
```

The `Serializable` interface is empty: it doesn't require us to write any methods at all. As a result, we often don't need to make any other changes to `MyClass` to make it serializable. However, there are two conditions that we need to check:

- If any of the instance variables in the class contain objects, these objects must belong to serializable classes.
- The class's direct superclass must have a no-arg constructor or be serializable.

 The compiler won't issue an error message if a program tries to write an object that's not serializable. Instead, a `NotSerializableException` will occur when the program is executed.

Writing Objects

In order to write objects to a file, we'll need to create an instance of the `ObjectOutputStream` class. This instance will be layered on top of an instance of the `FileOutputStream` class:

```
FileOutputStream fileOut = new FileOutputStream(fileName);
ObjectOutputStream out = new ObjectOutputStream(fileOut);
```

The argument to the `ObjectOutputStream` constructor can be any kind of output stream. The constructor may throw `IOException`.

Table 14.15 lists some of the methods provided by the `ObjectOutputStream` class. All methods in the table throw `IOException` if an error occurs.

Table 14.15
`ObjectOutputStream`
Methods

Description	*Action*
`void write(int data)`	Writes the value of `data` as a single byte.
`void write(byte[] b)`	Writes the bytes in the specified array.
`void write(byte[] b, int off, int len)`	Writes `len` bytes of the array `b`, starting at the position indicated by `off`.
`void writeBoolean(boolean data)`	Writes the value of `data` as a byte containing either 1 (`true`) or 0 (`false`).
`void writeByte(int data)`	Writes the value of `data` as a single byte.
`void writeBytes(String data)`	Writes the specified string as a sequence of bytes.
`void writeChar(int data)`	Writes the value of `data` as 2 bytes.
`void writeChars(String data)`	Writes the specified string as a sequence of two-byte Unicode characters.
`void writeDouble(double data)`	Writes the value of `data` as 8 bytes.
`void writeFloat(float data)`	Writes the value of `data` as 4 bytes.
`void writeInt(int data)`	Writes the value of `data` as 4 bytes.
`void writeLong(long data)`	Writes the value of `data` as 8 bytes.
`void writeObject(Object obj)`	Writes the specified object.
`void writeShort(int data)`	Writes the value of `data` as 2 bytes.
`void writeUTF(String data)`	Writes the specified string using UTF-8 encoding.

writeObject   Of all the methods in Table 14.15, the most important is `writeObject`, which is used to write an object to an `ObjectOutputStream`. Because the parameter to `writeObject` has type `Object`, we can supply any object at all to a call of `writeObject`. For example, strings are objects, and the `String` class implements the `Serializable` interface, so we could write a string by using the following call:

```
out.writeObject("Testing...");
```

Three different exceptions can arise as a result of this call:

- IOException—There's a problem with the underlying stream.
- InvalidClassException—There's a problem with the class to which the object belongs. The conditions that cause this exception to occur are fairly arcane (for example, the superclass is not serializable and lacks an accessible no-arg constructor).
- NotSerializableException—The object passed to writeObject doesn't belong to a class that implements the Serializable interface. (NotSerializableException can also occur if some object that needs to be serialized as a result of writing the original object doesn't belong to a class that implements the Serializable interface.)

Fortunately, we don't have to write catch blocks for all these exceptions. InvalidClassException and NotSerializableException are indirect subclasses of IOException, so a catch block for IOException will handle those as well.

The remaining methods in Table 14.15 are used to write other types of data, such as integers, floating-point numbers, and characters. These methods closely resemble DataOutputStream methods (Tables 14.8 and 14.9). By providing these methods, the ObjectOutputStream class lets us create a file containing a mixture of objects and values of the primitive types.

Reading Objects

To be able to read objects, we must first create an instance of the ObjectInput-Stream class:

```
FileInputStream fileIn = new FileInputStream(fileName);
ObjectInputStream in = new ObjectInputStream(fileIn);
```

The argument to the ObjectInputStream constructor can be any kind of input stream.

The ObjectInputStream constructor may throw IOException and StreamCorruptedException. We've never encountered StreamCorruptedException before; it indicates a problem with the format of the underlying file. (Trying to open a file that doesn't contain objects is a typical way to trigger this exception.) StreamCorruptedException is an indirect subclass of IOException, so a catch block for IOException can handle both exceptions.

Table 14.16 on the next page lists some of the methods provided by the ObjectInputStream class. All methods in the table throw IOException if an error occurs. If one of the read methods fails to read any input because it reaches the end of the file, it returns –1. Each of the methods whose name mentions a primitive type (readBoolean and readByte, for example) throws

Table 14.16
`ObjectInputStream`
Methods

Description	Action
`int read()`	Reads a byte, returning it in `int` form.

`int read(byte[] b,`
`          int off,`
`          int len)`
	Reads up to `len` bytes of data into the array b, starting at the position indicated by `off`. Returns the number of bytes read.

`boolean readBoolean()`	Reads a single byte. Returns `false` if the byte is 0; returns `true` otherwise.
`byte readByte()`	Reads a single byte and returns it.
`char readChar()`	Reads a 2-byte `char` value and returns it.
`double readDouble()`	Reads an 8-byte `double` value and returns it.
`float readFloat()`	Reads a 4-byte `float` value and returns it.
`int readInt()`	Reads a 4-byte `int` value and returns it.
`long readLong()`	Reads an 8-byte `long` value and returns it.
`Object readObject()`	Reads an object and returns it.
`short readShort()`	Reads a 2-byte `short` value and returns it.
`String readUTF()`	Reads a string and returns it. The string is assumed to be stored using UTF-8 encoding.

`EOFException` if it fails to read the necessary number of bytes because it has reached the end of the file.

readObject   Objects are read from an `ObjectInputStream` by calling the `read-Object` method. `readObject` returns an `Object` value, which can then be cast to the proper type:

```
String str = (String) in.readObject();
```

Five (yes, five!) exceptions can arise as a result of this call:

- `ClassNotFoundException`—The Java interpreter is unable to locate the class to which the object belongs. (This situation typically arises when a file is written on one computer and then read on a different computer.)
- `InvalidClassException`—There's a problem with the class to which the object belongs.
- `IOException`—There's a problem with the underlying stream.
- `OptionalDataException`—The `readObject` method encountered unexpected data—most likely, bytes belonging to a primitive type—while trying to read an object.
- `StreamCorruptedException`—The `readObject` method encountered an inconsistency in the data.

`InvalidClassException`, `OptionalDataException`, and `Stream-CorruptedException` are (indirect) subclasses of `IOException`, so a single `catch` block for `IOException` will handle four of the exceptions. `ClassNot-FoundException` is not a subclass of `IOException`, however, so it will need a separate `catch` block.

The remaining methods in Table 14.16 are used to read other types of data, such as integers, floating-point numbers, and characters. These methods closely resemble the `DataInputStream` methods (Table 14.10).

Reading and Writing Entire Data Structures

Data structures, such as arrays and vectors, are themselves objects, so we can write an entire data structure to a file with a single method call. Here's an example of writing an array to a file:

```
int[] a = {1, 2, 3};

try {
  FileOutputStream fileOut = new FileOutputStream(fileName);
  ObjectOutputStream out = new ObjectOutputStream(fileOut);
  out.writeObject(a);
  out.close();
} catch (IOException e) {
  System.out.println(e.getMessage());
}
```

Here's how we would read the array back in:

```
int[] a;

try {
  FileInputStream fileIn = new FileInputStream(fileName);
  ObjectInputStream in = new ObjectInputStream(fileIn);
  a = (int[]) in.readObject();
  in.close();
} catch (IOException e) {
  System.out.println(e.getMessage());
} catch (ClassNotFoundException e) {
  System.out.println(e.getMessage());
}
```

We could use similar code to write a vector or other data structure and then read it later. See the `PhoneDirectory2` program of Section 14.8 for an example.

When serializing a data structure, make sure that the elements of the data structure are serializable. If they're not, a `NotSerializableException` will occur when the program is executed.

Review Questions

1. What is the name of the process that Java uses to write objects to a file?

2. In order to be written to a file, an object must belong to a class that implements the _____ interface.

3. The `writeObject` method belongs to the _____ class.

4. True or false: An entire data structure can be written to a file with a single method call.

14.8   Case Study: A Phone Directory (Revisited)

In Section 5.8, we developed a program named PhoneDirectory that stores
names and telephone numbers. The program allows the user to enter new names
and numbers as well as look up existing names. The original program suffers
from a major flaw: the names and phone numbers are lost when the program terminates. In this section, we'll develop a modified version of PhoneDirectory that saves the names and numbers in a file when it terminates. When the
program is run the next time, it restores the names and numbers by reading from
the file.

The new version of PhoneDirectory will differ from the old one in two
other ways as well. First, it will store PhoneRecord objects in a vector rather
than an array. Using a vector lets us avoid placing a limit on the amount of data the
program can store. Second, the new program has been redesigned to use helper
methods instead of a single main method. The addNumber and findNumber
helper methods implement the a (add) and f (find) commands. The save-
Records method is called to save the records in a file when the program terminates. The readRecords method is called to read records from the same file
each time the program begins to execute.

The program will save the records in a file named records.dat. For simplicity, saveRecords will save the entire vector as a single object. If read-
Records is unable to read from the records.dat file (or the file doesn't
exist), the method will display a message and create an empty vector.

The PhoneRecord class will be almost the same as in Section 5.8. The only
difference is that we'll need to add the words implements Serializable to
the class declaration.

PhoneDirectory2.java

```
1   // Program name: PhoneDirectory2
2   // Author: K. N. King
3   // Written: 1999-12-22
4   //
5   // Stores names and telephone numbers and allows phone
6   // numbers to be looked up. The user is given a menu of
7   // three commands:
8   //
9   //    a - Add a new phone number
10  //    f - Find a phone number
11  //    q - Quit
12  //
13  // The "a" command prompts the user to enter a name and a
14  // number, which are then stored in the program's database.
15  //
16  // The "f" command prompts the user to enter a name; the
17  // program then displays all matching names in the database,
18  // along with the corresponding phone numbers. It is not
19  // necessary to enter the entire name; all names that begin
```

```
20   // with the specified characters will be displayed. The "f"
21   // command ignores the case of letters when looking for
22   // matching names.
23   //
24   // The "q" command causes the program to terminate. The names
25   // and numbers are saved in a file named "records.dat". When
26   // the program is run the next time, it will open the file
27   // and read the records.
28
29   import java.io.*;
30   import java.util.*;
31   import jpb.*;
32
33   public class PhoneDirectory2 {
34     // Class variables
35     private static final String DATA_FILE = "records.dat";
36     private static Vector records;
37
38     public static void main(String[] args) {
39       // Read records from data file
40       readRecords();
41
42       // Display list of commands
43       System.out.println("Phone directory commands:\n" +
44                          "  a - Add a new phone number\n" +
45                          "  f - Find a phone number\n" +
46                          "  q - Quit\n");
47
48       // Read and execute commands
49       while (true) {
50
51         // Prompt user to enter a command
52         SimpleIO.prompt("Enter command (a, f, or q): ");
53         String command = SimpleIO.readLine().trim();
54
55         // Determine whether command is "a", "f", "q", or
56         // illegal; execute command if legal.
57         if (command.equalsIgnoreCase("a")) {
58
59           // Command is "a". Call addNumber to add a new
60           // name and number to the database
61           addNumber();
62         } else if (command.equalsIgnoreCase("f")) {
63
64           // Command is "f". Call findNumber to find phone
65           // numbers that match the user's criteria.
66           findNumber();
67         } else if (command.equalsIgnoreCase("q")) {
68
69           // Command is "q". Save records in data file and
70           // terminate program.
71           saveRecords();
72           return;
73         } else {
```

```
74
75               // Command is illegal. Display error message.
76               System.out.println("Command was not recognized; " +
77                                  "please enter only a, f, or q.");
78            }
79
80         System.out.println();
81      }
82   }
83
84   //////////////////////////////////////////////////////////////
85   // NAME:       addNumber
86   // BEHAVIOR:   Prompts the user for a name and number,
87   //             then creates a phone record and stores it in
88   //             the records vector.
89   // PARAMETERS: None
90   // RETURNS:    Nothing
91   //////////////////////////////////////////////////////////////
92   private static void addNumber() {
93      SimpleIO.prompt("Enter new name: ");
94      String name = SimpleIO.readLine().trim();
95      SimpleIO.prompt("Enter new phone number: ");
96      String number = SimpleIO.readLine().trim();
97      records.addElement(new PhoneRecord(name, number));
98   }
99
100  //////////////////////////////////////////////////////////////
101  // NAME:       findNumber
102  // BEHAVIOR:   Prompts the user for a search key. Searches
103  //             the records vector for records whose names
104  //             begin with the search key. Prints these
105  //             names and the corresponding phone numbers.
106  // PARAMETERS: None
107  // RETURNS:    Nothing
108  //////////////////////////////////////////////////////////////
109  private static void findNumber() {
110     SimpleIO.prompt("Enter name to look up: ");
111     String key = SimpleIO.readLine().trim().toLowerCase();
112     for (int i = 0; i < records.size(); i++) {
113        PhoneRecord currentRecord =
114           (PhoneRecord) records.elementAt(i);
115        String name = currentRecord.getName().toLowerCase();
116        if (name.startsWith(key))
117           System.out.println(currentRecord.getName() + " " +
118                              currentRecord.getNumber());
119     }
120  }
121
122  //////////////////////////////////////////////////////////////
123  // NAME:       readRecords
124  // BEHAVIOR:   Restores the records vector to its previous
125  //             state by reading it (as a single object)
126  //             from the data file. Creates an empty vector
127  //             if the file does not exist or cannot be
```

```
128     //              read.
129     // PARAMETERS: None
130     // RETURNS:     Nothing
131     //////////////////////////////////////////////////////////
132     private static void readRecords() {
133       try {
134         FileInputStream fileIn = new FileInputStream(DATA_FILE);
135         ObjectInputStream in = new ObjectInputStream(fileIn);
136         records = (Vector) in.readObject();
137         in.close();
138       } catch (Exception e) {
139         System.out.println(DATA_FILE + " does not exist or " +
140                            "cannot be read\n");
141         records = new Vector();
142       }
143     }
144
145     //////////////////////////////////////////////////////////
146     // NAME:        saveRecords
147     // BEHAVIOR:    Saves the records vector (as a single
148     //              object) by writing it to the data file.
149     // PARAMETERS: None
150     // RETURNS:     Nothing
151     //////////////////////////////////////////////////////////
152     private static void saveRecords() {
153       try {
154         FileOutputStream fileOut =
155           new FileOutputStream(DATA_FILE);
156         ObjectOutputStream out =
157           new ObjectOutputStream(fileOut);
158         out.writeObject(records);
159         out.close();
160       } catch (IOException e) {
161         System.out.println("Error writing to " + DATA_FILE);
162       }
163     }
164   }
165
166   // Represents a record containing a name and a phone number
167   class PhoneRecord implements Serializable {
168     private String name;
169     private String number;
170
171     //////////////////////////////////////////////////////////
172     // NAME:        PhoneRecord
173     // BEHAVIOR:    Constructs a phone record containing the
174     //              specified name and phone number
175     // PARAMETERS: personName - name of a person
176     //              phoneNumber - phone number for that person
177     //////////////////////////////////////////////////////////
178     public PhoneRecord(String personName, String phoneNumber) {
179       name = personName;
180       number = phoneNumber;
181     }
```

```
182
183     ////////////////////////////////////////////////////////////
184     // NAME:         getName
185     // BEHAVIOR:     Returns the name stored in this record
186     // PARAMETERS:   None
187     // RETURNS:      The name stored in this record
188     ////////////////////////////////////////////////////////////
189     public String getName() {
190        return name;
191     }
192
193     ////////////////////////////////////////////////////////////
194     // NAME:         getNumber
195     // BEHAVIOR:     Returns the phone number stored in this
196     //               record
197     // PARAMETERS:   None
198     // RETURNS:      The phone number stored in this record
199     ////////////////////////////////////////////////////////////
200     public String getNumber() {
201        return number;
202     }
203  }
```

Q & A

Q: **What happens if a program terminates without closing all the files that it opened? [p. 606]**

A: Most operating systems will automatically close any files that are left open by a Java program. However, it's a good idea to close files explicitly, for several reasons. First, it makes it easier for someone reading the program to determine when the program stops using the file. Second, if the file is being used for output, closing the file also flushes the stream's buffer, ensuring that the file is intact in case the system should crash. Finally, closing a file releases system resources that may be needed for other purposes (such as opening additional files later in the program).

Q: **In Section 14.2, you entered c:\programs\lottery as input to the FileProperties program. Why didn't you have to use two backslashes? [p. 611]**

A: The backslash problem described in Section 14.2 only occurs when there are backslashes in *literal* strings, because the compiler will try to treat each backslash as the beginning of an escape sequence. Strings that are entered by the user don't have this problem because they don't occur in the program's source code and are never seen by the compiler.

Q: **When an int value (or value of another primitive type) is written to a file, in what order are the bytes written? [p. 626]**

A: That's an excellent question. Suppose that the value of the int variable n is 300. In binary, the value of n is 00000000 00000000 00000001 00101100. (I've added spaces to make the number more readable.) When n is written to a file, it will occupy four bytes.

There are two logical ways to store the value of n. One alternative is to write the leftmost byte first:

00000000	00000000	00000001	00101100

The other alternative is to write the bytes in the opposite order, with the rightmost byte first:

00101100	00000001	00000000	00000000

The first alternative is called *big-endian;* the second is known as *little-endian.* (The names come from Jonathan Swift's *Gulliver's Travels,* in which the Lilliputians were divided into two camps: those who opened their soft-boiled eggs on the big end and those who opened them on the little end.) Java's stream classes store data in big-endian order.

Byte ordering is an important issue for many programmers. As long as a file is written by a Java program and later read by a Java program, there's no problem. But if the file is written by a non-Java program and then read by a Java program, or vice versa, there could be a problem if the programs are expecting different byte orders.

Q: What does UTF-8 stand for? [p. 627]

A: I was afraid you were going to ask. UTF stands for *UCS Transformation Format,* and 8 is the number of bits used in the encoding. Your next question, of course, is: what does UCS stand for? UCS is an acronym for *Universal Character Set.* At around the same time Unicode was created by a consortium of software manufacturers, the International Organization for Standardization (ISO) began a similar effort to develop an international character set, which they called the Universal Character Set. UCS characters are 31 bits long, rather than 16 bits. Fortunately, Unicode and UCS are compatible.

Q: When an object is serialized, are the values of its class variables preserved? [p. 636]

A: No. Only the values of its instance variables are saved when an object is serialized.

Q: Is there some way to preserve only some of the instance variables in an object, rather than all the instance variables? [p. 636]

A: Yes. Any instance variables that have been declared transient (a Java keyword) won't be saved when an object is serialized.

Summary

- A file is a collection of related data that is given a name and placed on a storage medium of some sort.
- All files, regardless of the kind of data they contain, consist of bytes.
- Files fall into two categories: text files, in which the bytes represent characters, and binary files, in which bytes can represent other kinds of data.
- Text files are divided into lines, with one or two special characters at the end of each line.
- Some operating systems allow text files to contain a special end-of-file marker.
- A stream is an abstraction that represents any "file-like" source of input or destination for output.
- In Java, streams are represented by objects that belong to one of the classes in the `java.io` package. These classes have names that end with `Stream`, `Reader`, or `Writer`.
- Classes whose names end with `Reader` or `Writer` are designed specifically for text files. A reader object automatically converts bytes to Unicode characters. A writer object converts Unicode characters to single bytes.
- Opening a file is done by creating an instance of a stream, reader, or writer class. If the file is opened for input, it must already exist. If the file is opened for output, it will be truncated if it already exists; if it does not exist, the file will be created.
- Performing an operation on a file (such as reading input or writing output) is done by calling an instance method.
- When a program is finished with a file, it should close the file by calling the `close` method, which is supported by all stream, reader, and writer classes.
- Data written to a file normally goes into a buffer first. The buffer is flushed (written to the file) automatically when it's full or the file is closed.
- A file buffer can be flushed at any time by a call of the `flush` method, which is supported by all output stream and writer classes.
- Each open file has a file pointer, which keeps track of the current position within that file. As bytes are read from the file or written to the file, the file pointer advances automatically.
- It is necessary to test for the end-of-file condition each time input is read from a file.
- When a file is opened, the file pointer is normally at the beginning of the file. In some cases, however, a program will need to append data to the end of a file, rather than replacing the data that the file already contains.

- Sequential access to a file involves reading or writing bytes in sequence, from first to last. The alternative is random access: the program changes the file pointer at will, allowing immediate access to data in any part of the file.

- The `File` class provides methods for checking the properties of a file (`canRead`, `canWrite`, `exists`, `isDirectory`, `isFile`, `length`, and `list`) and performing a few basic file operations (`delete`, `mkdir`, and `renameTo`).

- The `list` method returns an array containing the names of all files in a particular directory.

- The `FileInputStream` and `FileOutputStream` classes provide methods for reading and writing bytes.

- The primary methods provided by `FileOutputStream` are named `write`. One version writes a single byte, another version writes an array of bytes, and the third version writes a portion of an array of bytes.

- The primary methods provided by `FileInputStream` are named `read`. One version of `read` reads a single byte, another version attempts to fill an array with bytes, and the third version reads a specified number of bytes into an array at a specified starting position.

- The exception classes are all subclasses (directly or indirectly) of a class named `Throwable`.

- `Throwable` has two direct subclasses: `Error` and `Exception`.

- Exception classes that extend `Error` represent unrecoverable errors, such as the Java interpreter failing to load a class or running out of memory.

- Exception classes that extend `Exception` represent problems that can potentially be handled within a program.

- One of the subclasses of `Exception` is named `RuntimeException`. Subclasses of `Error` or `RuntimeException` represent unchecked exceptions. Subclasses of `Exception` (but not `RuntimeException`) represent checked exceptions.

- If an exception is thrown inside a `try` block, the first `catch` block whose exception type is compatible with the type of the exception will be allowed to handle the exception.

- If the exception type in one `catch` block is a subclass of the exception type in another block, the `catch` block for the subclass must come first. Otherwise, that block can never be executed.

- A `catch` block for a superclass can catch exceptions that belong to all subclasses. In particular, a `catch` block for `Exception` can catch exceptions that represent all recoverable errors.

- A `finally` block is allowed at the end of a series of `catch` blocks. The `finally` block is executed after the `try` block terminates or the exception is caught by a `catch` block.

- The `finally` block must be executed even if the `try` block terminates prematurely because of a control statement (`break`, `continue`, or `return`).

- Instead of handling a checked exception, a method can ignore the exception and allow it to be handled where the method was called. The method's declaration must include the word `throws`, followed by the name of the exception.

- The `DataInputStream` and `DataOutputStream` classes allow specific data types to be read and written, not just bytes. These classes are designed for use with binary files, not text files.

- The methods in the `DataOutputStream` class can write data of specific types. In addition to the `write` methods, which can write a single byte or an array of bytes, methods include `writeBoolean`, `writeByte`, `writeChar`, `writeDouble`, `writeFloat`, `writeInt`, `writeLong`, and `writeShort`.

- `DataOutputStream` also has three methods for writing strings: `writeBytes`, `writeChars`, and `writeUTF`.

- The `writeBytes` method writes a string as a series of single bytes.

- The `writeChars` method writes a string as a series of Unicode characters, each of which requires two bytes.

- The `writeUTF` method uses an encoding scheme known as UTF-8 to write a string in such a way that it can be read later. If the string contains only ASCII characters, then its UTF-8 encoding consists of a two-byte integer containing the length of the string, followed by the characters in the string, each as a single byte.

- A `DataInputStream` object is used to read data that was written to a `DataOutputStream`.

- The methods in the `DataInputStream` class can read data of specific types. In addition to the `read` methods, which can read a single byte or an array of bytes, methods include `readBoolean`, `readByte`, `readChar`, `readDouble`, `readFloat`, `readInt`, `readLong`, `readShort`, and `readUTF`.

- A `FileWriter` object can be used to write characters to a text file. As it writes to a file, a `FileWriter` object automatically converts each Unicode character into a single byte.

- For efficiency, it's customary to create a `BufferedWriter` object that writes to the `FileWriter` object.

- The methods provided by `BufferedWriter` aren't very convenient, so programmers usually create a `PrintWriter` object that writes to the `BufferedWriter` object.

- The `PrintWriter` class provides methods named `print` and `println`.

- A `FileReader` object can be used to read characters from a text file. As it reads from a file, a `FileReader` object automatically converts each byte into the corresponding two-byte Unicode character.

- The `BufferedReader` class provides a convenient set of methods for reading from a text file, including `read` methods for reading a single character or an array of characters, and a `readLine` method that reads an entire line, returning it as a string.

- Objects can be stored in a file via a process known as serialization. During serialization, Java automatically adds information to identify the class to which each object belongs. If an object contains references to other objects, those objects are stored as well.

- When objects are serialized, each object is stored only once, regardless of the number of references to it.

- In order to be serialized, an object must belong to a class that implements the `Serializable` interface, or it must have a superclass that implements `Serializable`.

- The `ObjectOutputStream` class provides the `writeObject` method, which is used to write an object.

- Other `ObjectOutputStream` methods are designed to write strings and values of a primitive type. In addition to the `write` methods, which can write a single byte or an array of bytes, these methods include `writeBoolean`, `writeByte`, `writeBytes`, `writeChar`, `writeChars`, `writeDouble`, `writeFloat`, `writeInt`, `writeLong`, `writeShort`, and `writeUTF`.

- The `ObjectInputStream` class provides the `readObject` method, which is used to read an object.

- Other `ObjectInputStream` methods are designed to read strings and values of a primitive type. In addition to the `read` methods, which can read a single byte or an array of bytes, these methods include `readBoolean`, `readByte`, `readChar`, `readDouble`, `readFloat`, `readInt`, `readLong`, `readShort`, and `readUTF`.

- Data structures, such as arrays and vectors, are themselves objects, making it possible to write an entire data structure to a file with a single method call.

Exercises

Section 14.1

1. Suppose that a file consists of the following four bytes: 00000000 00000001 00000010 00000011. What value(s) does the file contain in each of the following cases:
   (a) Each byte represents an ASCII character.
   (b) Each pair of bytes represents a `short` value.
   (c) The bytes represent a single `int` value.

2. A text file containing the same data will have a different length in Windows than in Unix. Explain why.

3. Indicate whether each of the following files is more likely to contain text data or binary data:

   (a) A Java program in source code form
   (b) A Java class file
   (c) A file containing an image
   (d) An e-mail message sent from one computer to another
   (e) A file containing a sound

4. Suppose that we need to store 10000 int values in a file. Discuss the advantages and disadvantages of using a binary file versus a text file. (In a binary file, each int value would require exactly four bytes. In a text file, each int value would be stored as a series of digits, with each digit requiring one byte.)

Section 14.2

5. Write one or more statements that create a directory named temp inside a directory named java.

Section 14.3

6. Assume that buffer is an array of bytes. Construct a loop that writes the contents of buffer to a FileOutputStream object named out, with each pair of bytes written in reverse order. (In other words, the loop will write the elements of buffer in the order 1, 0, 3, 2, 5, 4, …)

Section 14.4

7. What's wrong with the catch blocks in the following statement?

```
try {
    ...
} catch (IOException e) {
    ...
} catch (EOFException e) {
    ...
}
```

Section 14.5

8. Assume that each of the following methods is called with 25 as its argument. What byte(s) would each method write to a DataOutputStream object? (Show the bytes in binary.)

   (a) writeByte
   (b) writeInt
   (c) writeLong
   (d) writeShort

9. Assume that each of the following methods is called with "Java" as its argument. What byte(s) would each method write to a DataOutputStream object? (Show the bytes in binary.)

   (a) writeBytes
   (b) writeChars
   (c) writeUTF

10. Table 14.8 lists a number of methods that write to a DataOutputStream. Why didn't the designers of Java use the name write for all these methods, instead of giving them individual names such as writeBoolean, writeByte, writeChar, and so on?

Section 14.6

11. Tables 14.12 and 14.13 list the print and println methods in the PrintWriter class. Explain why none of these methods has a byte or short parameter, although all the other primitive types are used as parameter types.

Programming Projects

1. Modify the SSNInfo program (Programming Project 1, Chapter 5) so that it reads the area numbers and locations from a file named ssn.dat. Each line in the file will contain a single area number and corresponding location, separated by a space:

    ```
    3 New Hampshire
    7 Maine
    9 Vermont
    ```

2. Modify the Bank program (Programming Project 8, Chapter 5) so that it saves the account data in a file named bank.dat when it terminates. When the program is run the next time, have it restore the accounts by reading from the file. Have the program save the accounts as individual BankAccount objects.

3. Modify the CourseAverage2 program (Section 7.7) so that it reads input data from a file, which is given to the program as a command-line argument. Each line of the file will have the following form:

    ```
    Smith,John,20,19,15,18.5,20,20,18,20,9,10,5.5,8,9.5,78,92,85
    ```

    The line begins with a last name and first name, followed by eight program scores (0–20), five quiz scores (0–10), two test scores (0–100), and a final exam score (0–100). There may be any number of lines in the file, with each line representing a different student. The output of the program will have the following form:

    ```
    Name            Average
    ----            -------
    Smith, John        88
    Jones, Mary        93
    ```

4. Modify the PrintCalendar program (Section 8.6) so that it writes 12 monthly calendars to a file. The user will specify the year and the file in which the calendars should be stored:

    ```
    java PrintCalendar 2000 calendar
    ```

    After the program is finished, the file named calendar will contain calendars for January 2000, February 2000, and so forth. There should be one blank line separating the calendars for consecutive months.

5. Modify the Rot13 program (Section 9.5) so that it obtains the message to be encrypted from a file and writes the encrypted message to another file. For example, the command

    ```
    java Rot13 original secret
    ```

    will encrypt the message stored in the file named original and store the result in a file named secret. The encrypted file will contain the same number of lines as the original file.

6. Modify the Personnel program (Programming Project 3, Chapter 11) so that it saves the employee records in a file named employees.dat when it terminates. When the program is run the next time, have it restore the records by reading from the file. Have the program save the data as individual HourlyEmployee and SalariedEmployee objects.

7. Modify the ShowDefinition program (Section 12.8) so that it reads the terms and their definitions from a file named defs.dat. Each line of the file will contain either a term or

its definition. The lines will alternate, with each term immediately followed by the definition of the term.

8. Modify the `ScrollingList` program (Programming Project 9, Chapter 12) so that it reads the words from a file named `words.dat`. Each line of the file will contain a single word.

9. Modify the `PhoneDirectory` program (Programming Project 10, Chapter 12) so that it saves the names and phone numbers in a file named `phone.dat` when it terminates. When the program is run the next time, have it restore the names and numbers by reading from the file. Each line of the file will contain either a name or a phone number. The lines will alternate, with each name immediately followed by the corresponding phone number.

10. Modify the `FindDistance` program (Section 13.1) so that it reads the city names and distances from a file named `cities.dat`. The first line in the file will contain the number of cities. The next group of lines will contain the city names, one per line. Each of the remaining lines will contain the distances from one of the cities to all the other cities, with adjacent distances separated by commas. For example, the `cities.dat` file might look like this:

```
8
Atlanta
Boston
Chicago
Houston
Los Angeles
New York
San Francisco
Washington
0,1110,710,790,2190,850,2480,620
1110,0,1000,1830,3020,210,3130,450
710,1000,0,1090,2050,810,2170,710
790,1830,1090,0,1540,1610,1910,1370
2190,3020,2050,1540,0,2790,390,2650
850,210,810,1610,2790,0,2930,240
2480,3130,2170,1910,390,2930,0,2840
620,450,710,1370,2650,240,2840,0
```

11. Modify the `SortLines` program (Section 13.4) so that it sorts a file specified by the user on the command line, putting the sorted lines back into the original file.

12. Modify the `AirMileage` program (Section 13.5) so that it reads the city names and mileages from a file named `mileage.dat`. The first line of the file will specify the number of cities. The remaining lines will contain either a city name or a mileage. The lines will alternate, with each city name immediately followed by the air mileage between that city and New York City.

13. Modify the `FindAnagrams` program (Section 13.8) so that it obtains the input words from a file specified by the user on the command line. Each line of the file will contain a single word.

14. Modify the `FileProperties` program (Section 14.2) so that it obtains the file name from the command line rather than by prompting the user to enter it.

15. Modify the `ListFiles` program (Section 14.2) so that it displays some of the properties of the files in the current directory. Here's an example of what we might see if the current

directory contains three ordinary files and two directories:

```
rw          965 index.html
drw           0 javalinks
drw           0 photos
rw         2969 programs.html
rw         3292 students.html
```

The letter d indicates a directory. r and w indicate that the file can be read and written, respectively. The numbers are the lengths of the files in bytes.

16. Write a program named DeleteTempFiles that deletes all files in the current directory whose extension is .tmp or .TMP.

17. Modify the CopyFile program (Section 14.3) so that it copies one byte at a time, rather than copying a block of bytes.

18. Modify the CopyFile program (Section 14.3) so that, if either the source file or destination file can't be opened, the program displays an error message containing the name of that file.

19. Modify the ConvertToHTML program (Section 14.6) so that it allows the user to specify the background color and font for the HTML file, in addition to the title. For example, suppose that the file demo.txt contains the following lines:

```
color=255,200,0
font=Verdana
title=Coming of Age in Electronic Commerce
...
```

After the program is finished, the file named demo.html will have the following form:

```
<HTML>
<HEAD>
<TITLE>Coming of Age in Electronic Commerce</TITLE>
</HEAD>
<BODY BGCOLOR="#ffc800">
<FONT FACE="Verdana">
<H2>Coming of Age in Electronic Commerce</H2>
...
</FONT>
</BODY>
</HTML>
```

The line

```
<BODY BGCOLOR="#ffc800">
```

specifies that the background color for the Web page will be ffc800, where ff is the hexadecimal code for the red component, c8 is the code for the green component, and 00 is the code for the blue component.

The first few lines of the original file may contain the following commands:

- color=*value,* where *value* consists of three integers between 0 and 255, with a comma between each pair of adjacent integers.
- font=*value,* where *value* is the name of a font.
- title=*value,* where *value* is the title of the Web page.

All three commands are optional. If color is omitted, then the

```
<BODY BGCOLOR="#ffc800">
```

line will be replaced by

```
<BODY>
```

If font is omitted, the <FONT ...> and </FONT> lines are not included in the HTML file. If the title command is omitted, then the <TITLE> and <H2> lines are not included in the HTML file. The order of the commands doesn't matter. There may be spaces before and after color, font, title, and *value*.

20.   Write a program named ViewFile that displays the contents of a file as bytes and as characters. For example, suppose that we execute the program by entering the command

```
java ViewFile JavaRules.java
```

where JavaRules.java is the program at the beginning of Section 2.1. ViewFile will display the following output on the screen:

```
Offset                  Bytes                 Characters
------  ------------------------------------  ----------
     0  2F 2F 20 44 69 73 70 6C 61 79  // Display
    10  73 20 74 68 65 20 6D 65 73 73  s the mess
    20  61 67 65 20 22 4A 61 76 61 20  age "Java
    30  72 75 6C 65 73 21 22 0D 0A 0D  rules!"...
    40  0A 70 75 62 6C 69 63 20 63 6C  .public cl
    50  61 73 73 20 4A 61 76 61 52 75  ass JavaRu
    60  6C 65 73 20 7B 0D 0A 20 20 70  les {..  p
    70  75 62 6C 69 63 20 73 74 61 74  ublic stat
    80  69 63 20 76 6F 69 64 20 6D 61  ic void ma
    90  69 6E 28 53 74 72 69 6E 67 5B  in(String[
   100  5D 20 61 72 67 73 29 20 7B 0D  ] args) {.
   110  0A 20 20 20 20 53 79 73 74 65  .    Syste
   120  6D 2E 6F 75 74 2E 70 72 69 6E  m.out.prin
   130  74 6C 6E 28 22 4A 61 76 61 20  tln("Java
   140  72 75 6C 65 73 21 22 29 3B 0D  rules!");.
   150  0A 20 20 7D 0D 0A 7D 0D 0A     .  }..}..
```

Each line shows 10 bytes from the file, as hexadecimal numbers and as characters. The number in the Offset column indicates the position within the file of the first byte on the line. Characters are displayed only if their decimal value is between 32 and 176 (inclusive). Characters outside this range are shown as periods.

21.   Write a program named SplitFile that splits a file into pieces of a specified size. For example, the command

```
java SplitFile demo 1024
```

would split the file named demo into smaller files, with each file (except possibly the last) containing 1024 bytes. The smaller files will have the same name as the original file, with an added extension of .1, .2, .3, and so on. For example, if demo has 3000 bytes, the smaller files would be named demo.1, demo.2, and demo.3. The first two files would contain 1024 bytes, and the third would contain 952 bytes.

22.   Write a program named CombineFiles that combines multiple files into a single file. For example, the command

```
java CombineFiles part1 part2 part3 demo
```

would combine part1, part2, and part3 into a new file named demo. (The last command-line argument is the name of the combined file.) The length of the file must be equal to the sum of the lengths of `part1`, `part2`, and `part3`.

23. Of the many techniques for compressing the contents of a file, one of the simplest and fastest is known as ***run-length encoding***. This technique compresses a file by replacing sequences of identical bytes by a pair of bytes: a repetition count followed by a byte to be repeated. For example, suppose that the file to be compressed begins with the following sequence of bytes (shown in hex):

    46 6F 6F 20 62 61 72 21 21 21 20 20 20 20 20

    The compressed file will contain the following bytes:

    01 46 02 6F 01 20 01 62 01 61 01 72 03 21 05 20

    Run-length encoding works well if the original file contains many long sequences of identical bytes. In the worst case (a file with no repeated bytes), run-length encoding can actually double the length of the file.

    (a) Write a program named `Compress` that uses run-length encoding to compress a file. To run `Compress`, we would use a command of the form

    ```
    java Compress demo
    ```

    where `demo` is the name of the file to be compressed. The program will write the compressed data to a file with the same name, but with `.rle` added as an extension (`demo.rle`, in this example). *Hint:* The `ViewFile` program of Programming Project 20 could be useful for debugging.

    (b) Write a program named `Uncompress` that reverses the compression performed by the `Compress` program. To run `Uncompress`, we would use a command of the form

    ```
    java Uncompress demo.rle
    ```

    where `demo.rle` is the name of the compressed file. The program will write the uncompressed data to a file with the same name as the compressed file, but without the `.rle` extension.

24. Write a program named `DisplayImage` that displays a gray-scale image stored in a file. The name of the file will be supplied as a command-line argument. The first line of the file will contain the number of rows in the image; the second line will contain the number of columns. Each subsequent line will contain n integers between 0 and 255, where n is the number of columns in the image, with commas separating adjacent integers. For example, consider the gray-scale image shown in Section 13.1. The file containing this image would have the following appearance:

    ```
    20
    16
    231,231,231,231,231,231,231,231,231,231,231,231,231,231,231,231
    ...
    138,109,161,109,177,255,231,7,23,231,255,161,231,177,161,138
    ```

    The program will display the image in a frame whose drawable area matches the size of the image. *Hint:* See Exercise 2 in Chapter 13.

25. Write a program named `TextStats` that displays statistics about a text file. For example, the command

    ```
    java TextStats demo
    ```

    might produce the following output:

    ```
    Number of characters: 506
    Number of words: 89
    Number of lines: 11
    ```

The character count does not include the end-of-line markers. A "word" is any sequence of non-white-space characters.

26. Write a program named `FormatText` that fills and justifies the paragraphs in a text file. To illustrate what the program does, assume that the file `java.txt` contains the following lines:[1]

```
We wanted to build a system that could be
programmed  easily without a lot of
   esoteric training and which  leveraged today's standard
practice.  Most programmers working these days use C,
      and  most   programmers  doing
object-oriented  programming  use C++. So even
 though we found  that C++  was unsuitable, we designed
   Java as closely to  C++ as possible
in order to make the system  more comprehensible.

Java  omits  many rarely   used, poorly
understood, confusing  features of C++ that in
   our experience bring more grief than benefit. These
 omitted features  primarily consist of operator
overloading   (although the  Java language does
      have method overloading),  multiple
inheritance, and extensive  automatic coercions.
```

To run the program, we'll use the following command

```
java FormatText java.txt javafmt.txt 60
```

where `java.txt` is the name of the original file, `javafmt.txt` is the name of the formatted file, and `60` is the desired number of characters per line. After the program has finished execution, `javafmt.txt` will contain the following lines:

```
We wanted to build a system that could be programmed  easily
without a lot  of  esoteric  training  and  which  leveraged
today's standard practice. Most  programmers  working  these
days use  C,  and  most  programmers  doing  object-oriented
programming use C++. So even though we found  that  C++  was
unsuitable, we designed Java as closely to C++  as  possible
in order to make the system more comprehensible.

Java omits many rarely used,  poorly  understood,  confusing
features of C++ that in our experience bring more grief than
benefit.  These  omitted  features  primarily  consist   of
operator overloading (although the Java language  does  have
method overloading),  multiple  inheritance,  and  extensive
automatic coercions.
```

The formatted file should be identical to the original file, except that extra spaces are deleted, and lines are filled and justified. "Filling" a line means adding words until one more word would cause the line to overflow. "Justifying" a line means adding extra spaces between words so that each line has the same length (60 characters in this example). Justification must be done so that the space between words in a line is equal (or as nearly equal as possible). The last line of each paragraph will not be justified. (A blank line in the original file is assumed to indicate the beginning of a new paragraph.)

---

[1]From "The Java Language: An Overview"

(*http://java.sun.com/docs/overviews/java/java-overview-1.html*)

Answers to Review Questions

Section 14.1
1. (e)
2. Text files and binary files
3. Stream
4. Java stores characters in Unicode, using two bytes per character, whereas most software requires ASCII characters, which are stored in single bytes.
5. Open
6. Append

Section 14.2
1. The `File` class is used for determining the properties of a file and performing a few basic file operations, including deleting a file and renaming a file.
2. `canWrite`
3. `list`
4. `mkdir`

Section 14.3
1. `FileOutputStream out = new FileOutputStream("records.dat", true);`
2. `IOException`
3. They return −1.

Section 14.4
1. `Throwable`
2. Subclasses of `Error` or `RuntimeException` represent unchecked exceptions. Subclasses of `Exception` (but not `RuntimeException`) represent checked exceptions.
3. Yes. The `catch` block for `FileNotFoundException` must come first. If the `IOException` block were to come first, it would catch `FileNotFoundException` as well, because `FileNotFoundException` is a subclass of `IOException`.
4. Write a `catch` block for `Exception`.

Section 14.5
1. Binary files
2. `DataInputStream` and `DataOutputStream` provide methods for reading and writing data of specific types, not just bytes.
3. As a sequence of individual bytes, as a sequence of two-byte Unicode characters, or using UTF-8 encoding
4. Seven

Section 14.6
1. Text files
2. `BufferedWriter`
3. `print` and `println`
4. `read` and `readLine`

Section 14.7
1. Serialization
2. `Serializable`
3. `ObjectOutputStream`
4. True

APPENDIX A
Setting Up Java

This appendix explains how to download and install the Java Development Kit (JDK) and the `jpb` package, which is used by many of the programs in this book. The instructions given are specific to the Windows platform, although the downloading and installation process is similar for other platforms.

The programs in this book are designed to work with version 1.1 of the JDK or any later version. Because version 1.1 can be downloaded faster than later versions, and provides all the capabilities we'll need, I've provided instructions for downloading this version. If you're installing a more recent version, you may need to make changes to the instructions. For updated instructions, please visit the *Java Programming: From the Beginning* Web site at *http://knking.com/books/java/*.

Downloading the JDK

1. Launch your browser and have it load the page at *http://java.sun.com/products/jdk/1.1/*.
2. Click on "JDK 1.1 Win32 Release."
3. Locate step 1, which is titled "Download JDK 1.1.8 Software for Windows 95 / 98 / NT 4.0." Press the "continue" button.
4. You will be shown a license agreement. Read it and then click on "Accept."
5. Press the button labeled "FTP download." You will be asked where the file should be saved on your computer. You can save the file anywhere you like. Make a note of where the file is saved so that you can find it later.
6. Wait patiently. Downloading may take an hour or so unless you have a fast connection to the Internet.

Although it's not strictly necessary, you might consider downloading the documentation that comes with the JDK. To download the documentation, go back to the page with the "continue" button and locate step 2, which is titled "Download JDK 1.1.8 Documentation." Click on the link and follow the instructions to download the documentation in HTML form. You can view this documentation using your Web browser; no connection to the Internet is necessary, because the files will be stored on your own computer. If you choose not to download the documentation, you can always view it at *http://java.sun.com/products/jdk/1.1/docs/index.html.*

Installing the JDK

1. Execute the file that you downloaded previously. There are several ways to do this. One is to click the Start button (normally located at the lower-left corner of the screen) and choose "Run..." from the menu. Press the "Browse..." button and locate the file that you downloaded. (The Windows version of JDK 1.1.8 is stored in a file named `jdk1_1_8-win.exe`.) Once the file name is displayed in the Run window, click the OK button.
2. An installation program will begin running. This program will give you the opportunity to specify where you want the JDK to be installed. (The default directory is `c:\jdk1.1.8`.) You'll also be asked which components of the JDK you want installed. The default setting shown by the installation program should be fine for our purposes.
3. After the installation is complete, you'll need to modify the `AUTOEXEC.BAT` file, which is normally stored in the root directory on the C: drive. Open a DOS window and enter the following command:

```
edit c:\autoexec.bat
```

(If you prefer, you can use Notepad to modify the `AUTOEXEC.BAT` file. To locate Notepad, click on the Start button, select Programs, and then select Accessories.) Here's what you'll see in the DOS window:

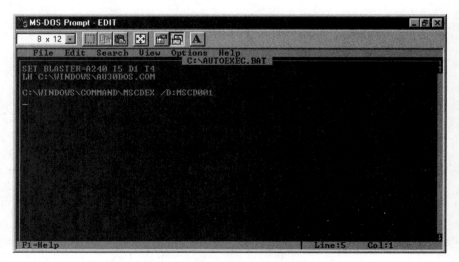

You probably won't see exactly the same lines in your AUTOEXEC.BAT file, because the contents of this file vary considerably from one PC to another.

4. Add the following line to the end of the AUTOEXEC.BAT file:

```
SET PATH=%PATH%;C:\JDK1.1.8\BIN
```

If you installed the JDK in a directory other than c:\jdk1.1.8, you should use the name of that directory instead. Be sure to include \bin at the end, however. Here's what you'll see on the screen now:

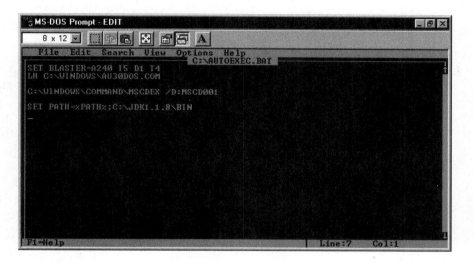

Installing the jpb package may also require changing the AUTOEXEC.BAT file, so you might want to make that change now. See the instructions under "Installing the jpb Package" on the next page.

5. Save the file by going to the File menu and selecting Save. Exit the edit program by going to the File menu and selecting Exit.

6. If you want to begin using the JDK without restarting your computer, you'll need to execute the AUTOEXEC.BAT file by entering

```
c:\autoexec
```

in the DOS window. If you won't be using the JDK immediately, this step isn't necessary. Each time you restart your computer, the commands in the AUTOEXEC.BAT file will be automatically executed, thereby adding C:\JDK1.1.8\BIN to the path, which allows Windows to locate the programs in the JDK.

7. You should be able to execute any program in the JDK now. See Chapter 2 for information on using javac (the Java compiler) and java (the Java interpreter). Appendix D describes how to use appletviewer, another program in the JDK.

Downloading the `jpb` Package

1. Create a directory named `jpb` somewhere on your hard drive. You might have already created a directory to store your Java programs (named `MyProgs`, let's say). If you have such a directory, put the `jpb` directory inside it.
2. Launch your browser and have it load the page at *http://knking.com/books/java/*.
3. Click on the link titled "Download the files in the `jpb` package."
4. You will see a page containing links to files named `Convert.java`, `DrawableFrame.java`, and `SimpleIO.java`. Follow the instructions on this page to download each of these files and save it in your `jpb` directory.

Installing the `jpb` Package

Once you have downloaded the files in the `jpb` package, you can begin using the package immediately. There's no need to compile the files in the package. They will be compiled automatically when you use them in your programs.

Any program that you put in the directory *above* the `jpb` directory will be able to use the `jpb` package. For example, if the `jpb` directory is located inside the `MyProgs` directory, then any program in `MyProgs` will be able to use the `jpb` package.

In order to be able to use the `jpb` package in *any* directory, you'll need to modify the `CLASSPATH` variable. The programs in the JDK use the `CLASSPATH` variable to locate classes that aren't in the current directory and aren't standard Java classes. Here's how to change `CLASSPATH`:

1. Open a DOS window and enter the following command:

```
edit c:\autoexec.bat
```

2. Add the following line to the end of the `AUTOEXEC.BAT` file:

```
SET CLASSPATH=.;C:\MyProgs
```

   I'm assuming that `MyProgs` contains the `jpb` directory. If you've put the `jpb` directory inside some other directory, use the name of that directory instead.
3. Save the file and exit the `edit` program.
4. If you want to begin using the `jpb` package without restarting your computer, you'll need to execute the `AUTOEXEC.BAT` file by entering

```
c:\autoexec
```

   in the DOS window. (See the discussion under step 6 of "Installing the Java Development Kit.")

Java Language Summary

This appendix provides a partial summary of the Java programming language. It also includes discussions of a few features that aren't covered in the main text.

In the description of a language construct, square brackets are used to indicate an optional item. An ellipsis (…) indicates that the preceding item can be repeated as many times as desired. For example, a local variable declaration has the following form:

type   variable-name [= *initializer*] [, *variable-name* [= *initializer*]] … ;

The declaration begins with a type, which is then followed by a variable name. The variable name can be followed by an equals sign and an initializer. (Both are optional, but if one is present, the other must also be present.) A second variable can then be declared by adding a comma and the name of the variable. That variable can also be followed by an equals sign and an initializer. The ellipsis indicates that the pattern used for the second variable can be repeated if additional variables are needed. The declaration ends with a semicolon.

For a more complete and precise description of Java, see *The Java Language Specification* by Gosling, Joy, and Steele (Addison-Wesley, 1996) or visit *http://java.sun.com/docs/books/jls/*.

Comments

Java has three kinds of comments. The first kind begins with // and ends at the end of the line:

```
// Comment style 1
```

The second kind begins with `/*`, ends with `*/`, and can be continued over any number of lines:

`/* Comment style 2 */`

The third kind (a "doc comment") begins with `/**`, ends with `*/`, and can be continued over any number of lines:

`/** Comment style 3 */`

Doc comments can be extracted by a special program, `javadoc`, to produce on-line documentation for a program.

Identifiers

Identifiers may contain letters (both uppercase and lowercase), digits, and underscores (_) but must not begin with a digit. Identifiers can have any length. A lowercase letter is not considered to be equivalent to the corresponding uppercase letter.

When an identifier consists of more than one word, the Java convention is to capitalize the first letter of each word after the first (`lastIndexOf`, for example). By convention, the name of a class begins with an uppercase letter (`Color`, for example). The name of a constant consists of all uppercase letters; if the name contains more than one word, underscores are used to separate the words (`WINDOW_SIZE`, for example).

Keywords

The keywords in Table B.1 are reserved and may not be used as identifiers.

Table B.1
Keywords

abstract	double	int	super
boolean	else	interface	switch
break	extends	long	synchronized
byte	final	native	this
case	finally	new	throw
catch	float	package	throws
char	for	private	transient
class	goto*	protected	try
const*	if	public	void
continue	implements	return	volatile
default	import	short	while
do	instanceof	static	

*Not currently used in Java.

The words `null`, `true`, and `false` are also reserved, although they aren't considered keywords.

Types

The primitive types consist of the integer types (`byte`, `short`, `int`, and `long`), the floating-point types (`float` and `double`), `boolean`, and `char`. All other types in Java are reference types. A variable of a reference type stores a reference to an object or array, not the object or array itself.

Integer Types

Table B.2 summarizes the integer types.

Table B.2
Integer Types

Type	Size	Smallest Value	Largest Value
byte	8 bits	−128	127
short	16 bits	−32,768	32,767
int	32 bits	−2,147,483,648	2,147,483,647
long	64 bits	-2^{63}	$2^{63}-1$

Integer literals can be written in octal (base 8), decimal (base 10), or hexadecimal (base 16). Octal literals must begin with `0` and contain only digits between `0` and `7`. Hexadecimal literals must begin with `0x` or `0X`, and may contain the letters `a` through `f` (or `A` through `F`) in addition to the decimal digits. By default, an integer literal has type `int`. An integer literal may end with the letter `l` (or `L`) to indicate that it has type `long`.

Floating-Point Types

Table B.3 summarizes the characteristics of the floating-point types.

Table B.3
Floating-Point Types

Type	Size	Smallest Positive Value	Largest Value	Precision
float	32 bits	1.40×10^{-45}	3.40×10^{38}	6 digits
double	64 bits	4.94×10^{-324}	1.79×10^{308}	15 digits

Floating-point literals may have an exponent (`3.94e-2`, for example). A floating-point literal that doesn't have an exponent must contain a decimal point or be followed by a suffix (`f`, `F`, `d`, or `D`). A floating-point literal that is followed by `f` or `F` has type `float`. A floating-point literal that is followed by `d` or `D` has type `double`. A floating-point literal without a suffix also has type `double`.

The `float` and `double` types include three special values: +∞, −∞, and NaN ("Not a Number"). If a program divides a positive number by zero, the result will be +∞. Dividing a negative number by zero yields −∞. NaN is the result of a mathematically undefined operation, such as dividing zero by zero.

The `boolean` Type

The `boolean` type has two values: `true` and `false`. The relational and equality operators produce `boolean` values. The logical operators (`&&`, `||`, and `!`) expect `boolean` operands and produce `boolean` results. When used with `boolean` operands, the `&` and `|` operators are similar to the `&&` and `||` operators, but don't perform short-circuit evaluation of their operands.

The `char` Type

Values of the `char` type are 16-bit Unicode characters. Table B.4 shows the first 128 values of the `char` type, which are identical to the ASCII character set.

Table B.4

ASCII Character Set

Decimal	Octal	Unicode	Char	Character							
0	\0	\u0000		*nul*	32		64	@	96	`
1	\1	\u0001		*soh* (^A)	33	!	65	A	97	a
2	\2	\u0002		*stx* (^B)	34	"	66	B	98	b
3	\3	\u0003		*etx* (^C)	35	#	67	C	99	c
4	\4	\u0004		*eot* (^D)	36	$	68	D	100	d
5	\5	\u0005		*enq* (^E)	37	%	69	E	101	e
6	\6	\u0006		*ack* (^F)	38	&	70	F	102	f
7	\7	\u0007		*bel* (^G)	39	'	71	G	103	g
8	\10	\u0008	\b	*bs* (^H)	40	(	72	H	104	h
9	\11	\u0009	\t	*ht* (^I)	41	)	73	I	105	i
10	\12	\u000a	\n	*lf* (^J)	42	*	74	J	106	j
11	\13	\u000b		*vt* (^K)	43	+	75	K	107	k
12	\14	\u000c	\f	*ff* (^L)	44	,	76	L	108	l
13	\15	\u000d	\r	*cr* (^M)	45	-	77	M	109	m
14	\16	\u000e		*so* (^N)	46	.	78	N	110	n
15	\17	\u000f		*si* (^O)	47	/	79	O	111	o
16	\20	\u0010		*dle* (^P)	48	0	80	P	112	p
17	\21	\u0011		*dc1* (^Q)	49	1	81	Q	113	q
18	\22	\u0012		*dc2* (^R)	50	2	82	R	114	r
19	\23	\u0013		*dc3* (^S)	51	3	83	S	115	s
20	\24	\u0014		*dc4* (^T)	52	4	84	T	116	t
21	\25	\u0015		*nak* (^U)	53	5	85	U	117	u
22	\26	\u0016		*syn* (^V)	54	6	86	V	118	v
23	\27	\u0017		*etb* (^W)	55	7	87	W	119	w
24	\30	\u0018		*can* (^X)	56	8	88	X	120	x
25	\31	\u0019		*em* (^Y)	57	9	89	Y	121	y
26	\32	\u001a		*sub* (^Z)	58	:	90	Z	122	z
27	\33	\u001b		*esc*	59	;	91	[	123	{
28	\34	\u001c		*fs*	60	<	92	\	124		
29	\35	\u001d		*gs*	61	=	93	]	125	}
30	\36	\u001e		*rs*	62	>	94	^	126	~
31	\37	\u001f		*us*	63	?	95	_	127	*del*

Character literals are enclosed within single quotes:

```
'a'   'z'   'A'   'Z'   '0'   '9'   '%'   '.'   ' '
```

Character literals (as well as string literals) may contain escape sequences, which are used primarily to represent nonprinting (invisible) characters. There are three kinds of escape sequences:

- ***Character escapes.*** A character escape consists of the \ character followed by one more character. The character escapes are \b (backspace), \f (form feed), \n (line feed), \r (carriage return), \t (tab), \\ (backslash), \' (single quote), and \" (double quote).

- ***Octal escapes.*** An octal escape begins with \, followed by an octal number, representing the value of the character in Unicode. The number in an octal escape must be between 0 and 377.

- ***Unicode escapes.*** A Unicode escape begins with \u, followed by a four-digit hexadecimal number, representing the value of the character in Unicode.

The char type is considered to be an integral type because Java allows arithmetic on characters.

Operators

Table B.5 on the next page lists all Java operators. The first column shows the relative precedence of each operator. Operators at level 1 take precedence over operators at level 2; those at level 2 take precedence over those at level 3; and so on. The last column indicates whether each operator is left associative or right associative.

Some of the operators in Table B.5 aren't discussed in any of the chapters. These operators fall into two groups: the shift operators (<<, >>, and >>>) and the bitwise operators (~, &, ^, and |). The compound assignment operators that combine these operations with assignment also are not discussed in the chapters.

Shift Operators

The ***shift operators*** (<<, >>, and >>>) can transform the binary representation of a number by shifting its bits to the left or right. The value of i << j is the result when the bits in i are shifted left by j places. For each bit that is "shifted off" the left end of i, a zero bit enters at the right. The value of i >> j is the result when i is shifted right by j places. The >> operator performs "sign extension," which means that if i is negative, the result of the shift will also be negative. The >>> operator is identical to the >> operator, except that it does not perform sign extension. For each bit that is shifted off the right end of i, a zero bit enters at the left.

The following examples illustrate the effect of applying the shift operators to the number 13:

Table B.5

Operators

Precedence	Name	Symbol(s)	Associativity
1	increment (postfix)	++	left
1	decrement (postfix)	--	left
2	increment (prefix)	++	right
2	decrement (prefix)	--	right
2	unary plus	+	right
2	unary minus	-	right
2	bitwise complement	~	right
2	logical negation	!	right
3	cast	( )	right
4	multiplicative	* / %	left
5	additive	+ -	left
6	shift	<< >> >>>	left
7	relational	< > <= >= instanceof	left
8	equality	== !=	left
9	bitwise *and*	&	left
10	bitwise exclusive *or*	^	left
11	bitwise inclusive *or*	|	left
12	logical *and*	&&	left
13	logical *or*	||	left
14	conditional	? :	right
15	assignment	= *= /= %= += -= <<= >>= >>>= &= ^= |=	right

```
int i, j;

i = 13;         // i = 00000000000000000000000000001101
j = i << 2;     // j = 00000000000000000000000000110100
j = i >> 2;     // j = 00000000000000000000000000000011
j = i >>> 2;    // j = 00000000000000000000000000000011
```

Notice that the `>>` and `>>>` operators give the same result when used to shift a positive number, such as 13. The difference between `>>` and `>>>` becomes apparent when the number being shifted is negative:

```
i = -13;        // i = 11111111111111111111111111110011
j = i << 2;     // j = 11111111111111111111111111001100
j = i >> 2;     // j = 11111111111111111111111111111100
j = i >>> 2;    // j = 00111111111111111111111111111100
```

The value of `j` after the last assignment is a very large number (1,073,741,820, to be precise). The sign bit switched from 1 (negative) to 0 (positive), causing this unusual result.

As these examples show, the shift operators don't modify their operands. To modify a variable by shifting its bits, a compound assignment operator (<<=, >>=, or >>>=) can be used:

```
i = 13;        // i = 00000000000000000000000000001101
i <<= 2;       // i = 00000000000000000000000000110100
i >>= 2;       // i = 00000000000000000000000000001101
i >>>= 2;      // i = 00000000000000000000000000000011
```

The operands for the shift operators may be of any integral type (byte, short, int, long, or char). If the left operand has type byte, short, or char, it is promoted to int. The type of the result is the type of the left operand after promotion.

Bitwise Operators

The *bitwise operators* (~, &, ^, and |) can be applied to boolean values, but typically they're used for performing Boolean operations on the bits in an integer.

The ~ operator, which is unary, produces the complement of its operand, with zeros replaced by ones and ones replaced by zeros. The & operator, which is binary, performs a Boolean *and* operation on all corresponding bits in its two operands. The ^ and | operators are similar (both perform a Boolean *or* operation on the bits in their operands); however, ^ produces 0 whenever both operands have a 1 bit, whereas | produces 1.

The following examples illustrate the effect of the ~, &, ^, and | operators:

```
int i, j, k;

i = 21;       // i = 00000000000000000000000000010101
j = 56;       // j = 00000000000000000000000000111000
k = ~i;       // k = 11111111111111111111111111101010
k = i & j;    // k = 00000000000000000000000000010000
k = i ^ j;    // k = 00000000000000000000000000101101
k = i | j;    // k = 00000000000000000000000000111101
```

The compound assignment operators &=, ^=, and |= correspond to the bitwise operators &, ^, and |:

```
i = 21;       // i = 00000000000000000000000000010101
j = 56;       // j = 00000000000000000000000000111000
i &= j;       // i = 00000000000000000000000000010000
i ^= j;       // i = 00000000000000000000000000101000
i |= j;       // i = 00000000000000000000000000111000
```

Implicit Conversions

Implicit conversions are performed in the following situations:

- When the operands in a numeric expression don't have the same type.
- When the type of the expression on the right side of an assignment doesn't

match the type of the variable on the left side.

- When the type of an argument in a method call doesn't match the type of the corresponding parameter.
- When a value needs to be converted to string form. (This type of conversion occurs when the expression "THX" + 1138 is evaluated, causing 1138 to be converted automatically to a String object.)

When the operands in a numeric expression don't have the same type, Java converts them to a common type via a process known as numeric promotion:

1. If either operand is of type double, the other is converted to double.
2. If either operand is of type float, the other is converted to float.
3. If either operand is of type long, the other is converted to long.
4. Otherwise, both operands are converted to int.

Numeric promotion doesn't apply to assignment. Instead, Java simply converts the expression on the right side of the assignment to the type of the variable on the left side, provided that the variable's type is at least as "wide" as the expression's type. The following list shows the numeric types, in order of increasing width:

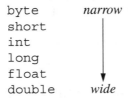

```
byte          narrow
short
int
long
float
double        wide
```

In addition, a char value can be assigned to a variable of type int, long, float, or double.

If the type of an argument in a method call doesn't match the type of the corresponding parameter, Java will attempt to convert the argument to the correct type, using rules similar to those for conversion during assignment.

Statements

Statements are commands to be performed when a Java program is executed. The simplest statements are:

- Expression statement—an expression followed by a semicolon
- Block—a series of statements enclosed in curly braces
- Empty statement—a semicolon

Other statements include local variable declaration statements, selection statements (if and switch), loop statements (do, for, and while), jump statements (break, continue, and return), and the try statement.

Local Variable Declaration Statements

A local variable declaration statement has the following form:

type variable-name [= *initializer*] [, *variable-name* [= *initializer*]] ... ;

The following statements declare three int variables and one String variable:

```
int i = 0, j = 1, k;
String userInput;
```

Local variable declaration statements are allowed at the top level of a method or within a block. A variable declared within a block can't have the same name as a variable declared in an enclosing block or method.

The word final can be added at the beginning of a variable declaration to indicate that the values of the variables being declared will not change:

```
final double FREEZING_POINT = 32.0, DEGREE_RATIO = 5.0 / 9.0;
```

The declaration of an array variable specifies the type of the array's elements and the number of dimensions, but not the size of each dimension:

```
int[] a;          // One-dimensional array of integers
String[][] b;     // Two-dimensional array of strings
```

Declaring an array variable doesn't cause Java to allocate any space for the array's elements. Allocation can be done later, using the new keyword:

```
a = new int[5];
b = new String[3][2];   // 3 rows, 2 columns
```

If desired, storage can be allocated at the time the array is declared:

```
int[] a = new int[5];
String[][] b = new String[3][2];
```

The elements of an array are given default values at the time storage for the array is allocated. Numbers are set to zero, boolean elements are set to false, and elements of a reference type are set to null.

Another way to allocate storage for an array is to provide an initializer in the declaration of the array. The compiler determines the size of the array from the number of elements in the initializer:

```
int[] a = {3, 0, 3, 4, 5};
String[][] b = {{"a", "b"}, {"c", "d"}, {"e", "f"}};
```

Selection Statements

Java's selection statements are the if and the switch (Table B.6 on the next page).

General Form	Example

`if ( `*expression*` )`
    statement
	`if (score > 100)`
	    `score = 100;`

`if ( `*expression*` )`
    statement
`else`
    statement
	`if (a > b)`
	    `larger = a;`
	`else`
	    `larger = b;`

`switch ( `*expression*` ) {`
    `case `*constant-expression*` : `*statements*
    `...`
    `case `*constant-expression*` : `*statements*
    `default : `*statements*
`}`
	`switch (day) {`
	    `case 1:`
	        `hoursOpen = 0;`
	        `break;`
	    `case 3: case 5:`
	        `hoursOpen = 10;`
	        `break;`
	    `case 7:`
	        `hoursOpen = 6;`
	        `break;`
	    `default:`
	        `hoursOpen = 8;`
	        `break;`
	`}`

Loop Statements

Java has three loop statements: `do`, `for`, and `while` (Table B.7).

General Form	Example

`do`
    statement
`while ( `*expression*` ) ;`
	`do {`
	    `numDigits++;`
	    `n /= 10;`
	`} while (n > 0);`

`for ( `*initialization*` ; `*test*` ; `*update*` )`
    statement
	`for (int i = 0; i < n; i++)`
	    `sum += i;`

`while ( `*expression*` )`
    statement
	`while (i < n)`
	    `i *= 2;`

The *initialization, test,* and *update* parts of a `for` statement are all optional. The control variable can be declared within the `for` statement itself (as in the example in Table B.7), or it can be declared prior to the `for` statement. The *initialization* and *update* parts may contain multiple expressions, separated by commas. Any number of expressions are allowed within *initialization* and *update*, provided that each can stand alone as a statement.

Jump Statements

Java's `break`, `continue`, and `return` statements (Table B.8 on the next page) are used to transfer control from one part of a program to another.

Table B.8
Jump Statements

General Form	*Example*

`break ;`	```for (int d = 2; d < n; d++)```
	``` if (n % d == 0)```
	``` break;```

`break` *identifier* `;`	```findLoop:```
	```for (int i = 0; i < a.length; i++)```
	``` for (int j = 0; j < a[0].length; j++)```
	``` if (a[i][j] == key)```
	``` break findLoop;```

`continue ;`	```for (int d = 2; d < n; d++) {```
	``` if (n % d == 0)```
	``` continue;```
	``` sum += d;```
	```}```

`continue` *identifier* `;`	```sumLoop:```
	```for (int i = 0; i < a.length; i++)```
	``` for (int j = 0; j < a[0].length; j++) {```
	``` if (a[i][j] == 0)```
	``` continue sumLoop;```
	``` sum += a[i][j];```
	``` }```

`return` *expression* `;`	```return x * x - 2 * x + 1;```

The `try` Statement

The `try` statement is used to handle exceptions. A `try` statement consists of a `try` block, followed by zero or more `catch` blocks, followed by an optional `finally` block:

```
try
   block
[catch ( exception-type identifier )
   block]
...
[finally
   block]
```

exception-type identifies what type of exception each `catch` block should handle. *identifier* is an arbitrary name used to identify the exception within the scope of a `catch` block.

The following `try` statement consists of a `try` block followed by two `catch` blocks:

```
try {
   quotient = Integer.parseInt(str1) / Integer.parseInt(str2);
} catch (NumberFormatException e) {
   System.out.println("Error: Not an integer");
```

```
} catch (ArithmeticException e) {
  System.out.println("Error: Division by zero");
}
```

Classes

A class declaration specifies which variables, constructors, and methods belong to the class. An instantiable class can be used to create objects.

Class Declarations

A class declaration has the following form:

```
[public] class class-name [extends superclass-name]
    [implements interface-name [, interface-name] …] {
  variable-declarations
  constructor-declarations
  method-declarations
}
```

If `public` is present, this class can be accessed by all other classes, even those not in the same package; otherwise, this class can be accessed only by other classes in the same package. If `extends` *superclass-name* isn't present, the class will have `Object` as its superclass. If `implements` is present, the class must provide all methods required by the interfaces whose names are listed.

The following examples declare classes named `Account`, `Savings-Account`, and `ButtonListener`:

```
public class Account {
  …
}
```

```
public class SavingsAccount extends Account {
  …
}
```

```
class ButtonListener implements ActionListener {
  …
}
```

Variable Declarations

A variable declaration within a class has the following form:

```
[access-modifier] [static] type variable-name [= initializer]
                         [, variable-name [= initializer]] … ;
```

The word `static` is used in declarations of class variables. If `static` is not present, the variables being declared are instance variables. The following examples declare an instance variable named `balance` and a class variable named `accountsOpen`:

```
private double balance;              // Instance variable
private static int accountsOpen = 0; // Class variable
```

Constructor Declarations

A constructor declaration has the following form:

[*access-modifier*] *class-name* ([*parameter-list*])
    [`throws` *exception-name* [, *exception-name*] ...] *body*

Parameter-list has the following form:

type parameter-name [, *type parameter-name*] ...

Each *exception-name* following `throws` is the name of a checked exception that the constructor might throw. *Body* is a series of statements enclosed in curly braces. The following example declares a constructor for the `Account` class:

```
public Account(double initialBalance) {
   balance = initialBalance;
   accountsOpen++;
}
```

Method Declarations

A method declaration has the following form:

[*access-modifier*] [`static`] *result-type method-name* ([*parameter-list*])
    [`throws` *exception-name* [, *exception-name*] ...] *body*

The word `static` is used in the declaration of a class method. If `static` is not present, the method is an instance method. *Result-type* is `void` if the method does not return a value. The following examples declare an instance method named `deposit` and a class method named `getAccountsOpen`:

```
public void deposit(double amount) {    // Instance method
   balance += amount;
}

public static int getAccountsOpen() {  // Class method
   return accountsOpen;
}
```

Access Modifiers

The declaration of a variable, constructor, or method usually begins with an access modifier, which specifies the amount of access to that entity. Table B.9 describes the meaning of each access modifier.

Table B.9

Access Modifiers

Access Modifier	Meaning
private	Can be accessed only in the same class
protected	Can be accessed in the same class, in a subclass, or in any class in the same package
public	Can be accessed in any class
None	Can be accessed in any class in the same package

Abstract Classes

The declaration of an abstract class must include the word `abstract`, which is usually placed just before the word `class`:

```
public abstract class Graphics {
    ...
}
```

Some of the methods in an abstract class may be abstract methods. The declaration of an abstract method must include the word `abstract`:

```
public abstract Color getColor();
```

An abstract method has no body; its declaration ends with a semicolon instead. It is illegal to create an instance of an abstract class.

Interfaces

An interface resembles a class, except that all its methods are abstract and the word `class` is replaced by `interface`. The word `abstract` is not required in method declarations within an interface. The following example declares an interface named `ActionListener`:

```
public interface ActionListener extends EventListener {
    public void actionPerformed(ActionEvent evt);
}
```

Any variables declared in an interface must be both `static` and `final`.

Final Classes and Methods

A class declaration may include the word `final` to indicate that the class can't be extended:

```
public final class Math {
   ...
}
```

Individual methods within a class can be declared `final` to indicate that they can't be overridden:

```
public final int read(byte[] b) throws IOException {
   ...
}
```

Methods that are declared either `static` or `private` are automatically final.

Creating Objects

Objects are created using the `new` keyword:

```
Account acct = new Account(1000.00);
```

The `acct` variable will store a reference to the new `Account` object.

Calling Instance Methods

An instance method call has the following form:

[*object* `.`] *method-name* ([*argument-list*])

Argument-list has the following form:

expression [`,` *expression*] ...

Object (and the period that follows) can be omitted if the method is being called by another instance method in the same class. In the following examples, the `acct` object is used to call the `deposit` and `close` instance methods:

```
acct.deposit(1000.00);
acct.close();
```

Calling Class Methods

A class method call has the following form:

[*class-name* `.`] *method-name* ([*argument-list*])

Class-name (and the period that follows) can be omitted if the method is being called by another method in the same class. The following statements call the `getAccountsOpen` method (from the `Account` class) and the `exit` method (from the `System` class):

```
int numAccounts = Account.getAccountsOpen();
System.exit(-1);
```

Packages

A package is a collection of classes. Every class belongs to a package. Any class with no package specified is automatically added to a default package that has no name.

To specify that a class belongs to a particular package, a package declaration must appear at the beginning of the file containing the class declaration. A package declaration has the form

```
package package-name ;
```

This line must come before any import declarations and before the class declarations themselves.

A public class that belongs to a named package can be accessed outside the package by writing *package-name . class-name*. An import declaration can be used to avoid having to specify the package name each time the class is used. The following import declaration imports all public classes in a package:

```
import package-name . * ;
```

It is also possible to import a single class:

```
import package-name . class-name ;
```

For example, a program that needs the `Button` class could import all classes in the `java.awt` package or just the `Button` class by itself:

```
import java.awt.*;        // Import all classes in java.awt
import java.awt.Button;   // Import only the Button class
```

APPENDIX C
Java API Summary

This appendix describes some of the most commonly used classes in the Java Application Programming Interface (API). In order to keep this appendix reasonably brief but still informative, I took the following approach:

- Only classes mentioned in this book are listed. Some classes were deliberately omitted, including exception and event classes, which require little documentation.

- Not all methods are listed for each class. I've included only the methods mentioned in this book, plus other major methods that don't require a lengthy description. I've omitted methods that exist only in the most recent versions of Java (JDK 1.2 and later). Nearly all protected methods are omitted, as are all "deprecated" methods, which are no longer recommended for use. Every class has methods named `equals` and `toString`, either declared in the class itself or inherited from a superclass, so I have omitted these methods except in the description of the `Object` class.

- The declarations of some methods have been simplified by omitting the keywords `native` and `synchronized`. These keywords aren't discussed in this book and don't affect the way methods are called. (Which methods are declared `synchronized` varies among different versions of the JDK, which is another reason for omitting this information.)

- Inherited methods aren't shown. If you don't find the method you're looking for in a particular class, try looking in its superclasses.

Complete descriptions of the Java API are available elsewhere. The entire API documentation can be viewed at *http://java.sun.com* or downloaded in HTML form. To view the API documentation on-line, use the following URL:

http://java.sun.com/products/jdk/?.?/docs/api/index.html

In this URL, *?.?* is a version of the Java Development Kit, such as 1.1, 1.2, or 1.3. For example, the API documentation for version 1.1 of the JDK is located at

http://java.sun.com/products/jdk/1.1/docs/api/index.html

The most thorough description of the API—with examples included—appears in the two-volume set *The Java Class Libraries, Second Edition* by Chan, Lee, and Kramer (Addison-Wesley, 1998). Chan's *The Java Developers Almanac* (Addison-Wesley, updated annually) is a highly condensed version of the API, with no descriptions of the methods.

Packages

The following is a list of the API classes described in this appendix, grouped by the package to which each belongs. The Java API has many other packages, and each package has additional classes that are not shown here.

`java.applet`

Provides support for writing applets—small programs that are designed to be embedded in Web pages.

Classes: `Applet`

`java.awt`

Provides classes that are used for displaying graphics and creating graphical user interfaces.

Classes: `BorderLayout, Button, Checkbox, CheckboxGroup, Choice, Color, Component, Container, Dimension, FlowLayout, Font, FontMetrics, Frame, Graphics, GridLayout, Label, List, Panel, Point, Polygon, Scrollbar, TextArea, TextComponent, TextField, Window`

`java.io`

Provides classes for performing input and output.

Classes: `BufferedReader, BufferedWriter, DataInputStream, DataOutputStream, File, FileInputStream, FileOutputStream, FileReader, FileWriter, ObjectInputStream, ObjectOutputStream, PrintStream, PrintWriter`

java.lang

Provides classes that are an integral part of the Java language.

Classes: `Boolean`, `Byte`, `Character`, `Double`, `Float`, `Integer`, `Long`, `Math`, `Object`, `Short`, `String`, `StringBuffer`, `System`

java.util

Contains a variety of useful utility classes, including data structure classes as well as date and time classes.

Classes: `BitSet`, `Calendar`, `GregorianCalendar`, `Vector`

Alphabetical List of Classes

The following is an alphabetical list of the major classes used in this book (and, in some cases, their superclasses). The first line of each entry gives the name of the class and the package to which it belongs. The next two lines show the super-classes of the class as well as the interfaces that it implements. For example, the entry for the `Checkbox` class begins with the following lines:

Checkbox	**java.awt**
`Object` → `Component` → `Checkbox` IMPLEMENTS `ItemSelectable`	

The first line indicates that `Checkbox` belongs to the `java.awt` package. The second shows that `Checkbox` is a subclass of `Component`, which in turn is a subclass of `Object`. The third line indicates that `Checkbox` implements the `ItemSelectable` interface. The declaration of the `Checkbox` class would have the following appearance:

```
public class Checkbox extends Component
                      implements ItemSelectable {
    ...
}
```

Applet   java.applet

`Object` → `Component` → `Container` → `Panel` → `Applet`

Applets are created by defining a subclass of the `Applet` class. Applets inherit a number of methods from the `Applet` class and its superclasses. These methods are invoked by a Web browser (or applet viewer) as needed. Many of the inherited methods (`init` and `paint`, for example) are designed to be overridden; in fact, some of them do nothing at all unless they are overridden.

Constructors

Applet   `public Applet()`

Methods

getParameter   `public String getParameter(String name)`
Returns the value associated with the specified name in the HTML file that contains this applet. The case of letters in the name does not matter.

init   `public void init()`
Called by the browser to notify this applet that it has been loaded. An applet should override this method if it has initialization to perform. Unless it is overridden, this method does nothing.

showStatus   `public void showStatus(String msg)`
Requests that the specified string be displayed in the browser's "status window." Typically, the string is displayed in a status line at the bottom of the browser window.

BitSet   `java.util`

`Object → BitSet`
IMPLEMENTS `Cloneable, Serializable`

A bit set behaves like a vector whose elements are `boolean` values. By setting some of the elements of a bit set to `true` and the others to `false`, we can use it to keep track of the elements in a set. Because the elements of a bit set have only two possible values (`true` or `false`), Java can store each element as a single bit (0 or 1). As a result, a bit set requires considerably less memory than an array or vector containing ordinary `boolean` values. A bit set will automatically increase its size as needed. If we change the value of a bit from `false` to `true`, and the position of that bit lies outside the bit set's current range, Java will increase the size of the bit set to accommodate the new bit.

Constructors

BitSet   `public BitSet()`
Creates a bit set. All bits are initially `false`.

BitSet   `public BitSet(int nbits)`
Creates a bit set whose initial size is the specified number of bits. All bits are initially `false`.

Methods

and   `public void and(BitSet set)`
Performs a logical *and* of this bit set with the argument. This bit set is modified so

that each bit has the value `true` if and only if it initially had the value `true` and the corresponding bit in the argument also had the value `true`.

clear   `public void clear(int bit)`
Sets the bit at the specified position to `false`.

get   `public boolean get(int bit)`
Returns the value of the bit at the specified position.

or   `public void or(BitSet set)`
Performs a logical *or* of this bit set with the argument. This bit set is modified so that each bit has the value `true` if and only if it already has the value `true` or the corresponding bit in the argument has the value `true`.

set   `public void set(int bit)`
Sets the bit at the specified position to `true`.

size   `public int size()`
Returns the number of bits currently in this bit set. The size is the capacity of the bit set, not the number of bits with the value `true`.

xor   `public void xor(BitSet set)`
Performs a logical exclusive *or* of this bit set with the argument. This bit set is modified so that each bit has the value `true` if and only if the bit initially has the value `true`, and the corresponding bit in the argument has the value `false`, or the bit initially has the value `false`, and the corresponding bit in the argument has the value `true`.

Boolean   `java.lang`

`Object → Boolean`
IMPLEMENTS `Serializable`

`Boolean` is a wrapper class. Each `Boolean` object contains a single `boolean` value, allowing it to be treated as an object. The class also provides utility methods for working with `boolean` values.

Constants

FALSE   `public static final Boolean FALSE`
The `Boolean` object corresponding to the primitive value `false`.

TRUE   `public static final Boolean TRUE`
The `Boolean` object corresponding to the primitive value `true`.

Constructors

Boolean   `public Boolean(boolean value)`
Creates a `Boolean` object containing the specified value.

Boolean   `public Boolean(String s)`
Creates a `Boolean` object containing the value `true` if the specified string is not null and is equal, ignoring case, to the string `"true"`. Otherwise, creates a `Boolean` object containing the value `false`.

Methods

booleanValue `public boolean booleanValue()`
Returns the `boolean` value stored in this object.

valueOf `public static Boolean valueOf(String s)`
Returns a `Boolean` object containing the value `true` if the specified string is not null and is equal, ignoring case, to the string `"true"`. Otherwise, returns a `Boolean` object containing the value `false`.

BorderLayout   `java.awt`

`Object → BorderLayout`
IMPLEMENTS `LayoutManager2, Serializable`

The `BorderLayout` layout manager supports the positioning of up to five components within a container. Components can be placed at the top of the container (`"North"`), the bottom (`"South"`), the right side (`"East"`), the left side (`"West"`), and the center (`"Center"`).

Constructors

BorderLayout `public BorderLayout()`
Creates a border layout with no gaps between components.

BorderLayout `public BorderLayout(int hgap, int vgap)`
Creates a border layout with the specified horizontal and vertical gaps between components.

Methods

getHgap `public int getHgap()`
getVgap `public int getVgap()`
Returns the horizontal and vertical gaps between components.

setHgap `public void setHgap(int hgap)`
setVgap `public void setVgap(int vgap)`
Sets the horizontal and vertical gaps between components.

BufferedReader   `java.io`

`Object → Reader → BufferedReader`

Using a `BufferedReader` object to read characters from a text file is more efficient than reading directly from a `FileReader` object. In addition, the `BufferedReader` class provides a method that reads entire lines, not just single characters. Each method listed here throws `IOException` if an input/output error occurs.

Constructors

BufferedReader `public BufferedReader(Reader in)`

Creates a buffered reader that reads from the specified reader, using a default buffer size.

BufferedReader   `public BufferedReader(Reader in, int sz)`
Creates a buffered reader that reads from the specified reader, using the specified buffer size. Throws `IllegalArgumentException` if the buffer size is less than or equal to zero.

Methods

close   `public void close() throws IOException`
Closes this stream.

read   `public int read() throws IOException`
Reads a single character, returning it as an `int` value. Returns –1 if no character could be read because the end of the file was reached.

read   `public int read(char[] cbuf, int off, int len)`
`    throws IOException`
Reads up to `len` characters, storing them in the specified array starting at the position indicated by `off`. Returns the number of characters read, or –1 if no characters could be read because the end of the file was reached.

readLine   `public String readLine() throws IOException`
Reads a line of input. A line is considered to be terminated by a line feed (`'\n'`), a carriage return (`'\r'`), or a carriage return followed immediately by a line feed. Returns the line, not including any line-termination characters; returns `null` if no characters could be read because the end of the file was reached.

BufferedWriter   `java.io`

`Object → Writer → BufferedWriter`

Using a `BufferedWriter` object to write characters to a text file is more efficient than writing directly to a `FileWriter` object. Each method listed here throws `IOException` if an input/output error occurs.

Constructors

BufferedWriter   `public BufferedWriter(Writer out)`
Creates a buffered writer that writes to the specified writer, using a default buffer size.

BufferedWriter   `public BufferedWriter(Writer out, int sz)`
Creates a buffered writer that writes to the specified writer, using the specified buffer size. Throws `IllegalArgumentException` if the buffer size is less than or equal to zero.

Methods

close   `public void close() throws IOException`
Closes this stream.

flush   `public void flush() throws IOException`
Flushes this stream.

newLine   `public void newLine() throws IOException`
Writes a line separator; which character(s) are written depends on the platform.

write   `public void write(int c) throws IOException`
Writes the specified character.

write   `public void write(char[] cbuf, int off, int len)`
`    throws IOException`
Writes `len` characters in the specified array, starting at the position indicated by `off`.

write   `public void write(String s, int off, int len)`
`    throws IOException`
Writes `len` characters in the specified string, starting at the position indicated by `off`.

Button   `java.awt`

`Object → Component → Button`

A button is a component that can be pressed by the user to trigger an action. A button may have a label.

Constructors

Button   `public Button()`
Creates a button with no label.

Button   `public Button(String label)`
Creates a button with the specified label.

Methods

addActionListener   `public void addActionListener(ActionListener l)`
Registers the specified action listener to receive action events from this button.

getActionCommand   `public String getActionCommand()`
Returns the command name of the action event fired by this button.

getLabel   `public String getLabel()`
Returns the label of this button.

setActionCommand   `public void setActionCommand(String command)`
Sets the command name of the action event fired by this button. By default, the command name is the same as the button's label.

setLabel   `public void setLabel(String label)`
Sets the label for this button.

Byte   `java.lang`

`Object → Number → Byte`

`Byte` is a wrapper class, similar to `Integer`. See the `Integer` class for descriptions of the constants, constructors, and methods in `Byte`.

Constants

MAX_VALUE	`public static final byte MAX_VALUE`
MIN_VALUE	`public static final byte MIN_VALUE`

Constructors

Byte	`public Byte(byte value)`
Byte	`public Byte(String s) throws NumberFormatException`

Methods

byteValue	`public byte byteValue()`
parseByte	`public static byte parseByte(String s)` `    throws NumberFormatException`
parseByte	`public static byte parseByte(String s, int radix)` `    throws NumberFormatException`
toString	`public static String toString(byte b)`
valueOf	`public static Byte valueOf(String s)` `    throws NumberFormatException`
valueOf	`public static Byte valueOf(String s, int radix)` `    throws NumberFormatException`

Calendar (abstract)   `java.util`

`Object → Calendar`
IMPLEMENTS `Cloneable, Serializable`

`Calendar` is an abstract class representing a date and time value. `Calendar` is abstract because there are several different calendars in use throughout the world. Each subclass of `Calendar` represents a specific calendar system. (Currently, `GregorianCalendar` is the only subclass provided in the Java API.) `Calendar` provides methods to get and set dates and times, as well as methods for changing dates and times.

Constants

JANUARY	`public static final int JANUARY`
FEBRUARY	`public static final int FEBRUARY`
MARCH	`public static final int MARCH`
APRIL	`public static final int APRIL`
MAY	`public static final int MAY`
JUNE	`public static final int JUNE`
JULY	`public static final int JULY`
AUGUST	`public static final int AUGUST`
SEPTEMBER	`public static final int SEPTEMBER`
OCTOBER	`public static final int OCTOBER`
NOVEMBER	`public static final int NOVEMBER`
DECEMBER	`public static final int DECEMBER`

UNDECIMBER	`public static final int UNDECIMBER`

These constants represent months of the year. They are intended to be supplied as arguments in calls of `GregorianCalendar` methods. `UNDECIMBER` is an artificial name representing a 13th month (used for lunar calendars).

SUNDAY	`public static final int SUNDAY`
MONDAY	`public static final int MONDAY`
TUESDAY	`public static final int TUESDAY`
WEDNESDAY	`public static final int WEDNESDAY`
THURSDAY	`public static final int THURSDAY`
FRIDAY	`public static final int FRIDAY`
SATURDAY	`public static final int SATURDAY`

These constants represent days of the week. They are intended to be supplied as arguments in calls of `GregorianCalendar` methods.

AM	`public static final int AM`
PM	`public static final int PM`

These constants represent 12-hour periods. They are intended to be supplied as arguments in calls of `GregorianCalendar` methods.

AM_PM	`public static final int AM_PM`
DATE	`public static final int DATE`
DAY_OF_MONTH	`public static final int DAY_OF_MONTH`
DAY_OF_WEEK	`public static final int DAY_OF_WEEK`
DAY_OF_WEEK_IN_MONTH	`public static final int DAY_OF_WEEK_IN_MONTH`
DAY_OF_YEAR	`public static final int DAY_OF_YEAR`
DST_OFFSET	`public static final int DST_OFFSET`
ERA	`public static final int ERA`
HOUR	`public static final int HOUR`
HOUR_OF_DAY	`public static final int HOUR_OF_DAY`
MILLISECOND	`public static final int MILLISECOND`
MINUTE	`public static final int MINUTE`
MONTH	`public static final int MONTH`
SECOND	`public static final int SECOND`
WEEK_OF_MONTH	`public static final int WEEK_OF_MONTH`
WEEK_OF_YEAR	`public static final int WEEK_OF_YEAR`
YEAR	`public static final int YEAR`
ZONE_OFFSET	`public static final int ZONE_OFFSET`

These constants represent time fields. They are intended to be supplied as arguments in calls of `Calendar` methods. `DATE` and `DAY_OF_MONTH` are equivalent; both represent the day of the month. The meaning of `ERA` is calendar-specific. (The Gregorian calendar has two eras: B.C. and A.D.) `HOUR` and `HOUR_OF_DAY` both represent the hour, but `HOUR` is used for the 12-hour clock and `HOUR_OF_DAY` is used for the 24-hour clock.

Methods

clear	`public final void clear()`

Clears the values of all the time fields.

clear	`public final void clear(int field)` Clears the value in the specified time field.
get	`public final int get(int field)` Returns the value for the specified time field in this calendar.
isLenient	`public boolean isLenient()` Returns `true` if this calendar has a lenient interpretation of dates and times. (See `setLenient`.)
isSet	`public final boolean isSet(int field)` Returns `true` if the specified time field has a value set.
set	`public final void set(int field, int value)` Sets the time field with the specified value.
set	`public final void set(int year, int month, int date)`
set	`public final void set(int year, int month, int date,` `        int hour, int minute)`

set	`public final void set(int year, int month, int date,`
	`        int hour, int minute, int second)`
	Sets values for the year, month, date, hour, minute, and second time fields. Month values are zero-based, so 0 represents January, 1 represents February, and so on.

setLenient	`public void setLenient(boolean lenient)` Specifies whether or not this calendar has a lenient interpretation of dates and times. A lenient interpretation causes dates such as March 40, 2000 to be adjusted to legal values automatically (April 9, 2000 in this case). If interpretation is not lenient, setting such a date causes an exception to be thrown.

Character   `java.lang`

`Object → Character`
IMPLEMENTS `Serializable`

`Character` is a wrapper class. Each `Character` object contains a single `char` value, allowing it to be treated as an object. The class also provides utility methods for working with `char` values, including methods for testing characters and changing their case.

Constants

MAX_RADIX	`public static final int MAX_RADIX` The largest radix available for converting a digit from character form to numeric form and vice versa.
MAX_VALUE	`public static final char MAX_VALUE` The largest value of type `char`.
MIN_RADIX	`public static final int MIN_RADIX` The smallest radix available for converting a digit from character form to numeric form and vice versa.
MIN_VALUE	`public static final char MIN_VALUE` The smallest value of type `char`.

Constructors

Character   `public Character(char value)`
Creates a `Character` object containing the specified value.

Methods

charValue   `public char charValue()`
Returns the `char` value stored in this object.

digit   `public static int digit(char ch, int radix)`
Returns the numeric value of the specified character in the specified radix. Returns −1 if the radix is not between `MIN_RADIX` and `MAX_RADIX` or if the character is not a valid digit in the specified radix.

forDigit   `public static char forDigit(int digit, int radix)`
Returns the character representation of the specified digit in the specified radix. Returns the null character if the radix is not between `MIN_RADIX` and `MAX_RADIX` or the digit is not between 0 and `radix`−1.

isDigit   `public static boolean isDigit(char ch)`
Returns `true` if the specified character is a digit.

isISOControl   `public static boolean isISOControl(char ch)`
Returns `true` if the specified character is an ISO control character.

isLetter   `public static boolean isLetter(char ch)`
Returns `true` if the specified character is a letter.

isLetterOrDigit   `public static boolean isLetterOrDigit(char ch)`
Returns `true` if the specified character is a letter or digit.

isLowerCase   `public static boolean isLowerCase(char ch)`
Returns `true` if the specified character is a lowercase character.

isSpaceChar   `public static boolean isSpaceChar(char ch)`
Returns `true` if the specified character is a Unicode space character.

isUpperCase   `public static boolean isUpperCase(char ch)`
Returns `true` if the specified character is an uppercase character.

isWhitespace   `public static boolean isWhitespace(char ch)`
Returns `true` if the specified character is a white-space character. White-space characters include the space character and certain control characters, such as horizontal tab, line feed, vertical tab, form feed, and carriage return.

toLowerCase   `public static char toLowerCase(char ch)`
Returns the lowercase equivalent of the specified character, if one exists. Otherwise, returns the character itself.

toUpperCase   `public static char toUpperCase(char ch)`
Returns the uppercase equivalent of the specified character, if one exists. Otherwise, returns the character itself.

Checkbox   `java.awt`

`Object → Component → Checkbox`
IMPLEMENTS `ItemSelectable`

A checkbox is a component with two states: "checked" and "not checked" (represented by `true` and `false`).

Constructors

Checkbox   public Checkbox()

Checkbox   public Checkbox(String label)

Checkbox   public Checkbox(String label, boolean state)

Checkbox   public Checkbox(String label, boolean state,
           CheckboxGroup group)

Checkbox   public Checkbox(String label, CheckboxGroup group,
           boolean state)
Creates a checkbox with the specified label and state, belonging to the specified checkbox group. By default, the label is empty and the state is `false`.

Methods

addItemListener   public void addItemListener(ItemListener l)
Registers the specified item listener to receive item events from this checkbox.

getCheckboxGroup   public CheckboxGroup getCheckboxGroup()
Returns the checkbox group to which this checkbox belongs.

getLabel   public String getLabel()
Returns the label of this checkbox.

getState   public boolean getState()
Returns the state of this checkbox.

setCheckboxGroup   public void setCheckboxGroup(CheckboxGroup g)
Sets the checkbox group to which this checkbox belongs.

setLabel   public void setLabel(String label)
Sets the label of this checkbox.

setState   public void setState(boolean state)
Sets the state of this checkbox.

CheckboxGroup   `java.awt`

Object → CheckboxGroup
IMPLEMENTS Serializable

A checkbox group is an object that connects several checkboxes so that only one can be selected at a time. (The checkboxes behave like "radio buttons.")

Constructors

CheckboxGroup   public CheckboxGroup()

Methods

getSelectedCheckbox   public Checkbox getSelectedCheckbox()
Returns the checkbox that is currently selected.

setSelectedCheckbox   public void setSelectedCheckbox(Checkbox box)

Forces the specified checkbox to be the one that is currently selected. There is no effect if the checkbox does not belong to this group.

Choice   java.awt

Object → Component → Choice
IMPLEMENTS ItemSelectable

A choice menu is a component that, when selected, displays a menu of choices. Once a selection has been made, it continues to be displayed after the menu itself has disappeared.

Constructors

Choice public Choice()

Methods

add public void add(String item)
addItem public void addItem(String item)
Adds an item to this choice menu. Throws NullPointerException if the item is null. (add and addItem are identical.)

addItemListener public void addItemListener(ItemListener l)
Registers the specified item listener to receive item events from this choice menu.

getItem public String getItem(int index)
Returns the item at the specified index in this choice menu.

getItemCount public int getItemCount()
Returns the number of items in this choice menu.

getSelectedIndex public int getSelectedIndex()
Returns the index of the currently selected item in this choice menu.

getSelectedItem public String getSelectedItem()
Returns the currently selected item in this choice menu.

insert public void insert(String item, int index)
Inserts the specified item into this choice menu at the specified position. Throws IllegalArgumentException if index is less than 0.

remove public void remove(int position)
Removes the item at the specified position from this choice menu.

remove public void remove(String item)
Removes the first occurrence of item from this choice menu. Throws Illegal-ArgumentException if the item doesn't exist in the choice menu.

removeAll public void removeAll()
Removes all items from this choice menu.

select public void select(int pos)
Selects the item at the specified position. Throws IllegalArgumentException if the position is invalid.

select public void select(String str)
Selects the item that matches the specified string.

Color

`java.awt`

Object → Color
IMPLEMENTS Serializable

A `Color` object represents a color, with the red, green, and blue components each represented by a number between 0 and 255.

Constants

black	`public static final Color black`
blue	`public static final Color blue`
cyan	`public static final Color cyan`
darkGray	`public static final Color darkGray`
gray	`public static final Color gray`
green	`public static final Color green`
lightGray	`public static final Color lightGray`
magenta	`public static final Color magenta`
orange	`public static final Color orange`
pink	`public static final Color pink`
red	`public static final Color red`
white	`public static final Color white`
yellow	`public static final Color yellow`

Constructors

Color   `public Color(int r, int g, int b)`
Creates a color with the specified red, green, and blue values, which must be in the range 0–255.

Methods

brighter   `public Color brighter()`
Returns a brighter version of this color.

darker   `public Color darker()`
Returns a darker version of this color.

getBlue   `public int getBlue()`
Returns the blue component of this color.

getGreen   `public int getGreen()`
Returns the green component of this color.

getRed   `public int getRed()`
Returns the red component of this color.

Component (abstract)

`java.awt`

Object → Component
IMPLEMENTS ImageObserver, MenuContainer, Serializable

A component is a visual object that has a position and size, can be painted on the screen, and can receive input events. Components are the building blocks of graphical user interfaces. The `Component` class is abstract; its subclasses represent specific types of components.

Methods

getBackground   `public Color getBackground()`
Returns the background color of this component. If the component does not have a background color, the background color of its parent is returned.

getFont   `public Font getFont()`
Returns the font of this component. If the component does not have a font, the font of its parent is returned.

getFontMetrics   `public FontMetrics getFontMetrics(Font font)`
Returns the font metrics for the specified font when displayed within this component.

getForeground   `public Color getForeground()`
Returns the foreground color of this component. If the component does not have a foreground color, the foreground color of its parent is returned.

getGraphics   `public Graphics getGraphics()`
Returns the graphics context for this component. Returns `null` if the component is not currently on the screen.

getLocation   `public Point getLocation()`
Returns a `Point` object containing the coordinates of this component's upper-left corner, measured in the coordinate space of the component's parent.

getPreferredSize   `public Dimension getPreferredSize()`
Returns the preferred size of this component.

getSize   `public Dimension getSize()`
Returns the current size of this component.

paint   `public void paint(Graphics g)`
Paints this component using the specified graphics context. This method is called when the component is first shown and whenever it needs to be refreshed.

setBackground   `public void setBackground(Color c)`
Sets the background color of this component.

setFont   `public void setFont(Font f)`
Sets the font for this component.

setForeground   `public void setForeground(Color c)`
Sets the foreground color for this component.

setLocation   `public void setLocation(int x, int y)`
setLocation   `public void setLocation(Point p)`
Moves this component so that its upper-left corner is positioned at the specified location. The coordinates of the new location are measured in the coordinate space of the component's parent.

setSize   `public void setSize(int width, int height)`
Resizes this component to the specified width and height.

setSize   `public void setSize(Dimension d)`
Resizes this component to the specified dimension.

setVisible   `public void setVisible(boolean b)`
Shows or hides this component, depending on whether `b` is `true` or `false`, respectively.

Container (abstract)   `java.awt`

`Object → Component → Container`

A container is an object that contains components. Each container may have an associated layout manager, which is responsible for determining the layout of the components within the container. Containers are themselves components, which allows nesting of containers. The `Container` class is abstract; its subclasses represent specific types of containers.

Methods

add   `public Component add(Component comp)`
add   `public Component add(String name, Component comp)`
Adds the specified component to this container. The `name` argument, if present, is given to the container's layout manager to specify the position of the component within the container.

getLayout   `public LayoutManager getLayout()`
Returns the layout manager for this container.

remove   `public void remove(Component comp)`
Removes the specified component from this container.

removeAll   `public void removeAll()`
Removes all components from this container.

setLayout   `public void setLayout(LayoutManager mgr)`
Sets the layout manager for this container.

DataInputStream   `java.io`

`Object → InputStream → FilterInputStream →`
`        DataInputStream`
IMPLEMENTS `DataInput`

The `DataInputStream` class provides methods for reading values of the primitive types from a binary file. In particular, these methods can be used to read data written by methods in the `DataOutputStream` class. Each method listed here throws `IOException` if an input/output error occurs.

Constructors

DataInputStream   `public DataInputStream(InputStream in)`
Creates a data input stream that reads from the specified input stream.

Methods

read   `public final int read(byte[] b) throws IOException`
Reads bytes into the specified array until it is full or the end of the file has been reached. Returns the number of bytes read, or –1 if no bytes could be read because the end of the file was reached.

read   `public final int read(byte[] b, int off, int len)`
`    throws IOException`
Reads up to `len` bytes, storing them in the specified array starting at the position indicated by `off`. Returns the number of bytes read, or –1 if no bytes could be read because the end of the file was reached.

readBoolean   `public final boolean readBoolean() throws IOException`
Reads a single byte. Returns `false` if the byte is 0; returns `true` otherwise. Throws `EOFException` if the end of the file is reached before the byte could be read.

readByte   `public final byte readByte() throws IOException`
readChar   `public final char readChar() throws IOException`
readDouble   `public final double readDouble() throws IOException`
readFloat   `public final float readFloat() throws IOException`
readInt   `public final int readInt() throws IOException`
readLong   `public final long readLong() throws IOException`
readShort   `public final short readShort() throws IOException`
Reads a value of a primitive type and returns it. Throws `EOFException` if the end of the file is reached before all the bytes in the value could be read.

readUTF   `public final String readUTF() throws IOException`
Reads a string and returns it. The string is assumed to be stored using UTF-8 encoding. Throws `EOFException` if the end of the file is reached before all the bytes in the string could be read.

DataOutputStream   `java.io`

`Object → OutputStream → FilterOutputStream →`
`        DataOutputStream`
IMPLEMENTS `DataOutput`

The `DataOutputStream` class provides methods for writing values of the primitive types from a binary file. The methods in the `DataInputStream` class can be used later to read the data from the file. Each method listed here throws `IOException` if an input/output error occurs.

Constructors

DataOutputStream   `public DataOutputStream(OutputStream out)`
Creates a data output stream that writes to the specified output stream.

Methods

flush   `public void flush() throws IOException`

	Flushes this stream.
write	`public void write(int b) throws IOException` Writes the specified byte.

write	`public void write(byte[] b, int off, int len)`
	   `throws IOException`
	Writes `len` bytes in the specified array, starting at the position indicated by `off`.

writeBoolean	`public final void writeBoolean(boolean v)`
	   `throws IOException`
	Writes the specified value as a byte containing either 1 (`true`) or 0 (`false`).

writeByte	`public final void writeByte(int v) throws IOException` Writes the specified value as a single byte.
writeBytes	`public final void writeBytes(String s) throws IOException` Writes the specified string as a sequence of bytes, using one byte per character.
writeChar	`public final void writeChar(int v) throws IOException` Writes the specified value as two bytes.
writeChars	`public final void writeChars(String s) throws IOException` Writes the specified string as a sequence of two-byte Unicode characters.
writeDouble	`public final void writeDouble(double v) throws IOException` Writes the specified value as eight bytes.
writeFloat	`public final void writeFloat(float v) throws IOException` Writes the specified value as four bytes.
writeInt	`public final void writeInt(int v) throws IOException` Writes the specified value as four bytes.
writeLong	`public final void writeLong(long v) throws IOException` Writes the specified value as eight bytes.
writeShort	`public final void writeShort(int v) throws IOException` Writes the specified value as two bytes.
writeUTF	`public final void writeUTF(String str) throws IOException` Writes the specified string using UTF-8 encoding.

Dimension   `java.awt`

`Object → Dimension`
IMPLEMENTS `Serializable`

A `Dimension` object contains a width and a height, both of which are stored in public variables.

Variables

height	`public int height`
width	`public int width`

Constructors

Dimension	`public Dimension()`
Dimension	`public Dimension(Dimension d)`

Dimension	`public Dimension(int width, int height)` Creates a `Dimension` object and initializes it to the specified width and height. If no width and height are specified, both are set to zero.

Double   `java.lang`

Object → Number → Double

`Double` is a wrapper class. Each `Double` object contains a single `double` value, allowing it to be treated as an object. The class also provides utility methods for working with `double` values.

Constants

MAX_VALUE	`public static final double MAX_VALUE` The largest positive value of type `double`.
MIN_VALUE	`public static final double MIN_VALUE` The smallest positive value of type `double`.
NaN	`public static final double NaN` A NaN (not a number) value of type `double`.
NEGATIVE_INFINITY	`public static final double NEGATIVE_INFINITY` The negative infinity of type `double`.
POSITIVE_INFINITY	`public static final double POSITIVE_INFINITY` The positive infinity of type `double`.

Constructors

Double	`public Double(double value)` Creates a `Double` object containing the specified value.
Double	`public Double(String s) throws NumberFormatException` Creates a `Double` object containing the `double` value corresponding to the specified string. Throws `NumberFormatException` if the string does not represent a legal `double` value. (See `valueOf` for a description of the format required for the string.)

Methods

doubleValue	`public double doubleValue()` Returns the `double` value stored in this object.
isInfinite	`public boolean isInfinite()` Returns `true` if the value stored in this object is either positive infinity or negative infinity.
isInfinite	`public static boolean isInfinite(double v)` Returns `true` if the specified number is either positive infinity or negative infinity.
isNaN	`public boolean isNaN()` Returns `true` if the value stored in this object is equal to NaN.
isNaN	`public static boolean isNaN(double v)` Returns `true` if the specified number is equal to NaN.

toString   `public static String toString(double d)`
Returns a string representation of the specified number. The string consists of a minus sign (if the number is negative), a sequence of digits, a period, another sequence of digits, and possibly an exponent. The values NaN, NEGATIVE_INFINITY, POSITIVE_INFINITY, –0.0, and +0.0 are represented by the strings `"NaN"`, `"-Infinity"`, `"Infinity"`, `"-0.0"`, and `"0.0"`, respectively.

valueOf   `public static Double valueOf(String s)`
      `throws NumberFormatException`
Returns a `Double` object containing the value represented by the specified string. The string must have one of the following formats (square brackets indicate optional portions):

[-] *digits* . [*digits*] [*exponent*]
[-] . *digits* [*exponent*]

Exponent is the letter e or E followed by an integer (which may begin with a plus or minus sign). Throws `NumberFormatException` if the string does not represent a legal `double` value.

File   `java.io`

`Object → File`
IMPLEMENTS `Serializable`

A `File` object represents a file stored on disk or some other medium. The `File` class provides methods to test the properties of a file and perform a few basic file operations, including deleting a file and renaming a file.

Constructors

File   `public File(File dir, String name)`
Creates a `File` object representing the file with the specified name, located in the directory specified by `dir`. If `dir` is `null`, the object represents a file in the current directory.

File   `public File(String path)`
Creates a `File` object representing the file with the specified path. Throws `NullPointerException` if the argument is `null`.

File   `public File(String path, String name)`
Creates a `File` object representing the file with the specified name, located in the directory specified by `path`.

Methods

canRead   `public boolean canRead()`
Returns `true` if the program can read from this file.

canWrite   `public boolean canWrite()`
Returns `true` if the program can write to this file.

delete	`public boolean delete()`
	Deletes this file. If this file is a directory, the directory must be empty. Returns `true` if the operation succeeds.
exists	`public boolean exists()`
	Returns `true` if this file exists.
getName	`public String getName()`
	Returns the name of this file.
getParent	`public String getParent()`
	Returns the parent of this file (the file's complete path, without the name of the file). Returns `null` if the file has no parent.
getPath	`public String getPath()`
	Returns the complete path for this file.
isDirectory	`public boolean isDirectory()`
	Returns `true` if this file is a directory.
isFile	`public boolean isFile()`
	Returns `true` if this file is normal (not a directory).
length	`public long length()`
	Returns the length of this file in bytes. Returns zero if the file does not exist.
list	`public String[] list()`
	Returns an array of strings containing the names of the files in this directory. The array does not include the current directory or the parent directory (`"."` and `".."`).
mkdir	`public boolean mkdir()`
	Creates a directory corresponding to this `File` object. Returns `true` if the operation succeeds.
mkdirs	`public boolean mkdirs()`
	Creates a directory corresponding to this `File` object, including any necessary parent directories. Returns `true` if the operation succeeds.
renameTo	`public boolean renameTo(File dest)`
	Renames this file to the name specified by `dest`. Returns `true` if the operation succeeds.

FileInputStream   java.io

`Object` → `InputStream` → `FileInputStream`

Creating a `FileInputStream` object opens a binary file for reading. The `FileInputStream` class itself has only a few methods for reading data, so programmers typically create another kind of stream object (a `DataInputStream` object, for example) from the `FileInputStream` object. Each method listed here throws `IOException` if an input/output error occurs.

Constructors

FileInputStream	`public FileInputStream(File file)` `    throws FileNotFoundException`

Creates a file input stream for the file represented by the specified `File` object. Throws `FileNotFoundException` if the file cannot be opened for reading.

FileInputStream
```
public FileInputStream(String name)
    throws FileNotFoundException
```
Creates a file input stream for the file with the specified name. Throws `FileNot-FoundException` if the file cannot be opened for reading.

Methods

close
```
public void close() throws IOException
```
Closes this stream.

read
```
public int read() throws IOException
```
Reads a single byte, returning it as an `int` value. Returns –1 if no byte could be read because the end of the file was reached.

read
```
public int read(byte[] b) throws IOException
```
Reads bytes into the specified array until it is full or the end of the file has been reached. Returns the number of bytes read, or –1 if no bytes could be read because the end of the file was reached.

read
```
public int read(byte[] b, int off, int len)
    throws IOException
```
Reads up to `len` bytes, storing them in the specified array starting at the position indicated by `off`. Returns the number of bytes read, or –1 if no bytes could be read because the end of the file was reached.

FileOutputStream   `java.io`

Object → OutputStream → FileOutputStream

Creating a `FileOutputStream` object opens a binary file for writing. The `FileOutputStream` class itself has only a few methods for writing data, so programmers typically create another kind of stream object (a `DataOutput-Stream` object, for example) from the `FileOutputStream` object. Each method listed here throws `IOException` if an input/output error occurs.

Constructors

FileOutputStream
```
public FileOutputStream(File file) throws IOException
```
Creates a file output stream for the file represented by the specified `File` object. Throws `IOException` if the file cannot be opened for writing.

FileOutputStream
```
public FileOutputStream(String name) throws IOException
```
Creates a file output stream for the file with the specified name. Throws `IOException` if the file cannot be opened for writing.

FileOutputStream
```
public FileOutputStream(String name, boolean append)
    throws IOException
```
Creates a file output stream for the file with the specified name. Data written to the file will be appended if `append` is `true`. Throws `IOException` if the file cannot be opened for writing.

Methods

close   ```
public void close() throws IOException
```
Closes this stream.

*write*    ```
public void write(int b) throws IOException
```
Writes the specified byte.

write   ```
public void write(byte[] b) throws IOException
```
Writes all bytes in the specified array.

*write*    ```
public void write(byte[] b, int off, int len)
    throws IOException
```
Writes `len` bytes in the specified array, starting at the position indicated by `off`.

FileReader   `java.io`

`Object → Reader → InputStreamReader → FileReader`

Creating a `FileReader` object opens a text file for reading. The `FileReader` class itself has no methods for reading data (although it inherits a few), so programmers typically create another kind of reader object (a `BufferedReader` object, for example) from the `FileReader` object.

Constructors

FileReader   ```
public FileReader(File file) throws FileNotFoundException
```
Creates a file reader for the file represented by the specified `File` object. Throws `FileNotFoundException` if the file cannot be opened for reading.

*FileReader*    ```
public FileReader(String fileName)
    throws FileNotFoundException
```
Creates a file reader for the file with the specified name. Throws `FileNotFoundException` if the file cannot be opened for reading.

FileWriter   `java.io`

`Object → Writer → OutputStreamWriter → FileWriter`

Creating a `FileWriter` object opens a text file for writing. The `FileWriter` class itself has no methods for writing data (although it inherits a few), so programmers typically create another kind of writer object (a `BufferedWriter` object, for example) from the `FileWriter` object.

Constructors

FileWriter   ```
public FileWriter(File file) throws IOException
```
Creates a file writer for the file represented by the specified `File` object. Throws `IOException` if the file cannot be opened for writing.

*FileWriter*    ```
public FileWriter(String fileName) throws IOException
```
Creates a file writer for the file with the specified name. Throws `IOException` if

the file cannot be opened for writing.

FileWriter
```
public FileWriter(String fileName, boolean append)
   throws IOException
```
Creates a file writer for the file with the specified name. Data written to the file will be appended if `append` is `true`. Throws `IOException` if the file cannot be opened for writing.

Float   `java.lang`

Object → Number → Float

`Float` is a wrapper class, similar to `Double`. See the `Double` class for descriptions of the constants, constructors, and methods in `Float`.

Constants

MAX_VALUE	`public static final float MAX_VALUE`
MIN_VALUE	`public static final float MIN_VALUE`
NaN	`public static final float NaN`
NEGATIVE_INFINITY	`public static final float NEGATIVE_INFINITY`
POSITIVE_INFINITY	`public static final float POSITIVE_INFINITY`

Constructors

Float	`public Float(float value)`
Float	`public Float(double value)`
Float	`public Float(String s) throws NumberFormatException`

Methods

floatValue	`public float floatValue()`
isInfinite	`public boolean isInfinite()`
isInfinite	`public static boolean isInfinite(float v)`
isNaN	`public boolean isNaN()`
isNaN	`public static boolean isNaN(float v)`
toString	`public static String toString(float f)`
valueOf	`public static Float valueOf(String s)`
	`   throws NumberFormatException`

FlowLayout   `java.awt`

Object → FlowLayout
IMPLEMENTS LayoutManager, Serializable

The `FlowLayout` layout manager supports the positioning of an unlimited number of components within a container. Components are laid out from left to right in rows, in the order in which they were added to the container. Each row contains as many components as will fit. By default, each row is centered within the container.

Constants

CENTER	`public static final int CENTER`
LEFT	`public static final int LEFT`
RIGHT	`public static final int RIGHT`

These constants can be supplied to the `FlowLayout` constructor to specify whether rows should be centered, left-aligned, or right-aligned.

Constructors

FlowLayout	`public FlowLayout()`
FlowLayout	`public FlowLayout(int align)`
FlowLayout	`public FlowLayout(int align, int hgap, int vgap)`

Creates a flow layout with the specified alignment and gap values. `align` must be one of `FlowLayout.CENTER`, `FlowLayout.LEFT`, or `FlowLayout.RIGHT`. `hgap` and `vgap` specify the horizontal and vertical gaps between components. By default, rows are centered, with five-pixel horizontal and vertical gaps.

Methods

getAlignment	`public int getAlignment()`

Returns the alignment value for this layout (either `FlowLayout.CENTER`, `FlowLayout.LEFT`, or `FlowLayout.RIGHT`).

getHgap	`public int getHgap()`
getVgap	`public int getVgap()`

Returns the horizontal and vertical gaps between components.

setAlignment	`public void setAlignment(int align)`

Sets the alignment value for this layout (either `FlowLayout.CENTER`, `FlowLayout.LEFT`, or `FlowLayout.RIGHT`).

setHgap	`public void setHgap(int hgap)`
setVgap	`public void setVgap(int vgap)`

Sets the horizontal and vertical gaps between components.

Font   `java.awt`

`Object → Font`
IMPLEMENTS `Serializable`

A `Font` object stores a font name, point size, and style. Fonts are platform-independent; they must be mapped to fonts that are actually available on a particular platform.

Constants

BOLD	`public static final int BOLD`
ITALIC	`public static final int ITALIC`
PLAIN	`public static final int PLAIN`

These constants are used to represent the style of a font. They may be added to create mixed styles (the only useful combination is `Font.BOLD + Font.ITALIC`, which yields a bold italic style).

Constructors

Font   `public Font(String name, int style, int size)`
Creates a font with the specified name, style, and point size. Supported font names are `"Serif"`, `"SansSerif"`, `"Monospaced"`, `"Dialog"`, `"Dialog-Input"`, and `"Symbol"`.

Methods

getFamily   `public String getFamily()`
Returns a string containing the platform-specific family name of this font. Use `getName` to get the logical name of the font.

getName   `public String getName()`
Returns the logical name of this font.

getSize   `public int getSize()`
Returns the point size of this font.

getStyle   `public int getStyle()`
Returns the style of this font.

isBold   `public boolean isBold()`
Returns `true` if this font is bold.

isItalic   `public boolean isItalic()`
Returns `true` if this font is italic.

isPlain   `public boolean isPlain()`
Returns `true` if this font is plain.

FontMetrics (abstract)   `java.awt`

`Object → FontMetrics`
IMPLEMENTS `Serializable`

A font metrics object is constructed from a particular font in order to provide measurements for text displayed in that font. Information is available for the following metrics:

- *Advance width*—the amount by which the current point is moved from one character to the next in a line of text.
- *Ascent*—the distance from the baseline to the top of most alphanumeric characters. (Some characters in the font may extend above this height.)
- *Descent*—the distance from the baseline to the bottom of most alphanumeric characters. (Some characters in the font may extend below this height.)
- *Leading*—the amount of space between the descent of one line of text and the ascent of the next line.
- *Height*—the distance between the baselines of adjacent lines of text. The height is the sum of the leading, ascent, and descent. There's no guarantee that

lines of text spaced at this distance will be disjoint; lines may overlap if some characters overshoot either the standard ascent or the standard descent.

Methods

bytesWidth
```
public int bytesWidth(byte[] data, int off, int len)
```
Returns the total advance width for displaying a series of bytes in the font. `data` is an array containing the bytes to be displayed, `off` is the position of the first byte to be displayed, and `len` is the number of bytes to be displayed.

charsWidth
```
public int charsWidth(char[] data, int off, int len)
```
Identical to `bytesWidth`, except that `data` is an array of characters.

charWidth
```
public int charWidth(char ch)
```
charWidth
```
public int charWidth(int ch)
```
Returns the advance width of the specified character in the font.

getAscent
```
public int getAscent()
```
Returns the ascent for the font.

getDescent
```
public int getDescent()
```
Returns the descent for the font.

getFont
```
public Font getFont()
```
Returns the font.

getHeight
```
public int getHeight()
```
Returns the height for the font.

getLeading
```
public int getLeading()
```
Returns the leading for the font.

getMaxAdvance
```
public int getMaxAdvance()
```
Returns the maximum advance width of any character in the font. Returns -1 if the maximum advance is not known.

getMaxAscent
```
public int getMaxAscent()
```
Returns the maximum ascent of all characters in the font. No character will extend further above the baseline than this distance.

getMaxDescent
```
public int getMaxDescent()
```
Returns the maximum descent of all characters in the font. No character will extend further below the baseline than this distance.

getWidths
```
public int[] getWidths()
```
Returns an array containing the advance widths of the first 256 characters in the font.

stringWidth
```
public int stringWidth(String str)
```
Returns the total advance width for displaying the specified string in the font.

Frame   java.awt

Object → Component → Container → Window → Frame
IMPLEMENTS MenuContainer

A frame is a top-level window with a title and a border. The default layout for a frame is `BorderLayout`.

Constructors

Frame   `public Frame()`
Frame   `public Frame(String title)`
Creates a frame. The frame is not visible when created. The `title` argument, if present, is displayed as the title of the frame.

Methods

getTitle   `public String getTitle()`
Returns the title of this frame.

isResizable   `public boolean isResizable()`
Returns `true` if the user can resize this frame.

setResizable   `public void setResizable(boolean resizable)`
Specifies whether or not this frame is resizable.

setTitle   `public void setTitle(String title)`
Sets the title for this frame.

Graphics (abstract)   `java.awt`

`Object → Graphics`

`Graphics` is an abstract class representing a graphics context (an image that's visible on the screen or stored in a buffer). The pixel at the upper-left corner of a graphics context has coordinates (0, 0). A number of `Graphics` methods require `x`, `y`, `width`, and `height` as arguments. These arguments describe a rectangle with the specified width and height whose upper-left corner lies at the point (x, y).

Methods

clearRect   `public abstract void clearRect(int x, int y, int width, int height)`
Clears the specified rectangle by filling it with the current background color.

copyArea   `public abstract void copyArea(int x, int y, int width, int height, int dx, int dy)`
Copies a rectangular area by a distance specified by `dx` and `dy` to the right and down (specifying a negative value for `dx` or `dy` copies to the left or upwards). The rectangular area is specified by `x`, `y`, `width`, and `height`.

drawArc   `public abstract void drawArc(int x, int y, int width, int height, int startAngle, int arcAngle)`
Draws an arc bounded by the specified rectangle, starting at `startAngle` and extending for `arcAngle`, using the current color. Both angles are measured in degrees; 0 degrees is at the 3-o'clock position. A positive arc angle indicates a counterclockwise rotation; a negative arc angle indicates a clockwise rotation.

drawBytes   `public void drawBytes(byte[] data, int offset, int length, int x, int y)`
Draws the text represented by the specified bytes using the current font and color. `data` is an array containing the bytes to be displayed, `off` is the position of the

first byte to be displayed, and `length` is the number of bytes to be displayed. `x` and `y` are the coordinates of the first character's baseline.

drawChars   `public void drawChars(char[] data, int offset,`
`        int length, int x, int y)`
Identical to `drawChars`, except that `data` is an array of characters.

drawLine   `public abstract void drawLine(int x1, int y1, int x2,`
`        int y2)`
Draws a line between the points (`x1`, `y1`) and (`x2`, `y2`) using the current color.

drawOval   `public abstract void drawOval(int x, int y, int width,`
`        int height)`
Draws the outline of an oval bounded by the specified rectangle, using the current color.

drawPolygon   `public abstract void drawPolygon(int[] xPoints,`
`        int[] yPoints, int nPoints)`
Draws the outline of a polygon using the current color. The *x* and *y* coordinates of the polygon's vertices are assumed to be stored in `xPoints` and `yPoints`, respectively. `nPoints` is the number of vertices. If the first and last vertices are different, the figure is automatically closed by drawing a line between the two.

drawPolygon   `public void drawPolygon(Polygon p)`
Draws the outline of a polygon defined by the specified `Polygon` object using the current color.

drawPolyline   `public abstract void drawPolyline(int[] xPoints,`
`        int[] yPoints, int nPoints)`
Identical to `drawPolygon`, except that the figure is not automatically closed if the first vertex is different from the last vertex.

drawRect   `public void drawRect(int x, int y, int width, int height)`
Draws the outline of the specified rectangle using the current color.

drawRoundRect   `public abstract void drawRoundRect(int x, int y,`
`        int width, int height, int arcWidth, int arcHeight)`
Draws the outline of the specified rounded-corner rectangle using the current color. `arcWidth` is the horizontal diameter of the arc at the four corners; `arcHeight` is the vertical diameter of the arc at the four corners.

draw3DRect   `public void draw3DRect(int x, int y, int width,`
`        int height, boolean raised)`
Draws a 3-D outline of the specified rectangle. The edges of the rectangle will be highlighted so that it appears as if the edges are beveled and lit from the upper-left corner. If `raised` is `true`, the rectangle will appear to be raised above the surface; otherwise, the rectangle will appear to be sunk into the surface.

drawString   `public abstract void drawString(String str, int x, int y)`
Draws the specified string using the current font and color. `x` and `y` specify the starting point of the string's baseline.

fillArc   `public abstract void fillArc(int x, int y, int width,`
`        int height, int startAngle, int arcAngle)`
Fills an arc bounded by the specified rectangle, starting at `startAngle` and extending for `arcAngle`, using the current color. (The result will resemble a pie

wedge.) Both angles are measured in degrees; 0 degrees is at the 3-o'clock position. A positive arc angle indicates a counterclockwise rotation; a negative arc angle indicates a clockwise rotation.

fillOval

```
public abstract void fillOval(int x, int y, int width,
    int height)
```

Fills an oval bounded by the specified rectangle, using the current color.

fillPolygon

```
public abstract void fillPolygon(int[] xPoints,
    int[] yPoints, int nPoints)
```

Fills a polygon using the current color. The *x* and *y* coordinates of the polygon's vertices are assumed to be stored in xPoints and yPoints, respectively. nPoints is the number of vertices.

fillPolygon

```
public void fillPolygon(Polygon p)
```

Fills the polygon defined by the specified Polygon object using the current color.

fillRect

```
public abstract void fillRect(int x, int y, int width,
    int height)
```

Fills the specified rectangle using the current color.

fillRoundRect

```
public abstract void fillRoundRect(int x, int y,
    int width, int height, int arcWidth, int arcHeight)
```

Fills the specified rounded-corner rectangle using the current color. arcWidth is the horizontal diameter of the arc at the four corners; arcHeight is the vertical diameter of the arc at the four corners.

fill3DRect

```
public void fill3DRect(int x, int y, int width,
    int height, boolean raised)
```

Draws a 3-D rectangle filled with the current color. The edges of the rectangle will be highlighted so that it appears as if the edges are beveled and lit from the upper-left corner. If raised is true, the rectangle will appear to be raised above the surface; otherwise, the rectangle will appear to be sunk into the surface.

getColor

```
public abstract Color getColor()
```

Returns the current color.

getFont

```
public abstract Font getFont()
```

Returns the current font.

getFontMetrics

```
public FontMetrics getFontMetrics()
```

Returns the font metrics of the current font.

getFontMetrics

```
public abstract FontMetrics getFontMetrics(Font f)
```

Returns the font metrics for the specified font.

setColor

```
public abstract void setColor(Color c)
```

Sets the current color.

setFont

```
public abstract void setFont(Font font)
```

Sets the current font.

GregorianCalendar `java.util`

```
Object → Calendar → GregorianCalendar
```

A GregorianCalendar object stores a date and time according to the Gregorian calendar, which is used in most of the world. See the `Calendar` class for names of time fields that can be passed to `GregorianCalendar` methods.

Constants

AD `public static final int AD`
BC `public static final int BC`
These constants represent possible values of the `Calendar.ERA` time field.

Constructors

GregorianCalendar `public GregorianCalendar()`
Creates a `GregorianCalendar` object containing the current time.
GregorianCalendar `public GregorianCalendar(int year, int month, int date)`
GregorianCalendar `public GregorianCalendar(int year, int month, int date,`
`    int hour, int minute)`
GregorianCalendar `public GregorianCalendar(int year, int month, int date,`
`    int hour, int minute, int second)`
Creates a `GregorianCalendar` object containing the specified year, month, date, hour, minute, and second time fields. Month values are zero-based, so 0 represents January, 1 represents February, and so on.

Methods

add `public void add(int field, int amount)`
Adds the specified amount of time to the specified time field, based on this calendar's rules. The amount may be either positive or negative. Throws `Illegal-ArgumentException` if the field is `DST_OFFSET` or `ZONE_OFFSET`.
after `public boolean after(Object when)`
Returns `true` if the time of this object is after the time represented by `when` (a `Calendar` object).
before `public boolean before(Object when)`
Returns `true` if the time of this object is before the time represented by `when` (a `Calendar` object).
getGreatestMinimum `public int getGreatestMinimum(int field)`
Returns the highest minimum value for the specified time field. (Returns the same value as `getMinimum`.)
getLeastMaximum `public int getLeastMaximum(int field)`
Returns the lowest maximum value for the specified time field. (For example, `getLeastMaximum(Calendar.DAY_OF_MONTH)` returns 28.)
getMaximum `public int getMaximum(int field)`
Returns the maximum value for the specified time field. (For example, `get-Maximum(Calendar.DAY_OF_MONTH)` returns 31.)
getMinimum `public int getMinimum(int field)`
Returns the minimum value for the specified time field. (For example, `get-Minimum(Calendar.DAY_OF_MONTH)` returns 1.)
isLeapYear `public boolean isLeapYear(int year)`
Returns `true` if the specified year is a leap year.

roll   `public void roll(int field, boolean up)`
If up is `true`, increases the specified time field by one unit. If up is `false`, decreases the specified time field by one unit. Other time fields will be adjusted if necessary. Throws `IllegalArgumentException` if the field is `DST_OFFSET` or `ZONE_OFFSET`.

GridLayout   `java.awt`

`Object → GridLayout`
IMPLEMENTS `LayoutManager, Serializable`

The `GridLayout` layout manager arranges components into a grid. Each cell in the grid has the same size, so `GridLayout` is best used with components of identical size. Components are laid out from left to right in rows, in the order in which they were added to the container.

Constructors

GridLayout   `public GridLayout()`
GridLayout   `public GridLayout(int rows, int cols)`
GridLayout   `public GridLayout(int rows, int cols, int hgap, int vgap)`
Creates a grid layout with the specified number of rows and columns and the specified horizontal and vertical gaps. The default value for rows and cols is 1. If rows is 0, there is no limit on the number of rows; the actual number of rows depends on the number of columns and the number of components in the container. Similarly, if cols is 0, there is no limit on the number of columns. Only one of rows and cols can be 0, not both. If no values are specified for the horizontal and vertical gaps, they default to 0. Throws `IllegalArgumentException` if the row and column values are invalid.

Methods

getColumns   `public int getColumns()`
Returns the number of columns in this layout.
getHgap   `public int getHgap()`
Returns the horizontal gap between components.
getRows   `public int getRows()`
Returns the number of rows in this layout.
getVgap   `public int getVgap()`
Returns the vertical gap between components.
setColumns   `public void setColumns(int cols)`
Sets the number of columns in this layout.
setHgap   `public void setHgap(int hgap)`
Sets the horizontal gap between components.
setRows   `public void setRows(int rows)`
Sets the number of rows in this layout.
setVgap   `public void setVgap(int vgap)`
Sets the vertical gap between components.

Integer   `java.lang`

Object → Number → Integer

`Integer` is a wrapper class. Each `Integer` object contains a single `int` value, allowing it to be treated as an object. The class also provides utility methods for working with `int` values.

Constants

MAX_VALUE   `public static final int MAX_VALUE`
The largest value of type `int`.

MIN_VALUE   `public static final int MIN_VALUE`
The smallest value of type `int`.

Constructors

Integer   `public Integer(int value)`
Creates an `Integer` object containing the specified value.

Integer   `public Integer(String s) throws NumberFormatException`
Creates an `Integer` object containing the int value corresponding to the specified string. Throws `NumberFormatException` if the string does not represent a legal `int` value.

Methods

intValue   `public int intValue()`
Returns the `int` value stored in this object.

parseInt   `public static int parseInt(String s)`
`        throws NumberFormatException`

parseInt   `public static int parseInt(String s, int radix)`
`        throws NumberFormatException`
Converts the specified string into `int` form and returns it. If the radix is not specified, it is assumed to be 10. Throws `NumberFormatException` if the string does not represent a legal `int` value.

toBinaryString   `public static String toBinaryString(int i)`
toHexString   `public static String toHexString(int i)`
toOctalString   `public static String toOctalString(int i)`
Returns a string representation of the specified number in either binary, hexadecimal, or octal.

toString   `public static String toString(int i)`
toString   `public static String toString(int i, int radix)`
Returns a string representation of the specified number. If the radix is not specified, it is assumed to be 10.

valueOf   `public static Integer valueOf(String s)`
`        throws NumberFormatException`

valueOf   `public static Integer valueOf(String s, int radix)`
`        throws NumberFormatException`

Returns an `Integer` object containing the value represented by the specified string. If the radix is not specified, it is assumed to be 10. Throws `Number-FormatException` if the string does not represent a legal `int` value.

Label   `java.awt`

`Object → Component → Label`

A label is a component containing a single line of text. The text can be changed by the program, but it can't be edited by the user.

Constants

CENTER `public static final int CENTER`
LEFT `public static final int LEFT`
RIGHT `public static final int RIGHT`
These constants represent possible alignments for a label.

Constructors

Label `public Label()`
Label `public Label(String text)`
Label `public Label(String text, int alignment)`
Creates a label containing the specified text and with the specified alignment. The default text is the empty string; the default alignment is `Label.LEFT`.

Methods

getAlignment `public int getAlignment()`
Returns the alignment of this label.
getText `public String getText()`
Returns the text of this label.
setAlignment `public void setAlignment(int alignment)`
Sets the alignment for this label. Throws `IllegalArgumentException` if an illegal alignment is specified.
setText `public void setText(String text)`
Sets the text for this label.

List   `java.awt`

`Object → Component → List`
IMPLEMENTS `ItemSelectable`

A list is a component that displays a list of strings, stacked vertically. If the number of strings in the list exceeds the number that can be displayed, a scrollbar automatically appears, allowing the user to scroll through the list.

   The user is allowed to select any single item from a list. (Multiple selections can be enabled if desired.) Clicking on an item selects it; clicking again deselects it. Clicking on a new item deselects any previously selected item. Clicking on an item causes an *item* event; double-clicking causes an *action* event. Pressing the Enter key after an item has been selected also causes an action event.

Constructors

List   `public List()`

List   `public List(int rows)`

List   `public List(int rows, boolean multipleMode)`
Creates a list with the specified number of visible lines. If `multipleMode` has the value `true`, multiple selections are allowed. By default, no lines are visible and multiple selections are not allowed.

Methods

add   `public void add(String item)`
Adds the specified item to the end of this list.

add   `public void add(String item, int index)`
Adds the specified item to this list at the specified position. Index values start at 0. If `index` is –1 or if it is greater than or equal to the number of items in the list, the item is added at the end.

addActionListener   `public void addActionListener(ActionListener l)`
Registers the specified action listener to receive action events from this list.

addItemListener   `public void addItemListener(ItemListener l)`
Registers the specified item listener to receive item events from this list.

deselect   `public void deselect(int index)`
Deselects the item at the specified index in this list.

getItem   `public String getItem(int index)`
Returns the item at the specified index in this list.

getItemCount   `public int getItemCount()`
Returns the number of items in this list.

getItems   `public String[] getItems()`
Returns an array containing all items in this list.

getRows   `public int getRows()`
Returns the number of visible lines in this list.

getSelectedIndex   `public int getSelectedIndex()`
Returns the index of the currently selected item in this list; returns –1 if no item is selected or more than one item is selected.

getSelectedIndexes   `public int[] getSelectedIndexes()`
Returns an array containing all selected indexes in this list.

getSelectedItem   `public String getSelectedItem()`
Returns the currently selected item in this list; returns `null` if no item is selected or more than one item is selected.

getSelectedItems   `public String[] getSelectedItems()`
Returns an array containing all selected items in this list.

getVisibleIndex   `public int getVisibleIndex()`
Returns the index of the item in this list that was last made visible by the method `makeVisible`.

isIndexSelected	`public boolean isIndexSelected(int index)`
	Returns `true` if the item at the specified index has been selected in this list.
isMultipleMode	`public boolean isMultipleMode()`
	Returns `true` if this list allows multiple selections.
makeVisible	`public void makeVisible(int index)`
	Forces the item at the specified index in this list to be visible.
remove	`public void remove(int position)`
	Removes the item at the specified position from this list.
remove	`public void remove(String item)`
	Removes the first occurrence of the specified item from this list. Throws `IllegalArgumentException` if the item isn't in the list.
removeAll	`public void removeAll()`
	Removes all items from this list.
replaceItem	`public void replaceItem(String newValue, int index)`
	Replaces the item at the specified index in this list by the specified string.
select	`public void select(int index)`
	Selects the item at the specified index in this list.
setMultipleMode	`public void setMultipleMode(boolean b)`
	Specifies whether this list should allow multiple selections.

Long   `java.lang`

`Object → Number → Long`

Long is a wrapper class, similar to `Integer`. See the `Integer` class for descriptions of the constants, constructors, and methods in Long.

Constants

MAX_VALUE	`public static final long MAX_VALUE`
MIN_VALUE	`public static final long MIN_VALUE`

Constructors

Long	`public Long(long value)`
Long	`public Long(String s) throws NumberFormatException`

Methods

longValue	`public long longValue()`
parseLong	`public static long parseLong(String s)`
	`    throws NumberFormatException`
parseLong	`public static long parseLong(String s, int radix)`
	`    throws NumberFormatException`
toBinaryString	`public static String toBinaryString(long i)`
toHexString	`public static String toHexString(long i)`
toOctalString	`public static String toOctalString(long i)`
toString	`public static String toString(long i)`

toString	`public static String toString(long i, int radix)`
valueOf	`public static Long valueOf(String s)`
	`    throws NumberFormatException`
valueOf	`public static Long valueOf(String s, int radix)`
	`    throws NumberFormatException`

Math

`java.lang`

Object → Math

The `Math` class provides methods that perform fundamental mathematical operations. `Math` also provides a couple of useful mathematical constants (*e* and π).

Constants

E   `public static final double E`
The best `double` approximation to *e*, the base of the natural logarithms.

PI   `public static final double PI`
The best `double` approximation to π, the ratio of the circumference of a circle to its diameter.

Methods

abs   `public static int abs(int a)`
abs   `public static long abs(long a)`
abs   `public static float abs(float a)`
abs   `public static double abs(double a)`
Returns the absolute value of the specified number.

acos   `public static double acos(double a)`
Returns the arc cosine of the specified number. The result is between 0.0 and π. If the argument is not between -1 and 1, the result is NaN.

asin   `public static double asin(double a)`
Returns the arc sine of the specified number. The result is between $-\pi/2$ and $\pi/2$. If the argument is not between -1 and 1, the result is NaN.

atan   `public static double atan(double a)`
Returns the arc tangent of the specified number. The result is between $-\pi/2$ and $\pi/2$.

atan2   `public static double atan2(double a, double b)`
Returns the arc tangent of a/b. This method is useful for converting from Cartesian coordinates to polar coordinates because it returns the value of the θ component of the point (r, θ) in polar coordinates that corresponds to the point (b, a) in Cartesian coordinates.

ceil   `public static double ceil(double a)`
Returns the smallest (closest to negative infinity) `double` value that is not less than the argument and is equal to a mathematical integer.

cos   `public static double cos(double a)`
Returns the cosine of the specified angle, which is measured in radians.

exp   `public static double exp(double a)`
Returns *e* raised to the specified power, where *e* is the base of the natural logarithms.

floor   `public static double floor(double a)`
Returns the largest (closest to positive infinity) `double` value that is not greater than the argument and is equal to a mathematical integer.

log   `public static double log(double a)`
Returns the natural logarithm (base *e*) of the specified number. Throws `ArithmeticException` if the argument is less than zero.

max   `public static int max(int a, int b)`
max   `public static long max(long a, long b)`
max   `public static float max(float a, float b)`
max   `public static double max(double a, double b)`
Returns the larger of the two specified numbers.

min   `public static int min(int a, int b)`
min   `public static long min(long a, long b)`
min   `public static float min(float a, float b)`
min   `public static double min(double a, double b)`
Returns the smaller of the two specified numbers.

pow   `public static double pow(double a, double b)`
Returns a raised to the power b. Throws `ArithmeticException` if a is equal to 0.0 and b is less than or equal to 0.0, or if a is less than or equal to 0.0 and b is not a whole number.

random   `public static double random()`
Returns a pseudorandom number that is greater than or equal to 0.0 and less than 1.0.

rint   `public static double rint(double a)`
Returns the integer closest to the argument. If two integers are equally close, `rint` returns the even one. Thus, `Math.rint(1.5)` and `Math.rint(2.5)` both return 2.0.

round   `public static int round(float a)`
Returns the value of the argument rounded to the nearest `int` value. Returns `Integer.MIN_VALUE` if the argument is negative infinity or a number less than or equal to `Integer.MIN_VALUE`. Returns `Integer.MAX_VALUE` if the argument is positive infinity or a number greater than or equal to `Integer.MAX_VALUE`.

round   `public static long round(double a)`
Identical to the previous `round` method, except that the argument has `double` type and the returned value has `long` type. Returns `Long.MIN_VALUE` or `Long.MAX_VALUE` if the argument is too small or too large.

sin   `public static double sin(double a)`
Returns the sine of the specified angle, which is measured in radians.

sqrt   `public static double sqrt(double a)`
Returns the square root of the specified number. Throws `ArithmeticException` if the number is negative.

tan   `public static double tan(double a)`
Returns the tangent of the specified angle, which is measured in radians.

Object   `java.lang`

`Object` is the superclass—directly or indirectly—of all other classes in Java. Every class inherits the methods that belong to `Object`, although these methods are often overridden.

Constructors

Object   `public Object()`

Methods

clone   `protected Object clone() throws CloneNotSupportedException`
Called by a subclass method to create a clone of this object (a new object whose instance variables are initialized to the values in this object). Throws `CloneNot-SupportedException` if the subclass does not implement the `Cloneable` interface. Throws `OutOfMemoryError` if there is not enough memory.

equals   `public boolean equals(Object obj)`
Returns `true` if this object is equal to the specified object. The default behavior is to return `true` if the objects have the same reference. This method is often overridden by subclasses.

toString   `public String toString()`
Returns a string representation of this object. The default behavior is to return a string containing the name of the class to which the object belongs, the @ character, and the object's hash code in hexadecimal. This method is normally overridden by subclasses.

ObjectInputStream   `java.io`

`Object → InputStream → ObjectInputStream`
IMPLEMENTS `ObjectInput, ObjectStreamConstants`

The `ObjectInputStream` class is used to read objects and other data that were previously written to a binary file by methods in the `ObjectOutputStream` class. Each method listed here throws `IOException` if an input/output error occurs.

Constructors

ObjectInputStream   `public ObjectInputStream(InputStream in)`
     `throws IOException, StreamCorruptedException`
Creates an object input stream that reads from the specified input stream. Reads a header from the underlying stream; throws `IOException` if the underlying stream throws an exception as the header is being read. Throws `Stream-`

CorruptedException if the stream has been corrupted (most likely, the data was not originally written by methods in the ObjectOutputStream class).

Methods

close   public void close() throws IOException
Closes this stream.

read   public int read() throws IOException
Reads a single byte, returning it as an int value. Returns –1 if no byte could be read because the end of the file was reached.

read   public int read(byte[] b, int off, int len)
    throws IOException
Reads up to len bytes, storing them in the specified array starting at the position indicated by off. Returns the number of bytes read, or –1 if no bytes could be read because the end of the file was reached.

readBoolean   public boolean readBoolean() throws IOException
Reads a single byte. Returns false if the byte is 0; returns true otherwise. Throws EOFException if the end of the file is reached before the byte could be read.

readByte   public byte readByte() throws IOException
readChar   public char readChar() throws IOException
readDouble   public double readDouble() throws IOException
readFloat   public float readFloat() throws IOException
readInt   public int readInt() throws IOException
readLong   public long readLong() throws IOException
Reads a value of a primitive type and returns it. Throws EOFException if the end of the file is reached before all the bytes in the value could be read.

readObject   public final Object readObject()
    throws OptionalDataException, ClassNotFoundException,
        IOException
Reads an object and returns it. Throws ClassNotFoundException if the Java interpreter can't locate the class to which the object belongs. (This situation typically arises when a file is written on one computer and then read on a different computer.) Throws InvalidClassException if there's a problem with the object's class. Throws StreamCorruptedException if there's an inconsistency in the data. Throws OptionalDataException if unexpected data is encountered (most likely, bytes belonging to a primitive type).

readShort   public short readShort() throws IOException
Reads a two-byte short value and returns it. Throws EOFException if the end of the file is reached before all the bytes in the value could be read.

readUTF   public String readUTF() throws IOException
Reads a string and returns it. The string is assumed to be stored using UTF-8 encoding. Throws EOFException if the end of the file is reached before all the bytes in the string could be read.

ObjectOutputStream   `java.io`

`Object → OutputStream → ObjectOutputStream`
IMPLEMENTS `ObjectOutput, ObjectStreamConstants`

The `ObjectOutputStream` class is used to write objects to a binary file via a process known as serialization. When an object is written to a file, Java automatically adds information to identify its class. If the object contains references to other objects, those objects are stored as well. Each object is stored only once, regardless of the number of references to it. Objects written to a file must belong to a class that implements the `Serializable` interface. The `ObjectOutput-Stream` class also provides methods for writing strings and values of the primitive types. The methods in the `ObjectInputStream` class can be used later to read values written using the `ObjectOutputStream` methods. Each method listed here throws `IOException` if an input/output error occurs.

Constructors

ObjectOutputStream `public ObjectOutputStream(OutputStream out)`
`    throws IOException`
Creates an object output stream that writes to the specified output stream. Writes a header to the underlying stream; throws `IOException` if the underlying stream throws an exception as the header is being written.

Methods

close `public void close() throws IOException`
Closes this stream.

flush `public void flush() throws IOException`
Flushes this stream.

write `public void write(int data) throws IOException`
Writes the specified byte.

write `public void write(byte[] b) throws IOException`
Writes all bytes in the specified array.

write `public void write(byte[] b, int off, int len)`
`    throws IOException`
Writes `len` bytes in the specified array, starting at the position indicated by `off`.

writeBoolean `public void writeBoolean(boolean data) throws IOException`
Writes the specified value as a byte containing either 1 (`true`) or 0 (`false`).

writeByte `public void writeByte(int data) throws IOException`
Writes the specified value as a single byte.

writeBytes `public void writeBytes(String data) throws IOException`
Writes the specified string as a sequence of bytes, using one byte per character.

writeChar `public void writeChar(int data) throws IOException`
Writes the specified value as two bytes.

writeChars	`public void writeChars(String data) throws IOException` Writes the specified string as a sequence of two-byte Unicode characters.
writeDouble	`public void writeDouble(double data) throws IOException` Writes the specified value as eight bytes.
writeFloat	`public void writeFloat(float data) throws IOException` Writes the specified value as four bytes.
writeInt	`public void writeInt(int data) throws IOException` Writes the specified value as four bytes.
writeLong	`public void writeLong(long data) throws IOException` Writes the specified value as eight bytes.

writeObject	`public final void writeObject(Object obj)`
	`    throws IOException`
	Writes the specified object. All instance variables not declared `transient` (including inherited instance variables) are written, along with information to identify the object's class. If the object contains references to other objects, those objects are written as well. Throws `InvalidClassException` if there's a problem with a class involved in the serialization. Throws `NotSerializable-Exception` if some object to be serialized doesn't belong to a class that implements the `Serializable` interface.

writeShort	`public void writeShort(int data) throws IOException` Writes the specified value as two bytes.
writeUTF	`public void writeUTF(String data) throws IOException` Writes the specified string using UTF-8 encoding.

Panel   `java.awt`

`Object → Component → Container → Panel`

A panel is a container with no visible border. Panels are used primarily to group several components into a single component for layout purposes. A panel must be nested within some other container, such as an applet or a frame.

Constructors

Panel	`public Panel()`
Panel	`public Panel(LayoutManager layout)` Creates a panel with the specified layout manager. The default layout for a panel is `FlowLayout`.

Point   `java.awt`

`Object → Point`
IMPLEMENTS `Serializable`

A `Point` object contains the *x* and *y* coordinates of a point in two-dimensional space. Both coordinates are stored in public variables.

Variables

x   `public int x`
y   `public int y`
The *x* and *y* coordinates of this point.

Constructors

Point   `public Point()`
Point   `public Point(Point p)`
Point   `public Point(int x, int y)`
Creates a point with the specified *x* and *y* coordinates. By default, both coordinates are 0.

Methods

move   `public void move(int x, int y)`
Changes this point to have the specified *x* and *y* coordinates.
translate   `public void translate(int x, int y)`
Translates this point by adding `x` and `y` to the stored *x* and *y* coordinates, respectively.

Polygon   `java.awt`

`Object → Polygon`
IMPLEMENTS `Shape, Serializable`

A `Polygon` object stores a series of points in two-dimensional space. The variables `npoints` (number of points), `xpoints` (*x* coordinates of the points), and `ypoints` (*y* coordinates of the points) are public.

Variables

npoints   `public int npoints`
Number of points in this polygon.
xpoints   `public int[] xpoints`
Array containing the *x* coordinates of the points in this polygon.
ypoints   `public int[] ypoints`
Array containing the *y* coordinates of the points in this polygon.

Constructors

Polygon   `public Polygon()`
Creates an empty polygon.
Polygon   `public Polygon(int[] xpoints, int[] ypoints, int npoints)`
Creates a polygon with specified number of points, which have the specified *x* and *y* coordinates.

Methods

addPoint   `public void addPoint(int x, int y)`
Appends a point with the specified *x* and *y* coordinates to this polygon.

contains	`public boolean contains(Point p)`
contains	`public boolean contains(int x, int y)`

Returns `true` if the specified point is inside this polygon.

translate	`public void translate(int deltaX, int deltaY)`

Translates all points in this polygon by adding `deltaX` to each *x* coordinate and `deltaY` to each *y* coordinate.

PrintStream   java.io

Object → `OutputStream` → `FilterOutputStream` → `PrintStream`

Writes data to a text stream, converting characters from Unicode to single bytes. The standard output stream (`System.out`) and standard error stream (`System.err`) are instances of `PrintStream`. The `PrintStream` class is not recommended for writing to a file; use the `PrintWriter` class instead.

Methods

close	`public void close()`

Closes this stream.

flush	`public void flush()`

Flushes this stream.

print	`public void print(boolean b)`
print	`public void print(char c)`
print	`public void print(int i)`
print	`public void print(long l)`
print	`public void print(float f)`
print	`public void print(double d)`

Converts the argument to string form and then writes it to the stream.

print	`public void print(char[] s)`

Writes the characters in the specified array.

print	`public void print(String s)`

Writes the characters in the specified string. If the value of the argument is `null`, writes `"null"`.

print	`public void print(Object obj)`

Writes the value returned by the object's `toString` method.

println	`public void println()`

Terminates the current output line.

println	`public void println(boolean x)`
println	`public void println(char x)`
println	`public void println(int x)`
println	`public void println(long x)`
println	`public void println(float x)`
println	`public void println(double x)`
println	`public void println(char[] x)`
println	`public void println(String x)`

println	`public void println(Object x)`

The `println` methods are identical to the corresponding `print` methods, except that `println` terminates the current output line after writing the specified value.

write	`public void write(int b)`

Writes the specified byte.

write	`public void write(byte[] buf, int off, int len)`

Writes `len` bytes in the specified array, starting at the position indicated by `off`.

PrintWriter   `java.io`

Object → Writer → PrintWriter

Writes data to a text stream. If automatic flushing is enabled, it will occur only when one of the `println` methods is called.

Constructors

PrintWriter	`public PrintWriter(OutputStream out)`

Creates a print writer that writes to the specified output stream. Automatic line flushing is not enabled.

PrintWriter	`public PrintWriter(OutputStream out, boolean autoFlush)`

Creates a print writer that writes to the specified output stream. Automatic line flushing is enabled if `autoFlush` is `true`.

PrintWriter	`public PrintWriter(Writer out)`

Creates a print writer that writes to the specified writer. Automatic line flushing is not enabled.

PrintWriter	`public PrintWriter(Writer out, boolean autoFlush)`

Creates a print writer that writes to the specified writer. Automatic line flushing is enabled if `autoFlush` is `true`.

Methods

close	`public void close()`

Closes this stream.

flush	`public void flush()`

Flushes this stream.

print	`public void print(boolean b)`
print	`public void print(char c)`
print	`public void print(int i)`
print	`public void print(long l)`
print	`public void print(float f)`
print	`public void print(double d)`

Converts the argument to string form and then writes it to the stream.

print	`public void print(char[] s)`

Writes the characters in the specified array.

print	`public void print(String s)`

Writes the characters in the specified string. If the value of the argument is `null`, writes `"null"`.

print   `public void print(Object obj)`
Writes the value returned by the object's `toString` method.

println   `public void println()`
Terminates the current output line.

println   `public void println(boolean x)`
println   `public void println(char x)`
println   `public void println(int x)`
println   `public void println(long x)`
println   `public void println(float x)`
println   `public void println(double x)`
println   `public void println(char[] x)`
println   `public void println(String x)`
println   `public void println(Object x)`
The `println` methods are identical to the corresponding `print` methods, except that `println` terminates the current output line after writing the specified value.

write   `public void write(int c)`
Writes the specified character.

write   `public void write(char[] buf, int off, int len)`
Writes `len` characters in the specified array, starting at the position indicated by `off`.

write   `public void write(char[] buf)`
Writes all characters in the specified array.

write   `public void write(String s, int off, int len)`
Writes `len` characters in the specified string, starting at the position indicated by `off`.

write   `public void write(String s)`
Writes all characters in the specified string.

Scrollbar   `java.awt`

`Object → Component → Scrollbar`
IMPLEMENTS `Adjustable`

A scrollbar is a horizontal or vertical sliding bar. Each scrollbar represents a number chosen from a range of integers. In a horizontal scrollbar, the minimum value is at the left end and the maximum value is at the right end. In a vertical scrollbar, the minimum value is at the top and the maximum value is at the bottom.

The sliding portion of the scrollbar (the "scroll box" or "bubble") must have a width of at least 1 (measured in the scrollbar's own units, not in pixels), but it can be wider if desired. The width of the scroll box affects the largest value that the user can select, which is the maximum value of the scrollbar's range minus the width of the scroll box. For example, if the scrollbar has a range of 0 to 100, and the scroll box has a width of 10, then the largest value that the user can select is 100 − 10 = 90.

The user can change the value of a scrollbar in several ways. One possibility is to drag the scroll box to a different position. Another is to click on the scrollbar's arrow buttons, which change the value of the scrollbar by a small amount, known as the "unit increment." (By default, the unit increment is 1.) Finally, by clicking in the area between an arrow button and the scroll box, the user can change the value of the scrollbar by a larger amount, known as the "block increment." (By default, the block increment is 10.) An adjustment event occurs when the value of a scrollbar is changed.

Constants

HORIZONTAL   `public static final int HORIZONTAL`
VERTICAL   `public static final int VERTICAL`
Used to specify the orientation of a scrollbar.

Constructors

Scrollbar   `public Scrollbar()`
Scrollbar   `public Scrollbar(int orientation)`
Scrollbar   `public Scrollbar(int orientation, int value,`
      `int visible, int minimum, int maximum)`
Creates a scrollbar. The value of `orientation` (either `Scrollbar.HORIZONTAL` or `Scrollbar.VERTICAL`) determines the scrollbar's orientation; the default is `Scrollbar.VERTICAL`. The values of `minimum` and `maximum` determine the range of integers that the scrollbar represents; the default values are 0 and 100, respectively. `value` determines the initial value of the scrollbar; the default is 0. The value of `visible` (measured in the scrollbar's own units) determines the width of the scroll box; the default value is 10. Throws `IllegalArgumentException` if the value of `orientation` is illegal.

Methods

addAdjustmentListener   `public void addAdjustmentListener(AdjustmentListener l)`
Registers the specified adjustment listener to receive adjustment events from this scrollbar.

getBlockIncrement   `public int getBlockIncrement()`
Returns the block increment for this scrollbar.

getMaximum   `public int getMaximum()`
Returns the maximum value of this scrollbar.

getMinimum   `public int getMinimum()`
Returns the minimum value of this scrollbar.

getOrientation   `public int getOrientation()`
Returns the orientation of this scrollbar.

getUnitIncrement   `public int getUnitIncrement()`
Returns the unit increment for this scrollbar.

getValue   `public int getValue()`
Returns the current value of this scrollbar.

getVisibleAmount	`public int getVisibleAmount()` Returns the visible amount of this scrollbar.
setBlockIncrement	`public void setBlockIncrement(int v)` Sets the block increment for this scrollbar.
setMaximum	`public void setMaximum(int newMaximum)` Sets the maximum value of this scrollbar.
setMinimum	`public void setMinimum(int newMinimum)` Sets the minimum value of this scrollbar.
setOrientation	`public void setOrientation(int orientation)` Sets the orientation of this scrollbar (`Scrollbar.HORIZONTAL` or `Scrollbar.VERTICAL`).
setUnitIncrement	`public void setUnitIncrement(int v)` Sets the unit increment for this scrollbar.
setValue	`public void setValue(int newValue)` Sets the value of this scrollbar. If this value is below the scrollbar's minimum value or above the scrollbar's maximum value minus the visible amount, then one of those values is used instead.

setValues	`public void setValues(int value, int visible,`
	`    int minimum, int maximum)`
	Sets the values for this scrollbar. This method enforces the following constraints by adjusting the values if necessary: `maximum` can't be less than `minimum`, and `value` must be greater than or equal to `minimum` and less than or equal to `maximum` minus `visible`.

setVisibleAmount	`public void setVisibleAmount(int newAmount)` Sets the visible amount of this scrollbar.

Short

`java.lang`

`Object → Number → Short`

`Short` is a wrapper class, similar to `Integer`. See the `Integer` class for descriptions of the constants, constructors, and methods in `Short`.

Constants

MAX_VALUE	`public static final short MAX_VALUE`
MIN_VALUE	`public static final short MIN_VALUE`

Constructors

Short	`public Short(short value)`
Short	`public Short(String s) throws NumberFormatException`

Methods

parseShort	`public static short parseShort(String s)` `    throws NumberFormatException`
parseShort	`public static short parseShort(String s, int radix)` `    throws NumberFormatException`

shortValue	`public short shortValue()`
toString	`public static String toString(short s)`
valueOf	`public static Short valueOf(String s)`
	`    throws NumberFormatException`
valueOf	`public static Short valueOf(String s, int radix)`
	`    throws NumberFormatException`

`String`   `java.lang`

`Object → String`
IMPLEMENTS `Serializable`

The `String` class supports the creation and manipulation of character strings. In addition to the methods listed here, Java also allows the use of the + operator to concatenate strings. The `String` class provides no methods for changing the contents of a string, because strings are immutable—they can't be changed after creation. To change a string, it's necessary to create a `StringBuffer` object containing the same characters as the original string, make the changes to that object, and then convert it back to a string.

Constructors

String   `public String()`
Creates a string containing no characters.

String   `public String(String value)`
Creates a string containing the same characters as the specified string.

String   `public String(char[] value)`
Creates a string containing the same characters as the specified array of characters.

String   `public String(char[] value, int offset, int count)`
Creates a string containing characters from the specified array. The string will consist of `count` characters from the array, starting with the character at position `offset`. Throws `StringIndexOutOfBoundsException` if `offset` and `count` refer to characters outside the bounds of the array.

String   `public String(StringBuffer buffer)`
Creates a string containing the same characters as the specified string buffer.

Methods

charAt   `public char charAt(int index)`
Returns the character at the specified index, a number between 0 and the string's length minus 1. Throws `StringIndexOutOfBoundsException` if the index is out of range.

compareTo   `public int compareTo(String anotherString)`
Compares this string with the specified string. Returns 0 if the strings are equal, a value less than 0 if this string is less than the specified string, and a value greater than 0 if this string is greater than the specified string. The comparison is done

character-by-character, using the Unicode values of the characters.

concat   `public String concat(String str)`
Returns a string containing the characters in this string followed by the characters in the specified string.

copyValueOf   `public static String copyValueOf(char[] data)`
Returns a string containing the characters in the specified array.

copyValueOf   `public static String copyValueOf(char[] data,`
      `int offset, int count)`
Returns a string containing characters from the specified array. The string will consist of `count` characters from the array, starting with the character at position `offset`. Throws `StringIndexOutOfBoundsException` if `offset` and `count` refer to characters outside the bounds of the array.

endsWith   `public boolean endsWith(String suffix)`
Returns `true` if the specified string is a suffix of this string.

equalsIgnoreCase   `public boolean equalsIgnoreCase(String anotherString)`
Returns true if this string contains the same characters as the specified string, ignoring the case of the characters in both strings.

getChars   `public void getChars(int srcBegin, int srcEnd,`
      `char[] dst, int dstBegin)`
Copies characters from this string into the specified character array. The first character to be copied is at index `srcBegin`; the last character to be copied is at index `srcEnd`–1. The characters are copied into `dst` starting at index `dstBegin`. Throws `StringIndexOutOfBoundsException` if `srcBegin` or `srcEnd` is out of range, or if `srcBegin` is greater than `srcEnd`.

indexOf   `public int indexOf(int ch)`
indexOf   `public int indexOf(int ch, int fromIndex)`
indexOf   `public int indexOf(String str)`
indexOf   `public int indexOf(String str, int fromIndex)`
Searches this string for the specified character or string. The search begins at the beginning of this string unless `fromIndex` is supplied, in which case the search begins at that position. Returns the index of the match; if no match is found, returns –1.

lastIndexOf   `public int lastIndexOf(int ch)`
lastIndexOf   `public int lastIndexOf(int ch, int fromIndex)`
lastIndexOf   `public int lastIndexOf(String str)`
lastIndexOf   `public int lastIndexOf(String str, int fromIndex)`
Searches this string for the last occurrence of the specified character or string. The search begins at the end of this string unless `fromIndex` is supplied, in which case the search begins at that position. Returns the index of the match; if no match is found, returns –1. If `fromIndex` is supplied, the value returned is always less than or equal to `fromIndex`.

length   `public int length()`
Returns the length of this string (the number of characters in the string).

replace   `public String replace(char oldChar, char newChar)`
Returns a new string resulting from replacing all occurrences of `oldChar` in this

string with newChar. If oldChar does not occur in the string, then the original string is returned.

startsWith   `public boolean startsWith(String prefix)`
Returns `true` if the specified string is a prefix of this string.

startsWith   `public boolean startsWith(String prefix, int toffset)`
Identical to the previous method, except that the `prefix` argument must match a substring of this string starting at position `toffset`.

substring   `public String substring(int beginIndex)`
Returns a substring of this string. The substring begins at the specified index and extends to the end of this string. Throws `StringIndexOutOfBoundsException` if the index is out of range.

substring   `public String substring(int beginIndex, int endIndex)`
Returns a substring of this string. The substring begins at `beginIndex` and ends at `endIndex–1`. Throws `StringIndexOutOfBoundsException` if `beginIndex` or `endIndex` is out of range.

toCharArray   `public char[] toCharArray()`
Returns a character array containing the characters in this string.

toLowerCase   `public String toLowerCase()`
Returns a string that is identical to this string, except that the characters have been converted to lower case.

toUpperCase   `public String toUpperCase()`
Returns a string that is identical to this string, except that the characters have been converted to upper case.

trim   `public String trim()`
Returns a string that is identical to this string, except that leading and trailing white-space characters have been removed. All characters with Unicode values less than or equal to the space character are considered to be white space.

valueOf   `public static String valueOf(Object obj)`
Returns a string representation of the specified object. If the argument is `null`, returns the string `"null"`; otherwise, returns the value of `obj.toString()`.

valueOf   `public static String valueOf(char[] data)`
Returns a string containing the same sequence of characters as the specified character array.

valueOf   `public static String valueOf(char[] data, int offset, int count)`
Returns a string containing the same sequence of characters as the specified character array, using only the portion of length `count`, starting at position `offset`.

valueOf   `public static String valueOf(boolean b)`
Returns the string `"true"` if b has the value `true`; returns `"false"` otherwise.

valueOf   `public static String valueOf(char c)`
Returns a string of length 1 containing the specified character.

valueOf   `public static String valueOf(int i)`
valueOf   `public static String valueOf(long l)`
valueOf   `public static String valueOf(float f)`

valueOf   `public static String valueOf(double d)`
Returns a string representation of the specified number. The value returned is identical to that returned by `Integer.toString`, `Long.toString`, `Float.toString`, or `Double.toString`.

StringBuffer   `java.lang`

`Object → StringBuffer`
IMPLEMENTS `Serializable`

The `StringBuffer` class allows the creation of "mutable" sequences of characters. `String` objects can't be modified, so changing a string requires creating a string buffer containing the same characters as the original string, making the changes to the buffer, and then converting the buffer back to a string using the `toString` method.

Each string buffer has a capacity—the maximum number of characters it can store. If an operation on the buffer causes the capacity to be exceeded, the capacity is increased automatically.

Constructors

StringBuffer   `public StringBuffer()`
Creates an empty string buffer with a capacity of 16 characters.

StringBuffer   `public StringBuffer(int length)`
Creates an empty string buffer with the specified capacity. Throws `Negative-ArraySizeException` if the argument is less than 0.

StringBuffer   `public StringBuffer(String str)`
Creates a string buffer containing the same sequence of characters as the specified string. The capacity of the string buffer is the length of the string plus 16.

Methods

append   `public StringBuffer append(Object obj)`
append   `public StringBuffer append(String str)`
append   `public StringBuffer append(char[] str)`
append   `public StringBuffer append(char[] str, int offset,`
`              int len)`
append   `public StringBuffer append(boolean b)`
append   `public StringBuffer append(char c)`
append   `public StringBuffer append(int i)`
append   `public StringBuffer append(long l)`
append   `public StringBuffer append(float f)`
append   `public StringBuffer append(double d)`
Converts the argument to string form (as if by a call of `String.valueOf`) and appends the resulting string to the end of the string stored in this string buffer. The capacity of the buffer is automatically increased if necessary. Returns this string buffer.

capacity   `public int capacity()`
Returns the current capacity of this string buffer.

charAt   `public char charAt(int index)`
Returns the character at the specified index in this string buffer. (The first character in a string buffer is located at index 0.) Throws `StringIndexOutOfBounds-Exception` if the index is less than 0 or greater than or equal to the length of the string stored in the buffer.

ensureCapacity   `public void ensureCapacity(int minimumCapacity)`
Increases the capacity of this string buffer, if necessary, to ensure that it can hold at least the specified number of characters. Returns without taking action if the argument is not a positive number.

getChars   `public void getChars(int srcBegin, int srcEnd,`
`    char[] dst, int dstBegin)`
Copies characters from this string buffer into the specified character array. The first character to be copied is at index `srcBegin`; the last character to be copied is at index `srcEnd-1`. The characters are copied into `dst` starting at index `dst-Begin`. Throws `StringIndexOutOfBoundsException` if `srcBegin` or `srcEnd` is out of range, or if `srcBegin` is greater than `srcEnd`.

insert   `public StringBuffer insert(int offset, Object obj)`
insert   `public StringBuffer insert(int offset, String str)`
insert   `public StringBuffer insert(int offset, char[] str)`
insert   `public StringBuffer insert(int offset, boolean b)`
insert   `public StringBuffer insert(int offset, char c)`
insert   `public StringBuffer insert(int offset, int i)`
insert   `public StringBuffer insert(int offset, long l)`
insert   `public StringBuffer insert(int offset, float f)`
insert   `public StringBuffer insert(int offset, double d)`
Converts the second argument to string form (as if by a call of `String.valueOf`) and inserts the resulting string into this string buffer starting at index `offset`. Characters at index `offset` and later are placed after the inserted string. The capacity of the buffer is automatically increased if necessary. Returns this string buffer. Throws `StringIndexOutOfBoundsException` if the value of `off-set` is less than 0 or greater than the length of the string stored in the buffer.

length   `public int length()`
Returns the length of the string stored in this string buffer.

reverse   `public StringBuffer reverse()`
Reverses the order of the characters stored in this string buffer and returns the buffer.

setCharAt   `public void setCharAt(int index, char ch)`
Sets the character at the specified index in this string buffer to the specified character. Throws `StringIndexOutOfBoundsException` if the index is out of range.

setLength   `public void setLength(int newLength)`
Sets the length of this string buffer. If the specified length is less than the current length of the string buffer, the string buffer is truncated. If the specified length is

greater than the current length, null characters are appended to the string buffer until the desired length is reached. Throws `StringIndexOutOfBounds-Exception` if the specified length is less than 0.

System   `java.lang`

`Object → System`

The `System` class provides class variables representing the standard streams, as well as a variety of system-related class methods.

Variables

err `public static final PrintStream err`
The standard error stream. Unless it has been redirected, this stream normally represents the user's screen. This stream is used to display error messages that should always appear on the screen, even if the user has redirected the standard output stream.

in `public static final InputStream in`
The standard input stream. Unless it has been redirected, this stream normally represents the user's keyboard.

out `public static final PrintStream out`
The standard output stream. Unless it has been redirected, this stream normally represents the user's screen.

Methods

arraycopy `public static void arraycopy(Object src, int src_position,`
   `Object dst, int dst_position, int length)`
Copies a portion of one array into another array. `src` is the array to be copied, and `src_position` is the position within `src` of the first element to be copied. `dst` is the array into which the elements are to be copied, and `dst_position` is the first element to be assigned a new value. `length` is the number of elements to be copied. Throws `ArrayStoreException` if `src` and `dst` are not arrays, or if the copied elements cannot be legally assigned to the elements of `dst`. Throws `ArrayIndexOutOfBoundsException` if the value of `src_position`, `dst_position`, or `length` would cause the copy to go out of bounds in either array.

exit `public static void exit(int status)`
Causes the program to terminate. The argument is a status code. By convention, zero indicates normal termination. Any value other than zero indicates abnormal termination.

TextArea   `java.awt`

`Object → Component → TextComponent → TextArea`

A text area is a component that displays one or more lines of text. If desired, the text can be edited by the user.

Constants

SCROLLBARS_BOTH   `public static final int SCROLLBARS_BOTH`

SCROLLBARS_HORIZONTAL_ONLY   `public static final int SCROLLBARS_HORIZONTAL_ONLY`

SCROLLBARS_NONE   `public static final int SCROLLBARS_NONE`

SCROLLBARS_VERTICAL_ONLY   `public static final int SCROLLBARS_VERTICAL_ONLY`

These constants are used to specify whether a text area is accompanied by a horizontal scrollbar, a vertical scrollbar, both, or neither.

Constructors

TextArea   `public TextArea()`
Creates a text area.

TextArea   `public TextArea(String text)`
Creates a text area containing the specified text.

TextArea   `public TextArea(int rows, int columns)`
Creates an empty text area with the specified number of rows and columns.

TextArea   `public TextArea(String text, int rows, int columns)`
Creates a text area with the specified text and number of rows and columns.

TextArea   `public TextArea(String text, int rows, int columns,`
`    int scrollbars)`
Creates a text area with the specified text, number of rows and columns, and scrollbar visibility (see the constants above).

Methods

append   `public void append(String str)`
Appends the specified text to the end of this text area.

getColumns   `public int getColumns()`
Returns the number of columns in this text area.

getRows   `public int getRows()`
Returns the number of rows in this text area.

getScrollbarVisibility   `public int getScrollbarVisibility()`
Returns a value indicating whether this text area is accompanied by a horizontal scrollbar, a vertical scrollbar, both, or neither (see the constants above).

insert   `public void insert(String str, int pos)`
Inserts the specified text at the specified position in this text area.

replaceRange   `public void replaceRange(String str, int start, int end)`
Replaces a portion of the text within this text area with the specified text. The portion replaced begins at the specified start index and ends just before the specified end index.

setColumns   `public void setColumns(int columns)`
Sets the number of columns for this text area. Throws `IllegalArgument-Exception` if the specified number is less than 0.

setRows	`public void setRows(int rows)`
	Sets the number of rows for this text area. Throws `IllegalArgumentException` if the specified number is less than 0.

TextComponent   `java.awt`

`Object → Component → TextComponent`

`TextComponent` is the direct superclass of `TextArea` and `TextField`. It provides methods that are common to both text areas and text fields.

Methods

addTextListener	`public void addTextListener(TextListener l)`
	Registers the specified text event listener to receive text events from this text component.
getCaretPosition	`public int getCaretPosition()`
	Returns the position of the text insertion caret for this text component.
getSelectedText	`public String getSelectedText()`
	Returns the currently selected text in this text component.
getSelectionEnd	`public int getSelectionEnd()`
	Returns the selected text's end position in this text component.
getSelectionStart	`public int getSelectionStart()`
	Returns the selected text's start position in this text component.
getText	`public String getText()`
	Returns a string containing all text in this text component.
isEditable	`public boolean isEditable()`
	Returns `true` if this text component is editable.
select	`public void select(int selectionStart, int selectionEnd)`
	Selects a portion of the text within this text component. The portion selected begins at the specified start index and ends just before the specified end index.
selectAll	`public void selectAll()`
	Selects all text in this text component.
setCaretPosition	`public void setCaretPosition(int position)`
	Sets the position of the text insertion caret for this text component. Throws `IllegalArgumentException` if the position is less than 0.
setEditable	`public void setEditable(boolean b)`
	Makes this text component editable or not editable, depending on whether b is `true` or `false`, respectively.
setSelectionEnd	`public void setSelectionEnd(int selectionEnd)`
	Sets the end of a selection in this text component. The new end position must be at or after the start of the current selection.
setSelectionStart	`public void setSelectionStart(int selectionStart)`
	Sets the start of a selection in this text component. The new starting position must be before or at the end of the current selection.

setText   `public void setText(String t)`
Sets the text of this text component.

TextField   `java.awt`

`Object → Component → TextComponent → TextField`

A text field is a component that displays one line of text. If desired, the text can be edited by the user.

Constructors

TextField   `public TextField()`
Creates a text field.

TextField   `public TextField(String text)`
Creates a text field containing the specified text.

TextField   `public TextField(int columns)`
Creates an empty text field with the specified number of columns.

TextField   `public TextField(String text, int columns)`
Creates a text field with the specified number of columns, containing the specified text.

Methods

addActionListener   `public void addActionListener(ActionListener l)`
Registers the specified action listener to receive action events from this text field.

getColumns   `public int getColumns()`
Returns the number of columns in this text field.

setColumns   `public void setColumns(int columns)`
Sets the number of columns for this text field. Throws `IllegalArgument-Exception` if the specified number is less than 0.

setText   `public void setText(String t)`
Sets the text of this text field.

Vector   `java.util`

`Object → Vector`
IMPLEMENTS `Cloneable, Serializable`

A vector is similar to an array, except that it can grow and shrink as elements are added and removed. The elements of a vector are accessed by position; the first element is at position 0. The elements of a vector must be objects. A value of a primitive type, such as `int` or `double`, can't be stored into a vector directly. Instead, it must be converted into an object by using a wrapper class, such as `Integer` or `Double`.

Each vector has a size, a capacity, and a capacity increment. The *size* of a vector is the number of elements currently stored in it. The *capacity* is the number of the elements that the vector currently has room to store. (The size is always less than or equal to the capacity.) The *capacity increment* is the amount by which the vector increases when it becomes full.

Constructors

Vector   `public Vector()`
Creates an empty vector.

Vector   `public Vector(int initialCapacity)`
Creates an empty vector with the specified initial capacity.

Vector   `public Vector(int initialCapacity, int capacityIncrement)`
Creates an empty vector with the specified initial capacity and capacity increment.

Methods

addElement   `public void addElement(Object obj)`
Adds the specified object to the end of this vector, increasing its size by one. The capacity of this vector is increased if its size becomes greater than its capacity.

capacity   `public int capacity()`
Returns the current capacity of this vector.

contains   `public boolean contains(Object elem)`
Returns `true` if the specified object is an element in this vector.

copyInto   `public void copyInto(Object[] anArray)`
Copies the elements of this vector into the specified array. The array must be big enough to hold all the objects in this vector.

elementAt   `public Object elementAt(int index)`
Returns the element at the specified index. Throws `ArrayIndexOutOf-BoundsException` if the index is less than 0 or greater than or equal to the vector's size.

ensureCapacity   `public void ensureCapacity(int minCapacity)`
Increases the capacity of this vector, if necessary, to ensure that it can hold at least the specified number of elements.

firstElement   `public Object firstElement()`
Returns the first element in this vector. Throws `NoSuchElementException` if this vector is empty.

indexOf   `public int indexOf(Object elem)`
Returns the index of the first occurrence of the specified object in this vector; objects are tested for equality using the `equals` method. Returns −1 if the object is not found.

indexOf   `public int indexOf(Object elem, int index)`
Identical to the previous version of `indexOf`, except that the search begins at `index`.

insertElementAt   `public void insertElementAt(Object obj, int index)`
Inserts the specified object into this vector at the specified index. Each element in this vector with an index greater or equal to the specified index is shifted to the next higher position. Throws `ArrayIndexOutOfBoundsException` if the index is less than 0 or greater than the vector's size.

isEmpty	`public boolean isEmpty()`
	Returns `true` if this vector has no elements.
lastElement	`public Object lastElement()`
	Returns the last element in this vector (the element at index `size()`−1). Throws `NoSuchElementException` if this vector is empty.
lastIndexOf	`public int lastIndexOf(Object elem)`
	Returns the index of the last occurrence of the specified object in this vector; objects are tested for equality using the `equals` method. Returns −1 if the object is not found.
lastIndexOf	`public int lastIndexOf(Object elem, int index)`
	Identical to the previous version of `lastIndexOf`, except that the value returned must be less than `index`.
removeAllElements	`public void removeAllElements()`
	Removes all elements from this vector and sets its size to zero.
removeElement	`public boolean removeElement(Object obj)`
	Removes the first occurrence of the specified object from this vector. Elements stored at subsequent positions are shifted to the next lower position, and the size of the vector decreases by one. Returns `true` if the object was found in the vector.
removeElementAt	`public void removeElementAt(int index)`
	Removes the element at the specified index. Elements stored at subsequent positions are shifted to the next lower position, and the size of the vector decreases by one. Throws `ArrayIndexOutOfBoundsException` if the index is less than 0 or greater than or equal to the vector's size.
setElementAt	`public void setElementAt(Object obj, int index)`
	Sets the element at the specified index to be the specified object. The value previously stored at that index is discarded. Throws `ArrayIndexOutOfBounds-Exception` if the index is less than 0 or greater than or equal to the vector's size.
setSize	`public void setSize(int newSize)`
	Sets the size of this vector. If the new size is greater than the current size, `null` elements are added to the end of the vector. If the new size is less than the current size, all elements at index `newSize` and greater are discarded.
size	`public int size()`
	Returns the number of elements in this vector.
trimToSize	`public void trimToSize()`
	Reduces the capacity of this vector to be the same as the vector's size.

Window   `java.awt`

`Object` → `Component` → `Container` → `Window`

A window has no borders. The default layout for a window is `BorderLayout`. `Window` is primarily important as the superclass for `Frame` and other window classes.

Constructors

Window   `public Window(Frame parent)`
Creates a window with the specified parent (a frame that "owns" the window). The window is not visible when created.

Methods

addWindowListener   `public void addWindowListener(WindowListener l)`
Registers the specified window listener to receive window events from this window.

dispose   `public void dispose()`
Disposes of this window. This method must be called to release the resources that are used for the window.

isShowing   `public boolean isShowing()`
Returns `true` if this window is visible on the screen.

pack   `public void pack()`
Sets the size of this window so that components within it are displayed at their preferred sizes.

show   `public void show()`
Makes this window visible on the screen. If the window is already visible, it will be brought to the front, on top of any overlapping windows.

toBack   `public void toBack()`
Places this window behind any overlapping windows.

toFront   `public void toFront()`
Places this window on top of any overlapping windows.

APPENDIX D
Applets

There are two primary types of Java programs: *applications* and *applets.* All the programs in the main text are applications. This appendix explains how applets are written and executed.

Although it's often possible to convert an application into an applet or vice versa, there are fundamental differences between the two kinds of programs:

- An application is a stand-alone program that can be launched from the command line. Executing an applet is a more-involved process: The applet must first be embedded in an HTML file. When the HTML file is loaded into a Web browser, the applet will begin to execute.

- An applet must extend the `Applet` class.

- An application must have a `main` method. An applet, on the other hand, has no `main` method. The behavior of an applet is controlled by the browser that is executing the applet.

- An application has no restrictions on what it can do. For security reasons, applets are subject to various restrictions. In particular, an applet can't normally read or write a file. (These restrictions can be circumvented if the user gives permission.)

Writing and Executing Applets

We already know how to write and execute an application. First, we create a file containing the program's source code. Next, we use `javac` to compile the program. Finally, we use the `java` interpreter to execute the program. The process is somewhat different for an applet. After we create a file containing the applet's source code, we will need to compile the applet. Next, we'll create an HTML file containing a special APPLET tag, thereby embedding the applet in the HTML file. Finally, we'll load the HTML file into a browser or a special "applet viewer." Let's look at each of these steps in detail.

Writing an Applet

An applet is a public class that extends the Applet class. (We'll need to import java.applet.* in order to get access to Applet. We'll usually import java.awt.* as well, because many applets need the Graphics class.) Inside the class, we'll put a method named paint. The paint method will have one parameter (a Graphics object) and a result type of void. Statements in the body of paint can call the drawing methods of Chapter 6 to display text and graphics.

Consider the JavaRules program of Section 2.1, which displays the message Java rules!. Here's what the program would look like as an applet:

JavaRules2.java

```
 1   // Displays the message "Java rules!"
 2
 3   import java.applet.*;
 4   import java.awt.*;
 5
 6   public class JavaRules2 extends Applet {
 7     public void paint(Graphics g) {
 8       g.drawString("Java rules!", 50, 25);
 9     }
10   }
```

The graphics context g represents a rectangular area within a browser window. The drawString method displays the message Java rules! at coordinates (50, 25) within this area. Notice that we don't call the paint method; paint will be called automatically when the applet begins to execute.

Embedding an Applet in an HTML File

Once we've entered the JavaRules2 program into a file, the next step is to compile the program. Applets are compiled in the same way as applications, using the javac compiler:

```
javac JavaRules2.java
```

If JavaRules2 were an application, we could now use the java interpreter to execute it. Applets can't be executed by java, however. Instead, we must embed the applet in an HTML file.

 Don't try to run an applet without first creating an HTML file. The java interpreter can't execute applets.

An HTML file contains text with interspersed formatting commands, known as *tags.* Here's an example of what an HTML file might contain:

```
<HTML>
<HEAD>
<TITLE>Bob's Bagels</TITLE>
</HEAD>
<BODY>
<H2>Bob's Bagels</H2>
<P>
Bob's Bagels--voted "Best In New York" four times since 1985.
<P>
Bob's Bagels are 100% natural and most are fat-free. Baked
daily for your eating pleasure!
</BODY>
</HTML>
```

Notice that tags often come in pairs, such as <HTML> and </HTML> or <HEAD> and </HEAD>. The tags indicate the structure of the document and provide information about how it should be displayed in a browser.

A typical HTML file has a head (indicated by the <HEAD> and </HEAD> tags) and a body (indicated by the <BODY> and </BODY> tags). Within the head is the title of the document (indicated by the <TITLE> and </TITLE> tags). The body of the document may include paragraphs (each marked with a <P> tag) and headings (marked with tags such as <H1>, <H2>, and so on, depending on the size of the heading). An HTML file normally begins with an <HTML> tag and ends with a </HTML> tag.

Other tags—not shown in this example—indicate which fonts to use, whether characters should be bold and/or italic, and where images should go. Tags are also used to embed links to other documents. A great deal of information about HTML is available in books and on the Web itself, so I won't go into any more detail.

Applets are embedded into HTML files using the <APPLET> tag. For example, to embed the JavaRules2 applet in an HTML file, we could use the following lines:

JavaRules2.html

```
1  <APPLET CODE="JavaRules2.class" WIDTH="250" HEIGHT="100">
2  </APPLET>
```

The WIDTH and HEIGHT attributes specify the size of the rectangular area that the browser should set aside for the applet. In this example, the applet area will be 250 pixels wide and 100 pixels high. The use of WIDTH and HEIGHT is mandatory, by the way; they have no default values.

Be careful that the <APPLET> tag is correct. In particular, make sure that the WIDTH and HEIGHT attributes are specified correctly. If there's an error in the <APPLET> tag, you'll get a series of mysterious error messages (or nothing at all) when you try to test the applet.

In order to test an applet, we'll need to create an HTML file containing the `<APPLET>` and `</APPLET>` tags. It's not necessary for the file to contain anything else, although it won't hurt. (For example, we could embed an applet into the Bob's Bagels HTML file shown earlier. The applet would go somewhere in the body, between the `<BODY>` and `</BODY>` tags.) If an applet is included in the same HTML file as text and images, the applet is treated as an image for layout purposes. For example, the `JavaRules2` applet would be treated as an image that's 250 pixels wide and 100 pixels high.

The HTML file can have any name we like; there's no requirement that it match the name of the applet. It's customary to use either `.html` or `.htm` as the file's extension, however. The HTML file will go in the same directory as the applet's `.class` file.

Executing an Applet

Once we've embedded an applet into an HTML file, we're ready to test the applet. One way to proceed is to load the HTML file into a "Java-aware" browser—a browser that's capable of executing Java applets. Most modern browsers—including Internet Explorer and Netscape Communicator—can handle Java.

It's not necessary to be connected to the Internet to load an HTML file. Just go to the File menu on the browser and select "Open..." (Internet Explorer) or "Open Page..." (in Netscape). Next, press the "Browse..." button (Internet Explorer) or the "Choose File..." button (Netscape), and locate the HTML file.

Once the HTML file has been loaded into the browser, the applet should begin to execute automatically. Here's what the `JavaRules2` applet looks like in Internet Explorer:

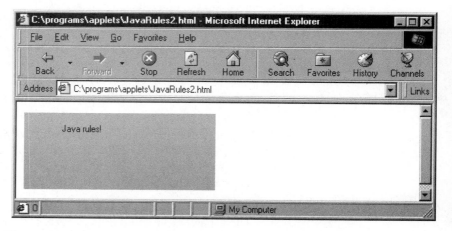

The applet shows up as a gray rectangle. The left edge of the letter J is 50 pixels from the left side of the applet, and the baseline of `Java rules!` is 25 pixels from the top of the applet.

Using a browser to test applets usually isn't the best technique. For one thing, most browsers won't detect any changes that you make to an applet during debugging. In order to get the browser to display an updated version of the applet, you'll need to close the browser and restart it, which is quite a nuisance.

 Most browsers won't reload an applet after it's been changed. To see an updated version of the applet, you may need to close the browser and restart it.

Fortunately, the JDK includes an "applet viewer" program, which makes testing applets much easier. This program, named `appletviewer`, will execute an applet embedded in an HTML file. Like the other tools in the JDK, `appletviewer` is executed from the command line. It requires that we specify the name of the HTML file containing the applet (*not* the name of the applet itself):

```
appletviewer JavaRules2.html
```

A window will now appear on the screen, displaying the applet:

Notice that the background of the applet is white in the applet viewer, but gray in Internet Explorer. To avoid this inconsistency, we can use the `setBackground` method to choose a background color for the applet. (The `StopSign2` program, which appears later in this appendix, illustrates the use of `setBackground`.)

The applet viewer discards the contents of the HTML file, displaying only the applet, not any text or graphics in the file. (To see the entire contents of the file, we'd have to use a browser.)

 Be sure that you compile an applet before you attempt to test it. If you try to execute an applet that hasn't been compiled yet, the browser or applet viewer will display a "class not found" error message.

Passing Parameters to Applets

A Java application can obtain information from the command line at the time the program is run. Applets have a similar ability: an applet can read parameters that are supplied in the HTML file that contains the applet. Each parameter is identified by a <PARAM> tag. There can be any number of <PARAM> tags. <PARAM> tags must be placed between the <APPLET> and </APPLET> tags.

For example, suppose that we want to make the JavaRules2 program more general, so that it displays an arbitrary message at an arbitrary position. We'll need three parameters: the message to be displayed, the *x* coordinate of the message, and the *y* coordinate of the message. Assuming that the new program is named Message, here's what the HTML will look like:

Message.html

```
1  <APPLET CODE="Message.class" WIDTH="250" HEIGHT="100">
2  <PARAM NAME="message" VALUE="Java rules!">
3  <PARAM NAME="x" VALUE="50">
4  <PARAM NAME="y" VALUE="25">
5  </APPLET>
```

Each <PARAM> tag must have a NAME attribute and a VALUE attribute. In this example, the first parameter is named message; its value is "Java rules!".

An applet can retrieve the value of one of its parameters by calling the get-Parameter method, which is inherited from the Applet class. To obtain the value of the message parameter, for example, the Message applet can use the following call of getParameter:

```
String message = getParameter("message");
```

The value of a parameter is always a string. To use a parameter value as an integer, we'll need to convert it to integer form by calling Integer.parseInt:

```
int x = Integer.parseInt(getParameter("x"));
```

Here's what the Message applet will look like:

Message.java

```
1  // Displays a message. The message and its coordinates are
2  // supplied as parameters.
3
4  import java.applet.*;
5  import java.awt.*;
6
7  public class Message extends Applet {
8    public void paint(Graphics g) {
9      String message = getParameter("message");
10      int x = Integer.parseInt(getParameter("x"));
11      int y = Integer.parseInt(getParameter("y"));
12      g.drawString(message, x, y);
13    }
14  }
```

Applet Methods

Every applet is a subclass of the Applet class. Applet itself has several super-classes:

Object → Component → Container → Panel → Applet

An applet inherits many methods from Applet (and the superclasses of Applet), some of which are designed to be overridden. Of these methods, init and paint are the most fundamental. Let's take a closer look at these two methods.

The paint Method

The paint method's job is to create an image for the browser to display. Whenever the browser needs to display the applet, it constructs a graphics context and passes it to paint. The paint method can then use any of the methods described in Chapter 6 to display text and/or graphics within the graphics context. The user sees the graphics context as a rectangle within the browser.

The paint method is called more often than you might think. paint is called not only when the applet is first displayed on the screen, but also when the window containing the applet is resized, when the applet becomes visible after having been covered by another window, and at other times when it becomes necessary to refresh the applet.

The following applet shows how paint works. The applet keeps track of the number of times paint has been called, using drawString to display the number to the user.

PaintCount.java

```
1   // Displays the number of times paint has been called.
2
3   import java.applet.*;
4   import java.awt.*;
5
6   public class PaintCount extends Applet {
7     private int count = 0;
8
9     public void paint(Graphics g) {
10       count++;
11       g.drawString("Number of times paint called: " + count,
12                  10, 20);
13     }
14   }
```

Here's the HTML file that accompanies the applet:

PaintCount.html

```
1   <APPLET CODE="PaintCount.class" WIDTH="200" HEIGHT="30">
2   </APPLET>
```

And here's what the applet looks like in the applet viewer:

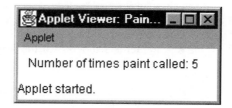

Try loading this applet into a browser and then resizing the browser window, minimizing and maximizing the browser window, and hiding the browser window underneath another window. The count will often increase to a surprisingly large number, as paint is called one or more times for each operation.

The `init` Method

Because paint is called more than once by the browser, it's a good idea to keep this method small. In particular, statements that need to be executed only once don't belong in paint. Instead, they should be put into a method named init. The init method, like the paint method, is called automatically by the browser. However, init is called only once, at the time the applet is created.

Consider the Message applet. The calls of getParameter don't need to be done in the paint method, because the parameters will never change once the applet has been loaded. These calls should go into the init method instead. Here's what the Message applet would look like with the getParameter calls moved to init:

Message2.java

```
1   // Displays a message. The message and its coordinates are
2   // supplied as parameters.
3
4   import java.applet.*;
5   import java.awt.*;
6
7   public class Message2 extends Applet {
8     private String message;
9     private int x, y;
10
11    // Called once, when the applet is created
12    public void init() {
13      message = getParameter("message");
14      x = Integer.parseInt(getParameter("x"));
15      y = Integer.parseInt(getParameter("y"));
16    }
17
18    // Called each time the applet needs to be redisplayed
19    public void paint(Graphics g) {
20      g.drawString(message, x, y);
21    }
22  }
```

`message`, `x`, and `y` are declared as instance variables, not local variables, so they'll be visible to both `init` and `paint`.

We can now more accurately describe what happens when we use a browser to execute an applet. When the browser loads an HTML file containing the `APPLET` tag, it reserves space for a rectangle of the size specified by the `WIDTH` and `HEIGHT` attributes, and loads the class file specified in the tag. The browser next creates an applet object—an instance of the class that's stored in the file—and calls the object's `init` method to allow the applet to initialize itself. It then calls the object's `paint` method, allowing the applet to display text or graphics in the rectangle.

`init` and `paint` aren't the only methods that are automatically called by the browser. There are several others, each designed for a specific purpose. Coverage of these methods is beyond the scope of this book, however.

Using Graphics in Applets

In Chapter 6, we saw how to use methods from the `Graphics` class to create a drawing within a `DrawableFrame` object. These same methods can be used to draw within an applet.

Consider the `StopSign` program of Section 6.4, which displays an octagonal stop sign. Here's the original program:

StopSign.java

```
1   // Displays a stop sign
2
3   import java.awt.*;
4   import jpb.*;
5
6   public class StopSign {
7     public static void main(String[] args) {
8       // Create drawable frame
9       DrawableFrame df = new DrawableFrame("Stop Sign");
10      df.show();
11      df.setSize(125, 125);
12
13      // Obtain graphics context
14      Graphics g = df.getGraphicsContext();
15
16      // Define coordinates of outer polygon (edge of sign) and
17      // inner polygon (red portion)
18      int[] xOuter = {36, 87, 123, 123, 87, 36, 0, 0};
19      int[] yOuter = {0, 0, 36, 87, 123, 123, 87, 36};
20      int[] xInner = {37, 86, 118, 118, 86, 37, 5, 5};
21      int[] yInner = {5, 5, 37, 86, 118, 118, 86, 37};
22
23      // Draw edge of sign in black
24      g.setColor(Color.black);
25      g.drawPolygon(xOuter, yOuter, xOuter.length);
```

```
26
27          // Fill interior of sign with red
28          g.setColor(Color.red);
29          g.fillPolygon(xInner, yInner, xInner.length);
30
31          // Display "STOP" in white
32          g.setColor(Color.white);
33          g.setFont(new Font("SansSerif", Font.BOLD, 36));
34          g.drawString("STOP", 13, 76);
35
36          // Repaint frame
37          df.repaint();
38        }
39    }
```

To convert this program to an applet, we can discard all statements that pertain to the DrawableFrame object and move the remaining statements into the paint method. (To keep paint as small as possible, we should declare the arrays as instance variables rather than local variables.) paint has one parameter, a Graphics object named g, which can be used in the same way as the object g in the original program. To make sure that the applet has a white background, we can put a call of setBackground (an inherited method) inside the init method. Here's the modified program:

StopSign2.java

```
1    // Displays a stop sign (applet version)
2
3    import java.applet.*;
4    import java.awt.*;
5
6    public class StopSign2 extends Applet {
7        // Coordinates of outer polygon (edge of sign) and inner
8        // polygon (red portion)
9        private int[] xOuter = {36, 87, 123, 123, 87, 36, 0, 0};
10       private int[] yOuter = {0, 0, 36, 87, 123, 123, 87, 36};
11       private int[] xInner = {37, 86, 118, 118, 86, 37, 5, 5};
12       private int[] yInner = {5, 5, 37, 86, 118, 118, 86, 37};
13
14       public void init() {
15           setBackground(Color.white);
16       }
17
18       public void paint(Graphics g) {
19           // Draw edge of sign in black
20           g.setColor(Color.black);
21           g.drawPolygon(xOuter, yOuter, xOuter.length);
22
23           // Fill interior of sign with red
24           g.setColor(Color.red);
25           g.fillPolygon(xInner, yInner, xInner.length);
26
27           // Display "STOP" in white
28           g.setColor(Color.white);
```

```
29        g.setFont(new Font("SansSerif", Font.BOLD, 36));
30        g.drawString("STOP", 13, 76);
31    }
32 }
```

Here's the HTML file that accompanies the applet:

StopSign2.html

```
1 <APPLET CODE="StopSign2.class" WIDTH="125" HEIGHT="125">
2 </APPLET>
```

And here's what the applet looks like in the applet viewer:

Writing GUI Applets

In Chapter 12, we saw how to create an application with a graphical user interface by extending the Frame class. Any subclass of Frame is a container class, allowing us to put GUI components into it.

Applets are also containers. In fact, applets and frames have much in common, thanks to the superclasses that they share. Here's the ancestry of the Frame class:

Object → Component → Container → Window → Frame

The Applet class is also a subclass of Component and Container:

Object → Component → Container → Panel → Applet

panels ➤ *12.6*

Because the Applet class is a subclass of Panel, applets behave much like panels. We can use the init method to create GUI components and add them to an applet.

In many cases, converting a GUI application to an applet is a simple process. Consider the PickColor program of Section 12.8. This program displays a frame containing three scrollbars. By moving the scrollbars, the user can experiment with different color combinations. Here's the code for the original program:

PickColor.java

```
1    // Allows the user to pick a color by moving three scrollbars
2
3    import java.awt.*;
4    import java.awt.event.*;
5
6    // Driver class
7    public class PickColor {
8      public static void main(String[] args) {
9        Frame f = new PickColorFrame("Pick Color");
10        f.setSize(150, 200);
11        f.setVisible(true);
12      }
13    }
14
15    // Frame class
16    class PickColorFrame extends Frame {
17      private Label redLabel =
18        new Label("Red = 128", Label.CENTER);
19      private Label greenLabel =
20        new Label("Green = 128", Label.CENTER);
21      private Label blueLabel =
22        new Label("Blue = 128", Label.CENTER);
23      private Scrollbar redBar =
24        new Scrollbar(Scrollbar.HORIZONTAL, 128, 1, 0, 256);
25      private Scrollbar greenBar =
26        new Scrollbar(Scrollbar.HORIZONTAL, 128, 1, 0, 256);
27      private Scrollbar blueBar =
28        new Scrollbar(Scrollbar.HORIZONTAL, 128, 1, 0, 256);
29
30      // Constructor
31      public PickColorFrame(String title) {
32        // Set title, background color, and layout
33        super(title);
34        setBackground(new Color(128, 128, 128));
35        setLayout(new GridLayout(6, 1));
36
37        // Create scrollbar listener
38        ScrollbarListener listener = new ScrollbarListener();
39
40        // Add red scrollbar and label to frame; attach
41        // listener to scrollbar
42        add(redBar);
43        redBar.addAdjustmentListener(listener);
44        add(redLabel);
45
46        // Add green scrollbar and label to frame; attach
47        // listener to scrollbar
48        add(greenBar);
49        greenBar.addAdjustmentListener(listener);
50        add(greenLabel);
51
52        // Add blue scrollbar and label to frame; attach
53        // listener to scrollbar
54        add(blueBar);
```

```
55        blueBar.addAdjustmentListener(listener);
56        add(blueLabel);
57
58        // Attach window listener
59        addWindowListener(new WindowCloser());
60     }
61
62     // Listener for all scrollbars
63     class ScrollbarListener implements AdjustmentListener {
64        public void adjustmentValueChanged(AdjustmentEvent evt) {
65           int red = redBar.getValue();
66           int green = greenBar.getValue();
67           int blue = blueBar.getValue();
68
69           redLabel.setText("Red = " + red);
70           greenLabel.setText("Green = " + green);
71           blueLabel.setText("Blue = " + blue);
72
73           Color newColor = new Color(red, green, blue);
74           redLabel.setBackground(newColor);
75           greenLabel.setBackground(newColor);
76           blueLabel.setBackground(newColor);
77        }
78     }
79
80     // Listener for window
81     class WindowCloser extends WindowAdapter {
82        public void windowClosing(WindowEvent evt) {
83           System.exit(0);
84        }
85     }
86  }
```

To convert this program into an applet, we'll need to get rid of the main method (and the entire driver class). We'll also need to have the remaining class extend Applet rather than Frame, move statements from the constructor into the init method, and get rid of the event listener for the window. Here's the resulting program:

PickColor2.java

```
1   // Allows the user to pick a color by moving three scrollbars
2   // (applet version)
3
4   import java.applet.*;
5   import java.awt.*;
6   import java.awt.event.*;
7
8   public class PickColor2 extends Applet {
9      private Label redLabel =
10        new Label("Red = 128", Label.CENTER);
11     private Label greenLabel =
12        new Label("Green = 128", Label.CENTER);
13     private Label blueLabel =
14        new Label("Blue = 128", Label.CENTER);
```

```
15     private Scrollbar redBar =
16       new Scrollbar(Scrollbar.HORIZONTAL, 128, 1, 0, 256);
17     private Scrollbar greenBar =
18       new Scrollbar(Scrollbar.HORIZONTAL, 128, 1, 0, 256);
19     private Scrollbar blueBar =
20       new Scrollbar(Scrollbar.HORIZONTAL, 128, 1, 0, 256);
21
22     public void init() {
23       // Set background color and layout
24       setBackground(new Color(128, 128, 128));
25       setLayout(new GridLayout(6, 1));
26
27       // Create scrollbar listener
28       ScrollbarListener listener = new ScrollbarListener();
29
30       // Add red scrollbar and label to frame; attach
31       // listener to scrollbar
32       add(redBar);
33       redBar.addAdjustmentListener(listener);
34       add(redLabel);
35
36       // Add green scrollbar and label to frame; attach
37       // listener to scrollbar
38       add(greenBar);
39       greenBar.addAdjustmentListener(listener);
40       add(greenLabel);
41
42       // Add blue scrollbar and label to frame; attach
43       // listener to scrollbar
44       add(blueBar);
45       blueBar.addAdjustmentListener(listener);
46       add(blueLabel);
47     }
48
49     // Listener for all scrollbars
50     class ScrollbarListener implements AdjustmentListener {
51       public void adjustmentValueChanged(AdjustmentEvent evt) {
52         int red = redBar.getValue();
53         int green = greenBar.getValue();
54         int blue = blueBar.getValue();
55
56         redLabel.setText("Red = " + red);
57         greenLabel.setText("Green = " + green);
58         blueLabel.setText("Blue = " + blue);
59
60         Color newColor = new Color(red, green, blue);
61         redLabel.setBackground(newColor);
62         greenLabel.setBackground(newColor);
63         blueLabel.setBackground(newColor);
64       }
65     }
66   }
```

Notice that a GUI applet doesn't need a `paint` method. An applet that doesn't provide its own `paint` method will inherit one from a superclass. The inherited version will take care of displaying any components that are added to the applet.

Here's the HTML file that accompanies the applet:

PickColor2.html

```
1   <APPLET CODE="PickColor2.class" WIDTH="150" HEIGHT="200">
2   </APPLET>
```

Here's what the applet looks like in the applet viewer:

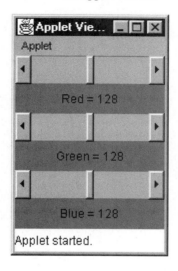

The `jpb` Package

Many of the programs in this book rely on the `jpb` package, which was created to make it easier for beginners to perform common tasks. There are only three classes in the `jpb` package: `Convert`, `DrawableFrame`, and `SimpleIO`. The `Convert` class provides methods for converting strings to `float` and `double` form. The `DrawableFrame` class makes it easy to display graphics in a frame. The `SimpleIO` class simplifies the task of obtaining keyboard input from the user.

In this appendix, we'll see how these classes work. We'll also see how to write programs that use only standard API classes, without relying on the `jpb` package.

The `Convert` Class

The `Convert` class provides methods named `toDouble` and `toFloat`, which convert a string to a `double` value or `float` value.

Convert.java

```
1   // Provides methods to convert a string containing a number
2   // to double or float form
3
4   package jpb;
5
6   public class Convert {
7     // Converts the string s to double form; terminates the
8     // program if s does not represent a valid double value
9     public static double toDouble(String s) {
10      double d = 0.0;
11      try {
12        d = Double.valueOf(s).doubleValue();
13      } catch (NumberFormatException e) {
```

```
14              System.out.println("Error in Convert.toDouble: " +
15                                  e.getMessage());
16              System.exit(-1);
17          }
18          return d;
19      }
20
21      // Converts the string s to float form; terminates the
22      // program if s does not represent a valid float value
23      public static float toFloat(String s) {
24          float f = 0.0f;
25          try {
26              f = Float.valueOf(s).floatValue();
27          } catch (NumberFormatException e) {
28              System.out.println("Error in Convert.toFloat: " +
29                                  e.getMessage());
30              System.exit(-1);
31          }
32          return f;
33      }
34  }
```

Double class ➤ *13.3*

The `toDouble` method uses the `Double.valueOf` method to create a `Double` object from the argument. It then calls the `doubleValue` method to extract the `double` value stored in the object. The `toFloat` method is similar.

If you're using version 1.1 of the Java Development Kit, you can replace calls of `Convert.toDouble` and `Convert.toFloat` as follows. Instead of

```
double d = Convert.toDouble(str);
```

where `str` is a `String` object, use

```
double d = Double.valueOf(str).doubleValue();
```

Instead of

```
float f = Convert.toFloat(str);
```

use

```
float f = Float.valueOf(str).floatValue();
```

If you're using version 1.2 or later of the JDK, it's even easier, because there are now methods that convert a string directly to a `double` or `float` value:

```
double d = Double.parseDouble(str);
float f = Float.parseFloat(str);
```

The `DrawableFrame` Class

The `DrawableFrame` class makes it easy to create a frame and display a drawing within it.

DrawableFrame.java

```java
1   // A frame in which drawings can be displayed
2
3   package jpb;
4
5   import java.awt.*;
6   import java.awt.event.*;
7
8   public class DrawableFrame extends Frame {
9     private Image imageBuffer = null;
10    private Insets insets;
11
12    // Constructor
13    public DrawableFrame(String title) {
14      super(title);
15      addWindowListener(new WindowCloser());
16    }
17
18    // Called automatically to display the contents of the
19    // frame
20    public void paint(Graphics g) {
21      if (imageBuffer != null)
22        g.drawImage(imageBuffer, insets.left, insets.top, null);
23    }
24
25    // Called automatically by repaint. Used to reduce flicker.
26    public void update(Graphics g) {
27      paint(g);
28    }
29
30    // Sets the size of the frame. The width and height
31    // parameters control the size of the drawable portion of
32    // the frame. The frame itself is somewhat larger.
33    public void setSize(int width, int height) {
34      insets = getInsets();
35      super.setSize(width + insets.left + insets.right,
36                    height + insets.top + insets.bottom);
37      imageBuffer = createImage(width, height);
38    }
39
40    // Returns the graphics context associated with the image
41    // buffer
42    public Graphics getGraphicsContext() {
43      return imageBuffer.getGraphics();
44    }
45
46    // Listener for window
47    class WindowCloser extends WindowAdapter {
48      public void windowClosing(WindowEvent evt) {
49        System.exit(0);
50      }
51    }
52  }
```

The DrawableFrame class provides four methods. Two of these, paint and `update`, are called automatically when needed. The other two, `setSize` and `getGraphicsContext`, are designed to be used by the programmer.

When the `setSize` method is called, it resizes the frame so that it's large enough to display graphics of the specified size. The frame itself needs to be larger than the arguments supplied to the `setSize` method in order to accommodate the border around the frame. `setSize` creates an `Insets` object to determine how much extra space is needed for the border (An `Insets` object has four instance variables—`left`, `right`, `top`, and `bottom`—which contain the sizes of a frame's borders.) This object is stored in an instance variable named `insets`. `setSize` also creates an "image buffer" whose size matches the arguments passed to `setSize`. This buffer is stored in an instance variable of type `Image`. (Instances of the `Image` class are used to represent images of all kinds.) The `Insets` class and the `Image` class aren't discussed in this book.

The `getGraphicsContext` method returns a graphics context that is connected to the image buffer. Any drawing done using this graphics context will be reflected in the image buffer.

The `paint` method is automatically called when the frame is first displayed on the screen or needs to be refreshed. (For example, `paint` is called when the frame is resized or needs to be redisplayed after being obscured by another window.) `paint` displays the image buffer within the frame (provided that the image buffer exists). The value of `insets` is used to make sure that the image buffer doesn't overlap the frame's borders.

The `update` method is harder to explain. The `DrawableFrame` class inherits a method named `repaint`, which can be called to force the frame to be refreshed. `repaint` should be called after a program has made changes to the drawing displayed within the frame; it is especially important during animation. Calling `repaint` triggers a call of `update`, which in turn calls `paint`. The `DrawableFrame` class would normally inherit `update`, just as it inherits `repaint`. However, the inherited version of `update` would clear the contents of the frame and then call `paint`, which can cause a noticeable flicker. By providing a version of `update` that calls `paint` without clearing the frame first, the `DrawableFrame` class avoids this problem.

There's no simple replacement for the `DrawableFrame` class. To use the `Graphics` methods in a GUI application, the best technique is to create a subclass of the `Canvas` class (not described in this book) and then create an instance of this class. An applet's `paint` method can use the `Graphics` methods directly, as described in Appendix D.

The `SimpleIO` Class

The Java API doesn't provide an easy way to obtain keyboard input from the user. As a result, authors of Java books typically create their own classes for this purpose. My class, which is named `SimpleIO`, has only two methods: `prompt` and `readLine`.

SimpleIO.java

```java
1   // Provides prompt and readLine methods for console input
2
3   package jpb;
4
5   import java.io.*;
6
7   public class SimpleIO {
8     private static InputStreamReader streamIn =
9       new InputStreamReader(System.in);
10    private static BufferedReader in =
11      new BufferedReader(streamIn, 1);
12
13    // Displays the string s without terminating the current
14    // line
15    public static void prompt(String s) {
16      System.out.print(s);
17      System.out.flush();
18    }
19
20    // Reads and returns a single line of input entered by the
21    // user; terminates the program if an exception is thrown
22    public static String readLine() {
23      String line = null;
24      try {
25        line = in.readLine();
26      } catch (IOException e) {
27        System.out.println("Error in SimpleIO.readLine: " +
28                                    e.getMessage());
29        System.exit(-1);
30      }
31      return line;
32    }
33  }
```

The `prompt` method displays a prompt on the screen and then calls `System.out.flush` to make sure that the prompt appears immediately. The `readLine` method reads a single line of input entered by the user. As is typical in Java, `SimpleIO` makes use of layered streams: Calling `SimpleIO.readLine`

BufferedReader class ➤ 14.6 causes a call of `in.readLine`, where `in` is a `BufferedReader` object. `in.readLine`, in turn, calls methods belonging to `InputStreamReader`.

System.in ➤ 7.5 These methods obtain data from `System.in`, the standard input stream. Using 1 as the second argument to the `BufferedReader` constructor (line 11) was done to work around a problem with some versions of the JDK.

To see how to read input without the `SimpleIO` class, let's turn to the `FtoC3` program of Section 2.10. Here's the original program:

FtoC3.java

```java
1   // Converts a Fahrenheit temperature entered by the user to
2   // Celsius
```

```
3
4    import jpb.*;
5
6    public class FtoC3 {
7      public static void main(String[] args) {
8        final double FREEZING_POINT = 32.0;
9        final double DEGREE_RATIO = 5.0 / 9.0;
10
11       SimpleIO.prompt("Enter Fahrenheit temperature: ");
12       String userInput = SimpleIO.readLine();
13       double fahrenheit = Convert.toDouble(userInput);
14       double celsius =
15         (fahrenheit - FREEZING_POINT) * DEGREE_RATIO;
16       System.out.println("Celsius equivalent: " + celsius);
17     }
18   }
```

Here's a version of the program that doesn't use SimpleIO; changes are marked in **bold:**

FtoC4.java

```
1    // Converts a Fahrenheit temperature entered by the user to
2    // Celsius
3
4    import java.io.*;
5    import jpb.*;
6
7    public class FtoC4 {
8      public static void main(String[] args) {
9        final double FREEZING_POINT = 32.0;
10       final double DEGREE_RATIO = 5.0 / 9.0;
11       InputStreamReader streamIn =
12         new InputStreamReader(System.in);
13       BufferedReader in = new BufferedReader(streamIn, 1);
14
15       System.out.print("Enter Fahrenheit temperature: ");
16       System.out.flush();
17       try {
18         String userInput = in.readLine();
19         double fahrenheit = Convert.toDouble(userInput);
20         double celsius =
21           (fahrenheit - FREEZING_POINT) * DEGREE_RATIO;
22         System.out.println("Celsius equivalent: " + celsius);
23       } catch (IOException e) {
24         System.out.println(e.getMessage());
25         System.exit(-1);
26       }
27     }
28   }
```

streamIn and in can be declared as class variables, making them available to other methods besides main. The try statement can be eliminated by declaring that main throws IOException.

throws clause ➤*14.4*

BIBLIOGRAPHY

Arnold, K., and J. Gosling, *The Java Programming Language,* Second Edition, Addison-Wesley, Reading, Mass., 1998. A concise introduction to the Java language cowritten by James Gosling, Java's chief designer. It's well written and manages to convey a lot of the thinking behind the design of Java. Coverage of the API is very limited, though, and there are few examples of complete programs.

Bentley, J., *Programming Pearls*, Second Edition, Addison-Wesley, Reading, Mass., 2000. Although it's not about Java, this book will be of great interest to Java programmers. The author emphasizes writing efficient programs, but he touches on other topics that are crucial for the professional programmer. His light touch makes the book as enjoyable to read as it is informative.

Chan, P., *The Java Developer's Almanac 2000*, Addison-Wesley, Reading, Mass., 2000. An extremely concise guide to the Java API. Not useful for learning how to use the classes in the API, but very handy for looking up small details, such as the name of a class or the parameters required by a method. Updated regularly, so make sure you get the latest edition.

Chan, P., R. Lee, and D. Kramer, *The Java Class Libraries, Second Edition, Volume 1: java.io, java.lang, java.math, java.net, java.text, java.util,* Addison-Wesley, Reading, Mass., 1998. The definitive reference for the Java API, with detailed descriptions and examples of nearly every class and method. Volume 1 covers six major API packages and two related packages. Amazingly detailed, with more than 2000 pages!

Chan, P., and R. Lee, *The Java Class Libraries, Second Edition, Volume 2: java.applet, java.awt, java.beans,* Addison-Wesley, Reading, Mass., 1998. The second volume of the Chan/Lee epic, with a mere 1682 pages.

Chan, P., R. Lee, and D. Kramer, *The Java Class Libraries, Second Edition, Volume 1: Supplement for the Java 2 Platform, Standard Edition, v1.2,* Addison-Wesley, Reading, Mass., 1999. Supplements *The Java Class Libraries, Second Edition, Volume 1* by describing the new classes in version 1.2 of the JDK.

Gosling, J., B. Joy, and G. Steele, *The Java Language Specification,* Addison-Wesley, Reading, Mass., 1996. A detailed description of the Java language. Not easy reading, but it's the most precise definition of Java currently available. Includes a description of the standard Java conventions. Available on the Web at *http://java.sun.com/docs/books/jls/.*

McConnell, S., *Code Complete: A Practical Handbook of Software Construction*, Microsoft Press, Redmond, Wash., 1993. An excellent handbook for programmers, regardless of which language they're using. Addresses nearly all the important issues that programmers face, including design, style, debugging, and maintenance.

Raymond, E. S., ed., *The New Hacker's Dictionary*, Third Edition, MIT Press, Cambridge, Mass., 1996. Not a Java book, but useful for understanding much of the jargon that programmers use.

INDEX